**SEVENTH EDITION**

# Advanced FINANCIAL ACCOUNTING

Thomas H. Beechy
SCHULICH SCHOOL OF BUSINESS, YORK UNIVERSITY

V. Umashanker Trivedi
SCHULICH SCHOOL OF BUSINESS, YORK UNIVERSITY

Kenneth E. MacAulay
GERALD SCHWARTZ SCHOOL OF BUSINESS,
ST. FRANCIS XAVIER UNIVERSITY

Toronto

Vice-President, Editorial Director: Gary Bennett
Editor-in-Chief: Nicole Lukach
Acquisitions Editor: Megan Farrell
Sponsoring Editor: Kathleen McGill
Marketing Manager: Claire Varley
Developmental Editor: Patti Sayle
Project Manager: Jessica Hellen
Manufacturing Specialist: Jane Schell
Production Editor: GEX Publishing Services
Copy Editor: Heather Sangster, Strong Finish
Proofreader: Sally Glover
Compositor: GEX Publishing Services
Permissions Researcher: PreMediaGlobal
Art Director: Julia Hall
Cover Designer: Julia Hall
Interior Designer: Cenveo/Nesbitt
Cover Image: Getty Images

Credits and acknowledgments of material borrowed from other sources and reproduced, with permission, in this textbook appear on the appropriate page within the text and on p. xiv.

If you purchased this book outside the United States or Canada, you should be aware that it has been imported without the approval of the publisher or author.

Previous editions published under the title *Canadian Advanced Financial Accounting* © 1994.

All CGA material adapted from *Financial Accounting: Consolidations & Advanced Issues (FA4) Exams,* published by the Certified General Accountants Association of Canada © 1997 to 2008 CGA-Canada. Reproduced with permission. Because of regular Tax Act updates, changes to IFRS and the CICA Handbook, the contents of these examinations may be out of date; therefore the accuracy of the contents is the sole responsibility of the user.

2 2020

**Library and Archives Canada Cataloguing in Publication**

Beechy, Thomas H., 1937-
   Advanced financial accounting / Thomas H. Beechy, V. Umashanker Trivedi, Kenneth E. MacAulay. -- 7th ed.

 First-3rd eds. published under title: Canadian advanced financial accounting.
Includes bibliographical references and index.
ISBN 978-0-13-292893-9
   1. Accounting--Textbooks.  I. MacAulay, Kenneth E. (Kenneth Eugene), 1962-
II. Trivedi, V. Umashanker (Viswanath Umashanker), 1965-  III. Beechy, Thomas H.,
1937- . Canadian advanced financial accounting.  IV. Title.

HF5636.B43 2013              657'.046              C2012-905111-X

ISBN 978-0-13-292893-9

# Brief Contents

# Contents

# About the Authors

## Thomas H. Beechy, DBA, CPA (Illinois)

Tom Beechy has been in the forefront of Canadian accounting publishing for many decades. This is the seventh edition of the first Canadian-authored advanced accounting university textbook, initially published in 1984. Professor Beechy also is co-author of a major Canadian intermediate accounting text, now in its sixth edition. Tom immigrated to Canada from the United States more than 40 years ago after acquiring degrees from George Washington University, Northwestern University, and Washington University (St. Louis) and after teaching at the Illinois Institute of Technology for 10 years. After his arrival in Canada, he joined the Schulich School of Business, where he is Professor Emeritus of Accounting as well as Director of International Academic Development. Tom loves to travel and can often be found in Europe or Asia (especially in China). He is a classical music fanatic, and also enjoys dance, theatre, movies, and novels.

## V. Umashanker Trivedi, PhD

V. Umashanker (Shanker) Trivedi is an Associate Professor of Accounting at the Schulich School of Business, York University. He is a chartered accountant from India and obtained his PhD from Arizona State University. Shanker's research interests are in financial accounting, the accounting profession, and tax. He has won research grants from the Canadian Institute of Chartered Accountants and the Canadian Academic Accounting Association. Shanker has published in journals such as *Experimental Economics, Accounting Organizations and Society, Behavioral Research in Accounting, Journal of Business Ethics,* and *Canadian Tax Journal.* Shanker has also published many cases in financial accounting. In the past 19 years Shanker's has taught at York University, McMaster University, and Arizona State University and at all levels; bachelors, masters, and doctoral. His service at York University includes serving on the Senate and as the Chairman of the Senate Appeals Committee. Shanker enjoys smooth jazz, new age, and classical music.

## Kenneth MacAulay, PhD, CA

Ken MacAulay is a Professor of Accounting in the Gerald Schwartz School of Business at St. Francis Xavier University. His research interests lie in the area of corporate governance and financial literacy. He has co-authored several university-level textbooks and published in journals such as *Journal of Multinational Financial Management* and *Quarterly Journal of Finance & Accounting.* He holds degrees from St. Francis Xavier University (BBA) and Queen's University (PhD). Before his academic career, Ken was a chartered accountant with Touche Ross (now Deloitte and Touche). He has continued to be active in the profession, having taught in the Atlantic School of Chartered Accountancy and having served on the Nova Scotia Securities Commission. He is a committed conservationist and can often be found fly-fishing for trout and salmon in his spare time.

# Preface

Welcome to the latest edition of *Advanced Financial Accounting!* Since 1984, this book has guided students through the complexities of business combinations, consolidations, and financial reporting for business enterprises, non-profit organizations, and governments. This book is about more than just technical knowledge. Our goal is to help students develop a professional approach to accounting issues.

To help students demonstrate their professional competencies, we offer a variety of cases at the end of each chapter as well as a range of numerical problems. The cases address advanced accounting issues within realistic contexts. Using these cases, students can practise exercising their professional judgment. Most chapters have at least one *multiple competency* case wherein students are encouraged to apply their technical knowledge in a real-world setting over a wide range of issues.

## New Features

In this edition, we have retained many pedagogic features of previous editions and added new features that will enhance students' learning experience:

- **Learning Objectives** will help to focus students' attention on the main issues of each chapter.
- The material in each chapter is **linked** to the Learning Objectives.
- **Reality Check** boxes highlight applications in practice as well as point out significant findings from empirical research.
- **Concept Check** boxes enable students to self-test their own understanding of important issues and concepts as they proceed through each chapter.
- **International Financial Reporting Standards** are explained and applied through examples in the main body of each chapter. **IFRS terminology** is used throughout.
- **Accounting standards for private enterprises (ASPE)** are explained in a separate section at the end of each chapter, whenever ASPE differs from IFRS.
- **Proposed Change boxes** highlight changes in accounting standards that are being considered by the IASB and that may become reality by the time students reach their professional examination stage.
- The **direct method** of consolidation is used more extensively in this edition, within each consolidation chapter. However, for those who find a worksheet approach more understandable, a worksheet solution for every chapter example is available online, on the book's **Companion Website (CW)**.
- The **MEAR steps for consolidation** provide students with an effective method for remembering the steps in the consolidation process; MEAR is introduced in Chapter 3 and further developed in the following consolidation chapters.
- **Graphic exhibits** in the consolidation chapters complement and highlight the discussion in these chapters in a visually appealing manner.
- The quantity of **self-study problems** has been increased.

- Marginal icons direct students to a greatly enhanced **Companion Website**.
- A list of **relevant IFRS and ASPE accounting standards** is provided at the end of each chapter.
- **Online appendices** discuss specialized aspects of consolidation that are less essential for a thorough professional understanding of those topics, as well as additional issues of fund accounting.

## Text Updating

**Synopsis.** **Chapter 1** presents the basic structure of accounting standards in Canada as they apply to all types of organizations, private and public. We explain the role of accounting objectives, and we stress the importance of accounting estimates. While most of the accounting standards discussed in this book eliminate any choice of accounting policy, the reality is that the standards allow for a lot of latitude in making estimates that ultimately can have a significant impact on reported financial results. The chapter also develops the theme of international comparability, or the lack thereof.

**Chapters 2 through 6** explain the complex issues and process of consolidation and accounting for business combinations. These chapters constitute the core of the book— for most people, this is what advanced accounting is all about. We have revised and updated these chapters, while ensuring the text remains highly readable.

The main focus of these chapters is on the *acquisition method* required under IFRS and particularly on the entity approach. This focus allows students first to obtain a clear and firm understanding of the consolidation process, and then to expand their understanding to the other complexities of consolidation. A supplementary discussion of the parent-company extension approach (an available option within IFRS) is included later in each chapter. Throughout these chapters, the equity method is compared to the results of consolidation.

The direct method of consolidation is used throughout the book. We use a unique step-by-step approach, the **MEAR steps to consolidation**, that we first introduced in the previous edition. This approach takes the student through a logical progression of steps that will work in all consolidation situations. The MEAR steps divide the consolidation process into self-contained parts, allowing students to approach the process of consolidation in an organized and structured manner. Thus, these steps allow students to focus on a specific task, such as the calculation of the amortization of fair value increments in later years, retained earnings, net income of the subsidiary, or non-controlling interest. These self-contained sections replicate the types of problems that students will often encounter on professional exams. We believe that students will find the *MEAR steps to consolidation* easy to follow and apply.

We believe that focusing on the direct method for illustrations within the text chapters is another feature that makes the difficult consolidation material manageable and easy to understand. However, the worksheet-method solutions for the chapter illustrations are now presented in the Companion Website for those students and instructors who prefer this method.

We have also incorporated new graphic exhibits in the consolidation chapters to complement and highlight the discussion in these chapters in a visually appealing manner. Further, the *Reality Check* boxes in each of the consolidation chapters have been carefully chosen to highlight the most recent examples from practice of how the material is implemented in real life as well as findings from current research on related topics.

**Chapter 7** steps back from the process of consolidation to look at its opposite—disaggregation. The chapter explains the issues involved in disaggregating consolidated reporting both for shorter periods and for separate business lines of a consolidated enterprise—interim and segmented reporting. The existing problem material in this chapter has been refreshed and several new problems have been added.

**Chapters 8 and 9** deal with the second most important topic in the book—the impact of foreign currency transactions and investments. We have updated our discussions to include the most recent IFRS standards that became effective in 2013.

Chapter 8 introduces the topic of hedging and the accounting for hedges generally. The specific topic of hedge accounting focuses on anticipated transactions. Fair value and cash flow hedges are reviewed and examples provided. Two methods of recording hedges (the gross method and the net method) are illustrated for all examples involving hedges in the chapter. In Chapter 9, the translation of foreign operations is examined using the IFRS functional currency concept.

Both Chapters 8 and 9 conclude with a discussion of Canadian accounting standards for private enterprise. Most of the problem material in these two chapters is either new or revised.

**Chapter 10** presents the latest developments and financial accounting standards for not-for-profit (NFP) organizations. The nature and characteristics of NFPs in Canada are introduced early in the chapter and used to provide additional insights in subsequent discussions of the accounting issues faced by NFPs. The basics of fund accounting and encumbrance accounting are also introduced in the chapter. In addition, the online Appendix 10A, "Fund Accounting," has been substantially lengthened to provide a fuller explanation of how fund accounting works. New material is introduced on recording encumbrances and budgetary accounts. In the appendix, we include a comprehensive problem illustrating the use of the restricted fund method.

**Chapter 11** discusses financial reporting for governments. Governmental reporting is very different from accounting for NFPs, and yet this is the only major advanced accounting text to clearly make this distinction and to provide a separate chapter on public sector accounting. Information on the nature and characteristics of governments is introduced early in the chapter and used to inform subsequent discussions. The types of government organizations and the major public sector accounting issues are discussed. The new *statement of remeasurement gains and losses* is also introduced. The chapter concludes with a presentation and discussion of a comprehensive example of government financial statements.

## Student Supplements

## Companion Website—www.pearsoned.ca/beechy

The book's Companion Website offers a considerable amount of additional assistance to students:

- **Excel® templates** for some problems.
- **Worksheet solutions** to supplement the direct method for all in-text consolidation examples.
- **Additional self-study problems,** with solutions.
- **Practice quizzes** for self-testing.
- **Appendices** of additional material on tangential issues that relate to some chapters.
- **IFRS Updates** as needed as the IASB reconsiders old standards and issues new ones.

**CourseSmart (ISBN: 978-0-13-313504-6).** CourseSmart goes beyond traditional expectations—providing instant, online access to the textbooks and course materials at a lower cost for students (average savings of 60%). With instant access from any computer and the ability to search the text, students will find the content they need quickly, no matter where they are. And with online tools like highlighting and note-taking, students can save time and study efficiently.

Instructors can save time and hassle with a digital eTextbook that allows them to search for the most relevant content at the very moment they need it. Whether it's about evaluating textbooks or creating lecture notes to help students with difficult concepts, CourseSmart can make life a little easier. See all the benefits at **www.coursesmart.com/instructors** or **www.coursesmart.com/students**.

## Instructor Supplements

**Instructor's Solutions Manual (ISBN: 978-0-13-313506-0).** This supplement contains an overview of each chapter's main concepts and assignment material, as well as solutions for all review questions, cases (including detailed case notes), and problems. The Instructor's Resource Manual with Solutions is available to download from Pearson Education Canada's online catalogue at **http://catalogue.pearsoned.ca**.

**Test Item File and TestGen Test Bank (TIF ISBN: 978-0-13-313508-4; TG ISBN: 978-0-13-313502-2).** An expanded and improved set of multiple choice and short answer test questions is available to instructors as a Test Item File in Microsoft® Word and as a computerized test bank in Pearson Education Canada's TestGen software. TestGen allows instructors to custom design, generate, edit, and save classroom tests. It provides many options for organizing and displaying tests, along with search and sort features. The Test Item File and TestGen test bank are available to download from Pearson Education Canada's online catalogue at **http://catalogue.pearsoned.ca**.

**PowerPoint® Presentations (ISBN: 978-0-13-313507-7).** Extensively revised for the seventh edition, these slides highlight all of the important concepts in the text. The PowerPoint Presentations are available to download from Pearson Education Canada's online catalogue at **http://catalogue.pearsoned.ca** and on the Instructor's Resource CD-ROM.

**Technology Specialists.** Pearson's Technology Specialists work with faculty and campus course designers to ensure that Pearson technology products, assessment tools, and online course materials are tailored to meet your specific needs. This highly qualified team is dedicated to helping schools take full advantage of a wide range of educational resources, by assisting in the integration of a variety of instructional materials and media formats. Your local Pearson Education sales representative can provide you with more details on this service program.

# Acknowledgments

As in the previous editions, much of the assignment material was drawn from the professional examination of Canada's three professional accounting bodies: CGA Canada, CICA, and SMA Canada. A few cases have also been included by the kind permission of the Institute of Chartered Accountants of Ontario. We are deeply indebted to all of these organizations for their cooperation and support in permitting us to use their copyrighted material. An acknowledgment appears at the end of each case or problem that was obtained from one of these four professional sources.

We are deeply indebted to the individuals who reviewed and provided valuable suggestions on the revision plan and the manuscript, including:

Pierre Hilal, Concordia University
Nathalie Johnstone, University of Saskatchewan
Jaime A. Morales, Trent University
Robert Maher, University of New Brunswick
Ann-Marie Cederholm, Capilano University
Eckhard Schuman, University of Toronto, Mississauga
Nicola M. Young, Saint Mary's University
Dr. Leslie Blyth, Grant MacEwan University
Betty Wong, Athabasca University
Keri Norrie, Camosun College

We are also grateful for the enthusiastic support and encouragement of the people at Pearson Canada. In particular, we would like to thank Nicole Lukach, Editor-in-Chief, Business and Economics; Megan Farrell, Acquisitions Editor; Kathleen McGill, Sponsoring Editor; Patti Sayle, Developmental Editor; Jessica Hellen, Project Manager; Claire Varley, Marketing Manager; Heather Sangster, Copy Editor; Sally Glover, Proofreader; and the team at GEX Publishing Services.

On a more personal note, we would like to thank our friends and families for their support and encouragement throughout the lengthy process of bringing this new edition to fruition.

## Corrections

Despite the efforts of many people and reviews by many sets of eyes, errors have a nasty way of creeping into all books. Of course, we authors bear the responsibility for any errors that you may come across. We would greatly appreciate your bringing any and all errors to our attention, no matter how minor. We will place these corrections in the online *errata* section of the Companion Website as they come to our attention. Your corrections will also enable us to eliminate those errors prior to the next printing of the book, thereby making life a little easier for future students and instructors.

Please report errors by email to tbeechy@schulich.yorku.ca, strivedi@schulich.yorku.ca, or kmacaula@stfx.ca.

Thank you for using *Advanced Financial Accounting*, Seventh Edition. We hope you will find it an enjoyable book from which to learn these complex topics.

## A Great Way to Learn and Instruct Online

The Pearson Canada Companion Website is easy to navigate and is organized to correspond to the chapters in this textbook. Whether you are a student in the class room or a   distance learner you will discover helpful resources for in-depth study and research that empower you in your quest for greater knowledge and maximize your potential for success in the course.

# www.pearsoned.ca/beechy

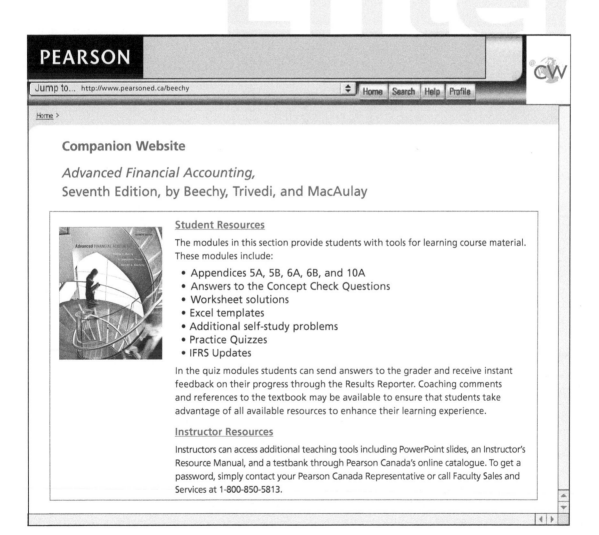

# Chapter 1
## Setting the Stage

## Learning Objectives

**After studying this chapter, you should be able to:**

LO ❶ identify the four different types of reporting entities and the distinguishing characteristics of each;

LO ❷ explain the origin and location of the different sets of accounting standards that apply to different types of organizations; and

LO ❸ identify the obstacles to international comparability under International Financial Reporting Standards.

## 1.1 WHAT IS ADVANCED ACCOUNTING?

**LO ❶**
Identify the four different types of reporting entities and the distinguishing characteristics of each

In previous accounting courses, you've learned how to apply most financial accounting reporting standards as they apply to profit-oriented enterprises, both public and private. However, there are a few complex topics that your earlier financial accounting courses touched upon very lightly, if at all. The purpose of *Advanced Financial Accounting* is to fill those knowledge gaps.

*Advanced Financial Accounting* is the detailed study of three major topics:

- accounting for business combinations and preparing consolidated financial statements;
- accounting for foreign currency transactions and foreign operations; and
- financial reporting by non-business organizations—not-for-profit organizations and governments.

In this introduction, we first will briefly introduce each of these topics. Then we will take a broader look at the full range of financial accounting standards in Canada.

### Consolidations

Almost certainly, every financial statement that you have ever seen is a *consolidated* statement. We're sure you've noticed the word "consolidated" in each statement title, such as *Consolidated Statement of Comprehensive Income*, and you undoubtedly have a general idea what it means: *consolidated statements include the assets, liabilities, revenues, expenses, and cash flows for the parent company plus all of its subsidiaries*. It may seem excessive to devote half (or more) of a course to this simple concept. However, that simple concept disguises the complexities that underlie consolidated statements.

Consolidated statements do not report on a "real" corporation. Instead, they report on all of the assets theoretically under control, directly or indirectly, by the shareholders of the parent company. The fictional entity portrayed in consolidated statements does not exist as an identifiable legal entity. Thus, consolidated statements are sometimes referred to as an *accounting fiction*. By this we don't mean that consolidated statements aren't useful, but simply that they are an abstract construction. As such, they must be used with caution.

Any professional accountant or qualified financial analyst should understand how consolidated statements are prepared. Many accounting estimates and assumptions are necessary to prepare financial statements for a "consolidated" entity that, legally, does not even exist! Although consolidated statements are an accounting fiction, every professional accountant must clearly understand why and how they are created. An accountant must also be able to explain the limitations of consolidated statements to potential users.

The process of consolidation can lead to a plethora of "What if?" questions. In this book, we try to resist pursuing obscure and/or improbable scenarios. Just as in other areas of financial accounting, it is not possible (or wise) to get into great detail. We all need to know the basic approaches and complexities of business combinations and consolidations, but we don't need to be experts at every detail, any more than we need to be experts at every possible facet of revenue recognition or pension accounting. In *Advanced Financial Accounting*, we will give you an overview, not an exhaustive reference book.

## International Operations

We all are aware that the scope of business is increasingly international. Even relatively small companies are affected by international trade, even if it's only by purchasing inventory or raw materials from foreign suppliers in a foreign currency. Most large companies have substantial operations in one or more foreign countries. For example, Montreal-based Bombardier had 2011 revenue of about $18 billion, but less than 6% of that revenue was from its Canadian operations. Bombardier does business around the world and operates factories in Germany, the United Kingdom, the United States, China, France, Spain, and many other countries.

How can Bombardier combine transactions and consolidate subsidiaries operating in US dollars, Canadian dollars, euros, British pounds sterling, and Chinese renminbi? Not only are Bombardier's many "offshore" companies operating in host countries with different currencies, but each subsidiary also is operating internationally itself. The impacts of foreign operations show up in many ways in consolidated financial statements, some of which represent genuine risk exposure and some of which are just the mechanical results of the consolidation process. You need to know the difference.

## Non-Business Organizations

What happens when a corporation or organization is not driven by the profit motive? When profit ceases to be the motivation for an organization's existence, neither its operations nor its financial statements are driven by "bottom line" thinking. Not-for-profit

(NFP) organizations and governments are substantial segments of the world's economic activity, contributing 20–30% of employment in most countries. An accountant's or financial analyst's knowledge is not complete until he or she understands the very significant differences between profit-oriented enterprises and non-business organizations.

It is likely that your accounting education so far has focused exclusively on business enterprises. All business enterprises have similar accounting and reporting needs and can use a common private-enterprise accounting framework. Businesses comprise most of the world's economic activity. In contrast, NFPs and governments operate in many different ways and are engaged a wide variety of activities that have no parallel in business.

An oft-heard comment is that "governments and NFPs should be run like a business." The difficulty with trying to run an NFP or government like a business is that they are *not* businesses. Business enterprises have identifiable products or services that are sold or delivered to specific, identifiable customers or clients. There is nothing so specific about NFPs or governments. Certainly, there are "products," such as cancer research and road repair, but there is no identifiable "customer" to whom these products are sold. Nor do the "customers" normally pay for the product, at least not directly. Thus, the essential cost–revenue link that underlies all business activity does not exist in NFPs or governments.

While it is true that some segments of NFP and government activity *are* like businesses, such as a museum gift shop or a city electrical utility, these activities are a minor part of both NFPs and governments. Those business-type enterprises can and should be accounted for as a business because they have the essential cost–revenue relationship.

Therefore the final two chapters discuss the nature of accounting for *non-business activities* of NFPs (Chapter 10) and governments (Chapter 11). Many accounting graduates will find themselves involved in non-business organizations as professional accountants, as advisors, as board members, or simply as educated citizens who should be fully aware of NFP and government accounting issues.

## Concept Check 1-1

1. Why might we refer to consolidated statements as *fictional* statements?
2. Why does an international corporation have greater accounting challenges than does a company operating in only one country?
3. Why is it a mistake to claim that a not-for-profit organization should be "run like a business"?

# 1.2 A NEW WORLD ORDER IN ACCOUNTING

The year 2011 was a pivotal year in accounting history. For the first time, most industrialized and developing countries began using International Financial Reporting Standards (IFRS). Nations (mostly in Europe) have been using IFRS for several years, but more joined the user group in 2011, including Canada.

This commonality sounds wonderfully simple and consistent. As we will discuss a little later, however, international accounting standards do not necessarily provide the consistency and comparability that we might assume they do.

As well, despite the appearance of widespread commonality among nations, IFRS may have quite limited application in many countries:

- IFRS usually is required only for preparing *consolidated* financial statements; a nation's laws may require parent corporations to issue their own separate-entity *non*-consolidated statements using that nation's legislated reporting framework.

- IFRS usually applies only to *publicly accountable* companies—primarily companies with debt or equity securities traded on public markets; private companies usually have a different reporting regime even though large private companies are competing for capital in the private capital markets.

- IFRS seldom is applied to not-for-profit organizations, although large-scale organizations may choose to use IFRS if it best satisfies the needs of that organization's financial statement users.

**LO ❷**

Explain the origin and location of the different sets of accounting standards that apply to different types of organizations

Indeed, Canada is one of the many nations that require IFRS only for certain companies, not for all. In the next section, we will review the current situation in Canada and the post-2011 role of the CICA's Accounting Standards Board.

## 1.3 ACCOUNTING STANDARDS IN CANADA

Prior to the adoption of IFRS, the *CICA Handbook* contained the accounting standards for all Canadian companies, public and private, as well as for not-for-profit organizations. Those standards of the Canadian Institute of Chartered Accountants (CICA) were generally applicable to all Canadian corporations because the national and provincial corporations acts require auditors to report in accordance with Generally Accepted Accounting Principles (GAAP), and GAAP was defined as compliance with the *CICA Handbook*.

For a long time, the CICA's Accounting Standards Board (AcSB) developed its own standards, although always with an eye on what other countries were doing, particularly the United States. For a while in the late twentieth century, the AcSB's official policy was to harmonize with the US standards. Keeping step with the USA's Financial Accounting Standards Board (FASB) was intended to make life much easier for the tiny proportion of Canadian companies that had to report to the US Securities and Exchange Commission (SEC) because their securities are traded in the USA. Those companies would then not have to reconcile their Canada-based statements with US standards.

Eventually, the AcSB realized that constantly adjusting Canadian standards to meet ever-changing US standards was a rather futile endeavour. Also, a series of huge US corporate accounting scandals (e.g., Enron, WorldCom) caused people around the world to realize that perhaps US standards weren't as "high quality" as had always been proclaimed. Simultaneously, the idea of worldwide acceptance of IFRS for multinational stock exchange listings began to take shape.

Consequently, the AcSB decided that Canada should also adopt IFRS. In a world increasingly characterized by international commerce, separate Canadian standards began to look like an anachronism. The year 2011 was chosen for full conversion to IFRS for Canadian publicly accountable enterprises, partially because several other countries had promised to convert in that same year.

Does that mean Canada is out of the standard-setting business? No. It does mean that Canada has fully adopted IFRS for publicly accountable enterprises; but public companies and other publicly accountable enterprises constitute a very small proportion of

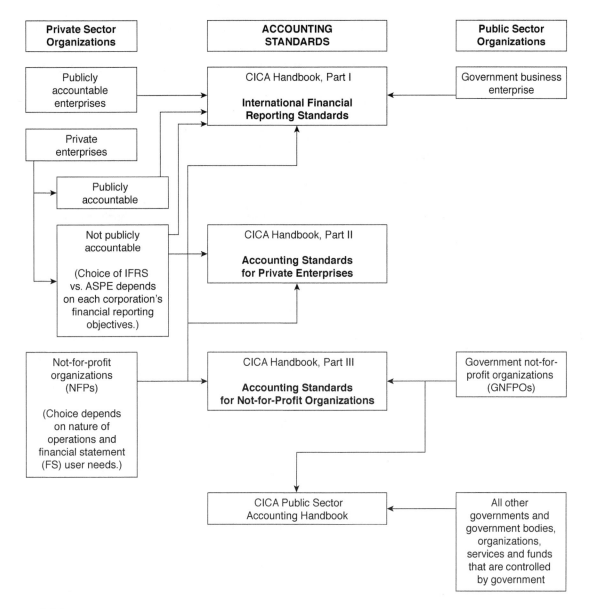

**Exhibit 1.1** Overview of Canadian Accounting Standards

Canadian corporations. Therefore, the CICA has a four-pronged approach to accounting standards:

1. Public and publicly accountable enterprises (e.g., fiduciary organizations such as investment funds and private banks) will follow IFRS for their consolidated, general-purpose, publicly issued financial statements. The standards for publicly accountable enterprises are included in the *CICA Handbook, Part I*. The standards in Part I are exactly the same, word for word, as the International Accounting Standards Board (IASB) standards. They are included in the *CICA Handbook* only to satisfy certain legal reporting requirements that are contained in the various corporations acts and securities acts of the federal and provincial governments.

2. Canadian accounting standards for private enterprise are contained in the *CICA Handbook, Part II*.

3. NFP accounting standards are contained in the *CICA Handbook, Part III*, as previously was the case, with special sections devoted to the unique reporting requirements and issues of NFPs.

4. The Public Sector Accounting Board (PSAB) will continue to make recommendations for both senior (i.e., national, provincial, and territorial) and municipal governments, which are published by the CICA in the *Public Sector Accounting Handbook*.

The relationships between organizational types and Canadian accounting standards are diagrammed in Exhibit 1.1.

The clearest relationship is for publicly listed corporations and publicly accountable private enterprises. They must report on the basis of IFRS; there is no option.

Private enterprises that are not publicly accountable have a choice. They can use either IFRS or Accounting Standards for Private Enterprises (ASPE). The choice will be based on the company's reporting objectives, which in turn are based on who are the most important users of the company's financial statements.

For example, if the company is competing for capital with publicly listed companies (e.g., through the private equity or debt markets), it makes sense to use the same reporting framework as its competition in the capital markets, that is, IFRS. Similarly, if a private enterprise's management is contemplating becoming a public company (via an initial public offering [IPO]) sometime in the future, the company should use IFRS so that the necessary financial reporting information is readily available.

Alternatively, if the company has little or no need for external capital, or if it is dealing with sophisticated Canadian institutional investors such as Canadian banks and pension funds, the simpler ASPE will usually be the preferred choice.

Not-for-profit organizations (NFP) have the choice of reporting under either (1) IFRS, (2) ASPE, or (3) the not-for-profit accounting standards in the *CICA Handbook, Part III*. As you will see in Chapter 10, there are also accounting choices to be made within the frame-work contained in Part III of the *CICA Handbook*, particularly between two basic reporting approaches: (1) the deferred revenue approach and (2) the restricted fund approach. The choice depends on the nature of the NFP's operations, the source of its funding, and the organization's reporting objectives.

Canadian governmental reporting standards are developed by the Public Sector Accounting Board. Unlike the CICA, the PSAB has no ability to impose its accounting and reporting recommendations on governments or governmental organizations. The PSAB standards are recommendations, rather than rules. Only the governmental legislatures can impose standards. However, the PSAB works closely with provincial Auditors General and ministers of finance in formulating the standards. Governmental reporting is discussed in Chapter 11.

An interesting aspect of government accounting is that different parts of a government may use different standards depending on their function. Some government enterprises function as a business, such as innovation centres or major public utilities, and such organizations should apply IFRS, since they are competing with profit-oriented business enterprises.

On the other hand, some units of the government are functioning as NFP organizations, in which case they may follow not-for-profit standards instead of PSAB standards.

All other components of government, including the general operations for the citizenry, should use the PSAB recommendations.

Over the next 11 chapters, this book will explain and illustrate the four threads of Canadian financial reporting.

## 1.4 THE ROLE OF REPORTING OBJECTIVES

Each reporting organization chooses its accounting and reporting policies by considering the often-conflicting needs of the statement users on the one hand, and the motivations of the preparers on the other. *Users* include shareholders, bankers, employees, creditors, Canada Revenue Agency, and regulatory agencies. The *preparers* are the managers, both senior managers and the accountants. The auditors are not the preparers—they audit what management has done. Auditors can and should challenge management to defend its accounting choices, and they can make recommendations. Nevertheless, it's the responsibility of managers to set accounting policy.[1]

In most of the topics covered in this book, there really is little or no choice available in accounting policy, except for a private enterprise's choice between IFRS and ASPE. Even then, the choice has little impact on business combinations, consolidations, foreign currency translation, and foreign operations. IFRS and ASPE are largely the same in these major areas.

Although the choice of *accounting policies* is highly constrained, a major area of discretion and judgment is in the many *accounting estimates* that management must make, especially when it involves business combinations, either domestic or foreign. As you will see in the coming chapters, fair values often must be "determined." But how is that determination made?

For example, when one corporation buys another, the initial measurement of the purchase price can have a substantial long-term effect on the consolidated earnings as amortization, depreciation, and successive-years' "fair values" are determined. Accounting policy choice may be limited by accounting standards, but measurement methods often are very imprecise and can be manipulated to suit the preparers' objectives and motivations.

As you learn about business combinations and consolidations in the following chapters, try to keep the role of estimates firmly in mind. Remember that they are always just that—estimates—and estimates are derived from expectations about future events. Think about the impact of different measurements and allocations on the financial statements, and thus on users' perceptions of the consolidated entity's financial health and prospects.

### Concept Check 1-2

1. What standard-setting approaches are used in Canada? What are the four "threads" of Canadian financial reporting?

2. When might a private enterprise choose to use IFRS instead of ASPE?

3. Can accounting standards completely eliminate the need for management judgment in accounting measurements? Explain.

---

[1] A discussion of both users' and preparers' reporting objectives is included in the Companion Website for this book. Refer to it if you feel the need for a review, or if you have not previously been exposed to reporting objectives.

# 1.5 INTERNATIONAL STANDARDS—AN ILLUSION OF COMPARABILITY

The driving force behind adopting international standards has been the *international financial markets*—to enable companies to list their securities on multiple exchanges around the world. The underlying logic is that if every country adopts international accounting standards, it will be easy to compare the financial results of companies based in different countries.

That logic is attractive. If we all use the same reporting standards, the barriers of diverse national standards will fall. And that logic is correct to a certain extent—and comparability is certainly much better with IFRS. However, interpretation of financial statements under international standards will still be difficult. To some extent, comparability is an illusion. A financial statement user must be aware of many factors in a corporation's host country that will affect the company's financial reporting. In the following sections, we will briefly discuss the following four limiting factors:

1. Some jurisdictions may accept IFRS, but not *all* of IFRS. Although IFRS is used in about 100 countries around the world, they are not applied to the same extent in every country.

2. The quality of the accounting infrastructure varies among nations. The quality of the accounting infrastructure is defined by the quality of the accounting and auditing profession in that country, as well as by the effectiveness of the country's financial reporting enforcement mechanisms.

3. National factors can have a significant effect on proper interpretation of financial statements. Even when the full IFRS are formally adopted by a nation, some standards will inevitably be applied differently in different nations due to local circumstances.

4. IFRS usually apply only to public corporations—those that come under the jurisdiction of national securities regulators. Public companies compete with large private companies for financing in the private debt and equity markets, but the two types of companies most likely will be using different reporting standards.

When each nation used home-grown financial standards, users were automatically forewarned that the statements were not directly comparable. Statements from other countries looked different, used different terminology, and were arranged differently. And some statements were "missing"—for example, a cash flow statement was not generally required outside of Anglo-Saxon countries such as the United States, United Kingdom, Canada, and Australia. The new hazard is that, with international standards, users will be misled into thinking that inter-nation comparison is simple.

Although we will discuss all four limiting factors, we will place primary emphasis on the fourth factor because the vast majority of corporations in Canada are private, not public.

## Uneven Adoption of IFRS

There are two basic ways in which national accounting standards are established:

1. By law or government regulation. Examples include most European countries, the EU, and China. These are known as *code-law* countries.

2. By the country's accounting profession or an independent non-government authority established within that country. Examples include the USA, UK, Canada, and Japan. These are known as *common-law* countries.

Under either approach, a nation may not adopt IFRS completely.

- In code-law countries, a change to international standards requires legislation. When the IASB changes or amends international standards, a code-law country must pass new legislation before the change can become effective. New legislation may be slow in coming or may not be proposed at all for some individual aspects of IFRS.

- In common-law countries, legislation is not required, but the local standard-setter may balk at one or more aspects of an international standard and refuse to put that standard into effect.

When acceptance of IFRS is incomplete, we really don't have truly international standards. Instead we have something a little different. For example, in the European Union, companies are required to report their consolidated financial statements on the basis of IFRS, but only after each new or revised standard is accepted by the EU Parliament. Not all provisions of every IFRS are accepted. Thus, a company following IFRS as accepted in the EU will be using accounting standards that are not the same as those being used in common-law countries such as Canada or Australia. Reality check 1-1 gives an example of a company that uses IFRS as adopted by the EU.

## Institutional Quality

To apply international standards effectively, a nation must have:

- professional and experienced preparers;
- quality auditing; and
- an effective enforcement mechanism.

### Reality Check 1–1

## Example of a Company Using EU IFRS

The 2011 annual report of the large mining group Rio Tinto discloses that the consolidated statements are prepared "in accordance with International Financial Reporting Standards (IFRS) as adopted by the European Union ("EU IFRS")."

Note 1 of the Rio Tinto financial statements lists the standards in which the EU IFRS differs in some respects from IASB IFRS:

- IAS 1 (amendment), "Presentation of financial statements"
- IAS 27 (revised), "Consolidated and separate financial statements"

- IAS 38 (amendment), "Intangible assets"
- IFRS 3 (amendment), "Business combinations"
- IFRS 5 (amendment), "Non-current assets held for sale and discontinued operations"
- Eligible Hedged Items (an amendment to IAS 39 Financial Instruments: Recognition and Measurement)
- IFRIC 17 Non cash distributions to owners
- IFRS 2 amendment, "Share-based payment"—Group cash-settled share-based payment transactions
- Improvements to IFRS 2009

As well, corporate senior managers must be honest and ethical, and not attempt to hide issues from the auditors (or internal auditors). If any one of these factors is missing, the financial statements may not be a fair and true indicator of the financial health of the company.

**Preparer Professionalism**  To apply complex international standards, preparers (i.e., internal accounting staff) must possess a high level of professional judgment. Preparers need to make many judgments concerning such issues as asset lives, residual values, fair values, impairments, account collectability, inventory obsolescence, and so forth. Professional judgment requires training and the internalization of judgmental criteria (e.g., reliability, verifiability, relevance); otherwise, there is no difference between *professional* judgment and *amateur* judgment.

In developing countries, professionally trained accountants often are in short supply. As a result, accounting estimates become inconsistent and/or arbitrary; international comparisons therefore may not be valid.

**Audit Quality**  Audits are not of consistently high quality around the world. It is easy to think of the "Big Four" auditing firms extending their knowledgeable and ethical arms around the world, but a majority of audits are not carried out by the Big Four. In any case, those large firms are not international partnerships; each one is an association of affiliated national partnerships, and not all of the national offices are equally strong.

For example, one of the Big Four firms was very embarrassed when its Italian affiliate failed to detect a massive fraud taking place in an Italy-based international dairy company, Parmalat SpA—the auditor didn't even discover the simple fact that a supposed $4 billion dollar bank account did not exist! Not surprisingly, the Big Four firm quickly disassociated itself from that Italian auditing affiliate.

A sophisticated auditing profession does not exist in many small countries. Even if well-trained auditors are imported from other countries to add expertise, those imported auditors may not understand the local environment and ways of doing business, which is fundamental to performing a good audit.

---

### Reality Check 1–2

## Importance of the Accounting Infrastructure

Some Chinese public companies prepare two sets of financial statements, for reporting to two different shareholder groups. An empirical study into financial reporting in China during the 1990s found large differences in reported net income *for the same company in the same year* depending on whether the audit was by (1) a local audit firm reporting to government and local investors, or (2) an international audit firm reporting to foreign investors. The researchers concluded that the disparity was due to the lack of "an effective financial-reporting infrastructure, including preparer professionalism, quality auditing, and effective enforcement. Developing countries often lack such infrastructure to make accounting standards work as originally intended."

Source: S. Chen, Z. Sun, and Y. Wang, "Evidence from China on Whether Harmonized Accounting Standards Harmonize Accounting Practices." *Accounting Horizons* 16:3 (September 2002) p. 193.

**Effective Enforcement**   What good are accounting standards if there is no one to enforce them? A nation must have a body that is responsible for reviewing and, if necessary, challenging a corporation's reported financial results.

Enforcement can be the responsibility of (1) an independent or semi-independent agency, usually in the form of a securities commission that supervises the securities exchanges in that country, or (2) a government department, such as a Ministry of Finance.

As examples, (1) in the US, the Securities and Exchange Commission is the enforcement agency for accounting standards for companies listed on US stock exchanges, while (2) Canadian enforcement has largely been carried out by the Ontario Securities Commission (OSC).

The effectiveness of an enforcement body is limited by two important factors:

- (1) the relative size of the budget that it has or is given to carry out its enforcement mandate.

- (2) its ability to enforce reporting standards of *all* companies that come under its jurisdiction.

For example, the SEC is effective if the US Congress appropriates a large enough budget to monitor all of the companies listed on the US stock exchanges and to launch effective investigations. The SEC can be weakened by inadequate financing, as happened in much of the latter part of the twentieth century prior to the major accounting scandals of Enron and WorldCom, among others. Inadequate financing is also alleged to have been the reason that a decade of SEC investigations of Bernard Madoff failed to reveal that he was running a giant pyramid (known as a Ponzi scheme) that bilked investors of an estimated US$48 *billion*.

Effective enforcement is likely only when a company is listed in the country of its operations. If a Tokyo-based company is listed on the Toronto Stock Exchange (TSX) but not in Japan and there is some question about its reporting, the primary enforcer must be in Japan because only an agency in the company's home country has the ability to subpoena documents and individuals.

## Reality Check 1–3

## Investigating an Overseas Corporation

In mid-2011, Muddy Waters LLC issued a report alleging that a TSX-listed company, Sino-Forest Corporation, was engaged in fraudulent reporting. Sino-Forest is a Chinese company; all of its operations and management are in China. The company is not listed in its home country (including Hong Kong), thereby leaving the OSC as the only possible enforcement agency. After Muddy Waters issued its report, the OSC (and, later, the Royal Canadian Mounted Police) launched an investigation. Although these Canadian investigations are underway, it is not possible for either the OSC or the RCMP to obtain any documents or to subpoena individuals in China unless they gain the cooperation of the Chinese authorities. Thus, the TSX is relatively ineffective agency in enforcing Chinese reporting or auditing standards; the OSC's only recourse is to suspend trading (which they did) and delist the company if the allegations turn out to be correct.

Since the true power of enforcement lay only in a public company's home country, one might venture the opinion that an investment in any company that is listed abroad *only*, and not in its home country, carries a higher risk level than may otherwise be apparent.

Regulators of other exchanges don't have the legal authority to investigate a company that is based in another jurisdiction. For example, the OSC does not have the right to investigate a company based in Russia, even if it is listed on the TSX; the OSC cannot subpoena documents and statements from outside Canada. Thus, reliable international accounting requires effective enforcement in all nations that have public companies.

## International Comparisons Made Simple—or Are They?

The primary driving force for adopting international standards was the internationalization of the securities markets. If companies use a common set of accounting standards, securities exchanges can solicit listings from companies anywhere in the world and not be restricted to listings only from domestic companies using local GAAP. International companies such as German auto giant Daimler AG could (and did) list its shares on dozens of exchanges around the world without using different accounting standards in each country. Thus, if German, American, Japanese, and Korean auto companies all use international standards, it theoretically should be possible to compare the financial statements of those companies without learning the accounting peculiarities of each nation.

However, it is not quite so simple. A common international set of accounting standards does achieve a surface similarity. Companies from all nations will have similar-looking financial statements, statement components, disclosures, and measurement methods. The invisible differences lie in the underlying economic, political, legal, and environmental differences between countries, as well as simply the ways of doing business.

**Legal Factors**   In many countries (e.g., Italy and France), taxable income must be the same as accounting net income. In other countries (e.g., Canada and the United States), taxable income can be different (in limited ways) from accounting income. When tax–book conformity is required, managers have strong motivation to use accounting options that reduce earnings. This can be accomplished via the range of accruals and estimates that are inherent in accounting and that you studied in intermediate accounting.

If an Italian company is following a tax-minimization reporting strategy while a competing UK company is using an income-maximization reporting strategy, it will impair a user who is trying to assess the relative performance of the two companies—even though both would be using IFRS.

Another entirely different type of legal factor may arise from religious considerations. Some countries require application of Islamic principles in business. Islamic principles forbid interest. Banks that follow Islamic principles earn their return by taking an equity stake instead of charging interest. The equity stake is designed to achieve essentially the same return as would interest, but without violating Islamic principles. The bank receives payment in the form of dividends or profit-sharing; no interest expense will appear on the books of the "borrower." Under such a system a calculation of "times interest earned" or similar ratios will be meaningless.

**Ways of Doing Business**   In Germany, employees and bankers play a major role in corporate management. Both have representatives on the board of supervisors (that is, directors). There are significant financial reporting implications. One major difference is in the way high debt is viewed. In North America, a high debt load is normally viewed as a bad indicator while a conservative no-debt structure indicates a safer company. In Germany, however, the presence of high debt and bank representation on the board indicates that the banks are supporting the company. In contrast, the absence of debt in a company's capital structure often indicates that the banks have no faith in that company—a very bad indicator.

Japan offers another example. In North America, publicly issued financial statements must be consolidated statements. Until recently, Japan did not issue consolidated statements. Now that Japan does require consolidated statements, it should be possible to see the resources under control of those huge corporate groups (such as Mitsubishi). Good step forward for comparability, right? Wrong!

Japanese corporate structure is very different from that in Western countries. Conglomerates in the United States, Canada, and Europe operate through a parent company and a multitude of controlled subsidiaries. In contrast, a Japanese conglomerate of hundreds of companies has no parent company. Instead, each company in the group owns a tiny percentage of the other companies in the group, no more than 2 or 3%. A majority of the shares of any one company is owned within the group through these multiple intercompany holdings, thereby rendering hostile takeovers impossible. But since there is no pyramid of companies with a parent company at the top, Japanese consolidated statements don't include the assets and liabilities of other companies in the group—they include only a miscellany of controlled subsidiaries, usually those in foreign countries.

**Economic and Political Factors**   When we compare the financial statements of Canadian companies we can be assured that the economic and political environment affects all companies more or less equally. When we compare across borders, that consistency may disappear. Inflation and exchange rate fluctuations vary by country. Even a relatively small difference in inflation rates can have a long-term impact on prospective earnings of companies in different countries. The higher the inflation rate, the more likely that assets will be revalued. Also, high inflation leads companies away from holding monetary investments, but may increase reliance on monetary liabilities, especially if financed from a low-inflation country.

Another important economic and political factor is the extent of state control or regulation in a company's home country. State control and/or regulation always entails prescriptive accounting, either directly or indirectly. An example of indirect accounting influence is regulatory rate-of-return guidelines. Rate-of-return regulations always base the permitted level of operating earnings on a percentage of the asset base. A company that is subject to rate-of-return limitations will (1) capitalize as many costs as possible, thereby increasing the asset base, and (2) use high levels of debt financing to increase the residual rate of return to shareholders.

Japan provides an example of accounting choice based on avoiding legislative sanction. Large companies are subject to regulatory oversight for violations of the anti-monopoly law. Therefore, companies may try to "lie low" by adopting accounting policies and estimates that make them seem less dominant and profitable. A comparative study of major construction companies in Japan and the United States discovered that while US companies almost always used percentage-of-completion accounting, Japanese companies used the completed-contract method to delay revenue recognition unless they were weak companies and were trying to reassure investors and banks with higher assets and earnings.[2]

---

[2]Kazuyuki Suda, "International Accounting Standards and Japanese Corporate Accounting: An Empirical Research of Accounting for Construction Contracts." *Kansai University Review of Economics and Business* 23:1–2 (March 1995), pp. 95–123. Completed-contract accounting is not permitted under IFRS; Japan committed to IFRS compliance by 2011.

# Evidence on the Limits of International Comparability

Empirical studies of cross-country accounting comparisons have always found that using a common set of standards does not completely solve the comparability problem. For example:

■ An extensive international interview study of international investors concluded that investors who make the effort to understand the firms in a foreign country on their own terms, that is, familiarize themselves with local environmental norms and develop skills in interpreting foreign accounts in their original form, are least likely to encounter problems caused by accounting differences.[a]

■ Another comparison of "matched" Japanese and American companies discovered that a common GAAP (US, in this study) didn't solve the problem of comparison between countries:

■ Analysts are likely to perceive inaccurately that the financial statements of Japanese companies listing in the United States are directly comparable to those of US companies because they are both based on US GAAP. . . . [R]estated Japanese numbers are easily misinterpreted, as US investors may not fully understand the difference in environmental factors and business practices between the two countries.[b]

■ Japanese financial statements, restated according to US GAAP, are more comparable to the financial statements of Japanese companies, using Japanese GAAP, than to the financial statements of US companies.[c]

In other words, it is possible to create uniform accounting standards, but not uniform economic, political, legal, or business environments. Financial reporting is a function of its environment, not just of accounting standards.

a Frederick D. S. Choi and Richard M. Levich, *The Capital Market Effects of International Accounting Diversity* (1990: Dow Jones-Irwin), p. 82.

b Don Herrmann, Tatsuo Inuoe, and Wayne B. Bertrand, "Are There Benefits to Restating Japanese Financial Statements According to US GAAP?", *The Journal of Financial Statement Analysis* (Fall 1996), p. 7.

c *Ibid.*

## Private Companies in Different Countries

Private companies have a much smaller and more easily identifiable user group than do public companies. Public companies are reporting to the worldwide community of investors, investors who have no other direct access to information about the company. In contrast, a private company is reporting to a small user group, often only to its bankers. Both banks and private equity investors (if any) have the ability to demand additional information directly from a company if they are not satisfied with the annual financial statements. Since the user group is easily identified and has more specific information needs, there is no need for a private corporation to issue "general purpose" financial statements.

Therefore, nations generally exempt private companies from applying IFRS, or at least from applying the full set of IFRS. In practice, there are five different possible sets of GAAP that a private company might use, depending on its home country:

1. IFRS for small and medium enterprises (SMEs);

2. full IFRS, the same as for public companies;

3. a national GAAP for SMEs or private companies;

4. a code-law requirement to satisfy legal reporting requirements; or

5. a disclosed basis of accounting.

The first category is used by countries that have no well-established standard-setting mechanism, which includes most of the world's smaller nations. The IASB has developed a somewhat simplified version of "IFRS for SMEs" (sometimes nicknamed "IFRS-lite"). IFRS-SME is based on full IFRS, but has less complex reporting requirements.

The second approach, to use full IFRS, is never a *requirement* but may be an appropriate *choice* by large private companies that are competing with public companies for debt or equity financing in the private financial markets. A large private company may fear that its cost of capital will be higher if it reports on a basis different from competing public companies.

Canada falls into the third category—countries that develop their own standards for private enterprises. While these national reporting standards have many similarities to IFRS, they usually are simpler and may provide additional guidance to special industries (e.g., mining) that the IFRS doesn't cover well currently.[3]

The fourth approach, following a country's legally required accounting requirements, may apply to smaller companies that do not need external capital. This choice may also be used for individual companies within a consolidated group to meet local reporting requirements.

The fifth approach applies in countries (such as the United States) that have no mandated reporting requirements for private companies. In these countries many companies may choose not to use IFRS or IFRS-SME, but instead use the fifth option—a disclosed basis of accounting (DBA). If there is no imposed set of GAAP for private companies, they can use accounting policies that are "tailored" to their needs, also known as tailored accounting policies (TAP).

DBA doesn't imply that a company can throw out all of general body of GAAP, but only that it may choose to modify or ignore some aspects of GAAP, such as accounting for deferred income taxes or employee retirement benefits. Large private companies need to keep their bankers and private investors happy, so they may prefer to use accounting that best serves the users' needs, such by stressing the transparency of cash flows rather than complex allocations. They may also choose to maintain all accounts on a historical cost basis and ignore fair values.

The point is that when we compare a public company with a private company, the two companies may be using different accounting principles, thereby partially defeating the broader purpose of international standards.

## Concept Check 1-3

1. Explain briefly why the effective application of IFRS depends on the quality of professional accountants worldwide.

2. Why is *enforcement* a major factor affecting the credibility of financial statements prepared in different countries, even when all are prepared on the basis of IFRS?

3. The wide acceptance of IFRS around the world is intended to improve comparability between companies based in different countries. Explain briefly which national and institutional factors may affect the *real* comparability as opposed to the *apparent* comparability.

4. If a private company is not required to use IFRS by law or by the national standard-setter in its home country, why would that company voluntarily adopt IFRS as its reporting basis?

---

[3]For example, IFRS deals with agriculture quite extensively, since agriculture looms large in the European consciousness. However, IFRS doesn't deal with gold or diamond mining or oil sands development at all because there aren't a lot of those things going on in Europe.

## 1.6 A NOTE ON IRFS VS. ASPE PRESENTATION IN THIS BOOK

As you proceed through this book, the chapters pertaining to business enterprises (Chapters 2–9) will present both IFRS and ASPE. To avoid jumping back and forth, we base the main body of each chapter on IFRS. At the end of each chapter you will find a section describing how Canadian ASPE differs from IFRS. The differences are always to make the accounting simpler, never more complex. Once you've learned IFRS, you only have to remember those few aspects that don't apply to private companies in Canada. We believe that you will not be confused by the differences.

## 1.7 A SPECIAL NOTE ON FINANCIAL STATEMENT PRESENTATION

The IASB is considering changes in the format of financial statement presentation. If and when they are adopted, the new formats will change presentation, but they will not affect the process and procedures of consolidation. Therefore, in this book, we continue to use the traditional North American financial statement formats. Learning about consolidations can be difficult enough without also having to cope with a new reporting format.

You will notice that we use "statement of financial position" (SFP) throughout the text, in conformity with IFRS terminology. This is not compulsory. "Balance sheet" will continue to be a completely acceptable statement title, and probably will continue to be the most commonly used title in Canada. Indeed, ASPE uses "balance sheet" as its dominant terminology.

## 1.8 SUMMARY OF KEY POINTS

1. There are four types of accounting standards in Canada: those for (1) publicly accountable enterprises, (2) private companies, (3) not-for-profit organizations, and (4) governments. The first three are included in different parts of the *CICA Handbook*, while governmental reporting standards are issued by the Public Sector Accounting Board. **LO 1**

2. International Financial Reporting Standards (IFRS) are developed by the international Accounting Standards Board (IASB). IFRS is the required basis of accounting for Canada-based companies that have publicly traded securities, and also for private companies that have a fiduciary responsibility, such as investment companies. **LO 1**

3. The primary impetus for the development and acceptance of international standards was the emergence of international financial markets, and especially of stock exchanges competing for company listings. **LO 2**

4. IFRS is designed for publicly accountable companies—those that have publicly issued equity and/or debt securities, plus other companies that have a fiduciary responsibility by holding resources belonging to others, such as banks, trust companies, and mutual

funds. However, private companies may also use IFRS if they choose, or if their home country requires them to use IFRS or the version of IFRS that is designed specifically for private enterprises. **LO 2**

5. Financial statement quality depends on the quality of the accounting infrastructure in the home country of the reporting company—an adequate supply of trained accountants, quality auditing, and effective enforcement. IFRS increases the importance of a strong accounting infrastructure. **LO 3**

6. Despite the general worldwide acceptance of IFRS, it is very difficult to compare companies across national borders. Nations have significantly differing legal, economic, and political environments, and different ways of doing business. Common standards do not adjust for different reporting environments. **LO 3**

7. Standards for private companies are established by their home country. Some nations may use the small and medium enterprise (SME) standards being developed by the IASB, while others may use full IFRS. Some other nations may use their own national standards. The CICA's Accounting Standards Board has developed Canadian accounting standards for private enterprise (ASPE) on the basis of the pre-2011 CICA *Handbook*, modified somewhat to be more consistent with IFRS. ASPE is a somewhat simplified version of pre-existing standards, based largely on historical cost, and contains fewer required disclosures than IFRS. **LO 3**

**Visit the text's website at** www.pearsoned.ca/beechy **for practice quizzes, additional problems, Excel® templates, answers to Concept Check questions, and important IFRS updates.**

## Review Questions

1. International standards are intended to provide uniformity, and yet some countries may not adopt IFRS in their entirety. Explain why this may happen.

2. What are the four "threads" of Canadian accounting standards?

3. Who issues governmental financial reporting standards in Canada? Are all governments in Canada required to abide by these standards? Explain.

4. Comment on the following quotation: "Some accounting standards offer no flexibility in accounting policy choice; every company must follow the same accounting policies. Therefore, there is no room for judgment when applying those standards."

5. What are the three components of a nation's accounting infrastructure? How can these components affect the quality of financial reporting in that country?

6. You wish to compare the financial statements of three automobile manufacturers, one each in the United States, Germany, and Japan. All use IFRS. What national business environment factors may make comparison difficult? Give at least two examples.

7. In Canada, what reporting options are available to non-publicly accountable enterprises? When would each be used?

# 1.9 CASES

## CASE 1-1 CAPRICORN CARPET CORPORATION

Capricorn Carpet Corporation (CCC) is a private enterprise manufacturer of broadloom carpeting. The company's head office and manufacturing facilities are located in Winnipeg, Manitoba. The company was founded 26 years ago by three entrepreneurs. In the second decade of CCC's operations, the founders sought a substantial amount of additional capital to expand production. The capital was obtained via a private-equity transaction with the venture capital unit of Professional Pension Plan (PPP), a large Canadian pension plan. In return for its investment, PPP received new shares amounting to 60% of the total outstanding shares. The other 40% continued to be held by the original founders, who now are retired from the business.

CCC enjoys a good reputation for its product, but unfortunately has not been very profitable in recent years owing to increasing imports of cheaper carpeting. To combat this threat, in 20X1, CCC invested substantial sums of money in new state-of-the-art equipment to improve efficiency. Again, the money for the equipment was provided by the venture capital unit of PPP, but this time via a private placement of secured debentures; the security was a lien on all of CCC's tangible capital assets.

Efficiency did improve significantly after CCC acquired the new equipment. Nevertheless, CCC still confronted intense competition from Asian competitors who had less efficient equipment but lower labour costs. The competitive environment for CCC continued to decline, largely because most of CCC's output had been destined for real estate property developers in the USA. These developers had little need for large-scale commercial and industrial carpeting due to the weak US economy. As a result, the non-US world market became especially important to CCC.

In late 20X3, PPP decided that CCC was too small to continue to compete effectively in the non-US world market. Therefore, in 20X4, PPP sold its 60% interest to Unified Enterprises Ltd. (UEL), a publicly traded British carpet manufacturer. UEL planned to integrate CCC into its own operations, so that CCC would both (1) manufacture certain types of carpet sold through UEL's overseas distributors and (2) be the North American distributor of UEL's British-made carpets. CCC would, of course, continue to be a Canadian corporation, with its own board of directors.

As a Canadian private enterprise, CCC has followed the CICA's Accounting Standards for Private Enterprises. In contrast, UEL was required to use IFRS as adopted in the EU.

Two months after UEL purchased control over CCC, the UEL financial vice-president sent a letter to David Blasé, the controller of CCC, in which he detailed three changes in accounting policy that CCC should institute to make its reporting practices consistent with those of UEL, for purposes of consolidation and divisional performance appraisal. Included in the letter were the following:

1. CCC should change its accounting policy for land and buildings from the historical cost method to the revaluation method, wherein each type of asset is revalued periodically to its estimated fair value.[4] Feasible methods of determining the fair values would include:

   (1) periodic assessment by professional appraisers;

   (2) indexing by reference to other property (for land and buildings) or to price indices;

   (3) resale value for assets with a resale market; and

   (4) replacement cost or reproduction cost, depreciated to reflect the age of CCCs assets.

   UEL should be consulted concerning values assigned to the various assets so that CCC's accounting reflects UEL's reporting objectives.

2. Carpeting sold to UEL and its other subsidiaries should be billed at standard cost plus 10%, rather than at full list price less 15%, as is now the case. In effect, the gross margin on the intercompany transfers would be reduced from 35% of cost to 10% of cost. Carpet purchased by CCC from the UEL group of companies would also be invoiced to CCC at cost plus 10%.

3. Depreciation on the equipment (at revalued amounts) should be increased from 8% per year (straight-line) to 12.5% per year. Standard costs would be adjusted to reflect the higher rate.

The financial vice-president, in his letter to Mr. Blasé, has asked for a report that specifically identifies and describes any problems that may arise in implementing the suggested changes in accounting, and provides solutions to any problems that exist.

## Required

Assume that you are David Blasé. Draft the report for the vice-president on the suggested changes to the accounting policies.

# CASE 1-2 SMITH AND STEWART

Smith and Stewart (Stewart) is a partnership of lawyers. It was recently formed from a merger of Becker & Brackman (Becker) and Copp & Copp (Copp). Stewart has 38 partners—including 6 from Becker and 32 from Copp—and 75 employees. At the date of the merger, Stewart purchased land and an office building for $2 million, and fully computerized its offices. The partners have agreed to have the annual financial statements audited even though this was not done in the past.

---

[4]Changes in value are reported as an item of other comprehensive income and as a separate component of owners' equity. Between revaluations, depreciation is based on the most recent valuation. The frequency of revaluation depends on the assets' value volatility; IFRS suggests one to five years.

*Case Continued >*

*Case Continued >*

The partnership agreement requires an annual valuation of the assets and liabilities of the firm. This valuation will be used to determine the amount an existing partner will receive from the partnership when exiting the partnership, and the amount a new partner will pay to enter the partnership.

The partners have been busy getting the new partnership up and running and have paid little attention to accounting policies.

Prior to the merger, Becker recorded revenue when it invoiced the client. Daily time reports were used to keep track of the number of hours worked for each client. This information was not recorded in the accounting system, and in general the accounting records were not kept up-to-date.

Copp also recorded revenue at the time the client was invoiced. This was based on partner hours, which were determined based on work in progress and recorded for employees at their regular billing rate, based on the hours worked. At year-end, an adjustment was made to reduce work in progress to reflect the actual costs incurred by Copp.

The new partnership agreement requires a valuation of work in progress at the merger date. This amount, which has yet to be determined, will be recorded as goodwill.

Stewart has arranged a line of credit with a bank that allows the partnership to borrow up to 75% of the carrying value of accounts receivable and 40% of the carrying value of work in progress based on the partnership's monthly financial statements. The bank has also provided mortgage financing of $950,000 for Stewart's land and building. The bank requires unaudited monthly financial statements as well as the annual audited financial statements.

As at the date of the merger, capital assets owned by the predecessor firms were transferred to the new partnership.

Each partner receives a monthly "draw" payment, which is an advance on his or her share of annual profit.

Your auditing firm has been hired by Stewart to prepare a report advising the partnership on accounting policies—identifying alternatives and making specific supported recommendations. A partner in your auditing firm has asked you to prepare the report. In addition, the partner has asked you to prepare a memo detailing the important auditing issues that are likely to arise and how they could be resolved.

### Required

Prepare the requested report and the memo.
[CICA, adapted]

## CASE 1-3 RENAUD DEVELOPMENT CORPORATION

Renaud Development Corporation (RDC) is a real estate development company that is 60% owned by Bertrand Renaud. RDC has three shareholders: (1) Bertrand Renaud, a major figure in real property development, owns 60%; (2) Ascher's Inc., a privately owned Canadian department store chain, owns 30%; and (3) the TransCanada Bank owns 10%. RDC engages in two types of development—residential land sites and commercial retail space.

Mr. Renaud has been considering issuing a new class of RDC non-voting common shares to a small group of private investors. The purpose would be to provide a larger equity base so that RDC could be more aggressive in its commercial division. Like all real estate development companies, RDC is very highly leveraged; about 80% of the assets are financed by debt, most of which is provided by or through TransCanada Bank. The issue price of the new shares would be determined on the basis of the net market value of the equity of the company's properties (that is, the total appraised values minus the company's outstanding debt). Since the company will continue to be private, a shareholders' agreement will govern the company's buyback of the new shares if any investor decides in the future to sell his or her shares. The buyback price of the non-voting shares is to be determined as the original issue price of the shares plus a proportionate share in the increase in the net book value of the common share equity from the date of issue to the date of repurchase, based on the most recent audited financial statements.

The shareholders' agreement places no restrictions on the potential resale price of the voting shares held by Mr. Renaud, Ascher's Inc., and the bank; should any of these shares be sold, they would be sold at their fair market value (which, for real estate developments, is normally based on the present value of future cash flows).

Mr. Renaud is interested in the implications of the proposed non-voting share issue for financial reporting. He is aware that Canada has recently moved to international accounting standards but is uncertain how or if the change will affect RDC. Therefore he has engaged an accounting advisor to offer advice on the most desirable general accounting approach as well as on the most suitable specific accounting policies. A description of the business of the company follows.

## RESIDENTIAL DEVELOPMENT

In the residential division, RDC buys large tracts of land near major Canadian cities and holds the land for a few years until the growth of the city makes the land attractive for residential development. The purchase of the land is financed at least 90% by bank loans, and the loans provide for a line of credit to enable the company to borrow from the bank to pay the interest on the loans for up to five years after the land purchase; this holding period is considered by the bank to be the development period. When the time seems right (but usually within five years), RDC develops the land by providing services (e.g., sewer, water, electrical, and telephone mains and connections), laying out roads, and subdividing the land into home sites. The development process takes less than a year.

The sites are then advertised and sold to customers; about 25% of the sales are for cash, but more often they are for a 10–20% down payment with RDC accepting a mortgage for the remainder. The mortgages are usually for a 5-year term and a 20-year amortization, bearing interest at a fixed rate that is one or two percentage points below the market rate of mortgage interest (but above the cost of RDC's borrowing). The prices charged to customers for the land vary within an individual tract. Some locations are considered more desirable than others and may therefore carry a price that is as much as double that of the less desirable locations within the same development.

RDC does no residential building; the company only sells the sites. Purchasers must arrange for construction of the houses themselves. Usually, however, RDC enters into an exclusive contract with one (or sometimes two) house builder(s) to construct houses

*Case Continued >*

*Case Continued >*

on the sites. The builders erect model homes on the front sites (i.e., on the major access road), and then negotiate individually with the customers for construction of their homes. RDC charges the builders rent for the properties occupied by the model homes. When sales of the sites are complete, RDC sells the property under the model homes to the purchasers of the model homes or to the builder.

RDC has been quite successful in its residential land development business. However, there is one land tract outside of Calgary that it has been unable to sell as quickly as desired. Purchased eight years ago and developed two years ago, only about 30% of the tract has been sold. Defaults by purchasers have been high, and the proceeds from the land sales have not been sufficient to pay the interest on the bank loan; the company has had to use cash from other developments to service the loan.

## COMMERCIAL DEVELOPMENT

The commercial division builds and leases retail developments in urban and suburban locations. Sometimes the shopping centres are built on a part of the residential development areas described above, but usually the sites are completely independent of the residential division.

There is little lag between acquisition and development of a retail site, although the project can take up to six years from land assembly to final grand opening. The acquisition and development costs are financed by the bank, although in very large developments the bank will syndicate its participation (that is, bring in other banks to share the cost and the risk). Syndicate members demand audited financial statements from RDC.

RDC's general policy is to hold and operate the properties, although the company will sell if the price is right. Each property usually has an Ascher's store as an "anchor" store (a major retailer that occupies a large space and provides much of the attractiveness of the development to shoppers and thereby to smaller retail lessees). There is a long-term lease agreement between the Ascher's store and RDC that locks the store into the development for at least 30 years. Similar leases bind other major anchor stores, but smaller retailers usually sign five-year leases that are cancellable by either party at the end of the lease term.

The long-term leases are for fixed lease payments, with provision for increases due to inflation and due to increases in operating costs. Shorter-term (e.g., five-year) leases are for a minimum monthly amount plus a percentage of the gross sales of the store. Smaller lessees also pay a large amount, equivalent to 50% of one year's minimum lease payments, at the inception of the lease; this payment is not repeated for lease renewals. RDC's cash flow from the lease payments is used to operate the developments and to service the bank debt that financed them. RDC has not had to pay any income taxes in the commercial division because capital cost allowance (CCA) on the properties is more than enough to offset lease income. Excess CCA from the commercial division cannot be used to offset profits in the residential division for income tax purposes, however.

Most of the retail developments have been very successful; the insurable value of the properties is, in aggregate, four times the depreciated historical cost of the properties. There are three recently built shopping centres that have not yet reached their full potential but are expected to do so within the next two years. Four other developments were built in recent years in parts of the country that were hit hard by the economic recession in those years, and they have never fully recovered; these properties are unable to recover their full operating and carrying costs.

## Required

Outline the accounting policies that would seem to best serve the reporting objectives of RDC, assuming that the new share issue is to occur. Your recommendations should include (but not be limited to) recognition of the revenues for each division, treatment of costs (including development costs and interest), and valuation of properties under development and after development. You also should advise Mr. Renaud as to whether RDC should follow international accounting standards from now on.

[Institute of Chartered Accountants of Ontario, adapted]

## CASE 1-4 W&K GARDENS

Lindsay Kay approached her friend Michael Wait about going into business together as co-owners of a gardening centre. Lindsay loved gardening and had some skills as an accountant. Michael was a landscape architect. Lindsay and Michael agreed to become business partners and open a new garden centre to be called W&K Gardens (W&K). There were only two existing nurseries in the local area, and Lindsay and Michael felt that there would be sufficient customer demand from continued residential expansion to support another gardening centre.

The pair decided that Lindsay would assume responsibility for the accounting and Michael would complete gardening layouts for customers. In addition, Michael would design a website where customers could order plants for pickup or delivery, and on which Lindsay could eventually provide online gardening tips and advice. Michael suggested that they initially pay a flat fee to an Internet service provider for hosting their website. Michael would register their Internet domain name, develop the webpage, and create the initial graphics.

They developed a business plan for the gardening centre, and Lindsay applied for a loan from the provincial Ministry of Agriculture and Education, which was offering forgivable loans for up to $500,000 to promote small businesses in the province. Lindsay and Michael soon received a letter from the provincial government that started with the words, "Congratulations—you have met all the criteria to receive a forgivable loan of $500,000." (Further details on the loan are provided in Exhibit A).

Although there were many details to work out, they felt that they could be open for business by the first week of June. They already had start-up funds from the forgivable loan, and a business plan. Michael knew of a large plot of land (20 hectares) with a small but suitable building in a nearby location that was available for lease. Lindsay and Michael reviewed the terms of the lease (Exhibit B) received from a real estate agent and agreed that although the payments were considerable, the location would be well worth it and they would have plenty of space to carry a full assortment of annuals, perennials, shrubs, trees, and garden accessories. They were willing to pay a higher fee for the ability to expand in the future. Lindsay's notes concerning the inventory of plants and care that would be needed are included in Exhibit C.

*Case Continued >*

The old building would have to be renovated before it could be used as a storefront, and they agreed to hire someone to complete the necessary work on time. They estimated the cost of the renovation to be about $125,000 but realized that they would have to meet with a contractor to get a formal estimate for the work to be done.

Lindsay also noted that they would need an operating loan for approximately $100,000 in addition to the government loan. Lindsay arranged to meet with her bank manager as soon as possible. With her business plan in hand, she was going to approach the bank for additional financing for the initial costs and purchase of inventory. Lindsay's personal borrowing rate was currently 11%. However, she had been advised that the new business would be able to borrow at 2% below this rate, assuming that W&K would be able to maintain an adequate amount of assets to cover liabilities by the second year of operation. Lindsay now began to gather the details needed to finalize the business plan for the bank.

Michael determined that they would have to purchase a small truck and some equipment to carry out the landscape design service. Since he had been in charge of purchasing at Green Thumb Landscapers, he had a good idea of the type and cost of this equipment (Exhibit D).

To provide income during the off-season, Michael suggested they submit a bid for a tender that he had seen advertised in the paper. The town was accepting bids for snow removal from municipal parking lots and storage of snow from street removal. Last year, the town had had difficulty finding contractors for the snow removal since it was a small job. The town also needed space to "store" the removed snow and, with this new location, Michael and Lindsay would certainly have the capability to store snow. Michael was concerned, though, that the snow would contain chemical contaminants acquired from the town's roads. Michael believed that they could win the snow removal contract for a flat fee of $30,000 and an additional flat fee of $50,000 for storage of snow for one "snow season."

Michael suggested that they should discuss the details of the business partnership at a meeting the following morning to avoid future disputes. They had already agreed that Michael would contribute his personally owned landscaping equipment (fair value $18,000), a small used truck (fair value $12,000), and cash of $5,000. Lindsay would contribute computer equipment (fair value $8,500), office furniture (fair value $6,500), and cash of $20,000. Each partner would receive an equal interest in both capital and income. Michael also stated that he wanted Lindsay's opinion on the appropriate accounting policies that should be selected so he could anticipate earnings. He also wanted an outline of any matters related to the set-up of the business and Lindsay's opinion about whether a partnership would be the best structure for their business.

## Required

Assume the role of Lindsay Kay. Prepare notes to summarize your analysis in preparation for a meeting between Lindsay and Michael.

## Exhibit A
## Forgivable Loan from Ministry of Agriculture and Education

Clause 1: Lindsay Kay will receive a forgivable loan of $500,000 for the development and operation of W&K Gardens as described in the attached business plan.

Clause 2: The government will provide $500,000 on May 20, 20X6, which is forgivable on May 20, 20X11, if the following conditions are met:

- three university students are hired for the period June 1 to August 31 each year;

- all produce is grown on-site or purchased from local growers; and

- audited financial statements are provided to the government three months after year-end.

Clause 3: If any of the above terms is not met, the loan is repayable with interest of 10% by the end of the fiscal year in which the term is broken.

Clause 4: The government has the right to inspect the premises and financial records to ensure that all conditions of the loan have been met at any time.

## Exhibit B
## Terms of the Lease

Addison Ltd. agrees to rent to W&K the land site and building that it requires in starting up its new business. The lease agreement calls for five annual lease payments of $300,000 (including executory costs of $19,506) at the beginning of each year. The details surrounding the agreement are as follows:

| | |
|---|---|
| Commissions and legal fees (incurred by Addison) | $ 60,000 |
| Building: | |
| Addison's carrying value of building | $ 340,000 |
| Fair value of the building | $ 400,000 |
| Economic life of building | 6 years |
| Guaranteed residual value at end of lease term | $ 75,000 |
| Land: | |
| Addison's carrying value of land | $ 375,000 |
| Fair value of the land | $1,000,000 |
| Residual value at end of lease term | $1,000,000 |
| Rate implicit in the lease (known by W&K) | 10% |

Addison contacted its building contractor, who promised to have the renovations completed on time at a price very close to the estimated amount of $125,000. The renovation work would have a useful life of approximately eight years.

Addison stated that the lease will be non-cancellable but is willing to provide an option to renew the lease at the end of the five-year term.

## Exhibit C
## Inventory Requirements

W&K would be open for business all year, but the amount and type of inventory would fluctuate depending on the time of the year. The garden centre would consist of a greenhouse, outdoor tents, a store, and a small outdoor nursery. The storefront would be open year-round and would sell fertilizers, planters, garden tools, and accessories. Gift baskets would be brought in for special occasions such as Mother's Day, Halloween, Thanksgiving, and Christmas.

To attract customers to the store, Michael would provide customized landscape designs for a flat fee of $500. The customer would then receive a credit for the same amount at the store. The credit would have no cash value, but could be used for the purchase of shrubs, flowers, and so forth, at the store over the next two years.

Annual plants (such as geraniums, petunias, and many more varieties) would be purchased from local growing farms each spring. These plants would all have to be sold before the end of summer. Perennial plants (including bellflowers, day lilies, and hostas) would be grown in W&K's greenhouse and transferred to the outdoor store protected by large tents. Those plants not sold by September 30 would be returned to the green-house for winter storage and care. It was expected that most perennial plants would be sold, especially if Lindsay discounted the price to encourage customers to buy and plant in the fall instead of waiting for the following spring.

Shrubs and trees would be purchased from local nurseries early in the spring. It was expected that about 80% of these purchases would be sold during the growing season. The remaining 20% would be transferred to the outdoor nursery to be replanted and would remain there until the next season. To be competitive with the other two garden centres, Lindsay thought that they should offer a one-year warranty on all shrubs and trees returned by customers with a valid sales receipt.

The outdoor nursery would be used primarily for Christmas trees, which would be grown from seedling stock and could remain in the ground for a number of years. In the initial years, mature trees would be bought from a local supplier.

## Exhibit D
## Capital Asset Requirements

Michael estimated that the following capital assets would be required for the first year of operations. Part of the government loan would be used to purchase these items.

| | |
|---|---|
| Three small used trucks (in addition to the one contributed by Michael) | $40,000 |
| Landscaping equipment (backhoe, Rototiller, etc.) | $60,000 |
| Small power tools | $15,000 |
| Display shelves for the store | $12,000 |

[Institute of Chartered Accountants of Ontario, adapted]

# Chapter 2

## Intercorporate Equity Investments: An Introduction

### Learning Objectives

**After studying this chapter, you should be able to:**

LO **1** explain the difference between passive investments and strategic investments;

LO **2** identify the proper accounting treatment for both passive and strategic investments;

LO **3** describe the basic principles of consolidation;

LO **4** apply both the direct and worksheet methods of consolidation in simple situations;

LO **5** explain the relationship between consolidation and equity reporting; and

LO **6** identify simple accounting treatments associated with changes in ownership.

## INTRODUCTION

Onex Corporation is a diversified Canadian company that has control or significant influence over a wide variety of operating companies. Onex has significant investments in 14 different companies, including Celestica (an Ontario-based global electronic systems company) and Hawker Beechcraft Corporation (a leading manufacturer of business, special-mission, and trainer aircraft).

The objective of financial reporting is to show the assets and liabilities that are under the control of the shareholders of a corporation. When a reporting entity such as Onex owns shares in other companies, the reporting entity may control not only the assets it legally owns, but also the assets that are owned by other companies in the group. How can financial statements reflect this economic reality underlying intercorporate share ownership? That is the main focus of this text.

## 2.1 CLASSIFICATION OF INTERCORPORATE INVESTMENTS

An **intercorporate investment** is any purchase by one corporation of the securities of another corporation. Broadly speaking, the investment may be in either debt securities or equity securities—preferred or common shares. You have already studied investments in debt securities in your intermediate accounting courses. Therefore, our focus in this text is on equity investments.

**LO 1**
Explain the difference between passive investments and strategic investments

**LO 2**
Identify the proper accounting treatment for both passive and strategic investments

The investment of a corporation in the equity of another corporation can broadly be classified as either passive or strategic:

1.  A **passive investment** is made to earn dividends or to earn profits by actively trading the investment for short-term profit.

2.  A **strategic investment** is made to *control* or *significantly influence* the operations of the investee corporation.

## Passive Investments

Accounting for passive investments poses no particular problems. They are initially recorded at cost and are reported at fair market value on each period's statement of financial position.

The treatment of gains and losses depends on how the company has elected to classify the investment—a choice that the reporting entity makes for each separate passive equity investment when the investment is first made. The choices available under IFRS 9, *Financial Instruments*, are to report the investment at either

1.  fair value through profit or loss (FVTPL), or

2.  fair value through other comprehensive income (FVTOCI).[1]

If an equity investment is classified as "fair value through profit and loss," both (1) dividends and (2) the change in fair value from one period to another are reported in the net income section of the statement of comprehensive income (SCI).

If, on the other hand, an equity investment is classified as "fair value through other comprehensive income," (1) dividends from that investment are recognized in net income, but (2) changes in the fair value of the investment are reported as *other comprehensive income* (OCI); the accumulated gains and losses are reported as a separate component of shareholders' equity. The choice to classify an equity investment as "fair value through other comprehensive income" is irrevocable—the classification cannot be changed subsequently.

The fair value gains and losses of FVTOCI investments can never be transferred from their separate component of equity to net income. However, the company can move the accumulated gains and losses *within* shareholders' equity. That means that the company can transfer the gains and losses directly to retained earnings at any time, *but not via the profit and loss section of the statement of comprehensive income*.

### Illustration of the accounting of an FVTPL investment

Little Financial Corporation (LFC) purchased 100 shares of Big Corporation (BC) for $20 each on January 1, 20X3. The brokerage commission/fee for the transaction was $10. LFC received dividends totalling $200 on these shares on April 30, 20X3. The market value of each

---

[1]The terms "held for trading" and "available for sale" were used previously under IAS 39 to refer to FVTPL and FVTOCI investments, respectively. IFRS 9, which replaces IAS 39, is likely to become mandatory in 2015; however, early adoption is permitted. Many Canadian public companies early-adopted IFRS 9, thereby avoiding the necessity of restating prior years' financial statements. While the accounting treatment applicable to held for trading and FVTPL investments are identical, the same is not the case for FVTOCI and available for sale investments. Therefore, in addition to illustrating the accounting treatment of FVTPL and FVTOCI investments in the text, we have also illustrated the accounting treatment of available for sale investments.

share of BC on December 31, 20X3, LFC's financial year-end, was $25. LFC sold all of its shares in BC on March 1, 20X4, for $28 each. LFC classified its investment in BC as a FVTPL investment for accounting purposes.

The investment is a FVTPL investment, and therefore incidental costs, such as brokerage commissions, represent normal operating expenses and are expensed immediately. LFC will make the following journal entry in its books at the time of the initial investment on January 1, 20X3:

| | | |
|---|---|---|
| Investment in BC Dr. | 2,000 | |
| Brokerage expense Dr. | 10 | |
| Cash Cr. | | 2,010 |

The receipt of the dividend revenue of $200 on April 30, 20X3, will be recorded as follows:

| | | |
|---|---|---|
| Cash Dr. | 200 | |
| Dividend Revenue Cr. | | 200 |

On December 31, 20X3, LFC will make the following journal entry to change the value of the investment in its books from carrying value to fair value on that day:

| | | |
|---|---|---|
| Investment in BC Dr. | 500 | |
| Holding gain on investment in BC Cr. | | 500 |

Finally, when the shares are sold on March 1, 20X4, LFC will make the following journal entry to remove the investment from its books and recognize any related gain or loss:

| | | |
|---|---|---|
| Cash Dr. | 2,800 | |
| Investment in BC Cr. | | 2,500 |
| Gain on sale of investment in BC Dr. | | 300 |

**Illustration of the accounting of an FVTOCI investment**   We will continue with the LFC example above, but now assume that its investment in BC is instead a FVTOCI investment. In the case of FVTOCI investments, incidental costs such as brokerage fees are treated as part of the initial cost of the investment and thus are not expensed. The journal entry on January 1, 20X3, for the investment in 100 shares of BC for $20 each, and for the associated brokerage cost of $10, is as follows:

| | | |
|---|---|---|
| Investment in BC Dr. | 2,010 | |
| Cash Cr. | | 2,010 |

The entry for the receipt of the dividend revenue of $200 on April 30, 20X3, remains the same as for the FVTPL case and is repeated below for convenience:

| | | |
|---|---|---|
| Cash Dr. | 200 | |
| Dividend Revenue Cr. | | 200 |

The entry required on December 31, 20X3, to change the value of the investment in LFC's books from carrying value to fair value on that day is slightly different from that for the FVTPL case we saw before, and is as follows:

| | | |
|---|---|---|
| Investment in BC Dr. | 490 | |
| OCI—holding gain on investment in BC Cr. | | 490 |

The accounting treatment to recognize the gain on sale of the investment in BC on March 1st, 20X4, is also slightly different from that required for the FVTPL case we saw earlier:

| | | |
|---|---|---|
| Cash Dr. | 2,800 | |
| Investment in BC Cr. | | 2,500 |
| OCI—gain on sale of investment in BC Cr. | | 300 |

**Illustration of the accounting of an available for sale investment**  When an available for sale investment is sold, IAS (International Accounting Standards) 39 requires all unrealized gains and losses accumulated in OCI to be removed from OCI and recognized in net income, along with any additional gains and losses. This process is called recycling. If we now assume that LFC's investment in BC is an available for sale investment and not a FVTOCI investment, the following entry is necessary at the time of the sale of its investment in BC on March 1, 20X4:

| | | |
|---|---|---|
| Cash Dr. | 2,800 | |
| OCI | 490 | |
| Investment in BC Cr. | | 2,500 |
| Realized gain on sale of investment in BC (taken to net income portion of SCI) Cr. | | 790 |

All other entries are identical to the FVTOCI case and therefore are not repeated here. You may have already realized that the ability to recycle gains/losses allows managers to manipulate the company's earnings by selectively identifying those investments to sell that have appreciated/depreciated so as to report gains/losses in net income as and when "needed" to hit earnings targets or reduce earnings volatility. Because the IASB realized this possibility, IFRS 9 no longer allows recycling of gains/losses from OCI to net income when FVTOCI investments are sold.

# Strategic Investments

Strategic investments provide a strategic or long-term advantage by giving the investor the ability to either significantly influence or control the operating or financing decisions of the investee. Strategic equity investments can take several different forms depending on the investor's strategic objectives:

- Controlled entities:
  - Subsidiaries
  - Structured entities

- Associated companies
- Joint ventures

Generally, investments are considered strategic if a company owns, either directly or indirectly, 20% or more of the voting shares of the investee, unless it can clearly be demonstrated that the investments are passive.

Debt instruments can also be used strategically, because they give the investor leverage over the investee corporation, especially in start-up or developing investee corporations. In those cases, the investor can provide capital to the investee while still gaining the greater security that comes with being a creditor rather than a shareholder. Although the investor may use debt instruments as an effective strategic tool, the investment in debt itself is not accounted for as a strategic investment, but instead is accounted for at amortized cost as an investment in debt securities being held to maturity.

In the following sections, we will explain these various types of strategic equity investments and the appropriate method of accounting for each. Along the way, we also will discuss the two basic concepts that underlie accounting for strategic investments—(1) control and (2) significant influence.

### Concept Check 2-1

1. Why are the two categories of passive and strategic used to classify equity investments?
2. What are the major types of strategic investments?

## 2.2 CONTROLLED ENTITIES

**LO ❶**
Explain the difference between passive investments and strategic investments

**LO ❷**
Identify the proper accounting treatment for both passive and strategic investments

According to IFRS 10, *Consolidated Financial Statements*, "control exists when one entity is exposed to, or has rights to, variable returns from its involvement with another entity and has the power over the other entity so as to affect such returns." All three elements—(1) power over the other entity; (2) exposure to, or rights over, the variable returns from involvement in the other entity; and (3) the ability to use the power over the other entity to affect the amount of the investor's returns—must be considered when determining whether or not control exists. Notice that the definition cites the power to control and does not require that the controlling entity actively use that power. Often, the controlling entity is quite happy to let the controlled entity continue to manage its own affairs without direct interference by the parent.

There are many aspects of control that accountants must be aware of. The two general types of controlled entities are *subsidiaries* and *structured entities*. We'll give a broad view of each type first, and then return later to examine some of the nuances of the concept of *control*.

### Subsidiaries

By far the most common type of controlled entity is a *subsidiary*. A **subsidiary** is a corporation (or an unincorporated entity such as a partnership or trust) that is controlled by a **parent** company that owns, usually, a majority of the voting shares/rights of the subsidiary. Since shareholders elect a corporation's board of directors, holding most of the shares enables the parent company to control the composition of the subsidiary's board.

## Example of Control and Reporting of Controlled Group—Onex Corporation

Onex Corporation obtained control of Crown Amusements Ltd. in the second quarter of 2011 by purchasing 100% of Crown's shares. Crown is the largest casino operator in the Alberta region. Onex's unaudited interim financial statements for the second quarter ended June 30, 2011, show the consolidated financial results under IFRS of the

Onex group, which includes, in addition to the financial results of Onex itself, the financial results of all the companies controlled by Onex, such as Crown Amusements.

Source: Onex Corporation, Q2 2011 Report, http://www.onex.ca/Assets/Downloads/Q2-11%20Onex%20Quarterly%20Report.pdf

Since the board has the power to determine a corporation's relevant activities, that is, the activities that significantly affect the returns of the investee, the parent corporation can control those activities through its power to elect the subsidiary's board.

Virtually all business corporations operate through a structure that consists of a parent company and many subsidiary corporations, the vast majority of which were formed by the parent company to carry out part of its business operations. A parent corporation will establish subsidiaries for three principal reasons:

1. To isolate risk; if one subsidiary fails, it does not jeopardize the overall corporate structure and functioning.

2. To develop different management teams for essentially different functions or types of business, such as manufacturing vs. sales.

3. To comply with local legal requirements, including tax compliance.

To the public the most "famous" subsidiaries are those that are the result of one corporation buying another, known as a *business combination*. Business combinations often get lots of public attention, and yet their number is really quite small when compared with the vast numbers of parent-founded subsidiaries. Onex Corporation, mentioned in this chapter, is an example of a company specializing in buying other companies; Onex is known as a *turn-around company*, whose specialty is buying faltering companies and restoring them to health.

Although business combinations are a relatively minor source of subsidiaries, they bring with them many accounting issues that will be explained in the following chapters further.

## Structured Entities

A second type of controlled enterprise is a *structured entity*, also known as a *variable interest entity* or a *special purpose entity*. IFRS 10 provides guidance on when a **structured entity** (SE) should be consolidated. An SE is set up by the reporting enterprise (or "sponsor") to perform a very specific and narrow function. The difference between a subsidiary and an SE is that an SE is not controlled through voting power. Indeed, an SE may not even be a corporation but could instead be a partnership. An SE also can be created simply by delegating specific powers to certain individuals to act on behalf of the "sponsoring" corporation—in effect, by creating a sort of "agency" relationship with individuals instead of corporate entities.

Three examples of SEs are:

■ A corporation (the "sponsor") may set up an SE to buy assets (e.g., buildings, equipment) on behalf of the sponsor. The SE will arrange the purchase financing and then collect rent from the sponsor for use of the assets (and thereby pay down the debt). This arrangement often is intended to keep both the assets and the related debt financing off the books of the sponsor, thereby achieving off-balance-sheet financing.

■ The controlling shareholders of a corporation may form a separate "lending agency" to provide secured loans to the corporation. The shareholders give their own money to the SE, which in turn lends it to the corporation. Effectively, the shareholders are contributing additional capital to the corporation, but instead of bearing risk, they are entitled to receive interest and loan repayments. If the corporation goes bankrupt, the shareholders get first claim on the assets (over other creditors) because they are secured.

■ A not-for-profit organization that is engaged in active public fundraising efforts may set up a separate not-for-profit SE, usually called a foundation. In the past, some NFPs have channelled major donations into a foundation instead of into the main organization so that the main organization appears to be less well funded than it really is.

All three of these examples have been used extensively by managers who aren't very attentive to ethical financial reporting standards.

On the other hand, there are uses for SEs that don't attempt to mislead anyone. For example, a separate corporation (i.e., an SE) may be established to *securitize* a company's receivables. **Securitization** is the process of transferring receivables into an SE and then issuing securities to private or public investors as a means of financing those receivables. That is, the company sells the receivables to an SE, and the SE gets the money (or the vast majority of the money) to pay for the receivables by selling bonds or similar financial instruments to other investors.

SEs are not usually controlled through shareholdings. Instead, control is exercised by other means, such as through contractual means or through interlocking management. The crucial questions in deciding on *control* are, "Who has the rights that provide power over the activities of the SE?" and "Who is affected most?" If the activities of an SE primarily affect the sponsoring corporation's, finances, operations, or financial reports, then the SE must be *consolidated* in the same manner as a subsidiary. This relatively recent requirement in accounting standards clearly tends to undercut the unethical use of SEs to manipulate a company's financial statements.

## Accounting for Controlled Entities

Under both IFRS and US standards, a corporation's publicly issued financial statements *must* be **consolidated**—all entities controlled by the reporting entity, including subsidiaries and controlled SEs, must be included in the consolidated statements. With consolidated statements, all of the assets and all of the liabilities are reported as a single *economic* entity, as though the combined companies were a single legal entity. However,

Daimler AG, the manufacturer of Mercedes-Benz vehicles, makes use of SEs for refinancing its financial services business. The company consolidates such SEs in its consolidated financial statements. The company's 2010 annual report states:

> As an additional funding source, Daimler transfers finance receivables, in particular receivables from the leasing and automotive business, to special purpose entities. Daimler thereby principally retains significant risks of the transferred receivables…,

these special purpose entities have to be consolidated by the transferor. The transferred financial assets remain on Daimler's consolidated statement of financial position.

In this note, Daimler is using an older term, special purpose entities, but the meaning is the same.

Source: Daimler AG, Note 1, Significant accounting policies, *Annual Report 2010*, p. 178, http://www.daimler.com/Projects/c2c/channel/documents/1985489_Daimler_Annual_Report_2010.pdf

the IASB is proposing to exempt investment entities (that is, entities that invest solely to obtain capital appreciation and dividend income from their investments) from being required to consolidate controlled entities. Instead, investment entities will be required to report entities that they control as FVTPL investments.

In many countries, such as New Zealand, Japan, Germany, and France, the parent company is permitted (or *required*) to issue its own separate-entity, unconsolidated statements. If you look at the financial statements of a company in these countries, be sure to find out whether you're looking at the consolidated statements or just at the parent company's separate-entity statements.

Consolidated financial statements are designed to report on the **economic entity** formed by the parent and all of its controlled entities (both subsidiaries and SEs). There is no legal entity that corresponds with a consolidated economic entity, and therefore consolidated statements are sometimes referred to as an *accounting fiction*. The word "fiction" here is not meant to be negative or derogatory—it merely is intended to convey the fact that the statements do not portray a "real" corporation but instead include the assets and liabilities of many separate controlled entities. Financial statement readers should be aware of this fact.

Understanding this accounting fiction is important for anyone who is lending money to (or doing business with) a parent company based on its consolidated statements. Lending agreements are with individual legal entities; the parent corporation may control its subsidiaries, but most of the assets on the consolidated statements are out of reach of the parent company's creditors because they don't legally belong to the parent company.

## Concept Check 2-2

1. What three factors determine the existence of control of subsidiaries and SEs?
2. What are the two major types of controlled entities?
3. How do publicly accountable entities commonly report entities controlled by them?
4. Why are SEs required to be consolidated?

## 2.3 ASSOCIATES

IAS 28, Investments in Associates, defines **associates** as companies (investees) over whom the investor has the ability to exert *significant influence* but not the ability to exert control, either solely or jointly with other entities. **Significant influence** is the ability to *participate* in the operating and financial policy decisions of the investee without being able to control them.

**LO ❶**
Explain the difference between passive investments and strategic investments

**LO ❷**
Identify the proper accounting treatment for both passive and strategic investments

## Significant Influence

A holding, either directly or indirectly through subsidiaries, of 20% or more of the voting shares of another entity is taken as evidence that significant influence exists, unless evidence exists to prove otherwise. Likewise, a holding of less than 20% of the voting shares is indicative of lack of significant influence unless evidence exists to prove otherwise.

The 20% threshold should not be given undue weight. A shareholding of 35% may not provide significant influence to an investor if the shareholder is prevented from exercising influence by another shareholder holding the remaining 65%. Conversely, the existence of another shareholder holding the majority of the shares of the investee may not preclude significant influence from existing. The following additional evidence should be considered for deciding whether or not significant evidence exists:

- representation on the board of directors or other equivalent governing body of the investee;
- participation in the policy-making process of the investee;
- significant and essential transactions between the investor and the investee;
- interchange of managerial personnel between the investor and investee; or
- provision of essential technical information by the investor to the investee.

Additionally, potential voting rights are a factor to be considered in deciding whether significant influence exists.

---

### Reality Check 2–3

### Applying the 20% Threshold—Onex Corporation

Onex Corporation has substantial investments in 14 operating companies. Of the 14, 10 are controlled through voting share ownership and are consolidated. The other 4 are as follows:

| Investee corporation | Onex ownership share |
| --- | --- |
| Tomkins Limited | 50% |
| RSI Home Products, Inc. | 50% |
| Hawker Beechcraft Corporation | 19% |
| Allison Transmission, Inc. | 15% |

Two of the four investments are below the normal 20% threshold, but are still treated as associates. The company states that "Onex has certain contractual rights and protections, including the right to appoint members to the Board of Directors, in respect of these entities."

Source: http://www.onex.ca/Assets/Downloads/Q2-11%20Onex%20Quarterly%20Report.pdf.

---

## Reporting Method

Significant influence gives the investor the power to play a major role in the investee's earnings process. Since the investor is a participant in the investee's earnings process, under IAS 28, the investor's proportionate share of the investee's earnings should be reported in the investor's SCI. This is known as the **equity method of reporting**. Under the equity method, the investor doesn't report dividends as income. Instead, the investor calculates its share of the associate's net income (or loss), and then adds that amount to the investment account and includes it in determining the investor's net income.

For example, assume that Helmut Corporation owns 25% of Aaron Ltd. Helmut's 25% share of Aaron's $400,000 in earnings is $100,000. At the end of the reporting period, Helmut will record the earnings as follows:

| | | |
|---|---|---|
| Investment in Aaron (SFP) | 100,000 | |
| Helmut share of earnings of Aaron (SCI, net income section) | | 100,000 |

If Aaron declares dividends of $60,000, Helmut will record its 25% share as a reduction in the investment account:

| | | |
|---|---|---|
| Dividends receivable (SFP) | 15,000 | |
| Investment in Aaron (SFP) | | 15,000 |

The receipt of dividends has no effect on Helmut's net income because Aaron's earnings have already been recognized in Helmut's accounts.

As you will see later, Helmut's share is not necessarily the same as Aaron's net income × 25%; there are usually some adjustments that must be made first. The equity method is illustrated further below.

### Concept Check 2-3

1. Why is a 20% or more shareholding in an entity insufficient by itself to determine whether or not significant influence exists?
2. Why are investments in associates reported under the equity method?

**LO 1**
Explain the difference between passive investments and strategic investments

**LO 2**
Identify the proper accounting treatment for both passive and strategic investments

## 2.4 JOINT VENTURES

## Types of Joint Ventures

A **joint venture** is defined in IFRS 11, *Joint Arrangements*, as an agreement between two or more entities whereby the parties that have *joint control* of the arrangement have rights to the net assets of the arrangement. Joint ventures are common in certain industries (such as resource exploration). They also are common in global competition when two otherwise competing companies join forces to establish operations in another country or when one company joins with the host country's government in establishing a new venture.

Under IFRS 11 there are two types of joint arrangements—*joint operations* and *joint ventures*. In **joint operations**, the entities having joint control have rights over individual assets and are obligated for individual liabilities of the joint operation. Therefore, each joint venturer should include on its respective financial statements its share of the assets, liabilities, revenues, and expenses of the joint operation.

In contrast, in a **joint venture**, the joint venturers have no rights over the individual assets nor have obligations toward the individual liabilities of the joint venture. Instead, like shareholders of a corporation, joint venturers have rights only over the *net assets* of the joint venture.

In the rest of the text we will restrict our discussion to joint ventures, given that, (1) compared to joint operations, joint ventures have far greater economic significance to society and (2) accounting for joint operations is relatively simple.

## Joint Venture Agreements

The **joint venture agreement** specifies each co-venturer's capital contribution, representation on the board of directors, and involvement in management, plus other relevant matters. An essential and distinguishing characteristic of a joint venture is that no one investor can make major strategic decisions unilaterally; major decisions require the consent of all of the co-venturers. This is known as **joint control**.

Usually joint ventures are carried on as separate private corporations. The joint venture agreement is similar to the shareholders' agreement in private corporations that clarifies the rights and responsibilities of the various shareholders. The difference is that, in private corporations, a single shareholder or a small group may exercise control. In a joint venture no one investor (or subgroup of investors) can control the joint venture, even though that investor may contribute a majority of the capital or hold the majority of shares. Joint ventures require agreement among the co-venturers, not voting power.

Joint control should not be confused with profit sharing. Control is joint, but profit sharing is not necessarily equal. The joint venture agreement stipulates how the risks and benefits of the venture will be shared, including the distribution of profits and dividends.

## Reporting Method

Under IFRS 11, joint ventures must be reported using the equity method. Another method, proportionate consolidation, had previously been widely used in Canada because so much of the resource industry is carried out through joint ventures. However, IFRS 11 removed proportionate consolidation as a reporting alternative since it does not accurately reflect the true economic interest that a joint venturer has in a joint venture.

The equity method has been discussed above, for associates. For joint ventures, it is applied in essentially the same manner.

### Concept Check 2-4

1. What differentiates an investment in a joint venture from investments in (1) an associate and (2) a subsidiary, respectively?

2. Why does the IASB feel that the equity method, compared with the proportionate consolidation method, is a better method for reporting an investment in a joint venture?

## 2.5 EQUITY INVESTMENTS AND REPORTING METHODS UNDER IFRS

Exhibit 2.1 provides the decision rules to be followed to classify equity investments and the method of their reporting under IFRS.

In the following sections, we will illustrate both consolidation and equity reporting.

As we review consolidation, it is crucial to understand that *reporting* is not the same as *recording*. Consolidated amounts *never appear on the parent company's books*—reported numbers are the result of spreadsheet analysis, either computer-based or manual.

Similarly, investments *reported* on the equity basis are usually *recorded* on the cost basis on the investor's books. The adjustments to determine the equity-basis investment amount for the SFP are normally made on the accountant's working papers but are not necessarily recorded on the parent's books. To convert the cost-basis investment account to the equity basis requires a simple adjusting entry at the end of each year (or quarter).

**LO ❸**
Describe the basic principles of consolidation

**LO ❹**
Apply both the direct and worksheet methods of consolidation in simple situations

## 2.6 ILLUSTRATION OF CONSOLIDATION

Consolidated statements are prepared from the point of view of the shareholders of the parent company. Consolidation adds the elements in the financial statements of subsidiaries and structured entities to those of the parent. On the SFP there will be no investment account for the controlled subsidiaries and SEs. Instead, the assets and liabilities of the controlled entities will be added to those of the parent to show the economic

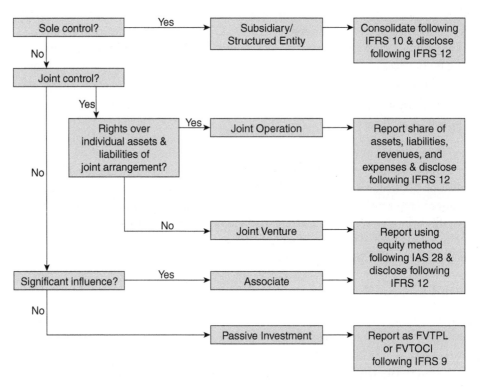

**Exhibit 2.1** Equity Investments and Reporting Methods Under IFRS

resources of the entire economic entity. On the SCI, the revenues and expenses will be the totals for each item for the parent plus the controlled entities. The effects of any and all intercompany transactions will be eliminated to avoid double-counting.

## Eliminations and Adjustments

To prepare its consolidated financial statements, a parent will add together the financial statement amounts for itself and its controlled entities. In the process, however, some changes to the pre-consolidation reported balances must be made. There are two types of changes that are made when statements are consolidated: (1) *eliminations* and (2) *adjustments*:

■ Eliminations are changes that prevent certain amounts on the separate-entity statements from appearing on the consolidated statements. Eliminations are necessary to avoid double-counting (such as intercompany sales) and to cancel out offsetting balances (such as intercompany receivables and payables).

■ Adjustments, on the other hand, are made to alter reported amounts to reflect the economic substance of transactions rather than their nominal amount.

## Direct Versus Worksheet Approach to Consolidation

**Direct Approach**   There are two general approaches to preparing consolidated financial statements, the direct approach and the worksheet approach. The **direct approach** prepares the consolidated statements by setting up the SCI and SFP formats and computing each consolidated balance directly. Each asset, liability, revenue, and expense is separately calculated and entered into the consolidated statement. The direct approach works from the separate-entity financial statements of the parent and the subsidiary.

**Worksheet Approach**   The alternative method is the **worksheet approach**. The worksheet (or spreadsheet) approach uses a multi-columnar worksheet to enter the trial balances of the parent and each subsidiary. Then eliminations and adjustments are entered onto the worksheet, and the accounts are cross-added to determine the consolidated balances. The finished consolidated statements are then prepared from the consolidated trial balance.

**Which Approach to Use?**   The direct approach is intuitively appealing because we are working directly with the statements and can see clearly what is happening to the consolidated statements as we make eliminations and adjustments. When the statements to be consolidated are fairly simple, it is quite feasible to compile the consolidated statements by the direct method. In more complex situations, it becomes difficult to keep track of the many adjustments, with the frustrating result that the financial statements won't balance!

The worksheet approach is less intuitive, but is more methodical and keeps better track of the eliminations and adjustments, some of which get very complicated. In complex situations, therefore, accountants in practice find it easier to use a worksheet (usually computerized) to summarize the necessary eliminations and adjustments. The worksheet also provides the management trail (or audit trail) that explains how the consolidated statements were derived.

In this chapter we will illustrate both approaches. The direct approach will be presented first and the worksheet approach second. Both approaches yield the same result. It doesn't matter which approach is used—what is important is the result, not the method used to derive the result. The worksheet approach becomes unwieldy to illustrate in the text when more complicated problems are involved (even though it helps keep better track of the various adjustments and eliminations). In later chapters of the text, therefore, we will only use the direct approach. However, this text's Companion Website will show the worksheet approach for all text examples that are in later chapters. The worksheet examples will be available online on the Companion Website for this text at www.pearsoned.ca/beechy.

LO ❸
Describe the basic principles of consolidation

## 2.7 CONSOLIDATION: COST METHOD RECORDING

## Consolidating a Parent-Founded Subsidiary—Simple Example

The condensed SFP of a parent before setting up its subsidiary is shown below.

| Parent Statement of Financial Position December 31, 20X9 | |
|---|---|
| **Assets** | |
| Cash | $10,000 |
| TOTAL ASSETS | $10,000 |
| | |
| **Liabilities and shareholders' equity** | |
| Share capital | $ 5,000 |
| Retained earnings | 5,000 |
| TOTAL LIABILITIES AND SHAREHOLDERS' EQUITY | $10,000 |

**New Subsidiary Founded** Assume that the parent founded a subsidiary by investing $1,000. The separate statements of financial position for each company are provided below. Notice that we introduced an "investment in subsidiary" account for $1,000 in the parent's SFP and a counterbalancing share capital account for $1,000 in the subsidiary's SFP. From the parent's point of view, no new owner's equity was created by the formation of the subsidiary. All that happened is that one asset (cash) decreased by $1,000, while another account, investment in subsidiary, increased by the same amount of $1,000. Its total equity continued to be $10,000.

| Separate Statements of Financial Position December 31, 20X9 | Parent | Subsidiary |
|---|---|---|
| **Assets** | | |
| Cash | $ 9,000 | $1,000 |
| Investment in subsidiary | 1,000 | — |
| TOTAL ASSETS | $10,000 | $1,000 |
| | | |
| **Liabilities and shareholders' equity** | | |
| Share capital | $ 5,000 | $1,000 |
| Retained earnings | 5,000 | — |
| TOTAL LIABILITIES AND SHAREHOLDERS' EQUITY | $10,000 | $1,000 |

# Direct Approach—Consolidation Immediately After Founding the Subsidiary

Both the investment in subsidiary account of $1,000 in the parent's SFP and the share capital account of $1,000 in the subsidiary's SFP are eliminated. From the consolidated perspective one asset, cash, went up $1,000, while another asset, investment in subsidiary, went down by $1,000. *The subsidiary's share capital is not added to the parent's share capital since it is already reflected in the parent's total equity of $10,000.* If we consolidate the subsidiary immediately after its creation, with the parent, we should get back the original SFP of the parent.

| Parent Consolidated Statement of Financial Position December 31, 20X9 | |
|---|---:|
| **Assets** | |
| Cash ($9,000 + $1,000) | $10,000 |
| Investment in subsidiary ($1,000 − **$1,000**) | 0 |
| **TOTAL ASSETS** | $10,000 |
| **Liabilities and shareholders' equity** | |
| Share capital | $ 5,000 |
| Retained earnings | 5,000 |
| **TOTAL LIABILITIES AND SHAREHOLDERS' EQUITY** | $10,000 |

# Worksheet Approach—Consolidation upon Founding the Subsidiary

The entries to eliminate the investment in subsidiary account in the parent's books and the share capital in the subsidiary's books and the parent's consolidation worksheet are provided below. The consolidated SFP under the worksheet approach will be identical to the SFP derived under the direct approach above.

| | | |
|---|---|---|
| Share capital (of subsidiary) | 1,000 | |
| Investment in subsidiary (of parent) | | 1,000 |

| December 31, 20X9 | | | | |
|---|---|---|---|---|
| | Trial Balances | | Adjustments | |
| | Parent | Subsidiary | Dr/(Cr) | Consolidated |
| Cash | $ 9,000 | $ 1,000 | — | $10,000 |
| Investment in subsidiary | 1,000 | — | $ (1,000) | 0 |
| Share capital | (5,000) | (1,000) | 1,000 | (5,000) |
| Retained earnings | (5,000) | — | — | (5,000) |
| | $ — | $ — | $ — | $ — |

# Example with Intercompany Transactions and Balances

Assume that Parco established a subsidiary in 20X0 by creating a new corporation named Subco. Subco issued 100 common shares to Parco in return for $80,000 cash paid by Parco for the shares. Parco has remained the sole shareholder of Subco in succeeding years.

On December 31, 20X8, a few years after the incorporation of Subco, the trial balances for the two companies are as shown in Exhibit 2.2. The 20X8 separate-entity financial statements of the two companies (derived from the trial balances) are presented in Exhibit 2.3, prior to any adjustments related to Parco's investment in Subco. In Exhibit 2.3, we have boldfaced and highlighted those elements that are of particular interest for consolidation purposes.

**Exhibit 2.2** Separate-Entity Trial Balances

| December 31, 20X8 | Parco | | Subco | |
|---|---|---|---|---|
| | Dr | Cr | Dr | Cr |
| Cash | $ 70,000 | | $ 40,000 | |
| Accounts receivable | 200,000 | | 110,000 | |
| Receivable from Subco | 60,000 | | — | |
| Inventories | 150,000 | | 120,000 | |
| Land | 100,000 | | — | |
| Buildings and equipment | 1,000,000 | | 450,000 | |
| Accumulated depreciation | | $ 300,000 | | $ 100,000 |
| Investment in Subco (at cost) | 80,000 | | | |
| Accounts payable | | 120,000 | | 80,000 |
| Due to Parco | | — | | 60,000 |
| Long-term notes payable | | — | | 300,000 |
| Deferred income taxes | | 140,000 | | 30,000 |
| Common shares | | 300,000 | | 80,000 |
| Dividends declared | 30,000 | | 20,000 | |
| Retained earnings, December 31, 20X7 | | 762,000 | | 60,000 |
| Sales revenue | | 800,000 | | 400,000 |
| Dividend income | | 20,000 | | — |
| Cost of sales | 480,000 | | 280,000 | |
| Depreciation expense | 130,000 | | 30,000 | |
| Income tax expense | 32,000 | | 20,000 | |
| Other expenses | 110,000 | | 40,000 | |
| | $ 2,442,000 | $ 2,442,000 | $ 1,110,000 | $ 1,110,000 |

To prepare the consolidated statements, we first need to know the nature and extent of financial interactions between the two. Important facts relating to the 20X8 statements are as follows:

1. Parco uses the *cost method* to account for its investment in Subco ($80,000). Under the **cost method**, the value of the investment is retained at the original cost paid for the investment, without adjusting it for the investor's share of the investee's earnings. Dividends received by the parent from the subsidiary are reported as income in the separate-entity SCI of the parent.

2. The two statements of financial position include $60,000 that is owed by Subco to Parco. The amount is a current asset for Parco and a current liability for Subco.

3. Dividends received from Subco during the year are shown as dividend income on Parco's SCI.

4. The sales of Parco include $100,000 of merchandise sold to Subco, all of which was sold by Subco to outside customers during the year.

## Overall Analysis of the Example
We can arrive at the following conclusions based on the facts provided in the example:

- In this example, consolidation requires only eliminations; adjustments are not required.

- We need to make eliminations to remove double-counting for the following two issues:

  - the sale of $100,000 by Parco to Subco; and
  - the dividend income of $20,000 of Parco received from Subco.

- We need to make eliminations to remove offsetting balances for the following two issues:

  - the investment in Subco of $80,000; and
  - $60,000 owed by Subco to Parco.

- *Finally, but very importantly, the retained earnings of Subco are not eliminated during the consolidation process.*

## In-Depth Analysis of the Example
We will elaborate on each of the above issues in further detail below:

- The sale of $100,000[a] by Parco to Subco.[2] When Parco sold these goods to Subco, it would have recognized a sale of $100,000 and the cost of purchasing those goods (amount not provided in the problem) as cost of goods sold in its SCI. Subco in turn sold the same goods to outsiders. Therefore, it would recognize the amount at which it sold the goods to outsiders (amount not provided in the problem) as a sale, while recognizing the cost of purchasing these goods from Parco at $100,000 as cost of goods sold in its SCI.

---

[2]The discussion in the text and the related adjustment under the direct method in the relevant table are linked using superscript letters. This practice will be followed in later examples in the text as well.

**Exhibit 2.3** Separate-Entity Financial Statements

### Statements of Financial Position
### December 31, 20X8

| Assets | Parco | Subco |
|---|---|---|
| Current assets: | | |
| Cash | $ 70,000 | $ 40,000 |
| Accounts receivable | 200,000 | 110,000 |
| Receivable | **60,000** | — |
| Inventories | 150,000 | 120,000 |
| | 480,000 | 270,000 |
| Property, plant, and equipment: | | |
| Land | 100,000 | — |
| Buildings and equipment | 1,000,000 | 450,000 |
| Accumulated depreciation | (300,000) | (100,000) |
| | 800,000 | 350,000 |
| Other assets: | | |
| Investment in Subco (at cost) | **80,000** | — |
| TOTAL ASSETS | $1,360,000 | $620,000 |
| Liabilities and shareholders' equity | | |
| Current liabilities: | | |
| Accounts payable | $ 120,000 | $ 80,000 |
| Due to Parco | — | **60,000** |
| | 120,000 | 140,000 |
| Long-term notes payable | — | 300,000 |
| Deferred income taxes | 140,000 | 30,000 |
| Total liabilities | 260,000 | 470,000 |
| Shareholders' equity: | | |
| Common shares | 300,000 | **80,000** |
| Retained earnings | 800,000 | 70,000 |
| Total shareholders' equity | 1,100,000 | 150,000 |
| TOTAL LIABILITIES AND SHAREHOLDERS' EQUITY | $1,360,000 | $620,000 |

### Statements of Comprehensive Income
### Year Ended December 31, 20X8

| | Parco | Subco |
|---|---|---|
| Sales revenue | $ 800,000 | $400,000 |
| Dividend income | **20,000** | — |
| | 820,000 | 400,000 |
| Operating expenses: | | |
| Cost of sales | 480,000 | 280,000 |
| Depreciation expense | 130,000 | 30,000 |
| Income tax expense | 32,000 | 20,000 |
| Other expenses | 110,000 | 40,000 |
| | 752,000 | 370,000 |
| NET INCOME | 68,000 | 30,000 |

### Statements of Changes in Equity-Retained Earnings Section
### Year Ended December 31, 20X8

| | | |
|---|---|---|
| Retained earnings, December 31, 20X7 | 762,000 | 60,000 |
| Net income | 68,000 | 30,000 |
| Dividends declared | (30,000) | **(20,000)** |
| Retained earnings, December 31, 20X8 | $ 800,000 | $ 70,000 |

Therefore, from a consolidated perspective, both the sales figure and the cost of goods sold figure are overstated by $100,000. Only the results of transactions with outsiders should be included in the consolidated financial statements. As a result, we need to subtract $100,000 from both sales and cost of goods sold when preparing the consolidated statements.

■ The dividend income of $20,000[b] of Parco received from Subco. This $20,000 is already included in Subco's income. Therefore, from a consolidated perspective, including the same $20,000 as both Parco's dividend income and as part of Subco's net income would be double-counting. Only the results of transactions with outsiders should be included in the consolidated financial statements.

Therefore, we need to subtract $20,000 from both dividend income and dividends declared. Doing so will decrease Parco's income by $20,000 but increase Subco's retained earnings by that amount. Since we are going to add Subco's retained earnings to Parco's retained earnings (as discussed in detail further below), the overall impact of this elimination on the consolidated retained earnings is nil.

■ The investment in Subco of $80,000.[c] The investment account is really just an aggregate that represents the net assets of the subsidiary; instead of showing the net investment in the subsidiary as an asset, the consolidated statements show all of the assets and liabilities of the subsidiary that underlie the investment. Parco accounts for its investment in Subco at cost. Therefore, the balance in the investment account will match the share capital of Subco. We need to eliminate both amounts.

As we pointed out in our first consolidation example, *the subsidiary's share capital is not added to the parent's share capital because Subco's net assets, equal to its share capital, are already included in the parent's total net assets (and shareholders' equity) of $1,100,000.* The net assets and shareholders' equity that will be shown in Parco's consolidated SFP will be the net assets (and shareholders' equity) *from the point of view of the Parco shareholders.* The common share equity that is outstanding for Parco is the $300,000 shown in Parco's SFP.

■ $60,000[d] owed by Subco to Parco. From a consolidated point of view you cannot lend and owe money to yourself. Therefore, "Receivable from Subco" and "Due to Parco" are both reduced by $60,000, respectively.

■ Retained earnings of Subco. Because Parco accounts for its investment in Subco at cost, Parco recorded only the dividend income received from Subco; Parco did not record the rest of Subco's earnings from the time of its establishment. Therefore, Parco's retained earnings do not reflect the retained earnings of Subco. Hence, during consolidation, Subco's retained earnings should be added to Parco's retained earnings.

We will modify this conclusion later (1) in the presence of non-controlling interest, (2) when the subsidiary is not established by the parent but is purchased, and (3) when the parent uses the equity method to record its subsidiary in its separate-entity financial statements. Stay tuned!

## Direct Approach—Consolidation Involving Intercompany Transactions and Balances

The Parco consolidated financial statements for 20X8 are shown in Exhibit 2.4. In this exhibit, the statements have been prepared by the direct method. The consolidated financial statements are obtained by (1) adding together the individual amounts on the parent and subsidiaries' financial statements; (2) subtracting amounts as necessary for

**Exhibit 2.4** Parco Consolidated Financial Statements

| Consolidated Statement of Financial Position<br>December 31, 20X8 | |
|---|---:|
| **Assets** | |
| Current assets: | |
| Cash [70,000 + 40,000] | $  110,000 |
| Accounts receivable [200,000 + 110,000] | 310,000 |
| Receivable from Subco [60,000 + 0 – **60,000**[d]] | — |
| Inventories [150,000 + 120,000] | 270,000 |
| | 690,000 |
| Property, plant, and equipment: | |
| Land [100,000 + 0] | 100,000 |
| Buildings and equipment [1,000,000 + 450,000] | 1,450,000 |
| Accumulated depreciation [300,000 + 100,000] | (400,000) |
| | 1,150,000 |
| Other assets: | |
| Investment in Subco (at cost) [80,000 + 0 – **80,000**[c]] | — |
| **TOTAL ASSETS** | $1,840,000 |
| **Liabilities and shareholders' equity** | |
| Current liabilities: | |
| Accounts payable [120,000 + 80,000] | $  200,000 |
| Due to Parco [0 + 60,000 – **60,000**[d]] | — |
| | 200,000 |
| Long-term notes payable [0 + 300,000] | 300,000 |
| Deferred income taxes [140,000 + 30,000] | 170,000 |
| Total liabilities | 670,000 |
| Shareholders' equity: | |
| Common shares [300,000 + 80,000 – **80,000**[c]] | 300,000 |
| Retained earnings [800,000 + 70,000] | 870,000 |
| Total shareholders' equity | 1,170,000 |
| **TOTAL LIABILITIES AND SHAREHOLDERS' EQUITY** | $1,840,000 |

| Consolidated Statement of Comprehensive Income<br>Year Ended December 31, 20X8 | |
|---|---:|
| Revenue: | |
| Sales revenue [800,000 + 400,000 – **100,000**[a]] | $1,100,000 |
| Dividend income [20,000 + 0 – **20,000**[b]] | — |
| | 1,100,000 |
| Operating expenses: | |
| Cost of sales [480,000 + 280,000 – **100,000**[a]] | 660,000 |
| Depreciation expense [130,000 + 30,000] | 160,000 |
| Income tax expense [32,000 + 20,000] | 52,000 |
| Other expenses [110,000 + 40,000] | 150,000 |
| | 1,022,000 |
| **NET INCOME** | $    78,000 |

| Statements of Changes in Equity-Retained Earnings Section<br>Year Ended December 31, 20X8 | |
|---|---:|
| Net income | $    78,000 |
| Retained earnings, December 31, 20X7 [762,000 + 60,000] | 822,000 |
| Dividends declared [30,000 + 20,000 – **20,000**[b]] | (30,000) |
| Retained earnings, December 31, 20X8 | $  870,000 |

eliminations; and then (3) entering the resulting amounts directly into consolidated financial statements.

### Worksheet Approach—Consolidation Involving Intercompany Transactions and Balances

Exhibit 2.5 illustrates a worksheet based on the separate-entity trial balances for each company. The trial balances of the parent and the subsidiary (or subsidiaries) are listed in the first columns of the worksheet, and the eliminations and adjustments are inserted in the next column. Cross-adding the rows yields the amounts that will be used to prepare the consolidated statements.

**Exhibit 2.5** Parco Consolidated Worksheet—Cost Basis of Recording

| December 31, 20X8 | Trial balances | | | |
|---|---|---|---|---|
| | Parco Dr/(Cr) | Subco Dr/(Cr) | Adjustments Dr/(Cr) | Parco consolidated trial balance |
| Cash | $ 70,000 | $ 40,000 | | $ 110,000 |
| Accounts receivable | 200,000 | 110,000 | | 310,000 |
| Receivable from Subco | 60,000 | — | $(60,000)[d] | — |
| Inventories | 150,000 | 120,000 | | 270,000 |
| Land | 100,000 | — | | 100,000 |
| Buildings and equipment | 1,000,000 | 450,000 | | 1,450,000 |
| Accumulated depreciation | (300,000) | (100,000) | | (400,000) |
| Investment in Subco (at cost) | 80,000 | — | (80,000)[c] | — |
| Accounts payable | (120,000) | (80,000) | | (200,000) |
| Due to Parco | — | (60,000) | 60,000[d] | — |
| Long-term notes payable | — | (300,000) | | (300,000) |
| Deferred income taxes | (140,000) | (30,000) | | (170,000) |
| Common shares | (300,000) | (80,000) | 80,000[c] | (300,000) |
| Dividends declared | 30,000 | 20,000 | (20,000)[b] | 30,000 |
| Retained earnings, December 31, 20X7 | (762,000) | (60,000) | | (822,000) |
| Sales revenue | (800,000) | (400,000) | 100,000[a] | (1,100,000) |
| Dividend income | (20,000) | — | 20,000[b] | — |
| Cost of sales | 480,000 | 280,000 | (100,000)[a] | 660,000 |
| Depreciation expense | 130,000 | 30,000 | | 160,000 |
| Income tax expense | 32,000 | 20,000 | | 52,000 |
| Other expenses | 110,000 | 40,000 | | 150,000 |
| | $ — | $ — | $ — | $ — |

The eliminations that were made in preparing Parco's consolidated statements can be summarized as follows, in general journal format. The parentheses indicate the company on whose statements the accounts being adjusted appear.

| | | |
|---|---|---|
| (a) Sales (Parco) | 100,000 | |
|     Cost of sales (Subco) | | 100,000 |
| (b) Dividend income (Parco) | 20,000 | |
|     Dividends declared (Subco) | | 20,000 |
| (c) Common shares (of Subco) | 80,000 | |
|     Investment in Subco (by Parco) | | 80,000 |
| (d) Due to Parco (Subco) | 60,000 | |
|     Receivable from Subco (Parco) | | 60,000 |

In each of the eliminations, one side eliminates an amount on Subco's financial statements, while the other side of the entry eliminates an amount on Parco's statements. There is no way that these entries can or should be recorded on either company's books. Consolidation elimination "entries" are entered only on working papers to prepare the consolidated statements, and they are never entered on the formal books of account of either the parent or the subsidiary.

LO ❸
Describe the basic principles of consolidation

## 2.8 REPORTING SUBSIDIARIES USING THE EQUITY METHOD

### Separate-Entity Financial Statements

The preparation of consolidated financial statements does not eliminate the need for each separate legal entity to prepare its own financial statements. Each corporation is taxed individually, and unconsolidated statements are necessary for income tax reporting if for no other purpose.

Consolidated statements may not be adequate for the needs of creditors or other users of financial statements. Creditors have claims on the resources of specific corporations, not on the resources of other corporations within a consolidated group of companies. Therefore it may be of little benefit to a creditor to see the consolidated assets and liabilities when the credit risk is associated with the financial position of a single company.

Under IFRS, when a parent prepares its separate-entity statements for public use, investments in unconsolidated subsidiaries are reported at cost or as financial instruments. However, often such investments may be reported on the equity basis when the separate-entity financial statements are prepared for the use of a specific user, such as a bank or other major lender, who is interested in the net assets, earnings, and cash flow of the individual corporation. The equity basis permits the financial statement user to discern the full economic impact of the operations of the overall economic entity (i.e., the parent corporation and its subsidiaries) and yet still see the assets, liabilities, results of operations, and cash flows for the parent company alone.

## Subsidiaries Recorded on the Cost Method but Reported by the Equity Method

A parent company almost invariably carries its subsidiaries' investment accounts on the cost basis, even if the investments will be reported on the equity method for unconsolidated reporting. The reason is that the process of consolidation is much simpler if the investments are carried at cost instead of equity. We shall illustrate this fact in a following section. Thus, normally, a parent company will choose to *record* its investment in a subsidiary using the cost method even if it *reports* unconsolidated subsidiaries on the equity method.

It is vital to remember that, with strategic investments, an investor's *recording* usually does not coincide with its *reporting*. Adjustments and eliminations appear only on working papers for preparing financial statements and are not recorded in the investor corporation's accounts.

In our present example, the following adjustments can be made *on Parco's working papers* to convert the investment in Subco from the cost to the equity method for *reporting* purposes:

| | | |
|---|---|---|
| Dividend income | 20,000 | |
|   Investment in Subco | | 20,000 |
|   (to eliminate the dividends recognized as income under the cost method) | | |
| Investment in Subco | 30,000 | |
|   Equity in earnings of Subco | | 30,000 |
|   (to recognize Parco's share of the subsidiary's current year's earnings as income) | | |
| Investment in Subco | 60,000 | |
|   Retained earnings | | 60,000 |
|   (to recognize Parco's share of the unremitted earnings of Subco from prior years) | | |

It is important to remember that these entries are worksheet entries only—they will not be recorded on Parco's books because the account is maintained on the cost basis.

## Recording a Subsidiary by the Equity Method

It is possible, but rare, for a parent company to carry a subsidiary's investment account on its books by using the equity basis. Therefore, for completeness, we will now assume that Parco does record its investment in Subco using the equity method.

Exhibit 2.6 shows the various components of the carrying value of Subco under the equity method of accounting. In the current year, the entries required in Parco's books relating to its share of Subco's earnings in the current year are as follows.

| | | |
|---|---|---|
| Investment in Subco | 30,000 | |
|   Equity in earnings of Subco | | 30,000 |
| Cash (or Dividends Receivable) | 20,000 | |
|   Investment in Subco | | 20,000 |

**Exhibit 2.6** Investment in Subco in Separate-Entity Financial Statements of Parco Using Equity Basis of Recording

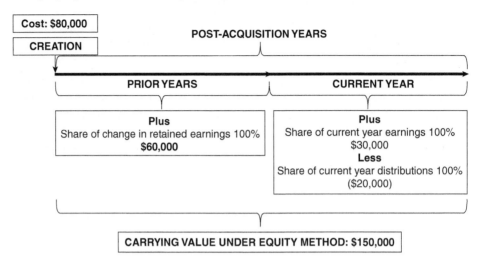

The first entry above recognizes Parco's 100% share of Subco's current year earnings of $30,000 and increases the investment in Subco's account by that amount. The equity in earnings of Subco will be included as an income item in Parco's current year SCI. The dividend of $20,000 is deducted from the investment in Subco account, offset by an increase in the cash (or dividends receivable) account.

Under the equity method, Parco would have made similar entries in earlier years to recognize its share of Subco's prior years' earnings. Thus, Parco's books will already reflect its share of Subco's unremitted earnings. Therefore, no further entries are required in the current year in relation to Subco's prior years' earnings.

Note that under the equity method it is *not* necessary to eliminate intercompany transactions such as the $100,000 sales by Parco to Subco. The necessary adjustments are only for items that affect net income—the intercompany transaction washes out in its effect on net income.

Explain the relationship between consolidation and equity reporting

## 2.9 COMPARISON OF COST, EQUITY, AND CONSOLIDATION METHODS

Exhibit 2.7 provides a comparison of the financial statements of Parco under the three different policies for reporting the investment in Subco. The first column shows Parco's separate-entity financial statements with the investment in Subco reported on the cost basis. These financial statements are derived from the first column of Exhibit 2.3.

The second column shows Parco's separate-entity financial statements prepared on the equity basis. Note that the first two columns are identical except for the investment in Subco and reported earnings from Subco. As a result, the reported net income and retained earnings of Parco differ significantly between the first and second columns.

The third column of Exhibit 2.7 shows Parco's consolidated financial statements. Almost all of the amounts in the third column are different from those in the first two

**Exhibit 2.7** Parco Financial Statements using Different Reporting Practices

### Statement of Financial Position
### December 31, 20X8

| | Cost basis | Equity basis | Consolidated |
|---|---|---|---|
| **Assets** | | | |
| Current assets: | | | |
| Cash | $ 70,000 | $ 70,000 | $ 110,000 |
| Accounts receivable | 200,000 | 200,000 | 310,000 |
| Receivable from Subco | 60,000 | 60,000 | — |
| Inventories | 150,000 | 150,000 | 270,000 |
| | 480,000 | 480,000 | 690,000 |
| Property, plant, and equipment: | | | |
| Land | 100,000 | 100,000 | 100,000 |
| Buildings and equipment | 1,000,000 | 1,000,000 | 1,450,000 |
| Accumulated depreciation | (300,000) | (300,000) | (400,000) |
| | 800,000 | 800,000 | 1,150,000 |
| Other assets: | | | |
| Investment in Subco | 80,000 | 150,000 | — |
| **TOTAL ASSETS** | $1,360,000 | $1,430,000 | $1,840,000 |
| **Liabilities and shareholders' equity** | | | |
| Liabilities: | | | |
| Current accounts payable | $ 120,000 | $ 120,000 | $ 200,000 |
| Long-term notes payable | — | — | 300,000 |
| Deferred income taxes | 140,000 | 140,000 | 170,000 |
| Total liabilities | 260,000 | 260,000 | 670,000 |
| Shareholders' equity: | | | |
| Common shares | 300,000 | 300,000 | 300,000 |
| Retained earnings | 800,000 | 870,000 | 870,000 |
| Total shareholders' equity | 1,100,000 | 1,170,000 | 1,170,000 |
| **TOTAL LIABILITIES AND SHAREHOLDERS' EQUITY** | $1,360,000 | $1,430,000 | $1,840,000 |

### Statement of Comprehensive Income
### Year Ended December 31, 20X8

| | Cost basis | Equity basis | Consolidated |
|---|---|---|---|
| Sales revenue | $ 800,000 | $ 800,000 | $1,100,000 |
| Operating expenses: | | | |
| Cost of sales | 480,000 | 480,000 | 660,000 |
| Depreciation expense | 130,000 | 130,000 | 160,000 |
| Income tax expense | 32,000 | 32,000 | 52,000 |
| Other expenses | 110,000 | 110,000 | 150,000 |
| | 752,000 | 752,000 | 1,022,000 |
| Net income from operations | 48,000 | 48,000 | 78,000 |
| Dividend income | 20,000 | | |
| Equity in earnings of Subco | — | 30,000 | — |
| **NET INCOME** | $ 68,000 | $ 78,000 | $ 78,000 |

### Statement of Changes in Equity-Retained Earnings Section
### Year Ended December 31, 20X8

| | Cost basis | Equity basis | Consolidated |
|---|---|---|---|
| Net income | $ 68,000 | $ 78,000 | $ 78,000 |
| Retained earnings, December 31, 20X7 | 762,000 | 822,000 | 822,000 |
| Dividends declared | (30,000) | (30,000) | (30,000) |
| Retained earnings, December 31, 20X8 | $ 800,000 | $ 870,000 | $ 870,000 |

columns. The assets, liabilities, revenues, and expenses include those of both Parco and Subco, while the investment account in Subco and the receivable from Subco accounts have disappeared and the long-term notes payable account has been added.

It is impossible to tell from the third column which of the assets and liabilities are those of Parco, since the two corporations are reported as a single economic entity. If a lender were to extend a line of credit to Parco based on (for example) 75% of Parco's accounts receivable, the lender would not be able to tell from the consolidated statements just how much of the $310,000 reported accounts receivable is an asset of Parco.

While most of the consolidated amounts differ from those in the first two columns of Exhibit 2.7, two items are the same in the second and third columns but different from the first column: *Retained earnings* and *Net income*. A basic and important attribute of the equity method is that the parent's reported net income and net assets (shareholders' equity) will be the same as when the subsidiaries are consolidated. The effect of consolidation is to disaggregate the net investment in the subsidiary into the component assets and liabilities, and to disaggregate the parent's equity in the earnings of the subsidiary into its components of revenue and expense.

The equity method is frequently referred to as **single-line consolidation** because the equity method and consolidation both result in the same net income and shareholders' equity for the parent. There is one line on the SFP that shows the net asset value of the subsidiary, and one line on the SCI that shows the net earnings derived from the subsidiary.[3]

The one-line adjustment to the parent's earnings is commonly known as the **equity pick-up** of the subsidiary's earnings.

### Concept Check 2-5

1. Why is the retained earnings balance of the subsidiary not eliminated during consolidation when a parent-founded subsidiary is recorded under the cost method?

2. Why are intercompany transactions and balances not eliminated under the equity method of reporting?

Describe the basic principles of consolidation

## 2.10 CONSOLIDATION: EQUITY METHOD RECORDING

In our earlier illustration of direct consolidation and of the consolidation worksheet, we assumed that the parent company carried the investment in Subco at cost. While the cost method is most commonly used for internal recordkeeping, the equity method may also be used. Therefore, we will now illustrate how consolidation works when Parco uses the equity method in its separate-entity financial statements to record its investment in Subco. Given that such a practice is rare in real life, later chapters will not illustrate consolidation under equity recording.

If Parco had been using the equity method, (1) the investment account would be $150,000 at the end of 20X8; (2) Parco's opening retained earnings would be $822,000

---

[3]An exception arises for the investor's share of any discontinued operations of the investee. The investor's proportionate share of discontinued operations will be reported net of related taxes on the investor's SCI after net income from continuing operations.

instead of $762,000; and (3) the SCI accounts would include the $30,000 equity in the earnings of Subco rather than dividend income of $20,000.

The first column of Exhibit 2.8 shows the condensed financial statements for Parco, assuming that the investment has been recorded using the equity method. The accounts and amounts that are affected by using the equity method rather than the cost method are highlighted in bold. When the eliminating entries are prepared, the two entries to eliminate the balance of the investment account differ from those shown in Exhibit 2.5 because the composition of the balance in the investment account is different.

Under the cost method, only the original cost of the investment is included in the investment account, and the only elimination necessary is to offset the cost of the investment against the common share account of the subsidiary.

**Exhibit 2.8** Parco Consolidation Worksheet—Equity Basis of Recording

| | December 31, 20X8 | | | |
| | Trial balances | | | |
| | Parco Dr/(Cr) | Subco Dr/(Cr) | Elimination and adjustments Dr/(Cr) | Parco Consolidated trial balance |
| --- | --- | --- | --- | --- |
| Cash | $ 70,000 | $ 40,000 | | $ 110,000 |
| Accounts receivable | 200,000 | 110,000 | | 310,000 |
| Receivable from Subco | 60,000 | — | $ (60,000)c | — |
| Inventories | 150,000 | 120,000 | | 270,000 |
| Land | 100,000 | — | | 100,000 |
| Buildings and equipment | 1,000,000 | 450,000 | | 1,450,000 |
| Accumulated depreciation | (300,000) | (100,000) | | (400,000) |
| **Investment in Subco** | | | | |
| **(at equity)** | **150,000** | — | (140,000)a (10,000)b | |
| Accounts payable | (120,000) | (80,000) | | (200,000) |
| Due to Parco | — | (60,000) | 60,000 c | — |
| Long-term notes payable | — | (300,000) | | (300,000) |
| Deferred income taxes | (140,000) | (30,000) | | (170,000) |
| Common shares | (300,000) | (80,000) | 80,000 | (300,000) |
| Dividends declared | 30,000 | 20,000 | (20,000) | 30,000 |
| **Retained earnings,** | | | | |
| **December 31, 20X7** | **(822,000)** | (60,000) | **60,000** a | (822,000) |
| Sales revenue | (800,000) | (400,000) | 100,000 d | (1,100,000) |
| Equity in earnings of Subco | **(30,000)** | — | **30,000** b | — |
| Cost of sales | 480,000 | 280,000 | (100,000)d | 660,000 |
| Depreciation expense | 130,000 | 30,000 | | 160,000 |
| Income tax expense | 32,000 | 20,000 | | 52,000 |
| Other expenses | 110,000 | 40,000 | — | 150,000 |
| | $ — | $ — | $ — | $ — |

Under the equity method, however, the investment account includes both the original cost of the investment and the unremitted earnings of the subsidiary. Both of these amounts must be eliminated. The parent's retained earnings under the equity method also include the earnings of the subsidiary, since the subsidiary's earnings are taken into the parent's income each year. If we now add the retained earnings of Subco to the retained earnings of Parco, as we did under the cost method, we would be double-counting Subco's retained earnings. Therefore, the worksheet entries to eliminate the investment account are shown as follows when the equity method of recording the investment has been used:

| | | |
|---|---|---|
| **(a)** Common shares (of Subco) | 80,000 | |
| Retained earnings (of Subco) | 60,000 | |
| Investment in Subco (by Parco) | | 140,000 |
| **(b)** Equity in earnings of subsidiary (of Parco) | 30,000 | |
| Dividends declared (by Subco) | | 20,000 |
| Investment in Subco (of Parco) | | 10,000 |

Worksheet entry (a) eliminates the original investment and the accumulated retained (and unremitted) earnings of Subco of prior years. Entry (b) eliminates the dividends and the double-counting of Subco's earnings for the current year. In effect, the two adjustments reverse the entries that were originally made by Parco to record its interest in the earnings of Subco and to record the original investment.

The process of consolidation cancels out entries made for the equity pick-up of the subsidiaries' earnings. This is why companies virtually always use the cost basis of recording their strategic investments—the process of consolidation requires that the equity-basis adjustments be eliminated, and thus most companies simply record the investment on the cost basis. It is simpler *not* to use the equity method for *recording* the investment. The remaining two eliminations, for the intercompany debt and the intercompany sales, are unaffected by the method of recording the investment.

The net effect of the eliminations to the SCI and retained earnings section of the statement of changes in equity (SCE/RE) is to reduce the combined ending retained earnings by $70,000, thereby preventing the double-counting of Subco's ending retained earnings. This net change of $70,000 is transferred to the SFP to complete the worksheet.

Exhibit 2.9 graphically depicts the impact on the separate-entity SCI and SFP of the parent of using the cost and equity method respectively to record its investment in its 100% owned subsidiary. Exhibit 2.9 also shows the impact of consolidation on the consolidated SCI and SFP. Further, Exhibit 2.9 briefly summarizes the changes needed to convert from the cost method of reporting the investment in the subsidiary to the equity method and consolidation, respectively, and likewise from the equity method to consolidation.

## Concept Check 2-6

1. When might a parent, which otherwise must consolidate its subsidiaries, report them under the equity method?

2. Why is the consolidated retained earnings balance of the parent equal to its retained earnings balance under the equity method of reporting investments in subsidiaries?

**Exhibit 2.9** Cost, Equity, and Consolidation Methods to Report
100% Owned Subsidiary

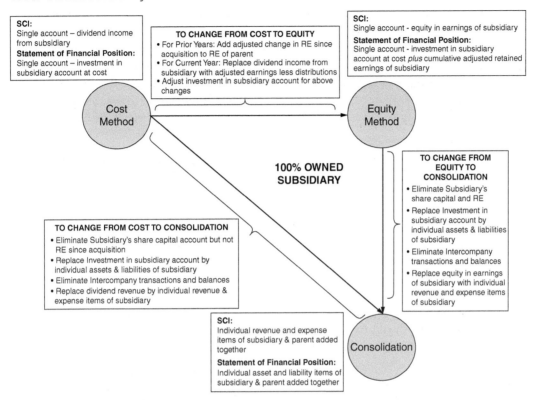

## 2.11 EQUITY METHOD: A CONCEPTUAL ELABORATION

Under the **equity method**, the investor records the investment initially at its cost or purchase price. Usually, the purchase price equals the fair or market value of the investment at the time of the purchase. The purchase price rarely is equal to the carrying value of the investment in the books of the investee. The difference between the carrying value of the investment in the books of the investee and the purchase price or cost paid by the investor is known as the purchase price discrepancy (PPD) or fair value adjustment (FVA).

In subsequent years, the carrying value of the investment is adjusted to recognize the investor's share of the investee's adjusted earnings after the date of acquisition. The investor makes two major types of adjustments to the investee's earnings before calculating its share of such earnings: (1) amortization of the PPD/FVA; and (2) elimination by reducing unrealized gains/losses on intercompany transactions.

The adjustments to the investee's earnings are similar to the adjustments required when consolidating the financial statements of subsidiaries with the financial statement of the parent; therefore, these adjustments are called **consolidating adjustments**. The carrying value of the investment is also reduced by any distributions, such as dividends, made by the investee.

LO **3**
Describe the basic principles of consolidation

LO **5**
Explain the relationship between consolidation and equity reporting

Exhibit 2.10 provides an overview of how the carrying value is calculated under the equity method, focusing on the most common adjustments (1) at time of acquisition, (2) in prior years, and (3) in the current year. These adjustments will be the subject of our discussion in the next few chapters.

The investor's share of the investee's adjusted net income or loss is included as a single line item of profit or loss in the investor's SCI. The investment is included at its carrying value as a single line item on the investor's SFP. Therefore, the equity method is also known as *single-line consolidation*. Additional adjustments to the carrying value of the investment are also necessary for the investor's proportionate share of the investee's OCI.

## Share of Losses Exceeds Investor's Interest in Associate or Joint Venture

Sometimes the investor's share of the adjusted losses of the investee (i.e., associate or joint venture) exceeds its interest in the investee. In such circumstances, the investor stops recognizing further losses in its net income. Here "investor's interest in the investee" refers to the carrying value of the investment in the investee, calculated using the equity method and including long-term interests in the investee that are deemed to constitute additional investments.

Examples of such long-term interests include preferred shares and long-term receivables. There should be no plans for settlement of such additional investments in the near future. If the investor provides further commitments or guarantees on behalf of the investee, losses are recognized only as provision (liability) to the extent of those commitments or guarantees. When the investee resumes making profits, the investor starts recognizing its portion of such profits only when they exceed the losses not recognized previously.

**Exhibit 2.10** Common Adjustments Under the Equity Method

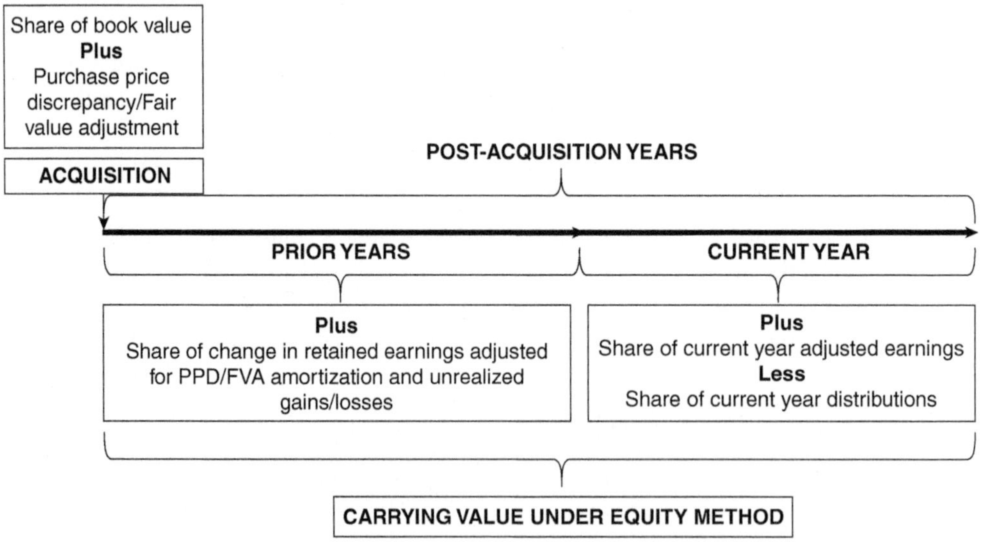

# 2.12 A CLOSER LOOK AT CONTROL

LO 3
Describe the basic principles of consolidation

A corporation's strategic activities are normally determined by its board of directors. The members of the board of directors are elected by the shareholders. Therefore, if an investor owns a majority of the voting shares, the investor normally will possess the power to elect a majority of the board of directors and thus will have the power of control.

Note that we said a majority of the *voting shares*. Many corporations, especially in Canada, have dual share structures wherein one class of common shares, called multiple voting shares, has more votes than the other, called subordinate shares. For example, Onex Corporation (as of the end of June 2011) owns only 8% of the total outstanding shares of Celestica Inc. but has 71% of the votes. Onex owns all of the approximately 19 million multiple voting shares of Celestica, which have 25 votes each, but owns less than 1% of the approximately 197 million subordinate voting shares, which have only one vote each.

Note also that having a majority of the votes does not always ensure control. An investor's ability to elect a majority of an investee's board of directors may be restricted by contractual agreements, regulatory requirements, or legal restrictions.

Determining whether control exists is not a formulaic process. Instead, the accountant must determine whether or not control exists by looking at many factors. Control may be direct or indirect, and may be exercised through factors other than just share ownership. For example, under IFRS 10, the following are some of the factors that must be considered, solely or jointly with other factors, while determining the presence or absence of control:

- Does the investor have a contractual agreement with other investors that guarantees control?

- Does the investor have the ability to appoint, hire, transfer, or fire key members of the investee's management?

- Do the investor and investee corporation have interlocking boards, wherein a majority of the board members are on both companies' boards?

- Does the investor provide retractable debt financing to the investee that is crucial to the investee's financial health?

## Indirect Control

Control need not be direct. **Indirect control** exists when a subsidiary is controlled by one or more other subsidiaries rather than by the parent company. Exhibit 2.11 shows three examples of indirect control.

In Case 1, the parent (**P**) controls subsidiary **A** by owning 70% of **A**'s voting shares, and **A** controls **C** by owning 60% of **C**'s voting shares. Since **P** controls **A**, **P** can control **A**'s votes for **C**'s board of directors. Therefore, **P** has indirect control of **C**. **C** is a subsidiary of **A**, and both **C** and **A** are subsidiaries of **P**.

Voting control is a yes–no matter, not multiplicative. **P** controls 60% of the votes for **C**'s board of directors, not just 42% (i.e., 70% × 60%). **P** controls **A**, and **A** controls **C**; therefore **P** controls **C**. Ownership of 60%, whether direct or indirect, gives **P** complete control over the strategic policies of **C**.

**Exhibit 2.11** Examples of Indirect Control

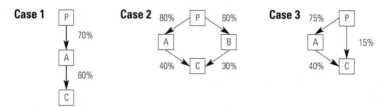

In Case 2, control of **P** over **C** is achieved indirectly through two direct subsidiaries of **P**: **A** and **B**. Neither **A** nor **B** has control of **C** because each has less than a majority of **C**'s voting shares. However, **P** can control **C** because **P** controls 70% of the votes in **C** through its control of **A** and **B** (40% + 30%). In this example, **A**, **B**, and **C** are all subsidiaries of **P**, but **C** is *not* a subsidiary of either **A** or **B**.

In Case 3, **P** has both direct and indirect ownership interests in **C**. Control is achieved only by virtue of the shares of **C** that are owned by both **P** and **A**, and thus **P**'s control of **C** is still indirect, despite **P**'s direct ownership of 15% of **C**'s voting shares. The sum of one corporation's direct and indirect interest in another corporation is known as the **beneficial interest**. **P** has a 55% beneficial interest in **C**. **A** and **C** are subsidiaries of **P**; **C** is *not* a subsidiary of **A**.

Other types of ownership arrangements can exist; these three examples are merely illustrative. Some intercorporate ownerships are very complex, and require careful analysis to determine who controls whom.

## Consolidation of Indirect Holdings

When there are several layers of subsidiaries, consolidated statements will normally be prepared at each level, particularly when there are non-controlling shareholders in the intermediate layers. For example, assume that Corporation A owns 70% of Corporation B, and Corporation B owns 60% of C. The following financial statements will be prepared:

- C will prepare its own separate-entity financial statements, which will be used by C's non-controlling shareholders and for C's income tax purposes.

- B will prepare separate-entity (i.e., non-consolidated) statements for its tax purposes, internal purposes, and perhaps for specific users, such as the bank. In the non-consolidated statements, the investment in C will be shown as an asset.

- For issuance to the general public, B will also prepare consolidated statements that include the assets, liabilities, revenue, expenses, and cash flows of C. These statements are relevant for B's non-controlling shareholders.

- A will prepare consolidated statements that include all of the assets, liabilities, revenues, expenses, and cash flows of the consolidated statements of B, which includes C. A's consolidated statements are relevant to the shareholders of A, *and of A only*. A will also prepare non-consolidated statements for its tax purposes and perhaps as special-purpose statements for bankers and creditors.

Non-controlling shareholders are interested only in the statements of the company in which they own shares. B's non-controlling shareholders are not entitled to the statements of A, even though B is controlled by A, because they are not shareholders of A.

## 2.13 PRIVATE ENTERPRISE REPORTING AND UNCONSOLIDATED STATEMENTS

LO **2**

Identify the proper accounting treatment for both passive and strategic investments

In addition to presenting accounting methods for publicly accountable enterprises, Exhibit 2.12 provides the private-enterprise reporting alternatives for various types of equity investments available under Canadian Accounting Standards for Private Enterprises. An investor corporation must use the chosen method of accounting uniformly for all investments within each category of investment (i.e., subsidiaries, controlled SEs, significantly influenced associate companies, joint ventures, and passive investments).

Private enterprises are not required to prepare consolidated statements. The users of private enterprise financial statements often prefer to see non-consolidated statements to evaluate the creditworthiness, management performance, or dividend-paying ability of the separate entity. If consolidated statements are forced upon these users, the additional costs of consolidation will be pointless and will violate the basic concept that user benefits should exceed the preparation cost.

Reporting requirements relating to equity investments under ASPE differ significantly from their IFRS counterparts and are as follows:

- Either the cost or equity method may be used to report non-consolidated subsidiaries and SEs of private enterprises. However, the cost method cannot be used for reporting a publicly traded subsidiary; it has to be reported at its quoted amount, with the associated gains/losses recognized in net income. A company cannot choose to consolidate some subsidiaries and not others. The investor corporation should use the same method to report all of its subsidiaries.

- For significant-influence investments, it is not necessary to use the equity method. The cost method may be used instead. However, the investor cannot use the cost method, but instead has to use the fair value method when the investee's shares are quoted in an active market. All investments in significantly influenced companies must be reported on the same basis, either all by the cost method or all by the equity method.

- For joint ventures, the investor can use proportionate consolidation, the cost method, or the equity method. All joint ventures must be reported on the same basis. Passive investments in equity can be valued at cost less impairment losses. However, when a quoted market price is available, passive investments have to be valued at fair value, with associated gains and losses being recognized in net income. The option of taking gains and losses to OCI is not available. Dividends are recognized as dividend income in net income.

Reality Check 2-4 provides findings from empirical research on the issue of proportionate consolidation versus the equity method.

# Proportionate Consolidation Versus Equity Method of Reporting

Even though proportional consolidation has been eliminated under IFRS as a reporting choice for reporting joint ventures, there is some empirical evidence suggesting that it provides useful information to investors that is lost with equity reporting. Under proportional consolidation, the investor's proportionate shares of the investee's assets and liabilities are brought onto the investor's statement of financial position. This is not required under the equity method of reporting. Therefore, the equity method of accounting can be used as an off-balance-sheet financing technique to reduce the debt-to-equity ratio of the investor. One study found that financial statements prepared using proportionate consolidation provide better predictions of future profitability than statements prepared using the equity method.[a] Another study, using US data, found that proportionately consolidated financial statements have greater relevance than statements using the equity method for explaining bond ratings.[b] Surprisingly, a third study, using Canadian data, found that financial statement measures based on the equity method are more relevant for bond ratings than are similar measures based on proportionate consolidation.[c]

The lack of information provided by the equity method of reporting can be alleviated by requiring the investor to provide adequate disclosure regarding its share of the investee's assets and liabilities. A UK study of mandated disclosures by UK firms of their share of the liabilities of their equity-accounted associates and joint ventures found that such disclosures are useful to the market when valuing the shares of the investing firms.[d] International accounting standards also require similar disclosures relating to the assets and liabilities of associates and joint ventures.

[a] R. C. Graham, R. D. King, and C. K. J. Morrill, "Decision usefulness of alternative joint venture reporting methods." *Accounting Horizons* 17:2 (June 2003), p. 123.

[b] M. P. Bauman, "Proportionate consolidation versus the equity method: Additional evidence on the association with bond ratings." *International Review of Financial Analysis* 16 (2007), p. 496.

[c] K. Kothavala, "Proportionate consolidation versus the equity method: A risk measurement perspective on reporting interests in joint ventures." *Journal of Accounting and Public Policy* 22 (2003), p. 517.

[d] J. O'Hanlon and P. Taylor, "The value relevance of disclosures of liabilities of equity-accounted investees: UK evidence." *Accounting and Business Research* 37:4 (2007), p. 267.

## 2.14 SUMMARY OF REPORTING METHODS

LO ❷

Identify the proper accounting treatment for both passive and strategic investments

Exhibit 2.12 summarizes the reporting methods for intercorporate equity investments applicable to publicly accountable and private enterprises, respectively.

**Exhibit 2.12** Accounting for Strategic Intercorporate Investments

| Investment Type | Publicly Accountable Enterprises | | | | Private Enterprises |
|---|---|---|---|---|---|
| | Method of Accounting | SFP | Impact on Net Income | OCI | |
| Fair value through profit and loss (FVTPL and FVTOCI) | Fair value | Fair value | Share of dividends and gain/loss on revaluation to fair value from carrying value | | Fair value if quoted market price available, otherwise can use cost; dividends and gains/losses in net income |
| Fair value through OCI | Fair value | Fair value | Share of dividends | Gain/loss on revaluation to fair value from carrying value | |
| Significantly influenced associate companies | Equity method | Initial cost plus adjusted cumulative unremitted earnings | Share of investee's earnings adjusted for amortizations and intercompany unrealized & realized profits, & realized gains/losses on sale (fair value—carrying value) | OCI items of investee added to OCI of investor | Equity method not required; can use the cost method or fair value if quoted price available; same method should be used for all investments |
| Joint ventures | Equity method | Same as above | Same as above for each method | Same as above | Proportionate consolidation, cost, or equity method; same method should be used for all joint ventures |
| Subsidiaries and controlled SEs | Consolidation | Investment account replaced by assets and liabilities of investee | Revenue and expense items of investee added to investor's revenue and expense items on SCI adjusted for amortizations and intercompany unrealized and realized profits | Same as above | In addition to consolidation, can use either the cost or equity method; fair value if quoted market price available; same method should be used for all subsidiaries |

# Relevant Standards

## International Accounting Standards Board

| | |
|---|---|
| **IAS 1** | Presentation of Financial Statements |
| **IAS 39** | Financial Instruments: Recognition and Measurement |
| **IFRS 3** | Business Combinations |
| **IFRS 9** | Financial Instruments |
| **IFRS 10** | Consolidated Financial Statements |
| **IAS 28** | Investments in Associates |
| **IFRS 11** | Joint Arrangements |
| **IFRS 12** | Disclosure of Interests in Other Entities |

## Accounting Standards for Private Enterprises

| | |
|---|---|
| **1582** | Business Combinations |
| **1601** | Consolidated Financial Statements |
| **1602** | Non-controlling Interests |
| **1590** | Subsidiaries |
| **3051** | Investments |
| **3055** | Joint Ventures |
| **3856** | Financial Instruments |

# 2.15 SUMMARY OF KEY POINTS

1. An intercorporate investment is any investment by one corporation in the debt or equity securities of another. **LO 1**

2. A passive investment is an intercorporate investment in debt, non-voting shares, or a relatively small number of voting shares in another corporation. Passive investments do not have the ability to influence the strategies of the investee corporation. All passive equity investments are reported at fair values. While all gains (realized as well as unrealized) relating to passive investments classified as "fair value through profit and loss" are taken to net income, all gains relating to passive investments irrevocably classified as "fair value through other comprehensive income" are taken directly to equity through other comprehensive income (OCI). Such gains can never be reclassified into net income. **LO 1 & 2**

3. A strategic intercorporate investment is intended to enable the investor to control or significantly influence the strategic activities of the investee. If the investor has the ability to determine the strategic operating and financing policies of the investee, then the investor controls the investee. The controlled company is deemed to be a subsidiary of the investor, or parent, corporation. **LO 1**

4. Most subsidiaries are created by the parent company to carry on some aspect of the company's business. These are known as parent-founded subsidiaries. Other subsidiaries are acquired by buying voting control from the subsidiary's former shareholders. When a parent controls a subsidiary by owning less than 100% of the shares, a non-controlling interest exists. **LO 1**

5. A structured entity (SE) is a business venture that is established by a corporation but that is not controlled by the corporation through share ownership. The decision of

whether or not an SE is controlled should be made on the same basis as the decision of whether or not a subsidiary is controlled. However, the specific facts used will differ, since control of SEs is achieved via contractual means rather than via ownership of voting shares. **LO 1**

6. Significant influence may exist if the investor holds less than voting control but more than a nominal amount. The general guideline is that ownership of between 20% and 50% of the voting shares gives the investor significant influence. Equity-basis reporting is normally used to report investments in significantly influenced companies. **LO 1 & 2**

7. A joint venture is a co-operative venture undertaken together with one or more other investors. No one investor controls a joint venture. All of the co-venturers must agree on strategic policies. Joint ventures are reported using the equity method. Equity-basis reporting is sometimes called one-line consolidation. **LO 1 & 2**

8. Parent companies should prepare consolidated statements that report on the total economic entity that is controlled by the parent. All controlled entities should be consolidated. **LO 1 & 2**

9. The recording and reporting of strategic intercorporate investments are two different things. Intercorporate investments are usually recorded on the books of the investor on the cost basis. If the equity basis is used for reporting, the adjustments from cost to equity are entered on working papers and are not recorded in the investor's books. Consolidated financial statements are always prepared on working papers. The working papers may use either a direct approach or a worksheet approach. It is not possible to record the adjustments needed for consolidation, because there is no set of books that corresponds to the consolidated economic entity. **LO 3, 4, & 5**

10. Canadian businesses commonly operate through a multi-corporate structure, with a parent company controlling several subsidiaries. Each legal corporate entity must prepare its own separate-entity financial statements for tax and other special purposes. Corporations that issue general purpose financial statements must issue only consolidated financial statements to the general public. **LO 3**

11. Control can be either direct or indirect. Indirect control exists when the parent company controls an intermediate company that controls another company. Control does not imply absolute control. The parent company can have complete control over the subsidiary only by owning 100% of the subsidiary's shares. **LO 3**

12. Exceptions to the consolidation policy can occur when the reporting enterprise is a private corporation (and not otherwise accountable to the public). **LO 3**

**Visit the text's website at** www.pearsoned.ca/beechy **for practice quizzes, additional problems, Excel® templates, answers to Concept Check questions, and important IFRS updates.**

# Self-Study Problems[4]

1. Bunker Ltd. is a wholly owned subsidiary of Archie Corp. Bunker was formed by Archie with an initial investment of $1,000,000. Bunker produces some of the merchandise sold by Archie in its retail stores. Bunker also sells some of its output to other, unrelated companies. The December 31, 20X6, trial balances for Archie and Bunker are shown in Exhibit 2.13. The condensed SFP, SCI, and the SCE/RE for both companies are shown in Exhibit 2.14. Additional information is as follows:

    a. During 20X6, Bunker sold goods with a production cost of $2,600,000 to Archie for $4,000,000. Archie subsequently sold the goods to its customers for $7,000,000.

    b. Included in Archie's current receivables is $80,000 in dividends receivable from Bunker.

    c. Included in Bunker's current receivables is $200,000 due from Archie for merchandise purchases.

    d. During 20X6, Archie declared dividends of $2,000,000 and Bunker declared dividends of $500,000.

Required

Prepare a consolidated SFP and a consolidated SCI and SCE/RE for Archie Corp. for the year ended December 31, 20X6. Use either the direct method or the worksheet method (or both!).

**Exhibit 2.13** Separate-Entity Trial Balances, December 31, 20X6

|  | Archie Corp. | | Bunker Ltd. | |
| --- | --- | --- | --- | --- |
|  | Dr | Cr | Dr | Cr |
| Cash and current receivables | $ 200,000 |  |  | $ 400,000 |
| Inventories | 900,000 |  |  | 500,000 |
| Furniture, fixtures, and equipment (net) | 2,000,000 |  |  | 1,700,000 |
| Buildings under capital leases (net) | 6,000,000 |  |  | 3,000,000 |
| Investment in Bunker Ltd. (at cost) | 1,000,000 |  |  |  |
| Current liabilities |  | 1,500,000 |  | 400,000 |
| Long-term liabilities |  | 4,000,000 |  | 2,000,000 |
| Common shares |  | 1,500,000 |  | 1,000,000 |
| Retained earnings, December 31, 20X5 |  | 2,100,000 |  | 1,600,000 |
| Dividends declared | 2,000,000 |  | 500,000 |  |
| Sales revenue |  | 13,000,000 |  | 5,000,000 |
| Dividend income |  | 500,000 |  | — |
| Cost of sales | 7,000,000 |  | 3,200,000 |  |
| Other expenses | 3,500,000 | — | 700,000 | — |
|  | $22,600,000 | $22,600,000 | $10,000,000 | $10,000,000 |

[4]The solutions to all of the Self-Study Problems are at the end of the text, following Chapter 11.

**Exhibit 2.14** Separate-Entity Financial Statements

| Statements of Financial Position December 31, 20X6 | | |
| --- | --- | --- |
| Assets | Archie Corp. | Bunker Ltd. |
| Cash and current receivables | $ 200,000 | $ 400,000 |
| Inventories | 900,000 | 500,000 |
| Furniture, fixtures, and equipment (net of accumulated depreciation) | 2,000,000 | 1,700,000 |
| Buildings under capital lease (net of related amortization) | 6,000,000 | 3,000,000 |
| Investment in Bunker Ltd. (at cost) | 1,000,000 | — |
| | $10,100,000 | $5,600,000 |
| Liabilities and shareholders' equity | | |
| Current liabilities | $ 1,500,000 | $ 400,000 |
| Long-term liabilities | 4,000,000 | 2,000,000 |
| Common shares | 1,500,000 | 1,000,000 |
| Retained earnings | 3,100,000 | 2,200,000 |
| | $10,100,000 | $5,600,000 |

| Statements of Comprehensive Income Year Ended December 31, 20X6 | | |
| --- | --- | --- |
| Revenue | Archie Corp. | Bunker Ltd. |
| Sales | $13,000,000 | $5,000,000 |
| Dividend income | 500,000 | — |
| | 13,500,000 | 5,000,000 |
| Expenses | | |
| Cost of sales | 7,000,000 | 3,200,000 |
| Other expenses | 3,500,000 | 700,000 |
| | 10,500,000 | 3,900,000 |
| Net income | $ 3,000,000 | $1,100,000 |

| Statements of Changes in Equity-Retained Earnings Section Year Ended December 31, 20X6 | | |
| --- | --- | --- |
| Net income | $ 3,000,000 | $1,100,000 |
| Retained earnings, December 31, 20X5 | 2,100,000 | 1,600,000 |
| Dividends declared | (2,000,000) | (500,000) |
| Retained earnings, December 31, 20X6 | $ 3,100,000 | $2,200,000 |

2. In 20X1, Brad Corporation established a wholly owned subsidiary, Pitt Limited, with an initial investment of $20,000,000. Brad is a Winnipeg-based appliance manufacturer. Brad established Pitt as a retail chain to sell Brad's appliances under several different brand names, as well as some lines of kitchen appliances imported from Europe. Both Brad and Pitt are Canadian corporations.

The separate-entity statements of comprehensive income and the retained earnings section of the statements of changes in equity for the year ended December 31, 20X7, are shown in Exhibit 2.15. The statements of financial position for December 31, 20X7, are shown in Exhibit 2.16. Additional information is as follows:

a. During 20X7, Pitt purchased merchandise from Brad for a total price of $1,400,000. Brad's cost of goods sold for this merchandise was $1,100,000. Pitt sold all of the merchandise to unrelated customers for $2,100,000.

b. At year-end 20X7, Pitt owed $200,000 to Brad for merchandise purchases.

c. On December 17, 20X7, Pitt's board of directors declared dividends of $100,000, payable on January 10, 20X8.

d. On July 1, 20X7, Pitt borrowed $1,000,000 from Brad, interest to be paid annually at a rate of 6% per annum.

e. Brad Corporation uses the cost method for recording the investment in Pitt Limited.

## Exhibit 2.15

### Statements of Comprehensive Income
### Year Ended December 31, 20X7
### (000 omitted)

|  | Brad Corp. | Pitt Ltd. |
|---|---|---|
| **Revenue** | | |
| Sales revenue | $ 7,100 | $3,400 |
| Other income | 235 | 840 |
| Total revenue | 7,335 | 4,240 |
| **Operating expenses** | | |
| Cost of goods sold | 4,175 | 1,900 |
| Selling expenses | 435 | 560 |
| General and administrative expenses | 995 | 770 |
| Interest and other expenses | 1,015 | 30 |
| Total operating expenses | 6,620 | 3,260 |
| **Earnings before income taxes** | 715 | 980 |
| Income tax expense | 215 | 290 |
| **Net earnings** | $ 500 | $ 690 |

### Statements of Changes in Equity—Retained Earnings Section
### Year Ended December 31, 20X7
### (000 omitted)

|  | Brad Corp. | Pitt Ltd. |
|---|---|---|
| Retained earnings, December 31, 20X6 | $39,500 | $6,410 |
| Net earnings | 500 | 690 |
| Dividends declared | (160) | (100) |
| Retained earnings, December 31, 20X7 | $39,840 | $7,000 |

## Required

Prepare a consolidated SFP at December 31, 20X7, and a consolidated SCI and SCE/RE for the year then ended.

## Exhibit 2.16

| Statements of Financial Position<br>December 31, 20X7 (000 omitted) | Brad Corp. | Pitt Ltd. |
|---|---|---|
| **Assets** | | |
| Cash and temporary investments | $ 1,500 | $ 450 |
| Current receivables and accrued expenses | 3,400 | 1,890 |
| Inventories | 10,640 | 5,210 |
| Current assets | 15,540 | 7,550 |
| Loan receivable | 1,000 | — |
| Land | 18,000 | — |
| Buildings and equipment (net) | 37,700 | 22,450 |
| Investment in Pitt Limited | 20,000 | — |
| Total assets | $92,240 | $30,000 |
| **Liabilities and shareholders' equity** | | |
| Current payables and accrued liabilities | $ 2,820 | $ 1,540 |
| Income tax payable | 180 | 85 |
| Current liabilities | 3,000 | 1,625 |
| Long-term debt payable | 33,750 | 1,000 |
| Deferred tax liability | 2,650 | 375 |
| Total liabilities | 39,400 | 3,000 |
| Common shares | 13,000 | 20,000 |
| Retained earnings | 39,840 | 7,000 |
| Total shareholders' equity | 52,840 | 27,000 |
| Total liabilities and shareholders' equity | $92,240 | $30,000 |

## Review Questions

1. What are the two types of passive equity investments? What is the appropriate method of accounting for these investments?

2. What is the difference between fair value through profit and loss (FVTPL) investments and fair value through other comprehensive income (FVTOCI) investments?

3. ABC Corporation owns 12% of XYZ's common shares. Is the cost method of reporting the investment necessarily appropriate? Explain.

4. What factors should be examined to determine whether significant influence exists?

5. What is a joint venture?

6. Is profit sharing equal in a joint venture? Explain.

7. How are dividends received from an investee corporation reported by an investor corporation by the investor under the equity method?

8. "The extent of share ownership does not necessarily coincide with the extent of control exercised." Explain.

9. Under what circumstance can one corporation control another without owning a majority of the controlled corporation's voting shares?

10. P Corporation owns 75% of S Corporation, and S Corporation owns 55% of T Corporation. Is T a subsidiary of P?

11. P Corporation owns 55% of Q Corp. and 58% of R Corp. Q and R each own 30% of W Ltd. Is W a subsidiary of one or more of the other three companies? If so, which one(s)?

12. Why do many parent corporations prefer to own 100% of the shares of their subsidiaries, rather than smaller proportions? What advantages are there to a parent in owning less than 100% of its subsidiaries?

13. Why do many corporations carry out their operations through multiple subsidiaries?

14. Why would a company purchase a subsidiary rather than simply establishing a new subsidiary of its own? Why would a corporation want to keep a purchased subsidiary as a separate legal entity?

15. Explain one legitimate use for a structured entity (SE).

16. When should an investor corporation report its investment in the shares of another corporation on the equity basis?

17. What is the objective of preparing consolidated financial statements?

18. Why might a corporation use the cost method of recording an intercorporate investment while using the equity method or consolidation for reporting?

19. What are the two general approaches to preparing consolidated financial statements? Do the different approaches provide different results?

20. When intercompany sales are eliminated during consolidation, why is cost of sales reduced by the amount of intercompany sales?

21. Are consolidation eliminating and adjusting entries entered on the books of the parent or of the subsidiary? Explain.

22. Why is the equity method often referred to as one-line consolidation?

23. Why might it be necessary for a parent company to prepare unconsolidated financial statements as well as consolidated statements?

24. How does the process of consolidation differ when the parent company has used the equity method of recording its investment in a subsidiary, as compared with consolidation, when the cost method of recording has been used?

25. When might consolidated statements be misleading?

26. Is it possible for a parent company to go bankrupt while its operating subsidiaries stay healthy?

27. To what extent do the creditors of a subsidiary have a claim on the assets of the parent company?

28. Why do users of private-company financial statements often prefer non-consolidated financial statements?

29. How are strategic investments reported under accounting standards for private enterprises?

30. Under what circumstances is the cost method used to account for strategic investments?

## 2.16 CASES

# CASE 2-1 MULTI-CORPORATION

Multi-Corporation has been following a growth and diversification strategy for the past two years. To accomplish this goal, it has been making a series of strategic investments. This growth has been financed through the bank and private investors. Next year, the company is going to issue shares to the public.

You have just finished a meeting with Catherine, the controller of Multi-Corporation. She has asked you to provide recommendations on how to report the following investments that were made in 20X6.

1. Multi-Corporation purchased all of the 100,000 outstanding B shares of Suds Limited. Each B share has one vote. The previous owner of the B shares, Megan, retained all of the 80,000 outstanding A shares of Suds Limited. Each A share also has one vote. To avoid sudden changes to the business, Megan stipulated in the sales agreement that she was to retain the right to refuse the appointment of management for Suds Limited and to approve any significant transactions of Suds Limited.

2. Multi-Corporation owns 37% of the voting common shares of Berry Corporation. The remaining 63% of the shares are held by members of the family of the company founder.

To date, the family has elected all members of the board of directors, and Multi-Corporation has not been able to obtain a seat on the board. Multi-Corporation is hoping eventually to buy a block of shares from an elderly family member and eventually to own 60% of the shares.

### Required

Provide a report to Catherine outlining the appropriate method of accounting for these investments.
[CICA, adapted]

# CASE 2-2 SALIERI LTD.

Salieri Ltd. is a manufacturer of musical instruments that is controlled by Tony Antonio. Salieri Ltd. was originally a private company, but it became public in 20X0 when a substantial public share issue occurred. The Antonio family now holds 68% of the shares of Salieri; the remaining 32% are widely distributed throughout Canada.

Although Salieri is an operating company, it also has substantial investments in a number of other Canadian corporations. One such investment is its ownership of 80% of the shares of Bach Burgers, Inc., a chain of fast-food outlets. Salieri acquired its shares in Bach from the original founder of the company, John Sebastian, in 20X9. Bach Burgers

*Case Continued >*

*Case Continued >* is run completely independently; Teresa Antonio, Tony's wife, is one of the members of Bach Burgers' 12-person board of directors, but otherwise Salieri exercises no direction over the operations of Bach Burgers.

Another investment of Salieri Ltd. is its 45% interest in Pits Mining Corporation. This investment was the outcome of a takeover attempt by Salieri two years ago. Salieri was frustrated in its attempt by a coalition of other companies in the extraction industry, which effectively blocked Salieri's bid for control. Salieri was left with the 45% interest that it had managed to acquire. Although Salieri's block of Pits shares is by far the largest single block, Salieri has not been able to gain representation on the Pits board of directors. Salieri Ltd. has instituted court action against Pits Mining to force the other shareholders to admit Salieri nominees to the board.

Mozart Piano Corporation is a piano manufacturer that is 20% owned by Salieri Ltd. Although Salieri does manufacture musical instruments, it does not produce pianos, and Salieri and Mozart frequently conduct joint marketing efforts because their products are complementary and not competitive. Mozart is a private company; all of the other shares are held by the Amadeus family. Mozart has an 80%-owned subsidiary, Leopold Klaviers, Inc., which manufactures harpsichords and clavichords to be sold domestically through Mozart and internationally through other agents.

Salieri Ltd. also owns 15% of Frix Flutes, Ltd. The 15% share was acquired several years ago to provide Frix with some new financing at a time when the company was experiencing financial difficulties. Salieri also assisted Frix by licensing to Frix the rights to use patents owned by Salieri. The licensing agreement can be cancelled by Salieri upon six months' written notice.

The only other corporate share investment held by Salieri is its 100% ownership of Salieri Acceptance Corporation (SAC). SAC was formed by Salieri to aid its customers in purchasing Salieri instruments on an instalment basis. Six of the nine SAC directors are also directors of Salieri Ltd. The other three are representatives of the financial institutions that finance SAC's operations.

### Required

Discuss the manner in which Salieri should account for its various investments when issuing its annual financial statements. Specify what additional information you would like to have, if any. Recommend an accounting approach for each investment, stating any assumptions that you made in arriving at your recommendations.

## CASE 2-3 HEAVENLY HAKKA, NATURE'S HARVEST, AND CRYSTAL

### Situation A

Vincent Hzu is the sole owner of a successful chain of Hakka Indian–Chinese restaurants, Heavenly Hakka Inc., in Canada. Vincent (through Heavenly Hakka) and his two friends, Ibrahim Khan and Venkat Gupta, started a company, Szechwan Samosas Inc. (SS), 15 years ago to manufacture and sell Hakka-style samosas. Heavenly Hakka, Ibrahim, and

Venkat each own one-third of the shares of SS. However, given Vincent's experience running restaurants, it was agreed that the profits would be shared as follows: Heavenly Hakka, 40%, and the other two friends, 30% each. Further, Heavenly Hakka is the sole supplier of all the Hakka-style filling that goes into the samosas of SS. SS has become a great success in Ontario, in no small part due to the invaluable contribution of Vincent and Heavenly Hakka. The relationship between the friends had, by and large, been friendly in the past. However, during the past year differences have cropped up among the three on the future direction of SS. Vincent feels that the successful concept of SS should be expanded to other provinces in Canada. In contrast, both Ibrahim and Venkat feel that doing so might divert their attention from the Ontario operation, thereby potentially jeopardizing it. In the interest of maintaining amity among friends, Vincent has not pressed on the issue of expansion. However, clearly, Vincent has been unhappy these past few months, so much so that he has stopped visiting the SS restaurants completely.

## Situation B

Nature's Harvest (NH) is a petroleum exploration company incorporated in Benezuela; 60% of its voting shares are owned by Mid-West Petroleum, a publicly listed, Alberta-based company. The new nationalistic government of Benezuela recently decided that Benezuelan companies should be managed by Benezuelans and that their profits should be reinvested within Benezuela. Consequently, the Benezuelan government nominated the majority of the board of directors of NH with its own appointees. However, two of Mid-West's nominees still continue on the board of directors of NH. Further, the government of Benezuela legislated a ban on the repatriation of profits by Benezuelan companies to their foreign shareholders. All technical expertise to NH is, however, still being provided by Mid-West.

## Situation C

Premier Inc., a Canada-based public limited company and one of the world's top manufacturers of manual scooters, holds a 19% equity interest in Crystal Inc., a manufacturer of automatic motor scooters. Premier is represented on Crystal's board of directors. Further, Premier also has veto and blocking rights in Crystal as set forth in the partnership agreement between them. Premier is planning to divest its shares in Crystal by the end of next year.

### Required

Discuss the accounting alternatives available to report the investment in each of the three independent situations above. Specify what additional information you would like to have, if any. Recommend an accounting approach and disclosures required for each investment, stating any assumptions that you make in arriving at your recommendations. Refer to appropriate standards for appropriate disclosures relating to each situation above.

# CASE 2-4 INTER-PROVINCIAL BANKING CORPORATION

Early in 20X3, Inter-Provincial Banking Corporation (IPBC), a Canadian public company, acquired 100% of the shares of an inactive "shell" corporation, Safe Investments Inc. (SIC) for a nominal amount. After the acquisition, IPBC re-sold 97% of the shares to the public via a secondary offering, retaining only 3% of the shares.

One of IPBC's business lines is issuing mortgages for both residential and business properties. The intent of IPBC's management is to use SIC to securitize IPBC's residential mortgages. IPBC sells mortgages it originates to SIC for cash. To finance its purchase of the mortgages, SIC issues debt securities to the general public. The mortgages act as security for this debt.

Most of the holders of SIC's debt and equity securities are IPBC's current deposit holders. These debt and equity investors made their investments based on a marketing blitz carried out by IPBC to promote SIC as a high-yield investment. IPBC's branch-level financial advisors also encouraged their clients to invest in SIC securities. Otherwise, IPBC has no role in and control over the day-to-day affairs of SIC. An independent board of trustees manages SIC. The direct and only economic exposure of IPBC to SIC is limited to its 3% share investment. IPBC's financial vice-president intends to disclose IPBC's relationship with SIC as a related party transaction.

IPBC is audited by Kindle & Kobol, CAs. Ken Trilley is a K&K staff auditor assigned to the IPBC audit. The K&K audit manager, Mr. Nook Simple, has asked Ken Trilley to review the relationship between IPBC and SIC, to consider reporting alternatives, and to recommend the appropriate treatment of SIC in IPBC's 20X3 annual financial statements.

### Required

Assume you are Ken Trilley. Prepare a report to your manager, fully substantiating your answer with appropriate support from accounting standards.

# CASE 2-5 EENY, MEENY, MINY, AND MOE; AND TICK, TACK, AND TOE

Consider the following two independent situations and provide the required answer:

## Situation A

Eeny, Meeny, Miny, and Moe created IT Company with the following voting share ownership: Eeny 40%, Meeny 15%, Miny 25%, and Moe 20%. The contractual arrangement among the four parties specifies that at least 65% of the voting rights are required to make decisions affecting IT Company. All parties have rights only to the net assets of IT Company. Profits from IT Company, however, are divided based on the individual share ownership of the four parties.

## Situation B

Tick, Tac, and Toe created Draw Ltd. with the following voting share ownership: Tick 40%, Tack 30%, and Toe 30%. The contractual arrangement among Tic, Tac, and Toe specifies that at least 70% of the voting rights are required to make decisions affecting Draw Ltd. Profits from Draw Ltd., however, are divided based on the individual share ownership of the three parties. All parties have rights only to the net assets of Draw Ltd.

### Required

Determine the nature of the arrangement which exists between the shareholders in each of the two independent situations above. Further, for each situation above, state how the concerned shareholders report their individual investments.

## CASE 2-6 XYZ LTD.

During 20X5, XYZ Ltd. purchased for cash all of the 100,000 Class B shares of Sub Limited. Each B share carries one vote. The previous owner, Mr. Bill, retained all 20,000 outstanding Class A shares of Sub Limited, each carrying four votes. To avoid sudden changes, Mr. Bill stipulated in the sale agreement that he was to retain the right to refuse the appointment of management for Sub Limited and to approve any significant transactions of Sub Limited.

### Required

Should XYZ Ltd. consolidate the operations of Sub Limited in its 20X5 financial statements, which are to be issued in accordance with IFRS? Provide support for your recommendation.
[CICA]

## CASE 2-7 JACKSON CAPITAL INC.

Jackson Capital Inc. (JCI) is a new private investment company that provides capital to business ventures. JCI's business mission is to support companies to allow them to compete successfully in domestic and international markets. JCI aims to increase the value of its investments, thereby creating wealth for its shareholders.

Funds to finance the investments were obtained through a private offering of share capital, conventional long-term loans payable, and a bond issue that is indexed to the TSX Composite. Annual operating expenses are expected to be $1 million before bonuses, interest, and taxes.

Over the past year, JCI has accumulated a diversified investment portfolio. Depending on the needs of the borrower, JCI provides capital in many different forms, including demand loans, short-term equity investments, fixed-term loans, and loans convertible

*Case Continued >*

*Case Continued >*

into share capital. JCI also purchases preferred and common shares in new business ventures where JCI management anticipates a significant return. Any excess funds not committed to a particular investment are held temporarily in money market funds.

JCI has hired three investment managers to review financing applications. These managers visit the applicant's premises to meet with management and review the operations and business plans. They then prepare a report stating their reasons for supporting or rejecting the application. JCI's senior executives review these reports at their monthly meetings and decide whether to invest and what types of investments to make.

Once the investments are made, the investment managers are expected to monitor the investments and review detailed monthly financial reports submitted by the investees. The investment managers' performance bonuses are based on the returns generated by the investments they have recommended.

It is now August 20X6. JCI's first fiscal year ended on June 30, 20X6. JCI's draft statement of financial position and other financial information is included in Exhibits A, B, and C. An annual audit is required under the terms of the bond issue. Potter and Cook, Chartered Accountants, has been appointed auditor of JCI. You are employed by Potter and Cook and are the in-charge accountant on this engagement. Mr. Potter has asked you to prepare a memo discussing the significant accounting issues, audit risks, and related audit procedures for this engagement.

Required

Prepare the memo requested by Mr. Potter.

---

## Exhibit A

### DRAFT SFP (JUNE 30, 20X6) (THOUSANDS)

**Assets**

| | |
|---|---:|
| Cash and marketable securities | $ 1,670 |
| Investments (at cost) | 21,300 |
| Interest receivable | 60 |
| Furniture and fixtures (net of amortization) | 50 |
| | $23,080 |

**Liabilities**

| | |
|---|---:|
| Accounts payable and accrued liabilities | $ 20 |
| Accrued interest payable | 180 |
| Loans payable | 12,000 |
| | $12,200 |

**Equity**

| | |
|---|---:|
| Share capital | $12,000 |
| Deficit | (1,120) |
| | $23,080 |

## Exhibit B
## SUMMARY OF INVESTMENT PORTFOLIO (JUNE 30, 20X6)

The SFP for June 30, 20X6, shows a total of $21.3 million in long-term investments. The breakdown of these investments is as follows:

| Investments | Cost |
| --- | --- |
| 15% common share investment in Fairex Resource Inc., a company listed on the TSX Venture Exchange. Management intends to monitor the performance of this mining company over the next six months and to make a hold/sell decision based on reported reserves and production costs. | $3.8 million |
| 25% interest in common shares of Hellon Ltd., a private Canadian real estate company, plus 7.5% convertible debentures with a face value of $2 million acquired at 98% of maturity value. The debentures are convertible into common shares at the option of the holder. | $6.2 million |
| Five-year loan denominated in Brazilian currency (reals) to Ipanema Ltd., a Brazilian company formed to build a power generating station. Interest at 7% per annum is due semi-annually. 75% of the loan balance is secured by the power generating station under construction. The balance is unsecured. | $8 million |
| 50% interest in Western Gas, a jointly owned gas exploration project operating in Western Canada. One of JCI's investment managers sits on the three-member board of directors. | $2 million |
| 50,000 stock warrants in Toronto Hydrocarbons Ltd., expiring March 22, 20X8. The underlying common shares trade publicly. | $1.3 million |

# Exhibit C
# CAPITAL STRUCTURE (JUNE 30, 20X6)

The SFP for June 30, 20X6, shows a total of $12 million in share capital and $12 million in loans payable.

## LOANS PAYABLE

The company has $2 million in demand loans payable with floating interest rates, and $4 million in loans due September 1, 20X8, with fixed interest rates.

In addition, the Company has long-term 5% stock-indexed bonds payable. Interest at the stated rate is to be paid semi-annually, commencing September 1, 20X6. The principal repayment on March 1, 20X9, is indexed to changes in the TSX Composite as follows: the $6 million original balance of the bonds at the issue date of March 1, 20X6, is to be multiplied by the stock index at March 1, 20X9, and then divided by the stock index as at March 1, 20X6. The stock-indexed bonds are secured by the company's investments.

## SHARE CAPITAL

Issued share capital consists of:

| | |
|---|---|
| – 1 million 8% Class A (non-voting) shares redeemable at the holders' option on or after August 10, 20X8 | $7 million |
| – 10,000 common shares | $5 million |

[CICA]

# Problems

**P2-1 (15 minutes, easy)**

Alex Corporation acquired a 40% interest in Calvin Company on June 1, 20X8, for $425,000. The management of Alex Corporation is now preparing the first set of financial statements since the acquisition and is unsure about the method of accounting most appropriate for the investment. You are asked for advice.

Required

**a.** Can Alex report the investment in Calvin using the equity method or the proportionate consolidation method? Under what circumstances would each be appropriate? Are there circumstances under which Alex can use the cost method to report its investment in Calvin? Finally, under which circumstances can Alex use the fair value method to report its investment in Calvin? In each case, fully support your answer by providing all supporting factors.

**b.** What are the circumstances under which it would be appropriate for Alex to prepare consolidated financial statements? Identify the extent of control that would be implied by the use of consolidation and give examples of factors that would make consolidation appropriate.

**P2-2 (20 minutes, easy)**

On January 1, 20X3, Rose Corporation purchased 25% of the outstanding shares of Jasmine Corporation at a cost of $150,000. No purchase price discrepancy/fair value adjustment arose in relation to the purchase. During the next two fiscal years, Jasmine reported net income and dividends as follows:

| Year | Net Income | Dividends | Fair value of investment in Jasmine at year-end |
|------|-----------|-----------|--------------------------------------------------|
| 20X3 | $40,000 | $30,000 | $180,000 |
| 20X4 | 30,000 | 40,000 | 160,000 |

Required

What income/gains and losses will Rose report from its investment in Jasmine in its net income from continuing operations and other comprehensive income for 20X3 and 20X4 respectively, and what would the balance be in the Jasmine account at the end of fiscal year 20X4, assuming that the investment is recorded and reported:

**a.** Under the cost method?

**b.** As a FVTPL investment?

**c.** As a FVTOCI investment?

**d.** Under the equity method?

## P2-3 (12 minutes, easy)

On April 30, 20X4, Huge Inc. established a 100%-owned subsidiary known as Tiny Inc. Huge invested $550,000 in the shares of Tiny. Tiny has no other shares outstanding. Since its establishment, Tiny has had the following earnings and paid the following dividends:

| Year | Net Income (Loss) | Dividends |
|------|-------------------|-----------|
| 20X4 | ($60,000) | — |
| 20X5 | 70,000 | $ 18,000 |
| 20X6 | 46,000 | 42,000 |
| 20X7 | 110,000 | 54,000 |
| Total | $166,000 | $114,000 |

### Required

a. Determine the amount of Tiny Inc.'s earnings that will be reported as investment income by Huge Inc. in 20X7, under the equity method.

b. Calculate the balance of the investment in Tiny Inc. account on Huge Inc.'s books at December 31, 20X7, assuming that Huge Inc. maintains the investment account on the equity basis.

c. Provide the adjusting entry Huge Inc. will have to make on December 31, 20X7, if it uses the cost method to record and the equity method to report its investment in Tiny Inc.

## P2-4 (25 minutes, medium)

Harry Inc., a publicly traded company, purchased 1,000 shares, constituting a 40% ownership interest, in Sally Inc. on January 1, 20X1, for $160,000. Harry uses the cost method to record its investment in Sally. Harry Inc.'s income under the cost basis for 20X2 is $100,000. Sally's income per its separate-entity financial statements is $20,000, and it paid a total dividend of $15,000 in 20X1. Both companies have the same year-end. At year-end, each share of Sally was trading at $100 in the market.

### Required

a. Based on the above information, calculate/show (1) journal entries made by Harry in its books relating to its investment in Sally, and (2) the balance in its investment in the Sally account at year-end, assuming that Harry treats its investment in Sally as (i) a FVTPL and alternatively as (ii) a FVTOCI investment.

b. **Now assume that Harry changed its mind at year-end and has decided to use the equity method to record and report its investment in Sally.** Calculate/show the (1) journal entries made by Harry in its books relating to its investment in Sally, (2) total income of Harry for the year, and (3) balance in its investment in the Sally account at year-end.

## P2-5 (20 minutes, easy)

Take Inc. invested $60,000 for its 20% share in Give Inc. on January 1, 20X1, by purchasing 10,000 shares of Give Inc. The following table provides pertinent details relating to Give Inc. for the next four years. Take Inc. has a December 31 year-end.

| Year | Income | Dividends Declared | Share Price on December 31 |
|------|--------|--------------------|----------------------------|
| 20X1 | $160,000 | $140,000 | $4.80 |
| 20X2 | 80,000 | 110,000 | 4.50 |
| 20X3 | 120,000 | 100,000 | 5.00 |
| 20X4 | 60,000 | 80,000 | 4.70 |

Required

Calculate the dividend income and unrealized gains/losses recognized by Take Inc. in each of the four years, and the carrying value of its investment in Give Inc. Assume that Take Inc. accounts for its investment in Give Inc. as a FVTOCI investment.

## P2-6 (30 minutes, medium)

In the simple consolidation problem in the chapter, we assumed that Parent Co. established Subsidiary Co. on December 31, 20X9, by investing $1,000 cash in it. Refer to p. 40 to 41 for the example and provide your answer for each of the following five cases:

**Case 1:** Subsidiary Co. earned $100 in cash during 20X10 but did not pay any dividends. Parent Co. earned no income of its own in 20X10. Continue to assume that Parent Co. uses the cost method to record its investment in Subsidiary Co. Prepare the consolidated SCI for 20X10 and consolidated SFP on December 31, 20X10, of Parent Co., and the associated adjusting entries.

**Case 2:** Subsidiary Co. earned $100 and paid dividends of $40, both in cash, during 20X10. Parent Co. earned no income of its own in 20X10. Continue to assume that Parent Co. uses the cost method to record its investment in Subsidiary Co. Prepare the consolidated SCI for 20X10 and consolidated SFP on December 31, 20X10, of Parent Co., and the associated adjusting entries.

**Case 3:** Continuing with Case 1, assume that instead of using the cost method to record its investment in Subsidiary Co., Parent Co. uses the equity method. Prepare the consolidated SCI for 20X10 and consolidated SFP on December 31, 20X10, of Parent Co., and the associated adjusting entries.

**Case 4:** Continuing with Case 2, assume that instead of using the cost method to record its investment in Subsidiary Co., Parent Co. uses the equity method. Prepare the consolidated SCI for 20X10 and consolidated SFP on December 31, 20X10, of Parent Co., and the associated adjusting entries.

**Case 5:** Continuing with Case 1, now assume that Parent Co. did not establish Subsidiary Co. on December 31, 20X9. Instead, assume that Parent Co. purchased all the shares of Subsidiary Co. from its shareholders on December 31, 20X10, by paying cash of $1,100 to them. Prepare the consolidated SCI for 20X10 and consolidated SFP on December 31, 20X10, of Parent Co. after the acquisition of Subsidiary Co., and the associated adjusting entries. What difference do you notice between the consolidated SFP in Case 1 and the consolidated SFP prepared by you now?

## P2-7 (10–15 minutes, medium)

Capital Investments Inc. purchased 40% of the outstanding shares of Deep Value Inc. on January 1, 20X3, for $10,000. Capital Investments has chosen to record its investment in Deep Value under the cost method. Deep Value earned $8,000 and $10,000 in 20X3 and 20X4, respectively. Further, Deep Value declared and paid dividends of $4,000 and $5,000 in 20X3 and 20X4, respectively.

### Required

Prepare the necessary adjusting entries required of Capital Investment in 20X3 and 20X4, respectively, if it wants to report its investment in Deep Value under the equity method.

## P2-8 (20 minutes, easy)

Max Corporation has a wholly owned subsidiary, Min Ltd., which was formed several years ago. Both Max and Min are in the same business, but in different geographic areas. Min's initial capital was provided by Max, which purchased all of Min's shares for $600,000. At December 31, 20X6, the SFP accounts of Max and Min appeared as follows:

| Statements of Financial Position of Max and Min as at December 31, 20X6 | | |
|---|---|---|
| | Max | Min |
| Cash | $ 90,000 | $ 30,000 |
| Accounts receivable | 220,000 | 150,000 |
| Receivable from Min | 100,000 | — |
| Property, plant, and equipment | 2,400,000 | 1,500,000 |
| Accumulated depreciation | (670,000) | (360,000) |
| Investment in Min | 600,000 | — |
| TOTAL ASSETS | $2,740,000 | $1,320,000 |
| Accounts payable | $ 340,000 | $ 200,000 |
| Payable to Max | — | 100,000 |
| Bonds payable | 1,000,000 | — |
| Deferred tax liability | 100,000 | 50,000 |
| Common shares | 400,000 | 600,000 |
| Retained earnings | 900,000 | 370,000 |
| TOTAL LIABILITIES AND EQUITY | $2,740,000 | $1,320,000 |

During 20X6, Min paid dividends of $100,000 to Max and purchased goods from Max at a total price of $1,200,000. All of the purchases from Max were subsequently sold to third parties during the year.

### Required

Prepare a consolidated SFP for Max Corporation at December 31, 20X6. Additionally, show the consolidation-related adjusting entries required for preparing the consolidated SFP.

## P2-9 (25 minutes, easy)

Hook Corp. is a wholly owned, parent-founded subsidiary of Chappell Inc. The unconsolidated statement of comprehensive income and the retained earnings section of the statement of changes in equity for the two companies for the year ended December 31, 20X6, are as follows:

| Separate-Entity Financial Statements<br>Statements of Comprehensive Income<br>Year Ended December 31, 20X6 | | |
| --- | --- | --- |
| | Chappell Inc. | Hook Corp. |
| **REVENUES** | | |
| Sales | $6,500,000 | $2,100,000 |
| Interest | 200,000 | 60,000 |
| Dividends | 110,000 | — |
| Total revenue | 6,810,000 | 2,160,000 |
| **EXPENSES** | | |
| Cost of goods sold | 3,300,000 | 1,300,000 |
| Depreciation expense | 600,000 | 160,000 |
| Administrative expense | 900,000 | 300,000 |
| Income tax expense | 780,000 | 170,000 |
| Other operating expenses | 290,000 | 40,000 |
| Total expense | 5,870,000 | 1,970,000 |
| **Net earnings** | $ 940,000 | $ 190,000 |
| **Statements of Changes in Equity—Retained Earnings Section**<br>**Year Ended December 31, 20X6** | | |
| Retained earnings, January 1, 20X6 | $1,920,000 | $ 520,000 |
| Net earnings | 940,000 | 190,000 |
| Dividends declared | (330,000) | (110,000) |
| Retained earnings, December 1, 20X6 | $2,530,000 | $ 600,000 |

### Additional Information

1. During the year, Hook acquired merchandise from Chappell at a total sale price of $1,000,000. None of the merchandise was in Hook's inventory at year-end.

2. At the beginning of the year, Hook borrowed $900,000 from Chappell at 10% interest per annum. The loan (and accrued interest) was still outstanding at the end of the year.

3. Chappell carries its investment in Hook at the cost basis in its accounts.

### Required

Prepare a consolidated statement of comprehensive income and the retained earnings section of the statement of changes in equity for Chappell Inc. for the year ended December 31, 20X6.

## P2-10 (35 minutes, medium)

Thorne Ltd. is a wholly owned subsidiary of Fellows Corporation. The SFP, statement of comprehensive income, and retained earnings section of the statement of changes in equity for each company are shown below. Additional information is as follows:

1. Thorne sells most of its output to Fellows. During 20X6, intercompany sales amounted to $3,500,000. Fellows has accounts payable to Thorne for $20,000.

2. Fellows owns the land on which Thorne's building is situated. Fellows leases the land to Thorne for $30,000 per month.

3. The long-term note payable on Thorne's books represents a loan from Fellows. The note bears interest at 10% per annum.

4. Both companies declare dividends quarterly. The last quarter's dividends were declared on December 31, 20X6, payable on January 10, 20X7.

5. Fellows uses the cost method to account for its investment in Thorne.

**Required**

a. Prepare a consolidated SFP, SCI, and SCE/RE for Fellows Corporation.

b. What are the adjusting entries required if Fellows wishes to convert from the cost to the equity method to account for its investment in Thorne? How would Fellows' separate-entity financial statements appear if it accounts for its investment in Thorne under the equity method?

c. Using Fellows' separate-entity financial statements under the equity method, prepare a consolidated SFP, consolidated SCI, and consolidated SCE/RE for Fellows Corporation.

### Separate-Entity Financial Statements
### Statements of Comprehensive Income
### Year Ended December 31, 20X6

|  | Fellows | Thorne |
|---|---|---|
| **REVENUES** | | |
| Sales | $5,600,000 | $4,700,000 |
| Interest, dividend, and lease | 850,000 | 15,000 |
|  | 6,450,000 | 4,715,000 |
| **EXPENSES** | | |
| Cost of goods sold | 4,400,000 | 2,500,000 |
| Interest expense | — | 70,000 |
| Other expenses | 1,300,000 | 1,795,000 |
|  | 5,700,000 | 4,365,000 |
| Net income | $ 750,000 | $ 350,000 |

### Statements of Changes in Equity—Retained Earnings Section
### Year Ended December 31, 20X6

|  | Fellows | Thorne |
|---|---|---|
| Retained earnings, January 1, 20X6 | $1,330,000 | $ 100,000 |
| Net income | 750,000 | 350,000 |
| Dividends declared | (700,000) | (200,000) |
| Retained earnings, December 31, 20X6 | $1,380,000 | $ 250,000 |

| Statements of Financial Position December 31, 20X6 | | |
|---|---|---|
| | Fellows | Thorne |
| **ASSETS** | | |
| Current assets | | |
| Cash | $ 180,000 | $ 25,000 |
| Accounts receivable | 700,000 | 135,000 |
| Temporary investments and accrued investment income | 360,000 | 90,000 |
| Inventories | — | 330,000 |
| | 1,240,000 | 580,000 |
| **PROPERTY, PLANT, AND EQUIPMENT** | | |
| Land | 900,000 | — |
| Buildings and equipment | — | 1,500,000 |
| Accumulated depreciation | — | 500,000) |
| | 900,000 | 1,000,000 |
| Long-term note receivable | 700,000 | — |
| Investment in Thorne | 500,000 | — |
| TOTAL ASSETS | $3,340,000 | $1,580,000 |
| **EQUITIES** | | |
| Current liabilities | | |
| Accounts payable and accrued liabilities | $ 240,000 | $ 80,000 |
| Dividends payable | 120,000 | 50,000 |
| | 360,000 | 130,000 |
| Long-term note payable | — | 700,000 |
| Total liabilities | 360,000 | 830,000 |
| **Shareholders' equity** | | |
| Common shares | 1,600,000 | 500,000 |
| Retained earnings | 1,380,000 | 250,000 |
| TOTAL LIABILITIES AND SHAREHOLDERS' EQUITY | $3,340,000 | $1,580,000 |

**P2-11 (20 minutes, medium)**

Empire Optical Co. Ltd. is a chain of eyeglass outlets. Empire owns 100% of Class Glass Ltd., a competing chain that Empire established to serve a different market segment. To obtain the best deal from suppliers, Empire buys most of the materials and frames for both chains, and resells to Class whatever that chain needs.

During 20X6, Empire sold materials costing $2,000,000 to Class at cost. At the end of the year, Class still owed Empire $250,000 for purchases of the materials.

Empire records its investment in Class on the equity basis. During 20X6, Class declared and paid dividends totalling $200,000. Empire has not yet recorded its equity in the earnings of Class for 20X6. The pre-consolidation trial balances for the two companies are shown below. An Excel spreadsheet relating to this problem appears on the Companion Website.

## Required

Prepare a consolidated SFP and SCI for Empire Optical Co. Ltd. for 20X6.

|  | Trial Balances Dr (Cr) | |
|---|---|---|
|  | Empire | Class |
| Cash | $ 400,000 | $ 50,000 |
| Accounts receivable | 300,000 | 150,000 |
| Inventory | 1,200,000 | 600,000 |
| Fixtures and equipment (net) | 5,000,000 | 1,400,000 |
| Investment in Class Glass Ltd. | 2,100,000 | — |
| Other investments | 500,000 | — |
| Accounts payable | (700,000) | (500,000) |
| Common shares | (1,600,000) | (1,000,000) |
| Retained earnings | (5,700,000) | (1,300,000) |
| Dividends paid | 600,000 | 200,000 |
| Sales | (16,000,000) | (7,100,000) |
| Cost of goods sold | 11,000,000 | 5,000,000 |
| Other operating expenses | 3,000,000 | 2,500,000 |
| Dividend and interest income | (100,000) | — |
|  | $ 0 | $ 0 |

# Chapter 3
## Business Combinations

## Learning Objectives

**After studying this chapter, you should be able to:**

LO**1**   define a business combination;

LO**2**   identify the different types of business combinations;

LO**3**   explain the general accounting approach to business combinations;

LO**4**   measure the fair values of the consideration transferred and the assets and liabilities acquired;

LO**5**   identify the different approaches to reporting mergers;

LO**6**   demonstrate the mechanics of consolidating a purchased subsidiary at the time of acquisition;

LO**7**   understand the disclosure requirements relating to business combinations;

LO**8**   explain push-down accounting; and

LO**9**   understand the method of reporting investments in associates and joint ventures.

## INTRODUCTION

Barrick Gold Corporation (Barrick), the biggest gold company in the world, announced on April 25, 2011, that it had agreed to acquire all of the outstanding shares of Equinox Minerals Limited for $7.32 billion in cash. The all-cash offer represented a 30% premium over Equinox's closing share price on February 25, 2011 (the last trading date before Equinox's own unsolicited and unsuccessful takeover bid for Lundin Mining Corporation). The cash offer also represented a 16% premium over a rival offer to take over Equinox by Minmetals Resources Limited. Purchasing Equinox gives Barrick control over the Lumwana mine in Zambia, representing the biggest foreign investment in that country, and Jabal Sayid, the largest copper project in Saudi Arabia.

In the previous chapter, we pointed out that most subsidiaries are established by the parent corporation to carry out some part of the parent's operations. The acquisition of Equinox by Barrick illustrates a different way of obtaining a subsidiary—by a business combination, where one corporation acquires another functioning business as a going concern. As the Barrick example also illustrates, the intense competition between potential acquirers during the acquisition process results in the final acquirer paying a significant premium to obtain control over the acquiree. Such a premium is often allocated to goodwill.

A second example of a business combination is the reverse merger in 2011 of Cabia Goldhills Inc. (Cabia), a private Canadian company, with Gee-Ten Ventures Inc. (Gee-Ten), listed on the TSX Venture Exchange. Cabia became a public company by merging with Gee-Ten and then changing the name of the merged company to Cabia Goldhills Inc., which trades on the TSX Venture Exchange under the symbol CGH. That's a quick way to become a public company.

In this chapter, we will discuss the various reasons why a parent may want to purchase a subsidiary. In addition, we will examine the accounting issues that arise when one corporation acquires another company as a going concern rather than by establishing a new subsidiary.

The consolidation procedures that we illustrate in this chapter are at the simplest level—a consolidated statement of financial position at the date of acquisition. However, consolidations after the acquisition date are much more complicated. Chapters 4, 5, and 6 will deal with these post-acquisition complexities.

Sources: Barrick, press release, April 25, 2011. http://www.barrick.com/Theme/Barrick/files/docs_pressrelease/2011/Barrick-announces-agreement-to-acquire-Equinox.pdf; Cabia Goldhills Inc., Press Release, October 21, 2011. http://www.cekoweb.com/~cabia/documents/en/2011-11-21_press_release.pdf.

LO **1**
Define a business combination

LO **2**
Identify the different types of business combinations

## 3.1 DEFINITION OF A BUSINESS COMBINATION

A **business combination** is a transaction or other event in which one corporate entity obtains control of one or more operating businesses. Not every type of combination is a *business combination* within the accounting definition. To understand what is meant by a business combination, we must further examine two key aspects of this definition: (1) What is meant by control? and (2) What constitutes a business?

The first key aspect of the definition is that the buyer obtains **control**. Control can usually be obtained either by:

1. buying the assets of an operating business directly, which automatically gives control of that operating business to the buyer, or

2. buying enough shares in the corporation that owns the assets to enable the investor to control the investee corporation, which makes the purchased corporation a subsidiary of the investor corporation.

Some combinations do not give control to the acquirer; these are *joint ventures* and were discussed in the previous chapter. As well, when two entities that already are under *common control* (discussed later in the chapter) combine, such a combination does not fit the definition of a business combination because control is not being acquired—it already existed prior to the combination.

The second key aspect of the definition is that the acquirer obtains control of a *business*. The term **business** means an organized group of activities and assets that can be carried on or managed for the purpose of providing returns. Returns can be in terms of dividends, lowering of costs, or other economic benefits to investors. Thus, a business consists of inputs (i.e., assets) and processes (i.e., organized group of activities) applied to those inputs that currently have the ability to create outputs or that can reasonably be expected to do so in the future.[1]

## Control via Acquisition of Assets

An acquired business does not need to be a separate corporate entity. An acquirer can buy a portion of a corporation, such as an operating division or a sales group that can function as a stand-alone business.

When the purchaser buys a group of assets that constitutes a business, there may or may not be liabilities attached, such as when one corporation sells an operating division to another company. Because this type of business combination is a direct purchase of net assets, the acquired assets and any related liabilities are recorded directly on the books of the acquirer, as we shall illustrate shortly.

Quite often, an acquirer will purchase a group of assets that does *not* meet the definition of a business combination. For example, a corporation may buy a disused factory from another company. The factory is not a "business" because it is not an operational unit that generates a return—it's just a bunch of assets. This kind of purchase is called an "asset group acquisition." When an asset group is acquired, the cost of purchasing the asset group is apportioned to the individual identifiable assets and liabilities on the basis of their individual fair values. This type of transaction is often called a "basket purchase" of assets. You will already have studied this type of asset acquisition in intermediate accounting.

## Control via Share Purchase

When an investor acquires *control* over another corporation via purchase of shares, liabilities are automatically part of the package. It is important to remember that in any discussion of business combinations, **net assets** equals assets minus any related liabilities.

However, the acquired assets and liabilities are *not* recorded on the books of the acquirer. Instead, the acquired company continues as its own separate legal entity, but now as a subsidiary of the acquiring corporation. The value of the net assets purchased will show on the parent's separate-entity books only as an investment account. The consolidation process occurs only when consolidated financial statements are needed at the end of a reporting period, to create the "accounting fiction" that we discussed in Chapter 1.

It is important to remember that not all business combinations result in a parent–subsidiary relationship. Exhibit 3.1 depicts graphically some common types of business combinations that do and do not lead to consolidation. We will discuss some of these business combinations as we proceed through this chapter.

---

[1] The presence of outputs is not essential for a business to exist; for example, a business in a developmental stage will not have outputs.

**Exhibit 3.1** Common Types of Business Combinations

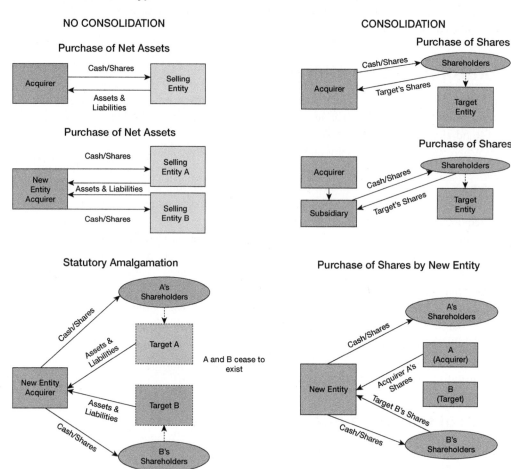

LO ❸
Explain the general accounting approach to business combinations

## 3.2 ACCOUNTING FOR BUSINESS COMBINATIONS— GENERAL APPROACH

There are several theoretically distinct methods for reporting business combinations. Various countries' national accounting standards have used some of these methods in the fairly recent past. Currently, however, IFRS 3, *Business Combinations*, requires the *acquisition method* to report all business combinations.

### The Acquisition Method

The acquisition method approaches a business combination from the point of view of the acquirer, the entity that obtains control of the other entity or entities in the business combination. Under the **acquisition method**, the buyer identifies all assets and liabilities and reports them on the consolidated SFP at their *fair values*.

A key word is *identify*. The acquiree's books normally will show only those assets that the acquiree purchased. However, there actually may be significant assets that are *not* reported on the acquired company's books. For example, there may well be other valuable

## Benefits of Mergers and Reasons for Mergers

Empirical research on mergers and acquisitions indicates that while mergers do appear to create value, most of the associated gains appear to go to the shareholders of the target company or acquiree. Mergers appear to occur in waves and to cluster by industry. This evidence suggests that mergers occur in reaction to sudden and unexpected shocks within a particular industry.

Empirical research also supports other theoretical reasons given for why mergers occur: (1) efficiency-related reasons, such as economies of scale or some other synergy; (2) creation of market power by forming monopolies or oligopolies; (3) market discipline in the form of the removal of incompetent target management, (4) self-serving reasons on the part of management, such as "empire building"; and (5) diversification to reduce risk.

In contrast, a survey of chief financial officers (CFOs) of US firms that had acquired other firms during the 1990–2001 period, the largest merger wave in history, found that the top-ranked reason given for mergers was operating synergies. It also found that CFOs viewed achieving diversification, especially as a means of reducing losses during economic downturns, as being a legitimate reason for mergers.

A. Gregor, M. Mitchell, and E. Stafford, "New evidence and perspectives on mergers." *The Journal of Economic Perspectives 15:2* (Spring 2001), p. 103.

T. K. Mukherjee, H. Kiymaz, and H. K. Baker, "Merger motives and target valuation: A survey of evidence from CFOs." *Journal of Applied Finance 14:2* (Fall 2004), p. 7.

*identifiable* assets (such as license rights or customer lists) that clearly have a fair value but are not reported on the acquired company's books.

A major advantage of recognizing these previously unidentified assets is that it will allow users to more accurately assess the value of the investment and its subsequent performance and compare it against other alternative investments or entities and their performance.

The acquisition method applies to accounting for both types of business combinations: (1) directly purchasing the net assets, or (2) obtaining control over the net assets of a corporation, usually through the purchase of shares. Application of the method is a five-step process:

1. identify the *acquirer*;
2. determine the *acquisition date*;
3. calculate the *fair value of the purchase consideration* transferred (i.e., the *cost* of the purchase);
4. recognize and measure the identifiable assets and liabilities of the acquired business; and
5. recognize and measure either *goodwill* or a *gain from a bargain purchase*, if either exists in the transaction.

If an acquirer gains control by purchasing less than 100% of the shares of the acquired entity, then the fourth step includes measuring and recognizing the *non-controlling interest*. We will delay our discussion of non-controlling interests until Chapter 5.

The *mechanics* of accounting for the acquisition will depend on the nature of the purchase, particularly on whether the purchase was of the net assets directly or of *control* over the net assets through acquisition of shares of the company that owns the assets. Let's look at the general features that apply to all business combinations before we worry about the acquisition method used.

## Identifying the Acquirer

The **acquirer** in a business combination is the corporation whose shareholders control the combined economic entity. When the purchase is for cash (or other assets or by incurring liabilities), the acquirer obviously is the company that buys the other (or the assets of the other). When the combination is effected by an exchange of shares, the acquirer may not be so obvious.

The corporation that issues the shares is usually, but not always, the acquirer. Therefore, it is necessary to examine which shareholder group gets control of the combined economic entity to determine who the acquirer is.

Voting control may appear to be evenly split between the shareholders of the two combining companies. If that is the case, other factors must be examined to determine who the acquirer is. Examples of other factors include:

- the relative voting rights in the combined entity of the owners of the combining entities;
- in the absence of any group with significant voting interest, the presence of a group with a large minority voting interest;
- the composition of the board of directors;
- the composition of the senior management team; and
- the terms relating to the exchange of the equity shares, with the group paying a premium being the acquirer.

## Determining the Acquisition Date

The acquisition date is the date on which the acquirer obtains control over the acquired company. Usually, the closing date, the date on which the purchase consideration is transferred and the assets and liabilities of the acquiree are acquired, constitutes the acquisition date. However, the acquirer and the acquiree can, through a written agreement, arrange for control to be transferred on a date other than the closing date. In such a case, the date on which the control is transferred, and not the closing date, will constitute the date of acquisition.

## Calculating the Fair Value of the Consideration

Usually the purchase consideration for the assets acquired is in the form of (1) cash and/or other assets, (2) shares issued by the acquirer, or (3) a combination of cash and shares. Specifically, the purchase consideration transferred can include cash, other assets, a business or a subsidiary, ordinary and preferred shares, options, warrants, liabilities incurred to former owners, or contingent consideration. On occasion, it is possible to acquire control without actually transferring any consideration, such as by contract alone.

The general principle is that the consideration transferred should be measured at its fair value on the *date of the acquisition*. When the purchase is by cash, it is not difficult to determine the fair value of the consideration transferred. When the purchase is paid for with other assets or with liabilities of the acquirer, the purchase consideration is measured by the fair value of those assets and liabilities on the date of the acquisition.

In many cases the acquirer issues its own shares in full or partial payment to acquire the net assets of another company. Theoretically, the value of the consideration is the market value of the shares issued by the acquirer. In practice, it may be a little more complicated. For example, the fair value of the *acquiree's* shares may be more reliably measurable than the fair value of the acquirer's shares. A prime example occurs when the acquiree is a public company but the acquirer is a private company. In such cases, fair value should be measured using the acquisition date fair value of the transferred equity interest of the acquiree.

**Acquisition-Related Costs**   **Acquisition-related costs** are costs incurred to achieve the business combination and are not considered part of the purchase consideration. These costs are treated as expenses of the period in which they are incurred and services are received. Examples of such costs are finder's fees; professional or consulting fees (e.g., advisory, legal, accounting, and valuation fees); and general administrative costs, including costs incurred for maintaining an acquisitions department. The exceptions are costs of issuing debt or shares. Costs of issuing debt are deducted from the value of the debt originally recognized. Transaction costs relating to the issue of shares are deducted from shareholders' equity, net of any related income tax benefit.

**Measurement Period**   The **measurement period** is a period after the acquisition date during which certain adjustments are permitted. The measurement period cannot be more than one year. Sometimes, it takes a while to determine the fair value of the acquiree's assets and liabilities. Indeed, it sometimes takes a while just to determine what all of the identifiable assets are, especially for intangible assets such as intellectual property and licence rights. The amount of purchase consideration may also be uncertain at the date of acquisition.

When it is not feasible to fully determine either the purchase price and/or the fair values at the date of acquisition, the acquiring company uses estimated values or *provisional amounts*. Once the acquirer does determine the consideration and/or fair values, these "final" amounts are used as though they had been known at the date of acquisition.

There always is some lag between the date of acquisition and final measurement because the acquirer has other things to worry about during the acquisition phase—fair values are assigned later. In most cases, the final measurements are determined by the time that the financial statements are prepared, two or three months after the end of the fiscal year. If final determination happens after financial statements for the acquisition date have been issued, some restatement of the acquisition year's statements may be necessary when the next period's statements are issued.

Reality Check 3-2 provides an example of how the measurement period was used by Lexmark International Inc., a US-based provider of printing and imaging products, software, solutions, and services, to finalize the purchase price allocation (PPA) relating to its purchase of Perceptive Software Inc., a provider of enterprise content management software and solutions.

**Contingent Consideration**   A business combination may include a provision for contingent consideration. **Contingent consideration** is an add-on to the base acquisition price that is based on events occurring or conditions being met some time after the purchase takes place. The amount of contingent consideration can be based on a number of factors, such as:

- a fuller assessment of the finances and operations of the acquired company;
- the outcome of renegotiating agreements with debt holders;
- achievement of stated earnings objectives in accounting periods *following* the change of control; or
- achievement of a target market price for the acquirer's shares by a specified future date.

Contingent consideration is paid in future periods but is considered as being part of the consideration transferred for the acquisition. The fair value of contingent consideration is estimated on the acquisition date and is included as part of the total consideration. The value of contingent consideration normally will change as the future unfolds.

Recognition of these changes depends on whether those changes relate to (1) additional information obtained *during* the measurement period, or (2) events occurring *after* the acquisition date. In the first instance, the changes are considered part of the original purchase consideration transferred, and the original accounting of the acquisition is adjusted accordingly. In the latter case, the changes are recognized separately from the business combination and usually are adjusted as gains or losses in the acquirer's SCI (net income section).

A recent empirical analysis of mergers and acquisitions indicates that contingent consideration has increased both as a percentage of the value of each merger and as a percentage of the overall value of mergers.[2] Reality Check 3-3 provides an example of an acquisition with a typical contingent consideration requirement.

**Business Combinations with No Transfer of Consideration**  A business combination can occur without the transfer of any consideration by the acquirer. Examples include such circumstances as:

- when the acquiree repurchases a sufficient quantity of its shares from other shareholders such that the acquirer, who previously was a minority owner of the acquiree, now is the majority shareholder of the acquiree and controls it;

---

[2]Sam Bridges, Contingent Consideration, *J. P. Morgan Mergers Insight* (March 4, 2011). http://www.jpmorgan.com/tss/DocumentForEmail/MandA_trends-contingent_earn-outs/1304257505366

- when the acquirer owns the majority of the acquiree's voting shares but had previously been prevented from exercising control by regulation or by contract—if that restriction lapses or is removed, the acquirer now gains control over the acquiree; and
- by contract alone.

A business combination by contract alone, as the name denotes, occurs when the acquirer and acquiree agree to a business combination solely via contract. No consideration is exchanged for obtaining control, and the acquirer does not own any equity interest in the acquiree, both previous to the acquisition and on the date of acquisition. For example, often companies that manage the medical practice of physicians enter into formal management agreements with physicians or with physician practice companies to manage the latter's medical practices. Such agreements give control of the medical practice to the management companies, despite the absence of any consideration being exchanged and the absence of share ownership. In such cases a business combination is deemed to have occurred solely via contract. Ownership of the medical practice stays with the original shareholders/physicians.

## Recognizing and Measuring Identifiable Assets and Liabilities

Under the acquisition method, the acquirer is required to:

1. *recognize* identifiable assets and liabilities separately from goodwill; and
2. *measure* such assets and liabilities at their fair values on the *date of the acquisition*.

A key word is **identifiable**. The acquirer may be able to identify many more assets and liabilities than those shown on the acquiree's SFP. This is particularly true for intangible assets. An identifiable intangible asset is one that either is *separable* or *arises from contractual rights*. In addition, the fair value of any identifiable intangible asset must be measurable. The acquirer should not ignore these assets and just assume they are part of the acquiree's goodwill.

Similarly, contingent liabilities should be separately identified if (1) they are a present obligation that arises from past events, and (2) their fair values can be reliably measured.

# Categorization and Measurement of Identifiable Intangibles

**Identification**   As pointed out earlier, an acquired company often has intangible assets that are not reported on its SFP because the acquired company did not originally incur a cost to buy those assets. For example, suppose that Snowball Corporation has developed a valuable trademark over the course of its business. That trademark has not been reported as an asset on Snowball's SFP because the company did not incur any direct cost to acquire it. Subsequently, Icicle Limited buys Snowball. The trademark "Snowball" has been purchased by Icicle as part of the basket of Snowball's net assets. Icicle must recognize the trademark even though it does not appear on Snowball's books or SFP.

In addition to the trademarks, other identifiable intangible assets, such as patents and copyrights, are often not shown on the acquired company's SFP. Easily overlooked assets also include customer lists, employment contracts, favourable lease agreements, secret formulas (e.g., Coca-Cola, KFC), Internet domain names, and order backlogs. Goodwill should not be used as a catch-all to include identifiable intangible assets.

IFRS 3 classifies intangibles assets into five types: artistic-related, contract-based, customer-related, market-related, and technology-based. IFRS 3 provides illustrative examples for each type. While these examples are not exhaustive, they do provide a useful structure for identifying intangible assets.

**Measurement**   The measurement principle requires that all identifiable assets and liabilities be measured at their fair values on the date of acquisition. Therefore, the carrying values of the acquired assets and liabilities are completely irrelevant to the acquiring corporation's consolidated financial statements. Fair value measurements clearly are judgmental, often being a combination of different methods of valuation—a bit of a hodgepodge, really. This problem is especially severe in the case of intangible assets. There are three general types of valuation methods or models used for valuing intangible assets:

1. *Market-based*—based on prices in an active market, or prices of similar assets (analogy or benchmark approach);

2. *Income-based*—based on future economic benefit derived from owning the asset; and

3. *Cost-based*, although the result may not reflect fair value.

The market-based approach is the best approach; however, such data frequently are not available. Therefore, the most often used methods are income-based. All of these methods provide a great deal of latitude for management judgment in determining such fair values, especially in the case of intangible assets. As we shall see in the next chapter, measurement judgments can have significant consequences for reporting in future periods.

**Exceptions to the Fair Value Measurement Principle**   There are some exceptions to the fair-valuation rule: (1) deferred income taxes, (2) employee benefits, (3) indemnification assets, (4) reacquired assets, (5) share-based payment awards, and (6) assets held for sale. Most of these items are measured in accordance with the usual requirements under other applicable IFRS standards. Therefore, except for deferred income taxes, we will not discuss them in further detail in the text.

The deferred tax amounts that appear on the acquiree's SFP are not assets and liabilities from the standpoint of the buyer, since they relate solely to the differences between tax bases and accounting carrying values on the books of the acquiree.[3] We don't escape the complications of income tax allocation, however. Deferred tax accounting is a factor in the purchaser's financial reporting for purchased subsidiaries. Acquiring companies must determine their own deferred tax balances based on the difference between the asset and liability values they show on their consolidated financial statements and the tax bases. Deferred tax considerations are not central to an understanding of the complex issues in business combinations and consolidations. Therefore, rather than divert attention away from the main issues, we treat deferred tax implications separately, in Appendix 3A.

## Measuring and Recognizing Goodwill or a Gain from a Bargain Purchase

The price paid for the operating unit will be determined in part by its earnings ability. The acquirer may or may not choose to continue to operate the unit in the same manner; but regardless of the acquirer's plans, the price to be paid will take into account the acquiree's estimated future net earnings stream.

If the unit has been successful and has demonstrated an ability to generate above-average earnings, then the acquirer may have to pay a price that is higher than the aggregate fair value of the identifiable net assets. On the other hand, if the unit has not been successful, the price may be less than the fair value of the net identifiable assets (but not normally less than the liquidating value of the net assets including tax effects).

The difference between the fair value of the net identifiable assets (identifiable assets acquired less liabilities assumed) and the purchase consideration transferred is known as **goodwill** when the purchase consideration is higher than the fair value of the net identifiable assets and as a **gain from a bargain purchase** (also commonly known as **negative goodwill**) when the purchase consideration is less.[4]

Goodwill acquired in a purchase of net assets is recorded on the acquirer's books, along with the fair values of the other assets and liabilities acquired. It is important to understand that goodwill *is* a purchased asset. The purchaser paid good money (or shares) for the goodwill just as surely as for buildings and inventory. In some circles, goodwill is called a "nothing," which derives from the fact that it does not represent any specific asset, either tangible or intangible. But the fact that we can't point at an object (as for a tangible asset) or a specific right (as for an intangible or financial asset) does not make its cost any less real.

---

[3]This refers to the results of the inter-period income tax allocation process—deferred tax accounting. Any current taxes receivable or payable are assigned their fair value.

[4]IFRS 3 distinguishes between a gain from a bargain purchase and negative goodwill. The latter is a remote possibility which can occur in the absence of the former, since, as discussed in the previous section, under IFRS 3, certain acquired assets and liabilities are measured at amounts different from their date-of-acquisition fair values. However, reflecting the common use of the term "negative goodwill" to refer to a gain from bargain purchase, in this text we will use "bargain purchase" and "negative goodwill" as synonymous terms.

The gain from a bargain purchase or negative goodwill is recognized by the acquirer as a gain in its consolidated SCI. A bargain purchase typically happens when there is a forced sale on the part of the seller who is acting under compulsion from creditors or courts. To ensure that a gain on a bargain purchase is genuine, the acquirer must review all the assets and liabilities acquired and identify and recognize any unrecognized assets and liabilities noted during the review.[5]

## Measurement Subjectivity

You may have already noticed that there is quite a lot of subjectivity involved in many, if not most, of the valuations discussed above. There is very little directly relevant objective evidence upon which to base many measurements.

**Fair Value of the Consideration**   If the consideration is cash then the fair value is quite clear. If the consideration is in the form of other assets, then how shall those assets be valued if they are not traded in an active market?

**Contingent Consideration**   The nature of contingent consideration is that the estimated amount will change as the contingency period elapses. The longer the period, the more the fluctuation. Changes in estimated contingent consideration that result from events following the acquisition are reported as gains/losses in net income. Thus, making a high initial estimate of the amount of contingent consideration (e.g., justified as "management conservatism") will increase the cost of the acquisition but can easily result in gains being recorded in future periods as the total estimate is lowered. Therein lies a potential for income manipulation.

**Recognizing and Measuring Identifiable Assets and Liabilities**   How shall the fair values at the date of acquisition be measured? Most assets on the acquiree's books don't have an active second-hand market. The fair values of property, plant, and equipment (PPE) can be estimated on the basis of equivalent used property of similar age and type, if there is such a market. Or perhaps the fair value can be measured by using the price of new property, depreciated for age and obsolescence. Or a price index can be used to remeasure the value of the assets. Or appraisers can be hired to give their expert opinions. All of these methods, and others, can be used, as appropriate.

The point, however, is that there will always be a feasible range of potential values even for physical assets, and management must choose an "appropriate" measurement. For intangible assets, the challenge is even greater because, almost by definition, intangible assets are unique to the company and are extremely challenging to value.

**Auditability and the Ethical Challenge**   Attaching values to all of the components of a business combination is a challenging task at best. In almost every instance, management will have to choose from among a range of "feasible" values. The way in which they allocate the purchase price to the many assets and liabilities will depend partly on reliability of measurement and the needs and objectives of financial reporting. A "conservative" valuation of assets will lead to a large amount of the purchase price being allocated to goodwill. Goodwill is not amortized. Therefore, the more that is allocated to goodwill, the less impact the valuation will have on future earnings.

---

[5]Negative goodwill is discussed more fully at the end of this chapter.

Auditors can and should challenge management to provide justification for the values they assign to the various assets, both tangible and intangible. However, given the range of possible values for each asset, the best that the auditors can do is to make sure there is justification for management's choices and that the values fall within the feasible range of values. Auditors cannot themselves change any estimates; they can only challenge management, not second-guess them.

Now that we have a good overview of the acquisition method we can next focus on the actual mechanics of accounting for business combinations. In the following two sections we will (1) illustrate the accounting of a direct purchase of net assets, and then (2) discuss and illustrate the accounting for purchase of shares.

## Concept Check 3-1

1. Under the acquisition method, what are the five steps required to be followed to account for business combinations?

2. Why is determining the acquisition date important under the acquisition method of accounting for business combinations?

## 3.3 ILLUSTRATION OF DIRECT PURCHASE OF NET ASSETS

LO ④
Measure the fair values of the consideration transferred and the assets and liabilities acquired

To illustrate the accounting for a direct purchase of net assets, assume that on December 31, 20X5, Purchase Ltd. acquires all of the assets and liabilities of Target Ltd. by issuing 40,000 Purchase Ltd. common shares to Target Ltd. Before the transaction, Purchase Ltd. had 160,000 common shares outstanding. After the transaction, 200,000 Purchase Ltd. shares are outstanding, of which Target Ltd. owns 20%. The pre-transaction statements of financial position of both companies are shown in Exhibit 3.2.

The estimated fair values of Target Ltd.'s assets and liabilities are shown at the bottom of Exhibit 3.2. Their aggregate fair value is $1,100,000. If we assume that the market value of Purchase Ltd.'s shares is $30 each, then the total purchase consideration transferred for the acquisition is $1,200,000. Therefore, the goodwill relating to the acquisition is $100,000. The transaction will be recorded *on the books of Purchase Ltd.* as follows:

| | | |
|---|---|---|
| Cash and receivables | 200,000 | |
| Inventory | 50,000 | |
| Land | 400,000 | |
| Buildings and equipment | 550,000 | |
| Goodwill | 100,000 | |
| Accounts payable | | 100,000 |
| Common shares | | 1,200,000 |

The selling company, Target Ltd., will record the transaction by writing off all of its assets and liabilities and entering the new asset of Purchase Ltd.'s shares, recognizing a gain of $400,000 on the transaction. Note that from the perspective of the

**Exhibit 3.2** Pre-Transaction Statements of Financial Position

| December 31, 20X5 | Purchase Ltd. | Target Ltd. |
|---|---|---|
| Cash | $ 1,000,000 | $ 50,000 |
| Accounts receivable | 2,000,000 | 150,000 |
| Inventory | 200,000 | 50,000 |
| Land | 1,000,000 | 300,000 |
| Buildings and equipment | 3,000,000 | 500,000 |
| Accumulated depreciation | (1,200,000) | (150,000) |
| Total assets | $ 6,000,000 | $ 900,000 |
| Accounts payable | $ 1,000,000 | $ 100,000 |
| Long-term notes payable | 400,000 | — |
| Common shares* | 2,600,000 | 200,000 |
| Retained earnings | 2,000,000 | 600,000 |
| Total liabilities and shareholders' equity | $ 6,000,000 | $ 900,000 |
| *for Purchase Ltd.—160,000 shares outstanding | | |
| **Fair values of Target Ltd.'s net assets:** | | |
| Cash | | $ 50,000 |
| Accounts receivable | | 150,000 |
| Inventory | | 50,000 |
| Land | | 400,000 |
| Buildings and equipment | | 550,000 |
| Accounts payable | | (100,000) |
| Total | | $1,100,000 |

parent, this same $400,000 represents the **purchase price discrepancy (PPD)**, i.e., the difference between the purchase consideration of $1,200,000 and the carrying value of the net identifiable assets acquired of $800,000. The difference of $400,000 also represents the **fair value adjustment (FVA)**, the difference between the fair value of all of the assets of Target Ltd., including goodwill purchased by Parent Ltd. of $1,200,000, and the carrying value of those assets in the books of Target Ltd. of $800,000.

The post-transaction statements of financial position for the two companies will appear as shown in Exhibit 3.3. Purchase Ltd.'s assets and liabilities increase by the amount of the fair values of the acquired assets and the goodwill arising from the purchase, while Target Ltd.'s previous net assets have been replaced by its sole remaining asset, the shares in Purchase Ltd. If the transaction had been for cash instead of Purchase Ltd. shares, Target Ltd.'s sole remaining asset would have been the cash received.

The purchase of Target Ltd.'s net assets by Purchase Ltd. is a business combination, but it is not an intercorporate investment by Purchase Ltd. because Purchase Ltd. is not investing in the *shares* of Target Ltd. Since Purchase Ltd. is acquiring the assets and liabilities directly instead of indirectly through the purchase of Target Ltd. shares, Purchase Ltd. records the assets and liabilities directly on its books and there is no need for consolidated statements; Target Ltd. is *not* a subsidiary of Purchase Ltd.

**Exhibit 3.3** Post-Transaction Statements of Financial Position

| December 31, 20X5 | Purchase Ltd. | Target Ltd. |
|---|---|---|
| Cash | $ 1,050,000 | $ — |
| Accounts receivable | 2,150,000 | — |
| Inventory | 250,000 | — |
| Land | 1,400,000 | — |
| Buildings and equipment | 3,550,000 | — |
| Accumulated depreciation | (1,200,000) | — |
| Goodwill | 100,000 | — |
| Investment in Purchase Ltd. shares | — | 1,200,000 |
| Total assets | $ 7,300,000 | $1,200,000 |
| Accounts payable | $ 1,100,000 | $ — |
| Long-term notes payable | 400,000 | — |
| Common shares* | 3,800,000 | 200,000 |
| Retained earnings | 2,000,000 | 1,000,000 |
| Total liabilities and shareholders' equity | $ 7,300,000 | $1,200,000 |

*for Purchase Ltd.—200,000 shares outstanding

After the net asset purchase has been recorded, Purchase Ltd. will account for the assets as it would for any new asset group. There is no special treatment required.

## 3.4 PURCHASE OF SHARES

Buying the *assets* (or *net assets*) of another company is one way to accomplish a business combination. However, a much more common method of acquiring control over the assets of another company is to buy the *voting shares* of the other business. If one company buys a controlling block of the shares of another company, then control over the assets has been achieved, and the acquirer has a new subsidiary.

An acquirer can obtain a controlling share interest by any one or a combination of three methods:

- buying sufficient shares on the open market;

- entering into private sale agreements with major shareholders; or

- issuing a public tender offer to buy the shares.

Regardless of the purchase method used, the acquirer buys shares already outstanding. *The transaction is with the existing shareholders, not with the target company.* The buyer does not need the co-operation of the acquired company itself. Sometimes the target company's board of directors opposes a takeover attempt and tries to persuade the shareholders not to sell their shares to the acquirer—the takeover attempt in this instance is known as a **hostile takeover**. Nevertheless, if the purchaser can convince enough of the target company's shareholders to sell their shares, a business combination will occur.

**LO 2**
Identify the different types of business combinations

**LO 3**
Explain the general accounting approach to business combinations

**LO 4**
Measure the fair values of the consideration transferred and the assets and liabilities acquired

Unlike a direct purchase of assets, a business combination that is achieved by an acquisition of shares has no impact on the asset and equity structure of the acquired company.[6] The acquired company continues to carry its assets and liabilities on its own books. The purchaser has acquired *control* over the assets, but has not acquired the assets themselves.

## Advantages of Share Purchase

The purchase of shares rather than assets has the obvious advantage that control can be obtained by buying considerably less than 100% of the shares. Thus control can be obtained at substantially less cost than if the acquirer were to purchase the assets directly.

There are several other advantages to buying shares rather than the net assets themselves.

■ The shares may be selling at a price on the market that is less than the fair value per share (or even the carrying value per share) of the net assets. The acquirer can therefore obtain control over the assets at a lower price than could be negotiated for the assets themselves.

■ By buying shares rather than assets, the acquirer ends up with an asset that is more easily saleable than the assets themselves, in case the acquirer later decides to divest itself of the acquired business, or a portion thereof.

■ The acquirer may prefer to retain the newly acquired business as a separate entity for legal, tax, and business reasons. The acquired business's liabilities need not be assumed directly, and there is no interruption of the business relationships built up by the acquired corporation.

■ Income tax impacts can be a major factor in the choice between purchasing assets and purchasing shares. A purchase of shares may benefit the seller because any gain to the seller on a sale of shares will be taxed as a capital gain. However, if the assets are sold, gains may be subject to tax at full rates, such as (1) capital cost allowance (CCA) recapture, (2) a sale of inventory, or (3) a sale of intangibles that were fully deducted for tax purposes when paid for initially. Also, the acquiree may have substantial tax loss carryforwards that the company is unlikely to utilize. The purchaser may be able to take advantage of these carryforwards, say by transferring income-bearing assets to the acquired subsidiary.

For the buyer, however, a purchase of assets may be more desirable than a purchase of shares from a tax viewpoint. When the assets are purchased directly, their cost to the acquiring company becomes the basis for their tax treatment. For example, depreciable assets are recorded on the acquiring company's books at fair values, and CCA will be based on those fair values. Similarly, goodwill purchased is treated as *eligible capital property* for tax purposes, and 75% of the goodwill is subject to CCA (the other 25% is not deductible).

If control over the assets is obtained via a share purchase, on the other hand, there is no change in the tax basis for the assets because there is no change in the assets'

---

[6]An exception occurs when "push-down" accounting is used. We will discuss this concept toward the end of the chapter.

ownership. Thus the buyer cannot take advantage of any increased tax shields if net assets are purchased at fair values that are greater than carrying values.

Another advantage of purchasing shares to obtain control of another company is that the acquirer does not automatically assume the contingent liabilities of the target company, such as lawsuits or environmental liabilities. If large unexpected liabilities arise, the controlling company can let the subsidiary go bankrupt—the parent loses its investment, but that's better than being pulled down by overwhelming and unexpected liabilities associated with assets purchased directly.

To summarize, the decision on acquisition method is subject to many variables. In a friendly takeover, the method of purchase and the purchase price are subject to negotiation, taking into account the various factors affecting both parties, including income tax. If the takeover is hostile, then a purchase of shares is the only alternative.

## Share Exchanges

There are many different ways in which shares can be exchanged to accomplish a business combination.[7] Some of the more common and straightforward methods include the following:

- **Direct exchange**. The acquirer issues new shares to the shareholders of the acquired company in exchange for the shares of the target company (the acquiree).
- **Indirect exchange**. *Subsidiaries* of the acquirer issue shares in exchange for the acquiree's shares.
- **Holding company**. A new corporation is formed; the new corporation issues shares to the shareholders of both the acquirer and the acquiree in exchange for the outstanding shares of both companies.
- **Statutory amalgamation**. The shareholders of the two corporations agree to a *statutory amalgamation*.
- **Reverse takeover**. The acquiree issues new shares to the shareholders of the acquirer in exchange for the acquirer's outstanding shares.

**Direct Exchange**   The first method listed above is the most common approach. What happens is that:

- the acquirer issues new shares to the shareholders of the acquiree and therefore has more shares outstanding after the acquisition than before the acquisition;
- the pre-acquisition shareholders of the acquiree become shareholders in the acquirer, so that the acquirer's post-acquisition shareholders consist of both its original shareholders *and* the former shareholders of the acquiree; and
- the acquiree's shares are now held by the acquiring *corporation* instead of by external shareholders.

**Indirect Exchange**   The second approach is similar to the first, except that the acquirer does not issue its own shares to acquire the company directly. Instead, the

---

[7]Some share exchanges may also include cash as part of the purchase consideration.

acquirer obtains indirect control by having its existing subsidiaries issue new shares to acquire the company. This approach is useful when the acquirer does not want to alter the ownership percentages of the existing shareholders by issuance of additional shares.

For example, if the controlling shareholder of the acquirer owns 51% of the acquirer's shares, the issuance of additional shares would decrease the controlling shareholder's interest to below 50%, and control could be lost. But if the acquirer has a subsidiary that is, say, 70% owned, quite a number of additional shares could be issued by the subsidiary without jeopardizing the parent's control.

In our introductory example, the actual takeover of Equinox was effected by Barrick Canada Inc., a subsidiary of Barrick. Barrick announced on July 19, 2011, that it and its *affiliates* had completed the acquisition of 100% of the outstanding shares of Equinox by that date.

**Holding Company**   Under the third method, a new company is created that will hold the shares of both of the combining companies. The holding company issues its new shares in exchange for the shares of both the acquiree and the acquirer. After the exchange, the shares of both operating companies are held by the holding company, while the shares of the holding company are held by the former shareholders of both the acquiree and the acquirer.

The third method is not likely to be used by public companies. If the acquirer has a stock exchange listing, that listing would not automatically transfer to the newly formed company. The new company would have to apply for a new listing, which would disrupt trading in the acquirer's shares. The interruption in trading would likely have an adverse effect on the acquirer's share price.

**Statutory Amalgamation**   In a statutory amalgamation, the shareholders of two or more corporations approve the combination, or amalgamation, of their companies into a single surviving corporation. Statutory amalgamations are governed by the provincial or federal corporations acts under which the companies are incorporated. For two or more corporations to amalgamate, they must be incorporated under the same act. The shareholders of the combined company are the former shareholders of the combining companies.

Statutory amalgamation is the only method of combination in which the combining companies cease to exist as separate legal entities. It is also the only method of share exchange in which the assets of both companies end up being recorded on the books of one company, similar to the recording of assets in a direct purchase of net assets.

In all other forms of share exchange, there is no transfer of assets and thus no recording of the acquiree's assets on the acquirer's books—the results of the combination are reported by means of consolidated financial statements, as we discussed in the previous chapter. In contrast, consolidated statements are not needed for the combined companies after a statutory amalgamation because only one company survives. Of course, if either amalgamating company has subsidiaries, it would still be necessary to prepare consolidated statements that includes those subsidiaries.

**Reverse Takeover**   In the previous four methods of exchanging shares, it is clear which corporation is the acquirer in the business combination. Simply, the acquirer is the corporation that obtains control over the other entity. However, it is possible to arrange the combination in such a way that the company that legally appears to be the acquirer is, in substance, the acquiree. This is the fifth method.

For example, suppose that SmallLimited has 100,000 shares outstanding before the combination, and issues 200,000 new shares to acquire all of BigCorp's shares. SmallLimited will own all of the shares of BigCorp and thus will legally control BigCorp. However, two-thirds of the shares of SmallLimited will be owned by the former shareholders of BigCorp, and the former shareholders of BigCorp will have voting control of SmallLimited after the combination. The substance of the combination is that control resides with BigCorp's shareholders even though the legal form of the combination is that SmallLimited acquired BigCorp. This form of business combination is called a **reverse takeover**.

After a reverse takeover, the consolidated financial statements will be issued under the name of the legal parent (in this example, SmallLimited) but should reflect the substance of the combination as a continuation of the financial statements of the legal subsidiary (i.e., BigCorp). Pre-combination comparative statements and historical data should be those of the legal subsidiary (and in-substance acquirer), rather than of the legal parent (and in-substance acquiree).[8]

Because of the potential confusion from reporting the substance of the activities of the legal subsidiary under the name of the legal parent, it is common for reverse takeovers to be accompanied by a company name change so that the name of the legal parent becomes almost indistinguishable from that of the legal subsidiary. This is what happened in the Cabia Goldhills Inc. example that we cited in the chapter introduction.

One of the main reasons for a reverse takeover is to acquire a stock exchange listing. If SmallLimited had a Toronto Stock Exchange listing and BigCorp wanted one, a reverse takeover would avoid the trouble and expense of applying to the Ontario Securities Commission and the TSX for a new listing. After a reverse takeover, SmallLimited would legally own BigCorp and could continue to use the TSX listing. However, to preserve the substance of the transaction as a continuance of BigCorp, SmallLimited would legally change its name to BigCorp and continue trading with the same TSX listing but under the name of the in-substance acquirer. The controversy in 2011–2012 surrounding Sino-Forest Inc. has highlighted how companies can use reverse takeovers to obtain stock exchange listings without facing the full scrutiny of a new stock listing.

In some instances, the legal acquirer (and in-substance acquiree) is just a **shell company** that has an exchange listing but no assets. In that case, no business combination has really occurred because the shell company is not a "business" within the definitions used for business combinations.

The accounting problem in any business combination is to report in accordance with the *substance* of the combination, and not to be misled by its legal form. Accountants must be sensitive to the objectives of managers and owners in arranging business combinations, and must examine the end result to determine who purchased what and for how much.

## Illustration of a Share Exchange

To illustrate the acquirer's accounting for a purchase of shares, assume that on December 31, 20X5, Purchase Ltd. acquires all of the outstanding shares of Target Ltd. by issuing 40,000 Purchase Ltd. shares with a market value of $30, or $1,200,000 total, in exchange.[9]

---

[8]A detailed description of reverse takeover accounting is beyond the scope of this book. IFRS 3 provides guidance on reverse takeovers.

[9]This transaction has the same value as the illustration used earlier in the chapter for a direct purchase of net assets.

After the exchange of shares, all of the Target Ltd. shares will be held by the corporate entity of Purchase Ltd., while the newly issued shares of Purchase Ltd. will be held by the former shareholders of Target Ltd. and *not* by Target Ltd. as a corporate entity. Target Ltd. will have no shareholders external to the combined entity, while the shareholder base and the number of shares outstanding for Purchase Ltd. have increased.

When Purchase Ltd. acquires the shares, the entry to record the purchase on the books of Purchase Ltd. will be as follows:

| | | |
|---|---|---|
| Investment in Target Ltd. | 1,200,000 | |
| Common shares | | 1,200,000 |

There will be no entry on Target Ltd.'s books, because Target Ltd. is not a party to the transaction; the transaction is with the shareholders of Target Ltd. and not with the company itself. After the original purchase is recorded, the investment is accounted for on Purchase Ltd.'s books by either the cost or the equity method, as discussed in Chapter 2.

Exhibit 3.4 shows the statements of financial position of Purchase Ltd. and Target Ltd. on December 31, 20X5, both before and after the purchase of Target Ltd.'s shares by Purchase Ltd. The pre-transaction amounts are the same as were shown in Exhibit 3.2, when Purchase Ltd. purchased the net assets of Target Ltd.

The post-transaction amounts on Purchase Ltd.'s separate-entity SFP differ from the pre-transaction amounts in only one respect—Purchase Ltd. now has an account, "Investment in Target Ltd.," that reflects the cost of buying Target Ltd.'s shares, offset by an equal increase in Purchase Ltd.'s common share account. The purchase price was $1,200,000, determined by the value of the 40,000 Purchase Ltd. common shares given to Target Ltd.'s shareholders in exchange for their shares in Target Ltd.

**Exhibit 3.4** Statements of Financial Position, December 31, 20X5

| | Before the exchange of shares | | After the exchange of shares | |
|---|---|---|---|---|
| | Purchase Ltd. | Target Ltd. | Purchase Ltd. | Target Ltd. |
| Cash | $ 1,000,000 | $ 50,000 | $ 1,000,000 | $ 50,000 |
| Accounts receivable | 2,000,000 | 150,000 | 2,000,000 | 150,000 |
| Inventory | 200,000 | 50,000 | 200,000 | 50,000 |
| Land | 1,000,000 | 300,000 | 1,000,000 | 300,000 |
| Buildings and equipment | 3,000,000 | 500,000 | 3,000,000 | 500,000 |
| Accumulated depreciation | (1,200,000) | (150,000) | (1,200,000) | (150,000) |
| Investment in Target Ltd. | — | — | 1,200,000 | — |
| TOTAL ASSETS | $ 6,000,000 | $ 900,000 | $ 7,200,000 | $ 900,000 |
| Accounts payable | $ 1,000,000 | $ 100,000 | $ 1,000,000 | $ 100,000 |
| Long-term notes payable | 400,000 | — | 400,000 | — |
| Common shares* | 2,600,000 | 200,000 | 3,800,000 | 200,000 |
| Retained earnings | 2,000,000 | 600,000 | 2,000,000 | 600,000 |
| TOTAL LIABILITIES AND SHARE EQUITY | $ 6,000,000 | $ 900,000 | $ 7,200,000 | $ 900,000 |

*For Purchase Ltd., 160,000 shares before the exchange; 200,000 shares after the exchange.

*Target Ltd.'s SFP is completely unaffected by the exchange of shares.* Target Ltd.'s *owner* has changed, but nothing has changed in the company's accounts. Target Ltd.'s net asset carrying value was $800,000 prior to the change of ownership, and remains $800,000 after the change of ownership.

However, Target Ltd. is now a subsidiary of Purchase Ltd., and therefore Purchase Ltd. will prepare consolidated financial statements for public reporting purposes. The preparation of consolidated statements for a purchased subsidiary is somewhat more complex than for parent-founded subsidiaries, and involves choices from among several optional approaches. Consolidation of a purchased subsidiary at the date of acquisition will be illustrated shortly.

## Concept Check 3-2

1. Why would a company buy the shares of another company to obtain control of the net assets of that company rather than directly buying the net assets of that company?

2. What are the common methods of share exchange used in business combinations?

# 3.5 ALTERNATIVE APPROACHES TO REPORTING MERGERS

LO ⑤
Identify the different approaches to reporting mergers

Alternative Approaches to Reporting Business CombinationsIn Chapter 2, we demonstrated the preparation of consolidated statements for Parco. To obtain the Parco consolidated SFP, we simply added the balances of Subco's assets and liabilities to those of Parco, after eliminating the intercompany balances. It might seem logical to use the same procedure to prepare Purchase Ltd.'s consolidated SFP, adding the carrying values of the two companies' assets and liabilities together to get the consolidated amounts.

However, in Chapter 2 we were demonstrating consolidation of a *parent-founded* subsidiary. In wholly owned parent-founded subsidiaries, the carrying values of the subsidiary's net assets represent the costs of the assets to the consolidated economic entity, because it was the parent's investment that provided the funds to purchase the assets. When a subsidiary is purchased, however, the purchase price of the net assets acquired will almost certainly be different from the carrying value of those assets on the subsidiary's books.

Theoretically, there are three general alternative approaches to consolidation in a business combination in addition to the acquisition method that is current prescribed by both IFRS and ASPE.

**Pooling-of-Interests Method**  The **pooling-of-interests method** involves adding together the *carrying values* of the assets and liabilities of the two companies. The assumption underlying the pooling method is that the combined economic entity is a continuation under common ownership of two previously separate going concerns, and that the operations of both companies will continue without substantial change, and no synergy is created by the merger. If the companies continue to function as separate entities—although now under common ownership—then it is presumed that there should be no change in the basis of accounting for the assets and liabilities as a result of the combination. The pooling method completely ignores the fair value of both companies' assets and liabilities. As a result, its use can have a significant impact on the results reported in the company's financial statements.

**Purchase Method**   The **purchase method** adds the *purchase cost allocated* to Target Ltd.'s assets and liabilities at the date of acquisition to the *carrying values* of Purchase Ltd.'s assets and liabilities. Notice the subtle distinction between this method and the acquisition method. The acquisition method uses fair values, while the purchase method uses the purchase cost allocation to the acquiree's assets and liabilities. In the case of a *wholly owned subsidiary*, the purchase method will be identical to the acquisition method when the purchase price is equal to or greater than the fair values of the net identifiable assets of Target Ltd.

For non-wholly owned subsidiaries, however, the purchase method can yield results quite different from the acquisition method because of the difference between the two methods in how the non-controlling interest is valued.

**New-Entity Method**   The acquisition and purchase methods can be criticized because the consolidated SFP contains a mixture of old carrying values (for Purchase Ltd.'s assets) and date-of-acquisition fair values (for Target Ltd.'s assets). One can argue that when a business combination occurs, a new economic entity is formed, and that a new basis of accountability should be established for *all* of the assets.

Under the **new-entity method**, all of the assets and liabilities of *both* Target Ltd. and Purchase Ltd. are revalued to fair value, so that the consolidated SFP will disclose the current fair values (on the date of the combination) of all of the assets for the combined entity.

Under certain circumstances, there is merit in the arguments for the new-entity method. If the combining enterprises are of roughly comparable size, and if the operations of the newly combined enterprises are going to be substantially different from the predecessor operations, then a case can be made for establishing a new basis of accountability. However, there are significant practical problems in implementing the method. Obtaining fair values for all of the assets is likely to be an expensive and time-consuming project unless the acquiring company already uses current values for internal reporting purposes. In addition, an even higher degree of subjectivity would inevitably exist in the fair value determination than exists in the acquisition method.

## Summary of Methods

The two variables that vary among the four methods are (1) the valuation of the parent's net assets; and (2) the valuation of the subsidiary's net assets. The alternatives can be summarized as follows:

Although the acquisition method is now the "approved" method of accounting for business combinations, it is useful to be able to at least recognize the names of the alternative approaches. Accounting for business combinations has been contentious for a long time—it's never really been a settled issue. Indeed, standard-setters had quite recently given serious consideration to the new entity method, but eventually settled on the acquisition method. Who knows what may lie ahead?

| Method | Net Assets of Parent Company | Net Assets of Subsidiary | Applicability of Method in Canada |
|---|---|---|---|
| Pooling of interests | Carrying value | Carrying value | Prior to 2001 in limited cases |
| Acquisition | Carrying value | Fair value | Mandatory after January 1, 2011 |
| Purchase | Carrying value | Purchase price paid* | Widely used prior to January 1, 2011 |
| New entity | Fair value | Fair value | Discussed, but never used in practice |

*In the case of a 100%-owned subsidiary, if purchase price paid is equal to or greater than the fair value of the net identifiable assets of the subsidiary, the purchase and acquisition methods are identical.

With one exception, we will not discuss or illustrate the application of the alternative approaches because they are not currently used for business combinations. However, the pooling-of-interests approach is used in corporate restructurings. We will discuss pooling briefly in the next section, and then move on to applying the acquisition method for business combinations.

## Corporate Restructurings

The acquisition-method requirement of IFRS 3 does not apply to combinations of companies under **common control**, wherein two or more subsidiaries are controlled by the same owners both before and after the combination. The owners can be either the same parent company or the same controlling shareholders. The primary type of control is a parent company that combines two or more of its controlled subsidiaries. Common control can also be exerted through contractual arrangements.[10] *Common control transactions* are also commonly known as **corporate restructurings**.

A parent company (or its owners) may decide to rearrange the intercorporate ownerships of the economic entity comprising the parent and its several subsidiaries. New subsidiaries may be formed, or parts of the economic entity may be combined or otherwise regrouped or redefined. When a corporate restructuring takes place, it is not an arm's-length transaction because all of the individual corporations are ultimately controlled by the same shareholders. Since there is no arm's-length transaction, the assets cannot be revalued for reporting on either the separate-entity or the consolidated financial statements.

Common control transactions are quite common in both public and private companies in Canada. There is no guidance in IFRS for how such transactions should be reported because these corporate reshufflings have no impact on *consolidated* statements. Corporate restructurings are accounted for in the same manner as pooling of interests; since there is no substantive change to control or ownership interests, a corporate restructuring is accounted for strictly on the basis of carrying values—fair values are never used because they are not arm's-length transactions. Therefore, it is necessary to understand the general nature of the pooling method even though it is not used for business combinations.

---

[10]Sometimes, pursuant to contractual agreements, a group of individuals may collectively control two companies by having the power over their financial and operating policies and thereby obtaining returns from the activities of those companies. A combination of these two companies will not, therefore, lead to a change in the ultimate collective control over the combined entity. Therefore, such a combination will be deemed to be a common control transaction and not a business combination.

### Concept Check 3-3

1. What general alternative approaches to reporting business combinations are available, and how do they differ from each other?
2. How do corporate restructurings differ from business combinations?

**LO 6**
Demonstrate the mechanics of consolidating a purchased subsidiary at the time of acquisition

## 3.6 CONSOLIDATION PROCEDURES USING THE ACQUISITION METHOD

### General Approach

Before plunging into the greater complexities of consolidation in the following chapters, we will more carefully illustrate the general procedure for consolidating subsidiaries that were acquired through a business combination. The key factor that differentiates the procedure is that, for business combinations, consolidation mechanics must adjust for fair values, whereas fair values are not an issue for parent-founded subsidiaries.

The reporting objective is *substance over form*. Although the parent and its subsidiaries are separate *legal* entities and prepare separate, individual financial statements, the overall *economic* entity is the group of companies. Indeed, consolidated statements are called **group accounts** in most parts of the world, even though there are no formal "accounts" for the group—just consolidation working papers and financial statements.

In theory, acquisition-method accounting combines the carrying values of the parent with the fair values (*at date of acquisition*) of the purchased subsidiaries. In practice, consolidation actually begins with *carrying values* of both companies. At the date of acquisition, it is clear that the carrying values and the fair values relate to the same assets and liabilities. As time moves on, however, assets will enter and leave the SFP of the purchased subsidiary, and the asset base will change.

Therefore, broadly speaking, consolidation takes the carrying values of both companies and adds the fair value adjustment (FVA) relating to each asset. A **fair value adjustment**, which can be either a fair value increment or a fair value decrement, is the difference between the carrying values and fair values of the acquiree's identifiable assets and liabilities at the date of acquisition, plus any goodwill. Specifically, the FVA is first allocated to the various identifiable assets and liabilities of the acquiree to the *full extent* of their *fair value increments (or decrements)*. Any excess of the FVA after the allocation process is allocated to goodwill.

In this and the later chapters, chapter, we follow a sequence of steps that we call the MEAR steps to consolidation. MEAR is a mnemonic (a memory aid) that stands for the four steps required in a typical consolidation: **M**easure, **E**liminate, **A**mortize FVAs, and **R**ecognize non-controlling interest's share of earnings. We hope that this simple memory device will help you to remember the sequence in the consolidation process, which can become rather complex at times.

The MEAR steps to consolidation help us approach the consolidation process in a systematic and organized fashion, qualities indispensable for solving the more complicated consolidation problems that will come later in the text. Hopefully, they will save you countless hours of frustration. In our experience, students who approach consolidations systematically obtain a better understanding of the topic and consequently also perform better on exams. At the same time, these steps are like the training wheels on a bicycle. They are

**Exhibit 3.5** MEAR Steps to Consolidation—Phase 1

| Consolidation Steps | At Acquisition |
|---|---|
| 1. Measure | ▪ Calculate cost and fair value adjustments (FVA) |
|  | ▪ Allocate FVA |
| 2. Eliminate | ▪ Eliminate parent's investment account and sub's share equity accounts |

needed at the beginning when you are becoming comfortable with the consolidation process. However, you may feel comfortable enough to dispense with them in the course of time.

We will develop the full sequence of steps (and sub-steps) in subsequent chapters. However, since this chapter focuses only on consolidation at the date of acquisition, we need be concerned here with only the first two steps, **M**easure and **E**liminate. These steps are always required at the date of acquisition, as well as for all subsequent reporting dates. Exhibit 3.5 elaborates on the steps required under **M**easure and **E**liminate.

## Illustration

An analysis of the purchase price for Target Ltd. is illustrated in Exhibit 3.6. Of the $1,200,000 purchase price, $800,000 is attributed to the carrying value of the net assets acquired, and the difference of $400,000 represents the FVA. The FVA of $400,000 is allocated to the various identifiable assets of Target Ltd. to the extent of the total of their fair value increment of $300,000, the residual of $100,000 being allocated to goodwill.

Sometimes the PPD is less than the total of the fair value adjustments relating to the net identifiable assets. In such a case we have a negative goodwill or a bargain purchase. In such a situation, the difference is recognized as a gain from a bargain purchase in the consolidated financial statements by the acquirer, as discussed in further detail below. Irrespective of the presence or absence of a bargain purchase, the allocation of the FVA to the various assets and liabilities acquired is carried out as usual following the **M**easure step of the MEAR steps to consolidation.

Exhibit 3.7 shows the derivation of Purchase Ltd.'s consolidated SFP at December 31, 20X5, using the direct method. For each item on the SFP, we take the carrying value for Purchase Ltd., add the carrying value of Target Ltd., and add the fair value adjustment.

There is one aspect of Exhibit 3.7 that merits explanation. You'll notice that *accumulated depreciation* is calculated by adding the two companies' amounts together, and then *subtracting Target Ltd.'s accumulated depreciation at the date of acquisition*. We subtract Target Ltd.'s accumulated depreciation because we want to show the fair value of Target Ltd.'s depreciable assets at the date of acquisition. This amount is included in the capital asset account itself. If we carried Target's accumulated depreciation forward, we would be reducing the fair value. In effect, we would be combining fair value in the asset account with written-off cost in the accumulated depreciation.

Although we have indicated which adjustments on Exhibit 3.7 are for fair value adjustments and which are eliminations, bear in mind that these purchase adjustments and eliminations are not independent. Essentially, all of the adjustments shown in Exhibit 3.7 are allocations of the $1,200,000 fair value. In future years, all of the components of this fair value adjustment must be made simultaneously, as we will illustrate in the following chapters.

**Exhibit 3.6** Allocation of Fair Value Adjustment

| | | 100% Purchase of Target Ltd., December 31, 20X5 | | | |
|---|---|---|---|---|---|
| Purchase price | | | | | $1,200,000 |
| Less carrying value of Target's net identifiable assets (100%) | | | | | (800,000) |
| = Fair value adjustment, allocated below | | | | | 400,000 |
| | Carrying value (a) | Fair value (b) | Fair value adjustment (c) = (b) – (a) | FVA allocated | |
| Cash | $ 50,000 | $ 50,000 | — | | |
| Accounts receivable | 150,000 | 150,000 | — | | |
| Inventory | 50,000 | 50,000 | — | | |
| Land | 300,000 | 400,000 | $100,000 | $100,000 | |
| Buildings and equipment | 500,000 | 550,000 | 50,000 | 50,000 | |
| Accumulated depreciation | (150,000) | — | 150,000 | 150,000 | |
| Accounts payable | (100,000) | (100,000) | — | | |
| Total fair value adjustment | | | | | (300,000) |
| Net asset carrying value | $ 800,000 | | | | |
| Fair value of assets acquired | | $1,100,000 | | | |
| Balance of FVA allocated to goodwill | | | | | $ 100,000 |

The consolidation procedures under the worksheet method are provided on this textbook's Companion Website.

## Concept Check 3-4

1. What consolidation procedures are required at the time of acquisition under the acquisition method?

2. Under the acquisition method, why must fair value adjustments be allocated to various assets and liabilities?

**LO ⑥**
Demonstrate the mechanics of consolidating a purchased subsidiary at the time of acquisition

# 3.7 NEGATIVE GOODWILL

In the business combination used in the previous example, control over net assets with a fair value of $1,100,000 was acquired for $1,200,000. The difference between the purchase price and the fair value of the acquired net assets is treated as goodwill.

It is not unusual, however, for the total fair value of the assets and liabilities to be *greater* than the purchase price. This excess of fair values over the purchase price is commonly known as negative goodwill, although the term is not particularly indicative of the accounting treatment of the amount. The total of the net debits (to record the fair values) is greater than the credits (to record the consideration paid), and therefore there are more debits than credits in the consolidated statements—not a tolerable situation in a double-entry system. The task is to correct the balance by either increasing the credits or decreasing the debits.

**Exhibit 3.7** Purchase Ltd. Consolidated SFP

| Consolidated Statement of Financial Position | |
|---|---|
| December 31, 20X5 | |
| **ASSETS** | |
| Current assets: | |
| Cash [1,000,000 + 50,000] | $1,050,000 |
| Accounts receivable [2,000,000 + 150,000] | 2,150,000 |
| Inventory [200,000 + 50,000] | 250,000 |
| | 3,450,000 |
| Property, plant, and equipment: | |
| Land [1,000,000 + 300,000 + **100,000[a]**] | 1,400,000 |
| Buildings and equipment [3,000,000 + 500,000 + **50,000[a]**] | 3,550,000 |
| Accumulated depreciation [1,200,000 + 150,000 − **150,000[a]**] | (1,200,000) |
| | 3,750,000 |
| Other Assets: | |
| Investment in Target Ltd. [1,200,000 − **400,000[a]** − **800,000[b]**] | — |
| Goodwill [+ **100,000[a]**] | 100,000 |
| **TOTAL ASSETS** | $7,300,000 |
| **LIABILITIES AND SHAREHOLDERS' EQUITY** | |
| Liabilities: | |
| Current: accounts payable [1,000,000 + 100,000] | $1,100,000 |
| Long-term: notes payable [400,000 + 0] | 400,000 |
| | 1,500,000 |
| Shareholders' equity: | |
| Common shares [3,800,000 + 200,000 − **200,000[b]**] | 3,800,000 |
| Retained earnings [2,000,000 + 600,000 − **600,000[b]**] | 2,000,000 |
| | 5,800,000 |
| **TOTAL LIABILITIES AND SHAREHOLDERS' EQUITY** | $7,300,000 |

[a]Indicates the fair value (and goodwill) adjustments.

[b]Indicates elimination Purchase Ltd.'s investment account and Target's shareholders' equity accounts.

In previous years, it was common practice to increase the credits by establishing an account to credit for the amount of negative goodwill. It was not normally called "negative goodwill," of course. Usually a more opaque title was chosen, such as "excess of fair value over cost of assets acquired." This was prohibited by recent Canadian standards and is also prohibited under IFRS. Instead of creating a credit for negative goodwill, debits and credits must be balanced by recognizing a *gain on bargain purchase* in the acquirer's consolidated SCI.

A bargain purchase is possible for a variety of reasons. If the acquisition is by a purchase of shares, then the market price of the acquiree's shares may be lower than the net asset value per share. Or if the acquiree is a private company, an acquirer may make a bargain purchase if the present owners are anxious to sell, perhaps due to the death of the founder-manager, a divorce, changed family financial position, or simply an inability to manage effectively—family-owned businesses are infamous for failing after the third generation takes over.

Continuing our example, suppose that Purchase Ltd. acquired all of the shares of Target Ltd., as above, but at a cost of only $1,050,000. Since the fair value of Target's net assets is $1,100,000, negative goodwill of $50,000 exists. Under the acquisition method, the identifiable assets and liabilities of the acquiree are *always* reported at their fair values, regardless of the purchase consideration transferred.

Therefore, in our example, Target Ltd.'s assets and liabilities will be reported on Purchase Ltd.'s consolidated SFP at a total amount of $1,100,000, which is their fair value. The PPD in this case will be $250,000 ($1,050,000 purchase consideration less $800,000 carrying value of the net identifiable assets). However, the fair value adjustment continues to be $300,000. The difference of $50,000 ($300,000 fair value increment less $250,000 PPD) represents a negative goodwill and will be recognized as a gain on bargain purchase in the consolidated SCI issued by Purchase Ltd.

LO ❼
Understand the disclosure requirements relating to business combinations

## 3.8 DISCLOSURE

Business combinations are significant events. They often change the nature of operations of a company and thus change the components of the earnings stream. All users' financial reporting objectives are affected by substantial business combinations. At a minimum, the asset and liability structure of the reporting enterprise is changed. Disclosure of business combinations therefore is quite important.

IFRS 3 requires a long list of disclosures for business combinations completed during a reporting period. The acquirer is required to disclose information that enables users to evaluate:

- the nature and financial effect of business combinations that occurred either during the reporting period or after the end of the reporting period but before the date on which the financial statements for that period are authorized for issue; and

- the financial effects of the adjustments made in the current reporting period relating to a business combination that occurred either in that reporting period or in previous reporting periods.

We will not reproduce the complete list of disclosures here; the more essential aspects include:

- a description, including the name of the acquired subsidiary, the date of acquisition, percentage of the voting shares acquired, primary reason for the business combination, and how control was obtained;

- a qualitative description of the factors giving rise to the goodwill and intangible assets not separately identifiable from goodwill;

- the amount of any contingent consideration recognized, and the arrangement and basis for arriving at such amount;

- amounts of the major classes of assets and liabilities acquired;

- fair value on the acquisition date of the purchase consideration transferred and of each major class of consideration;

- the amount and reason for a gain from bargain purchase if present; and

- the amount and measurement basis of the non-controlling interest if less than 100% of the acquiree is acquired.

For acquisitions that are individually immaterial, similar information should be disclosed in the aggregate.

Exhibit 3.8 shows the first quarter 2012 disclosure note relating to business combinations made by SAP AG, the Germany-based provider of enterprise software. Exhibit 3.8 focuses mainly on SAP's acquisition of SuccessFactors Inc., a USA-based provider of cloud-based human capital management solutions. Notice that there are several pieces of information in this note:

- SAP made several acquisitions during the year; the most significant acquisition (SuccessFactors) is the main focus of the note, while the rest, being immaterial, are shown in aggregate.

- SAP's consolidated financial statements are prepared in accordance with IFRS; therefore, while the disclosure note is silent on the method of accounting applied to its acquisitions, it appears reasonable to assume that such accounting is consistent with the requirements of IFRS 3.

- Goodwill relates mainly to the synergies and the skills and technical talent of SuccessFactors' workforce.

- The initial allocation of the fair values relating to the acquisition in the first-quarter financial statements is provisional because SAP is still validating its valuation assumptions.

- SuccessFactors is a publicly listed company in the United States (its New York Stock Exchange [NYSE] symbol is SFSF). SAP did not buy the assets and liabilities of SuccessFactors directly. Instead, it bought 90% of the share capital of SuccessFactors and obtained control of SuccessFactors on February 21, 2012. Subsequently, SAP purchased the remaining shares for the same US$40 per share price that was paid for the original 90% of the shares.

- The purchase was for cash, and the total purchase consideration paid was cash of €2,659 million. Note that the costs associated with the acquisition of €10 million have not been capitalized but have instead been expensed as part of general and administrative expenses on the SCI. This is consistent with IFRS 3, which does not allow these costs to be added to the cost of the acquisition, but, rather, requires them to be expensed by the acquirer in the year they are incurred and the services are received.

- Of the total cost, €2,112 million was allocated to goodwill, which is 79.43% of the total purchase price.

**Exhibit 3.8** Disclosure of Acquisitions

SAP AG

## Note (4) Business Combinations

We acquired the following businesses during the first quarter in 2012:

| Acquired Businesses | Sector | Acquisition Type | Acquired Voting Interest | Acquisition Date |
|---|---|---|---|---|
| Purisma Inc, Short Hills, NJ, USA | Master Data Management Solution Business | Asset Deal | n/a | January 18, 2012 |
| datango AG, Berlin, Germany | Solution for Workforce Performance Support | Asset Deal | n/a | February 7, 2012 |
| SuccessFactors Inc, San Mateo, CA, USA | Provider of cloud-based human capital management (HCM) solutions | Share Deal | 100% | February 21, 2012 |

We acquire businesses in specific areas of strategic interest to us. The acquisitions during the first quarter of 2012 were not material to SAP except for the acquisition of SuccessFactors, for which additional information is provided below.

In the first quarter, our acquisitions are recorded with provisional estimates.

Acquisitions of the prior year are described in the Consolidated Financial Statements in our 2011 Annual Report.

Material Business Combinations

On February 21, 2012, we acquired more than 90 per cent of the outstanding ordinary shares of SuccessFactors, Inc. (NYSE: SFSF) and obtained control of SuccessFactors. Subsequent to the acceptance of the tender offer we effected a short-form merger and acquired the remaining shares for the same US$40.00 per share price that was paid in the cash tender offer.

SuccessFactors is a provider of cloud-based human capital management (HCM) solutions. As a result of the acquisition, we expect to significantly accelerate our momentum as a provider of cloud applications, platforms and infrastructure and to establish an advanced end-to-end offering of cloud and on-premise solutions for managing all relevant business processes.

The initial accounting for the business combination is provisional in our financial statements as of March 31, 2012 as we are still validating our valuation assumptions. The following table summarizes the consideration paid, provisional estimates of the acquisition-related costs and provisional values for assets acquired and liabilities assumed which were recognized at the acquisition date.

## FINANCIAL IMPACT FROM THE ACQUISITION OF SUCCESSFACTORS AS OF THE CLOSING DATE

| € millions | Total |
|---|---|
| Consideration | |
| Value of acquired shares outstanding paid | 2,543 |
| Value of acquired accelerated options, stock appreciation rights and restricted stock units | 116 |
| Total Cash payment | 2,659 |
| Value of earned portion of converted unvested restricted stock units, restricted stocks and performance stock (valued in accordance with IFRS 2) | 58 |
| Total Consideration transferred | 2,717 |
| | |
| Acquisition related costs (included in general and administrative expenses in our income statement) | |
| Acquisition-related costs incurred in 2011 | 4 |
| Acquisition-related costs recognized in 2012 | 6 |
| Total acquisition-related costs | 2,727 |
| | |
| Amounts of identifiable assets acquired and liabilities assumed expected to be recognized | |
| Cash and cash equivalents | 80 |
| Other financial assets | 10 |
| Trade and other receivables (net of € 2 millions reserves) | 58 |
| Other non-financial assets | 11 |
| Property, plant, and equipment | 10 |
| Intangible assets | 783 |
| Thereof customer relationship and other intangibles | 490 |
| Customer relationship | 466 |
| Tradename | 24 |
| Thereof acquired technology | 290 |
| Thereof software and database licenses | 3 |
| Current and deferred tax assets | 7 |
| Total assets | 959 |
| | |
| Trade accounts payable | −49 |
| Financial liabilities | −1 |
| Current and deferred tax liabilities | −166 |
| Provisions and other non-financial liabilities | −66 |
| Deferred revenue | −130 |
| Total liabilities | −412 |
| | |
| Total identifiable net assets | 547 |
| | |
| Recognized Goodwill | 2,112 |

The goodwill arising from the acquisition consists largely of the synergies and the skills and technical talent of SuccessFactors' workforce. The goodwill recognized is not expected to be deductible for income tax purposes. The goodwill assignment to our segments has not been finalized yet.

We are still evaluating contingent liabilities but do not expect to record material amounts.

Source: SAP AG, Note 4, Business Combinations, to the group first quarter consolidated interim financial statements of SAP AG for the period ended March 31, 2012. Consolidated Interim Financial Statements, p. 33. http://www.sap.com/corporate-en/investors/reports/quarterlyreport/2012/pdf/SAP-2012-Q1-Interim-Report.pdf

# 3.9 FAIR VALUES, REVALUATIONS, AND PUSH-DOWN ACCOUNTING

We have emphasized that when an acquirer purchases the shares of an acquiree, the fair values of the net assets of the acquiree are never recorded in the books of the acquirer; the full purchase price is simply recorded in an investment account on the acquirer's books. We have also stated that when a business combination is accomplished by a purchase of shares (rather than by a direct purchase of assets), the acquiree continues to exist as a separate legal and reporting entity. The carrying values of the acquiree's net assets are not affected by the acquisition or by the fair values attributed to the assets by the acquirer. However, there are two exceptions to this general rule.

## Revaluation Accounting

IAS 16 allows entities to choose between the cost model and the revaluation model to measure property, plant, and equipment after initial recognition. The revaluation model can be used for PPE whose fair value can be measured reliably. The choice between the two models must be made for an entire class of PPE.

Under the revaluation model, the assets are carried at their revalued amount, which is their fair values at the date of the revaluation minus any subsequent accumulated depreciation and impairment losses. Importantly, under the revaluation model, the assets have to be revalued with sufficient regularity to ensure that their carrying values are not materially different from their values if fair values were used at the end of the reporting period.

Similarly, IAS 38 also allows the use of the revaluation model to measure intangible assets that have an active market. Therefore, when a subsidiary chooses the revaluation model to measure its assets, the difference between the carrying values of its assets on its books and their corresponding acquisition date fair values may be minor or immaterial. If the parent and the subsidiary adopt the revaluation model for the latter's assets, the carrying values of those assets in the subsidiary's books will remain identical to their values on the consolidated financial statements. This practice will achieve results similar to the results obtained under push-down accounting, described below.

## Push-Down Accounting

An exception to the general rule that the acquiree's carrying values are unaffected by the purchase also may arise when the acquirer directs the acquiree to restate its assets to fair value. This practice is known as **push-down accounting** because the fair values are "pushed down" to the acquiree's books. The net effect is the same as though the acquirer had formed a new subsidiary, which then purchased all of the assets and liabilities of the acquiree.

While IFRS does not address the issue of push-down accounting, in the United States the SEC *requires* its registrants to use the practice when an acquired subsidiary is "substantially" wholly owned (95%) and there are no publicly held debt or senior shares. The SEC permits the use of push-down accounting in case of ownership between 80–95% of the subsidiary and prohibits such use if the ownership is less than 80% of the subsidiary. Push-down accounting was allowed but not required in Canada before the adoption of international standards. In any event, if push-down accounting was used by a Canadian company previously, such push-down accounting values can be used as **deemed cost** while it adopts IFRS for the first time.

**Advantages of Push-Down Accounting** There are two advantages to push-down accounting. The first is that the financial position and results of operations of the acquiree will be reported on the same economic basis in both the consolidated statements and its own separate-entity statements. Without push-down accounting, for example, it would be possible for the subsidiary to report a profit on its own and yet contribute an operating loss to the parent's consolidated results if the consolidation adjustments were sufficient to tip the balance between profit and loss.

The second advantage is that the process of consolidation will be greatly simplified for the parent. Since the carrying values will be the same as the acquisition fair values, there will be no need for many of the consolidation adjustments that otherwise would be required every time consolidated statements are prepared.

A special case of push-down accounting arises in a reverse takeover. In a reverse takeover, it is the legal acquirer that is really the in-substance acquiree—the fair values reported on the consolidated statements will be those of the company issuing the statements (the legal parent but in-substance subsidiary). In that case, it makes little sense for the in-substance acquiree to be carrying its assets and liabilities at carrying values that will never be reported in its own financial statements. It is more logical simply to put the fair values on the books of the in-substance acquiree.

## 3.10 EQUITY METHOD OF ACCOUNTING OF INVESTMENTS IN ASSOCIATES AND JOINT VENTURES

LO 9
Understand the method of reporting investments in associates and joint ventures

IAS 28, *Investments in Associates and Joint Ventures*, requires the allocation of the fair value adjustment arising at the time of the investment in the associate or joint venture to the various identified assets and liabilities of that entity. This allocation process is broadly similar to the process discussed by us previously in the chapter in relation to an investment in a subsidiary.

However, in the case of an investment in an associate or joint venture, this allocation process is carried out only to the extent of the investor's share of ownership in the investee. Further, any excess fair value adjustment remaining after the allocation process is not allocated to goodwill. Rather, the goodwill relating to the investment in the associate or joint venture is included in the carrying amount of the investment in that entity. Conversely, a gain from a bargain purchase is included as part of the investor's equity in the earnings of the investee in the year the investment is made. Since no goodwill is recognized under the equity method, the value of the investment calculated under that method is instead tested for impairment.

## 3.11 CANADIAN ACCOUNTING STANDARDS FOR PRIVATE ENTERPRISES

LO 5
Identify the different approaches to reporting mergers

Prior to Canada's move to IFRS, the *CICA Handbook* had already been harmonized with IFRS 3. Therefore, the basic definitions and reporting approaches described above, specifically the requirement to use the acquisition method to report business combinations, apply to private enterprises as well. However, there still are some significant differences that reflect the fact that, by definition, a private enterprise is not issuing general-purpose financial statements. The significant differences are as follows:

- Private enterprises are not required to issue consolidated statements. Consolidated reporting is a *choice*, not a requirement. When subsidiaries are not consolidated, they can be reported on either the cost or the equity basis. However, all subsidiaries should be reported on the same basis. A company cannot choose to consolidate some subsidiaries but not others.

- Sometimes, a private enterprise will have a subsidiary that is a public company. For example, a private company may own a majority of the public company's shares. In that case, the subsidiary's shares may be reported either (1) by the equity method or (2) at fair value with gains and losses from changes in fair value taken directly into earnings. If the equity method is chosen, the parent must disclose the fair value of the investment in the notes.

  If the class of shares owned by the parent (e.g., a special class of multiple-voting shares) are not traded publicly, then the equity method of reporting should be used.

- Both investments in and earnings from non-consolidated subsidiaries should be separately disclosed in the parent's financial statements.

### Concept Check 3-5

1. How does negative goodwill arise? How does negative goodwill affect the allocation of the PPD?
2. Explain what is meant by "push-down accounting." What are two possible benefits that arise from using this method?
3. Suppose that a private company holds a controlling interest in a public company. How, if at all, should the fair value of those shares be reported in the private company's financial statements?

## Relevant Standards

### IASB

**IFRS 3**  Business Combinations
**IAS 16**  Property, Plant and Equipment
**IFRS 10** Consolidated Financial Statements
**IAS 38**  Intangible Assets

### ASPE

**Section 1590** Subsidiaries
**Section 1601** Consolidated Financial Statements
**Section 3051** Investments
**Section 3051** Interests in Joint Ventures
**Section 3064** Goodwill and Intangible Assets

## 3.12 SUMMARY OF KEY POINTS

1.  A business combination is the acquisition of net assets or *control* over net assets that constitute a functioning business. Control over net assets is usually obtained by buying a majority of the shares in the company that owns the assets. The actual business combination transaction can be of many types. When control is acquired, the acquired net assets remain the property of the controlled subsidiary. Therefore, consolidated financial statements are necessary. **LO 1 & 2**

2.  Business combinations have to be accounted using the acquisition method, which requires five steps: (1) identify the acquirer, (2) determine the acquisition date, (3) calculate the fair value of the purchase consideration transferred, (4) recognize and measure net identifiable assets acquired and liabilities assumed, and (5) measure and recognize goodwill or a gain from a bargain purchase.

    The acquired identifiable assets and liabilities are recognized at their fair values. If the purchase price is less than the aggregate fair value of the net assets, negative goodwill or gain from bargain purchase arises. A gain from a bargain purchase is recognized in the consolidated SCI issued by the acquirer in the period of the acquisition. **LO 3**

3.  A purchase of net assets may be accomplished (1) by paying cash or other assets or (2) by issuing shares. A combination of cash and shares may be used. When shares are issued, the purchase price is based on the market value of the shares on the acquisition date. **LO 4**

4.  If the net assets are purchased directly, the fair values of the acquired assets and liabilities are recorded on the books of the acquirer. There is no parent–subsidiary relationship because the acquirer did not buy another corporation; it bought the net assets instead. **LO 4**

5.  Acquisition of majority control through the purchase of shares of another company enables the investor to obtain control over the assets without having to pay the full fair value of the assets. Shares can be purchased for cash or other assets. Alternatively, the purchaser can issue its own shares in exchange for the shares of the acquiree. If there is an exchange of shares, the acquirer does not have to give up any cash. The previous holders of the acquiree's shares now hold shares in the acquirer instead. **LO 4**

6.  Theoretically, there are three alternative approaches to reporting consolidated financial statements following purchase of control over another corporation in addition to IFRS 3's acquisition accounting: pooling of interests, purchase accounting, and new-entity method.

    (a) Under pooling of interests, the carrying values of the parent and the subsidiary are simply added together and reported as the consolidated amounts.

    (b) Under purchase accounting, the subsidiary's assets and liabilities are added to the parent's carrying values at the purchase price paid for them. If the purchase price is equal to or greater than the date-of-acquisition fair values of the subsidiary's identifiable assets and liabilities, then such assets and liabilities are added at their fair values to the parent's carrying values. In this latter situation, the purchase method of consolidation gives the same results as if the net assets had been purchased directly. When the purchase price paid is greater than the fair value of the identifiable assets and liabilities, the difference constitutes goodwill.

(c) With the new-entity method, the fair values of the parent and the subsidiary are added together to form a new basis of accountability for the ongoing economic entity. **LO 5 & 6**

7.  The pooling method is not permitted for arm's-length business combinations by International Financial Reporting Standards. However, the pooling method must be applied to non-arm's-length corporate restructurings, including the combining of companies under common control. **LO 5**

8.  Business combinations are significant events affecting all users' objectives. Disclosure of business combination therefore is quite important. IFRS 3 requires significant disclosures relating to business combination to enable users of financial statements to identify their nature and financial impact. **LO 7**

9.  Normally, fair values are not recorded on the books of the acquiree; adjustments are made solely on working papers to prepare consolidated financial statements. However, fair values may be recorded on the books of the acquired company if the investor corporation has acquired substantially all of the shares of the subsidiary. This practice is known as *push-down accounting*. Push-down accounting was allowed in the past in Canada and continues to be allowed in the United States. IFRS is silent on push-down accounting. Nevertheless, if push-down accounting was used previously by a Canadian entity, the push-down accounting values can be used as deemed cost while it adopts IFRS for the first time. **LO 8**

 Visit the text's website at www.pearsoned.ca/beechy **for practice quizzes, additional problems, Excel® templates, answers to Concept Check questions, and important IFRS updates.**

# Self-Study Problem

**1.** Ace Corporation acquired Blue Corporation on August 31, 20X6. Both corporations have fiscal years ending on August 31. Exhibit 3.9 shows the SFP for each corporation as of August 31, 20X6, immediately *prior* to the combination, and net income amounts for each corporation for the fiscal year ended August 31, 20X6.

The fair values of the assets and liabilities of the two companies at the date of acquisition are shown in Exhibit 3.10. The deferred development costs represent the unamortized balance of the development costs of the companies' leading-edge products. There is no observable market value for this identifiable intangible asset, but Ace expects to fully recover the costs in future years.

Before the combination, Ace had 1,200,000 common shares issued and outstanding. Blue had 750,000 common shares issued and outstanding.

**Required**

Prepare the Ace Corporation post-combination SFP under each of the following *independent* situations:

**a.** Ace Corporation purchased the assets and assumed the liabilities of Blue Corporation by paying $2,000,000 cash and issuing long-term instalment notes payable of $18,000,000.

**Exhibit 3.9** Pre-Combination Statements of Financial Position, August 31, 20X6

|  | Ace | Blue |
|---|---|---|
| Cash and cash equivalents | $ 2,350,000 | $ 1,200,000 |
| Accounts receivable | 2,000,000 | 1,800,000 |
| Land | 5,000,000 | — |
| Machinery and equipment (net) | 13,500,000 | 8,400,000 |
| Deferred development costs | 600,000 | 3,100,000 |
|  | $23,450,000 | $14,500,000 |
| Accounts payable | $ 650,000 | $ 1,100,000 |
| Notes payable, long-term | 2,000,000 | 1,000,000 |
| Common shares | 15,000,000 | 6,950,000 |
| Retained earnings | 5,800,000 | 5,450,000 |
|  | $23,450,000 | $14,500,000 |
| **Net income, year ended August 31, 20X6** | $ 2,450,000 | $ 1,300,000 |

**Exhibit 3.10** Fair Values, August 31, 20X6

|  | Ace | Blue |
|---|---|---|
| Cash and cash equivalents | $ 2,350,000 | $ 1,200,000 |
| Accounts receivable | 2,000,000 | 1,800,000 |
| Land | 8,500,000 | — |
| Machinery and equipment (net) | 11,000,000 | 11,000,000 |
| Deferred development costs | 750,000 | 4,000,000 |
| Accounts payable | (650,000) | (1,100,000) |
| Notes payable, long-term | (2,000,000) | (900,000) |
| Net asset fair value | $21,950,000 | $16,000,000 |

**b.** Ace issued 400,000 common shares for all of the outstanding common shares of Blue. The market value of Ace's shares was $50 per share.

**c.** Ace purchased 100% of Blue's outstanding common shares from Blue's previous shareholders. As consideration, Ace issued 270,000 common shares and paid $1,000,000 in cash. The market value of Ace's shares was $50 per share.

2. On January 1, 20X6, Patricia Ltd. acquired 100% of the shares of Shelley Inc. The acquisition took place by issuing new Patricia Ltd. shares to the Shelley Inc. shareholders in a one-to-one exchange for their shares of Shelley Inc. The value of the newly issued Patricia Ltd. shares was estimated at $850,000. At the date of acquisition, the statements of financial position for the companies were as shown in Exhibit 3.11.

At the date of acquisition, the fair values of Shelley's assets and liabilities differed from carrying values as follows:

|  | Carrying value | Fair value |
|---|---|---|
| Land | $180,000 | $300,000 |
| Buildings | 430,000 | 450,000 |
| Equipment | 120,000 | 180,000 |

## Required

Prepare the post-acquisition consolidated SFP for Patricia Ltd. at January 1, 20X6, using the acquisition method.

**Exhibit 3.11** Pre-Combination Statements of Financial Position, January 1, 20X6

|  | Patricia Ltd. | Shelley Inc. |
|---|---|---|
| **Assets** | | |
| Cash | $ 80,000 | $ 55,000 |
| Accounts receivable | 220,000 | 135,000 |
| Inventories | 100,000 | 90,000 |
| Total current assets | 400,000 | 280,000 |
| Land | 800,000 | 180,000 |
| Buildings (net) | 1,100,000 | 430,000 |
| Equipment (net) | 720,000 | 120,000 |
| Total assets | $3,020,000 | $1,010,000 |
| **Liabilities and shareholders' equity** | | |
| Accounts payable | $ 120,000 | $ 140,000 |
| Long-term debt payable | 400,000 | 420,000 |
| Total liabilities | 520,000 | 560,000 |
| Common shares | 1,000,000 | 200,000 |
| Retained earnings | 1,500,000 | 250,000 |
| Total shareholders' equity | 2,500,000 | 450,000 |
| Total liabilities and shareholders' equity | $3,020,000 | $1,010,000 |

# Review Questions

1. Describe the two basic types of acquisitions that can result in a business combination.

2. What consideration can be used in a business combination?

3. When one corporation buys the assets or assets and liabilities of another company, at what values are the acquired items recorded on the buyer's books?

4. In general, how would fair values be determined for productive assets?

5. In general, how would fair values be determined for liabilities?

6. What is *negative goodwill*? How should it be reported in the consolidated statements?

7. When an acquirer buys the net assets of another company by issuing shares, what is the relationship between the two companies after the transaction has taken place?

8. What are the advantages for the acquirer of obtaining control over assets by a purchase of shares rather than by a direct purchase of assets?

9. What are the disadvantages for the acquirer of obtaining control by a purchase of shares?

10. How can an acquirer obtain control if the management of the acquiree is hostile to the business combination?

11. From an income tax standpoint, what may be the disadvantages for an acquirer in obtaining control through a purchase of shares rather than by a direct purchase of net assets?

12. If an acquirer issues a tender offer, is it necessary for the offering company to buy all of the shares tendered?

13. Company P issues its shares in exchange for the shares of Company S. After the exchange, who owns the newly issued shares of P?

14. In an exchange of shares, how can the acquirer be identified?

15. What is the most common reason for a combination of a public company and a private company accomplished by means of a reverse takeover?

16. In consolidated statements following a reverse takeover, which company's net assets are reported at fair values: the legal acquirer's or the legal subsidiary's?

17. Why is a reverse takeover often immediately followed by a name change of the legal parent corporation?

18. In what form(s) of business combination do(es) the combining companies cease to exist as separate legal entities?

19. What is a corporate restructuring? How are restructurings accounted for?

20. Under what circumstances is push-down accounting most likely to be used?

## 3.13 CASES

### CASE 3-1 AMES BROTHERS LTD.

Ames Brothers Ltd. (ABL) is a relatively small producer of petrochemicals located in Sarnia, Ontario. The common shares of the firm are publicly traded on the Toronto Stock Exchange, while the non-voting preferred shares are traded on the over-the-counter market. Because of the strategic competitive position of the firm, there was considerable recent interest in the shares of the company. During 20X6, much active trading occurred, pushing the price of the common shares from less than $8 to more than $20 by the end of the year. Similarly, the trading interest in the preferred shares pushed the dividend yield from 12% to only 9%.

Shortly after the end of 20×6, three other firms made public announcements about the extent of their holdings in ABL shares. Silverman Mines announced that it had acquired, on the open market, 32% of the common shares of ABL; Hislop Industries announced that it had acquired 24% of ABL's common shares in a private transaction with an individual who had previously been ABL's major shareholder; and Render Resources announced that it had accumulated a total of 58% of ABL's preferred shares.

However, Silverman Mines and Hislop Industries are related. The Patterson Power Corporation owns 72% of the voting shares of Silverman Mines and 38% of the voting shares of Hislop Mines. There are no other large holdings of stock of either Silverman or Hislop. Render Resources is not related to Silverman, Hislop, or Patterson.

#### Required

a. Has a business combination occurred in 20X6, with respect to ABL, as the term "business combination" is used in IFRS? Explain fully.

b. What implications do the various accumulations of ABL shares have for the financial reporting (for 20X6 and following years) for:

　1. Silverman Mines

　2. Hislop Industries

　3. Render Resources

　4. Patterson Power Corporation

### CASE 3-2 SUDAIR LTD. AND ALBERTAIR LTD.

On February 7, 20X6, Sudair Ltd. and Albertair Ltd. jointly announced a merger of the two regional airlines. Sudair had assets totalling $500 million and 1,000,000 common shares outstanding. Albertair had assets amounting to $400 million and 600,000 shares outstanding. Under the terms of the merger, Sudair will issue two new Sudair shares for each share of Albertair outstanding. The two companies will then merge their administrative and operating structures and will coordinate their routes and schedules to improve interchange between the two lines and to enable the combined fleet of nine jet aircraft to be more efficiently used. Both companies are publicly owned.

**Required**

How should the merger of Sudair and Albertair be reported?

## CASE 3-3 POOL INC. AND SPARTIN LTD.

Pool Inc. and Spartin Ltd. are both public companies. The common shares of Pool have been selling in a range of $30 to $43 per share over the past year. Spartin's common shares have been selling at between $18 and $23.

The two companies are in related lines of business. In view of the increasing exposure of the companies to world competition arising from the reduction in tariff barriers, the boards of directors have approved an agreement in principle to combine the two businesses. The boards have also agreed that the combination should take the form of a share exchange, with one share of Pool equivalent to two shares of Spartin in the exchange. On the date of acquisition each share of Pool was worth $33, while each share of Spartin was worth $20.

The manner of executing the combination has not yet been decided. Three possibilities are under consideration:

1. Pool could issue one new share in exchange for two of Spartin's shares.

2. Spartin could issue two new shares in exchange for each of Pool's shares.

3. A new corporation could be formed, PS Enterprises Inc., which would issue one share in exchange for each share of Spartin and two shares in exchange for each share of Pool.

The directors are uncertain as to the accounting implications of the three alternatives. They believe that the fair values of the assets and liabilities of both companies are approximately equal to their carrying values. They have asked you to prepare a report in which you explain how the accounting results would differ under the three share exchange alternatives. They have provided you with the condensed statements of financial position of both companies, as shown in Exhibit A. Pool Inc. currently has 1,600,000 common shares outstanding, and Spartin Ltd. has 1,200,000 shares outstanding.

**Required**

Prepare the report requested by the boards of directors.

**Exhibit A**

**Condensed Statements of Financial Position of Pool Inc. and Spartin Ltd.**

|  | Pool Inc. | Spartin Ltd. |
|---|---|---|
| Current assets | $ 7,000,000 | $ 4,500,000 |
| Capital assets | 63,000,000 | 22,500,000 |
|  | $70,000,000 | $27,000,000 |
| Current liabilities | $ 6,000,000 | $ 1,500,000 |
| Long-term debt | 14,000,000 | 5,500,000 |
| Common shares | 17,000,000 | 16,000,000 |
| Retained earnings | 33,000,000 | 4,000,000 |
|  | $70,000,000 | $27,000,000 |

# CASE 3-4 BOATSMAN BOATS LIMITED AND STICKNEY SKATE CORPORATION

Boatsman Boats Limited (BBL) is a dealer in pleasure boats located in Kingston, Ontario. The company is incorporated under the *Ontario Business Corporations Act* and is wholly owned by its founder and president, Jim Boatsman. In 20X5, BBL had revenues of $2,500,000, with total assets of about $1,000,000 at year-end.

Late in 20X6, Jim Boatsman reached an agreement with Clyde Stickney for the combination of BBL and Stickney Skate Corporation (SSC). SSC is a manufacturer of ice skates and is located in Ottawa, Ontario. SSC's 20X5 revenue totalled $2,000,000, and year-end assets totalled $1,500,000. Clyde Stickney is president and general manager of SSC, and he owns 65% of the SSC shares. The other 35% is owned by Clyde's former partner, who left the business several years previously because of a policy disagreement with Clyde.

Clyde and Jim decided to combine the two businesses because their seasonal business cycles were complementary. Common ownership would permit working capital to be shifted from one company to the other, and the larger asset base and more stable financial performance of the combined company would probably increase the total debt capacity.

Under the terms of the agreement, BBL would issue common shares to Clyde Stickney in exchange for Clyde's shares in SSC. As a result of the exchange, Jim's share of BBL would drop to 60% of the outstanding BBL shares, and Clyde would hold the remaining 40%. Clyde and Jim signed a shareholders' agreement that gave each of them equal representation on the BBL board of directors.

As the end of 20X6 approached, Jim, Clyde, and CA (the BBL auditor) were discussing the appropriate treatment of the business combination on BBL's 20X6 financial statements. Clyde was of the opinion that CA should simply add together the assets and liabilities of the two companies at their carrying values (after eliminating intercompany balances and transactions, of course). Jim, on the other hand, thought that the combination had resulted in a new, stronger entity, and that the financial statements should reflect that fact by revaluing the net assets of both BBL and SSC to reflect fair values at the date of the combination. CA, however, insisted that only SSC's net assets should be revalued, and then only to the extent of the 65% of the assets that were represented by BBL's shareholdings in SSC.

While Jim and Clyde disagreed with each other on the appropriate valuation of the assets, both disagreed with CA's proposal. Jim and Clyde clearly controlled SSC through BBL, they argued; that was the whole point of the combination. In their opinion it would be inappropriate to value the same assets on two different bases, 65% current value and 35% carrying value. If only SSC's assets were to be revalued, then they reasoned that the assets at least should be valued consistently, at 100% of fair value.

In an effort to resolve the impasse that was developing, Jim and Clyde hired an independent consultant to advise them. The consultant was asked (1) to advise the shareholders on the pros and cons of each alternative in BBL's specific case, and (2) to make a recommendation on a preferred approach. The consultant was supplied with the condensed statements of financial position of BBL and SSC, as shown in Exhibit B, and with CA's estimate of fair values (Exhibit C).

Required

Prepare the consultant's report. Assume that the business combination took place on December 31, 20X6.

---

## Exhibit B
## Condensed Statements of Financial Position of BBL and SSC

### Condensed Statements of Financial Position
### December 31, 20X6

| | Boatsman Boats Ltd. | Stickney Skate Corp. |
|---|---|---|
| Current assets | $ 600,000 | $ 350,000 |
| Land | — | 250,000 |
| Buildings and equipment | — | 2,500,000 |
| Accumulated depreciation | — | (1,500,000) |
| Furniture and fixtures | 800,000 | 300,000 |
| Accumulated depreciation | (330,000) | (100,000) |
| Investment in Stickney Skate Corp. | 1,300,000 | — |
| TOTAL ASSETS | $2,370,000 | $1,800,000 |
| Current liabilities | $ 370,000 | $ 400,000 |
| Long-term liabilities | 300,000 | 900,000 |
| Common shares | 1,500,000 | 200,000 |
| Retained earnings | 200,000 | 300,000 |
| TOTAL LIABILITIES AND EQUITIES | $2,370,000 | $1,800,000 |

## Exhibit C
## Estimated Fair Values of BBL and SSC

| | Net Asset Fair Values December 31, 20X6 | |
|---|---|---|
| | Boatsman Boats Ltd. | Stickney Skate Corp. |
| Current assets | $ 600,000 | $ 350,000 |
| Land | — | 700,000 |
| Buildings and equipment: | | |
| estimated replacement cost new | — | 5,000,000 |
| less depreciation | — | (3,000,000) |
| Furniture and fixtures: | | |
| estimated replacement cost new | 1,300,000 | 500,000 |
| less depreciation | (520,000) | (240,000) |
| Current liabilities | (370,000) | (400,000) |
| Long-term liabilities* | (270,000) | (930,000) |
| Net asset fair value | $ 740,000 | $ 1,980,000 |

* Discounted at current long-term interest rates.

[ICAO, Adapted]

# CASE 3-5 GROWTH INC. AND MINOR LTD.

Growth Inc. has just acquired control of Minor Ltd. by buying 100% of Minor's outstanding shares for $6,500,000 cash. The condensed SFP for Minor on the date of acquisition is shown below.

Growth is a public company. Currently, it has two bank covenants. The first requires Growth to maintain a specific debt-to-equity ratio and the second requires a specific current ratio. If these covenants are violated, the bank loan will be payable on demand. Growth is in a very competitive business. To encourage its employees to stay, it has adopted a new business plan that provides managers with a bonus based on a percentage of net income.

The president of Growth Inc., Teresa, has hired you, CA, to assist her with the accounting for Minor.

To account for the acquisition, Growth's management has had all of Minor's capital assets appraised by two separate, independent engineering consultants. One consultant appraised the capital assets at $7,800,000 in their present state. The other consultant arrived at a lower figure of $7,100,000, based on the assumption that imminent technological changes would soon decrease the value-in-use of Minor's capital assets by about 10%.

The asset amount for the leased building is the discounted present value of the remaining lease payments on a warehouse that Minor leased to Growth Inc. five years ago. The lease is non-cancellable, and title to the building will transfer to Growth at the end of the lease term. The lease has 15 years yet to run, and the annual lease payments are $500,000 per year. The interest rate implicit in the lease was 9%.

Minor's debentures are thinly traded on the open market. Recent sales have indicated that these bonds are currently yielding about 14%. The bonds mature in 10 years.

The deferred income tax balance is the accumulated balance of CCA/depreciation temporary differences. The management of Minor sees no likelihood of the balance being reduced in the foreseeable future, because projected capital expenditures will enter the CCA classes in amounts that will more than offset the amount of depreciation for the older assets.

The carrying value of Minor's inventory appears to approximate replacement cost. However, an overstock of some items of finished goods may require temporary price reductions of about 10% to reduce inventory to more manageable levels.

Required

Provide a report for Teresa outlining how the assets of Minor Ltd. should be valued for purposes of preparing consolidated financial statements. She wants you to identify alternatives and support your decision.

| Minor Ltd. | |
|---|---|
| Condensed Statement of Financial Position | |
| Cash | $ 200,000 |
| Accounts receivable | 770,000 |
| Inventories | 1,000,000 |
| Capital assets (net) | 5,000,000 |
| Leased building | 4,030,000 |
| TOTAL ASSETS | $11,000,000 |
| Accounts payable | $ 300,000 |
| 8% debentures payable | 7,000,000 |
| Deferred income taxes | 700,000 |
| Common shares | 1,000,000 |
| Retained earnings | 2,000,000 |
| TOTAL LIABILITIES AND EQUITIES | $11,000,000 |

# CASE 3-6 WONDER AMUSEMENTS

Wonder Amusements Limited (WAL) was incorporated more than 40 years ago as an amusement park and golf course. Over time, a nearby city has grown to the point where it borders on WAL's properties. In recent years, WAL's owners, who are all members of one family, have seen WAL's land values increase significantly. WAL's majority shareholder, Howard Smith, owns 55% of the outstanding shares and is not active in WAL's day-to-day activities.

Last year, Howard hired a new chief executive officer, Leo Titan, who has a reputation for being an aggressive risk taker. Howard is committed to supporting Leo's plans, and he has the personal financial resources required.

Eight months ago, WAL became the successful bidder for a new sports franchise, in conjunction with a minority partner. Under the terms of the franchise agreement, WAL is required to build a sports arena, which is currently being constructed on a section of the amusement park. Another section of the amusement park is being relocated to ensure that the entrances to the arena are close to public transportation and parking. Consequently, some of the rides will be relocated. WAL is the sole owner of the arena at present.

The sports franchise is separately incorporated as Northern Sports Limited (NSL); WAL holds 75% of the shares in the company. Another bid is being prepared by NSL to obtain a second sports franchise so that the arena can be used more often. NSL will be required to lease space from WAL when the arena is completed, in about 22 months.

For the first two sports seasons, NSL will have to lease arena space from Aggressive Limited (AL). During this time, NSL does not expect to be profitable because:

■ it may take time to build a competitive team;

■ AL is charging a high rent and is not giving NSL a share of concession revenue;

■ AL cannot make the better dates (e.g., Saturday nights) available to NSL to attract sports fans; and

■ as a newcomer to the league, NSL is restricted with regard to the players who are available to it and the days of the week it can play in its home city.

Consequently, NSL has arranged to borrow funds from WAL and from others to finance costs and losses.

Your employer, Fabio & Fox, Chartered Accountants, has conducted the audit of WAL for several years. WAL has tended to be marginally profitable one year and then have losses the next year. The company has continued to operate because the directors knew the real estate holdings were becoming increasingly valuable.

Leo is expected to oversee the expanded accounting and finance functions in the company. Leo has met with you and the partner in charge of the WAL audit and has discussed various issues related to the year ending September 30, 20X6. His comments are provided in Exhibit D.

You have been asked by the partner to prepare for him a report, which will be used for the next meeting with Leo. He would like you to discuss the accounting and audit implications related to your discussion with Leo. The partner wants a thorough analysis of all important issues, as well as support for your position.

In your review of documents, and as a result of various conversations, you have learned the following:

1. The arena will be mortgaged, but only for about 50% of its expected cost. Lenders are concerned about the special-use nature of the arena and whether it will be successfully rented for other events, such as concerts.

2. The mortgage lenders to WAL and the minority shareholders in NSL are both expected to want to see appraisals and financial statements before deciding to invest. Covenants will be required by the lenders to ensure that excessive expenditures are not undertaken and that cash is preserved.

3. Leo does not intend to consolidate NSL until it is profitable. The investment in NSL will be reported on WAL's financial statements at cost. Thus, the WAL financial statements will also be used for income tax purposes.

4. WAL's minority shareholders are not active in the business and want quarterly financial statements to monitor progress and assess Leo's performance. The minority shareholders have all expressed concern over Leo's growth strategy over the past year. Many are approaching their retirement years and are relying on WAL to supplement their retirement income.

Required

Prepare the report.

[ICAO, Adapted]

---

## Exhibit D
## Notes from Discussions with Leo Titan

1. To build a road to the arena's parking lot, two holes of the 18-hole golf course will be relocated next spring. Costs of $140,000 are expected to be incurred this year in design, tree planting, ground preparation, and grass seeding to have the arena ready for next spring. These costs are to be capitalized as part of the golf course lands, along with the related property taxes of $13,000 and interest of $15,000.

2. In May 20X6, WAL acquired for $4.25 million all of the shares of an amusement park in a different city, when its land lease expired. The amusement park company was wound up, and the equipment, rides, concessions, and other assets are being transported to WAL at a cost of $350,000. The estimated fair value of the assets and liabilities (according to Leo) is as follows:

*Exhibit Continued >*

| | |
|---|---:|
| Concession prizes (e.g., stuffed animals) | $ 22,500 |
| Rides and games | 4,200,000 |
| Equipment and parts | 1,650,000 |
| Electrical supplies | 75,000 |
| Lighting and signs | 100,000 |
| Estimated present value of tax loss carryforward | 700,000 |
| | 6,747,500 |
| Liabilities | 1,200,000 |
| Net Assets | $5,547,500 |

WAL expects to spend approximately $400,000 in getting the assets in operating order and $500,000 on foundations and site preparations for the rides. Leo wants to "capitalize as much as possible."

3.  Approximately $600,000 will be used to relocate rides that are currently on land that is needed for the arena. This amount is to be capitalized, net of scrap recovery on dismantled and redundant equipment of $60,000. Virtually all of the rides were fully depreciated years ago.

4.  To assist in financing the new ventures, WAL sold excess land to developers who intend to construct a shopping centre, office buildings, and expensive homes that will be adacent to the golf course and away from the amusement park. The developers and WAL agreed to the following terms:

| | |
|---|---:|
| Paid to WAL on May 1, 20X6 | $ 6,000,000 |
| To be paid to WAL on March 1, 20X7 | 10,000,000 |
| To be paid to WAL on March 1, 20X8 | 8,000,000 |
| | $24,000,000 |

The land is to be turned over to the developers on or about February 1, 20X7, but the sale is to be reported in 20X6.

5.  An additional "contingent profit" will accrue to WAL if the developers earn a return on investment of more than 25% when they resell the newly constructed buildings. Leo wants a note to the 20X6 financial statements that describes the potential of a contingent gain.

6.  The excess land that was sold to the developers was carried on WAL's books at $1.35 million, on a pro rata cost basis. Leo would like to revalue the remaining land from $5.4 million to about $100 million in the 20X6 financial statements.

7.  The golf course has been unprofitable in recent years. However, green fees are to be raised and specific tee-off times will be allotted to a private club that is currently being organized. Members of the private club will pay a non-refundable entrance fee of $2,000 per member plus $100 per month for five years. The $2,000 is to be recorded as revenue on receipt. Approximately $350,000 is to be spent to upgrade club facilities.

8.  Leo wants to capitalize all costs of NSL on NSL's books until it has completed its first year of operations. In addition to the franchise fee, $20 million will have to be spent on the following:

| | |
|---|---|
| Acquisition of player contracts | $12,000,000 |
| Advertising and promotion | 1,500,000 |
| Equipment | 3,200,000 |
| Wages, benefits, and bonuses | 6,800,000 |
| Other operating costs | 3,300,000 |
| | 26,800,000 |
| Less: | |
| Revenue—ticket sales | (6,000,000) |
| Revenue—other | (800,000) |
| | $20,000,000 |

The value of players can change quickly, depending on their performance, injuries, and other factors.

9.  The new sports arena will have private boxes in which a company can entertain groups of clients. The boxes are leased on a five-year contract basis, and they must be occupied for a minimum price per night. To date, 12 boxes have been leased for $15,000 per box for a five-year period, exclusive of nightly charges. A down payment of $3,000 was required; the payments have been recorded as revenue.

10. Three senior officers of WAL, including Leo, receive bonuses based on income before income taxes. The three have agreed to have their fiscal 20X6 bonus accrued in 20X7, along with their 20X7 bonuses. Actual payments to them are scheduled for January 20X8.

11. Insurance premiums on the construction activity that is taking place total $1.4 million in fiscal 20X6, and to date they have been capitalized.

12. A $500,000 fee was paid to a mortgage broker to arrange financing for WAL. This amount has been recorded as "other assets." No financing has been arranged to date.

[ICAO, Adapted]

## CASE 3-7 MAJOR DEVELOPMENTS CORPORATION

John "Calc" Gossling is one of Canada's foremost real estate investment analysts. He works for the firm of Bouchard Wiener Securities Inc. (BWS). His job is to do research and make recommendations on the stock of publicly traded companies, independent of any interest his employer may have in the companies. The research gets published and is used by investors in making their investment decisions. He is noted for his superb number-crunching ability, scathing comments, and accurate analysis. In late 19X4, he correctly predicted the end of the real estate bubble, which occurred about two years later. His writing style is in marked contrast to the traditional dry prose of most investment analysts.

Major Developments Corporation (Major) is a publicly traded company operating primarily in the real estate sector. Major has a March 31 year-end and in 20X5 reported revenues of $704 million and after-tax income of $118 million. The company buys and sells commercial real estate properties and manufactures commercial elevator components (its original business before it got into real estate). Major survived the recession of the 19X0s, and during that time purchased a number of commercial "jewels" at bargain prices. In 20X4, Major ventured overseas, acquiring properties in three Asian countries.

Major's share price climbed steadily from 19X9 until July 11, 20X5. On that date BWS released a stunning research report by Gossling on Major (see extracts in Exhibit E). The report caused an uproar, as it claimed that many of Major's accounting policies in 20X5 were misleading and therefore not in accordance with IFRS principles. It further claimed that the company was overvalued and had poor prospects because of its real estate portfolio mix.

The stock had been trading in the $15–$16 range but immediately dropped to around $9. BWS profited from the decline in the stock price because it held a significant short position in Major's stock. Within four days, lawyers working for Major launched a legal suit against BWS, claiming damages plus a full retraction of all statements made, to be published in a national newspaper.

BWS's legal counsel is now examining various courses of action. To help prepare for the case, counsel has hired Brick & Mortar, Chartered Accountants, to provide a report on the validity of the positions of each of the parties on the disagreements over accounting policies, as well as any other relevant advice. You, CA, work for Brick & Mortar. You have obtained a copy of Major's 20X5 annual report (see extracts in Exhibit F). Major's lawyers have provided the information in Exhibit G.

### Required

Prepare a draft report to legal counsel for the partner to review.
[CICA]

## Exhibit E
## Extracts from John Gossling's Research Report

— I have done a detailed review of Major's 20X5 annual report. I approached management of the company with a detailed list of further questions, but management did not respond in the four days that I gave them.

— It is my contention that in 20X5, Major clearly violated IFRS principles on a number of issues. I am saying that the accounting is wrong, not just aggressive.

— Major's accounting for its real estate loans really takes the cake for non-compliance. The company consolidates the assets and results of two corporations to whom it has granted loans when it does not own any shares in either of the two companies.

— I don't like the accounting in Major's non-real-estate business. There is no question it is misleading. Starting in 20X5, the company specifically states in the financial statement notes that revenue (and profit, I might add) is recognized on product that is still sitting in the company's warehouse.

— How can Rely Holdings—a company that lost $750,000, in which Major had acquired an additional 25% interest for $5 million—be valued at over $29 million? The valuation of Rely Holdings makes no sense.

— How can a company capitalize costs incurred for properties that were never acquired? Clearly these costs cannot be considered assets, and it is misleading to do so.

— It is absurd that Major continues to recognize the revenue from properties in certain economically unstable Asian countries. It is unlikely that the money will be collected. Major should write off these buildings immediately instead of recognizing revenue from them.

| Recommendation on Major Developments Corp. | |
| --- | --- |
| Price earnings multiplier based on last fiscal year | 12.7 |
| Overall rating on their stock | underperform |
| Recommendation | sell |

## Exhibit F
## Extracts from Major Developments Corporation's 20X5 Annual Report

### NOTE 1: ACCOUNTING POLICIES

The company incurs significant costs in investigating new properties for purchase. Costs incurred in investigating any and all properties, whether or not these properties are ultimately purchased by the company, are capitalized as part of the cost of properties actually acquired. These costs are amortized over the useful lives of the properties acquired.

*Exhibit Continued >*

*Exhibit Continued >*

Economic problems in certain Asian countries where the company owns properties have made collection of rental revenues from these properties difficult at this time. The company expects that, once the difficulties in these countries have been resolved, amounts owed will be collected in full. It is the company's policy to accrue the revenue from these properties.

Revenue on product sales is recognized when the goods are shipped to the customer. In the case of "bill and hold" sales, revenue is recognized when the goods are placed in the company's designated storage area.

The consolidated financial statements include the accounts of Major and its majority-owned subsidiaries and, commencing prospectively in fiscal 20X5, the accounts of companies in which Major has no common share ownership but to which it has advanced loans that are currently in default. The equity method is used for investments in which there is significant influence, considered to be voting ownership of 20% to 50%.

## NOTE 14: INVESTMENTS

|  | 20X5 | 20X4 |
|---|---|---|
| Rely Holdings Inc. | $29,640,000 | $25,000,000 |

In 20X0, Major purchased an additional 25% interest in Rely Holdings Inc. for $5 million. Major now owns 48% of Rely Holdings Inc. Major accounts for its investment on an equity basis. In 20X5, Major recorded a loss of $750,000 from Rely Holdings Inc.

---

## Exhibit G
## Extracts from Information Provided by Major's Lawyers

1. Major's auditor has always provided an unqualified report on the audited financial statements of Major, including the 20X5 financial statements.

2. Major has a legal opinion that the two loans are in default (Item A), and a third-party opinion (Item B) that the default permits consolidation of these companies.

   **Item A** ". . . In my opinion, loan 323 to Skyscraper Inc. and loan 324 to Wenon Corporation are in default as of February 1, 20X4, under the aforesaid terms of default of the respective loan agreements, dated the 12th day of August, 20X1. The lender has the right under law and contract to repossess said aforementioned properties, for the purposes of realization on the loans, subject to restrictions of right under clause 43.(b) . . . " [Matthew Krebs, Q.C.]

   **Item B** "Based on facts set out in the attached document, we concur that it is acceptable, under international standards, for Major to consolidate Skyscraper Inc. and Wenon Corporation." [Jesse & Mitchell, Chartered Accountants]

3. "Bill and hold" refers to a practice whereby a customer purchases goods but the seller retains physical possession until the customer requests shipment. Delivery is delayed at the purchaser's request, but the purchaser accepts both the title to the goods and the related billing.

## Problems

**P3-1 (30 minutes, easy)**

Prairie Ltd. and Savannah Inc. have reached agreement in principle to combine their operations. However, the boards of directors are undecided as to the best way to accomplish the combination. Several alternatives are under consideration:

1. Prairie acquires the net assets of Savannah (including the liabilities) for $1,900,000 cash.

2. Prairie acquires all of the assets of Savannah (but not the liabilities) for $2,850,000 cash.

3. Prairie acquires the net assets of Savannah by issuing 120,000 shares in Prairie, valued at $1,900,000.

4. Prairie acquires all of the shares of Savannah by exchanging them for 120,000 newly issued shares in Prairie.

The reported carrying values of Prairie and Savannah are shown below, together with the fair values at the date of combination. Prior to the combination, Prairie has 480,000 shares outstanding and Savannah has 60,000 shares outstanding.

Required

**a.** In a comparative, columnar format, show how the consolidated SFP of Prairie Ltd. would appear immediately after the combination under each of the four alternatives using the acquisition method.

**b.** For each of the four alternatives, briefly state who owns the shares of each corporation and whether Prairie Ltd. and Savannah Inc. are related companies.

| | Condensed Statements of Financial Position (thousands of dollars) | | | |
|---|---|---|---|---|
| | Prairie Ltd. | | Savannah Inc. | |
| | Carrying values | Fair values | Carrying values | Fair values |
| Current assets | $ 8,000 | $ 8,000 | $ 600 | $ 550 |
| Capital assets | 12,000 | 16,000 | 800 | 1,450 |
| Investments | — | — | 600 | 350 |
| | $20,000 | | $2,000 | |
| Current liabilities | $ 4,000 | 6,000 | $ 200 | 150 |
| Long-term liabilities | 6,000 | 6,000 | 800 | 800 |
| Deferred income taxes | 2,000 | 2,000 | 200 | — |
| Common shares | 1,500 | | 400 | |
| Retained earnings | 6,500 | | 400 | |
| | $20,000 | | $2,000 | |

**P3-2 (20 minutes, easy)**

Information relating to six independent cases has been provided below.

| | Case | | | | | |
|---|---|---|---|---|---|---|
| | A | B | C | D | E | F |
| Purchase price | $120 | $120 | $100 | $ 80 | $100 | $ 80 |
| Fair value of net identifiable assets | 100 | 80 | 120 | 120 | 80 | 100 |
| Carrying value of net identifiable assets | 80 | 100 | 80 | 100 | 120 | 120 |

**Required**

1. Using the information provided for each case above, calculate the:
2. the net fair value adjustment;
3. the fair value adjustment allocated to net identifiable assets; and
4. the goodwill/gain from bargain purchase.

**P3-3 (20 minutes, easy)**

East Ltd. acquired 100% of the voting shares of West Ltd. In exchange, East Ltd. issued 60,000 common shares, with a market value of $10 per share, to the common shareholders of West Ltd. Both companies have a December 31 year-end, and this transaction occurred on December 31, 20X6. The outstanding preferred shares of West Ltd. did not change hands. The call price of the West Ltd. preferred shares is equal to their carrying value.

Following are the statements of financial position of the two companies at December 31, 20X6, before the transactions took place:

| Statements of Financial Position December 31, 20X6 | | | | |
|---|---|---|---|---|
| | East Ltd. | | West Ltd. | |
| | Carrying values | Fair values | Carrying values | Fair values |
| Current assets | $ 200,000 | $200,000 | $200,000 | $250,000 |
| Capital assets (net) | 900,000 | 820,000 | 750,000 | 850,000 |
| Goodwill | 100,000 | | — | |
| TOTAL | $1,200,000 | | $950,000 | |
| Current liabilities | $ 90,000 | $ 90,000 | $140,000 | 175,000 |
| Long-term liabilities | 200,000 | 520,000 | 150,000 | 220,000 |
| Preferred shares | — | | 250,000 | 250,000 |
| Common shares | 700,000 | | 115,000 | |
| Retained earnings | 210,000 | | 295,000 | |
| TOTAL | $1,200,000 | | $950,000 | |

**Required**

Prepare the consolidated SFP for the date of acquisition, December 31, 20X6, under the acquisition method.

**P3-4 (20 minutes, easy)**

On December 31, 20X6, the statements of financial position of Prosper Ltd. and Succeed Corp. are as follows:

| | Prosper Ltd. | Succeed Corp. |
|---|---|---|
| Cash | $ 400,000 | $ 780,000 |
| Accounts receivable | 1,600,000 | 2,000,000 |
| Inventories | 1,000,000 | 520,000 |
| Plant and equipment (net) | 3,500,000 | 5,450,000 |
| TOTAL ASSETS | $6,500,000 | $8,400,000 |
| Current liabilities | $ 600,000 | $ 310,000 |
| Long-term liabilities | 900,000 | 610,000 |
| Common shares | 2,500,000 | 1,000,000 |
| Retained earnings | 2,500,000 | 6,480,000 |
| TOTAL LIABILITIES AND EQUITIES | $6,500,000 | $8,000,000 |

Prosper Ltd. has 100,000 common shares outstanding, and Succeed Corp. has 45,000 shares outstanding. On January 1, 20X7, Prosper Ltd. issues an additional 90,000 common shares to Succeed Corp., at $100 per share, in return for all of the assets and liabilities of that company. Succeed Corp. distributes Prosper Ltd.'s common shares to its shareholders in return for their outstanding common shares, and ceases to exist as a separate legal entity. At the time of this transaction, the cash, accounts receivable, inventories, and current liabilities of both companies have fair values equal to their carrying values. The plant and equipment and long-term liabilities have fair values as follows:

|  | Prosper Ltd. | Succeed Corp. |
|---|---|---|
| Plant and equipment (net) | $3,900,000 | $5,450,000 |
| Long-term liabilities | 600,000 | 510,000 |
| In addition, Succeed Corp. has a patent worth $110,000. | | |

**Required**

a. What is the amount of goodwill that would be recorded for this business combination?

b. In completing the fair value adjustment allocation, what other intangible assets could potentially exist that a value could be allocated to instead of (or in addition to) goodwill?

c. Prepare an SFP at January 1, 20X7, for Prosper Ltd., that is, after the purchase.

**P3-5 (20 minutes, easy)**

Amber Corporation (Amber), a public corporation, has concluded negotiations with Beryl Corporation (Beryl) for the purchase of all of Beryl's net assets at fair value, effective January 1, 20X7. An examination at that date by independent experts disclosed that the fair value of Beryl's inventories was $250,000; the fair value of its machinery and equipment was $370,000.

**Additional Information:**

- The fair value of the patent was $77,000. The values of the accounts receivable and of the current and long-term liabilities were equal to their carrying value.

- The purchase agreement stated that the purchase price of all the net assets will be $582,000 payable in cash.

- Both corporations have December 31 year-ends. The statements of financial position of both corporations, as at the date of the implementation of the purchase agreement (January 1, 20X7), are as follows:

|  | Amber Corp. | Beryl Corp. |
|---|---|---|
| Cash | $ 800,000 | $100,000 |
| Accounts receivable | 275,000 | 250,000 |
| Inventories at cost | 250,000 | 200,000 |
| Machinery and equipment (net) | 450,000 | 250,000 |
| Patent | — | 55,000 |
| TOTAL ASSETS | $1,775,000 | $855,000 |
| Current liabilities | 75,000 | 120,000 |
| Long-term liabilities | 555,000 | 350,000 |
| Capital–common shares | 200,000 | 100,000 |
| Retained earnings | 945,000 | 285,000 |
| TOTAL LIABILITIES AND SHAREHOLDERS' EQUITY | $1,775,000 | $855,000 |

**Required**

**a.** Calculate the goodwill arising from the business combination.

**b.** Prepare Amber's SFP at January 1, 20X7, after its acquisition of Beryl's net assets.

**P3-6 (15 minutes, easy)**

Pristine Ltd. purchased 100% of the voting shares of Serene Ltd. for $1,500,000 on October 1, 20X6. The SFP of Serene Ltd. at that date was as follows:

| Serene Ltd.<br>Statement of Financial Position<br>October 1, 20X6 | | |
|---|---|---|
| | Net carrying value | Fair value |
| Cash | $ 330,000 | $330,000 |
| Receivables | 390,000 | 350,000 |
| Inventory | 580,000 | 770,000 |
| Capital assets (net) | 1,200,000 | 900,000 |
| | $2,500,000 | |
| Current liabilities | $ 350,000 | 380,000 |
| Long-term liability | 690,000 | 690,000 |
| Common shares | 360,000 | |
| Retained earnings | 1,100,000 | |
| | $2,500,000 | |

**Required**

Provide the eliminations and adjustments required *at the date of acquisition* that are necessary to prepare the consolidated SFP of Pristine Ltd. on Oct. 1, 20X6.

**P3-7 (20 minutes, easy)**

On December 31, 20X6, Profound Limited acquired 100% of the outstanding voting shares of Subtle Limited for $2.2 million in cash. The statements of financial position of Profound and Subtle and the fair values of Subtle's identifiable assets and liabilities immediately before the acquisition transaction were as follows:

| | Profound Limited | Subtle Limited | |
|---|---|---|---|
| | | Carrying value | Fair value |
| **ASSETS** | | | |
| Cash | $ 2,300,000 | $ 110,000 | $ 110,000 |
| Accounts receivable | 600,000 | 350,000 | 350,000 |
| Inventory | 500,000 | 580,000 | 650,000 |
| Land | 1,000,000 | 820,000 | 950,000 |
| Buildings and equipment | 6,200,000 | 1,350,000 | 1,150,000 |
| Accumulated depreciation | (3,000,000) | (380,000) | |
| Patents | — | 210,000 | 160,000 |
| | $ 7,600,000 | $3,040,000 | |

| LIABILITIES AND SHAREHOLDERS' EQUITY | | | |
|---|---|---|---|
| Accounts payable | $1,100,000 | $ 460,000 | $460,000 |
| Long-term debt | 2,100,000 | 980,000 | 850,000 |
| Common shares | 1,550,000 | 1,000,000 | |
| Retained earnings | 2,850,000 | 600,000 | |
| | $7,600,000 | $3,040,000 | |

**Required**

Prepare the consolidated SFP for Profound Limited immediately following the acquisition of Subtle Limited.

**P3-8 (30 minutes, easy)**

On January 4, 20X7, Pradeesh Corp. acquired 100% of the outstanding common shares of Serena Inc. by a share-for-share exchange of its own shares, valued at $1,200,000. Each share of Pradeesh had a fair value of $6 on January 4, 20X7. The statements of financial position of both companies just prior to the share exchange are shown below. Serena has patents that are not shown on the SFP, but that have an estimated fair value of $250,000 and an estimated remaining productive life of five years. Serena's buildings and equipment have an estimated fair value that is $250,000 in excess of carrying value, and the deferred charges are assumed to have a fair value of zero. Serena's buildings and equipment are being depreciated on the straight-line basis and have a remaining useful life of 10 years. The deferred charges are being amortized over the following four years. Please note that the spreadsheet relating to the problem is available on the Companion Website for this text.

| Statements of Financial Position December 31, 20X6 | | |
|---|---|---|
| | Pradeesh | Serena |
| Cash | $ 110,000 | $ 85,000 |
| Accounts and other receivables | 140,000 | 80,000 |
| Inventories | 110,000 | 55,000 |
| Buildings and equipment | 1,500,000 | 800,000 |
| Accumulated depreciation | (700,000) | (400,000) |
| Deferred charges | — | 120,000 |
| | $1,160,000 | $740,000 |
| Accounts and other payables | $ 200,000 | $100,000 |
| Bonds payable | — | 200,000 |
| Deferred income taxes | 60,000 | 40,000 |
| Common shares* | 600,000 | 150,000 |
| Retained earnings | 300,000 | 250,000 |
| | $1,160,000 | $740,000 |
| *Pradeesh = 300,000 shares; Serena = 150,000 shares. | | |

**Required**

Prepare a consolidated SFP for Pradeesh Corp., immediately following the share exchange.

## P3-9 (35 minutes, difficult)

On January 1, 20X1, Rodriguez Inc. purchased 100% of the common shares of Teresa Inc., for $325,000. On that date the following differences were observed with regard to specific net assets of Teresa Inc.:

|  | Fair value–carrying value differences |
|---|---|
| Land | ($75,000) |
| Buildings (net) | 35,000 |
| Equipment (net) | (45,000) |
| Notes payable | 15,000 |

The separate entity SFP of Teresa and the consolidated SFP of Rodriguez Inc. on January 1, 20X1, are presented below. The consolidated SFP of Rodriguez was prepared following the acquisition method.

|  | Teresa | Consolidated |
|---|---|---|
| Cash | 25,000 | 70,000 |
| Accounts receivable | 72,500 | 197,500 |
| Inventory | 129,000 | 234,000 |
| Land | 125,000 | 280,000 |
| Buildings (net) | 60,000 | 720,000 |
| Equipment (net) | 48,000 | 338,000 |
| Goodwill | 0 | 50,000 |
| TOTAL ASSETS | 409,500 | 1,889,500 |
| Accounts payable | 6,000 | 131,000 |
| Notes payable | 3,500 | 572,500 |
| Common stock | 310,000 | 380,000 |
| Retained earnings | 140,000 | 806,000* |
| TOTAL LIABILITIES AND SHAREHOLDERS' EQUITY | 409,500 | 1,889,500 |

*The consolidated retained earnings include a gain from bargain purchase of Teresa of $25,000.

### Required

Prepare the January 1, 20X1, separate-entity SFP of Rodriguez Inc. Show all supporting calculations.

# Chapter 4

## Wholly Owned Subsidiaries: Reporting Subsequent to Acquisition

## Learning Objectives

**After studying this chapter, you should be able to:**

LO **1** consolidate wholly owned subsidiaries in the first and second years after acquisition;

LO **2** eliminate transactions that occur between a parent and its subsidiaries;

LO **3** eliminate unrealized gains on upstream and downstream sales of inventory and capital assets between a subsidiary and a parent;

LO **4** recognize profits realized in the current year on upstream sale of inventory in the previous year;

LO **5** amortize fair value adjustments; and

LO **6** report non-consolidated subsidiaries on the equity basis.

## INTRODUCTION

Following the global financial crisis of the late 2000s, the financial sector witnessed hectic merger and acquisition activity. Canadian banks, being relatively unscathed by the financial crisis, took advantage of this crisis by being major acquirers of financial institutions in the United States. For example, Bank of Montreal (BMO) completed the acquisition of Marshall and Iisley Corporation on July 5, 2011, for $3.99 billion in an all-stock deal. BMO allocated $4.62 billion to identifiable intangible assets and goodwill.

All those acquired intangible assets either are amortizable or must be tested for impairment, or both. Not all of the amortization and/or impairment losses will be recorded on the subsidiary's books because most of the fair value appears only on BMO's *consolidated* statements—because Marshall and Iisley continue to amortize its assets at their carrying values on its books. Therefore, BMO must make consolidation-related amortization and impairment adjustments. BMO describes the amortization of the acquired intangible assets as follows:

> As part of this acquisition, we acquired a core deposit intangible asset that is being amortized on an accelerated basis over a period of 10 years, a customer relationship intangible asset that is being amortized on an accelerated basis over a period of 15 years, a credit card portfolio intangible asset that is being amortized on an accelerated basis

over a period of 15 years, and a trade name intangible asset that is being amortized on an accelerated basis over a period of five years.

Source: BMO Financial Group, Note 12, Acquisition, to the group financial statements of BMO Financial Group for the period ended October 31, 2011. Annual Report and Financial Statements, p. 145. http://www.bmo.com/ar2011/downloads/bmo_ar2011.pdf.

**LO ❶**

Consolidate wholly owned subsidiaries in the first and second years after acquisition

## 4.1 GENERAL APPROACH

After an acquirer obtains control over a subsidiary, the acquirer must prepare its subsequent consolidated statements on the basis of the fair values allocated to the acquiree's assets and liabilities. Those fair values do not reside permanently on the SFP. Short-term items such as inventories flow through the consolidated statement of comprehensive income; most long-term assets are depreciated or amortized. As well, the acquired assets must be written down if they are impaired (i.e., they have declined to below their consolidated carrying value).

Date-of-acquisition consolidation happens only once, and then only for internal reporting. The real issues arise in post-acquisition consolidation. In this chapter, things get more realistic—and much more complex! This chapter explains the basics of consolidation for the SCI and SFP after acquisition. We will do so in the context of wholly owned subsidiaries. We will illustrate the following aspects of consolidation for the first and second years after acquisition:

- eliminating transactions that occur between a parent and its subsidiaries;

- eliminating unrealized profit on intercompany sales of inventory;

- recognizing profit realized in the current year on upstream sales of inventory in the previous year;

- amortizing fair value adjustments; and

- reporting non-consolidated subsidiaries on the equity basis.

Exhibit 4.1 provides a pictorial overview of the common consolidation-related adjustments and eliminations made when consolidating at the end of the first and second years after acquisition.

We will, as usual, illustrate only the direct method in the text. For the worksheet method, refer to the text's Companion Website.

In the main body of the chapter, we focus on the core issues of post-acquisition consolidation of a wholly owned subsidiary, illustrated for the first and second reporting periods following its creation or acquisition. This chapter also has two appendices. The appendices cover issues that are relevant only for subsidiaries acquired in a business combination:

- deferred tax calculations (Appendix 4A)

- goodwill impairment testing (Appendix 4B)

Bear in mind that the vast majority of subsidiaries are parent-founded. These two issues do not arise when consolidating parent-founded subsidiaries because any deferred taxes and/or impairment losses, including impairment losses relating to the carrying value

**Exhibit 4.1** Adjustments and Eliminations Required at the End of the First and Second Years After Acquisition

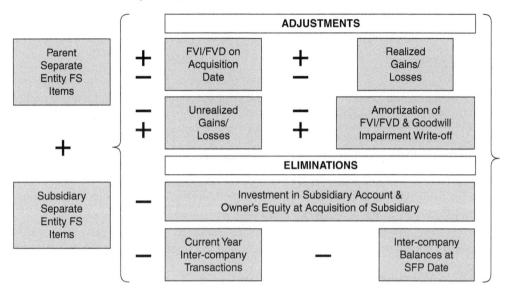

of goodwill present on the books of the subsidiary, will already have been recorded directly on the subsidiaries' books. The process of consolidation makes no changes in the values of a parent-founded subsidiary's assets or liabilities.

In this chapter, we deal only with wholly owned subsidiaries. Subsequent chapters will relax that simplifying assumption, thereby introducing further complexities.

Now, fasten your seat belt, pay attention, and enjoy the ride!

## 4.2 CONSOLIDATION ONE YEAR AFTER ACQUISITION

Before we begin, we must point out that the separate-entity financial statements of each corporation in the group—the parent and each of its subsidiaries—will include any and all intercompany transactions that occurred between companies in the group; for example, sales of inventory by one company to the other will be reported as revenue by the selling company and as inventory purchases by the other.

When we talk about *consolidated* statements, we are referring to the set of statements that a publicly held parent company prepares for distribution to its shareholders in accordance with GAAP. For a public company in Canada, the relevant GAAP is IFRS. These statements are based on the concept of the *economic entity*—there is no corresponding legal entity. Keep in mind that consolidated statements comprise only one set of financial statements, intended for a specific purpose—every corporation still prepares its own individual statements for the tax authorities, for its bankers, for its internal performance evaluation, and so forth.

**LO ❶**
Consolidate wholly owned subsidiaries in the first and second years after acquisition

**LO ❷**
Eliminate transactions that occur between a parent and its subsidiaries

**LO ❸**
Eliminate unrealized gains on upstream and downstream sales of inventory and capital assets between a subsidiary and a parent

**LO ❺**
Amortize fair value adjustments

**LO ❻**
Report non-consolidated subsidiaries on the equity basis

Chapter 3 used an example of Purchase Ltd.'s acquisition of 100% of the shares of Target Ltd. To prepare Purchase Ltd.'s consolidated financial statements *after* the date of acquisition, we will need four types of information:

1.  the details of the purchase transaction;

2.  the amortization or depreciation policy for capital assets;

3.  the nature and extent of intercompany transactions between the two companies, including intercompany receivables and payables and unrealized and realized profits in inventory transactions; and

4.  the disposition of assets that have been sold intercompany (including the assets in the original acquisition).

Over this and the following two chapters, we will add various types of transactions to our basic example of Purchase Ltd. and Target Ltd. We will not attempt to be exhaustive—this is an advanced accounting text, not an all-inclusive consolidation handbook. By the time you finish these first six chapters, however, you should have a thorough understanding of the consolidation process and of the types of interactions that must be accounted for.

## Basic Information

Assume that on December 31, 20X5, Purchase Ltd. purchased all of the outstanding shares of Target Ltd. by issuing 40,000 new shares of Purchase Ltd. in exchange for the shares of Target Ltd. The newly issued Purchase Ltd. shares had a market value of $30 per share—a total purchase cost of $1,200,000. The total cost was allocated to the fair values of Target Ltd.'s assets and liabilities and to goodwill *at the date of acquisition* as shown in Exhibit 4.2.[1] These fair values and goodwill are the same amounts used in the illustration in the previous chapter.

At every reporting date after December 31, 20X5, Purchase Ltd. will have to include the fair value adjustments and goodwill in its *consolidated* net assets. However,

- the carrying values of most fair-valued assets flow to net income, either directly through cost of sales (for current assets such as inventories) or indirectly through amortization or depreciation for tangible and intangible capital assets (except goodwill and other intangible assets with indefinite lives); and

- assets included in the purchase transaction may have been sold or retired at some time following Purchase's acquisition of Target.

When either of these events happens, we must make adjustments to the initial FVAs at every reporting date.

Other adjustments are needed to eliminate, or "back out," intercompany transactions. For the year ended December 31, 20X6, we will assume the following:

1.  Target Ltd.'s buildings and equipment will be depreciated over 10 years after the date of acquisition, using straight-line depreciation.

---

[1]Note that Exhibit 4.2 is identical to Exhibit 3.6. The same example is used throughout Chapters 3 to 5 to help you with comparisons and to make it easier for you to see the influence of additional complexities.

**Exhibit 4.2** Allocation of Purchase Price

| 100% Purchase of Target Ltd., December 31, 20X5 | | | | | |
|---|---|---|---|---|---|
| Purchase price | | | | | $1,200,000 |
| Less carrying value of Target's net identifiable assets (100%) | | | | | (800,000) |
| = Fair value adjustment, allocated below | | | | | 400,000 |
| | Carrying value (a) | Fair value (b) | Fair value adjustment (c) = (b) − (a) | FVA allocated | |
| Cash | $ 50,000 | $ 50,000 | — | | |
| Accounts receivable | 150,000 | 150,000 | — | | |
| Inventory | 50,000 | 50,000 | — | | |
| Land | 300,000 | 400,000 | $ 100,000 | $ 100,000 | |
| Buildings and equipment | 500,000 | 550,000 | 50,000 | 50,000 | |
| Accumulated depreciation | (150,000) | — | 150,000 | 150,000 | |
| Accounts payable | (100,000) | (100,000) | — | | |
| Total fair value adjustment | | | | | (300,000) |
| Net asset carrying value | $ 800,000 | | | | |
| Fair value of assets acquired | | $ 1,100,000 | | | |
| Balance of FVA allocated to goodwill | | | | | $ 100,000 |

2. During 20X6, Target Ltd. sold goods of $55,000 to Purchase Ltd. Target Ltd.'s gross margin is 40% of sales.

3. On December 31, 20X6, $20,000 of the goods acquired by Purchase Ltd. from Target Ltd. are still in Purchase Ltd.'s inventory.

4. During 20X6, Target Ltd. paid dividends totalling $30,000 to Purchase Ltd., Target Ltd.'s sole shareholder. Purchase Ltd. maintains its investment in Target Ltd.'s account on the cost basis, and therefore the dividends received were recorded as dividend income.

Chapter 2 illustrated the basic approach to eliminating intercompany transactions and balances. Chapter 3 explained the eliminations that are required when a subsidiary is purchased. The example in this chapter will combine these two types of adjustments and will add four more issues that are essential to understanding consolidations:

1. amortization of fair value adjustments;

2. impairment testing for goodwill;

3. elimination of unrealized profit on intercompany sales; and

4. recognition of the profit realized in the current year on intercompany sales made in the previous year.

The following three sections will discuss the first three issues in succession, while discussion of the fourth issue will be deferred until a little later in the chapter.

## Amortization/Impairment of Fair Value Adjustments

When a company directly purchases assets, it will amortize them at their fair values, which, at the time of purchase, are equal to the purchase price. Therefore, if, instead of buying the assets directly, the company chooses to acquire the company that owns those assets, the amortization relating to the underlying assets should continue to follow the same principle—that is, it should be based on the fair values of those assets. The form of the purchase—direct purchase of assets versus purchase of the company owning the assets—does not change the fair value of the assets.

When an acquiring company purchases the company owning the assets, the newly-acquired subsidiary will continue to amortize the underlying assets at the carrying values as shown on the subsidiary's books. Therefore, on the consolidated statements, we need to amortize the difference between the carrying and fair values of the assets in order to correctly recognize amortization based on the full fair values of the acquired assets.

As the survey of US business combinations summarized in Reality Check 4–1 shows, often a very large part of the purchase price in a business combination is allocated to fair value adjustments by companies.

Therefore, amortization and impairment of fair value adjustments is likely to significantly affect consolidated earnings subsequent to the purchase. Each major category of assets is discussed below.

**Inventory**   Fair value adjustments for inventory will flow through cost of sales to affect net income when the inventory is sold to third parties. In the period in which the inventory is sold, which typically is assumed to be the period after acquisition, the fair value adjustment is transferred from inventory and added to or subtracted from cost of sales on the consolidation working papers.

**Tangible Capital Assets**   A purchased subsidiary will continue to amortize the depreciable capital assets that are recorded on its books. However, the subsidiary's depreciation will be based on the *carrying value* of the assets on its books. The depreciation on the *subsidiary's separate-entity* financial statements will not reflect the prices paid by the parent in the business combination.

Reality Check 4–1

## Allocation of Purchase Price to Fair Value Adjustments

A study of 756 US business combinations carried out during the "dot-com" acquisition frenzy of the late 1990s revealed that the purchase price discrepancy—fair value adjustments and goodwill—equalled, on average, almost 200% of carrying value. The aggregate purchase price was $404 billion, comprising $137 billion in net asset carrying value and $267 billion in purchase price discrepancy.[a]

The same situation exists currently as internet companies and suppliers gobble each other up. Think about Apple—if Apple were to be purchased, almost all of the purchase price would be for intangibles, since Apple is not a manufacturing company.

[a]Benjamin C. Ayers, Craig E. Lefanowicz, and John R. Robinson, "The Financial Statement Effects of Eliminating the Pooling-of-Interest Method of Acquisition Accounting," *Accounting Horizons, 14*:1 (March 2000), pp. 1–19.

When the *parent's consolidated statements* are prepared, the fair value adjustments on depreciable assets must be amortized in accordance with the depreciation policy being used by the subsidiary. If, for example, a building has a 20-year estimated remaining useful life from the date of the business combination, the fair value adjustment must be amortized over the 20-year remaining period.

Suppose a subsidiary has a four-year-old asset with an original cost of $100,000. This asset is being amortized on the subsidiary's books by the straight-line method over 20 years. At the date on which the parent bought the subsidiary, the carrying value of the asset was as follows:

| | |
|---|---|
| Cost | $100,000 |
| Accumulated amortization [($100,000 ÷ 20) × 4] | 20,000 |
| | $ 80,000 |

Fair value at the date of acquisition was $120,000. Therefore, the fair value increment is $40,000. Following acquisition, the subsidiary will continue to amortize the asset at $5,000 per year: $100,000 ÷ 20 = $5,000. The fair value increment will be amortized over the remaining expected useful life of the asset, which is 16 years following acquisition: ($120,000 − $80,000) ÷ 16 = $2,500 per year. Amortization of this asset on the *consolidated* SCI will be $7,500.

| | | |
|---|---|---|
| Subsidiary's amortization | $100,000 ÷ 20 = | $5,000 |
| Fair value increment | $40,000 ÷ 16 = | 2,500 |
| Consolidated amortization | | $7,500 |

Exhibit 4.3 shows the portion of the fair value of the asset amortized on the subsidiary's books and the consolidated statements, respectively.

**Exhibit 4.3** Amortization of Asset Fair Values

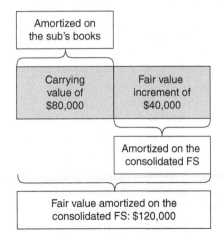

**Intangible Capital Assets**   A company recognizes an intangible asset on its books only when the asset has been purchased or when capitalizable costs were incurred to develop the asset. As a result, a company often has intangible assets that are not reported on its books. Examples include trademarks, customer lists, and franchises. When one company is acquired by another in a business combination, the acquirer should identify any specific intangible assets that have not been reported on the acquiree's SFP. When intangible assets can be identified, *whether or not they appear on the acquired company's SFP*, they must be assigned a fair value.

After initial recognition, an intangible asset is carried on the consolidated SFP at cost less any accumulated amortization and impairment losses. Thereafter, the accounting is as follows:

- If the intangible asset's life is indefinite, it is not amortized but tested for impairment.
- If the identifiable intangible asset is already reported on the subsidiary's SFP, the fair value adjustment is accounted for in the same way.
- If the intangible asset is not already reported on the subsidiary's SFP, the asset's useful life must be determined.
- If the asset's life is not indefinite, the fair value adjustment is amortized over its useful life.
- If it becomes apparent that an intangible asset's value has become impaired (i.e., has declined to below its consolidated carrying value), fair value must be written down to the impaired value.

**Goodwill**   *Goodwill is not amortized.* Since goodwill is not amortized, it must be subjected to an annual impairment test. To apply the impairment test, goodwill must be attributed to each **cash-generating unit** or group of cash-generating units, provided that each unit (or group of units) (1) constitutes the lowest level within the entity at which goodwill is monitored for internal management purposes, and (2) is not larger than the related operating segment as reported in the annual disclosure of operating segments.[2]

A cash-generating unit is not necessarily the same as a corporate entity. Therefore, when goodwill arises in a business combination, that goodwill must be allocated to individual cash-generating units if there is more than one within the acquired corporation.

Once goodwill has been attributed to cash-generating units, an impairment test for each unit is applied by comparing the recoverable amount of the unit with its carrying value, including goodwill. Any excess of carrying value over the recoverable amount is treated as an *impairment loss* in the consolidated SCI.

Clearly, the impairment test involves a lot of management estimation and judgment. Recoverable value of a cash-generating unit is a function of its future earnings, and there is a great deal of subjectivity to estimating future earnings. The application of impairment tests for goodwill seems to give management a lot of opportunity for write-downs to contribute to a "big bath" or to otherwise "manage" earnings through controlling the amount and timing of impairment losses.

Appendix 4B explains the IFRS impairment test more extensively.

---

[2]Segments and segment reporting are discussed in Chapter 7.

# Unrealized Profits

One of the more challenging aspects of consolidated statements is that we must keep track of assets that were sold by one company in the group to another. Sales from a parent to a subsidiary are **downstream sales**, while sales from a subsidiary to a parent are called **upstream sales**. Sales between two subsidiaries are treated as *upstream* sales.

In the facts for Purchase Ltd. and Target Ltd. listed above, there are three points relating to intercompany sales:

- Target Ltd. had sales to Purchase Ltd. (i.e., upstream sales) of $55,000;
- $20,000 of those goods are still in Purchase Ltd.'s inventory at year-end; and
- Target Ltd.'s gross margin on sales is 40%.

The $20,000 of goods in Purchase Ltd.'s inventory are recorded at their acquisition price to Purchase Ltd. However, Target Ltd.'s cost to produce the goods is much less. Target Ltd.'s gross margin is 40%, which means that the $20,000 inventory contains a gross profit margin of $20,000 × 40% = $8,000; the goods cost $12,000 to produce.

*Consolidated statements must show only the results of transactions between the consolidated entity and those companies and individuals outside the combined economic entity.* In substance, the $8,000 gross profit is only an internal, not an external, transaction. Therefore, consolidated inventory must be reduced by eliminating the $8,000 *unrealized profit* on the upstream sales of inventory. This treatment remains the same regardless of whether the sale is made by a 100%-, or wholly, owned subsidiary or by a *non*-wholly owned subsidiary to its parent. We always eliminate the entire unrealized profit relating to any intercompany sale during consolidation.

So the consolidated inventory must be reduced by $8,000. But what happens to the offset? When we compute cost of sales, beginning inventory and purchases are added together and ending inventory is subtracted. The SCI effect of an *overstated ending inventory* is to *understate cost of sales*. Therefore, we must not only reduce consolidated inventory by $8,000, but also increase cost of sales by $8,000. If this seems confusing, just remember that *increasing* a cost will *reduce* net income, thereby eliminating the unrealized profit.

In summary, two adjustments are necessary:

1. eliminate the intercompany sale transaction; and
2. eliminate the unrealized profit.

We will illustrate these two adjustments shortly.

Unrealized profit arises any time one corporation sells assets to another and those assets stay within the consolidated economic entity instead of being sold externally. Inventory is the most common type of intercompany sale, but capital assets or investments may also be sold. The same principles apply, regardless of the nature of the asset(s) involved.

# Direct Method

The unconsolidated financial statements for Purchase Ltd. and Target Ltd. are shown in Exhibit 4.4. We have assumed that Purchase Ltd. *records* its investment in Target Ltd. on the cost basis in its accounts, as is almost always the case. Therefore, the separate-entity financial statements show (1) the investment at the purchase price of $1,200,000 and (2) the dividends of $30,000 received by Purchase Ltd. from Target Ltd. as dividend income.

**Exhibit 4.4** Separate-Entity Financial Statements for 20X6

### Statements of Comprehensive Income
### Year Ended December 31, 20X6

| | Purchase Ltd. | Target Ltd. |
|---|---|---|
| **Revenue:** | | |
| Sales | $2,400,000 | $ 300,000 |
| Dividend income | 30,000 | — |
| | 2,430,000 | 300,000 |
| **Expense:** | | |
| Cost of sales | 1,750,000 | 180,000 |
| Depreciation expense | 100,000 | 35,000 |
| Other expenses | 250,000 | 20,000 |
| | 2,100,000 | 235,000 |
| **NET INCOME** | $ 330,000 | $ 65,000 |

### Statements of Changes in Equity—Retained Earnings Section
### Year Ended December 31, 20X6

| | Purchase Ltd. | Target Ltd. |
|---|---|---|
| Retained earnings, December 31, 20X5 | $2,000,000 | $ 600,000 |
| Net income | 330,000 | 65,000 |
| Dividends declared | — | (30,000) |
| Retained earnings, December 31, 20X6 | $2,330,000 | $ 635,000 |

### Statements of Financial Position December 31, 20X6

| | Purchase Ltd. | Target Ltd. |
|---|---|---|
| **ASSETS** | | |
| **Current Assets:** | | |
| Cash | $ 980,000 | $ 100,000 |
| Accounts receivable | 2,200,000 | 250,000 |
| Inventory | 250,000 | 70,000 |
| | 3,430,000 | 420,000 |
| **Property, plant, and equipment:** | | |
| Land | 1,000,000 | 300,000 |
| Buildings and equipment | 3,000,000 | 500,000 |
| Accumulated depreciation | (1,300,000) | (185,000) |
| | 2,700,000 | 615,000 |
| **Other assets:** | | |
| Investments (at cost) | 1,200,000 | — |
| **TOTAL ASSETS** | $7,330,000 | $1,035,000 |
| **LIABILITIES AND SHAREHOLDERS' EQUITY** | | |
| **Liabilities:** | | |
| Current: accounts payable | $800,000 | $200,000 |
| Long-term: notes payable | 400,000 | — |
| | 1,200,000 | 200,000 |
| **Shareholders' equity:** | | |
| Common shares | 3,800,000 | 200,000 |
| Retained earnings | 2,330,000 | 635,000 |
| | 6,130,000 | 835,000 |
| **TOTAL LIABILITIES AND SHAREHOLDERS' EQUITY** | $7,330,000 | $1,035,000 |

**MEAR Steps to Consolidation—Phase 2**  In Chapter 3, we introduced the MEAR approach to consolidating subsidiaries that were acquired via a business combination. In that chapter, we introduced the **M**easure step and, to a limited extent, the **E**liminate step. In this chapter, we extend the MEAR concept further. We will enlarge upon the **E**liminate step and introduce the **A**mortize step. Indeed, you may already have noticed that we expanded the **E**liminate step when we discussed intercompany transactions in the preceding section; intercompany transactions and unrealized profits must be eliminated.

Exhibit 4.5 shows the MEAR steps to consolidation required at the end of the first year following acquisition.

The **M**easure step and part of the **E**liminate step are sufficient when consolidation is occurring on the date of acquisition, since both relate solely to acquisition-related adjustments and eliminations. However, when consolidation is occurring in the first year subsequent to the date of acquisition, we need to add additional steps to the **E**liminate step and add the **A**mortize step. Note that throughout the chapters on consolidation we will present the consolidation process in terms of the MEAR steps. As we cover new issues, existing MEAR steps will be amplified and new steps will be added. The last step of every iteration will always be to consolidate the statements.

In our current example, the **E**liminate and **A**mortize steps relate to current year adjustments and eliminations. Specifically:

1. The **E**liminate step requires us to:
   **a.** identify and eliminate all intercompany transactions and balances; and
   **b.** calculate and eliminate any *unrealized* profit (or loss) relating to the intercompany sale of inventory and other assets in the current period.

**Exhibit 4.5** MEAR Steps to Consolidation at the End of the First Year
Following Acquisition

| Consolidation Steps | Acquisition-Related | Relating to First Year Following Acquisition |
|---|---|---|
| 1. Measure | ■ Calculate cost and fair value adjustments (FVA) <br> ■ Allocate FVA | |
| 2. Eliminate | ■ Eliminate parent's investment account and subsidiary's share equity accounts | |
| | | ■ Eliminate intercompany transactions and balances <br> ■ Eliminate unrealized profits |
| 3. Amortize | | ■ Amortize FVAs <br> ■ Recognize impairments |

2. The **A**mortize step requires us to:
   a. amortize the FVA allocated to the various identifiable assets and liabilities, as appropriate;
   b. write off any impairment of goodwill and other intangible assets with indeterminate useful lives; and
   c. determine the balance of the FVA allocated that remains unamortized or unimpaired at the end of the period.

Exhibit 4.2 already illustrates the **M**easure step for our example, as well as the first aspect of **E**liminate. We will now illustrate the additional steps of **E**liminate and **A**mortize.

## Eliminate

**Intercompany Transactions and Balances**    There were two intercompany transactions in 20X6 requiring eliminations:[3]

| Upstream sale by Target Ltd. | (55,000) |
|---|---|
| Dividend income of Purchase Ltd. and dividends declared by Target Ltd. | (30,000) |

These both must be eliminated. The first item relates to the sale by Target Ltd. of $55,000 worth of goods to Purchase Ltd. We need to eliminate $55,000 from both sales (of Target) and cost of goods sold (of Purchase). The second item relates to Purchase Ltd.'s *share* of $30,000 of the dividends declared by Target Ltd. that have been recognized by Purchase Ltd. as dividend income. Since Purchase owns 100% of Target, we must eliminate $30,000 from both dividend income (of Purchase) and dividends declared (by Target).

Notice that each of these eliminations is two-sided; each involves (1) eliminating something recorded on Target's books, offset by (2) eliminating something on Purchase's books. This should reinforce for you the fact that consolidation adjustments cannot be recorded on any company's books—*these are purely worksheet adjustments for consolidated financial reporting*. You also should always keep in mind that nothing that we do during consolidation affects anything on the books of either company. Their individual separate-entity statements are not affected at all.

**Unrealized Profits**    In our example there is only one source of unrealized profits, unrealized profit on the upstream sale of inventory. As we explained earlier, we need to increase cost of goods sold and decrease ending inventory by that amount.

| Unrealized profit on upstream sale of inventory | (8,000) |
|---|---|

---

[3]In this and remaining consolidation-related chapters in the text, eliminations and negative adjustments are set in parentheses.

**Amortize**   Before we start adjusting for amortization and depreciation, it is helpful to prepare a schedule of what we need to do. A schedule for Purchase Ltd.'s acquisition of Target Ltd. would be as follows:

| | FVA allocated | Amortization period | Amortization per year | Amortization/ impairment loss during 20X6 | Balance of FVA remaining at the end of 20X6 |
|---|---|---|---|---|---|
| Land | $100,000 | — | | — | $100,000 |
| Building & equipment | 200,000 | 10 | $20,000 | $20,000 | 180,000 |
| Goodwill | 100,000 | — | | — | 100,000 |
| Total | $400,000 | | | $20,000 | $380,000 |

From the schedule above, we know that we need to recognize a total amortization/ impairment loss adjustment of $20,000 in the 20X6 consolidated financial statements. This adjustment pertains to the depreciation expense relating to the fair value increment allocated to property, plant, and equipment.

We also know from the schedule/table above that we need to add an adjustment of $380,000 to the 20X6 year-end carrying values on the consolidated SFP. This total consists of an increase to land for $100,000, to building and equipment for $180,000, and to goodwill for $100,000. Note that the adjustment for building and equipment of $180,000 is the result of the initial FVA allocated to buildings and equipment of $200,000, minus the $20,000 depreciation adjustment required in the current year.

**Prepare the Consolidated Statements**   We can start the consolidation process by adding the carrying values of both companies and making the various adjustments and eliminations identified in the previous steps. We need to make appropriate adjustments to:

- eliminate the accumulated depreciation of the subsidiary as of the date of acquisition; and
- eliminate the common shares of $200,000 and retained earnings at the time of acquisition of $600,000 of Target Ltd., and the investment cost of $1,200,000.

To do this, we can go down the SCI and SFP and insert the correct amounts on a line-by-line basis. In Exhibit 4.6, we have added together the separate-entity amounts and made the required additional adjustments and eliminations. These adjustments and eliminations are listed below once again, now by each financial statement, starting with the SCI.

The starting point, as always, is to enter the carrying values of both companies' assets, liabilities, and shareholders' equity. Then we can add/subtract the FVAs, eliminate the investment (and Target's share equity accounts), and proceed with our other eliminations and adjustments.

**Exhibit 4.6** Purchase Ltd. Consolidated Financial Statements (Direct Method)

## Consolidated Statement of Comprehensive Income
### Year Ended December 31, 20X6

Revenue:

| | |
|---|---|
| Sales revenue [2,400,000 + 300,000 − **55,000**$^U$] | $2,645,000 |
| Dividend income [30,000 + 0 − **30,000**] | — |

Operating expenses

| | |
|---|---|
| Cost of sales [1,750,000 + 180,000 − **55,000**$^U$ + **8,000**$^U$] | 1,883,000 |
| Depreciation expense [100,000 + 35,000 + **20,000**] | 155,000 |
| Other expenses [250,000 + 20,000] | 270,000 |
| | 2,308,000 |
| NET INCOME AND CONSOLIDATED NET INCOME | $  337,000 |

## Consolidated Statement of Changes in Equity—Retained Earnings Section
### Year Ended December 31, 20X6

| | |
|---|---|
| Retained earnings, December 31, 20X5 [2,000,000 + 600,000 − **600,000**] | $2,000,000 |
| Consolidated net income | 337,000 |
| Dividends declared [0 + 30,000 − **30,000**] | — |
| Retained earnings, December 31, 20X6 | $2,337,000 |

## Consolidated Statement of Financial Position
### December 31, 20X6

ASSETS

Current assets:

| | |
|---|---|
| Cash [980,000 + 100,000] | $1,080,000 |
| Accounts receivable [2,200,000 + 250,000] | 2,450,000 |
| Inventory [250,000 + 70,000 − **8,000**$^U$] | 312,000 |
| | 3,842,000 |

Property, plant, and equipment:

| | |
|---|---|
| Land [1,000,000 + 300,000 + 100,000] | 1,400,000 |
| Buildings and equipment [3,000,000 + 500,000 + **50,000**] | 3,550,000 |
| Accumulated depreciation [1,300,000 + 185,000 − **150,000** + 20,000] | (1,355,000) |
| | 3,595,000 |

Other assets:

| | |
|---|---|
| Investments [1,200,000 + 0 − **1,200,000**] | — |
| Goodwill [100,000] | 100,000 |
| TOTAL ASSETS | $7,537,000 |

LIABILITIES AND SHAREHOLDERS' EQUITY

Liabilities:

| | |
|---|---|
| Current: accounts payable [800,000 + 200,000] | $1,000,000 |
| Long-term: notes payable [400,000 + 0] | 400,000 |
| | 1,400,000 |

Shareholders' equity

| | |
|---|---|
| Common shares [**Purchase Ltd. shares only**] | 3,800,000 |
| Retained earnings | |
| [2,330,000 + 635,000 − **600,000** − 8,000$^U$ − 20,000] | 2,337,000 |
| | 6,137,000 |
| TOTAL LIABILITIES AND SHAREHOLDERS' EQUITY | $7,537,000 |

Note: $^U$ = Upstream

You will notice that we placed a superscript letter U for upstream next to both (1) the eliminated $55,000 upstream inventory sale and cost of goods and (2) the $8,000 unrealized gain relating to the sale, both on the SFP and the SCI. This is to help us keep track of what we're doing. As we build additional complexities into our example, anything we can do to remind ourselves of what the adjustments are for will help us be clear about what we're doing (including also placing a subscript letter D for downstream).

## SCI and SCE/RE

- *Sales revenue*. The combined sales total is $2,700,000. We must eliminate the intercompany sales of $55,000$^U$. The result is consolidated sales of $2,645,000.

- *Dividend income*. We need to eliminate the entire $30,000 dividend income both from the dividend income line item on the SCI and from the dividend declared line item in the retained earnings section of the SCE/RE.

- *Cost of sales*. The combined unadjusted cost of sales is $1,750,000 + $180,000 = $1,930,000. This amount must be decreased by the full amount of the intercompany sales of $55,000$^U$ and increased by the unrealized profit of $8,000$^U$ that is in Purchase Ltd.'s ending inventory.

- *Depreciation expense*. The depreciation expense amount should be increased by the $20,000 depreciation of the fair value increment allocated to Target Ltd.'s buildings and equipment.

- The combined, unadjusted net income of the two companies is $330,000 + $65,000 = $395,000. After adjustment for amortization of fair value adjustments, and after eliminating unrealized profit, consolidated net income drops to $337,000. The total reduction is $58,000. Remember this number—you will see it again shortly!

## Statement of Financial Position

- *Inventory*. Combined inventories must be reduced by the unrealized profit of $8,000$^U$ from intercompany sales.

- *Land*. The fair value increment of $100,000 must be added.

- *Buildings and equipment*. The total fair value increment for Target Ltd.'s buildings and equipment is $200,000. The increase is recognized in the consolidated statements by (1) eliminating Target Ltd.'s date-of-acquisition accumulated depreciation of $150,000 and (2) increasing the buildings and equipment asset account by $50,000. Therefore, only $50,000 is added to the asset account.

- *Accumulated depreciation*. Target Ltd.'s accumulated depreciation at December 31, 20X6, is $185,000. This amount includes the $150,000 accumulated at the date of acquisition plus $35,000 additional depreciation expense for 20X6. The $150,000 must be eliminated—the acquired company's accumulated depreciation at the date of acquisition should not be carried forward. The $35,000 remains, because it represents depreciation *after* the date of acquisition. But the $35,000 represents depreciation on Target Ltd.'s *carrying value*. To reflect depreciation on the *fair* value, the $20,000 amortization of the fair value increment must be added.

■ *Investments.* The investment account must be reduced by the cost of Purchase Ltd.'s investment in Target Ltd. In this example, there are no other investments. In many situations, however, there will be other investments that will *not* be eliminated.

■ *Common shares.* Only Purchase Ltd.'s common shares are included.

■ *Retained earnings* (at year-end). This is the challenging one! We start by adding the two companies' retained earnings together. Next, we must eliminate Target Ltd.'s date-of-acquisition retained earnings ($600,000). Then we make the adjustments that were necessary for the consolidated SCI:

  ■ eliminate the unrealized profit of $8,000$^U$; and
  ■ reduce retained earnings by the amount of additional fair value amortization—$20,000.

There is one SCI adjustment that is missing from the list above relating to the ending retained earnings—dividend income. The reason that it doesn't show up among our adjustments on the retained earnings line of the SFP is that the amount has already washed out. Our adjustment relating to dividend income decreased both the dividend income amount on the SCI by $30,000 and the dividend declared amount in the SCE/RE by $30,000. The net impact on the consolidated ending retained earnings is zero, and thus there is no need for an adjustment to the ending retained earnings balance on the SFP.

Remember the $58,000 decrease in net income from separate-entity to consolidated net income? That consists of two amounts: $30,000 dividend income shown as revenue to Purchase Ltd. but *not as an expense to Target Ltd.*, plus the $28,000 (i.e., $8,000$^U$ + $20,000) in other adjustments to consolidated net income. *When deriving consolidated retained earnings on the SFP, all adjustments on the consolidated SCI and consolidated SCE/RE are made* except *for intercompany dividends.*

You may wonder why we don't simply take the ending consolidated retained earnings amount from the statement of changes in retained earnings and put that amount in the SFP. The answer is that we always must be able to derive the retained earnings independently, to make sure that the statements balance and that we haven't overlooked anything.[4]

## Worksheet Approach

For the illustration of how the worksheet approach applies to our example, please refer to the Companion Website.

---

[4]From a very practical student standpoint, it is also useful to be able to derive consolidated retained earnings without having to work through a consolidated statement of comprehensive income. That is a favourite examination question, both in coursework and in professional examinations!

# Equity-Basis Reporting of Non-Consolidated Subsidiaries

A Canadian publicly accountable parent company will issue *only* consolidated statements as its general purpose financial statements. A private company may or may not choose to issue consolidated statements to its limited group of statement users.

In addition to the consolidated statements, every parent company will also prepare non-consolidated statements. Non-consolidated statements are used for income tax reporting, for a bank's credit analysis, and for the shareholders of a private company.

In non-consolidated statements, the subsidiaries can be reported on either the cost or the equity basis. When the equity method of reporting is used, the parent corporation includes in its net income the parent's share of the subsidiary's earnings. Target Ltd.'s 20X6 separate-entity net income is $65,000, as shown in Exhibit 4.4. Using the equity method, Target Ltd.'s net income (after adjustment) will be reported in Purchase Ltd.'s SCI as a single amount.

The Target Ltd. net income cannot be reported by Purchase Ltd. simply as $65,000, because to do so would ignore the substance of the purchase transaction. Since Purchase Ltd. has acquired control over the assets and liabilities of Target Ltd., the earnings of Target Ltd. must be reported in Purchase Ltd.'s statements *as though the net assets of Target Ltd. had been purchased directly by Purchase Ltd.*

If the assets and liabilities had been purchased directly, then they would have been recorded at their fair values, and goodwill of $100,000 would have been recorded. The fair values are amortized, and any transactions between the Target Ltd. division and the rest of the company will not appear on the financial statements of Purchase Ltd. In other words, it is necessary to adjust the earnings of Target Ltd. to reflect *all of the same adjustments that would be made if Target Ltd. were consolidated.*

Part A of Exhibit 4.7 shows the computation of Target Ltd.'s adjusted earnings. Starting with the Target Ltd. reported net income of $65,000, deductions are made for (1) depreciation of the fair value increment on buildings and equipment, and (2) elimination of the unrealized profit on intercompany sales.

The adjusted Target Ltd. earnings amount to $37,000. Purchase Ltd. owns 100% of the shares of Target Ltd., so Purchase Ltd. will report this entire amount on Purchase Ltd.'s SCI as equity in the earnings of Target Ltd. (the *equity pick-up*).

Part B of Exhibit 4.7 summarizes the impact of the equity method on the investment account. The year-end balance of $1,207,000 will be reported on Purchase Ltd.'s unconsolidated SFP. The investment account reflects (1) the cost of the investment plus (2) the cumulative amount of unremitted adjusted earnings since the date of acquisition.

The adjustments made to Target Ltd.'s net income are made only for *reporting* on Purchase Ltd.'s statements. Target Ltd. will report net income of $65,000 on its own separate-entity financial statements, even though Purchase Ltd.'s equity-basis SCI will report the lesser amount of $37,000 in earnings from Target Ltd.

**Exhibit 4.7** Equity-Basis Reporting of Purchase Ltd.'s Investment in Target Ltd.

| Year Ended December 31, 20X6 | |
| --- | --- |
| **A. Equity in earnings of Target Ltd.:** | |
| Earnings as reported by Target | $ 65,000 |
| Adjustments: | |
| 1. Amortization of fair value increment on buildings and equipment: $200,000 ÷ 10 years | (20,000) |
| 2. Elimination of unrealized profit on upstream sales: $20,000 × 40% gross margin | (8,000) |
| Adjusted Target Ltd. earnings, equity basis | $ 37,000 |
| **B. Investment in Target Ltd.** | |
| Balance, December 31, 20X5 | $1,200,000 |
| Plus Purchase's share of Target's equity basis earnings: | |
| $37,000 × 100% | 37,000 |
| Less dividends received from Target | (30,000) |
| Balance, December 31, 20X6 | $1,207,000 |

Purchase Ltd. may choose to *record* the equity-basis earnings of Target in its accounts, in which case the adjustment will appear as follows:

| | | |
| --- | --- | --- |
| Investment in Target Ltd. | 37,000 | |
| Equity in earnings of Target Ltd. | | 37,000 |

The credit to the SCI account is offset by a debit to increase the investment account. When Target Ltd. declares dividends, the declaration will be recorded as follows:

| | | |
| --- | --- | --- |
| Dividends receivable | 30,000 | |
| Investment in Target Ltd. | | 30,000 |

When the dividends are received, Purchase Ltd. will debit cash and credit the dividends receivable account.

Bear in mind that Purchase Ltd. may not *record* its investment in Target Ltd. on the equity basis, even when it *reports* the investment on the equity basis. As a bookkeeping convenience, the investor usually carries the investment account on the cost basis in its own separate-entity SFP.

**Comparison of Consolidation Versus Equity Reporting** Exhibit 4.8 shows the SFP and SCI for Purchase Ltd. for the year ended December 31, 20X6. The first column shows the results of reporting Target on the equity basis, while the second column shows consolidated statements.

In Purchase Ltd.'s unconsolidated statements, the assets and liabilities are only those of Purchase Ltd., and the revenues and expenses are also only those generated or incurred by Purchase Ltd. One of the assets of Purchase Ltd. is the investment in Target Ltd., which appears as a non-current asset on the SFP. Similarly, the SCI shows Purchase Ltd.'s equity in the earnings of Target Ltd. as a separate item.

**Exhibit 4.8** Comparing Equity-Basis Reporting and Consolidation

| Purchase Ltd. Statement of Consolidated Income Year Ended December 31, 20X6 | Equity basis | Consolidated |
|---|---|---|
| Sales revenue | $2,400,000 | $2,645,000 |
| Equity in earnings of Target Ltd. | 37,000 | — |
| | 2,437,000 | 2,645,000 |
| Operating Expenses: | | |
| Cost of sales | 1,750,000 | 1,883,000 |
| Depreciation expense | 100,000 | 155,000 |
| Other expenses | 250,000 | 270,000 |
| | 2,100,000 | 2,308,000 |
| NET INCOME | $ 337,000 | $ 337,000 |

**Statement of Changes in Equity—Retained Earnings Section**
**Year Ended December 31, 20X6**

| | | |
|---|---|---|
| Retained earnings, December 31, 20X5 | $2,000,000 | $2,000,000 |
| Net income | 337,000 | 337,000 |
| Dividends declared | — | — |
| Retained earnings, December 31, 20X6 | $2,337,000 | $2,337,000 |

| Purchase Ltd. Statement of Financial Position December 31, 20X6 | Equity basis | Consolidated |
|---|---|---|
| **ASSETS** | | |
| Current assets: | | |
| Cash | $ 980,000 | $1,080,000 |
| Accounts receivable | 2,200,000 | 2,450,000 |
| Inventory | 250,000 | 312,000 |
| | 3,430,000 | 3,842,000 |
| Property, plant, and equipment: | | |
| Land | 1,000,000 | 1,400,000 |
| Buildings and equipment | 3,000,000 | 3,550,000 |
| Accumulated depreciation | (1,300,000) | (1,355,000) |
| | 2,700,000 | 3,595,000 |
| Other Assets: | | |
| Investments | 1,207,000 | — |
| Goodwill | — | 100,000 |
| TOTAL ASSETS | $7,337,000 | $7,537,000 |
| **LIABILITIES AND SHAREHOLDERS' EQUITY** | | |
| Liabilities: | | |
| Current: accounts payable | $ 800,000 | $1,000,000 |
| Long-term: notes payable | 400,000 | 400,000 |
| | 1,200,000 | 1,400,000 |
| Shareholders' equity: | | |
| Common shares | 3,800,000 | 3,800,000 |
| Retained earnings | 2,337,000 | 2,337,000 |
| | 6,137,000 | 6,137,000 |
| TOTAL LIABILITIES AND SHAREHOLDERS' EQUITY | $7,337,000 | $7,537,000 |

When we consolidate Purchase Ltd. and Target Ltd., however, we eliminate the investment in the Target Ltd. account on the SFP and instead show all of the individual assets and liabilities of Target Ltd. that the investment represents. The shareholders' equity accounts are exactly the same in both columns. The total net asset value of Purchase Ltd. is not altered by the process of consolidation; all that happens is that the investment account is disaggregated so that the readers of Purchase Ltd.'s financial statements can see the total resources (of both Purchase Ltd. and Target Ltd.) that are under the control of the management of Purchase Ltd.

The unconsolidated SCI includes the net equity-basis earnings of Target Ltd. on a single line. Upon consolidation, that line disappears and the net amount thereof ($37,000) is disaggregated by including the revenues and expenses of Target Ltd. in the main body of the statement, along with those of Purchase Ltd. The consolidated net income is exactly the same as the unconsolidated net income of Purchase Ltd., since the investment in Target Ltd. has been reported on the equity basis.

The equity-basis investment account is increased by the $37,000 equity pick-up of Target Ltd.'s earnings, minus the $30,000 dividends received from Target Ltd. As a result, the investment account is shown at $1,207,000 in the equity-basis column.

The equity-basis investment account and equity-in-earnings account summarize the investor's interest in the net assets and earnings from operations of the investee corporation in a single line on the financial statements of the investor. Therefore the equity method is often referred to as **one-line consolidation** and also as the *consolidation method of equity reporting*. The comprehensive income and the shareholders' equity are the same on the equity-basis unconsolidated statements as they are on the consolidated statements.

### Concept Check 4-1

1. Why should acquisition-related fair value adjustments be amortized in subsequent consolidated financial statements?

2. Why does the unrealized profit on the intercompany sale of assets have to be eliminated when we prepare consolidated financial statements?

LO **1**
Consolidate wholly owned subsidiaries in the first and second years after acquisition

LO **6**
Report non-consolidated subsidiaries on the equity basis

## 4.3 DISCONTINUED OPERATIONS

Under the equity method of accounting, an investor is required to include its share of the profit or loss of its associates as a separate line item in its SCI. Similarly, the investor's share of its associates' other comprehensive income must also be shown separately in the investor's statement of other comprehensive income.

However, it would be rare for an associate company's discontinued operation to qualify as a discontinued operation of the investor. Under IFRS 5, a discontinued operation is defined as a component of an entity that either (1) has been disposed of or (2) is classified as held for sale, *and*

1. represents a separate major line of business or geographical area of operations; or

2. is part of a single coordinated plan to dispose of a separate major line of business or geographical area of operations; or

3. is a subsidiary acquired exclusively with a view to resale.

Therefore, the discontinued operations of an associate will not normally constitute a discontinued operation of the investor. Nevertheless, to provide users of financial statements with adequate information, IAS 28 requires an investor to separately disclose its share of any discontinued operations of its associates.

Similarly, the discontinued operations of a subsidiary should be reported separately *only if the items represent discontinued operations to the parent*, by satisfying the requirements at the level of the parent.

Suppose that a subsidiary discontinues its major line of business. The subsidiary will report the gain or loss as a discontinued operation in its own separate-entity SCI. However, suppose also that the parent company has similar operations of its own or in other subsidiaries. From the point of view of the parent corporation, the subsidiary's discontinuance is just one of many similar lines of business. In that case, the parent would report the gain or loss as a normal operating activity.

For example, think about a parent company that has several retail clothing subsidiaries. If one subsidiary ceases operations, that is big news for the subsidiary but not for the parent. The parent will still be in the retail clothing business, even though one subsidiary has left the business. The retail clothing business line continues for the parent and therefore is not a discontinued operation for consolidated financial reporting.

In contrast to the discontinued operations of a subsidiary discussed above, the complete discontinuance of business by an associate or subsidiary may very well satisfy the requirements for treatment as a discontinued operation of the parent. In such cases, the discontinued operation of the associate or subsidiary is presented separately as a discontinued operation in the parent's financial statements.

## 4.4 CONSOLIDATION IN SECOND SUBSEQUENT YEAR

### Basic Information

Before we generalize the approach to preparing consolidated financial statements (in Chapter 6), we will extend this example for one more year. The two companies' financial statements for the year ended December 31, 20X7, are shown in Exhibit 4.9. Additional information is as follows:

1. Target Ltd. had sales of $60,000 to Purchase Ltd. (i.e., upstream); Target Ltd.'s 20X7 gross margin was 45%; $10,000 (sales price) of the goods are in Purchase Ltd.'s inventory on December 31, 20X7. Unrealized upstream profit therefore is $10,000 × 45% = $4,500^U$.

2. Purchase Ltd. had sales of $20,000 to Target Ltd. (i.e., downstream); Purchase Ltd.'s 20X7 gross margin was 30%; $6,000 (sales price) of the goods sold to Target Ltd. are in Target Ltd.'s 20X7 ending inventory. Unrealized downstream profit is $6,000 × 30% = $1,800_D$.

3. Purchase Ltd. borrowed $500,000 from Target Ltd. on December 29, 20X7. Both companies have reported this as a current amount on their individual separate-entity SFPs.

4. Target Ltd. sold its land to Purchase Ltd. for $450,000. The land originally cost Target Ltd. $300,000, and its fair value at the date of Purchase Ltd.'s acquisition of Target Ltd. was $400,000. The gain on the sale ($150,000^U$) is separately disclosed as an item of revenue on Target Ltd.'s SCI.

LO **1**
Consolidate wholly owned subsidiaries in the first and second years after acquisition

LO **2**
Eliminate transactions that occur between a parent and its subsidiaries

LO **3**
Eliminate unrealized gains on upstream and downstream sales of inventory and capital assets between a subsidiary and a parent

LO **4**
Recognize profits realized in the current year on upstream sale of inventory in the previous year

LO **5**
Amortize fair value adjustments

LO **6**
Report non-consolidated subsidiaries on the equity basis

**Exhibit 4.9** Separate-Entity Financial Statements for 20X7

## Statements of Comprehensive Income
### Year Ended December 31, 20X7

| | Purchase Ltd. | Target Ltd. |
|---|---|---|
| Revenue: | | |
| Sales | $3,000,000 | $ 400,000 |
| Dividend income | 20,000 | — |
| Gain on sale of land | — | 150,000 |
| | 3,020,000 | 550,000 |
| Expenses: | | |
| Cost of sales | 2,100,000 | 220,000 |
| Depreciation expense | 100,000 | 35,000 |
| Other expenses | 440,000 | 75,000 |
| | 2,640,000 | 330,000 |
| NET INCOME | $ 380,000 | $ 220,000 |

## Statements of Changes in Equity—Retained Earnings Section
### Year Ended December 31, 20X7

| | Purchase Ltd. | Target Ltd. |
|---|---|---|
| Retained earnings, December 31, 20X6 | $2,330,000 | $ 635,000 |
| Net income | 380,000 | 220,000 |
| Dividends declared | (135,000) | (20,000) |
| Retained earnings, December 31, 20X7 | $2,575,000 | $ 835,000 |

## Statements of Financial Position December 31, 20X7

| | Purchase Ltd. | Target Ltd. |
|---|---|---|
| ASSETS | | |
| Current assets: | | |
| Cash | $ 490,000 | $ 70,000 |
| Accounts receivable | 1,900,000 | 275,000 |
| Note receivable | — | 500,000 |
| Inventory | 300,000 | 60,000 |
| | 2,690,000 | 905,000 |
| Property, plant, and equipment: | | |
| Land | 1,450,000 | |
| Buildings and equipment | 3,800,000 | 500,000 |
| Accumulated depreciation | (1,400,000) | (220,000) |
| | 3,850,000 | 280,000 |
| Other assets: | | |
| Investments (at cost) | 1,200,000 | — |
| TOTAL ASSETS | $7,740,000 | $1,185,000 |

| LIABILITIES AND SHAREHOLDERS' EQUITY | | |
|---|---|---|
| Current liabilities: | | |
| Accounts payable | $ 515,000 | $ 150,000 |
| Note payable | 500,000 | — |
| Long-term: notes payable | 350,000 | — |
| | 1,365,000 | 150,000 |
| Shareholders' equity | | |
| Common shares | 3,800,000 | 200,000 |
| Retained earnings | 2,575,000 | 835,000 |
| | 6,375,000 | 1,035,000 |
| TOTAL LIABILITIES AND SHAREHOLDERS' EQUITY | $7,740,000 | $1,185,000 |

Our current example on consolidation (that is, at the end of the second year following acquisition), in addition to illustrating all the eliminations and adjustments discussed previously, will also illustrate the following two consolidation-related issues:

- elimination of unrealized profit on downstream sales; and
- recognition of the profit realized in the current year on upstream sales made in the previous year.

These issues will expand our MEAR analysis by another step. The next two sections will discuss these two issues.

## Eliminating Unrealized Profit on Downstream Sales

No special complication arises when a downstream sale is made by a parent to its 100%-owned subsidiary. In such a case, the treatment accorded to the unrealized profit is identical to the treatment, discussed previously, accorded to unrealized profits relating to upstream sales of assets. Things get a bit more complicated when there is a downstream sale by a parent to a *non*-wholly owned subsidiary. We will discuss this issue in greater depth in Chapter 5, when we discuss consolidation of non-wholly owned subsidiaries.

## Recognition of Profit Realized in Current Year on Intercompany Sales Made in Previous Year

In our example on consolidation at the end of 20X6, we had an $8,000 unrealized gain on the upstream sale of inventory. The continuation of our example in 20X7 is silent on what happened to the unsold portion of the inventory and to the related $8,000 unrealized gain during 20X7. That does not pose a problem. As a computational convenience, unrealized intercompany profits on inventory at the end of one year are automatically assumed to have been fully realized during the following year.

Therefore, a suitable adjustment to recognize this profit realization should be made as of the *beginning* of the second year. To the extent that unrealized profits from year-end

20X6 remain in the ending inventory of 20X7, the independent adjustment at the *end* of the second year will take care of unrealized profits remaining at the end of 20X7 regardless of whether those unrealized profits arose from 20X6 intercompany sales or from 20X7 sales. Consequently, the related profit, which was treated as *unrealized* during consolidation in the previous year, should now be treated as having been *realized* in the current year.

We increased the cost of goods sold account by $8,000 in 20X6 to reflect the fact that the $8,000 was unrealized at the end of the year. Now that the $8,000 is assumed to be realized, we should reflect that fact by decreasing the cost of goods sold by $8,000. What about the offset?

To find the answer to this question, remember that consolidation-related eliminations and adjustments are made only in working papers and are not recorded anywhere. Hence, they do not carry over to later years. Consequently, in these later years, we have to capture the cumulative impact of consolidation-related adjustments and eliminations made in earlier years.

In our example, we increased the cost of goods sold of 20X6 by $8,000, which had the effect of decreasing net income by $8,000 and, consequently, the ending SCE/RE of 20X6 by $8,000. The adjustment necessary now, in 20X7, to capture the cumulative impact of the above adjustment made in 20X6, requires us to decrease SCE/RE by $8,000. Therefore, the offset for decreasing the cost of goods sold of 20X7 by $8,000 will be to decrease beginning SCE/RE of 20X7 by $8,000.

Unrealized gains can also arise from intercompany sales of assets other than inventory. The treatment of such other unrealized gains is similar to the treatment of unrealized inventory gains. We will discuss this issue later in the chapter as we further develop our continuing example. However, the main discussion of unrealized gains on assets other than inventory is deferred to Chapter 6.

## Direct Method

The MEAR steps listed previously in Exhibit 4.5 relate to acquisition and current-period adjustments and eliminations. These steps are no longer sufficient when consolidation is occurring in the second or later years after acquisition. Now we have to make adjustments and eliminations relating to three time periods: (1) the period of acquisition; (2) the period(s) following acquisition but prior to the current period; and (3) the current period. To achieve the above objective we need a modified set of MEAR steps for phase 3. Exhibit 4.10 shows the MEAR steps modified for consolidating a wholly owned subsidiary in the second or later year following acquisition.

The **M**easure step remains unchanged and we will not repeat it here. However, the **E**liminate and **A**mortize steps will produce different results since we are now consolidating at the end of the *second* year after acquisition. The current year now is 20X7, while 20X6 is the previous year. In contrast, in our previous example, 20X6 was the current year. Therefore, at this stage of our example, the **E**liminate and **A**mortize steps relate to current year *as well as prior year(s)* adjustments and eliminations. Specifically:

1. The **E**liminate step adds a third step to the two from before:

    **a.** Identify and eliminate all intercompany transactions and balances.

**Exhibit 4.10** MEAR Steps to Consolidation at the End of the Second Year or Later Years Following Acquisition

| Consolidation Steps | Acquisition-Related | Relating to First Year Following Acquisition | Relating to Following Years |
|---|---|---|---|
| 1. Measure | ■ Calculate cost and fair value adjustments (FVA) <br> ■ Allocate FVA | | |
| 2. Eliminate and recognize | ■ Eliminate parent's investment account and subsidiary's share equity accounts | | |
| | | ■ Eliminate intercompany transactions and balances <br> ■ Eliminate unrealized profits | |
| | | | ■ Recognize realized profits |
| 3. Amortize | | ■ Amortize FVAs <br> ■ Recognize impairments | |
| | | | ■ Recognize cumulative Impairments |

b. Calculate and eliminate the *unrealized* profit (or loss) relating to the sale of inventory and other assets in the current period.

c. Calculate and recognize the profit (or loss) realized in the current year on the sale of inventory and other assets in previous periods.

2. The **A**mortize step now requires that we:

a. Amortize the FVA allocated to the various identifiable assets and liabilities (i.e., the fair value adjustments relating to those assets and liabilities) in the current and previous periods.

b. Write off any impairment of goodwill and other intangible assets with indeterminate useful lives in the current and previous periods.

c. Find the balance of the allocated FVA remaining unamortized or unimpaired at the end of the current period.

We will now perform these two steps for consolidation at the end of the second year after acquisition.

## Eliminate

**Intercompany Transactions and Balances**   The schedule of adjustments for 20X7 is as follows:

| | |
|---|---|
| Upstream sale by Target Ltd. | (60,000) |
| Downstream sale by Purchase Ltd. | (20,000) |
| Dividend income of Purchase Ltd. and dividends declared by Target Ltd. | (20,000) |
| Note receivable of Target Ltd. and note payable of Purchase Ltd. | (500,000) |

In our illustration, in 20X7, there are four intercompany items that need to be eliminated.

1. Target Ltd. sold $60,000 worth of goods to Purchase Ltd. We need to eliminate $60,000 from both sales and cost of goods sold.

2. Purchase Ltd. sold $20,000 worth of goods to Target Ltd. We need to eliminate this $20,000 from both sales and cost of goods sold.

3. Purchase Ltd. recognized its share of $20,000 of the dividends declared by Target Ltd. as dividend income. In this example, Target is a 100%-owned subsidiary, and thus the entire $20,000 dividend is Target Ltd.'s "share." We must eliminate this $20,000 from both dividend income and dividends declared.

4. Purchase Ltd. borrowed $500,000 from Target Ltd. on December 29, 20X7. We need to eliminate the associated note receivable and note payable at the time of consolidation. The example does not mention any interest rate attached to the loan. Furthermore, the loan occurred only on December 29. Therefore, we can disregard any associated interest as immaterial. Otherwise, we would have had to eliminate the associated interest income and interest expense that may have been recognized by Target Ltd. and Purchase Ltd., respectively.

## Unrealized and Realized Profits

| | |
|---|---|
| Realized profit on upstream sale of inventory in the previous year | 8,000 |
| Unrealized profit on upstream sale of inventory in the current year | (4,500) |
| Unrealized profit on downstream sale of inventory in the current year | (1,800) |
| Unrealized gain on sale of land by Target Ltd. to Purchase Ltd. | (150,000) |

In our illustration, we have one source of realized profit, two sources of unrealized profit, and one source of unrealized gain. Remember that in 20X6 we had $8,000 of unrealized profit on the upstream sale of inventory, which we eliminated by increasing the cost of goods sold of 20X6 and decreasing the ending inventory of 20X6, respectively, by that amount. The profit was unrealized because the corresponding goods were still with Purchase Ltd. at the end of the year. Now, in 20X7, these goods are assumed to have been sold to an outside party and therefore the associated profits are now realized.

The ending 20X6 inventory is also the beginning 20X7 inventory. Purchase Ltd. would have included the unadjusted beginning inventory in its cost of sales calculation in the current year; from the consolidation point of view, that results in *overstating* opening inventory by $8,000 and, consequently, *overstating* cost of sales by the same amount. Therefore, we must *reduce* consolidated cost of sales by $8,000 to account for the realization of the profits in 20X7.

We should increase the cost of goods sold of 20X7 and decrease the ending inventory of 20X7 by $4,500 and $1,800 to eliminate the unrealized profits on the upstream and downstream sale of inventory, respectively, this year. The underlying logic is identical to the logic underlying the elimination of the unrealized profit on the upstream sale of inventory in 20X6.

Finally, Target Ltd. sold its land to Purchase Ltd. during the year for a gain of $150,000. However, the land is still owned within the consolidated entity; the associated gain is unrealized and therefore has to be eliminated.

## Amortize

| | FVA allocated | Amortization period | Amortization per year | Amortization/ impairment loss during previous periods | Amortization/ impairment loss during 20X7 | Balance of FVA remaining at the end of 20X7 |
|---|---|---|---|---|---|---|
| Land | $100,000 | — | | | — | $100,000 |
| Building and equipment | 200,000 | 10 | $20,000 | $20,000 | $20,000 | 160,000 |
| Goodwill | 100,000 | — | | | — | 100,000 |
| Total | $400,000 | | | $20,000 | $20,000 | $360,000 |

From the schedule above, we can see that we need to recognize a total amortization/ impairment loss adjustment of $20,000 in the previous year (as explained in greater detail below) and a similar adjustment in the current year.

We can also see that the balance of the FVA adjustment to be added to the carrying values of the parent and subsidiary is $360,000, consisting of increases to land of $100,000, to building and equipment of $160,000, and to goodwill of $100,000. Note that the adjustment for building and equipment of $160,000 is the result of the initial FVA allocated to building and equipment of $200,000 minus the $40,000 depreciation adjustment required in total over the previous and current year.

Recall that in our earlier discussion we said that all consolidation-related adjustments or eliminations are made only in the consolidation-related working papers and are not recorded on either company's books. Therefore, these adjustments do not carry over to later years. Consequently, every time we consolidate subsequent to the date of acquisition, we need to either (1) replicate those adjustments and eliminations made in previous years, or (2) capture their cumulative impact with suitable but different cumulative adjustments.

Now we will illustrate the second type of adjustments—adjustments required to capture the cumulative impact of adjustments and eliminations made in prior years. Such adjustments are naturally made to the opening retained earnings of the year, since retained earnings represent the cumulative impact of prior years' operations.

In our current example, we have to adjust the opening retained earnings for the impact of two prior years' adjustments, as follows:

| | |
|---|---|
| Amortization/impairment loss adjustment of $20,000 pertaining to 20X6 | (20,000) |
| Unrealized profit on upstream sale of inventory in 20X6 | (8,000) |

**Amortization/Impairment Loss Adjustment**  The first item is the $20,000 amortization or depreciation expense adjustment made in 20X6 relating to the fair value increment allocated to buildings and equipment. This amortization expense adjustment would have decreased the consolidated income of 20X6 and, consequently, the ending consolidated retained earnings of 20X6 by $20,000. However, this decrease will not be reflected in the opening book retained earnings in 20X7 of either Target Ltd. or Purchase Ltd.

Therefore, at the time of consolidation in 20X7, to capture the impact of this prior-year amortization adjustment, we now have to adjust the beginning consolidated retained earnings of 20X7 by $20,000. If we were to extend our example to 20X8, and the facts remained the same, we would need to adjust the consolidated opening retained earnings balance of 20X8 by $40,000: $20,000 for the amortization expense adjustment relating to 20X6 and another $20,000 for the amortization expense adjustment relating to 20X7.

**Unrealized Profit**   The schedule above relates to the elimination of the unrealized profit of $8,000 on the upstream sale of inventory in 20X6. This elimination would have reduced the consolidated income of 20X6 and the ending retained earnings of 20X6 by $8,000. Again, to capture the impact of this prior-year elimination, we have to adjust the opening retained earnings of 20X7 by $8,000.

Recall that we adjusted the 20X7 cost of goods sold by reducing it by the same $8,000. We did this because the inventory in question was sold in 20X7 and thus the $8,000 became realized in 20X7. The impact will be to increase both (1) 20X7 consolidated income and (2) 20X7 ending retained earnings by $8,000. The net effect of the combination of the $8,000 reduction of the opening retained earnings balance and the increase by $8,000 of the ending retained earnings balance on the final ending retained earnings balance on the SFP is zero.

The impact of the series of adjustments relating to the upstream sale of inventory in 20X6 was to defer recognizing the profits relating to such inventory from 20X6 to 20X7, the period in which the profit was actually realized by the consolidated entity. This is an example of the interperiod allocation of profits.

Now we have all the ingredients required to carry out the actual consolidation. Again, we will go down the SCI and SFP and insert the correct amounts on a line-by-line basis.

**SCI and SCE/RE**   The consolidated statement of comprehensive income is shown in Exhibit 4.11. The amounts that require adjustment are as follows:

■ *Sales*. The two companies' combined sales of $3,400,000 must be adjusted for the intercompany sales. In 20X7, there were upstream sales (Target Ltd. to Purchase Ltd.) of $60,000 and downstream sales (Purchase Ltd. to Target Ltd.) of $20,000. The sum of these amounts must be removed from sales revenue: $60,000^U + $20,000_D = $80,000.

■ *Dividend income*. We need to eliminate the entire $20,000 dividend income both from the dividend income line item on the SCI and from the dividend declared line item on the SCE/RE.

■ *Gain on sale of land*. The $150,000^U unrealized gain on the sale of land by Target Ltd. to Purchase Ltd. in 20X7 must be eliminated.

■ *Cost of sales*. Cost of sales must also be reduced by the $80,000 ($60,000^U + $20,000_D) of intercompany sales. Some of the goods sold from one company to the other are still in inventory. Therefore, we must also adjust cost of sales by increasing it for the unrealized profit of $4,500^U in Purchase Ltd.'s year-end inventory and of $1,800_D in Target Ltd.'s year-end inventory. Finally, we must adjust cost of sales by decreasing it for the realized profit of $8,000^U from the previous year's upstream sale of inventory.

■ *Depreciation expense*. We must continue to amortize the fair value increment on Target Ltd.'s buildings and equipment. As in 20X6, the amortization is $200,000 ÷ 10 years, or $20,000. This amount is added to the depreciation expense.

■ *Dividends declared*. Target Ltd.'s $20,000 in dividends paid to Purchase Ltd. must be eliminated.

**Exhibit 4.11** Purchase Ltd. Statement of Comprehensive Income (Direct Method)

| Consolidated Statement of Comprehensive Income Year Ended December 31, 20X7 | |
|---|---:|
| **Revenue:** | |
| Sales revenue [3,000,000 + 400,000 − **60,000$^U$ − 20,000$_D$**] | $3,320,000 |
| Dividend income [20,000 + 0 − **20,000**] | — |
| Gain on sale of land [0 + 150,000 − **150,000$^U$**] | — |
| | 3,320,000 |
| **Operating expenses:** | |
| Cost of sales | |
| [2,100,000 + 220,000 − **60,000$^U$ − 20,000$_D$ + 4,500$^U$ + 1,800$_D$ − 8,000$^U$**] | 2,238,300 |
| Depreciation expense [100,000 + 35,000 **+ 20,000**] | 155,000 |
| Other expenses [440,000 + 75,000] | 515,000 |
| | 2,908,300 |
| **NET INCOME AND COMPREHENSIVE INCOME** | $ 411,700 |
| **Consolidated Statement of Changes in Equity—Retained Earnings Section Year Ended December 31, 20X7** | |
| Retained earnings, December 31, 20X6 | |
| [2,330,000 + 635,000 − **600,000 − 20,000 − 8,000$^U$**] | $2,337,000 |
| Comprehensive income | 411,700 |
| Dividends declared [135,000 + 20,000 − **20,000**] | (135,000) |
| Retained earnings, December 31, 20X7 | $2,613,700 |
| $_D$ = Downstream | |
| $^U$ = Upstream | |

■ *Opening retained earnings.* The opening balances (i.e., the December 31, 20X6, balances) must be adjusted for two things: (1) Target Ltd.'s retained earnings balance at the date of acquisition and (2) adjustments to earnings since the date of acquisition to December 31, 20X6. The 20X6 earnings adjustments were for $20,000 amortization of the fair value increment and for $8,000$^U$ unrealized profit on intercompany inventory sales in that year. Both of these amounts are subtracted from the opening retained earnings to get the correct, adjusted beginning balance.

**Statement of Financial Position** The consolidated SFP is shown in Exhibit 4.12. Adjustments are as follows:

■ *Note receivable.* The intercompany receivable of $500,000 that is included on Target Ltd.'s books must be eliminated.

■ *Inventory.* The unrealized profits from the upstream and downstream sales of $4,500$^U$ and $1,800$_D$, respectively, embedded in the closing inventory of Purchase Ltd. and Target Ltd., respectively, must be eliminated.

■ *Land.* Target Ltd.'s land has been sold to Purchase Ltd. Target Ltd. recorded a gain of $150,000$^U$ on the sale. This is an intercompany unrealized profit that must be eliminated. However, there was a fair value increment of $100,000 on the land at the date of purchase. This FVI still must be added, even though legal title to the land has now been transferred from Target Ltd. to Purchase Ltd. In a consolidated statement, it doesn't matter which company actually owns it.

**Exhibit 4.12** Purchase Ltd. Consolidated Statement of Financial Position (Direct Method)

| Consolidated Statement of Financial Position December 31, 20X7 | |
|---|---:|
| ASSETS | |
| Current assets: | |
| Cash [490,000 + 70,000] | $ 560,000 |
| Accounts receivable [1,900,000 + 275,000] | 2,175,000 |
| Note receivable [0 + 500,000 – **500,000**] | — |
| Inventory [300,000 + 60,000 – **4,500$^U$** – **1,800$_D$**] | 353,700 |
| | 3,088,700 |
| Property, plant, and equipment: | |
| Land [1,450,000 + 0 + **100,000** – **150,000$^U$**] | 1,400,000 |
| Buildings and equipment [3,800,000 + 500,000 + **50,000**] | 4,350,000 |
| Accumulated depreciation [1,400,000 + 220,000 – **150,000** + **40,000**] | (1,510,000) |
| | 4,240,000 |
| Other assets: | |
| Investments [1,200,000 + 0 – **1,200,000**] | — |
| Goodwill | 100,000 |
| TOTAL ASSETS | $7,428,700 |
| Liabilities and shareholders' equity | |
| Current liabilities: | |
| Accounts payable [515,000 + 150,000] | $ 665,000 |
| Note payable [500,000 + 0 – **500,000**] | — |
| Long-term liability: notes payable [350,000 + 0] | 350,000 |
| | 1,015,000 |
| Shareholders' Equity: | |
| Common shares [Purchase Ltd. shares only] | 3,800,000 |
| Retained earnings [2,575,000 + 835,000 – **600,000** – **150,000$^U$** – **4,500$^U$** – **1,800$_D$** – (20,000 × 2)] | 2,613,700 |
| | 6,413,700 |
| TOTAL LIABILITIES AND SHAREHOLDERS' EQUITY | $7,428,700 |

$_D$ = Downstream
$^U$ = Upstream

- *Buildings and equipment.* The date-of-acquisition FVI of $50,000 must be added, just as in 20X6.

- *Accumulated depreciation.* Target Ltd.'s date-of-acquisition accumulated depreciation of $150,000 is eliminated; two years' worth of FVI amortization of $20,000 per year is added.

- *Current note payable.* Purchase Ltd.'s payables include the $500,000 owed to Target Ltd. This intercompany balance must be eliminated.

- *Common shares.* As usual, only the parent's shares are reported on the consolidated statement of financial position.

■ *Retained earnings*. Consolidated retained earnings is calculated by starting with the book balances of the two companies and then:

1. subtracting Target Ltd.'s date-of-acquisition retained earnings;

2. subtracting year-end unrealized profits; and

3. subtracting the cumulative amount of FVI amortization since the date of acquisition (i.e., $20,000 × 2 years).

Notice, as we discussed earlier, that it is not necessary to adjust for the unrealized profit in the beginning inventory when we compute the ending consolidated retained earnings. Target Ltd.'s separate-entity retained earnings already includes the $8,000 previously unrealized profit from 20X6, and by *not* making any adjustment, we permit it to flow through to consolidated retained earnings as a now-realized amount.

Of course, we are assuming that the beginning inventory has been sold during the period. This is the normal assumption; we only need to be told how much of the intercompany sales is still in *ending* inventory each year (and the relevant gross margin percentage) to make the adjustments for unrealized year-end profit, regardless of which year the intercompany sales occurred.

**"Proving" Retained Earnings**   It is wise to calculate the closing balance of the consolidated retained earnings on the SFP at the time of every consolidation. As we observed earlier in the chapter, we could have obtained the year-end consolidated retained earnings from the bottom of the statement of changes in retained earnings, or simply by treating retained earnings as a "plug" once we had calculated all of the other balances.

However, it is useful to be able to derive closing retained earnings directly from information given, rather than going through the whole process of constructing a consolidated SCI. And "plugs" are always dangerous—there is no way to tell if the SFP really is in balance. Purchase Ltd.'s consolidated retained earnings figure for December 31, 20X7, is as follows:

| | |
|---|---:|
| Purchase Ltd.'s separate-entity retained earnings | $2,575,000 |
| Target Ltd.'s separate-entity retained earnings | 835,000 |
| Target Ltd.'s date-of-acquisition retained earnings | (600,000) |
| Unrealized profit on sale of land | (150,000) |
| Unrealized upstream profit in ending inventory | (4,500) |
| Unrealized downstream profit in ending inventory | (1,800) |
| Two years' amortization of FVI in buildings and equipment | (40,000) |
| Purchase Ltd.'s consolidated retained earnings | $2,613,700 |

## Worksheet Approach

As usual, the worksheet approach of consolidation two years after acquisition is available on the Companion Website.

## Completed Consolidated Financial Statements

Exhibit 4.13 and Exhibit 4.14 present the complete consolidated financial statements for Purchase Ltd. as of December 31, 20X7. Since financial statements should be comparative statements, the 20X7 statements also include the amounts for 20X6. A complete set of financial statements must include a cash flow statement. Exhibit 4.15 illustrates a cash flow statement.

The preparation of a consolidated cash flow statement involves no particular challenges. The statement can be prepared by combining the cash flow statements of the separate entities and eliminating intercompany transactions. Alternatively, you can prepare the statement directly from the consolidated SCI, SFP, and SCE/RE in exactly the same manner as you would from any other set of financial statements.

## Note Disclosure

While Exhibit 4.13 through Exhibit 4.15 do present the complete set of statements, they do not present the notes thereto. The notes should contain detailed disclosure of Purchase Ltd.'s acquisition of Target Ltd., as we discussed at the end of Chapter 3.

In practice, there is considerable variation in the extent of disclosure made by Canadian companies about business combinations. One possible reason for the relative lack of disclosure could be the absence of materiality. Reality Check 4–2 summarizes results from a research study on the various reasons and causes of management's disclosures relating to business combinations.

## Equity-Basis Reporting in Second Subsequent Year

When a subsidiary is reported under the equity method in the second subsequent year after acquisition, in addition to suitably accounting for the equity in the current year's earnings of the subsidiary, we need to suitably adjust the opening retained earnings of the parent for the adjusted change in retained earnings of the subsidiary in the previous year. Exhibit 4.16 shows all necessary computations relating to the reporting of Target Ltd. in 20X7 under the equity method.

**Exhibit 4.13** Purchase Ltd. Consolidated SCI and SCE/RE

| Consolidated Statement of Comprehensive Income Years Ended December 31 | | |
| --- | --- | --- |
| | 20X7 | 20X6 |
| SALES REVENUE | $3,320,000 | $2,645,000 |
| Operating expenses: | | |
| Cost of sales | 2,238,300 | 1,883,000 |
| Depreciation expense | 155,000 | 155,000 |
| Other expenses | 515,000 | 270,000 |
| | 2,908,300 | 2,308,000 |
| NET INCOME AND COMPREHENSIVE INCOME | $ 411,700 | $ 337,000 |
| Consolidated Statement of Changes in Equity—Retained Earnings Section Years Ended December 31 | | |
| | 20X7 | 20X6 |
| Retained earnings, January 1 | $2,337,000 | $2,000,000 |
| Comprehensive income | 411,700 | 337,000 |
| Dividends declared | (135,000) | — |
| Retained earnings, December 31 | $2,613,700 | $2,337,000 |

**Exhibit 4.14** Purchase Ltd. Consolidated Statement of Financial Position

| Consolidated Statement of Comprehensive Income<br>Years Ended December 31 | | |
| --- | --- | --- |
| | 20X7 | 20X6 |
| ASSETS | | |
| Current assets: | | |
| Cash | $ 560,000 | $1,080,000 |
| Accounts receivable | 2,175,000 | 2,450,000 |
| Inventory | 353,700 | 312,000 |
| | 3,088,700 | 3,842,000 |
| Property, plant, and equipment: | | |
| Land | 1,400,000 | 1,400,000 |
| Buildings and equipment | 4,350,000 | 3,550,000 |
| Accumulated depreciation | (1,510,000) | (1,355,000) |
| | 4,240,000 | 3,595,000 |
| Other assets: | | |
| Goodwill | 100,000 | 100,000 |
| TOTAL ASSETS | $7,428,700 | $7,537,000 |
| Liabilities and shareholders' equity | | |
| Liabilities: | | |
| Current: accounts payable | $ 665,000 | $1,000,000 |
| Long-term: notes payable | 350,000 | 400,000 |
| | 1,015,000 | 1,400,000 |
| Shareholders' equity: | | |
| Common shares | 3,800,000 | 3,800,000 |
| Retained earnings | 2,613,700 | 2,337,000 |
| | 6,413,700 | 6,137,000 |
| TOTAL LIABILITIES AND SHAREHOLDERS' EQUITY | $7,428,700 | $7,537,000 |

Part A of Exhibit 4.16 shows the computation of Target's adjusted earnings in 20X7. Target Ltd.'s reported earnings of $220,000 is adjusted for (1) the amortization in 20X7 of the fair value increment allocated to buildings; (2) profit realized in 20X7 on the upstream sale of inventory made in 20X6; (3) unrealized profit on the upstream and downstream sales of inventory in 20X7; and (4) unrealized gain on the upstream sale of land in 20X7. Since Purchase Ltd. owns 100% of Target Ltd., Purchase Ltd. will report in its separate-entity SCI 100% of the adjusted earnings of Target Ltd. of $51,700 as equity in the earnings of Target Ltd.

Part B of Exhibit 4.16 shows the computation of the separate-entity net income of Purchase Ltd. under the equity method. Notice that the separate-entity net income of

**Exhibit 4.15** Consolidated Cash Flow Statement

| Years Ended December 31 | | |
|---|---|---|
| | 20X7 | 20X6 |
| OPERATING ACTIVITIES | | |
| Consolidated net income, as reported | $ 411,700 | $ 337,000 |
| Add expenses not requiring cash: | | |
| Depreciation on capital assets | 155,000 | 155,000 |
| Changes in working capital items | | |
| Current accounts receivable | 275,000 | (300,000) |
| Inventory | (41,700) | (62,000) |
| Accounts payable | (335,000) | (100,000) |
| Net cash from operating activities | 465,000 | 30,000 |
| FINANCING ACTIVITIES | | |
| Decrease in long-term notes payable | (50,000) | — |
| Dividends declared and paid | (135,000) | — |
| | (185,000) | — |
| INVESTING ACTIVITIES | | |
| Purchase of buildings and equipment | (800,000) | — |
| Increase (decrease) in cash | $(520,000) | $ 30,000 |
| Cash at the beginning of the year | 1,080,000 | 1,050,000 |
| Cash at the end of the year | 560,000 | 1,080,000 |

Purchase Ltd. under the equity method of $41,700 is identical to the consolidated net income of Purchase Ltd. in Exhibit 4.11. This fact is not surprising, since, under the equity method, also known as one-line consolidation, we carry out the same adjustments as those required for calculating consolidated net income.

The computation of the adjusted change in retained earnings of Target Ltd. in 20X7 is provided in Part C of Exhibit 4.16. The two adjustments relating to (1) the amortization in 20X6 of the fair value increment allocated to buildings and equipment and (2) unrealized profit on the upstream sale of inventory in 20X6 are identical to the adjustments we made in Part A of Exhibit 4.7 while arriving at the equity in the earnings of Target Ltd. for 20X6. Given that these adjustments pertain to 20X6 and given that we are now in 20X7, the two adjustments are now made to the change in retained earnings in 20X6 of Target Ltd. Purchase Ltd. owns all of Target Ltd., therefore, 100% of the adjusted change in the retained earnings of Target Ltd. in 20X6 of $7,000 is added to the opening retained earnings of Purchase Ltd.

Finally, Part D of Exhibit 4.16 provides the computation of the balance in the investment in Target Ltd.'s account at the end of 20X7 under the equity method. The initial cost of acquisition of Target Ltd. of $1,200,000 on December 31, 20X5, is adjusted for (1) the adjusted change in retained earnings of Target Ltd. in 20X6 of $7,000; (2) equity in the earnings of Target Ltd. in 20X7 of $51,700; and (3) dividends received from Target Ltd. of $20,000 in 20X7.

## Management's Disclosures About Business Combinations

The 2007 edition of *Financial Reporting in Canada* reported that about 45% of 200 companies surveyed disclosed business combinations in each of the five years over the period 2002–2006, ranging from 42.5% in 2005 and 2006 to 47.5% in 2003. Most disclosures were made about the cost of the purchase, followed by disclosures of the name of the acquiree and of the fair value of the major class of assets and liabilities acquired, respectively.[a]

This study is the most recent such statistical study available in Canada. Although it was conducted some years ago, there is no evidence that the reporting situation has changed significantly in recent years.

A somewhat more recent empirical analysis of business combination disclosure found that management's level of disclosure decreases when an abnormally high level of the purchase price is allocated to goodwill. Goodwill is the residual remaining after allocating the purchase price to net identifiable assets. Therefore, if an acquirer overpays for an acquisition, the excess is absorbed by goodwill. Furthermore, since goodwill is not subject to amortization, increasing the portion of the purchase price allocated to goodwill reduces the amount allocated to assets that are subject to amortization and thereby increases future earnings.

The research also found that the level of disclosure appears to be related to two measures of earnings management, namely, (1) the frequency of unexpected accruals and (2) the frequency of exactly meeting quarterly analysts' forecasts in the five years leading up to the business combination. Better disclosure of business combinations was also found to be related to a more positive change in return on assets in the two years following the business combination, as well as to increased stock returns.

The author's analysis also indicates that investors do not fully adjust for the difference in disclosure levels; that is, they seem to be fooled by the level of accounting disclosures provided on business combinations by the managers.[b]

[a]*Financial Reporting in Canada* 2007, Thirty-second Edition (Toronto: CICA, 2007).
[b]R. Shalev, "The information content of business combination disclosure level," *The Accounting Review 84*:1 (2009), p. 239.

You may be wondering how an investment in an associate or joint venture is reported under the equity method. While we will discuss this issue in greater detail in Chapter 5, it is worth noting here that the computations required for reporting an investment in an associate or joint venture under the equity method are identical to the computations provided in Exhibit 4.7 and Exhibit 4.16, except that they are carried out only to the extent of the investor's proportionate share of ownership or profits in the associate or joint venture.

## Consolidating Parent-founded Subsidiaries

The example used throughout this chapter is that of a business combination. Purchase Ltd. acquired control over the net assets of Target Ltd. at a price that included both fair value adjustments and goodwill. By using a business combination as the basis for the example, we can fairly comprehensively illustrate the major types of adjustments that may be required when consolidated statements are prepared.

However, we pointed out in Chapter 2 that most subsidiaries are not the result of one corporation's acquiring another in a business combination. Instead, most subsidiaries are formed by their parent to conduct or facilitate some component of the parent's business. The process of consolidation for a subsidiary that was founded and wholly owned by its parent is much easier than for a subsidiary that was acquired as a going concern.

Since the investment by the parent was directly in the subsidiary (rather than by buying the subsidiary's shares from another shareholder), the paid-in capital accounts of

**Exhibit 4.16** Equity-Basis Reporting of Target Ltd. in 20X7

| Year Ended December 31, 20X7 | |
|---|---:|
| **A. Equity in earnings of Target Ltd.:** | |
| Earnings as reported by Target in 20X7 | $ 220,000 |
| Adjustments: | |
| 1. Amortization of fair value increment on buildings & equipment: $200,000/10 years | (20,000) |
| 2. Elimination/recognition of unrealized/realized profit on intercompany sales: | |
| Realized profit on upstream sale of inventory in the previous year | 8,000 |
| Unrealized profit on upstream sale of inventory in the current year | (4,500) |
| Unrealized profit on downstream sale of inventory in the current year | (1,800) |
| Unrealized gain on sale of land by Target Ltd. to Purchase Ltd. | (150,000) |
| Adjusted Target Ltd. earnings, equity basis | $ 51,700 |
| **B. Separate-entity net income of Purchase Ltd. in 20X7, equity basis:** | |
| Separate-entity net income of Purchase Ltd. under cost method | $ 380,000 |
| Less dividend revenue received from Target Ltd. | (20,000) |
| Add adjusted Target Ltd. earnings, equity basis, from A above | 51,700 |
| Separate-entity net income of Purchased Ltd., equity basis | $ 411,700 |
| **C. Adjusted change in retained earnings of Target Ltd. in 20X6:** | |
| Retained earnings balance of Target Ltd. on Dec. 31, 20X6 | $ 635,000 |
| Less retained earnings balance of Target Ltd. at time of acquisition | (600,000) |
| Less amortization of fair value increment on buildings & equipment: $200,000/10 years | (20,000) |
| Less unrealized profit on upstream sale of inventory in 20X6 | (8,000) |
| Adjusted change in retained earnings of Target Ltd. in 20X6 | $ 7,000 |
| **D. Investment in Target Ltd.:** | |
| Balance, December 31, 20X5 | $1,200,000 |
| Add adjusted change in retained earnings of Target in 20X6 from C above | 7,000 |
| Add adjusted Target Ltd. earnings, equity basis, in 20X7 from A above | 51,700 |
| Less dividends received from Target in 20X7 | (20,000) |
| Balance, December 31, 20X7 | $1,238,700 |

the subsidiary directly offset the original investment in the investment account of the parent. There are no fair value increments or goodwill to worry about. The lack of fair value increments means that there is no periodic amortization of those amounts to adjust for. Consolidating a wholly owned, parent-founded subsidiary simply requires:

1. adjusting for intercompany transactions;
2. eliminating any unrealized profits or losses; and
3. eliminating intercompany receivable and payable balances.

## Indirect Holdings

In Chapter 2 we pointed out that a A parent company might control a subsidiary indirectly through other subsidiaries, rather than by direct ownership. When the parent prepares its consolidated financial statements, both the direct and the indirect subsidiaries are consolidated.

Procedurally, indirect subsidiaries can be consolidated in either of two ways. The first is to consolidate by steps, from the bottom up. If P controls A, and A controls B and C, then consolidated statements for A can be prepared that include its direct subsidiaries, B and C. A's consolidated statements will then include all of the assets and liabilities of B and C just as if A owned them directly, and the investment accounts will have been eliminated. The next step is then to consolidate A's *consolidated* statements with P's statements. If the consolidation is being performed by the direct approach without a worksheet, then the step method is almost certainly the best one to use.

The second approach is to perform the consolidation of all subsidiaries, direct and indirect, on a single worksheet. A single-step worksheet approach may be easiest for those who are performing the consolidation on a computer spreadsheet, since it is relatively easy to include all of the subsidiaries on the worksheet with adequate space for explanatory notes.

Whichever procedural approach is used, the elimination and adjustment process is no different from that illustrated in this chapter for directly owned subsidiaries.

IFRS 10 requires that consolidated financial statements be prepared using uniform accounting policies for like transactions and events of similar nature. It simplifies the process of consolidation when all subsidiaries use the same accounting policies as the parent. When the same accounting policies are used, there will be no need for the parent to adjust the accounts of the subsidiaries for accounting policy differences. This is fairly easily accomplished with wholly owned subsidiaries—the parent company's management can specify the subsidiaries' accounting policies. Otherwise, appropriate adjustments must be made in the financial statements while preparing consolidated financial statements.

### Concept Check 4-2

1. What is the current-year adjustment for the unrealized profit on the intercompany sale of inventory in the previous year? What is the underlying rationale for such a treatment?

2. What, in general, is the current-year adjustment for consolidation-related adjustments and eliminations made in previous year(s)?

## 4.5 ACCOUNTING STANDARDS FOR PRIVATE ENTERPRISES

### Consolidation and the Use of the Equity Method Subsequent to Acquisition

The process of preparing consolidated financial statements and the use of the equity method to report an investment in an associate or joint venture under ASPE is identical to that required under IFRS. All the consolidation-related adjustments and eliminations required of public companies by IFRS, discussed previously in the chapter, are required under ASPE of private companies consolidating their subsidiaries or accounting for their interest in an associate or joint venture. All intercompany transactions and balances should be eliminated at the time of consolidation. Unrealized gains and losses on transactions between a parent and its subsidiary are required to be eliminated completely. Unrealized gains and losses on transactions between an investor and its associate or joint venture are required to be eliminated only to the extent of the investor's ownership of those entities.

**LO ⑤**
Amortize fair value adjustments

## Impairment Testing of Goodwill

Private enterprises (i.e., companies without public accountability) are not required to apply an annual impairment test. Private companies should apply an impairment test only when a specific event or circumstance indicates that impairment might have happened. Further, the impairment test need be performed only at the *reporting unit* level, rather than at the level of the cash-generating unit.

Basically, a *reporting unit* is defined by the internal reporting system of the corporation. A **reporting unit** is any part of the corporation that is evaluated regularly by the corporation's principal decision maker (normally the chief operating officer) for resource allocation decisions. Appendix 4B provides further details on the requirements for impairment testing of goodwill under ASPE.

## Relevant Standards

### IFRS

| | |
|---|---|
| **IFRS 5** | Non-current Assets Held for Sale and Discontinued Operations |
| **IFRS 8** | Operating Segments |
| **IFRS 10** | Consolidated Financial Statements |
| **IAS 1** | Presentation of Financial Statements |
| **IAS 28** | Investments in Associates |
| **IAS 36** | Impairment of Assets |

### ASPE

| | |
|---|---|
| **Section 1400** | General Standards of Financial Statement Presentation |
| **Section 1590** | Subsidiaries |
| **Section 1601** | Consolidated Financial Statements |
| **Section 3051** | Investments |
| **Section 3051** | Interests in joint ventures |
| **Section 3475** | Disposal of Long-lived Assets and Discontinued Operations |
| **Section 3063** | Impairment of Long-lived Assets |

## 4.6 SUMMARY OF KEY POINTS

1. The parent company and each of its subsidiaries will prepare individual, separate-entity financial statements. These statements are independent of the consolidated statements. Consolidated statements are prepared only for the shareholders of the parent company. The existence of consolidated statements does not eliminate the need for separate-entity statements. **LO 1**

2. Only a statement of financial position is necessary when a parent and its purchased subsidiary are consolidated at the date of acquisition. At all subsequent reporting dates, consolidation involves a full set of financial statements. **LO 1**

3. At reporting dates following acquisition, intercompany balances and transactions must be eliminated and consolidated net income must be adjusted for amortization of fair value adjustments, adjustments to goodwill, and elimination and recognition of unrealized and realized profits on intercompany sales. Amortization of fair value adjustments on tangible and intangible assets should be based on the estimated remaining useful life of the asset. Goodwill must be written down if its value for generating future earnings is impaired. **LO 1, 2, 3, 4, & 5**

4. Sales of current and non-current assets between a parent and its subsidiaries, or between subsidiaries, should be eliminated. Profits on intercompany sales of assets should be eliminated unless the assets have been sold to outside third parties. **LO 3**

5. If consolidated statements are not prepared, the parent can report its investment in the subsidiary on either the cost or the equity basis. If the equity basis is used for reporting non-consolidated subsidiaries, the parent company's reported net income and retained earnings will be exactly the same as though the statements had been consolidated. **LO 6**

6. A subsidiary's discontinued operation will not normally constitute a discontinued operation for the parent in a consolidated SCI. Discontinued operations arising in consolidated subsidiaries are reported as such in the parent's SCI only *if the items qualify as discontinued operations to the parent.* **LO 1**

7. A complete set of consolidated financial statements should include a cash flow statement. The cash flow statement can be prepared for consolidated statements in exactly the same manner as for separate-entity statements. **LO 1**

Visit the text's website at www.pearsoned.ca/beechy for practice quizzes, additional problems, Excel® templates, answers to Concept Check questions, and important IFRS updates.

## Self-Study Problems

**1.** Situation A: In 20X5, Primary Co. purchased inventory at a cost of $100,000 and sold it at a sale price of $200,000 to Stranger Co, an unrelated third-party company. This was the only sale made by Primary during the year.

Situation B: Now assume instead that in 20X5, Primary Co. purchased inventory at a cost of $100,000 and sold it at a sale price of $150,000 to a 100%-owned subsidiary, Secondary Co. Further assume that in 20X5, Secondary sold the entire inventory purchased from Primary to Stranger Co., an unrelated third-party company, at a sale price of $200,000.

**Required**

**a.** Provide the journal entries required in situation A by Primary to recognize the sale and cost of goods sold to Stranger in 20X5. What are the sale, cost of goods sold, and gross profit amounts?

**b.** Provide the journal entries required in situation B by Primary and Secondary, respectively, to recognize the sale and cost of goods sold by them in 20X5. Further, provide the consolidation-related adjusting entries that Primary has to make in relation to the intercompany sale between itself and Secondary in 20X5. Assuming that these were the only sales made by Primary and Secondary in 20X5, what are the consolidated sales, cost of goods sold, and gross profit amounts in 20X5? How do the consolidated amounts in situation B compare with the amounts calculated by you in situation A? Provide an explanation for the comparative numbers.

**2.** Refer to Self-Study Problem 1 above. Now assume in situation A that Primary sold only 40% of the inventory purchased in 20X5 to Stranger Co., at a gross profit of 50% on sales. Likewise, assume in situation B that while Primary sold 100% of the inventory purchased by it in 20X5 to Secondary, at a gross profit of 33.33% on sales that year, Secondary could sell only 40% of the inventory purchased from Primary to Stranger Co., at a gross profit of 25% of sales in 20X5.

**Required**

Provide the same information as required in Self-Study Problem 1 above.

**3.** Early in 20X5, Parco acquired 100% of the shares of Subco by issuing Parco shares worth $10 million. The carrying value of Subco's net assets at the date of acquisition was $7,000,000. The fair values of Subco's assets were deemed to be equal to their carrying values on Subco's books with one exception: The aggregate fair value of Subco's buildings was $1,400,000 higher than their carrying value.

Parco and Subco enjoyed a trading relationship for many years prior to the combination. In 20X4, for example, Subco had sold $1 million of goods to Parco (at a gross margin of 20% on sales) and Parco had billed Subco $300,000 for management services. However, the two companies had no common ownership interest and were not related companies prior to the 20X5 business combination.

In 20X5, following the business combination, Subco had sales of $1.2 million to Parco. Subco's gross margin remained at 20%. Of the amount sold, $200,000 remained in Parco's inventory at the end of 20X5. Parco billed Subco $400,000 for management fees, of which $100,000 remained unpaid at the end of the year. Other information is as follows:

- Subco reported separate-entity net income of $350,000 for 20X5. Subco declared and paid dividends of $150,000 during the year.
- Parco reported separate-entity net income of $680,000 for 20X5, including the dividend income from Subco. Parco declared dividends of $200,000, of which one-quarter were unpaid at year-end.
- Retained earnings at the date of acquisition were $3,450,000 for Parco and $1,250,000 for Subco.

- Subco's buildings have an estimated remaining useful life of 14 years. Subco uses straight-line depreciation.
- There has been no impairment of goodwill.

Required

Determine the following amounts:

a. Parco's consolidated net income for the year ended December 31, 20X5

b. Parco's consolidated retained earnings at December 31, 20X5

c. Parco's equity-basis earnings from Subco for 20X5

4. On January 1, 20X8, Parent Ltd. (Par) bought 100% of the shares of Subsidiary Inc. (Sub) for $1,084,000 cash. Sub's statement of financial position at the date of acquisition is shown in Exhibit 4.17, together with the estimated fair values of Sub's assets and liabilities.

   Additional information is as follows:
   - Sub depreciates its tangible capital assets over 10 years on a straight-line basis, assuming zero residual value.
   - During 20X9, Par sold goods with a cost of $300,000 to Sub for $390,000. At the end of 20X9, 20% of those goods remain in Sub's inventory.
   - Sub sold goods costing $100,000 to Par for $150,000 in 20X9. At the end of the year, 40% of these goods remain in Par's inventory.
   - Par sold land to Sub on January 1, 20X9, for $710,000. The original cost of the land was $500,000 to Par. The gain was netted to "other expenses."
   - On January 1, 20X9, Par had inventory on hand that it had bought from Sub for $45,000. Intercompany profit of $12,000 was included in that price.

The separate-entity financial statements for Par and Sub for the year ended December 31, 20X9, are shown in Exhibit 4.18.

Required

Prepare the consolidated financial statements for 20X9.

**Exhibit 4.17** Subsidiary Inc. Statement of Financial Position

| January 1, 20X8 | Carrying values | Fair values |
|---|---|---|
| Cash | $ 80,000 | $ 80,000 |
| Accounts receivable | 99,000 | 99,000 |
| Inventory | 178,000 | 195,000 |
| Property, plant, and equipment | 800,000 | 740,000 |
| Accumulated depreciation | (200,000) | |
| Total assets | $957,000 | |
| Accounts payable | $ 70,000 | 70,000 |
| Long-term notes payable | 200,000 | 200,000 |
| Common shares | 250,000 | |
| Retained earnings | 437,000 | |
| Total liabilities and shareholders' equity | $957,000 | |

**Exhibit 4.18** Separate-Entity Financial Statements for 20X9

### Statements of Comprehensive Income
### Year Ended December 31, 20X9

| | Parent Ltd. | Subsidiary Inc. |
|---|---|---|
| Sales revenue | $1,200,000 | $ 987,000 |
| Cost of goods sold | (800,000) | (650,000) |
| | 400,000 | 337,000 |
| Other operating expenses | (235,000) | (147,000) |
| NET INCOME | $ 165,000 | $ 190,000 |

### Statements of Changes in Equity—Retained Earnings Section
### Year Ended December 31, 20X9

| | Parent Ltd. | Subsidiary Inc. |
|---|---|---|
| Retained earnings, December 31, 20X8 | $1,153,000 | $ 330,000 |
| Net income | 165,000 | 190,000 |
| Retained earnings, December 31, 20X9 | $1,318,000 | $ 520,000 |

### Statements of Financial Position December 31, 20X9

| | Parent Ltd. | Subsidiary Inc. |
|---|---|---|
| **ASSETS** | | |
| **Current assets:** | | |
| Cash | $ 120,000 | $ 110,000 |
| Accounts receivable | 150,000 | 135,000 |
| Inventory | 240,000 | 195,000 |
| | 510,000 | 440,000 |
| Property, plant, and equipment | 1,400,000 | 910,000 |
| Accumulated depreciation | (510,000) | (320,000) |
| | 890,000 | 590,000 |
| **Other assets:** | | |
| Investments (at cost) | 1,084,000 | — |
| Goodwill | 76,000 | — |
| | 1,160,000 | — |
| **TOTAL ASSETS** | $2,560,000 | $1,030,000 |
| **LIABILITIES AND SHAREHOLDERS' EQUITY** | | |
| **Liabilities:** | | |
| Accounts payable | $ 142,000 | $ 60,000 |
| Long-term notes payable | 600,000 | 200,000 |
| | 742,000 | 260,000 |
| **Shareholders' Equity** | | |
| Common shares | 500,000 | 250,000 |
| Retained earnings | 1,318,000 | 520,000 |
| | 1,818,000 | 770,000 |
| **TOTAL LIABILITIES AND SHAREHOLDERS' EQUITY** | $2,560,000 | $1,030,000 |

# Review Questions

1. What is accomplished by the acquisition adjustment when consolidated statements are prepared?

2. How would the acquisition adjustment for an acquired subsidiary differ from that for a parent-founded subsidiary?

3. How is goodwill arising from a business combination accounted for in years following the combination?

4. Why are the fair value adjustments on depreciable capital assets amortized? What is the basis for determining the amount of amortization?

5. When is it necessary to eliminate the profit on intercompany transactions?

6. How does management judgment impact on the impairment test for goodwill?

7. What is the reporting option available to private enterprises for the goodwill impairment test?

8. Explain why the adjustment for unrealized profit in ending inventories appears to *increase* cost of goods sold.

9. Explain the difference between the acquisition adjustment and the operations adjustments.

10. Why is the equity method of reporting sometimes called the consolidation method of equity reporting?

11. How does a parent company's total net assets amount differ under consolidated reporting as compared with equity reporting for a subsidiary?

12. Under equity reporting, how do discontinued operations of an investee corporation affect the SCI of the investor corporation?

13. How does unrealized profit in the beginning inventories affect the consolidated net income if the inventories have been sold during the year?

14. What disclosure should be made in the financial statements of an acquirer as to the details of a business combination?

15. In what general ways will consolidation of a parent-founded subsidiary differ from consolidation of a purchased subsidiary?

16. Are consolidated statements required after one corporation directly acquires the net assets of another corporation?

## 4.7 CASES

### CASE 4-1 GROWTH LIMITED

You are the CA appointed as the new auditor of Growth Limited (GL), a private company, for the next three years. The requirement for an audit is specified in GL's debt covenant with the bank. This is the first year that an audit will be completed.

As part of an ongoing expansion program, GL added two new sizes to its line of fish-crate products. The president of GL is pleased with the continuing expansion program. Annual sales are $1,800,000, the highest level in GL's history, and a real achievement for a firm of its size. The president, who attributes the increase in sales to the exacting standards of quality incorporated in its new products, made the following comments:

"We have never amortized or tested goodwill for impairment, since goodwill is being built up in our business, not used. In fact, I can never see it going down in value, because our business is continuing to grow. This year for the first time we acquired another company that provides additional products to add to our line. That increased our goodwill even more.

"We also wrote off the deferred tax balance this year because it doesn't mean anything. In fact, our banker adds the accumulated deferred tax balance to retained earnings when he reviews our annual financing proposals. I just couldn't think of any reason why we should pay you to calculate deferred taxes when no one uses them."

Required

Discuss the president's comments.

[CICA]

### CASE 4-2 PELICAN SYSTEMS INC.

Pelican Systems Inc. (PSI), a public company, develops and manufactures equipment that is sold to technology, communications, and airline enterprises, and designs and installs customized information networks for customers. The chief executive officer (CEO) of PSI retired on December 31, 20X4, and Gerald Cinco was hired as his replacement. An executive search firm recommended Cinco, and he signed a three-year employment contract with PSI that includes performance bonuses. At the annual shareholders' meeting held on March 6, 20X5, Cinco predicted strong growth in revenue and in earnings per share, which would result in a healthy increase in the value of PSI's shares.

Cinco's predictions were validated by PSI's results as reflected in its audited financial statements for the fiscal year ended December 31, 20X5, and a substantial increase in the share value from the preceding year-end share value.

Following its policy of appointing new auditors every five years, at the annual shareholders' meeting held on March 5, 20X6, PSI appointed Sharp & Ipson, Chartered Accountants LLP (S&I), as auditor for the year ending December 31, 20X6.

It is now March 17, 20X6. You are a CA with S&I and have been assigned the responsibility for the PSI audit engagement. You have obtained the extracts from the consolidated financial statements for the year ended December 31, 20X5 (Exhibit A), information pertaining to the operations and accounting policies of PSI gathered through interviews with company employees (Exhibit B), and extracts from the audit working papers prepared by the predecessor auditor (Exhibit C).

The partner responsible for the PSI audit will be attending a meeting of the board of directors on March 26, 20X6. The partner has asked you to prepare a memo to help her understand the impact of the accounting policies followed in the prior year.

Required

Prepare the memo requested by the partner.

---

## Exhibit A
## Extracts from Consolidated Financial Statements

### Pelican Systems Inc.
### Consolidated Statement of Financial Position, December 31
### (in thousands of dollars)

| | 20X5 | 20X4 |
|---|---|---|
| **ASSETS** | | |
| **Current assets** | | |
| Cash | $ 2,080 | $ 1,090 |
| Accounts receivable | 11,300 | 10,200 |
| Inventory | 8,400 | 7,350 |
| Prepaids | 720 | 690 |
| | 22,500 | 19,330 |
| Property, plant, and equipment (net) | 40,400 | 44,800 |
| Deferred charges | 2,604 | 870 |
| Goodwill and other intangible assets | 3,956 | — |
| | $71,960 | $65,000 |
| **LIABILITIES AND SHAREHOLDERS' EQUITY** | | |
| **Current liabilities** | | |
| Bank indebtedness | $8,850 | $12,000 |
| Accounts payable and accruals | 3,110 | 3,160 |
| Current portion of long-term debt | 4,750 | 4,000 |
| | 16,710 | 19,160 |
| Long-term debt | 33,250 | 28,000 |
| Deferred income taxes | 1,090 | 980 |
| | 51,050 | 48,140 |
| Common shares | 12,000 | 12,000 |
| Retained earnings | 8,910 | 4,860 |
| | 20,910 | 16,860 |
| | $71,960 | $65,000 |

### Pelican Systems Inc.
### Consolidated Statement of Comprehensive Income
### Years Ended December 31 (in thousands of dollars)

| | 20X5 | 20X4 |
|---|---|---|
| Revenues | $80,000 | $73,000 |
| Cost of generating revenues | 49,600 | 44,100 |
| Gross margin | 30,400 | 28,900 |
| Selling, general, and administrative expenses | 14,400 | 14,600 |
| Interest and financing charges | 2,650 | 2,380 |
| Depreciation expense | 5,850 | 6,420 |
| | 22,900 | 23,400 |
| Income before taxes | 7,500 | 5,500 |
| Income taxes | 2,850 | 2,090 |
| Net income | $ 4,650 | $ 3,410 |

## Exhibit B

## Information Pertaining to the Operations and Accounting Policies of PSI

### SALES LEASING PROGRAM

To stimulate sales, PSI sells customized equipment on a leasing basis, whereby an unrelated financial institution purchases the equipment from PSI and leases this equipment to PSI's customers. PSI arranges sales on this basis for higher-credit-risk customers. This sales practice was adopted effective April 1, 20X5, as directed by the CEO "to expand our customer base to meet our objective of sales and earnings growth."

PSI pays a financing arrangement fee of 10% of the selling price of the equipment to the financial institution as compensation for extending a lower interest rate to the customer than would be typical for the credit risk related to the customer. PSI guarantees the payments of the customers. The financial institution holds title to the equipment until the final lease payment is made, at which time title is transferred to the lessee. PSI has the right to purchase each of the lease receivables from the financial institution at any time for the amount of the outstanding balance. The financing arrangement fee is not refundable.

During the fiscal year ended December 31, 20X5, sales totalling $12,000,000 were made under the terms of this leasing program, which provided PSI with a cash flow of $10,800,000 net of the financing arrangement fee paid to the financial institution. PSI's gross margin on these sales, before the financing arrangement fee, was $5,400,000.

PSI's director of marketing stated that, in January 20X6, the financial institution advised PSI that $1,600,000 of the $2,000,000 principal portion of the payments due by December 31, 20X5, had been made by the lessees and requested compensation of $400,000 plus interest of $24,000 for payments in arrears.

### ACQUISITION OF EQUIPMENT

On July 1, 20X5, PSI acquired state-of-the-art technology equipment that is being used to manufacture a new product line under a special financing arrangement. PSI is required to pay to the seller 15% of the profit, defined as gross margin, realized from sales of this product line during the three years ending August 31, 20X8. PSI is required to remit the amount due annually no later than November 30 of each year, with the amount supported by "a certification by PSI's auditor that PSI has remitted in full the amount due under the terms of the financing arrangement."

According to PSI's director of procurements, the cost to PSI to purchase the equipment for cash would have been $3,000,000. Revenue from sales of the new product line is projected to total $65,000,000 for the three years ending August 31, 20X8, as follows: first year, $19,500,000; second year, $27,300,000; third year, $18,200,000. For the fourth and fifth years combined, it is projected to be $25,000,000. The life of the product line is estimated to be five years. The projected gross margin is 40%. Sales of the new product line commenced on September 1, 20X5, totalled $6,500,000 for the four months ended December 31, 20X5, and generated a gross margin of $2,600,000.

This product line is often included in a "bundle of equipment" sold to customers, and a portion of the selling price of the "bundle" is allocated internally to this product line.

PSI's accounting policy is to recognize the amount payable to the seller annually on August 31 as a charge to the cost of generating revenues. No amount was accrued at December 31, 20X5.

## SALE OF SUBSIDIARY

On November 1, 20X5, PSI sold a wholly owned subsidiary, Ersatz Technologies Inc. (ETI), and realized a gain of $1,600,000 on the sale. The gain was included in selling, general, and administrative expense (SG&A) in PSI's SCI and was not separately disclosed. PSI's annual report for fiscal 20X5 included a statement that the corporation had "achieved its goal of improvements in efficiency and cost control by reducing SG&A to 18% of sales revenue from its previous level of 20%."

## INVESTMENT IN HOPE & PRATT

In February 20X5, PSI invested $2,500,000 in Hope & Pratt Ltd. (H&P), a publicly traded dot-com enterprise. This represented a 10% stake in the 25,000,000 shares issued. By May 20X5, H&P's shares were trading at a market price of $60 per share. On December 31, 20X5, H&P's shares were trading at $20 per share, and they had dropped to $5 per share by February 1, 20X6, as a result of financial warnings issued by H&P. H&P's shares are currently trading at $4 per share. H&P reported a loss of $9,800,000 for the year ended December 31, 20X5.

## ACQUISITION OF ATI

Effective September 1, 20X5, PSI acquired 100% ownership of AvanTemps Inc. (ATI) at a cost of $6,000,000. PSI determined its offering price as follows:
- fair value of ATI's net tangible assets, $2,044,000;
- $1,500,000 payment to Ethan Brodsky (who owned 51% of the shares of ATI, is the founder of ATI, and is responsible for the development of ATI's advanced technologies) for entering into a three-year employment contract with PSI;
- $456,000 for unused non-capital losses totalling $1,200,000 at a tax rate of 38%; and
- $2,000,000 to reflect the value of ATI's business.
  Brodsky was also granted stock options for shares of PSI.

Based on ATI's profitability in the first quarter of fiscal 20X6 and on projected profitability in the future, the treasurer advised you that the benefit of the unused tax losses will be recognized as a reduction in income tax expense in fiscal 20X6.

> **Exhibit C**
>
> **Extracts from Working Papers Prepared by Predecessor Auditor**
>
> 1. Materiality was set at $1,000,000 based on projected revenue for fiscal 20X5.
> 2. Inherent risk was noted as "greater than in previous years for fiscal 20X5 because of the new CEO's objective of reporting earnings growth and because of the risk of manipulation of earnings to maximize his bonus."
> 3. The working papers pertaining to the new sales leasing program include the following information:
>    - PSI's accounting policy is to recognize the profit on these sales at the date of sale to the financial institution that acts as a lessor to PSI's customers and to recognize the cost of the payment guarantees as paid to the financial institution. PSI accrued a $424,000 liability on December 31, 20X5, and included this amount in accounts payable based on notification by the financial institution of customer payments in arrears. PSI remitted this amount, which includes interest of $24,000, to the financial institution on January 31, 20X6. The CA concluded that PSI's accounting policy is acceptable because title to the equipment is transferred to the financial institution and the cost of the payment guarantee is reflected in PSI's financial statements.
>    - PSI's accounting policy is to defer and amortize the financing arrangement fee over the three-year term of the leases. Amortization of $200,000 of the $1,200,000 in fees incurred in fiscal 20X5 is included in the "interest and financing charges" SCI account, and the unamortized balance of $1,000,000 is included in the "deferred charges" SFP account.
> 4. A working paper noted that the determination of the gain on the sale of ETI had been verified and that PSI had received the full amount of the proceeds from the sale.
> 5. A working paper noted that the treasurer had informed the auditor that "it is too early to determine whether or not the loss in value of the H&P investment is other than a temporary decline." He is hopeful for a turnaround by H&P.
> 6. A working paper pertaining to the acquisition of ATI includes the following information: "An intangible asset in the amount of $1,500,000 has been recognized for the employment contract and is considered to have an indefinite life until such time as Brodsky announces his intention to leave PSI."
>    [ICAO]

# CASE 4-3 BRAND DRUG LIMITED

In the course of the audit of Brand Drug Limited (BDL), the chartered accountant (CA), while reviewing the draft financial statements for the year ended August 31, 20X6, noticed that BDL's investment in National Pharmaceuticals Limited (NPL) was valued on the cost basis. In 20X5, it had been valued on the equity basis. Representing a 22% interest in NPL, this investment had been made 10 years ago to infuse fresh equity into NPL, with a view to protecting BDL's source of supply for drugs.

BDL's controller informed the CA that NPL had suffered a large loss in 20X6, as shown by the May interim financial statements. BDL's representative on NPL's board of directors had resigned because BDL's purchases from NPL now constituted less than 5% of its total purchases. In addition, NPL had been unco-operative in providing profit data in time to make the year-end equity adjustment. Consequently, BDL's controller had revised the method of accounting for the investment in NPL.

The CA then found out that BDL's managers are planning a share issue in 20X7 and do not want their earnings impaired by NPL's poor performance. However, they are reluctant to divest themselves of NPL in case the rumoured development by NPL of a new drug to reduce the impact of colitis materializes.

When the CA approached NPL's managers, they refused to disclose any information on NPL's operations. The CA then learned from a stockbroker friend that NPL's poor results were due to its market being undercut by generic drug manufacturers. The loss had been increased when NPL's management wrote off most of NPL's intangible assets. The CA summarized the relevant information on the treatment of the investment for her audit file (Exhibit D).

Required

Discuss the matters raised above.

[CICA]

---

## Exhibit D
## CA's Notes on Investment in NPL's Shares

Extracts from BDL's draft financial statements for the year ended August 31, 20X6, in thousands of dollars:

|  | 20X6 (draft) | 20X5 (actual) |
|---|---|---|
| INVESTMENT IN NPL (NOTE 3) | $25,000  (1) | $27,400  (2) |
| Retained earnings: |  |  |
| Opening balance | $ 6,500 | $ 2,350 |
| plus: net earnings | 4,500 | 7,300 |
|  | 11,000 | 9,650 |
| less: prior period adjustment (Note 1) | (2,400) | — |
| Dividends | (2,250) | (3,150) |
| Closing balance | $ 6,350 | $ 6,500 |

**Note 1:** Represents original cost. The 20X5 balance has been reduced by the amount of previously recorded equity interest of $2.4 million. In the nine months ended May 31, 20X6, NPL reported a net loss of $140 million after writing off development and patent costs as extraordinary items.

**Note 2:** Valued on equity basis. Equity adjustment for 20X5 involved the elimination of $5.5 million unrealized profit included in ending inventory, on sales from NPL to BDL. The unrealized profit in BDL's ending inventory for 20X6 amounts to $1.5 million.

**Note 3:** Stock market trading in NPL's common shares has been heavy in 20X6. Prices for the year are as follows:

| August 31, 20X5 | $22.00 |
|---|---|
| February 28, 20X6 | $ 4.00 |
| August 31, 20X6 | $12.00 |

BDL owns 2,000,000 common shares of NPL; in neither 20X5 nor 20X6 did NPL declare or pay any dividends.

# CASE 4-4 EXOTIC BEAN BAGS INC.

Ada Vidal established Exotic Bean Bags Inc. (EBBI) in 20X2 to distribute exotic bean bags featuring colourful ethnic motifs and designs. EBBI also customizes its bean bags to match the decor and design requirements of individual customers and businesses. Ada designs the bags in Canada, but the bags are manufactured in the Republic of Chola (Chola). A parent-created subsidiary in Chola, EBB Chola Ltd. (EBBCL), is responsible for all manufacturing-related activities, such as inviting bids from manufacturers, choosing a manufacturer, and ensuring quality. Once EBBCL receives the manufactured bags from the manufacturer(s), it ships them to EBBI's warehouse in Calgary.

Until the end of 20X7, EBBI sold the bags through two of its own company-owned retail outlets in the Calgary area, as well as (1) through many other retail stores across Canada; (2) online via its website, www.exoticbeanbags.com, and; (3) for custom orders, directly to individuals or businesses.

Late in 20X7, Ada realized that her core competency lay in designing bean bags and in obtaining contracts for customized bean bags from businesses and individuals. Therefore, she decided to sell the two retail outlets to a prospective buyer. Erin Mazur, a wealthy acquaintance of Ada, agreed to buy the two retailing facilities from EBBI. EBBI created a company called Exotic Retailing Inc. (ERI) on December 31, 20X7, and transferred the two retail outlets to ERI on that date. EBBI Canada sold 80% of the shares of ERI to Erin on December 31, 20X7, while retaining the remaining 20%. Erin paid EBBI $1,200,000 for her 80% share ownership of ERI.

The agreement between EBBI and ERI stipulates the following:

- EBBI will be the exclusive bean bags supplier to ERI. All bean bags sold by ERI must be EBBI bean bags. However, ERI is free to sell products other than bean bags that are supplied by other companies.
- For 20X8 only, EBBI will guarantee that ERI's income before taxes as a percentage of sales is equal to or greater than EBBI's 20X8 income before taxes as a percentage of sales on its consolidated SCI. If not, EBBI must pay ERI the deficiency.
- To preserve the monopoly of ERI in the Calgary area, EBBI is prohibited from selling its bags to other retailers in Calgary.
- In determining EBBI's profit percentage, a qualified professional accountant must prepare EBBI's consolidated statement of comprehensive income under IFRS.

It is now January 20X9, and Ada wants to obtain a loan from EBBI's bank so that she can fund the expansion of EBBI's wholesale operations as well as the expansion of EBBI's sales of customized bean bags to individuals and businesses directly. The bank has asked Ada to provide EBBI's consolidated statement of comprehensive income for 20X8, prepared following international standards by a qualified accountant. Together, Ada and Erin approached a partner of Accounting Experts LLP (AE) to prepare the consolidated statement of comprehensive income of EBBI for 20X8. Ada and Erin provided AE with the additional information shown below, including the separate-entity financial statements for EBBI, EBBCL (translated into Canadian dollars), and ERI.

You recently joined AE as a staff accountant. The AE partner has assigned you the responsibility of preparing the EBBI consolidated statement and then drafting a report with recommendations to Ada and Erin.

Additional Information:

- The relevant financial statements of EBBCL, converted into Canadian dollars, are provided in Exhibit E.

- Erin notes that ERI's profit before taxes as a percentage of sales is less than the comparable figure on EBBI's separate-entity SCI. She had assumed that if such a comparison were to be made using the consolidated SCI of EBBI instead, the result would be similar. They need to understand the reasons for any difference and they also need to know if they should adjust their operating agreement for the future.

- EBBCL makes all of its sales to EBBI. EBBCL remits excess cash as dividends to EBBI in *four equal instalments, each instalment at the end of each quarter*.

- Ada thinks it is good for her business that the Chola kas has depreciated in value significantly vis-à-vis the Canadian dollar. This has reduced her cost of goods sold while having no impact on her sale prices in Canada, since EBBI has no competition in its niche in Canada. She does not expect the kas to recover in value compared with the Canadian dollar any time soon.

# Exhibit E

# Financial Statements for EBB Chola Ltd.

## Statement of Comprehensive Income Year Ended December 31, 20X8

|  | Can$ |
|---|---|
| Sales | $ 2,343,750 |
| Cost of goods sold | 1,771,758 |
| Gross profit | 571,992 |
| Salaries | 164,063 |
| Rent | 235,726 |
| Depreciation on furniture & fixtures | 115,000 |
| Overheads | 98,438 |
| Exchange loss on net monetary assets | 68,814 |
| Net income before taxes | (110,048) |
| Local income taxes | 83,320 |
| Net income and comprehensive income | $ (193,368) |

## Statement of Changes in Shareholders' Equity—Retained Earnings Section Year Ended December 31, 20X8

|  | Can$ |
|---|---|
| Retained earnings, December 31, 20X7 | $ 771,032 |
| Comprehensive income (loss) for the year | (193,368) |
| Dividends for the year | (343,536) |
| Retained earnings, December 31, 20X8 | $ 234,128 |

## Statement of Financial Position December 31, 20X8

| ASSETS | Can$ |
|---|---|
| Cash | $ 247,148 |
| Inventory | 170,625 |
| Pre-paid rent | 29,167 |
| Furniture & fixtures (net) | 920,000 |
| TOTAL ASSETS | $1,366,940 |
| LIABILITIES AND SHAREHOLDERS' EQUITY |  |
| Accounts payable | $ 182,813 |
| Common shares | 950,000 |
| Retained earnings | 234,128 |
| TOTAL LIABILITIES AND SHAREHOLDERS' EQUITY | $1,366,940 |

Additional information pertaining to Exotic Bean Bags Chola Ltd.:

■ All sales made to EBB Inc. Canada by EBB Chola Ltd. are made at the same gross profit percentage on sales.

## Exhibit F

## Financial Statements for Exotic Bean Bags Inc. (Canada)

### Statement of Comprehensive Income Year Ended December 31, 20X8

|  | Can$ |
|---|---|
| Sales | $ 2,734,375 |
| Cost of goods sold | 1,640,625 |
| Gross profit | 1,093,750 |
| Salaries | 240,625 |
| Depreciation, building | 337,500 |
| Depreciation, furniture & fixtures | 225,000 |
| Overheads | 142,188 |
| Dividend income from EBB Chola Ltd. | 343,536 |
| Net income before taxes | 491,974 |
| Canadian income taxes | 93,729 |
| Net income and comprehensive income | $    398,245 |

### Statement of Changes in Shareholders' Equity—Retained Earnings Section
### Year Ended December 31, 20X8

|  | Can$ |
|---|---|
| Beginning retained earnings | $ 4,911,905 |
| Comprehensive income (loss) for the year | 398,245 |
| Dividends for the year | 0 |
| Ending retained earnings | $ 5,310,150 |

### Statement of Financial Position December 31, 20X8

|  | Can $ |
|---|---|
| **ASSETS** |  |
| Cash | $   635,150 |
| Inventory | 703,125 |
| Furniture & fixtures (net) | 1,350,000 |
| Buildings (net) | 2,025,000 |
| Investment in EBB Chola Ltd. | 950,000 |
| Investment in Exotic Retailing Inc. | 300,000 |
| TOTAL ASSETS | $ 5,963,275 |
| **LIABILITIES AND SHAREHOLDERS' EQUITY** |  |
| Expenses and salaries payable | $   153,125 |
| Common shares | 500,000 |
| Retained earnings | 5,310,150 |
| TOTAL LIABILITIES AND OWNERS' EQUITY | $ 5,963,275 |

Additional information pertaining to Exotic Bean Bags Inc.:

- EBBI Canada had no inventory on January 1, 20X8, since the entire inventory received from EBB Chola Ltd. was in ER Inc.'s retail facilities on that date.
- All sales made to ER Inc. by EBBI Canada are made at the same gross profit percentage on sales.

The carrying and fair values of ER's net identifiable assets on January 1, 20X8, were as shown in Exhibit G.

## Exhibit G

## Financial Statements for 20X8 and Additional Information Relating to Exotic Retailing Inc. (Canada)

| | Carrying value | Fair value | Remaining life |
|---|---|---|---|
| Cash | $100,000 | $100,000 | |
| Inventory | 200,000 | 330,000 | |
| Building | 200,000 | 600,000 | 15 years, straight-line depreciation |
| Furniture & fixtures (net) | 200,000 | 500,000 | 15 years, straight-line depreciation |
| Bond payable | 200,000 | 200,000 | |

### Statement of Comprehensive Income Year Ended December 31, 20X8

| | Can$ |
|---|---|
| Sales | $3,996,394 |
| Cost of goods sold | 2,597,656 |
| Gross Profit | 1,398,738 |
| Salaries | 419,621 |
| Depreciation, building | 13,333 |
| Depreciation, furniture & fixtures | 13,333 |
| Overheads including interest on bonds payable | 349,684 |
| Net Income before taxes | 602,765 |
| Canadian income taxes | 210,968 |
| Net income and comprehensive income | $ 391,798 |

### Statements of Financial Position Years Ended December 31

| | 20X8 (Can$) | 20X7 (Can$) |
|---|---|---|
| **ASSETS** | | |
| Cash | $ 581,745 | $100,000 |
| Inventory | 136,719 | 200,000 |
| Furniture & fixtures (net) | 186,667 | 200,000 |
| Building | 186,667 | 200,000 |
| TOTAL ASSETS | $1,091,798 | $700,000 |
| **LIABILITIES AND SHAREHOLDERS' EQUITY** | | |
| Bonds payable | $ 200,000 | $200,000 |
| Common stock | 500,000 | 500,000 |
| Retained earnings | 391,798 | 0 |
| TOTAL LIABILITIES AND OWNERS' EQUITY | $1,091,798 | $700,000 |

Additional information pertaining to Exotic Retailing Inc.:

■ The buildings and furniture and fixtures had a further useful life of 15 years on January 1, 20X8. They are being depreciated on a straight-line basis assuming no salvage value.

■ No dividends were declared by ER during the year.

Required

Draft a report for the AE partner that includes the required financial statements, all associated calculations, and the analysis and recommendations for Ada and Erin.

# Problems

## P4-1 (20 minutes, easy)

Okavango Ltd. sold goods at a sale price of $10,000 to its 100%-owned subsidiary Serengeti Ltd. in 20X5 at a gross profit percentage of 50%. At the end of 20X5, 40% of the goods purchased from Okavango remained unsold in the ending inventory of Serengeti. These goods were sold by Serengeti to an outside party in 20X6.

### Required

**a.** Provide all the necessary consolidation-related adjusting entries in 20X5 and 20X6 in relation to the sale of inventory by Okavango Ltd. to Serengeti.

**b.** Would your answer have been different if the sale of the inventory had instead been by Serengeti to Okavango? Explain the rationale for your answer.

## P4-2 (30 minutes, medium)

OfficePlus Corporation is a retailer of office supplies and equipment in Vancouver. On March 5, 20X6, OfficePlus formed a new corporation in Calgary to operate the same type of business. OfficePlus invested $250,000 cash in exchange for 10,000 common shares in the new subsidiary, to be known as Plus Limited.

During 20X6, Plus Limited commenced operations. Most of Plus's initial inventory came from OfficePlus. In total, goods that had cost OfficePlus $200,000 were sold to Plus at an assigned value of $300,000. These goods were re-priced by Plus to sell for $500,000 at retail. At year-end, 30% of the merchandise acquired from OfficePlus was still in Plus's inventory.

OfficePlus also extended a loan to Plus to finance the start-up costs. A total of $150,000 was lent during the year, of which $90,000 was still owing at year-end. Interest of $10,000 on the loan had been accrued by both companies, of which only $5,000 had actually been paid during 20X6.

Condensed statements of financial position and statements of comprehensive income of the two companies are presented below, as of December 31, 20X6.

### Required

Prepare a consolidated SFP and SCI for OfficePlus Corporation at December 31, 20X6.

| Statements of Financial Position December 31, 20X6 | | |
|---|---|---|
| | OfficePlus | Plus |
| Cash | $ 85,000 | $ 40,000 |
| Accounts and other receivables | 275,000 | 150,000 |
| Inventories | 440,000 | 60,000 |
| Capital assets | 500,000 | 400,000 |
| Accumulated depreciation | (200,000) | (30,000) |
| Investment in Plus (at cost) | 250,000 | — |
| | $ 1,350,000 | $ 620,000 |
| Accounts and other payables | $ 320,000 | $ 150,000 |
| Long-term liabilities | 300,000 | 200,000 |
| Common shares | 50,000 | 250,000 |
| Retained earnings | 680,000 | 20,000 |
| | $ 1,350,000 | $ 620,000 |

*Continued >*

*Continued >*

### Statements of Comprehensive Income
### Year Ended December 31, 20X6

| | OfficePlus | Plus |
|---|---|---|
| Sales | $ 2,000,000 | $ 600,000 |
| Other income | 70,000 | — |
| | 2,070,000 | 600,000 |
| Expenses | 1,700,000 | 540,000 |
| Net income and comprehensive income | $ 370,000 | $ 60,000 |

### Statements of Changes in Equity—Retained Earnings Section
### Year Ended December 31, 20X6

| | OfficePlus | Plus |
|---|---|---|
| Retained earnings, December 31, 20X5 | $ 510,000 | — |
| Comprehensive income | 370,000 | $ 60,000 |
| Dividends | (200,000) | (40,000) |
| Retained earnings, December 31, 20X6 | $ 680,000 | $ 20,000 |

**P4-3 (40 minutes, medium)**

At the end of 20X7, the condensed statements of financial position and statements of comprehensive income of OfficePlus Corporation and Plus Limited were as they appear below. Intercompany activities were as follows:

1. Plus sold all of its opening (i.e., December 31, 20X6) inventory, including that acquired from OfficePlus (see P 4-2).

2. Plus purchased merchandise from OfficePlus for $400,000. This price included a 25% gross profit on the sale price to OfficePlus. At year-end, 40% of these goods were still in Plus's inventory.

3. Plus sold to OfficePlus some merchandise for $127,000. Plus had acquired the merchandise for $100,000. The merchandise was all in OfficePlus's inventory at year-end, but is expected to sell for $150,000 in 20X8.

4. Plus fully repaid OfficePlus the $90,000 loan that had been outstanding at the beginning of the year, plus $10,000 in interest ($5,000 of the interest pertained to 20X6).

5. OfficePlus purchased a plot of land in Calgary for $110,000 and resold it to Plus for $150,000.

Required

Prepare a consolidated statement of income and retained earnings and a consolidated SFP for OfficePlus Corporation for 20X7.

## Statements of Financial Position December 31, 20X7

|  | OfficePlus | Plus |
|---|---|---|
| Cash | $ 50,000 | $ 60,000 |
| Accounts and other receivables | 210,000 | 60,000 |
| Inventories | 440,000 | 195,000 |
| Capital assets | 560,000 | 520,000 |
| Accumulated depreciation | (230,000) | (60,000) |
| Investment in Plus | 250,000 | — |
| Other investments | 140,000 | — |
|  | $1,420,000 | $ 725,000 |
| Accounts and other payables | $ 360,000 | $ 250,000 |
| Long-term liabilities | 250,000 | 230,000 |
| Common shares | 50,000 | 250,000 |
| Retained earnings | 760,000 | 45,000 |
|  | $1,420,000 | $ 725,000 |

## Statements of Comprehensive Income
### Year Ended December 31, 20X7

|  | OfficePlus | Plus |
|---|---|---|
| Sales | $2,300,000 | $ 720,000 |
| Other income | 100,000 | — |
|  | 2,400,000 | 720,000 |
| Expenses | 2,100,000 | 650,000 |
| Net income | $ 300,000 | $ 70,000 |

## Statements of Changes in Equity—Retained Earnings Section
### Year Ended December 31, 20X7

|  | OfficePlus | Plus |
|---|---|---|
| Retained earnings, December 31, 20X6 | $ 680,000 | $ 20,000 |
| Net income | 300,000 | 70,000 |
| Dividends | (220,000) | (45,000) |
| Retained earnings, December 31, 20X7 | $ 760,000 | $ 45,000 |

**P4-4 (40 minutes, medium)**

On January 1, 20X6, Big Inc. acquired 100% of the outstanding shares of Small Corp. for $15,000,000 in cash. On this date, Small had shareholders' equity of $12,000,000, including $6,000,000 in retained earnings. Small had buildings and equipment that had a fair value of $1,800,000 less than carrying value, inventory that had a fair value of $450,000 greater than carrying value, and investments that had a fair value of $1,950,000 greater than carrying value.

The statements of financial position of the two companies on December 31, 20X6, are shown below.

Additional Information:

1.  The goodwill on Small's books arose from the purchase of another company several years ago, a company that has since been amalgamated into Small. The goodwill was assumed to have a fair value of zero on January 1, 20X6.

2.  Small's plant and equipment have an estimated average remaining life of 10 years from January 1, 20X6. The net carrying value of the plant and equipment was $15,000,000 on that date, after deducting $6,000,000 of accumulated depreciation.

3. On January 1, 20X6, Big held inventory of $1,200,000 that had been purchased from Small. Small had sold the merchandise to Big at a 50% gross profit on the sale price.

4. On December 31, 20X6, Big held inventory of $1,500,000 that had been purchased from Small during 20X6 at a 50% gross profit on the sale price.

5. At the end of 20X6, Big owed Small $600,000 for merchandise purchased on account.

6. During 20X6, Small sold an investment for $1,200,000. The investment had cost Small $540,000, and had a fair value of $900,000 on January 1, 20X6.

7. Big's retained earnings on December 31, 20X6, include dividend income received from Small. Small declared dividends of $600,000 in 20X6.

Required

Prepare a consolidated statement of financial position for Big Inc. at December 31, 20X6.

| Statements of Financial Position December 31, 20X6 | | |
|---|---|---|
| | Big | Small |
| Cash | $ 3,000,000 | $ 900,000 |
| Accounts receivable | 4,800,000 | 1,200,000 |
| Inventories | 7,200,000 | 2,100,000 |
| Plant and equipment | 63,000,000 | 21,000,000 |
| Accumulated depreciation | (18,000,000) | (7,500,000) |
| Goodwill | — | 1,200,000 |
| Long-term investments (cost) | 15,000,000 | 4,800,000 |
| Total assets | $75,000,000 | $23,700,000 |
| Accounts payable | $ 9,000,000 | $ 1,500,000 |
| Bonds payable | 15,000,000 | 9,000,000 |
| Common shares | 21,000,000 | 6,000,000 |
| Retained earnings | 30,000,000 | 7,200,000 |
| | $75,000,000 | $23,700,000 |

P4-5 (60 minutes, medium)

On January 1, 20X6, Parent Ltd. purchased 100% of the outstanding voting common shares of Sub Ltd. for $1,400,000. The depreciable assets of Sub have a future useful life of 10 years and are being depreciated using straight-line depreciation.

During 20X6, the following events occurred:

1. Neither Parent nor Sub paid any dividends.

2. Sub Ltd. sold inventory costing $247,000 to Parent Ltd. for $341,000, 30% of which was not sold at year-end.

3. All of the current assets of Sub at the time of acquisition were sold to outside parties or were collected.

4. Parent Ltd. uses the cost method to record the investment in Sub. Condensed trial balance information for Sub Ltd. and Parent Ltd. is shown below.

Required

Prepare a consolidated statement of comprehensive income and retained earnings and a consolidated statement of financial position for Parent Ltd. for the year ended December 31, 20X6.

| | Post-closing trial balance January 1, 20X6 | Sub Limited fair market value January 1, 20X6 | Pre-closing trial balance December 31, 20X6 |
|---|---|---|---|
| Cash | $ 92,500 | $ 92,500 | $ 67,500 |
| Accounts receivable, net | 216,000 | 225,000 | 192,500 |
| Inventory | 345,000 | 365,000 | 365,000 |
| Land | 255,000 | 285,000 | 255,000 |
| Buildings and equipment, net | 487,000 | 425,000 | 481,500 |
| Goodwill | 55,000 | — | 55,000 |
| | $1,450,500 | | $ 1,416,500 |
| Current liabilities | $ 160,000 | $ 160,000 | $ 155,000 |
| Bonds payable, 10% | 107,500 | 107,500 | 107,500 |
| Common shares | 200,000 | — | 200,000 |
| Retained earnings | 983,000 | — | 983,000 |
| Sales | — | — | 715,000 |
| Cost of goods sold | — | — | (433,500) |
| Depreciation | — | — | (5,500) |
| Other expenses | — | — | (294,250) |
| Bond interest expense | — | — | (10,750) |
| | $1,450,500 | | $1,416,500 |

| Parent Ltd. Pre-closing Trial Balance December 31, 20X6 | |
|---|---|
| Cash | $ 137,500 |
| Accounts receivable, net | 192,000 |
| Marketable securities | 64,500 |
| Inventory | 430,000 |
| Land | 365,000 |
| Buildings and equipment, net | 431,000 |
| Goodwill* | 70,000 |
| Investment in Sub Ltd. | 1,400,000 |
| | $ 3,090,000 |
| Current liabilities | $ 197,500 |
| Bonds payable | 342,500 |
| Common shares | 550,000 |
| Retained earnings | 1,878,500 |
| Sales | 965,000 |
| Cost of goods sold | (731,500) |
| Depreciation | (13,500) |
| Other expenses | (101,725) |
| Bond interest income | 3,225 |
| | $ 3,090,000 |

*Does not relate to the acquisition of Sub Ltd.

P4-6 (90 minutes, difficult)

Plain Ltd. acquired 100% of the voting shares of Stylish Ltd. on January 1, 20X3, for $1,500,000. The financial statement of Stylish Ltd. on the date of acquisition was as follows:

| Stylish Ltd. Statement of Financial Position January 1, 20X3 | | |
|---|---|---|
| | Carrying value | Fair market value |
| Cash | $ 50,000 | $ 50,000 |
| Accounts receivable | 115,000 | 140,000 |
| Inventory | 300,000 | 280,000 |
| Land | 300,000 | 420,000 |
| Depreciable capital assets | 580,000 | 500,000 |
| Accumulated depreciation | (120,000) | |
| Total | $1,225,000 | |
| Current liabilities | 275,000 | 250,000 |
| Common shares | 450,000 | — |
| Retained earnings | 500,000 | — |
| Total | $1,225,000 | |

The inventory will be sold and the accounts receivable will be collected within 20X3, and the depreciable capital assets will be depreciated over 10 years, straight-line, with no salvage value.

During 20X3, Stylish Ltd. sold inventory to Plain Ltd. for $180,000, with a 20% gross profit on the sale price. At the end of 20X3, $30,000 (at sale price) of these goods were still in the inventory of Plain Ltd. Plain Ltd. sold goods at $200,000 to Stylish Ltd. during 20X3, with a 30% gross profit on the sale price, and $50,000 (at sale price) of these goods were still in the inventory of Stylish Ltd. at the end of 20X3. All of these goods remaining in inventory were sold during 20X4.

During 20X4, Plain Ltd. sold $150,000 of goods to Stylish Ltd., with a 25% gross profit on sale price, and $50,000 (at sale price) of these goods were in the inventory of Stylish at the end of 20X4. In addition, Stylish Ltd. sold goods to Plain Ltd. for $250,000, with a 20% gross profit on sale price, and $100,000 (at sale price) of these goods were still in the inventory of Plain Ltd. at the end of 20X4.

While Plain paid $20,000 as dividends in 20X3, Stylish paid $15,000. Similarly, while Plain paid dividends of $25,000 in 20X4, Stylish paid $20,000.

The retained earnings balance of Plain on January 1, 20X3, was $1,650,000. The following are the financial statements of the two companies at December 31, 20X4:

| Statements of Financial Position December 31, 20X4 | | |
|---|---|---|
| | Plain Ltd. | Stylish Ltd. |
| Cash | $ 60,000 | $ 80,000 |
| Accounts receivable | 150,000 | 251,000 |
| Inventory | 420,000 | 350,000 |
| Land | 680,000 | 385,000 |
| Depreciable capital assets | 1,200,000 | 580,000 |
| Accumulated depreciation | (300,000) | (236,000) |
| Investment in Stylish Ltd. | 1,500,000 | — |
| Total | $3,710,000 | $ 1,410,000 |

## Statements of Financial Position
### December 31, 20X4

| | | |
|---|---|---|
| Current liabilities | $ 250,000 | $ 180,000 |
| Common shares | 1,460,000 | 450,000 |
| Retained earnings | 2,000,000 | 780,000 |
| Total | $3,710,000 | $ 1,410,000 |

### Statements of Comprehensive Income Year Ended December 31, 20X4

| | Plain Ltd. | Stylish Ltd. |
|---|---|---|
| Sales | $1,000,000 | $ 900,000 |
| Cost of goods sold | 640,000 | 550,000 |
| Depreciation | 120,000 | 58,000 |
| Other expenses | 130,000 | 162,000 |
| Total expenses | 890,000 | 770,000 |
| Net income | $ 110,000 | $ 130,000 |

### Required

Calculate the following under the entity method, considering all dates carefully:

**a.** Equity in the earnings of Stylish using the equity method for 20X3

**b.** The adjusted earnings of Plain for 20X3

**c.** Consolidated net income for 20X4

**d.** Consolidated retained earnings balance at the end of 20X4

**e.** Investment in Stylish account balance at the end of 20X3 under the equity method

**f.** Consolidated gross depreciable assets, accumulated depreciation, and net depreciable assets at December 31, 20X4

**g.** Consolidated balance of inventory at December 31, 20X4

### P4-7 (90 minutes, medium)

On January 4, 20X7, Pradeesh Corp. acquired 100% of the outstanding common shares of Serena Inc. by a share-for-share exchange of its own shares, valued at $1,000,000. The statements of financial position of both companies just prior to the share exchange are shown below. Serena had patents, not shown on the SFP, that had an estimated fair value of $200,000 and an estimated remaining productive life of four years. Serena's buildings and equipment had an estimated fair value $300,000 in excess of carrying value, and the deferred charges were assumed to have a fair value of zero. Serena's buildings and equipment are being depreciated on the straight-line basis and have a remaining useful life of 10 years. The deferred charges are being amortized over three years.

During 20X7, the year following the acquisition, Serena borrowed $100,000 from Pradeesh; $40,000 was repaid, and $60,000 is still outstanding at year-end. No interest is being charged on the loan. Through the year, Serena sold goods to Pradeesh totalling $400,000. Serena's gross margin is 40% of selling price. Three-quarters of these goods were resold by Pradeesh to its customers, for $450,000. Dividend declarations amounted to $80,000 by Pradeesh and $50,000 by Serena. There were no other intercompany transactions. The year-end 20X7 SFPs and SCIs for Pradeesh and Serena are shown below.

## Statements of Financial Position
## December 31, 20X6

| | Pradeesh | Serena |
|---|---|---|
| Cash | $ 110,000 | $ 85,000 |
| Accounts and other receivables | 140,000 | 80,000 |
| Inventories | 110,000 | 55,000 |
| Buildings and equipment | 1,500,000 | 800,000 |
| Accumulated depreciation | (700,000) | (400,000) |
| Deferred charges | — | 120,000 |
| | $ 1,160,000 | $ 740,000 |
| Accounts and other payables | $ 200,000 | $ 100,000 |
| Bonds payable | — | 200,000 |
| Deferred income taxes | 60,000 | 40,000 |
| Common shares* | 600,000 | 150,000 |
| Retained earnings | 300,000 | 250,000 |
| | $ 1,160,000 | $ 740,000 |

*Pradeesh = 300,000 shares; Serena = 150,000 shares.

## Required

**a.** How would the SCI and SFP for Pradeesh Corp. differ from those shown below if Pradeesh reported its investment in Serena on the equity basis? Show all calculations.

**b.** Prepare a complete set of consolidated financial statements for Pradeesh Corp. for 20X7. Show all calculations.

## Statements of Financial Position December 31, 20X7

| | Pradeesh | Serena |
|---|---|---|
| Cash | $ 50,000 | $ 25,000 |
| Accounts and other receivables | 240,000 | 90,000 |
| Inventories | 150,000 | 80,000 |
| Buildings and equipment | 1,300,000 | 900,000 |
| Accumulated depreciation | (570,000) | (445,000) |
| Land | — | 60,000 |
| Investment in Serena (at cost) | 1,000,000 | — |
| Other investments | 70,000 | 30,000 |
| Deferred charges | — | 80,000 |
| | $ 2,240,000 | $ 820,000 |
| Accounts and other payables | $ 150,000 | $ 180,000 |
| Bonds payable | — | 170,000 |
| Deferred income taxes | 70,000 | 45,000 |
| Common shares | 1,600,000 | 150,000 |
| Retained earnings | 420,000 | 275,000 |
| | $ 2,240,000 | $ 820,000 |

| Statements of Comprehensive Income Year Ended December 31, 20X7 | | |
|---|---|---|
| | Pradeesh | Serena |
| Sales | $ 1,500,000 | $ 900,000 |
| Dividend income | 50,000 | — |
| | 1,550,000 | 900,000 |
| Cost of sales | 1,000,000 | 540,000 |
| Depreciation expense | 70,000 | 45,000 |
| Amortization expense | — | 40,000 |
| Income tax expense | 50,000 | 25,000 |
| Other expenses | 230,000 | 175,000 |
| | 1,350,000 | 825,000 |
| Net income and comprehensive income | $ 200,000 | $ 75,000 |

### Statements of Changes in Equity—Retained Earnings Section
### Year Ended December 31, 20X7

| | Pradeesh | Serena |
|---|---|---|
| Retained earnings, December 31, 20X6 | $ 300,000 | $ 250,000 |
| Net income | 200,000 | 75,000 |
| Dividends declared | (80,000) | (50,000) |
| Retained earnings, December 31, 20X7 | $ 420,000 | $ 275,000 |

P4-8 (120 minutes, difficult)

Refer to P4-7. During 20X8, the following events occurred:

1. Serena Inc. had sales of $800,000 to Pradeesh Corp. Serena's gross margin was still 40% of selling price. At year-end, $120,000 of these goods were still in Pradeesh's inventory.

2. On October 1, 20X8, Serena sold its land to Pradeesh for $185,000 (on which income taxes were due for $20,000). Pradeesh paid Serena $85,000 and gave a promissory note for $100,000 that was due in three years at 10% interest per year, simple interest to be paid at maturity.

3. The $60,000 that Serena owed to Pradeesh at the beginning of the year was repaid during 20X8.

4. Pradeesh paid dividends of $100,000 during the year; Serena paid dividends of $70,000.

The pre-closing trial balances of Pradeesh and Serena at December 31, 20X8, are shown below.

Required

a. Determine Pradeesh Corp.'s equity in the earnings of Serena Inc. for 20X8. Determine the balance of the investment in the Serena account on Pradeesh's books at December 31, 20X8, assuming that Pradeesh recorded its investment on the equity basis. Show all calculations.

b. Prepare a comparative consolidated SFP and SCI for Pradeesh Corp. for 20X8. Show all calculations.

| Trial Balances December 31, 20X8 | Pradeesh | Serena |
|---|---|---|
| Cash | $ 55,500 | $ 45,000 |
| Accounts and other receivables | 160,000 | 116,000 |
| Inventories | 140,000 | 75,000 |
| Buildings and equipment | 1,700,000 | 900,000 |
| Accumulated depreciation | (655,000) | (495,000) |
| Land | 185,000 | — |
| Investment in Serena | 1,000,000 | — |
| Due from Pradeesh | — | 102,500 |
| Other investments | 100,000 | 50,000 |
| Deferred charges | — | 40,000 |
| Accounts and other payables | (225,000) | (215,000) |
| Payable to Serena | (102,500) | — |
| Deferred income taxes | (75,000) | (47,500) |
| Common shares | (1,800,000) | (150,000) |
| Retained earnings | (420,000) | (275,000) |
| Dividends paid | 100,000 | 70,000 |
| Sales | (1,680,000) | (1,200,000) |
| Cost of sales | 1,120,000 | 720,000 |
| Depreciation expense | 85,000 | 50,000 |
| Amortization expense | — | 40,000 |
| Income tax expense | 31,000 | 57,000 |
| Other expenses | 351,000 | 244,500 |
| Gain on sale of land | — | (125,000) |
| Other income | (70,000) | (2,500) |
| | $ 0 | $ 0 |

P4-9 (60 minutes, medium)

On January 1, 20X5, Piper Ltd. purchased 100% of the shares of Sutton Ltd. for $1,085,000. At that time Sutton Ltd. had the following SFP:

| Sutton Ltd. | | |
|---|---|---|
| Statement of Financial Position January 1, 20X5 | | |
| | Net carrying value | Fair value |
| Cash | $ 60,000 | $ 60,000 |
| Accounts receivable | 120,000 | 150,000 |
| Inventory—FIFO | 180,000 | 230,000 |
| Capital assets, net | 1,500,000 | 1,350,000 |
| Goodwill | 100,000 | — |
| | $ 1,960,000 | |
| | | |
| Current liabilities | $ 140,000 | 140,000 |
| Bonds payable | 800,000 | 850,000 |
| Common shares | 400,000 | — |
| Retained earnings | 620,000 | — |
| | $ 1,960,000 | |

The bonds were issued at par and will mature in 10 years. Sutton Ltd. has a receivables and inventory turnover of greater than six times per year. The capital assets have an average of 10 years of remaining life and are being amortized straight-line.

In 20X5, Sutton Ltd. sold inventory to Piper Ltd. for $260,000; the inventory had cost $320,000. At the end of 20X5, 25% was still in Piper's inventory, but it was all sold in 20X6.

In 20X6, Piper Ltd. sold inventory to Sutton Ltd. for $275,000; the inventory had cost $200,000. At the end of 20X6, 35% was left in Sutton's inventory.

During 20X5, the subsidiary earned $875,000 and paid dividends of $50,000. During 20X6, the subsidiary incurred a loss of $172,000 and paid dividends of $60,000.

Piper uses the cost method for the investment in subsidiary and nets almost everything to "Other expenses."

At December 31, 20X6, the following financial statements were available:

| Statements of Financial Position December 31, 20X6 | | |
|---|---|---|
| | Piper Ltd. | Sutton Ltd. |
| Cash | $ 290,000 | $ 75,000 |
| Accounts receivable | 850,000 | 179,000 |
| Inventory | 970,000 | 245,000 |
| Capital assets, net | 2,631,000 | 1,863,000 |
| Goodwill | — | 100,000 |
| Investment in Sutton Ltd. | 1,085,000 | — |
| | $ 5,826,000 | $ 2,462,000 |
| Current liabilities | $ 450,000 | $49,000 |
| Bonds payable | — | 800,000 |
| Common shares | 1,000,000 | 400,000 |
| Retained earnings | 3,026,000 | 1,385,000 |
| Net income (loss) | 1,350,000 | (172,000) |
| | $ 5,826,000 | $ 2,462,000 |

| Statement of Comprehensive Income Year Ended December 31, 20X6 | | |
|---|---|---|
| | Piper Ltd. | Sutton Ltd. |
| Sales | $ 9,865,000 | $ 1,650,000 |
| Cost of sales | 8,040,000 | 1,140,000 |
| Gross profit | 1,825,000 | 510,000 |
| Depreciation | (106,000) | (96,000) |
| Other expenses | (369,000) | (816,000) |
| Gain on sale of building | — | 230,000 |
| Net income and comprehensive income | $ 1,350,000 | $ (172,000) |

Required

a. Prepare a consolidated statement of comprehensive income for 20X6.

b. Calculate the amounts that would appear on the consolidated SFP at December 31, 20X6, for:

  i) capital assets, net

  ii) bonds payable

  [CGA–Canada, adapted]

P4-10 (120 minutes, difficult)

Parent Corp. purchased 100% of the outstanding shares of Subsidiary Corp. on January 1, 20X1, for $1,000,000. The Statement of Financial Position (SFP) of Subsidiary Corp. and the fair values of the different accounts are provided below.

| Subsidiary Co. Statement of Financial Position January 1, 20X1 | | |
|---|---|---|
| | Net carrying value | Fair value |
| Cash | $  250,000 | $  250,000 |
| Accounts receivable | 150,000 | 150,000 |
| Inventory | 175,000 | 250,000 |
| Land & buildings | 550,000 | 550,000 |
| Less accumulated depreciation | (250,000) | |
| Investments | 115,000 | 150,000 |
| Goodwill | 160,000 | — |
| TOTAL ASSETS | $1,150,000 | $1,350,000 |
| | | |
| Accounts payable | $  225,000 | $  200,000 |
| Long-term debt | 325,000 | 325,000 |
| Shareholders' equity | | |
| Contributed capital | 450,000 | |
| Retained earnings | 150,000 | — |
| TOTAL LIABILITIES & OWNERS' EQUITY | $1,150,000 | $  525,000 |

The buildings are being depreciated using straight-line depreciation and had a future life of five years on the date of acquisition. All current assets and liabilities turned over by the end of 20X1.

The separate-entity financial statements of Parent Corp. and Subsidiary Corp. for 20X2 are provided below.

| Parent Corp. Statement of Financial Position December 31, 20X2 | |
| --- | --- |
| Cash | $1,155,000 |
| Accounts Receivable | 100,000 |
| Inventory | 300,000 |
| Land & buildings | 650,000 |
| Less accumulated depreciation | (580,000) |
| Investments | 145,000 |
| Investment in subsidiary | 1,000,000 |
| Goodwill | 250,000 |
| TOTAL ASSETS | $3,020,000 |
| | |
| Accounts payable | $ 350,000 |
| Long-term debt | 750,000 |
| Shareholders' equity | |
| Contributed capital | 750,000 |
| Retained earnings | 1,170,000 |
| TOTAL LIABILITIES & OWNERS' EQUITY | $3,020,000 |

| Parent Company Statement of Comprehensive Income, Year Ended December 31, 20X2 | |
| --- | --- |
| Sales | $4,500,000 |
| Dividend income | 100,000 |
| Total revenues | 4,600,000 |
| | |
| Cost of goods sold | 3,600,000 |
| Depreciation expense | 90,000 |
| Interest expense | 37,500 |
| Administrative expenses | 275,000 |
| Other expenses | 55,000 |
| Income tax expense | 122,500 |
| Total expenses | 4,180,000 |
| Net income and comprehensive income | $ 420,000 |

| Parent Company Statement of Changes in Equity—Retained Earnings Section Year Ended December 31, 20X2 | |
| --- | --- |
| Beginning retained earnings | $ 900,000 |
| Add net income during the year | 420,000 |
| Less dividends declared | (150,000) |
| Ending retained earnings | $1,170,000 |

## Subsidiary Co.
### Statement of Financial Position December 31, 20X2

| | |
|---|---:|
| Cash | $ 650,000 |
| Accounts receivable | 175,000 |
| Inventory | 185,000 |
| Land & buildings | 550,000 |
| Less accumulated depreciation | (360,000) |
| Investments | 0 |
| Goodwill | 250,000 |
| TOTAL ASSETS | $1,450,000 |
| | |
| Accounts payable | $ 275,000 |
| Long-term debt | 300,000 |
| Shareholders' equity | |
| Contributed capital | 450,000 |
| Retained earnings | 425,000 |
| TOTAL LIABILITIES & OWNERS' EQUITY | $1,450,000 |

## Subsidiary Company
### Statement of Comprehensive Income
### Year Ended December 31, 20X2

| | |
|---|---:|
| Sales | $2,750,000 |
| Dividend income | 15,000 |
| Gain on sale of investments | 30,000 |
| Total revenues | 2,795,000 |
| | |
| Cost of goods sold | 2,150,000 |
| Depreciation expense | 55,000 |
| Interest expense | 15,000 |
| Administrative expenses | 196,000 |
| Other expenses | 24,000 |
| Income tax expense | 105,000 |
| Total expenses | 2,545,000 |
| Net income and comprehensive income | $ 250,000 |

### Subsidiary Company Statement of Changes in Equity—Retained Earnings Section
### Year Ended December 31, 20X2

| | |
|---|---:|
| Beginning retained earnings | $ 275,000 |
| Add net income during the year | 250,000 |
| Less dividends declared | (100,000) |
| Ending retained earnings | $ 425,000 |

Additional information:

- Subsidiary Corp. sold goods worth $300,000 at a gross profit of 25% to Parent Corp. in 20X0 (the year before 20X1). All of these goods remained unsold in Parent Corp.'s ending inventory at the end of year 20X0. Half of these goods were sold in 20X1, and the remaining half was sold in 20X2 to outsiders by Parent Corp.

- Subsidiary Corp. sold goods worth $250,000 at a gross profit of 30% to Parent Corp. in 20X1. One-third of these goods remained unsold with Parent Corp. at the end of 20X1. Parent Corp. sold goods worth $300,000 at a gross profit of 25% to Subsidiary Corp. in 20X1. Half of these goods remained unsold with Subsidiary Corp. at the end of 20X1.

- Subsidiary Corp. sold goods worth $200,000 at a gross profit of 30% to Parent Corp. in 20X2. Half of these goods remained unsold with Parent Corp. at the end of 20X2. Parent Corp. sold goods worth $350,000 at a gross profit of 25% to Subsidiary Corp. in 20X2. Forty percent of these goods remained unsold with Subsidiary Corp. at the end of 20X2.

- Subsidiary Corp. sold all of its investments in 20X2 to Parent Corp. for $145,000.

Required

Note: No financial statements are required.

a. Show the purchase price allocation calculations required at the time of acquisition and the goodwill balance at the time of acquisition.

b. Show all necessary consolidation adjustments required in 20X2 relating to 20X1 and 20X2 (i.e., show the remaining adjustments other than the acquisition-related adjustments required in item a, necessary under the MEAR steps).

c. Calculate the consolidated retained earnings balance at the end of 20X1.

d. Calculate the adjusted income of Subsidiary Corp. and the adjusted income of Parent Corp. for 20X2.

e. Calculate the consolidated income in 20X2.

f. Calculate the consolidated retained earnings balance at the end of 20X2.

g. Calculate the consolidated gross (i.e., original cost) and net balance (i.e., after deducting accumulated depreciation) of the buildings account at the end of 20X2.

h. Calculate the consolidated goodwill balance at the end of 20X2.

i. Calculate the consolidated investment account balance at the end of 20X2.

# APPENDIX 4A Income Tax Allocation Subsequent to Acquisition

## 4A.1 INTRODUCTION AND REVIEW

Appendix 3A on the Companion Website discussed the issue of income tax allocation in a business combination and illustrated the calculation of deferred tax at acquisition. The essence of tax allocation for business combinations is that the buyer, *on its consolidated SFP*, must calculate DT as part of the purchase equation. The DT for each asset and liability is based on its temporary difference. The temporary difference is the difference between (1) the tax basis of the asset to the *subsidiary* and (2) the fair value of the asset as it is included on the *parent's* consolidated statement.

For the purchase transaction in Chapter 3, which also pertains to this chapter, the amounts are as follows:

| | Target Ltd.'s carrying value (1) | Tax basis for Target (2) | Fair value to Purchase (3) | Temporary difference (3) – (2) |
|---|---|---|---|---|
| Land | $300,000 | $300,000 | $400,000 | $100,000 |
| Buildings and equipment | 350,000 | 250,000 | 550,000 | 300,000 |
| Total | $650,000 | $550,000 | $950,000 | $400,000 |

Target Ltd.'s carrying values are included as column (1), but they really are irrelevant for determining the amount of DT. They are irrelevant because we need to compare the fair values with the assets' *tax bases*, not with their carrying values on the subsidiary's books. We have put them in the table to emphasize that the tax bases of Target Ltd.'s assets may be different from their carrying values. For tax allocation, the relevant figures are those in columns (2) and (3).

The temporary differences are shown in the last column. The tax basis for each asset is subtracted from its fair value. If we assume that Purchase Ltd.'s income tax rate is 40%, we must include $400,000 × 40% = $160,000 as a DT liability when we allocate the purchase price. As we explained in Appendix 3A, the effect of including the DT liability is to increase the amount of the purchase price that is allocated to goodwill.

## 4A.2 POST-ACQUISITION TAX ACCOUNTING FOR FAIR VALUE ADJUSTMENTS

The balance in the DT account is a function of the temporary differences at each SFP date. In a business combination, the temporary difference is the difference between the tax basis of an asset to the tax-paying entity (that is, to the *subsidiary* that legally owns the asset and that deducts the CCA) and its value as reported *on the parent company's consolidated SFP*.

In a business combination, we must focus on the fair value adjustments relating to amortizable capital assets, both tangible and intangible. Residual goodwill in a purchase of shares is not a capital asset, and it is not deductible for tax purposes.

For amortizable capital assets, in years subsequent to the acquisition, (1) the fair value adjustments are amortized and flow into expense, thereby reducing their carrying value, and (2) the assets' tax bases change as the assets are recognized in taxable income (e.g., through CCA). Therefore, the temporary differences change. The change in temporary differences arising from fair value adjustment (FVA) amortization must be recognized on the consolidated SFP.

In this chapter, we amortized the fair value increment relating to buildings and equipment. The amortization for each of 20X6 and 20X7 was $20,000. Therefore, the fair value increment declined from $200,000 at the date of acquisition to $180,000 at the end of 20X6 and $160,000 at the end of 20X7.

The change in the FVI is only half of the situation. The other half is the tax basis. The tax basis changes because Target Ltd. continues taking CCA on its buildings and equipment. The overall temporary difference depends on both the FVI amortization and the change in the tax basis. Fortunately, however, we really don't need to know the tax basis of all of the subsidiary's assets to adjust for the change in temporary differences during each year.

Remember that the starting point for consolidation is the companies' separate-entity financial statements (or trial balances). The subsidiary will be using tax allocation procedures on its own books. Therefore, the subsidiary will already have recorded the DT that relates to temporary differences between its assets' tax bases and their carrying values. All we have to do for consolidation is to supplement that already-reported DT amount by recognizing the additional change to the temporary difference that relates to the FVI:

| | |
|---|---|
| Tax basis of Target assets | Recorded on Target's books |
| Carrying value on Target's books | |
| Consolidation value = carrying value + FVI | Added as a consolidation adjustment |

In essence, therefore, we only have to make a DT adjustment for the change in the temporary difference that is caused by the FVI amortization. In each of 20X6 and 20X7, the amortization is $20,000. At an assumed income tax rate of 40%, each year's worksheet adjustment for the additional change in consolidated DT will be:

| | | |
|---|---|---|
| Deferred tax liability—long-term | 8,000 | |
|    Income tax expense ($20,000 × 40%) | | 8,000 |

The adjustment always will be to *reduce* the DT liability because FVIs will never increase—they will only decrease. This does not mean that the *overall* temporary difference may not increase. Instead, it means that an increase that might have been recorded on Target Ltd.'s books will be reduced by the additional adjustment in consolidation.

For example, suppose that in 20X6, Target Ltd. recorded depreciation of $35,000 on its buildings and equipment and took CCA of $65,000. The carrying value of buildings and equipment *on Target Ltd.'s books* will be $350,000 − $35,000 = $315,000. The tax basis will be $250,000 - $65,000 = $185,000$. The changes can be summarized as follows:

|  | 20X5 | 20X6 |
| --- | --- | --- |
| Tax basis | $250,000 | $185,000 |
| Target's carrying value | 350,000 | 315,000 |
| Temporary difference | $100,000 | $130,000 |

From 20X5 to 20X6, Target Ltd.'s temporary difference for the buildings and equipment increased by $30,000. Target Ltd. will have *recorded* the appropriate increase in the DT liability of $12,000 (that is, $30,000 \times 40\% = \$12,000$) resulting from the increase in the temporary difference.

Looking now at Purchase Ltd.'s consolidated amounts (i.e., including FVI), the consolidated temporary difference is as follows:

| Tax basis | $250,000 | $185,000 |
| --- | --- | --- |
| Purchase's consolidated value | 550,000 | 495,000 |
| Temporary difference | $300,000 | $310,000 |

The consolidated value of the buildings and equipment acquired in the business combination was initially a Target Ltd. carrying value of $350,000 plus FVI of $200,000, for a total fair value of $550,000. One year later, the Target Ltd. carrying value has been depreciated to $315,000 and the FVI has been amortized to $180,000—the sum of these two amounts equals the $495,000 shown above.

Overall, the temporary difference relating to the fair values shown on Purchase Ltd.'s consolidated SFP is increased by $10,000. The related increase in the consolidated DT liability is $10,000 \times 40\% = \$4,000$. The change in consolidated DT liability relating to Target Ltd.'s buildings and equipment can be summarized as follows:

|  | Temporary difference | Deferred tax liability |
| --- | --- | --- |
| Increase recorded on Target Ltd.'s books | $30,000 | $12,000 Cr |
| Decrease from FVI amortization upon consolidation | 20,000 | 8,000 Dr |
| Net change in consolidated amounts | $10,000 | $ 4,000 Cr |

Therefore, when we make the consolidation adjustments relating to DT, we need only concern ourselves with the changes in the fair value adjustments. We can safely assume that the subsidiary has already recorded the DT arising from the timing differences between the tax basis and the carrying value of its assets and liabilities.

## 4A.3 UNREALIZED PROFIT

The only other income tax aspect that we need to worry about is that relating to unrealized profit. At the end of 20X6, there is unrealized upstream profit of $8,000 in inventory. This profit is unrealized only from the viewpoint of the consolidated entity. As far as the

Canada Revenue Agency is concerned, Target Ltd. has earned this profit and will be taxed on it in 20X6. The tax, at 40%, will amount to $3,200.

On consolidation, the unrealized profit is eliminated. Since the profit is removed from net income, tax allocation requires that the related taxes also be removed from net income. The adjustment to achieve this is quite straightforward:

| | | |
|---|---|---|
| Deferred tax | 3,200 | |
| Income tax expense ($8,000 × 40%) | | 3,200 |

All unrealized profit eliminations must be accompanied by an adjustment for income tax, deferring recognition of the income taxes paid by the selling company to the period in which the profit is realized.

In 20X7, the beginning-of-year unrealized profit is recognized in consolidated net income, and therefore the income tax expense also is recognized. However, since consolidation-related adjustments do not carry over, the impact of the entry made in 20X6 relating to the removal of taxes has to be first captured before the entry relating to the recognition of the income tax expense in 20X7 is made:

| | | |
|---|---|---|
| Deferred tax ($8,000 × 40%) | 3,200 | |
| Beginning retailed earnings | | 3,200 |

| | | |
|---|---|---|
| Income tax expense ($8,000 × 40%) | 3,200 | |
| Deferred tax | | 3,200 |

Or, in net, the entry required in 20X7 is:

| | | |
|---|---|---|
| Income tax expense ($8,000 × 40%) | 3,200 | |
| Beginning retailed earnings | | 3,200 |

Of course, the year-end 20X7 unrealized profit must be eliminated, and those eliminations must be accompanied by adjustments to defer recognition of the related income tax expense.

## 4A.4 SUMMARY

Income tax allocation affects consolidation in two ways:

1. Amortization of the fair value adjustments changes the consolidated reporting values of tangible and intangible capital assets (except land), and therefore the temporary differences are affected.

2. The tax relating to unrealized profits must be removed from consolidated net income and deferred as part of the DT balance(s) on the SFP.

Fortunately, we need not worry about making the full adjustment for the changes in consolidated temporary differences for capital assets. The subsidiary company will have recorded the effects of changes in temporary differences between their carrying values and the tax bases. On consolidation, we need only adjust for the income tax effect of the FVI amortization.

# Self-Study Problem

1. The only asset of T Ltd. is a building that had a carrying value of $150,000 on January 1, 20X2. The SFP of T Ltd. on that date is provided below:

| Building | $150,000 | Deferred tax liability | $ 20,000 |
|---|---|---|---|
| | | Owner's equity | 130,000 |
| | | **TOTAL LIABILITIES AND** | |
| TOTAL ASSETS | $150,000 | **SHAREHOLDERS' EQUITY** | $150,000 |

P Ltd. purchased all of the shares of T Ltd. on January 1, 20X2, for $260,000. The building of T Ltd. had a fair value of $250,000 on that date. The building has a future life of 10 years on January 1, 20X2, and is being depreciated on the straight-line basis.

During 20X2, T Ltd. sold goods with a sale price of $100,000 at a gross profit of 25% to P Ltd. At the end of 20X2, half of these goods remained unsold and in the ending inventory of P Ltd.

### Required

Following the MEAR steps, calculate all consolidation-related adjustments required at the end of 20X2 and show all supporting calculations. Assume a future tax rate of 40%.

## Problems

### P4A-1 (25 minutes, medium)

Okavango Ltd. sold goods at a sale price of $10,000 to its 100%-owned subsidiary Serengeti in 20X5 at a gross profit percentage of 50%. At the end of 20X5, 40% of the goods purchased from Okavango remained unsold in the ending inventory of Serengeti. These goods were sold by Serengeti to an outside party in 20X6. The applicable future tax rate is 20%.

### Required

a. Provide all the necessary consolidation-related adjusting entries, including deferred tax entries, in 20X5 and 20X6 in relation to the sale of inventory by Okavango Ltd. to Serengeti.

### P4A-2 (90 minutes, difficult)

Refer to P4-7. Now assume Pradeesh Corp. acquired 100% of the outstanding common shares of Serena Inc. by a share-for-share exchange of its own shares, valued at $1,000,000. The statements of financial position of both companies just prior to the share exchange are shown below. Serena had patents, not shown on the SFP, that had an estimated fair value of $200,000 and an estimated remaining productive life of four years. Serena's buildings and equipment had an estimated fair value $300,000 in excess of carrying value, and the deferred charges were assumed to have a fair value of zero. Serena's buildings and equipment are being depreciated on the straight-line basis and have a remaining useful life of 10 years. The deferred charges are being amortized over three years.

| Statements of Financial Position December 31, 20X6 | | |
|---|---|---|
| | Pradeesh | Serena |
| Cash | $ 110,000 | $ 85,000 |
| Accounts and other receivables | 140,000 | 80,000 |
| Inventories | 110,000 | 55,000 |
| Buildings and equipment | 1,500,000 | 800,000 |
| Accumulated depreciation | (700,000) | (400,000) |
| Deferred charges | — | 120,000 |
| | $1,160,000 | $ 740,000 |
| Accounts and other payables | $ 200,000 | $ 100,000 |
| Bonds payable | — | 200,000 |
| Deferred income taxes | 60,000 | 40,000 |
| Common shares* | 600,000 | 150,000 |
| Retained earnings | 300,000 | 250,000 |
| | $1,160,000 | $ 740,000 |

*Pradeesh = 300,000 shares; Serena = 150,000 shares

During 20X7, the year following the acquisition, Serena borrowed $100,000 from Pradeesh; $40,000 was repaid, and $60,000 is still outstanding at year-end. No interest is being charged on the loan. Through the year, Serena sold goods to Pradeesh totalling $400,000. Serena's gross margin is 40% of selling price. Three-quarters of these goods were resold by Pradeesh to its customers, for $450,000. Dividend declarations amounted to $80,000 by Pradeesh and $50,000 by Serena. There were no other intercompany transactions. The year-end 20X7 SFPs and SCIs for Pradeesh and Serena are shown below.

| Statements of Financial Position December 31, 20X7 | | |
|---|---|---|
| | Pradeesh | Serena |
| Cash | $ 50,000 | $ 25,000 |
| Accounts and other receivables | 240,000 | 90,000 |
| Inventories | 150,000 | 80,000 |
| Buildings and equipment | 1,300,000 | 900,000 |
| Accumulated depreciation | (570,000) | (445,000) |
| Land | — | 60,000 |
| Investment in Serena (at cost) | 1,000,000 | — |
| Other investments | 70,000 | 30,000 |
| Deferred charges | — | 80,000 |
| | $2,240,000 | $ 820,000 |
| Accounts and other payables | $ 150,000 | $ 180,000 |
| Bonds payable | — | 170,000 |
| Deferred income taxes | 70,000 | 45,000 |
| Common shares | 1,600,000 | 150,000 |
| Retained earnings | 420,000 | 275,000 |
| | $2,240,000 | $ 820,000 |

### Statements of Comprehensive Income Year Ended December 31, 20X7

|  | Pradeesh | Serena |
|---|---|---|
| Sales | $1,500,000 | $900,000 |
| Dividend income | 50,000 | — |
|  | 1,550,000 | 900,000 |
| Cost of sales | 1,000,000 | 540,000 |
| Depreciation expense | 70,000 | 45,000 |
| Amortization expense | — | 40,000 |
| Income tax expense | 50,000 | 25,000 |
| Other expenses | 230,000 | 175,000 |
|  | 1,350,000 | 825,000 |
| Net income and comprehensive income | $ 200,000 | $ 75,000 |

### Statements of Changes in Equity—Retained Earnings Section Year Ended December 31, 20X7

|  | Pradeesh | Serena |
|---|---|---|
| Retained earnings, December 31, 20X6 | $ 300,000 | $250,000 |
| Net income | 200,000 | 75,000 |
| Dividends declared | (80,000) | (50,000) |
| Retained earnings, December 31, 20X7 | $ 420,000 | $275,000 |

Assume that the relevant future income tax rate is 25%.

**Required**

**a.** How would the SCI and SFP for Pradeesh Corp. differ from those shown in P4-7 if Pradeesh reported its investment in Serena on the equity basis and after adjusting for all relevant deferred tax implications? Show all calculations.

**b.** Prepare a complete set of consolidated financial statements for Pradeesh Corp. for 20X7 after making suitable adjustments for all relevant deferred tax implications. Show all calculations.

**P4A-3 (150 minutes, difficult)**

Refer to P4-8. Now assume the following events occurred:

**1.** Serena Inc. had sales of $800,000 to Pradeesh Corp. Serena's gross margin was still 40% of selling price. At year-end, $120,000 of these goods were still in Pradeesh's inventory.

**2.** On October 1, 20X8, Serena sold its land to Pradeesh for $185,000 (on which income taxes were due for $20,000). Pradeesh paid Serena $85,000 and gave a promissory note for $100,000 that was due in three years at 10% interest per year, simple interest to be paid at maturity.

**3.** The $60,000 that Serena owed to Pradeesh at the beginning of the year was repaid during 20X8.

**4.** Pradeesh paid dividends of $100,000 during the year; Serena paid dividends of $70,000.

The pre-closing trial balances of Pradeesh and Serena at December 31, 20X8, are shown below.

| Trial Balances December 31, 20X8 | Pradeesh | Serena |
|---|---|---|
| Cash | $ 55,500 | $ 45,000 |
| Accounts and other receivables | 160,000 | 116,000 |
| Inventories | 140,000 | 75,000 |
| Buildings and equipment | 1,700,000 | 900,000 |
| Accumulated depreciation | (655,000) | (495,000) |
| Land | 185,000 | — |
| Investment in Serena | 1,000,000 | — |
| Due from Pradeesh | — | 102,500 |
| Other investments | 100,000 | 50,000 |
| Deferred charges | — | 40,000 |
| Accounts and other payables | (225,000) | (215,000) |
| Payable to Serena | (102,500) | — |
| Deferred income taxes | (75,000) | (47,500) |
| Common shares | (1,800,000) | (150,000) |
| Retained earnings | (420,000) | (275,000) |
| Dividends paid | 100,000 | 70,000 |
| Sales | (1,680,000) | (1,200,000) |
| Cost of sales | 1,120,000 | 720,000 |
| Depreciation expense | 85,000 | 50,000 |
| Amortization expense | — | 40,000 |
| Income tax expense | 31,000 | 57,000 |
| Other expenses | 351,000 | 244,500 |
| Gain on sale of land | — | (125,000) |
| Other income | (70,000) | (2,500) |
| | $　　　0 | $　　　0 |

Assume that the relevant future income tax rate is 25%.

Required

1. Determine Pradeesh Corp.'s equity in the earnings of Serena Inc. for 20X8 after adjusting for all relevant deferred tax implications. Determine the balance of the investment in the Serena account on Pradeesh's books at December 31, 20X8, assuming that Pradeesh recorded its investment on the equity basis after adjusting for all relevant deferred tax implications. Show all calculations.

2. Prepare a comparative consolidated SFP and SCI for Pradeesh Corp. for 20X8 after making suitable adjustments for all relevant deferred tax implications. Show all calculations.

# APPENDIX 4B Goodwill Impairment Test

## 4B.1 ALLOCATION OF GOODWILL TO CASH-GENERATING UNITS

Goodwill does not generate cash flows on its own, but contributes to the cash-generation potential of other assets or groups of assets. Therefore, the *recoverable value* of goodwill cannot be calculated independently of the *recoverable value* of other assets or groups of assets. To facilitate subsequent impairment testing of goodwill, acquisition-related goodwill must be allocated to each of the corporation's *cash-generating units*, or *groups* of cash-generating units, that are expected to profit from the synergies of the business combination. This requirement must be followed even if none of the acquiree's other assets or liabilities are allocated to such unit(s).

The unit or groups of units to which goodwill is allocated should (1) be the lowest level within the corporation at which goodwill is monitored internally, and (2) not be larger than an operating segment as reported in the annual financial statements.[1] The allocation process ensures that testing for impairment of goodwill occurs at a level at which the corporation manages its operations and to which goodwill can naturally be associated.

For impairment testing, goodwill should be allocated to each of a company's cash-generating units from the date of acquisition. However, if the initial allocation of goodwill cannot be completed by the end of the year in which the business combination occurs, the allocation of goodwill to cash-generating units should be completed before the first annual period beginning after the acquisition date (that is, by the end of the subsequent annual period).

## 4B.2 APPLYING THE IMPAIRMENT TEST

The impairment test for goodwill is conducted by comparing the carrying value of the related *cash-generating unit*(s), including the goodwill allocated, with their *recoverable values*. If the *recoverable value* is greater than the carrying value, including goodwill, there is no impairment. Conversely, if the *recoverable value* is less than the carrying value, there is an impairment loss. Such an impairment loss is used to reduce the carrying values of the goodwill and the other assets in the *cash-generating unit*(s) in the following order:

- first to reduce the carrying value of the goodwill allocated to the cash-generating unit or group of units; and
- next to reduce the other assets of the unit or group of units on a prorated basis, based on the carrying value of each such asset.

Impairment losses should be recognized immediately in profit or loss unless such losses relate to revalued assets. In the latter case, the impairment losses are treated as a revaluation decrease and are recognized in other comprehensive income to the extent that the

---

[1] The classification and reporting of segments is discussed in Chapter 7.

losses do not exceed the revaluation surplus relating to the same asset. Impairment losses reduce the value of the revaluation surplus for that asset.

A **cash-generating unit** is the corporation's smallest identifiable group of assets that generates cash inflows that are largely independent of the cash inflows of other assets or groups of assets. Goodwill often contributes to the cash-generation potential of multiple units as opposed to that of a single unit. Therefore, in such circumstances it may not be possible to allocate goodwill in a non-arbitrary manner to a single cash-generating unit to which it relates but only to a group of such cash-generating units.

Impairment testing of goodwill is carried out at the level of the group of cash-generating units to which the goodwill has been allocated. However, before doing so, you should first test the individual cash-generating unit to which the goodwill relates (but to which goodwill could not be allocated) for impairment. The impairment test should be conducted by comparing the carrying value of the unit, disregarding any related goodwill, to its recoverable value. Impairment testing of the goodwill allocated is carried out next in the usual fashion, as described in the previous paragraph.

Here, **recoverable value** of a cash-generating unit represents the higher of its (1) fair value less costs to sell and (2) *value in use*. **Value in use** of the cash-generating unit represents the present value of the estimated future cash flows expected to be generated from the continuing use of the unit, and from its disposal at the end of its useful life. It is not necessary for a corporation to determine both the fair value less costs to sell and the value in use of a cash-generating unit. As long as one of these values exceeds the carrying value of the unit, including the allocated goodwill, there is no impairment.

The most recent detailed calculation from the preceding period of the recoverable value of the cash-generating unit(s) to which goodwill has been allocated can be used in the current period (instead of making a fresh calculation) if *all* of the following three criteria are satisfied:

1. the cash-generating unit's assets and liabilities have not changed significantly since the most recent calculation of the recoverable value; *and*

2. the most recent recoverable value estimate exceeds the carrying amount of the unit by a substantial amount; *and*

3. events and circumstances since the most recent recoverable value estimation indicate that the probability of impairment is remote.

An impairment loss recognized in relation to goodwill cannot be reversed in later periods.

## 4B.3 TIMING OF IMPAIRMENT TESTS

Goodwill acquired in relation to a business combination should be tested for impairment annually regardless of whether or not there is any indication of impairment. While the annual impairment test can be conducted at any time in the year, it should be performed at the same time every year.

To test for impairment in goodwill, the cash-generating units(s) to which goodwill has been allocated must be tested for impairment. The impairment testing of the cash-generating unit(s), in addition to being carried out annually, should be done whenever there is an indication that the unit(s) may be impaired.

## 4B.4 PRIVATE ENTERPRISES

Accounting standards for private enterprises require a private corporation that is not otherwise publicly accountable to test goodwill for impairment only when events or changes in circumstances indicate that the carrying value of a *reporting unit* to which the goodwill has been assigned exceeds its fair value. Thus, private enterprises are exempt from the burden of conducting an annual test of impairment of goodwill. Further, the testing of impairment at the reporting unit level obviates the need to allocate fair values to individual assets. Examples of events and circumstances indicating that the carrying value exceeds the fair value include:

- a significant change in the legal or business environment of the enterprise;

- an unfavourable assessment or action by a regulator;

- unexpected competition;

- loss of key personnel;

- a more likely than not probability that a significant portion or all of a *reporting unit* will be sold or otherwise disposed of;

- testing for impairment or write-down of a significant asset group within a *reporting unit*; or

- recognition of a goodwill impairment loss by a subsidiary that is a component of the *reporting unit* in its separate-entity financial statements.

Notice that the requirements for impairment testing of goodwill under accounting standards for private enterprises differ from their counterparts under international standards in:

1. the use of the term *reporting unit* instead of *cash-generating unit*; and

2. the use of *fair value* instead of *recoverable value*.

The reason for these differences can be attributed to the fact that accounting standards for private enterprises are based on Canadian GAAP in existence before the adoption of international standards.

When the carrying value of a reporting unit, including the allocated goodwill, exceeds its fair value, such excess should be recognized as an impairment loss in the period in which such impairment occurs. Impairment losses, once recognized, cannot be reversed when the fair value of the related reporting unit increases in value subsequently.

## Relevant Standards

### IFRS

IAS 36   Impairment of Assets

### ASPE

Section 3064     Goodwill and Intangible Assets

# Chapter 5
## Consolidation of Non-Wholly Owned Subsidiaries

## Learning Objectives

**After studying this chapter, you should be able to:**

**LO①** explain why some subsidiaries are not wholly owned;

**LO②** identify the conceptual alternatives for consolidating non-wholly owned subsidiaries;

**LO③** describe the different principles of accounting provided by IFRS and/or ASPE for reporting non-wholly owned subsidiaries, associates, and joint ventures; and

**LO④** consolidate a non-wholly owned subsidiary:

   a. at the date of acquisition;

   b. one year after acquisition; and

   c. two years after acquisition.

## INTRODUCTION

Barrick Gold Corporation (Barrick), the biggest gold company in the world, states its consolidation policy as follows in its 2011 annual report:

> These consolidated financial statements include the accounts of Barrick and its subsidiaries.... We consolidate subsidiaries where we have the ability to exercise control.... Control is normally achieved through ownership, directly or indirectly, of more than 50 percent of the voting power. Control can also be achieved through power over more than half of the voting rights by virtue of an agreement with other investors or through the exercise of de facto control. For non wholly-owned subsidiaries, the net assets attributable to outside equity shareholders are presented as "non-controlling interests" in the equity section of the consolidated balance sheet. Profit for the period that is attributable to non-controlling interests is calculated based on the ownership of the minority shareholders in the subsidiary.

Barrick provides the following information relating to entities in which it has less than 100% ownership:

| | Entity type at December 31, 2011 | Economic interest at December 31, 2011[1] | Method |
|---|---|---|---|
| Marigold Mine | JCA | 33% | Proportional |
| Round Mountain Mine | JCA | 50% | Proportional |
| Turquoise Ridge Mine | JCA | 75% | Proportional |
| Kalgoorlie Mine | JCA | 50% | Proportional |
| Porgera Mine | JCA | 95% | Proportional |
| African Barrick Gold Plc[2,3] | Subsidiary, publicly traded | 73.9% | Consolidation |
| Pueblo Viejo Project[3] | Subsidiary | 60% | Consolidation |
| Cerro Casale Project[3] | Subsidiary | 75% | Consolidation |
| Donlin Gold Project[5] | JCE | 50% | Equity Method |
| Reko Diq Project[4,5] | JCE | 37.5% | Equity Method |
| Kabanga Project[5] | JCE | 50% | Equity Method |
| Highland Gold Plc | Associate, publicly traded | 20.4% | Equity Method |

[1]Unless otherwise noted, all of our joint ventures are funded by contributions made by their partners in proportion to their economic interest.

[2]In 2010, we completed an initial public offering ("IPO") for a non-controlling interest in our African gold mining operations. As a result of this transaction, our economic interest in the North Mara, Bulyanhulu and Buzwagi gold mines reduced from 100% to 73.9% and our economic interest in the Tulawaka gold mine was reduced from 70% to 51.7%.

[3]We consolidate our interests in Pueblo Viejo, Cerro Casale and ABG and record a non-controlling interest for the 40%, 25% and 26.1%, respectively, that we do not own.

[4]We hold a 50% interest in Atacama Copper, which has a 75% interest in the Reko Diq project.

[5]Our jointly controlled entities are all early stage exploration projects and, as such, do not have any significant assets, liabilities, income, contractual commitments or contingencies. Expenses are recognized through our equity pick-up (loss). Refer to note 14 for further details.

Not all of the subsidiaries of Barrick are 100% owned. Such subsidiaries are known simply as **non-wholly owned subsidiaries**. As we will see in this chapter, there are often good reasons for owning less than 100% of a subsidiary. Also notice that Barrick uses the proportional method of consolidation to report its interest in joint ventures and the equity method to report its interests in associates.

The previous two chapters dealt with the preparation of consolidated statements when the parent company owns 100% of the shares of the subsidiary. This chapter focuses on the consolidated statements of a parent that owns less than 100% of its subsidiary and also continues our discussion of accounting for interests in joint ventures and associates.

The numerical example in this chapter exactly parallels the example we used in Chapters 3 and 4, except that now we assume the parent buys *less* than 100% of the subsidiary's shares.

Source: Barrick, Annual Report (2011), pp. 112–113. http://www.barrick.com/Theme/Barrick/files/docs_annual/2012/Barrick-Annual-Report-2011.pdf.

LO **1**

Explain why some
subsidiaries are not
wholly owned

## 5.1 WHY OWN LESS THAN 100%?

A parent's ownership interest may be less than 100% for either of two reasons:

■  in a business combination, the acquiring company (the parent) may buy a majority of the shares, but less than 100%; or

■  a parent may form a new subsidiary with the involvement of a non-controlling partner who is providing specialized expertise, management ability, market access, governmental support, and so forth.

Some parent corporations prefer to purchase significantly less than 100% of the shares in a business combination. The parent then need not invest the full value of the subsidiary's net assets. A less-than-100% investment conserves the parent's liquid resources (if the purchase was for cash) or reduces its share dilution (if the purchase was an exchange of shares). In addition, the maintenance of a significant **non-controlling interest (NCI)** in the subsidiary can spread the ownership risk, can provide valuable links with other corporate shareholders, and can maintain a market for the subsidiary's shares.

Non-controlling interests may also exist if the parent initially establishes the subsidiary, but subsequently sells shares in the subsidiary to others. The sale may be of shares originally owned by the parent (i.e., a secondary offering by the parent) or of new shares (i.e., a direct or primary offering by the subsidiary). In either case, the parent ends up holding less than 100% of the subsidiary. Later changes in ownership interest are discussed in Appendices 5A and 5B on the Companion Website.

LO **2**

Identify the conceptual
alternatives for
consolidating non-wholly
owned subsidiaries

LO **3**

Describe the different
principles of accounting
provided by IFRS and/or
ASPE for reporting non-
wholly owned subsidiaries,
associates, and joint
ventures

## 5.2 CONCEPTUAL ALTERNATIVES

As is the case with most aspects of accounting, there is no single theoretical approach to accounting for subsidiaries when an NCI exists. Three consecutive questions arise.

1.  Should the NCI's share of net assets be included in the consolidated statement of financial position (SFP)?

2.  If it is included, should the net assets be shown at their carrying value on the subsidiary's books (i.e., carrying value) or at their fair value as of the date of acquisition?

3.  If the NCI's share of net assets is included at fair value, should such net assets also include the NCI's share of goodwill?

The answers to these three questions flow from two major competing theories of consolidation applicable to non-wholly owned subsidiaries—the *proprietary theory* and the *entity theory*.

The **proprietary theory** views the consolidated group from the viewpoint of the owners of the parent. Therefore, the goal of consolidation is to report only the total interest owned by the shareholders of the parent. The **proportionate consolidation method** is an application of proprietary theory.

In contrast, the **entity theory** views the consolidated group as a single economic entity, and the goal of consolidation is to report all of the interests *controlled* by that entity, regardless of the interest owned by the shareholders of the parent. The **entity method** (also known as *full goodwill method*) of consolidation is an application of entity theory.

Two other methods of consolidation lie between the proprietary and entity methods—the *parent-company method* and the *parent-company extension method*. The **parent-company method** consolidates (1) the parent's share of the *fair values* of the subsidiary's assets and liabilities plus (2) the NCI's share of the *carrying values* of the subsidiary's assets and liabilities. The **parent-company extension method** (also known as the *purchased goodwill method*) includes 100% of the *fair value* of the subsidiary's net identifiable assets and liabilities, but only the parent's share of goodwill. The four alternatives are summarized below. Exhibit 5.1 summarizes them pictorially.

1. **Proportionate consolidation method:** Include only the parent's share of the fair value of the subsidiary's assets, liabilities, revenues, and expenses (i.e., exclude the NCI entirely). The consolidated SCI would include only the parent's share of the subsidiary's revenues and expenses.

2. **Parent-company method:** Include the parent's share of the fair values of the subsidiary's assets and liabilities, plus the carrying value (i.e., book value) of the NCI's share. The consolidated SCI would include 100% of the subsidiary's revenues and expenses.

3. **Parent-company extension or purchased goodwill method:** Include 100% of the *fair value* of the subsidiary's net identifiable assets and liabilities, but only the parent's share of goodwill, and 100% of all revenues and expenses. Thus, under this method only the goodwill on the portion paid by the parent in excess of the proportionate net

**Exhibit 5.1** Consolidation Approaches to Reporting NCI

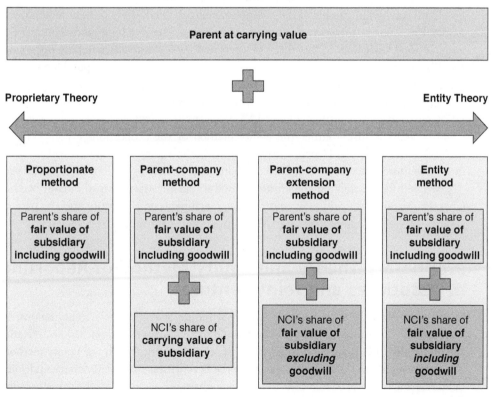

fair value acquired is included. On the SFP, the non-controlling interest is valued at its proportionate share of the fair value of the net identifiable assets of the subsidiary.

4.  **Entity** or **full goodwill method:** Include 100% of the *fair value* of the subsidiary's assets and liabilities *and goodwill*, and 100% of all revenues and expenses. This method includes the entire implicit goodwill for the enterprise as a whole, including the NCI's share. On the SFP, the NCI is valued at its proportionate share of the full fair value of the subsidiary.

Note that the parent's assets and liabilities are always brought onto the consolidated statements at their carrying values on the date of consolidation. The four alternatives summarized above differ only on the issue of whether, and to what extent, the NCI's share of the subsidiary should be included in the consolidated statements.

## Required Methods for Reporting Business Combinations

In principle, the IASB believes that the only correct method of measuring NCI is the fourth method above—that is, the entity, or full goodwill method. The board also believes that allowing alternative methods of measurement reduces comparability. Nevertheless, because not enough members of the IASB supported method 4 above, IFRS 3, *Business Combinations*, allows the use of either method 3 or method 4 above on a transaction-by-transaction basis. That is, each business combination can be viewed as a separate transaction that can be accounted for by either method. Consistency is not required.

Until recently, a variant of the parent-company method, the **purchase method**, was required in Canada to report business combinations. The purchase method limits the assigned total fair values of the acquired assets and liabilities to the purchase price paid. Pre-2011 business combinations that were initially reported using the purchase method can continue to be reported using that method.

The proportionate consolidation method was required in the past in Canada to report investments in joint ventures. Under IAS 31, *Interests in Joint Ventures*, joint ventures could be reported using either the equity method or the proportionate consolidation method. However, IFRS 11 permits only the use of the equity method to report interests in joint ventures after January 1, 2013. Proportionate consolidation is no longer allowed.

We will focus solely on the entity method in our illustrations in the main body of Chapters 5 and 6. We will point out the difference between the entity and the parent-company extension method in a separate section toward the end of each chapter.

## Proprietary Theory and Equity Method of Reporting of Associates and Joint Ventures

IFRS 3 favours the use of the entity theory while reporting business combinations. In contrast, IAS 28 (*Investments in Associates*) and IFRS 11 (*Joint Arrangements*) both require the proprietary theory for reporting associates and joint ventures on the equity method. The rationale for the divergence appears to be that in the case of associates and joint ventures, since control or sole control is lacking, there is less chance of the investor being able to manipulate profits reported by it by suitably arranging intercompany transactions

## Application of the Proprietary Theory While Reporting Associates and Joint Ventures Under the Equity Method

Transactions eliminated on consolidation

Unrealized gains arising from transactions with equity-accounted investees and joint ventures are eliminated against the investment to the extent of the Company's interest in the associate or the

joint venture. Unrealized losses are eliminated in the same manner as unrealized gains, but only to the extent that there is no evidence of impairment.

Source: Cameco, Annual Report (2011), p. 11.

with such entities. Therefore, under IFRS, the investing entity includes its share of the net income of the associate adjusted *only* for its share of any unrealized or realized gains and losses. Reality Check 5–1 provides the relevant extract from the 2011 annual report of Cameco, the world's largest publicly traded producer of uranium, located in Saskatoon, Saskatchewan, to illustrate such an application of the proprietary theory.

As the extract in Reality Check 5–1 demonstrates, when unrealized gains (and losses) exist on transactions between an entity and its associates and joint ventures, such gains and losses are eliminated *only* to the extent of the entity's ownership interest. It does not matter whether the transaction is downstream from the entity to its associates/joint ventures or upstream from the associates/joint ventures to the entity. This is a clear example of the application of the proprietary theory.

However, as you will discover later in the chapter, unrealized gains/losses on downstream sales are not treated the same as unrealized gain/losses on upstream sales when such sales occur between an entity and its non-wholly owned subsidiaries. The entity theory applies in the latter case. We will elaborate on these differences in greater detail further into the chapter.

### Concept Check 5-1

1. How do the four methods of consolidation (proportionate, parent-company, parent-company extension, and entity) apply the two theories of consolidation (proprietary and entity)?

2. Why does IFRS require the use of the entity theory while consolidating *subsidiaries* but require the use of the proprietary theory while reporting an *associate* or *joint venture* under the equity method?

## 5.3 CONSOLIDATION AT DATE OF ACQUISITION

LO **4a**

Consolidate a non-wholly owned subsidiary at the date of acquisition

To illustrate consolidation of a non-wholly owned subsidiary at the date of acquisition, we will use the same basic facts as we used in the Chapter 3 example.

Assume that Purchase Ltd. buys only 70% of the outstanding shares of Target Ltd. on December 31, 20X5, giving 28,000 Purchase Ltd. shares in exchange. If we assume that the market value of Purchase Ltd.'s shares is $30 per share, then the total cost of the

**Exhibit 5.2** Business Combination—Purchase of 70% of Target

| | Purchase Ltd. | Target Ltd. | Target Ltd. fair values |
|---|---|---|---|
| **Post-Acquisition Asset Positions, December 31, 20X5 Statements of Financial Position** | | | |
| Cash | $1,000,000 | $ 50,000 | $ 50,000 |
| Accounts receivable | 2,000,000 | 150,000 | 150,000 |
| Inventory | 200,000 | 50,000 | 50,000 |
| Land | 1,000,000 | 300,000 | 400,000 |
| Buildings and equipment | 3,000,000 | 500,000 | 550,000 |
| Accumulated depreciation | (1,200,000) | (150,000) | |
| Investment in Target Ltd. | 840,000 | | |
| Total assets | $6,840,000 | $900,000 | |
| Current: accounts payable | $1,000,000 | $100,000 | (100,000) |
| Long-term: notes payable | 400,000 | — | |
| Common shares | 3,440,000 | 200,000 | |
| Retained earnings | 2,000,000 | 600,000 | |
| Total liabilities and shareholders' equity | $6,840,000 | $900,000 | |
| Net fair value of Target Ltd. assets and liabilities | | | $1,100,000 |

acquisition is $840,000. The post-acquisition SFP of Purchase Ltd. and Target Ltd., and the fair values of Target Ltd.'s assets and liabilities, are shown in Exhibit 5.2.

We will use our MEAR steps for consolidation under the direct method from Chapter 4, now modified for consolidating a non-wholly owned subsidiary. The updated MEAR steps are presented in Exhibit 5.3.

Since we are now consolidating at the time of acquisition, we need to carry out only those adjustments and eliminations listed under the column titled "Acquisition-related," in Exhibit 5.3. Exhibit 5.4 applies the first step of **M**easure, which requires us to calculate the purchase price, the 100% fair value, and FVA—first allocating the FVA to the various identifiable assets and liabilities, while allocating the balance to goodwill. To reiterate, under the entity method, the goodwill of $100,000 represents the sum of Purchase Ltd.'s share of $70,000 and the NCI's share of $30,000.

You will notice that in Exhibit 5.4 we calculate 100% of the fair value of Target Ltd. based on the purchase price of $840,000 paid by Purchase Ltd. for its 70% share. This is a very quick and uncomplicated method of calculating the full fair value of the acquisition. However, this calculation won't yield the correct result if the buyer pays less than its proportionate fair value of the target company's net assets, which is known as a **bargain purchase**. We will illustrate the correct method for a bargain purchase in a separate section toward the end of this chapter.

Under the entity method, the NCI is measured at its share of 100% of the fair value of Target Ltd., including the full value of goodwill—that is, 30% of $1,200,000, or $360,000. Included in the $360,000 is the NCI's share of goodwill, which is 30% of $100,000, or $30,000.

**Exhibit 5.3** MEAR Steps for Consolidating a Non-Wholly Owned Subsidiary

| Consolidation Steps | Acquisition-related | Relating to First Year Following Acquisition | Relating to Following Years |
|---|---|---|---|
| 1. Measure | ■ Calculate cost and fair value adjustments (FVA) <br> ■ Allocate FVA <br> ■ Determine NCI balance | | |
| 2. Eliminate and recognize | ■ Eliminate parent's investment account and sub's share equity accounts | | |
| | | ■ Eliminate intercompany transactions and balances <br> ■ Eliminate unrealized profits | |
| | | | ■ Recognize realized profits |
| 3. Amortize | | ■ Amortize FVAs <br> ■ Recognize impairments | |
| | | | ■ Recognize cumulative amortization of FVAs <br> ■ Recognize cumulative impairments |
| 4. Recognize NCI share of earnings | | ■ Recognize NCI share of earnings <br> ■ Calculate NCI SFP balance <br> ■ Calculate RE balance | |
| 5. Check | ■ Independent calculation of RE balances <br> ■ Independent calculation of NCI balances | | |

We are now ready to prepare the consolidated SFP at the date of acquisition for our illustration. Exhibit 5.5 shows the Purchase Ltd. consolidated SFP immediately after the business combination, prepared (by the direct approach) using the entity method.

The derivation of Purchase Ltd.'s consolidated SFP at December 31, 20X5, in Exhibit 5.5 is very similar to the derivation in Exhibit 3.10 of Chapter 3. For each item on the SFP, we take the carrying value for Purchase Ltd., add the carrying value of Target Ltd., and add the fair value adjustment. The fair value adjustment (and goodwill) is indicated with a superscript letter a. Also, as required under the **E**liminate step applicable to consolidation at the time of acquisition, we must eliminate Purchase Ltd.'s investment account and Target's shareholders' equity accounts, indicated with a superscript letter b.

**Exhibit 5.4** Allocation of Fair-Value Adjustment

| 70% Purchase of Target Ltd., December 31, 20X5 | | | | | |
|---|---|---|---|---|---|
| Purchase price | | | | $840,000 | |
| 100% fair value based on purchase price [$840,000 × (100% / 70%)] | | | | | $1,200,000 |
| Less carrying value of Target's net identifiable assets | | | | | (800,000) |
| = Fair-value adjustment, allocated below | | | | | 400,000 |
| | Carrying value (a) | Fair value (b) | Fair-value adjustment (c) = (b) – (a) | FVA allocated | |
| Cash | $ 50,000 | $ 50,000 | — | | |
| Accounts receivable | 150,000 | 150,000 | — | | |
| Inventory | 50,000 | 50,000 | — | | |
| Land | 300,000 | 400,000 | $100,000 | $100,000 | |
| Buildings and equipment | 500,000 | 550,000 | 50,000 | 50,000 | |
| Accumulated depreciation | (150,000) | — | 150,000 | 150,000 | |
| Accounts payable | (100,000) | (100,000) | — | | |
| Total fair value adjustment | | | | | (300,000) |
| Net asset carrying value | $ 800,000 | | | | |
| Fair value of assets acquired | | $1,100,000 | | | |
| Balance of FVA allocated to goodwill @ 100% | | | | | $ 100,000 |

In Chapter 3, Target Ltd. was a wholly owned subsidiary of Purchase Ltd. In the present illustration, Purchase Ltd. owns only 70% of Target Ltd. Nevertheless, the consolidated total assets and total liabilities and shareholders' equity are the same in both cases—namely, $7,300,000. Under the entity method we need to include the full fair value of Target Ltd.'s assets and liabilities in the Purchase Ltd. consolidated SFP, rather than just the fair value adjustments that relate to Purchase Ltd.'s 70% share.

Therefore, to balance the SFP, we need to allocate to the NCI its 30% share of the carrying value (i.e., $800,000 × 30% = $240,000) and fair value adjustment ($400,000 × 30% = $120,000, including goodwill) of Target Ltd.'s net assets.

The total fair value of Target Ltd.'s identifiable net assets is $1,100,000, as shown in Exhibit 5.2. The total amount of Purchase Ltd.'s identifiable net assets is increased by that amount upon consolidation. The total goodwill of $100,000 relating to the acquisition of Target Ltd. is made up of the $70,000 paid by Purchase Ltd. for its 70% share and $30,000, the NCI's share allocated to it. Therefore, the non-controlling interest is $360,000, calculated as (30% × $1,100,000) + (30% × $100,000).

**Exhibit 5.5** Consolidation at Date of Acquisition, Non-Wholly Owned Subsidiary

| Purchase Ltd. Consolidated Statement of Financial Position December 31, 20X5 | |
|---|---:|
| **ASSETS** | |
| Current assets: | |
| Cash [1,000,000 + 50,000] | $1,050,000 |
| Accounts receivable [2,000,000 + 150,000] | 2,150,000 |
| Inventory [200,000 + 50,000] | 250,000 |
| | 3,450,000 |
| Property, plant, and equipment: | |
| Land [1,000,000 + 300,000 + **100,000**[a]] | 1,400,000 |
| Buildings and equipment [3,000,000 + 500,000 + **50,000**[a]] | 3,550,000 |
| Accumulated depreciation [1,200,000 + 150,000 − **150,000**[a]] | (1,200,000) |
| | 3,750,000 |
| Other assets: | |
| Investment in Target Ltd. [840,000 − **560,000**[b] − **280,000**[b]] | — |
| Goodwill [+ **100,000**[a]] | 100,000 |
| **TOTAL ASSETS** | $7,300,000 |
| **LIABILITIES AND SHAREHOLDERS' EQUITY** | |
| Liabilities: | |
| Current: accounts payable [1,000,000 + 100,000] | $1,100,000 |
| Long-term: notes payable [400,000 + 0] | 400,000 |
| | 1,500,000 |
| Shareholders' equity: | |
| Common shares [3,440,000 + 200,000 − **200,000**[b]] | 3,440,000 |
| Retained earnings [2,000,000 + 600,000 − **600,000**[b]] | 2,000,000 |
| NCI [+ **240,000**[a] + **120,000**[a]] | 360,000 |
| | 5,800,000 |
| **TOTAL LIABILITIES AND SHAREHOLDERS' EQUITY** | $7,300,000 |

[a] = the fair value adjustment (and goodwill)
[b] = elimination of parent's investment account and NCI's shareholders' equity accounts

Assigning goodwill to the non-controlling shareholders' interest can be defended because, if 70% of Target Ltd. is worth $840,000, then 30% must be worth three-sevenths of that amount, or $360,000. Canadian securities laws give some support to this approach. When there has been a block purchase of shares in certain publicly traded companies,[1] an offer to buy non-controlling shareholders' shares must be at least as attractive as the price paid for the majority shares.

---

[1] For example, those covered by the *Ontario Securities Act* (Section 91).

## Amortization in Subsequent Years

In Chapter 4, the parent owned 100% of the subsidiary. Therefore, we amortized 100% of the fair value adjustments over the expected useful lives of the assets. We also would have recognized losses resulting from the impairment of the full value of the goodwill.

Under the entity method, even when the parent does not own 100% of the subsidiary, the consolidated assets and liabilities (and consequently the NCI) continue to include the NCI's share of the subsidiary's fair value adjustments, including goodwill. Therefore, we should continue to amortize 100% of the fair value adjustments and recognize a loss on the impairment of 100% of the goodwill. However, to the extent these expenses and losses relate to the NCI's share in the subsidiary, we need to charge such expenses and losses against the NCI's interest on the consolidated SFP.

We will now illustrate consolidation of a non-wholly owned subsidiary (1) one year after acquisition and (2) two years after acquisition.

### Concept Check 5-2

1. For the same subsidiary, how would the consolidated SFP at the date of acquisition differ if the subsidiary were non-wholly owned rather than wholly owned?

2. Under the entity method, what does the value of the NCI on the consolidated SFP represent?

LO **4b**

Consolidate a non-wholly owned subsidiary one year after acquisition

# 5.4 CONSOLIDATION ONE YEAR AFTER ACQUISITION

## Basic Information

For the year ended December 31, 20X6 (i.e., one year following the business combination), the following occurred:

- Target Ltd.'s buildings and equipment will be depreciated over 10 years after the date of acquisition, using straight-line depreciation.

- During 20X6, Target sold goods of $55,000^U$ to Purchase Ltd. Target Ltd.'s gross margin is 40% of sales.

- On December 31, 20X6, $20,000 of the goods acquired by Purchase Ltd. from Target Ltd. are still in Purchase Ltd.'s inventory. Unrealized profit is $20,000 \times 40\% = \$8,000^U$.

- During 20X6, Target Ltd. paid dividends totalling $30,000. Of this amount, 70% (i.e., $21,000) were received by Purchase Ltd. Purchase Ltd. maintains its investment in Target Ltd. on the cost basis; therefore, the dividends were recorded as dividend income.

# Direct Method

Exhibit 5.6 shows the separate-entity financial statements for 20X6. We assume that Purchase Ltd. is using the cost basis of *recording* its investment in Target Ltd. These statements are very similar to those shown in Exhibit 4.2. The differences are due to two factors:

1. Purchase Ltd. acquired 70% instead of 100%, and, therefore:
   - investment in Target Ltd. is smaller by $360,000 (i.e., $1,200,000 − $840,000); and
   - Purchase Ltd.'s common share account is less by $360,000 due to the lower value of the shares issued in the acquisition.

2. Although Target declared and paid $30,000 in dividends (just as in 20X6 in Chapter 4), Purchase Ltd. received only 70% of Target Ltd.'s dividends. Therefore, Purchase Ltd.'s dividend income, closing retained earnings, and cash balance are all less by 30% × $30,000 = $9,000.

Since consolidation is now occurring in the first year after acquisition, we must carry out all the adjustments and eliminations required under the column titled "Relating to First Year Following Acquisition," in Exhibit 5.3. Exhibit 5.4 has already illustrated the first step, of **M**easure. Therefore, we will not repeat that step here. Now, we will go ahead and illustrate the remaining steps.

## Eliminate

### Intercompany Transactions and Balances

| | |
|---|---|
| Upstream sale by Target Ltd. | (55,000) |
| Dividends declared by Target Ltd. | (30,000) |

In our illustration, there are two intercompany items that need to be eliminated. The first item relates to the sale by Target Ltd. of $55,000$^U$ worth of goods to Purchase Ltd. Our analysis relating to the sale of $55,000$^U$ remains unchanged from our analysis in Chapter 4. We need to eliminate $55,000$^U$ from both sales and cost of goods sold.

The second item relates to the $30,000 worth of dividends declared by Target Ltd. Our analysis and conclusion relating to this item will now differ slightly compared with our analysis in Chapter 4. Remember that of the $30,000 dividends declared by Target Ltd., Purchase Ltd.'s share is only $21,000; the remaining $9,000 belongs to the NCI. Therefore, while we eliminate the dividends declared amount of $30,000, we need to eliminate only $21,000 from dividend income. The NCI's share of $9,000 will be subtracted from the NCI balance on the SFP.

### Unrealized and Realized Profits

| | |
|---|---|
| Unrealized profit on upstream sale of inventory | (8,000) |

There is only one adjustment required to eliminate unrealized earnings—the same adjustment as the one in Chapter 4 required for eliminating the unrealized profit on upstream sale of inventory. As we explained earlier, we need to increase cost of goods

**Exhibit 5.6** Separate-Entity Financial Statements for 20X6

## Statements of Comprehensive Income
### Year Ended December 31, 20X6

|  | Purchase Ltd. | Target Ltd. |
|---|---|---|
| **Revenue:** |  |  |
| Sales | $2,400,000 | $ 300,000 |
| Dividend income | 21,000 | — |
|  | 2,421,000 | 300,000 |
| **Expenses:** |  |  |
| Cost of sales | 1,750,000 | 180,000 |
| Depreciation expense | 100,000 | 35,000 |
| Other expenses | 250,000 | 20,000 |
|  | 2,100,000 | 235,000 |
| **NET INCOME AND COMPREHENSIVE INCOME** | **$ 321,000** | **$ 65,000** |

## Statement of Changes in Equity—Retained Earnings Section
### Year Ended December 31, 20X6

|  | Purchase Ltd. | Target Ltd. |
|---|---|---|
| Retained earnings, December 31, 20X5 | $2,000,000 | $ 600,000 |
| Net income | 321,000 | 65,000 |
| Dividends declared | — | (30,000) |
| Retained earnings, December 31, 20X6 | $2,321,000 | $ 635,000 |

## Statements of Financial Position
### December 31, 20X6

|  | Purchase Ltd. | Target Ltd. |
|---|---|---|
| **ASSETS** |  |  |
| **Current assets:** |  |  |
| Cash | $ 971,000 | $ 100,000 |
| Accounts receivable | 2,200,000 | 250,000 |
| Inventory | 250,000 | 70,000 |
|  | 3,421,000 | 420,000 |
| **Property, plant, and equipment:** |  |  |
| Land | 1,000,000 | 300,000 |
| Buildings and equipment | 3,000,000 | 500,000 |
| Accumulated depreciation | (1,300,000) | (185,000) |
|  | 2,700,000 | 615,000 |
| **Other assets:** |  |  |
| Investments (at cost) | 840,000 | — |
| **TOTAL ASSETS** | **$6,961,000** | **$1,035,000** |
| **LIABILITIES** |  |  |
| **Liabilities and shareholders' equity** |  |  |
| Current liability: accounts payable | $ 800,000 | $ 200,000 |
| Long-term liability: note payable | 400,000 | — |
|  | 1,200,000 | 200,000 |
| **Shareholders' equity** |  |  |
| Common shares | 3,440,000 | 200,000 |
| Retained earnings | 2,321,000 | 635,000 |
|  | 5,761,000 | 835,000 |
| **TOTAL LIABILITIES AND SHAREHOLDERS' EQUITY** | **$6,961,000** | **$1,035,000** |

sold and decrease ending inventory by that amount. Since this is the first year after acquisition, there are no profits on intercompany sales of inventory or other assets in prior period(s) that have been realized in the current period.

## Amortize

| | FVA allocated | Amortization period | Amortization per year | Amortization/ impairment loss during 20X6 | Balance of FVA remaining at the end of 20X6 |
|---|---|---|---|---|---|
| Land | $100,000 | — | | — | $100,000 |
| Building and equipment | 200,000 | 10 | $20,000 | $20,000 | 180,000 |
| Goodwill | 100,000 | — | | — | 100,000 |
| Total | $400,000 | | | $20,000 | $380,000 |

The schedule above is identical to the schedule in Chapter 4. Therefore, the inferences we can draw from it are identical to the ones in Chapter 4. Specifically, from the schedule above we know that there is a $20,000 amortization/impairment loss; this loss must be recognized in the consolidated financial statements in the current period. This adjustment pertains to the depreciation expense relating to the fair value increment allocated to property, plant, and equipment.

We also know from the schedule above that the balance of the FVA adjustment that needs to be added to the carrying values of the parent and subsidiary is $380,000, made up of an increase to land for $100,000, to buildings and equipment for $180,000, and to goodwill for $100,000.

Note that the adjustment for buildings and equipment of $180,000 is the result of the initial FVI allocated to buildings and equipment of $200,000 less the $20,000 depreciation adjustment required in the current year.

**Recognize NCI Share of Earnings**  In every consolidation of a controlled subsidiary, 100% of the subsidiary's revenues and expenses are added to those of the parent. The consolidated SCI shows the total combined revenues and expenses and, by extension, the total net income for the entire economic entity.

However, if all of the subsidiary's earnings were distributed to the shareholders as dividends, the parent would receive only the proportion relating to its ownership interest in the subsidiary—the remainder would go to the people or institutions that hold the remaining (or non-controlling) shares. Therefore, we need to show the parent's shareholders the portion of consolidated net income that belongs to them and the portion that "belongs" to the NCI. This is done by allocating the net income between the parent's shareholders and the NCI. This allocation will appear immediately below the net income line item on the consolidated SCI whenever the parent owns less than 100% of the shares. The net income allocated to the NCI represents the net income accruing to the minority interests, or NCI.

Be careful here—*accrue* and *belong* in this sense do not mean that the earnings are recorded on anyone's books the way we usually use the word. Each term is used simply to indicate that the parent corporation does not have the right to receive the benefits of shares it does not own.

Note that the amount apportioned as the non-controlling share is based on the subsidiary's separate-entity net income, *adjusted for unrealized profits and other expenses*. However, the consolidated SCI of Purchase Ltd. will provide only a final net income number for the consolidated entity as a whole. It will not provide us with a breakdown of that amount, such that we can identify the amount of the adjusted income of Target Ltd. Without this detail we cannot apportion the consolidated net income amount between the shareholders of Purchase Ltd. and the NCI.

From the previous steps we already know the various adjustments required to be made to Target Ltd.'s income. Further, Target Ltd.'s income on its separate-entity financial statements is $65,000. Therefore, we have all the information necessary to calculate the amount of income to be apportioned to the NCI on the SCI, as shown in the schedule below:

| Details | Amount |
|---|---|
| Net income of Target Ltd. for 20X6 (from separate-entity financial statement) | $ 65,000 |
| Less: | |
|   Unrealized gains on upstream sale of inventory | (8,000) |
|   Amortization of fair value adjustment during the year | (20,000) |
| **Adjusted net income of Target Ltd. for 20X6** | **37,000** |
| **NCI's share @ 30%** | 11,100 |
| **Purchase Ltd.'s share @ 70%** | $ 25,900 |

In the schedule above, we start with the unadjusted net income of Target Ltd. for the year 20X6, taken from its separate-entity financial statements. Target Ltd. reported separate-entity earnings of $65,000. Before calculating the NCI's share of Target Ltd.'s earnings, we need to adjust the $65,000 amount for the unrealized profits and amortization expenses identified in the previous steps.

Specifically, there are two adjustments to the net income of Target Ltd.—(1) elimination of the unrealized gain of $8,000$^U$ on the upstream sale of inventory, and (2) recognition of a $20,000 expense relating to the amortization of the fair value adjustment during the year. Both of these adjustments reduce the net income of Target Ltd., which results in an adjusted net income of $37,000.

On Purchase Ltd.'s consolidated SCI, 30% of this amount (i.e., $11,100) should be allocated to the NCI as its share of income for the year. Naturally, the remaining 70% of the adjusted net income of Target Ltd. for 20X6—that is, $25,900 ($37,000 – $11,100)—flows to the benefit of Purchase Ltd. shareholders.

### Why Reduce NCI's Earnings?

You may be wondering, why do the earnings of the NCI get reduced just because Purchase Ltd. failed to sell its entire inventory and also get reduced for the excess amortization relating to the fair value adjustment? They don't! These deductions for NCI have nothing to do with the NCI's real entitlement to the subsidiary's earnings and dividends. The non-controlling shareholders will look at the *subsidiary's* financial statements and receive the *subsidiary's* dividends, not those of the parent company.

In preparing Purchase Ltd.'s *consolidated* statements, we adjusted the consolidated cost of sales and depreciation expense for 100% of the unrealized profit and amortization of fair value adjustment. Now we need to reduce the NCI by the NCI's 30% share of the unrealized upstream profit and the amortization expense so that only 70% of that effect shows up in Purchase Ltd.'s consolidated earnings. Bear in mind that the calculation of NCI is an adjustment only to the *parent's* consolidated statements, not to the subsidiary's separate-entity statements.

**Prepare the Consolidated Statements**   We now have all the information necessary for preparing the consolidated financial statements of Purchase Ltd. at the end of 20X6. Therefore, we will now prepare the consolidated statement of income and the retained earnings section of the consolidated statement of changes in equity and the consolidated SFP for Purchase Ltd. for the year 20X6. We start the consolidation process by adding the carrying values of both companies and making the various adjustments identified in the previous steps. We also must remember to eliminate the common shares of $200,000 and retained earnings at the time of acquisition of $600,000 of Target Ltd., and the investment at cost of $840,000.

To do the above, following our practice in earlier chapters, we can go down the SCI and SFP and insert the correct amounts on a line-by-line basis. In Exhibit 5.7, we have added together the separate-entity amounts, and made the required additional adjustments and eliminations. The necessary adjustments and eliminations are listed below once again, now by each financial statement, starting with the SCI. Exhibit 5.7 illustrates consolidation under the entity method.

**Exhibit 5.7** Purchase Ltd. Consolidated Financial Statements

| Purchase owns 70% of Target Ltd. (Direct Method)<br>Consolidated Statement of Comprehensive Income<br>Year Ended December 31, 20X6 | |
| --- | --- |
| Sales revenue [2,400,000 + 300,000 − 55,000$^U$] | $2,645,000 |
| Dividend income [21,000 + 0 − **21,000**] | |
| Operating expenses: | |
| Cost of sales [1,750,000 + 180,000 − 55,000$^U$ + **8,000**$^U$] | 1,883,000 |
| Depreciation expense [100,000 + 35,000 + **20,000**] | 155,000 |
| Other expenses [250,000 + 20,000] | 270,000 |
| | 2,308,000 |
| NET INCOME AND COMPREHENSIVE INCOME | $  337,000 |
| Net income attributable to: | |
| Owners of the parent | $  325,900 |
| Non-controlling interests | 11,100 |

*Exhibit Continued >*

### Consolidated Statement of Changes in Equity—Retained Earnings Section
### Year Ended December 31, 20X6

| | |
|---|---|
| Retained earnings, December 31, 20X5 [2,000,000 + 600,000 − **600,000**] | 2,000,000 |
| Net income | 325,900 |
| Dividends declared [0 + 30,000 − **30,000**] | — |
| Retained earnings, December 31, 20X6 | $2,325,900 |

### Consolidated Statement of Financial Position
### December 31, 20X6

**Assets**

**Current assets:**

| | |
|---|---|
| Cash [971,000 + 100,000] | $1,071,000 |
| Accounts receivable [2,200,000 + 250,000] | 2,450,000 |
| Inventory [250,000 + 70,000 − **8,000**$^U$] | 312,000 |
| | 3,833,000 |

**Property, plant, and equipment:**

| | |
|---|---|
| Land [1,000,000 + 300,000 + **100,000**] | 1,400,000 |
| Buildings and equipment [3,000,000 + 500,000 + **50,000**] | 3,550,000 |
| Accumulated depreciation [1,300,000 + 185,000 − **150,000** + 20,000] | (1,355,000) |
| | 3,595,000 |

**Other assets:**

| | |
|---|---|
| Investments [840,000 + 0 − **840,000**] | — |
| Goodwill [0 + **100,000**] | 100,000 |
| TOTAL ASSETS | $7,528,000 |

**LIABILITIES AND SHAREHOLDERS' EQUITY**

**Liabilities:**

| | |
|---|---|
| Current: accounts payable [800,000 + 200,000] | $1,000,000 |
| Long-term: notes payable [400,000 + 0] | 400,000 |
| | 1,400,000 |

**Shareholders' equity:**

| | |
|---|---|
| Common shares [**Purchase Ltd. shares only**] | 3,440,000 |
| Retained earnings [2,321,000 + 635,000 − **600,000** − **10,500** − (**8,000**$^U$ × 70%) − (20,000 × 70%)]* | 2,325,900 |
| | 5,765,900 |
| NCI in net assets of Target Ltd. [**360,000** + **11,100** − **9,000**] | 362,100 |
| Total equity | 6,128,000 |
| TOTAL LIABILITIES AND SHAREHOLDERS' EQUITY | $7,528,000 |

*The $10,500 is the portion of the increase in retained earnings that is allocable to the NCI. Retained earnings increased by $35,000 ($635,000 − $600,000), and 30% of this increase is $10,500 ($35,000 × 30%). The adjustments to retained earnings are explained in more detail later.

## SCI and SCE/RE

- *Sales.* The upstream intercompany sales of $55,000^U$ are eliminated.

- *Dividend income.* The dividends paid by Target Ltd. to Purchase Ltd. are eliminated: $30,000 \times 70\% = \$21,000$.

- *Cost of sales.* Cost of sales is reduced by $55,000^U$ to avoid counting the intercompany sales in cost of goods sold twice. However, this elimination is partly offset by the unrealized profit in Purchase Ltd.'s ending inventory: $20,000 \times 40\% = \$8,000^U$.

- *Depreciation expense.* As usual, the FVI for buildings and equipment must be amortized. The amortization is of the full FVI of $200,000. The FVI amortization therefore is $200,000 \div 10 = \$20,000$.

- *Allocation of net income.* The net income of $337,000 has to be allocated between the owners of the parent and the NCI. Note, however, that only the NCI's share of the adjusted income of Target Ltd. is allocated to it. The NCI does not share in the profits from the operations of Purchase Ltd. Further, as pointed out earlier, this allocation process is done solely for the purpose of reporting the financial affairs of Purchase Ltd. to its shareholders. The NCI shareholders of Target Ltd. will not be using the financial statements of Purchase Ltd. Instead, they will use the separate-entity financial statements issued by Target Ltd. to its shareholders. The NCI's share of the adjusted income of Target Ltd. of $11,100 is allocated to it, while Purchase Ltd.'s income from its operations and its share of the adjusted income of Target Ltd., totalling $325,900, is allocated to its owners.

- *Beginning consolidated retained earnings.* The beginning consolidated retained earnings balance includes the retained earnings of only Purchase Ltd., since the beginning retained earnings balance of Target Ltd. represents its retained earnings on the date of its acquisition by Purchase Ltd.

## Statement of Financial Position

- *Inventory.* Inventory is reduced by the $8,000^U$ unrealized profit on upstream sales. This adjustment is the counterpart of the $8,000^U$ increase to cost of goods sold on the SCI. Therefore, in essence what we have done is that we first reduced the ending inventory value by $8,000^U$ and, next, treated such a reduction as an expense on the SCI by appropriately increasing the cost of goods sold. Alternatively, we can arrive at the same conclusion by using the following equation:

> Beginning Inventory + Purchases = Cost of Goods Sold + Ending Inventory

If we hold constant the beginning inventory and purchases, to maintain equality, any decrease in the ending inventory must be matched by an equal increase in the cost of goods sold account.

- *Land.* The FVI of $100,000 is added.

- *Buildings and equipment.* Buildings and equipment is *increased* by $50,000 to reflect the fair value at the date of acquisition, as was the case for consolidation at the date of acquisition.

- *Accumulated depreciation.* Target Ltd.'s date-of-acquisition accumulated depreciation is not carried forward on the consolidated SFP. The elimination is for the full amount of the date-of-acquisition accumulated depreciation of $150,000. There are two effects to this adjustment:
  - The net date-of-acquisition value assigned to Target Ltd.'s buildings and equipment is increased by $200,000 (that is, $150,000 + $50,000): (1) the elimination of accumulated depreciation plus (2) the increase in value assigned to the asset account.
  - The amount remaining in Target Ltd.'s accumulated depreciation is only the depreciation taken *since the date of acquisition*, which is one year's amortization of the FVI: $200,000 ÷ 10 = $20,000.
- *Investment in Target Ltd.* This account is eliminated completely, of course.
- *Common shares.* Only Purchase Ltd.'s shares are included.
- *Retained earnings.* Refer to the double-check step below for a detailed discussion of the calculation of the ending consolidated retained earnings balance.
- *Non-controlling interest.* Again, refer to the double-check step below for a detailed discussion of the calculation of the ending balance of the NCI.

**Classification of NCI on the SFP**   Throughout this text, following IFRS 10, the NCI will be shown on the SFP within equity, but separately from the parent shareholders' equity.

In the past, North American practice was to present the NCI on the SFP as a separate mezzanine item between liabilities and shareholders' equity. However, in the accounting profession worldwide, there was always some unease about this method of presenting the NCI. Theoretically, items on the equities side of the SFP should be a part of either creditors' equity (i.e., liabilities) or shareholders' equity. Having an unidentified floating object between liabilities and shareholders' equity seems contrary to the basic concept of the SFP. The present practice of presenting the NCI within equity removes this source of unease. It also is the method previously used in Japan, as well as in some other countries.

**Check**   We automatically arrived at the NCI and retained earnings balances at the end of 20X6 during the consolidation process. However, it is prudent to independently calculate the NCI and retained earnings balances at the end of the year as a double-check. We will first start with the NCI balance.

To do so, we update the beginning NCI balance with all items affecting NCI that occurred during the year. The NCI balance at the beginning of 20X6 is $360,000. In our example, there are two items pertaining to 20X6 that affect the NCI balance—(1) the net income allocated to the NCI as calculated previously, and (2) the NCI's share of the dividends declared by Target Ltd. As the schedule below demonstrates, it is relatively straightforward to calculate the ending NCI balance using the above information:

| NCI Balance at the End of 20X6 | |
| --- | --- |
| Balance of NCI at the time of acquisition | $360,000 |
| Add: NCI's share of Target Ltd.'s adjusted net income in 20X6 | 11,100 |
| Less: NCI's share of dividends declared by Target Ltd. in 20X6 | (9,000) |
| Ending balance of NCI in 20X6 | $362,100 |

Similarly, it is relatively straightforward to calculate the retained earnings balance of Purchase Ltd. on the date of consolidation, as demonstrated below:

| | |
|---|---:|
| Ending retained earnings balance of Purchase Ltd. from its separate-entity SFP | $2,321,000 |
| Less dividend income from Target Ltd. | (21,000) |
| = Adjusted separate-entity ending retained earnings balance of Purchase Ltd. | 2,300,000 |
| Add Purchase Ltd.'s share of Target Ltd.'s adjusted income | 25,900 |
| Ending consolidated retained earnings of Purchase Ltd. | $2,325,900 |

We will demonstrate an alternative calculation of ending consolidated retained earnings a little later in the chapter, one that begins with beginning *consolidated* retained earnings rather than ending *separate-entity* retained earnings. For professional examination purposes, it is useful to understand both approaches, depending on the format of the information presented in an examination question.

Notice that the first thing we did in the schedule above while calculating the ending retained earnings was to subtract the $21,000 dividend income recognized in the separate-entity financial statements of Purchase Ltd., under the cost method. In contrast, the consolidated retained earnings balance of Purchase Ltd. will include the full portion of Purchase Ltd.'s share of the adjusted income of Target Ltd. of $25,900, not just the portion distributed as dividends. Therefore, to avoid double-counting, we need to first subtract the dividend income recognized, before adding $25,900 to get the ending consolidated retained earnings of Purchase Ltd. of $2,325,900.

An alternative method of calculating the ending consolidated retained earnings balance is provided below. During consolidations there are conceptually different methods of calculating a particular answer. The suitability of a particular method will depend on the information available. You should try to understand the various alternative methods available to arrive at an answer. Such an exercise will go a long way in furthering your understanding of the consolidation process.

In the alternative method, we first start with Purchase Ltd.'s separate-entity retained earnings of $2,321,000. To this amount we need to add Purchase Ltd.'s share of the change in the separate-entity retained earnings of Target Ltd. from the time of acquisition to the date of consolidation—that is, during 20X6, which is $635,000 – $600,000 – $10,500; $10,500 represents the NCI's 30% share of the change in the separate-entity retained earnings of Target Ltd. of $35,000 ($635,000 – $600,000).

Additionally, we need to adjust Purchase Ltd.'s share of the change in the separate-entity retained earnings of Target Ltd. with Purchase Ltd.'s share of the unrealized profit on upstream sales of $5,600[U] and of the 20X6 amortization of FVI on buildings and equipment of $14,000. The result represents the consolidated retained earnings balance on December 31, 20X6, of $2,325,900. We have used this alternative method while preparing the consolidated financial statements below.

| | | |
|---|---|---:|
| Purchase's separate-entity retained earnings | | $2,321,000 |
| Purchase's share of increase in Target's retained earnings | | |
| Target's separate-entity retained earnings | 635,000 | |
| Less Target's date-of-acquisition retained earnings | (600,000) | |
| Less the NCI's portion of Target's increased retained earnings [(635,000 − 600,000) × 30%] | (10,500) | |
| Net increase to Purchase | | 24,500 |
| Purchase's share of unrealized upstream profit (8,000 × 70%) | | (5,600) |
| Purchase's share of 20X6 amortization of FVI on buildings and equipment ($20,000 × 70%) | | (14,000) |
| Consolidated retained earnings, December 31, 20X6 | | $2,325,900 |

## Worksheet Approach

For the illustration of how the worksheet approach applies to our example, please refer to the Companion Website.

### Concept Check 5-3

1. In the case of non-wholly owned subsidiaries, why are the eliminations relating to unrealized gains/losses on downstream transactions different from the eliminations relating to unrealized gains/losses on upstream transactions?

2. During the consolidation process, why does the NCI get allocated its share of the net income of the subsidiary and its share of the adjustments to the net income of the subsidiary?

LO **4c**

Consolidate a non-wholly owned subsidiary two years after acquisition

## 5.5 CONSOLIDATION IN SECOND SUBSEQUENT YEAR

The separate-entity financial statements for the two companies are shown in Exhibit 5.8. Assume that during 20X7, the following occurred:

1. Target Ltd. had sales of $60,000[U] to Purchase Ltd.; Target Ltd.'s 20X7 gross margin was 45%; $10,000 (sales price) of the goods is in Purchase Ltd.'s inventory on December 31, 20X7. Unrealized upstream profit therefore is $10,000 × 45% = $4,500[U].

2. Purchase Ltd. had sales of $20,000[D] to Target Ltd.; Purchase Ltd.'s 20X7 gross margin was 30%; $6,000 (sales price) of the goods sold to Target Ltd. is in Target Ltd.'s 20X7 ending inventory. Unrealized downstream profit is $6,000 × 30% = $1,800[D].

3. Purchase Ltd. borrowed $500,000 from Target Ltd. on December 29, 20X7. Both companies have reported this as a current item on their separate-entity statements of financial position.

4. Target Ltd. sold its land to Purchase Ltd. for $450,000. The land originally cost Target Ltd. $300,000, and its fair value at the date of Purchase Ltd.'s acquisition of Target Ltd. was $400,000. The gain on the sale ($150,000[U]) is separately disclosed on Target Ltd.'s SCI as an unusual item.

These facts are exactly the same as those used in Chapter 4; they are repeated here for your convenience.

**Exhibit 5.8** Separate-Entity Financial Statements for 20X7

## Statements of Comprehensive Income
### Year Ended December 31, 20X7

| | Purchase Ltd. | Target Ltd. |
|---|---|---|
| Revenue: | | |
| Sales | $3,000,000 | $400,000 |
| Dividend income | 14,000 | — |
| Gain on sale of land | — | 150,000 |
| | 3,014,000 | 550,000 |
| Expenses: | | |
| Cost of sales | 2,100,000 | 220,000 |
| Depreciation expense | 100,000 | 35,000 |
| Other expenses | 440,000 | 75,000 |
| | 2,640,000 | 330,000 |
| NET INCOME AND COMPREHENSIVE INCOME | $ 374,000 | $220,000 |

## Statements of Changes in Equity—Retained Earnings Section
### Year Ended December 31, 20X7

| | Purchase Ltd. | Target Ltd. |
|---|---|---|
| Retained earnings, December 31, 20X6 | $2,321,000 | $635,000 |
| Net income | 374,000 | 220,000 |
| Dividends declared | (135,000) | (20,000) |
| Retained earnings, December 31, 20X7 | $2,560,000 | $835,000 |

## Statements of Financial Position
### December 31, 20X7

| | Purchase Ltd. | Target Ltd. |
|---|---|---|
| ASSETS | | |
| Current assets: | | |
| Cash | $ 475,000 | $ 70,000 |
| Accounts receivable | 1,900,000 | 275,000 |
| Note receivable | — | 500,000 |
| Inventory | 300,000 | 60,000 |
| | 2,675,000 | 905,000 |
| Property, plant, and equipment | | |
| Land | 1,450,000 | — |
| Buildings and equipment | 3,800,000 | 500,000 |
| Accumulated depreciation | (1,400,000) | (220,000) |
| | 3,850,000 | 280,000 |
| Other assets | | |
| Investments (at cost) | 840,000 | — |
| TOTAL ASSETS | $7,365,000 | $1,185,000 |
| LIABILITIES AND SHAREHOLDERS' EQUITY | | |
| LIABILITIES: | | |
| Current liabilities | | |
| Accounts payable | $ 515,000 | $ 150,000 |
| Note payable | 500,000 | — |
| Long-term: note payable | 350,000 | — |
| | 1,365,000 | 150,000 |
| Shareholders' equity | | |
| Common shares | 3,440,000 | 200,000 |
| Retained earnings | 2,560,000 | 835,000 |
| | 6,000,000 | 1,035,000 |
| TOTAL LIABILITIES AND SHAREHOLDERS' EQUITY | $7,365,000 | $1,185,000 |

# Direct Method

In our illustration, we are now at the end of the second year after acquisition. Therefore, we must now carry out all the adjustments and eliminations listed under the last column, titled "Relating to Following Years," in Exhibit 5.3.

The first step, of **M**easure, remains unchanged from what it was earlier in the chapter when we illustrated consolidation at the time of acquisition; therefore, we will not repeat it here. Instead, we will now move to the next step of **E**liminate.

## Eliminate

### Eliminate Intercompany Transactions and Balances

| | |
|---|---:|
| Upstream sale by Target Ltd. | (60,000) |
| Downstream sale by Purchase Ltd. | (20,000) |
| Dividends declared by Target Ltd. | (20,000) |
| Note receivable of Target Ltd., and note payable of Purchase Ltd. | (500,000) |

In 20X7 there are four intercompany items. Our analysis of these steps remains unchanged from our analysis in Chapter 4 in relation to consolidation in the second subsequent year, except for the dividends declared by Target Ltd.

1. Target Ltd. sold $60,000^U$ worth of goods to Purchase Ltd. We need to eliminate $60,000^U$ from both sales and cost of goods sold.

2. Purchase Ltd. sold $20,000_D$ worth of goods to Target Ltd. We must eliminate $20,000_D$ from both sales and cost of goods sold as well.

3. Dividends of $20,000 were declared by Target Ltd. Our analysis of the dividends of $20,000 declared by Target Ltd. in 20X7 is the same as our analysis of the dividends declared in 20X6. Of the $20,000 dividends declared by Target Ltd. in 20X7, Purchase Ltd.'s share is only $14,000; the remaining $6,000 belongs to the NCI. Therefore, while we eliminate the dividends declared amount of $20,000, we need to eliminate only $14,000 from dividend income. The NCI's share of $6,000 will be subtracted from the NCI balance on the SFP.

4. Purchase Ltd. borrowed $500,000 from Target Ltd. on December 29, 20X7. We need to eliminate Target Ltd.'s note receivable and Purchase Ltd.'s note payable at the time of consolidation. The loan occurred at the end of the year, and thus we can disregard any associated interest as immaterial. Otherwise, we would have had to eliminate the associated interest income and interest expense that may have been recognized by Target Ltd. and Purchase Ltd., respectively.

### Unrealized and Realized Profits

| | |
|---|---:|
| Realized profit on upstream sale of inventory in previous year | 8,000 |
| Unrealized profit on upstream sale of inventory in the current year | (4,500) |
| Unrealized profit on downstream sale of inventory in the current year | (1,800) |
| Unrealized gain on sale of land by Target Ltd. to Purchase Ltd. | (150,000) |

Again, the unrealized and realized profits are the same as in Chapter 4 in the year 20X7. We have one source of realized profit, two sources of unrealized profit, and one source of unrealized gain. Remember that in 20X6 we had $8,000^U$ of unrealized profit on the upstream sale of inventory, which we eliminated by increasing the cost of goods sold of 20X6 and decreasing the ending inventory of 20X6, respectively, by that amount. The profit was unrealized because the corresponding goods were still with Purchase Ltd. at the end of the year. These adjustments would have decreased ending retained earnings and NCI by $5,600^U$ and $2,400^U$, respectively. Now, in 20X7, these goods have been sold to an outside party and therefore the associated profits are now realized.

The ending 20X6 inventory is also the beginning 20X7 inventory. Purchase Ltd. would have included the unadjusted beginning inventory in its cost of sales calculation in the current year; from the consolidation point of view that results in *overstating* opening inventory by $8,000^U$ and *overstating* cost of sales by the same amount. Therefore, we must *reduce* consolidated cost of sales by $8,000^U$ to account for the realization of the profits in 20X7. In summary, therefore, we should decrease the opening retained earnings and NCI balance of 20X7 by $5,600^U$ and $2,400^U$, respectively, while decreasing cost of goods sold of 20X7 by $8,000^U$.

We should increase the cost of goods sold of 20X7 and decrease the ending inventory of 20X7 by $4,500^U$ and $1,800_D$ to eliminate the unrealized profits on the upstream and downstream sales of inventory, respectively, this year. The underlying logic is identical to the logic underlying the elimination of the unrealized profit on the upstream sale of inventory in 20X6.

Finally, Target Ltd. sold its land to Purchase Ltd. during the year for a gain of $150,000^U$. However, the land is still owned within the consolidated entity; therefore, the associated gain is unrealized, and must be eliminated.

**Amortize**  The step of **A**mortize will produce different results in 20X7 as compared with the results in 20X6 in this chapter; however, the results will be the same as those obtained in 20X7 in Chapter 4.

| | FVA allocated | Amortization period | Amortization per year | Amortization/ impairment loss during previous periods | Amortization/ impairment loss during 20X7 | Balance of FVA remaining at the end of 20X7 |
|---|---|---|---|---|---|---|
| Land | $100,000 | — | | | — | $100,000 |
| Building and equipment | 200,000 | 10 | $20,000 | $20,000 | $20,000 | 160,000 |
| Goodwill | 100,000 | — | | | — | 100,000 |
| Total | $400,000 | | | $20,000 | $20,000 | $360,000 |

The inferences from the schedule above remain identical to those obtained in Chapter 4 for the second subsequent year. From the schedule above we can see that we need to recognize a total amortization/impairment loss adjustment of $20,000 in the previous year (as explained in greater detail in the following section) and a similar adjustment in the current year.

We can also see from the schedule above that the balance of the FVA adjustment that needs to be added to the carrying values of the parent and subsidiary is $360,000, made up of an increase to land for $100,000, to buildings and equipment for $160,000, and to goodwill for $100,000. Note that the adjustment for buildings and equipment of $160,000 is the result of the initial FVI allocated to buildings and equipment of $200,000 minus the $40,000 depreciation adjustment required in total over the previous and current years.

**Recognize NCI Share of Earnings**   Before we can determine our year-end balance in retained earnings and NCI, we must first determine how much of the subsidiary's net income is to be allocated to the NCI. The process is relatively simple. We start by calculating the adjusted income of the subsidiary. The income is adjusted to remove profits that are unrealized in the current year and to include profits unrealized in previous years that have been realized in the current year. In addition, any amortization or impairment of FVA has to be subtracted from the subsidiary's income. This will provide a measure of the subsidiary's adjusted income. After determining the adjusted income, we calculate the NCI's share of the adjusted income.

With the NCI's share of the adjusted income known, it is again a relatively simple process to determine the ending balance in NCI. We simply start with the balance in the NCI at the beginning of the year and add to it its share of the adjusted income and subtract its share of the dividends declared by the subsidiary. These steps are illustrated in detail below for our example.

We will first focus on the NCI's share of Target's adjusted income in 20X7. We already know the various adjustments that need to be made to the earnings of Target Ltd. in 20X7. We also know that Target Ltd.'s income in 20X7 is $220,000. Therefore, we can easily calculate the share of income that should be apportioned to the NCI. The calculation of the adjusted net income of Target Ltd. in 20X7, and the NCI's share of adjusted income, is presented in the schedule below:

| Details | Amount |
| --- | --- |
| Net income of Target Ltd. for 20X7 (from separate-entity financial statement) | $ 220,000 |
| Add: | |
| Realized profit on upstream sale of inventory in previous year | 8,000 |
| Less: | |
| Unrealized profit on upstream sale of inventory in the current year | (4,500) |
| Unrealized gain on sale of land by Target Ltd. to Purchase Ltd. | (150,000) |
| Amortization of FVA during the year | (20,000) |
| Adjusted net income of Target Ltd. for 20X7 | $   53,500 |
| NCI's share @ 30% | $   16,050 |

In the schedule above we start with the unadjusted net income of Target Ltd. for the year 20X7 of $220,000, taken from its separate-entity financial statements. Before calculating the NCI in Target Ltd.'s earnings, we need to adjust the $220,000 amount for realized and unrealized profits and other expenses.

Specifically, there are four adjustments required to be made to the net income of Target Ltd.—one relating to a realized profit, two related to unrealized profit amounts, and one related to the amortization of the fair value adjustment. All four of these adjustments were already identified in the previous **E**liminate and **A**mortize steps.

Note that we did not include the unrealized profit on the downstream sale of inventory of $1,800$_D$, identified in the **E**liminate step. This profit exists in the hands of

Purchase Ltd., and not in the hands of Target Ltd. Therefore, following entity theory, the NCI balance should not be adjusted for this amount. Instead of adjusting the net income of Target Ltd., we should adjust the separate-entity income of Purchase Ltd. by the $1,800_D$ unrealized gain relating to the downstream sale of inventory.

The adjusted net income of Target Ltd. for 20X7, after making all the above adjustments, is $53,500. Therefore, the NCI's share is $16,050. Naturally, Purchase Ltd.'s share of Target Ltd.'s adjusted income is $37,450. We also need to adjust Purchase Ltd.'s separate-entity net income by the $1,800_D$ unrealized gain relating to the downstream sale of inventory.

It is now easy to calculate the ending balance in the NCI, as demonstrated below. Note that our beginning balance of NCI is obtained from last year's consolidated financial statements, which we completed earlier in the chapter.

| NCI Balance at the End of 20X7 | |
| --- | --- |
| Balance of NCI at the beginning of 20X7 | $362,100 |
| Add: NCI's share of Target Ltd.'s adjusted net income in 20X7 | 16,050 |
| Less: NCI's share of dividends declared by Target Ltd. in 20X7 | (6,000) |
| Ending balance of NCI in 20X7 | $372,150 |

It is also relatively easy to calculate the ending balance in retained earnings. Again we start with the beginning balance in retained earnings, obtained from last year's consolidated financial statements. To it we add the parent's net income and the parent's share of its subsidiary's net income. Note that both the income of the parent and the income of the subsidiary have been adjusted for the various items we discussed above. You should also note that because we recorded our investment in Target using the cost method, we will have to reduce Purchase's net income by the amount of dividends that were received from Target and included in net income.

| Consolidated Retained Earnings Balance at the End of 20X7 | | |
| --- | --- | --- |
| Beginning balance of consolidated retained earnings | | $2,325,900 |
| Add: Purchase Ltd.'s adjusted income | | |
| Purchase Ltd.'s net income | | 374,000 |
| Less unrealized profit on downstream sale of inventory | | (1,800) |
| Less dividend income from Target Ltd. | | (14,000) |
| Purchase Ltd.'s adjusted income | | 358,200 |
| Add: Purchase Ltd.'s share of Target Ltd.'s adjusted income: | | |
| Adjusted net income of Target Ltd. for 20X7 | 53,500 | |
| Purchase Ltd.'s share @ 70% | | 37,450 |
| Less: Dividends declared by Purchase Ltd. | | 135,000 |
| Ending balance of consolidated retained earnings | | $2,586,550 |

The opening NCI and consolidated retained earnings balances for 20X7 were obtained from the ending NCI and consolidated retained earnings balances for 20X6, calculated previously. If all that we wanted was these balances and if we would always have problems that provided us with these balances, then, when using the direct method, we could stop here.

However, we will rarely encounter a problem that requires consolidation for two successive years, much less for the first two years after consolidation.

Instead, most problems will require consolidation a few years after acquisition, and these problems usually do not provide the ending consolidated balances of NCI and retained earnings from the previous year. In such a case, we will need the information necessary to calculate the opening NCI and retained earnings balances for that year without being able to refer to the ending balances of the previous year. The calculations that follow illustrate that process.

In this case, given that we already know these balances, we can view these calculations as a double-check on the beginning balances. Furthermore, the same process can be used in any year to check that the ending balances calculated for NCI and retained earnings are correct. However, it is important to remember that if the beginning balances are not provided, then these calculations become a necessary step in the consolidation process using the direct method.

### Information Necessary for Calculating NCI and Retained Earnings at the Beginning of the Year

There is no NCI balance on the separate-entity financial statements of the parent. Therefore, we will have to re-calculate the beginning NCI balance every year when we prepare consolidated financial statements of the parent. As we will see, we need to allocate to the NCI its share of the adjusted earnings of the subsidiary for previous years to be able to calculate the beginning NCI and retained earnings balances.

### Recognize NCI Share of Prior-Year Earnings

To calculate the NCI balance at the beginning of 20X7, we need to allocate to it its share of the adjusted change in the retained earnings of the subsidiary in the prior year of 20X6.

The opening retained earnings balance of Target Ltd. on its separate-entity SFP for 20X7 is $635,000. The retained earnings balance of Target Ltd. at the time of its acquisition is $600,000. Therefore, the change in the retained earnings of Target Ltd. from the time of acquisition until the beginning of 20X7 is $35,000. The NCI's share is $10,500. Therefore, the NCI balance at the beginning of 20X7 will be $370,500 before allocating to it its share of the consolidation-related adjustments and eliminations pertaining to prior years.

Recall our earlier statement that every time we consolidate subsequent to the date of acquisition, we need to either (1) repeat the individual adjustments and eliminations made in each previous year, or (2) capture their cumulative impact with cumulative adjustments. We will focus on the second type of adjustments—cumulative adjustments.

We are consolidating a non-wholly owned subsidiary. Therefore, the cumulative adjustments in 20X7 required to capture the cumulative impact of adjustments and eliminations made in prior years will have an impact not only on the opening retained earnings of the year, but also on the opening balance of NCI.

In our current example, we must adjust the opening retained earnings and the opening NCI for the impact of two prior years' adjustments:

| | |
|---|---|
| Amortization/impairment loss adjustment of $20,000 pertaining to 20X6 | (20,000) |
| Unrealized profit on upstream sale of inventory in 20X6 | (8,000) |

The first item is the $20,000 amortization or depreciation expense adjustment made in 20X6 relating to the fair value increment allocated to buildings and equipment. This amortization expense adjustment would have decreased the consolidated income of 20X6 and consequently decreased the 20X6 ending consolidated retained earnings by $14,000 and the ending NCI by $6,000. However, this decrease will not be reflected in the opening retained earnings in 20X7 of the separate-entity statements of either Target Ltd. or Purchase Ltd. As well, there is no NCI account in either of the separate-entity statements of financial position of Purchase Ltd. or Target Ltd.

Therefore, we now have to adjust the 20X7 beginning consolidated retained earnings by $14,000 and the beginning NCI by $6,000. If we were to extend our example to 20X8 and the facts remained the same, we would need to adjust the 20X8 opening consolidated retained earnings balance by $28,000: $14,000 for the amortization expense adjustment relating to 20X6 and another $14,000 for the amortization expense adjustment relating to 20X7. Similarly, the 20X8 opening NCI would need to be adjusted by $12,000: $6,000 for the amortization expense adjustment relating to 20X6 and another $6,000 for the amortization expense adjustment relating to 20X7.

| NCI Balance at the Beginning of 20X7 | | |
|---|---|---|
| Balance of NCI at the time of acquisition | | $ 360,000 |
| Add: NCI's share of the adjusted change in retained earnings in prior years: | | |
| Retained earnings balance of Target Ltd. at the end of 20X6 | $635,000 | |
| Retained earnings balance of Target Ltd. at the time of acquisition | 600,000 | |
| Change in carrying value of Target Ltd. in previous years | 35,000 | |
| Less: | | |
| Amortization of fair value adjustment in previous years | (20,000) | |
| Unrealized profit on upstream sale of inventory in 20X6 | (8,000) | |
| Adjusted change in retained earnings of Target Ltd. in prior years | 7,000 | |
| NCI's share @ 30% | | 2,100 |
| Opening balance of NCI on January 1, 20X7 | | $ 362,100 |
| **Opening Consolidated Retained Earnings Balance at the Beginning of 20X7** | | |
| Opening retained earnings balance from separate-entity financial statements of Purchase Ltd. on January 1, 20X7 | | $2,321,000 |
| Add: Purchase Ltd.'s share of the adjusted change in retained earnings in prior years: | | |
| Cumulative adjusted change in retained earnings of Target Ltd. in prior years (as calculated in the first section above) | $ 7,000 | |
| Purchase Ltd.'s share @ 70% | | 4,900 |
| Opening consolidated retained earnings balance on January 1, 20X7 | | $2,325,900 |

In addition, we will use the same process to calculate the beginning balances of retained earnings and NCI for the consolidated financial statements of Purchase Ltd. for 20X7. Furthermore, we already know the share of the adjusted income attributable to

Purchase Ltd. and the NCI for 20X7. Therefore, we now have all the ingredients required to carry out the consolidation. Again, we will go down the SCI and SFP and insert the correct amounts on a line-by-line basis.

**Consolidated SCI and SCE/RE**   The consolidated statement of comprehensive income and SCE/RE are as shown in Exhibit 5.9. The amounts that require adjustment are as follows:

- *Sales.* The two companies' combined sales of $3,400,000 are adjusted for the $80,000 ($60,000$^U$ + $20,000$_D$) in intercompany sales.

- *Dividend income.* The intercompany dividends are eliminated.

- *Gain on sale of land.* The $150,000$^U$ unrealized gain is eliminated.

- *Cost of sales.* The combined cost of goods sold is adjusted for the intercompany sales of $80,000 ($60,000$^U$ + $20,000$_D$). The unrealized profit adjustments to cost of sales are identical to those shown in Chapter 4 for 20X7. The entire unrealized profit in opening inventory ($8,000$^U$) must be subtracted from cost of sales (thereby increasing net income), and the unrealized profits in the ending inventory ($4,500$^U$ + $1,800$_D$) must be added.

- *Depreciation expense.* Amortization of the FVI on Target Ltd.'s buildings and equipment is added to the carrying amount of depreciation. As in 20X6, the amortization is $200,000 over 10 years, or $20,000.

- *Allocation of net income.* The net income of $411,700 must be allocated between the owners of the parent and the NCI. Remember that the NCI is entitled only to its proportionate share of Target Ltd.'s adjusted income. Therefore, we allocate $16,050 to NCI and $395,650 to Purchase Ltd.'s owners.

- *Opening retained earnings.* The 20X7 opening retained earnings is, by definition, the same as the year-end 20X6 retained earnings. The sum of the carrying balances is reduced by (1) Target Ltd.'s date-of-acquisition retained earnings; (2) NCI's share of Target Ltd.'s unadjusted earnings since acquisition; (3) Purchase Ltd.'s share of unrealized upstream profits; and (4) Purchase Ltd.'s share of pre-20X7 amortization of FVA. Note that we have used the same information here as we will in the check step later on in the chapter to calculate the retained earnings balances; it's just arranged differently here.

- *Dividends declared.* Target Ltd.'s declared dividends of $20,000 are eliminated. This reduction is matched by the elimination of the $14,000 dividend income of Purchase Ltd. and the $6,000 reduction that we will make to the NCI balance on the SFP.

**Statement of Financial Position**   The consolidated SFP is shown in Exhibit 5.10. Adjustments are as follows:

- *Note receivable.* The intercompany note receivable of $500,000 is eliminated.

- *Inventory.* The unrealized profits from both the upstream and downstream sales are eliminated: $4,500$^U$ and $1,800$_D$.

- *Land.* We add the FVI for land, and then subtract the $150,000$^U$ unrealized gain on the intercompany sale.

- *Buildings and equipment.* The balance is increased by $50,000, to reflect fair value.

**Exhibit 5.9** Purchase Ltd. Consolidated SCI (Direct Method) and SCE/RE

| | |
|---|---:|
| **Purchase Ltd.** | |
| **Consolidated Statement of Comprehensive Income** | |
| **Year Ended December 31, 20X7** | |
| Revenue: | |
| Sales revenue [3,000,000 + 400,000 − **60,000**$^U$ − **20,000**$_D$] | $3,320,000 |
| Dividend income [14,000 + 0 − **14,000**] | — |
| Gain on sale of land [0 + 150,000 − **150,000**$^U$] | — |
| | 3,320,000 |
| Operating expenses: | |
| Cost of sales [2,100,000 + 220,000 − **60,000**$^U$ − **20,000** − **8,000**$^U$ | |
|     + **4,500**$^U$ + **1,800**$_D$] | 2,238,300 |
| Depreciation expense [100,000 + 35,000 + **20,000**] | 155,000 |
| Other expenses [440,000 + 75,000] | 515,000 |
| | 2,908,300 |
| NET INCOME AND COMPREHENSIVE INCOME | $ 411,700 |
| Net income attributable to: | |
| Owners of the parent | $ 395,650 |
| Non-controlling interest | 16,050 |
| **Purchase Ltd.** | |
| **Consolidated Statement of Changes in Equity—Retained Earnings Section** | |
| **Year Ended December 31, 20X7** | |
| Retained earnings, December 31, 20X6 [2,321,000 + 635,000 − | |
|     **600,000** − (**35,000** × 0.30) − (**8,000**$^U$ × 0.70) − (**20,000** × 0.70) | $2,325,900 |
| Net income | 395,650 |
| Dividends declared [135,000 + 20,000 − 20,000] | (135,000) |
| Retained earnings, December 31, 20X7 | $2,586,550 |

- *Accumulated depreciation.* Target Ltd.'s date-of-acquisition accumulated depreciation of $150,000 is eliminated; two years' worth of FVI amortization of $20,000 per year is added.

- *Investments.* Purchase Ltd.'s $840,000 investment in Target Ltd. is eliminated.

- *Note payable.* The intercompany balance of $500,000 is eliminated.

- *Common shares.* Only Purchase Ltd.'s shares are included.

- *Retained earnings.* We start with the carrying balances of the two companies, and then we:

  1. subtract Target Ltd.'s date-of-acquisition retained earnings;

  2. subtract the NCI's share of the change in retained earnings since the date of acquisition: ($835,000 − $600,000) × 30% = $70,500;

  3. subtract Purchase Ltd.'s 70% share of upstream unrealized profits in land and in ending inventory;

**4.** subtract 100% of unrealized downstream profits and

**5.** subtract Purchase Ltd.'s 70% share of the cumulative amount of FVA amortization since the date of acquisition (i.e., $20,000 \times 70\% \times 2$ years).

**Exhibit 5.10** Purchase Ltd. Consolidated Statement of Financial Position (Direct Method)

| Statement of Financial Position December 31, 20X7 | |
|---|---:|
| **ASSETS** | |
| **Current assets:** | |
| Cash [475,000 + 70,000] | $ 545,000 |
| Accounts receivable [1,900,000 + 275,000] | 2,175,000 |
| Note receivable [0 + 500,000 − **500,000**] | — |
| Inventory [300,000 + 60,000 − **4,500**$^U$ − **1,800**$_D$] | 353,700 |
| | 3,073,700 |
| **Property, plant, and equipment:** | |
| Land [1,450,000 + 0 + **100,000** − **150,000**$^U$] | 1,400,000 |
| Buildings and equipment [3,800,000 + 500,000 + **50,000**] | 4,350,000 |
| Accumulated depreciation [1,400,000 + 220,000 − **150,000** + **20,000** + **20,000**] | (1,510,000) |
| | 4,240,000 |
| **Other assets** | |
| Investments [840,000 + 0 − **840,000**] | — |
| Goodwill | 100,000 |
| **TOTAL ASSETS** | $7,413,700 |
| **LIABILITIES AND SHAREHOLDERS' EQUITY** | |
| **Current liabilities:** | |
| Accounts payable [515,000 + 150,000] | $ 665,000 |
| Note payable [500,000 + 0 − **500,000**] | — |
| Long-term liability: notes payable [350,000 + 0] | 350,000 |
| | 1,015,000 |
| **Shareholders' Equity:** | |
| Common shares [**Purchase Ltd. shares only**] | 3,440,000 |
| Retained earnings [2,560,000 + 835,000 − **600,000** − (235,000 × 0.30) − (150,000$^U$ × 0.70) − (4,500$^U$ × 0.70) − 1,800$_D$ − (20,000 × 0.70 × 2)] | 2,586,550 |
| | 6,026,550 |
| NCI [**360,000 + 2,100 + 16,050 − 6,000**] | 372,150 |
| **TOTAL SHAREHOLDERS' EQUITY** | 6,398,700 |
| Total liabilities and shareholders' equity | $7,413,700 |

Again, we used the same information as we will use in the double-check step later, but arranged differently, to arrive at the closing consolidated retained earnings balance.

■ *Non-controlling interest.* We start with the NCI balance at the time of acquisition, and then we:

1. add the NCI's share of the adjusted change in the retained earnings of Target Ltd. in the prior year of 20X6 of $2,100;

2. add the NCI's share of the adjusted income of Target Ltd. in the current year of $16,050 and

3. subtract the NCI's share of the dividends declared by Target Ltd. of $6,000.

**Check** The NCI and retained earnings balances calculated below provide independent checks of the ending NCI and ending consolidated retained earnings. These will be useful checks of the accuracy of our work.

| NCI Balance at the End of 20X7 | | |
|---|---:|---:|
| Balance of NCI at the time of acquisition | | $ 360,000 |
| Add: NCI's share of the adjusted change in retained earnings in prior years | | |
| Retained earnings balance of Target Ltd. at the end of 20X7 | $835,000 | |
| Retained earnings balance of Target Ltd. at the time of acquisition | 600,000 | |
| Change in carrying value of Target Ltd. since acquisition | 235,000 | |
| Less: | | |
| Amortization of fair value adjustment | (40,000) | |
| Unrealized profit on upstream sale of inventory in 20X7 | (4,500) | |
| Unrealized gain on sale of land in 20X7 | (150,000) | |
| Adjusted change in retained earnings of Target Ltd. since acquisition | 40,500 | |
| NCI's share @ 30% | | 12,150 |
| Ending balance of NCI on December 31, 20X7 | | $372,150 |
| Consolidated Retained Earnings Balance at the End of 20X7 | | |
| 20X7 separate-entity ending retained earnings balance of Purchase Ltd. | | $2,560,000 |
| Less unrealized profit on downstream sale of inventory | | (1,800) |
| Adjusted separate-entity retained earnings balance of Purchase Ltd. | | 2,558,200 |
| Add: Purchase Ltd.'s share of the adjusted change in retained earnings since acquisition | | |
| Adjusted change in retained earnings of Target Ltd. since acquisition (as calculated in the section just above) | $ 40,500 | |
| Purchase Ltd.'s share @ 70% | | 28,350 |
| 20X7 ending consolidated retained earnings balance of Purchase Ltd. | | $2,586,550 |

Notice that there is one new adjustment required for calculating the adjusted separate-entity retained earnings of Purchase Ltd.—the adjustment relating to the unrealized profit on the downstream sale of inventory. As we pointed out earlier, this profit is unrealized in the hands of Purchase Ltd., and therefore should be fully attributed to Purchase Ltd.'s shareholders.

There is a relatively simple explanation for the remaining $28,350 adjustment required to obtain the ending consolidated retained earnings. We already know that the adjusted change in the retained earnings of Target Ltd. to December 31, 20X7, is $40,500. Therefore, Purchase Ltd.'s share of that amount is 70%, or $28,350. Consequently, we also don't need to make an eliminating adjustment for the $14,000 dividend income already recognized by Purchase Ltd. in 20X7. The consolidated retained earnings balance of Purchase Ltd. at the end of 20X7 is therefore $2,586,550.

### Concept Check 5-4

1. How do the adjustments relating to prior periods differ when a subsidiary is non-wholly owned compared to similar adjustments when a subsidiary is wholly owned?

2. What is the rationale for reporting the NCI as part of equity on the SFP?

LO ❸
Describe the different principles of accounting provided by IFRS and/or ASPE for reporting non-wholly owned subsidiaries, associates, and joint ventures

LO ❹a–c
Consolidate a non-wholly owned subsidiary: at the date of acquisition; one year after acquisition; and two years after acquisition

## 5.6 OTHER ISSUES

## Consolidated Statements under the Parent-Company Extension Method

In our illustration, under the entity method the NCI was allocated its implicit "share" of $30,000 of the goodwill of $100,000 based on the $70,000 paid by Purchase Ltd. for its share of the goodwill. However, an acquiring company may be willing to pay a bonus to gain control, and it may be *control* of the assets that gives rise to goodwill. That control gives rise to goodwill is shown by the fact that many takeover bids propose a high price, but offer to buy only enough of the outstanding shares (e.g., 51%) to gain control.

Therefore, when control of assets is what gives rise to goodwill, it may not be appropriate to attribute goodwill to the NCI. Even otherwise, the full value of the goodwill of Target Ltd. and the NCI's share of goodwill may not bear a linear relationship to the price paid by the parent for its share of goodwill. Therefore, in such a circumstance, given the uncertainty surrounding the value of the NCI's share of the goodwill, it may be prudent to include only the parent's portion of the goodwill in the consolidated SFP and not the entire 100% value of the goodwill. The parent-company extension method below follows this approach.

**Parent-Company Extension Method**   The parent-company extension method is identical to the entity method except that only the goodwill actually purchased by the parent is shown on the consolidated SFP—no goodwill is assigned to the NCI. Therefore, in our illustration, under the parent-company extension method, at the time of acquisition (1) the amount shown for goodwill will be $70,000 and (2) the NCI will be valued at its share of the fair value of the net identifiable assets—that is, at $330,000 (30% of $1,100,000).

Since under the parent-company extension method the goodwill on the consolidated SFP represents only the parent's share of goodwill, it naturally follows that any loss related to the impairment of the goodwill should be attributed solely to the parent. The NCI should not bear any impairment losses.

Of course, the amortization expenses relating to the NCI's share of fair value adjustments should continue to be charged against the NCI on the consolidated SFP. In our illustration, there was no impairment in the value of the goodwill in either 20X6 or 20X7. Therefore, for our illustration, the only differences to the consolidated financial statements under the parent-company extension method at all three points in time—at the time of acquisition, one year, and two years after acquisition—will be: (1) goodwill at $70,000 instead of at $100,000, and (2) an NCI balance lower by $30,000.

## Bargain Purchase

The acquisition method requires the acquiree to be valued at its full fair value on the date of its acquisition. When there is a bargain purchase, the purchase consideration paid by the parent for its share of the acquiree will be less than the fair value of its share. Therefore, in such a case, the full fair value of the acquiree cannot be determined by simply grossing up the purchase price paid by the parent. Consequently, the **M**easure step in our MEAR steps to consolidation is inappropriate when there is a bargain purchase. We will now provide an alternative calculation for the **M**easure step where there is a bargain purchase.

Let us alter our illustration by assuming that Purchase Ltd. paid only $759,500 for its 70% share of Target Ltd. in a bargain purchase. However, Purchase Ltd.'s share of the fair value of the net identifiable assets of Target Ltd. is $1,100,000 × 70% = $770,000. Therefore, the gain on the bargain purchase is $10,500, as calculated below:

| | |
|---|---:|
| Purchase Ltd.'s share of fair value of net identifiable assets [$1,100,000 × 70%] | $770,000 |
| Purchase price | 759,500 |
| Gain on bargain purchase allocated fully to Purchase Ltd. | $ 10,500 |

This gain on the bargain purchase belongs fully to Purchase Ltd. and is recognized as a gain in the consolidated SCI issued by Purchase Ltd. in the year of acquisition. Since we cannot assume that the NCI has bought or will also be capable of buying its share at a bargain, we cannot attribute a similar gain to the NCI. The correct value of NCI is calculated by ignoring the bargain purchase and is therefore 30% of $1,100,000—that is, $330,000.[2]

Since goodwill is absent, the fair value of 100% of Target Ltd. is equal to the full value of its net identifiable assets of $1,100,000. Therefore, the fair value adjustment is $300,000, which is fully allocated to the various identifiable assets and liabilities in the usual manner, as demonstrated in Exhibit 5.11.

The remaining MEAR steps to consolidation remain unchanged, and thus can be followed while consolidating a subsidiary purchased in a bargain purchase.

**Exhibit 5.11** Allocation of Fair Value Adjustment

| 70% Bargain Purchase of Target Ltd., December 31, 20X5 | | | | | |
|---|---|---|---|---|---|
| 100% fair value of Target Ltd. | | | | | $1,100,000 |
| Less carrying value of Target's net identifiable assets | | | | | (800,000) |
| = fair value adjustment, allocated below | | | | | 300,000 |
| | Carrying value (a) | Fair value (b) | Fair value adjustment (c) = (b) – (a) | FVA allocated | |
| Cash | $ 50,000 | $ 50,000 | — | | |
| Accounts receivable | 150,000 | 150,000 | — | | |
| Inventory | 50,000 | 50,000 | — | | |
| Land | 300,000 | 400,000 | $100,000 | $100,000 | |
| Buildings and equipment | 500,000 | 550,000 | 50,000 | 50,000 | |
| Accumulated depreciation | (150,000) | — | 150,000 | 150,000 | |
| Accounts payable | (100,000) | (100,000) | — | | |
| Total fair value adjustment | | | | | (300,000) |
| Net asset carrying value | $800,000 | | | | |
| Fair value of assets acquired | | $1,100,000 | | | |
| Balance of FVA | | | | | $ — |

---

[2] You will notice that the calculated value of $330,000 of NCI is identical to its value under the parent-company extension method. This is no coincidence; it is due to the fact that in both cases NCI's value depends only on the fair value of the net identifiable assets of Target Ltd. Specifically, in the case of a bargain purchase, the NCI is calculated ignoring any gain on such bargain purchase, while in the case of the parent-company extension method, it is calculated ignoring the value of goodwill.

# Application of Proprietary Theory When Using Equity Method to Report Associates and Joint Ventures

If Target Ltd. were an associate or joint venture instead of being a subsidiary of Purchase Ltd., IFRS would require us to use the proprietary theory while reporting Purchase Ltd.'s share of Target Ltd.'s adjusted net income under the equity method. The altered calculation required under the proprietary theory is provided below:

| Details | Amount |
| --- | ---: |
| Net income of Target Ltd. for 20X7 (from separate-entity financial statement) | $220,000 |
| Add: | |
|   Realized profit on upstream sale of inventory in previous year | 8,000 |
| Less: | |
|   Unrealized profit on upstream sale of inventory in the current year | (4,500) |
|   **Unrealized profit on downstream sale of inventory in the current year** | **(1,800)** |
|   Unrealized gain on sale of land by Target Ltd. to Purchase Ltd. | (150,000) |
|   Amortization of FVA during the year | (20,000) |
| Adjusted net income of Target Ltd. for 20X7 | $51,700 |
| Purchase's share @ 70% | $ 36,190 |

The only difference now, highlighted in bold above, is that while calculating Purchase Ltd.'s 70% share of Target Ltd.'s adjusted income, we also include the $1,800_D$ unrealized gain on the downstream sale. Therefore, Purchase Ltd.'s share is reduced by only its 70% share and not by the full amount of the unrealized gain of $1,800_D$, as was done previously in our main example, when Target was assumed to be a subsidiary. Thus, in our example, for the same set of facts, Purchase Ltd. will recognize an extra $540 in income if Target is its associate or joint venture instead of being its subsidiary.

## Concept Check 5-5

1. How is the value of the NCI on the SFP different under the parent-company extension method as compared to its value under the entity method?

2. Why is the calculation of the gain on a bargain purchase different from the calculation of goodwill in the absence of a bargain purchase?

3. How is the treatment of unrealized gains and losses different under the proprietary theory compared with under the entity theory?

Reality Check 5–2 provides findings from academic studies on the prevalence and implications of the existence of differences between ownership and control.

LO **2**
Identify the conceptual alternatives for consolidating non-wholly owned subsidiaries

LO **4**
Consolidate a non-wholly owned subsidiary: at the date of acquisition; one year after acquisition; and two years after acquisition

## 5.7 ACCOUNTING STANDARDS FOR PRIVATE ENTERPRISES

As discussed previously in Chapter 4, the ASPE reporting requirements for investments in subsidiaries, associates, and joint ventures are identical to those under IFRS.

■ Non-controlling interest at the time of acquisition can be valued either at its fair value or at its proportionate share of the acquiree's net identifiable assets.

■ Unrealized gains on downstream sales must be completely eliminated against the parent's shareholders.

■ Unrealized gains on upstream sales must be completely eliminated, but they do need to be allocated to the parent's shareholders and the NCI based on their respective ownership share.

■ Unrealized gains on downstream and upstream sales between an investor and its associate or joint venture are eliminated only to the extent of the investor's interest in the associate or joint venture.

## 5.8 THE NEXT STEPS

Chapters 4 and 5 have worked methodically through the consolidation process at three points in time: the date of acquisition, one year after acquisition, and two years after acquisition. Chapter 4 assumed that the parent owned 100% of the subsidiary shares. Chapter 5 illustrated consolidation when the subsidiary is *not* wholly owned. Through the course of these two chapters, most of the major aspects of consolidation have been illustrated.

The next chapter covers the one remaining major aspect of consolidations—intercompany sale of depreciable or amortizable assets. In fact, it is quite possible that an item that is an inventory item to the seller is a depreciable asset to the buyer. Don't worry, however; we will not be discussing this issue in the text!

Chapter 6 also presents a general set of steps to approach the consolidation process that can be used at any point in time, freeing us from the methodical process of year-by-year consolidations. We also will take a third and final look at the equity basis of reporting. We bet you can hardly wait!

# Ownership Versus Control

The common perception about corporations is that their ownership is widely held. However, research has found that this holds true only for large firms in the richest common-law countries.[a] In their analysis of the shareholding pattern of the largest corporations in 23 wealthy countries, the authors find that outside of the United States, especially in countries with poor shareholder protection, even the largest firms have controlling shareholders—sometimes it is the state but often it is the family of the founder. The authors find that the controlling shareholders typically have power over the firm significantly in excess of their ownership rights (excess control), typically through the use of pyramids (a chain of companies) and participation in management.

Another study found that even in developed countries there is diversion of corporate resources from the corporation and non-controlling shareholders to the controlling shareholders (known as tunnelling).[b] They also find that most of the tunnelling is legal, using mechanisms such as expropriation of corporate opportunities, favour-able transfer pricing, transferring assets at non-market prices, and loans at non-market rates. They also find in their analysis of law cases that civil-law countries, compared with common-law countries, are less protective of non-controlling shareholders.

Finally, a third study analyzed the ultimate shareholding pattern of a large sample of publicly traded firms in Canada and found that small investors in publicly traded firms are vulnerable to the expropriation of the resources of those firms because of excess control.[c] This problem is especially severe in Quebec, which follows civil law, as compared with the rest of Canada, which follows common law.

a. R. La Porta, F. Lopez-de-Silanes, and A. Shleifer. "Corporate ownership around the world." *The Journal of Finance* 54: 2 (April 1999), p. 471.
b. S. Johnson, R. La Porta, F. Lopez-de-Silanes, and A. Shleifer. "Tunneling." *The American Economic Review* 90: 2 (May 2000), p. 22.
c. N. Attig, "Excess control and the risk of corporate expropriation: Canadian evidence." *Canadian Journal of Administrative Sciences* 24: 2 (June 2007), p. 94.

## Relevant Standards

### IFRS

**IFRS  3**  Business Combinations
**IFRS 10**  Consolidated Financial Statements
**IFRS 11**  Joint Arrangements
**IAS  28**  Investments in Associates

### ASPE

**Section 1590**  Subsidiaries
**Section 1601**  Consolidated Financial Statements
**Section 1602**  Non-controlling Interests
**Section 3051**  Investments
**Section 3051**  Interests in Joint Ventures

## 5.9 SUMMARY OF KEY POINTS

1. When a parent company purchases control of a subsidiary but acquires less than 100% of the subsidiary's shares, the portion not owned by the parent is called the non-controlling interest (NCI). **LO 1**

2. Different conceptual alternatives exist for accounting for the NCI in the consolidated financial statements of the parent. These alternatives flow from two major competing theories of consolidation, which are at either end of a continuum—the proprietary theory and the entity theory. **LO 2**

3. Based on the degree to which each of these two theories of consolidation—the proprietary theory and the entity theory—are applied, we have four methods of consolidating a non-wholly owned subsidiary—proportionate method, parent-company method, parent-company extension method, and entity method. **LO 2**

4. IFRS requires either the *entity* or the *parent-company extension* method to be used on a transaction-by-transaction basis for consolidating non-wholly owned subsidiaries. Under the entity method, the subsidiary's assets and liabilities are consolidated with those of the parent at 100% of their fair values. In contrast, under the parent-company extension method, the subsidiary's assets and liabilities, *excluding the NCI's share of goodwill*, are consolidated with those of the parent at 100% of their fair values. Under both methods, the parent's assets and liabilities are consolidated at their carrying value on the parent's separate-entity SFP. **LO 3**

5. IFRS requires the application of the proprietary theory when reporting investments in an associate or joint venture under the equity method. Consequently, unrealized gains or losses on intercompany transactions between an entity and its associates or joint ventures are eliminated *only* to the extent of the entity's ownership share in those associates/joint ventures. **LO 3**

6. All of the subsidiary's assets and liabilities are consolidated on the parent's SFP, but part of those net assets represents the equity of the non-controlling interest. On the parent's SFP, there must be an amount shown for the NCI's share of the subsidiary's net assets. IFRS requires this amount to be shown under the equity section, separately from the parent's shareholders' equity. **LO 3**

7. All of the subsidiary's revenues and expenses are included in the parent's SCI, but part of the subsidiary's earnings accrues to the NCI. Therefore, the parent must allocate such share to the NCI on the consolidated SCI. **LO 4**

8. All unrealized gains relating to transactions between the parent and the subsidiary have to be eliminated, and the NCI's share of such gains should be allocated to it. **LO 4**

---

**Visit the text's website at** www.pearsoned.ca/beechy **for practice quizzes, additional problems, Excel® templates, answers to Concept Check questions, and important IFRS updates.**

---

# Self-Study Problems

1. In 20X5, Primary Co. purchased inventory at a cost of $100,000 and sold it at a sale price of $150,000 to Secondary Co. In 20X5, Secondary sold 40% of the inventory purchased from Primary to Stranger Co., an unrelated third-party company, at a gross profit on sales of 25%. The remaining inventory purchased from Primary was still in Secondary's inventory at the end of 20X5.

Required

Calculate the unrealized gain at the end of 20X5 on the intercompany sale for each of the following independent situations. In the case of transactions between a parent and its subsidiary, also provide all consolidation-related adjustments.

    **a.** Secondary is a 80%-owned subsidiary of Primary.

    **b.** Secondary is a 80%-owned associate of Primary.

    **c.** Assume instead that the intercompany sale is upstream from Secondary, a 80%-owned subsidiary, to its parent, Primary.

    **d.** Assume instead that the intercompany sale is upstream from Secondary, a 80%-owned associate, to Primary.

2. On January 10, 20X5, Regina Ltd. acquired 60% of the shares of Dakota Ltd. by issuing common shares valued at $150,000. Prior to the acquisition of Dakota, Regina's SFP appeared as shown in Exhibit 5.12. The SFP of Dakota Ltd. at the date of acquisition is shown in Exhibit 5.13.

**Exhibit 5.12** Regina Ltd.

| Statement of Financial Position<br>December 31, 20X4 | |
|---|---:|
| **Current assets:** | |
| Cash | $ 50,000 |
| Accounts and other receivables | 70,000 |
| Inventory | 80,000 |
| | 200,000 |
| **Capital assets:** | |
| Building | 260,000 |
| Accumulated depreciation | (40,000) |
| Equipment | 175,000 |
| Accumulated depreciation | (70,000) |
| | 325,000 |
| **TOTAL ASSETS** | $525,000 |
| **Liabilities:** | |
| Current accounts payable and accrued liabilities | $ 80,000 |
| **Shareholders' equity:** | |
| Common shares | 220,000 |
| Retained earnings | 225,000 |
| | 445,000 |
| **TOTAL LIABILITIES AND SHAREHOLDERS' EQUITY** | $525,000 |

**Exhibit 5.13** Dakota Ltd.

| Statement of Financial Position January 10, 20X5 | | |
|---|---|---|
| | Carrying value | Fair value |
| **Current assets:** | | |
| Cash | $ 10,000 | $ 10,000 |
| Accounts and other receivables | 20,000 | 20,000 |
| Inventory | 30,000 | 30,000 |
| | 60,000 | |
| **Capital assets:** | | |
| Land | 45,000 | 80,000 |
| Building | 150,000 | 130,000 |
| Accumulated depreciation | (50,000) | |
| Equipment | 130,000 | 10,000 |
| Accumulated depreciation | (80,000) | |
| | 195,000 | |
| **TOTAL ASSETS** | $255,000 | |
| **Liabilities:** | | |
| Current accounts payable | $ 40,000 | 40,000 |
| Long-term debenture payable | 50,000 | 50,000 |
| | 90,000 | |
| **Shareholders' equity:** | | |
| Common shares | 100,000 | |
| Retained earnings | 65,000 | |
| | 165,000 | |
| **TOTAL LIABILITIES AND SHAREHOLDERS' EQUITY** | $255,000 | |

**Required**

Prepare a consolidated SFP for Regina Ltd. as it would appear immediately following the acquisition of Dakota.

3.  During 20X5, the following transactions occurred between Regina Ltd. and Dakota Ltd. (see SSP2):

    **a.** Regina lent $50,000 at 10% interest to Dakota Ltd. on July 1, 20X5, for one year. The interest was unpaid at December 31, 20X5.

    **b.** During 20X5, Regina purchased inventory from Dakota at a cost of $400,000; $100,000 of that amount was still in Regina's inventory at the end of 20X5. (Hint: look at Dakota's SCI to compute Dakota's gross profit percentage.)

    **c.** During 20X5, Dakota purchased inventory of $200,000 from Regina; $40,000 of that amount was still in Dakota's inventory at the end of 20X5.

**Exhibit 5.14** Regina Ltd. and Dakota Ltd., SFP, SCI, and SCE/RE

## Statements of Financial Position
### December 31, 20X5

| | Regina Ltd. | Dakota Ltd. |
|---|---|---|
| **Current assets:** | | |
| Cash | $ 28,000 | $ 10,000 |
| Accounts and other receivables | 110,000 | 30,000 |
| Inventories | 160,000 | 60,000 |
| | 298,000 | 100,000 |
| **Capital assets:** | | |
| Land | — | 135,000 |
| Buildings | 300,000 | 150,000 |
| Accumulated depreciation | (45,000) | (60,000) |
| Equipment | 200,000 | 130,000 |
| Accumulated depreciation | (80,000) | (90,000) |
| | 375,000 | 265,000 |
| **Other assets:** | | |
| Investment in Dakota Ltd. (at cost) | 150,000 | — |
| **TOTAL ASSETS** | $823,000 | $365,000 |
| **Liabilities:** | | |
| Current accounts payable and accrued liabilities | $ 40,000 | $ 80,000 |
| Long-term liabilities | 65,000 | 50,000 |
| | 105,000 | 130,000 |
| **Shareholders' equity** | | |
| Common shares | 370,000 | 100,000 |
| Retained earnings | 348,000 | 135,000 |
| | 718,000 | 235,000 |
| **TOTAL LIABILITIES AND SHAREHOLDERS' EQUITY** | $823,000 | $365,000 |

## Statements of Comprehensive Income
### Year Ended December 31, 20X5

| | Regina Ltd. | Dakota Ltd. |
|---|---|---|
| Sales | $2,000,000 | $1,000,000 |
| Dividend income | 24,000 | — |
| Other income | 7,000 | — |
| | 2,031,000 | 1,000,000 |
| Cost of sales | 1,000,000 | 600,000 |
| Other operating expenses | 886,000 | 280,000 |
| Interest expense | 2,000 | 10,000 |
| | 1,888,000 | 890,000 |
| **NET INCOME AND COMPREHENSIVE INCOME** | $ 143,000 | $ 110,000 |

## Statements of Changes in Equity—Retained Earnings Section
### Year Ended December 31, 20X5

| | Regina Ltd. | Dakota Ltd. |
|---|---|---|
| Retained earnings, December 31, 20X4 | $ 225,000 | $ 65,000 |
| Net income | 143,000 | 110,000 |
| Dividends declared | (20,000) | (40,000) |
| Retained earnings, December 31, 20X5 | $ 348,000 | $ 135,000 |

Other Information

**d.** Dakota's building and equipment were estimated to have remaining useful lives from January 10, 20X5, of 10 and 5 years, respectively. Straight-line depreciation is being used.

**e.** There has been no impairment of goodwill.

**f.** No fixed assets were sold or written off during 20X5.

The December 31, 20X5, separate-entity financial statements for both companies are shown in Exhibit 5.14.

Required

Prepare the consolidated statement of income and retained earnings and the consolidated SFP for Regina Ltd. for the year ended December 31, 20X5.

**4.** Regina Ltd. owns 60% of the common shares of Dakota Ltd., acquired on January 10, 20X5. The details of the purchase are given in Self-Study Problem 2, and the trial balances for December 31, 20X5, and selected transactions for 20X5 are shown in Self-Study Problem 3. The financial statements of both companies (unconsolidated) at December 31, 20X6, are shown in Exhibit 5.15.

Additional Information

**1.** At the beginning of 20X6, unrealized upstream profits in inventory amounted to $40,000 held in Regina's inventory (i.e., from upstream sales) and $20,000 in Dakota's inventory (i.e., from downstream sales).

**2.** During 20X6, Dakota sold inventory to Regina for $160,000 at the normal gross margin. One-half of that amount is still in Regina's inventory at year-end.

**3.** Late in 20X6, Regina sold inventory to Dakota at a special price of $40,000. All of these goods are still in Dakota's inventory on December 31, 20X6. The cost to Regina of the goods sold to Dakota was $20,000, a 50% gross margin on the selling price.

**4.** The one-year, $50,000 loan that Regina extended to Dakota on July 1, 20X5, was extended for two more years (to July 1, 20X8). Simple interest (at 10%) has been accrued by both companies, but no interest will be paid until the principal is repaid.

Required

Calculate the following amounts for the year ended December 31, 20X6:

**a.** NCI in earnings (i.e., on Regina's consolidated SCI).

**b.** NCI (on Regina's consolidated SFP), December 31, 20X6.

**c.** Regina's year-end consolidated retained earnings.

**Exhibit 5.15** Regina Ltd. and Dakota Ltd.

## Statements of Financial Position
### December 31, 20X6

| | Regina Ltd. | Dakota Ltd. |
|---|---|---|
| **Current assets:** | | |
| Cash | $ 63,800 | $ 52,500 |
| Accounts and other receivables | 120,000 | 77,000 |
| Inventories | 130,000 | 55,000 |
| | 313,800 | 184,500 |
| **Capital assets:** | | |
| Land | — | 135,000 |
| Buildings | 380,000 | 150,000 |
| Accumulated depreciation | (56,200) | (70,000) |
| Equipment | 230,000 | 170,000 |
| Accumulated depreciation | (68,000) | (47,000) |
| | 485,800 | 338,000 |
| **Other assets:** | | |
| Investment in Dakota Ltd. (at cost) | 150,000 | — |
| **TOTAL ASSETS** | $949,600 | $522,500 |
| **Liabilities:** | | |
| Current accounts payable and accrued liabilities | $ 51,600 | $ 97,500 |
| Long-term liabilities | 180,000 | 120,000 |
| | 231,600 | 217,500 |
| **Shareholders' equity:** | | |
| Common shares | 370,000 | 100,000 |
| Retained earnings | 348,000 | 205,000 |
| | 718,000 | 305,000 |
| **TOTAL LIABILITIES AND SHAREHOLDERS' EQUITY** | $949,600 | $522,500 |

## Statements of Comprehensive Income
### Year Ended December 31, 20X6

| | Regina Ltd. | Dakota Ltd. |
|---|---|---|
| Sales | $2,200,000 | $1,100,000 |
| Dividend income | 36,000 | — |
| Gain on sale of equipment | 10,000 | — |
| Other income | 12,000 | — |
| | 2,258,000 | 1,100,000 |
| Cost of sales | 1,300,000 | 660,000 |
| Other operating expenses | 864,000 | 292,000 |
| Interest expense | 20,000 | 18,000 |
| | 2,184,000 | 970,000 |
| **NET INCOME AND COMPREHENSIVE INCOME** | $ 74,000 | $ 130,000 |

## Statements of Changes in Equity—Retained Earnings Section
### Year Ended December 31, 20X6

| | Regina Ltd. | Dakota Ltd. |
|---|---|---|
| Retained earnings, December 31, 20X5 | $ 348,000 | $ 135,000 |
| Net income | 74,000 | 130,000 |
| Dividends declared | (74,000) | (60,000) |
| Retained earnings, December 31, 20X6 | $ 348,000 | $ 205,000 |

## Review Questions

1. Define the following terms:
   a. NCI
   b. Minority interest
   c. Proportionate consolidation
   d. Parent-company method
   e. Parent-company extension method
   f. Entity method

2. Why do some corporations prefer to control their subsidiaries with less than full ownership?

3. How can the inclusion of 100% of a subsidiary's assets on the consolidated SFP be justified when the parent owns less than 100% of the subsidiary's shares?

4. When all of a non-wholly owned subsidiary's revenues and expenses are consolidated, what recognition is given to the fact that the parent's share of the subsidiary's earnings is less than 100%?

5. Under the entity approach of reporting non-controlling interest, what value is assigned to goodwill?

6. How does the parent-company extension method modify the entity approach? What is the rationale for this modification?

7. Explain why a subsidiary's assets and liabilities are consolidated using two different valuations (fair value and carrying value) under the parent-company method.

8. At the date of acquisition, how is the amount of non-controlling interest measured under the entity method and the parent-company extension method, respectively?

9. One year after the date of acquisition, how is the amount of non-controlling interest on the SFP measured under the entity method and the parent-company extension method, respectively?

10. How do unrealized profits on upstream sales affect the non-controlling interest's share of a subsidiary's earnings?

11. How do unrealized profits on downstream sales affect the non-controlling interest's share of a subsidiary's earnings?

12. How are non-controlling shareholders likely to react to the reduction of their share of the subsidiary's earnings as a result of unrealized profits?

13. What is the impact on the non-controlling interest of unrealized profits in *beginning* inventories?

14. Why are a non-wholly owned subsidiary's dividend payments completely eliminated even though the parent does not receive all of the dividends?

15. Under the parent-company and parent-company extension methods, all of a subsidiary's assets and liabilities are consolidated regardless of the ownership percentage of the parent. Nevertheless, the ownership percentage may affect the amount of the reported (consolidated) assets. Explain.

# 5.9 CASES

## CASE 5-1 METRO UTILITY WORKERS' UNION

Metro Utility Workers' Union (MUWU) is a registered not-for-profit organization that represents the workers of Metro Gas, a natural gas distribution company serving a metropolitan area in southern Alberta. The MUWU chief economist has retained Françoise Dubois to provide accounting advice in preparation for the union's forthcoming spring 20X9 labour contract negotiations. The chief economist has provided Ms. Dubois with the information that follows.

MUWU has provided you with the separate entity financial statements of Metro Utility for 20X8 and also for a natural gas–producing company, Oshkosh Utility. Metro Utility has a 40% ownership in Oshkosh. These financial statements had been provided to MUWU by Metro Utility in good faith prior to the start of negotiations. Metro Utility made its investment in OshKosh Utility at the end of 20X5. Metro Utility has not yet issued its annual report for 20X8. Therefore, the separate entity financial statements of Metro Utility are preliminary and not necessarily what will eventually be released to the public.

Metro Utility made its investment in Oshkosh Utility at the end of 20X5. Metro Utility's top management earns bonuses as a percentage of the net income for the year. One of the eight board members of Oshkosh Utility is a Metro Utility representative.

Metro Utility has typically purchased 70% of the natural gas produced by Oshkosh Utility, selling the gas to its customers throughout the metropolitan area. However, recently, competition for natural gas has been heating up due to rising demand. Since natural gas can be piped from southern Alberta to the northwestern USA, it will become relatively easy for Oshkosh Utility to sell its natural gas to other customers in North America who are willing to pay a higher price.

Both Metro Utility and Oshkosh Utility are public companies trading on the TSX. Both utilities pay regular dividends; many of the investors in both companies are retired individuals.

Information relating to Oshkosh Utility at the time of Metro Utility's 40% investment is as follows:

|                       | 20X5 Year-End Cost | 20X5 Year-End FMV |
|-----------------------|--------------------|-------------------|
| Cash                  | $ 50,000           | $ 50,000          |
| Accounts receivable   | 75,000             | 75,000            |
| Inventory             | 65,000             | 97,500            |
| Capital assets        | 200,000            | 280,000           |
| Patents               |                    | 50,000            |
| Current liabilities   | 40,000             | 40,000            |
| Long-term liabilities | 200,000            | 200,000           |

- Metro Utility paid $180,000 for its investment in Oshkosh Utility.

- At the end of 20X5, when Metro Utility made its investment in Oshkosh Utility, the capital assets had a useful life on average of 10 years, while the patents had a useful life of five years.

Oshkosh Utility's financial statements for 20X6–20X8 are as shown below:

| | 20X6 | 20X7 | 20X8 |
|---|---|---|---|
| Revenues | $200,000 | $225,000 | $275,000 |
| Production cost of gas sold | 135,000 | 185,000 | 200,000 |
| Gross profit | 65,000 | 40,000 | 75,000 |
| Depreciation | 30,000 | 25,000 | 25,000 |
| Other expenses | 15,000 | 20,000 | 18,000 |
| Interest expense | 16,000 | 16,000 | 16,000 |
| Gain/loss on sale of capital asset | | 20,000 | |
| Net income before taxes | $ 4,000 | ($1,000) | $ 16,000 |
| Income taxes | 1,200 | | 4,800 |
| Net income and comprehensive income | $ 2,800 | ($1,000) | $ 11,200 |
| Retained earnings, January 1 | 85,000 | 77,800 | 56,800 |
| Dividends | (10,000) | (20,000) | (20,000) |
| Retained earnings, December 31 | $ 77,800 | $ 56,800 | $ 48,000 |

| Oshkosh Utility—Separate-Entity Statements of Financial Position | | | | |
|---|---|---|---|---|
| | 20X5 | 20X6 | 20X7 | 20X8 |
| ASSETS | | | | |
| Cash | $ 50,000 | $ 82,800 | $105,550 | $124,250 |
| Accounts receivable | 75,000 | 50,000 | 56,250 | 68,750 |
| Inventory | 65,000 | 75,000 | 85,000 | 80,000 |
| Capital assets | 200,000 | 170,000 | 95,000 | 70,000 |
| TOTAL ASSETS | $390,000 | $377,800 | $341,800 | $343,000 |
| | | | | |
| LIABILITIES AND SHAREHOLDERS' EQUITY | | | | |
| Current liabilities | $ 40,000 | $ 35,000 | $ 20,000 | $ 30,000 |
| Long-term liabilities | 200,000 | 200,000 | 200,000 | 200,000 |
| Shareholders' equity | 65,000 | 65,000 | 65,000 | 65,000 |
| Retained earnings | 85,000 | 77,800 | 56,800 | 48,000 |
| TOTAL LIABILITIES AND SHAREHOLDERS' EQUITY | $390,000 | $377,800 | $341,800 | $343,000 |

■ A capital asset that had a net book value of $50,000 was sold to Metro Utility for $70,000 at the end of 20X7. At the time of this sale the asset had a future life of five more years. This asset had a carrying value equal to fair market value at the time of acquisition.

Metro Utility's cost-based preliminary separate-entity financial statements are as follows:

| Metro Utility—Separate-Entity Statement of Comprehensive Income for 20X8 | |
|---|---|
| Revenues | $800,000 |
| Cost of goods sold | 625,000 |
| Gross profit | $175,000 |
| Depreciation | 50,000 |
| Other expenses (including bonuses) | 45,000 |
| Interest expense | 50,000 |
| Dividend income | 8,000 |
| Net income before taxes | 38,000 |
| Taxes | 11,400 |
| Net income and comprehensive income | $ 26,600 |
| Beginning retained earnings | 188,400 |
| Dividends | 15,000 |
| Ending retained earnings | $200,000 |

| Metro Utility—Separate-Entity Statement of Financial Position December 31, 20X8 | |
|---|---|
| ASSETS | |
| Cash | $ 300,000 |
| Accounts receivable | 225,000 |
| Inventory | 95,000 |
| Loan to Oshkosh Utility | 200,000 |
| Capital assets | 450,000 |
| Investment in Oshkosh Utility | 180,000 |
| TOTAL ASSETS | $1,450,000 |
| LIABILITIES | |
| Current liabilities | $400,000 |
| Long-term liabilities | 600,000 |
| Shareholders' equity | 250,000 |
| Retained earnings | 200,000 |
| TOTAL LIABILITIES AND SHAREHOLDERS' EQUITY | $1,450,000 |

■ The beginning inventory of Metro Utility in 20X8 includes $55,000 worth of goods at sale price from Oshkosh Utility.

■ Half of Metro Utility's ending inventory of $95,000 in 20X8 was purchased from Oshkosh Utility.

### Required

Françoise Dubois has asked you to provide a report that covers the following:

- statement of comprehensive income and statement of financial position for Metro Utility for the current year—that is, 20X8—appropriately accounting for its investment in Oshkosh Utility under IFRS

- a clear explanation for your choice of accounting for Metro Utility's investment in Oshkosh Utility

- analysis of the resulting financial statements and advice on the financial situation of Metro Utility such that MUWU is properly prepared to get the best wage settlement from Metro Utility. Ms. Dubois also wants you to discuss the different motivating factors (users, objectives, etc.) and the impact these might have on how Metro Utility will account for its affairs in the consolidated financial statements that it will issue shortly.

## CASE 5-2 MCINTOSH INVESTMENTS LTD.

McIntosh Investments Ltd. (MIL) is a diversified public company. Loraine McIntosh, the president, owns 40% of the common shares of MIL. Another 30% are owned jointly by Loraine's brothers, Blair and Bill. The 70% ownership by Loraine and her brothers gives her control of the company. The remaining 30% of the shares are widely distributed.

On April 1, 20X6, the first day of MIL's fiscal year, Loraine succeeded in negotiating the acquisition by MIL of 30% of the outstanding common shares of Efrim Auto Parts, Inc. (EAPI). EAPI was an important supplier of parts to Candide Cars Corporation (CCC), a maker of specialty automobiles ("the best of all possible cars"), which was 40% owned by MIL. Loraine was particularly pleased at being able to arrange the purchase of the shares of EAPI because she was certain that great efficiency could be obtained by having the operations of EAPI and CCC more closely coordinated.

The EAPI shares were purchased from a descendant of the founder of EAPI, Jeffrey Efrim. The shares were purchased for a consideration of $600,000 cash and the issuance of 10,000 shares of MIL common stock. MIL shares were currently being traded on the TSX at $40 per share. Exhibit A presents the SFP of EAPI as of March 31, 20X6, the end of EAPI's fiscal year.

During the following year, Loraine and her fellow managers took an active interest in the affairs of both CCC and EAPI. CCC became EAPI's major customer, and it purchased $2,000,000 of parts from EAPI during fiscal 20X7. At the end of fiscal 20X7, CCC had parts in inventory that were purchased from EAPI at a cost (to CCC) of $300,000, as compared with only $100,000 of such parts in inventory a year earlier. The attention of MIL management had increased EAPI's efficiency, so that average gross profit on sales rose to 35% in fiscal 20X7. EAPI's net income after tax in fiscal 20X7 reached a record high of $300,000 after tax, enabling EAPI to declare a dividend of $1.50 per common share on March 31, 20X7.

### Required

Determine what impact MIL's investment in EAPI shares and EAPI's fiscal 20X7 activities will have on the financial statements of MIL. Where alternatives are possible, state them and briefly explain the alternatives you chose. State any assumptions that you find it necessary to make.

## Exhibit A
## EAPI Statement of Financial Position

### Statement of Financial Position
### March 31, 20X6

|  | Carrying value | Fair value |
|---|---|---|
| Cash | $ 200,000 | $ 200,000 |
| Accounts receivable | 300,000 | 300,000 |
| Inventories | 400,000 | 440,000 |
| Equipment (net) | 2,100,000 | 2,400,000 |
| Long-term investment (cost) | 300,000 | 360,000 |
|  | $3,300,000 |  |
| Accounts payable and accrued liabilities | 600,000 | 500,000 |
| Debentures outstanding | 700,000 | 600,000 |
| Common shares (60,000 shares) | 500,000 | — |
| Retained earnings | 1,500,000 | — |
|  | $3,300,000 |  |

# CASE 5-3 SIMPSON LTD.

Simpson Ltd. is a private Ontario corporation controlled by Ted Simpson. The company owns a series of chocolate chip cookie stores throughout Ontario, and also has a wholly owned Quebec subsidiary that operates stores in Montreal and Quebec City. Because of its lack of stores in Western Canada and its managers' lack of knowledge about that part of the country, Simpson Ltd. has just acquired 70% of the outstanding class A voting shares of Ong Inc. for $6,000,000 cash. Ong Inc. is another cookie store chain, which is headquartered in Vancouver and has stores throughout Vancouver and Victoria, as well as in Edmonton, Saskatoon, and Winnipeg.

Ted expects that the acquisition will greatly help the Simpson Ltd. "bottom line," which in turn will help Simpson Ltd. to obtain expanded debt financing because of the greater net income and cash flow. The management of Ong Inc. will not change as a result of the purchase; the former sole owner, John Ong, retains the remaining 30% of the Ong Inc. shares and has agreed to continue as CEO of Ong Inc. for at least five years after the change in control. The president and chief operating officer, Travis Hubner, will also stay on, so there is no reason that the acquired company should not continue to be highly profitable. The condensed SFP of Ong Inc. at the date of acquisition is shown in Exhibit B.

The acquisition was financed mainly by debt; $4,500,000 was borrowed by Simpson Ltd. from the Western Bank of British Columbia, secured by the assets of both Simpson Ltd. and Ong Inc. The bank has requested audited financial statements of both companies on an annual basis, supplemented by unaudited quarterly statements.

## Exhibit B
## Ong Inc. Condensed Statement of Financial Position

### Condensed Statement of Financial Position
### May 8, 20X5

**Assets**

| | | |
|---|---|---|
| Cash | | $ 200,000 |
| Accounts receivable | | 100,000 |
| Inventories—raw materials and supplies | | 1,200,000 |
| Buildings | $7,000,000 | |
|   Accumulated depreciation | (1,400,000) | 5,600,000 |
| Equipment | 3,000,000 | |
|   Accumulated depreciation | (1,200,000) | 1,800,000 |
| **TOTAL ASSETS** | | $8,900,000 |

**LIABILITIES AND SHAREHOLDERS' EQUITY**

Liabilities:

| | | |
|---|---|---|
|   Accounts payable | $ 350,000 | |
|   Accrued expenses | 50,000 | |
|   Total current liabilities | | $ 400,000 |
|   Bank loan payable, due May 3, 20X7 | | 2,700,000 |
| Deferred income taxes | | 1,100,000 |
| Total liabilities | | 4,200,000 |
| **Shareholders' equity:** | | |
|   Common shares—Class A voting | 1,000,000 | |
|   Retained earnings | 3,700,000 | 4,700,000 |
| **TOTAL LIABILITIES AND SHARE EQUITY** | | $8,900,000 |

Ong Inc. owns the buildings in which some of its stores are located, but most are leased. None of the land is owned. The buildings are being depreciated over 30 years. John has obtained two separate appraisals of the owned buildings; one appraisal firm has placed the aggregate current value at $9,500,000, while the second firm arrived at a value of $8,400,000. Ong Inc. owns all of the equipment in its stores; the equipment is being depreciated over 10 years and is, on average, 40% depreciated. It would cost $3,300,000 to replace the existing equipment with new equipment of similar capacity. Inventories are generally worth their carrying values, except that the replacement cost of the stock of imported Belgian chocolate in the Vancouver warehouse is $20,000 less than carrying value because of the strengthening Canadian dollar. On the other hand, the accounts payable shown in Exhibit B include an unrealized gain of $10,000 because much of the liability is denominated in euros.

### Required

Determine, on a line-by-line basis, the impact on Simpson Ltd.'s consolidated assets and liabilities as a result of the acquisition, in accordance with Ted Simpson's objectives in acquiring Ong Inc. Where alternative values could be used, explain the reasons for your selection.

    [ICAO]

# CASE 5-4 PROCTOR INDUSTRIES

You, CA, are the senior in charge of an audit of Proctor Industries (PI), a public company in the business of selling plumbing parts wholesale. It is now November 3, 20X5—five weeks after PI's year-end of September 30, 20X5, and one week before your firm has been asked to discuss the financial statements for PI, including any significant accounting issues, with PI's audit committee.

PI's unconsolidated annual sales approximate $36 million. It operates through six regional branches, with approximately equal sales volumes at each branch.

PI has a 60% interest in Minor Inc. (MI), a company located in the United Kingdom. Minor Inc. also has a September 30 year-end and is audited by a firm of chartered accountants in the United Kingdom.

You are at the client's premises reviewing the year-end working papers for Proctor Industries, and you note the following items:

1. PI's unconsolidated net income before income taxes is normally about $2 million.

2. The allowance for doubtful accounts in PI is $200,000. Based on the work performed in this section of the audit, the audit assistant concluded that the allowance should be at least $250,000, and could be as high as $350,000.

3. You have contacted the auditors for Minor Inc. to obtain its financial statements. However, they are unable to provide you with the audited financial statements because the president of MI refused to sign the management representation letter. He disagrees with the revenue recognition policy insisted on by the auditors of MI and intends to obtain opinions from other audit firms on this issue. The financial statements, under the policy supported by the auditors, show a net loss of $320,000 for the year. MI's current policy for revenue recognition is when items are produced, based on the support that there is a ready market for MI's supplies, which are currently in short supply. PI's revenue recognition policy is when goods are shipped to the customer.

4. There is a new item on PI's SFP called "Investments." The working papers indicate that this represents a cash payment in June 20X5 of $100,000 for all the common shares of Chemicals Inc. (CI). This company has an August 31 year-end. Although CI has previously never been audited, PI requested, and you have completed, an audit of CI for its August 31, 20X5, year-end. The audited financial statements for CI appear in Exhibit C. CI manufactures household cleaning products. The equipment used in the manufacturing process is not complex and is inexpensive to replace. CI has earned large profits in the past, mainly from government contracts. This year, the financial statements show an after-tax profit of $100,000.

5. An extract of the agreement to purchase CI states that if the company earns more than $1 million per year in any of the next five years, the vendor may buy back the common shares for a price to be determined.

6. One of the legal letters for PI was returned with the following comment:

   Chemicals Inc. may be liable for damages arising from the alleged dumping of hazardous chemicals from its Bedford plant into the nearby Black River. As of the current date, a statement of claim has been filed. CI denies these allegations.

Extracts from Audited Statement of Financial Position
as at August 31, 20X5

**Assets**

| | |
|---|---|
| Accounts receivable | $ 900,000 |
| Prepaid expenses | 100,000 |
| Inventory | 400,000 |
| Capital assets, net | 400,000 |
| | $1,800,000 |

**Liabilities and shareholders' equity**

| | |
|---|---|
| Accounts payable | $500,000 |
| Common shares (100 issued) | 50,000 |
| Retained earnings | 1,250,000 |
| | $1,800,000 |

The partner has asked you to prepare a memo on the above items for his use in discussions with the audit committee.

Required

Prepare the memo requested by the partner.

    [CICA]

# Problems

## P5-1 (25 minutes, easy)

Information relating to six independent cases has been provided below.

| | Case | | | | | |
|---|---|---|---|---|---|---|
| | A | B | C | D | E | F |
| Purchase price | $120 | $120 | $100 | $80 | $100 | $80 |
| Percentage of subsidiary acquired | 100% | 80% | 100% | 80% | 100% | 80% |
| Fair value of net identifiable assets | 100 | 80 | 120 | 120 | 80 | 100 |
| Carrying value of net identifiable assets | 80 | 100 | 80 | 100 | 120 | 120 |

### Required

Using the information provided for each case above, calculate:

**a.** the gain from bargain purchase, if present;

**b.** the net fair value adjustment;

**c.** the fair value adjustment allocated to net identifiable assets; and

**d.** the goodwill.

## P5-2 (25 minutes, easy)

Jaguar Company purchased 25,000 common shares (20 percent) of Panther Company on January 1, 20X1, for $500,000. On that day, the difference between the carrying value and fair value of Panther's assets of $300,000 was fully attributable to patents, which had a usual life of six years. Additional information on Panther Company for the three years ending December 31, 20X3, is as follows:

| Year | Net income | Dividends paid | Market value per share at Dec. 31 |
|---|---|---|---|
| 20X1 | $400,000 | $200,000 | $22 |
| 20X2 | (100,000) | 80,000 | 21 |
| 20X3 | 250,000 | 150,000 | 23 |

On December 31, 20X3, Jaguar Company sold its investment in Panther Company for $575,000.

### Required

**a.** Compute the balance in the investment account at the end of 20X1 assuming that the investment is classified as:

   **i.** an FVTPL investment;

   **ii.** an investment in an associate; and

   **iii.** a FVTOCI investment.

**b.** Calculate how much total income will be reported in net income and OCI by Jaguar in relation to its investment in Panther in 20X1, 20X2, and 20X3, respectively, assuming the investment is classified as:

   **i.** a FVTPL investment;

   **ii.** an investment in an associate; and

   **iii.** a FVTOCI investment.

## P5-3 (50 minutes, medium)

On December 30, 20X5, the statements of financial position of the Perk Company and the Scent Company are as follows:

|  | Perk Company | Scent Company |
|---|---|---|
| Cash | $ 7,000,000 | $ 200,000 |
| Accounts receivable | 1,000,000 | 600,000 |
| Inventory | 1,300,000 | 800,000 |
| Capital assets, net | 6,700,000 | 3,400,000 |
|  | $16,000,000 | $5,000,000 |
| Current liabilities | $ 3,000,000 | $200,000 |
| Long-term liabilities | 4,000,000 | 800,000 |
| Common shares | 5,000,000 | 1,000,000 |
| Contributed surplus | — | 1,000,000 |
| Retained earnings | 4,000,000 | 2,000,000 |
|  | $16,000,000 | $5,000,000 |

For both companies, the fair values of their identifiable assets and liabilities are equal to their carrying values except for the following fair values:

|  | Perk | Scent |
|---|---|---|
| Inventories | $1,000,000 | $ 600,000 |
| Capital assets (net) | 7,000,000 | 5,000,000 |
| Long-term liabilities | 3,800,000 | 1,100,000 |

The following cases are *independent*:

1.  On December 31, 20X5, Perk Company purchases the net assets of Scent Company for $5.5 million in cash. Scent Company distributes the proceeds to its shareholders in return for their shares, cancels the shares, and ceases to exist as a separate legal entity.

2.  On December 31, 20X5, Perk Company purchases 75% of the outstanding voting shares of Scent Company for $4.5 million in cash. Scent Company continues to operate as a separate legal entity.

### Required

For each of the two independent cases, prepare a consolidated SFP for Perk Company at December 31, 20X5, subsequent to the business combination. For the second case, prepare a consolidated SFP using *each* of the following four methods:

a.  proportionate consolidation;

b.  parent-company;

c.  parent-company extension; and

d.  entity.

[SMA, adapted]

P5-4 (15 minutes, easy)

Zoe Ltd. has the following SFP at December 31, 20X5:

| Zoe Ltd. | | |
|---|---|---|
| Statement of Financial Position | | |
| December 31, 20X5 | | |
| Current assets | | $80,000 |
| Capital assets: | | |
| Land | $ 30,000 | |
| Building, net | 100,000 | |
| Equipment, net | 50,000 | 180,000 |
| Goodwill | | 20,000 |
| | | $280,000 |
| Current liabilities | | $ 55,000 |
| Bonds payable | | 80,000 |
| Common shares | | 100,000 |
| Retained earnings, January 1, 20X5 | | 60,000 |
| Net loss for 20X5 | | (15,000) |
| | | $280,000 |

On December 31, 20X5, Halifax Ltd. bought 70% of the outstanding shares of Zoe Ltd. and paid $190,000. The current fair values of the net assets of Zoe Ltd. on December 31, 20X5, are:

| Current assets | $ 80,000 | Current liabilities | $55,000 |
|---|---|---|---|
| Land | 180,000 | Bonds payable | 70,000 |
| Building | 160,000 | | |
| Equipment | 20,000 | | |

Halifax Ltd. is an investment company that has assets composed only of cash and short-term marketable investments.

Required

Calculate the following items as they would appear on the Halifax Ltd. consolidated SFP at December 31, 20X5, under the entity method and the parent-company extension method, respectively:

a. land;

b. goodwill; and

c. NCI.
    [CGA-Canada, adapted]

P5-5 (15 minutes, easy)

Red Deer Ltd. acquired a subsidiary, Lethbridge Ltd., on July 1, 20X5, by paying $315,000 for 70% of the outstanding shares. The fiscal year-end for both companies is December 31. The statements of financial position of Lethbridge Ltd. and Red Deer Ltd. are shown below.

## Required

Prepare the consolidated SFP as at July 1, 20X5, for Red Deer Ltd. under the entity method and the parent-company extension method, respectively.

### Lethbridge Ltd.
### Statement of Financial Position
### July 1, 20X5

|  | Carrying value | Fair market value |
|---|---|---|
| Current assets | $210,000 | $210,000 |
| Capital assets: |  |  |
| Land | 135,000 | 225,000 |
| Building, net | 322,500 | 300,000 |
| Equipment, net | 90,000 | 135,000 |
|  | $757,500 |  |
| Current liabilities | $105,000 | 105,000 |
| Bonds payable | 315,000 | 337,500 |
| Common shares | 150,000 |  |
| Retained earnings, January 1, 20X5 | 105,000 |  |
| Net income (January 1–July 1) | 82,500 |  |
|  | $757,500 |  |

### Red Deer Ltd.
### Statement of Financial Position
### July 1, 20X5

|  | Carrying value | Fair market value |
|---|---|---|
| Current assets | $ 210,000 | $ 150,000 |
| Capital assets: |  |  |
| Land | 600,000 | 1,050,000 |
| Building, net | 825,000 | 600,000 |
| Equipment, net | 540,000 | 300,000 |
| Investment in Lethbridge Ltd. | 315,000 |  |
| Goodwill | 600,000 |  |
|  | $3,090,000 |  |
| Current liabilities | $90,000 | 90,000 |
| Bonds payable | 300,000 | 2550,000 |
| Common shares | 1,500,000 |  |
| Retained earnings, July 1, 20X5 | 1,200,000 |  |
|  | $3,090,000 |  |

P5-6 (25 minutes, easy)

Maui Ltd. has the following SFP at December 31, 20X5.

| Maui Ltd.<br>Statement of Financial Position<br>December 31, 20X5 | | |
|---|---|---|
| Current assets | | $170,000 |
| Capital assets: | | |
| Land | $ 60,000 | |
| Building, net | 240,000 | |
| Equipment, net | 100,000 | 400,000 |
| Goodwill | | 100,000 |
| | | $670,000 |
| Current liabilities | | $130,000 |
| Bonds payable, 18-year duration, due 2X23 | | 140,000 |
| Common shares | | 240,000 |
| Retained earnings, January 1, 20X5 | | 280,000 |
| Net loss for 20X5 | | (120,000) |
| | | $670,000 |

On January 1, 20X6, Oahu Ltd., whose assets are composed entirely of share investments and cash, paid $371,000 for 70% of the outstanding shares of Maui Ltd. The current fair values of the net assets of Maui Ltd. on January 1, 20X6, were:

| | | | |
|---|---|---|---|
| Current assets | $170,000 | Current liabilities | $130,000 |
| Land | 150,000 | Bonds payable | 140,000 |
| Building (net) | 360,000 | | |
| Equipment (net) | 60,000 | | |

Oahu Ltd. had the following shareholders' equity on January 1, 20X6:

| | |
|---|---|
| Common shares | $ 960,000 |
| Retained earnings | 1,420,000 |
| | $2,380,000 |

Required

a. Assume that a consolidated SFP is prepared on January 1, 20X6. Calculate the dollar amounts for the following items as they would appear on that consolidated SFP under the entity method:

   i. goodwill;

   ii. land;

   iii. equipment;

   iv. common shares;

   v. retained earnings; and

   vi. NCI.

**b.** What does NCI represent on the consolidated SFP?
[CGA-Canada, adapted]

**P5-7 (20 minutes, medium)**

On January 1, 20X5, Huge Ltd. purchased 80% of the shares of Tiny Ltd. for $2,100,000 and, on the same day, Tiny Ltd. purchased 60% of the shares of Tinier Ltd. for $1,395,000. Any fair value increment/decrement was fully allocated to land.

| At January 1, 20X5 | Huge Ltd. | Tiny Ltd. | Tinier Ltd. |
|---|---|---|---|
| Shares | $2,925,000 | $2,400,000 | $ 750,000 |
| Retained earnings | 3,450,000 | 2,865,000 | 1,095,000 |
| | $6,375,000 | $5,265,000 | $1,845,000 |
| **During 20X5** | | | |
| Net income (cost basis) | $1,200,000 | $ 900,000 | $ 450,000 |
| Dividends paid | 180,000 | 150,000 | 60,000 |

There were no intercompany transactions.

**Required**

Calculate the balance of non-controlling interest as it would be shown on the consolidated SFP of Huge Ltd. at December 31, 20X5, under the entity method.

**P5-8 (25 minutes, easy)**

Parent Ltd. pays $553,000 cash for 70% of the outstanding voting shares of Sub Ltd. on January 1, 20X5. The following information was available:

| Sub Ltd. Statement of Financial Position January 1, 20X5 | Carrying value | Fair value |
|---|---|---|
| Cash | $ 40,000 | $ 40,000 |
| Inventory | 40,000 | 30,000 |
| Equipment, net | 120,000 | 100,000 |
| Building, net | 300,000 | 360,000 |
| Land | 50,000 | 160,000 |
| | $550,000 | |
| Liabilities | $ 10,000 | 14,000 |
| Common shares | 250,000 | — |
| Retained earnings | 290,000 | — |
| | $550,000 | |

During 20X5, Sub Ltd. earned $180,000 and paid no dividends. The inventory on hand at January 1, 20X5, was sold during 20X5. The equipment will be depreciated over 10 years straight-line; the building will be depreciated over 20 years straight-line. The liabilities were paid during 20X5. Parent Ltd. uses the cost method of accounting for its investment.

## Required

Prepare the consolidation-related eliminations required at December 31, 20X5, based on the above information under the entity method.

[CGA-Canada, adapted]

**P5-9 (40 minutes, medium)**

On January 1, 20X5, Par Ltd. purchased 80% of the voting shares of Sub Ltd. for $906,400. The SFP of Sub Ltd. on that date was as follows:

| Sub Ltd Statement of Financial Position January 1, 20X5 | Net carrying value | Fair value |
|---|---|---|
| Cash | $ 160,000 | $160,000 |
| Accounts receivable | 200,000 | 240,000 |
| Inventory | 300,000 | 380,000 |
| Capital assets, net | 900,000 | 750,000 |
| | $1,560,000 | |
| Current liabilities | $ 150,000 | 130,000 |
| Bonds payable | 362,000 | 362,000 |
| Common shares | 200,000 | — |
| Retained earnings | 848,000 | — |
| | $1,560,000 | |

The accounts receivable, inventory, and current liabilities have "turned over" by December 31, 20X5, and the net capital assets will be amortized over 10 years, on a straight-line basis.

### Additional Information

1.  During 20X5, Par Ltd. sold goods costing $100,000 to Sub Ltd. for $140,000. At December 31, 20X5, 20% of these goods were still in the inventory of Sub Ltd.

2.  In 20X5, Sub Ltd. sold goods costing $200,000 to Par Ltd. for $250,000. At December 31, 20X5, 30% of these goods were still in the inventory of Par Ltd.

3.  In 20X5, Sub Ltd. sold land to Par Ltd. for $300,000. The land had cost Sub $240,000.

4.  Both companies pay income taxes at the rate of 40%.

The statements of financial position and statements of comprehensive income for Par Ltd. and Sub Ltd. at December 31, 20X5, are presented below.

| Statements of Financial Position December 31, 20X5 | Par Ltd. | Sub Ltd. |
|---|---|---|
| Cash | $ 200,000 | $ 140,000 |
| Accounts receivable | 300,000 | 190,000 |
| Inventory | 500,000 | 460,000 |
| Buildings and equipment (net) | 1,200,000 | 900,000 |
| Investment in Sub Ltd. | 906,400 | — |
| Other investments | 417,600 | — |
| TOTAL ASSETS | $3,524,000 | $1,690,000 |
| Current liabilities | $ 300,000 | $ 206,000 |
| Bonds payable | 513,000 | 362,000 |
| Common shares | 500,000 | 200,000 |
| Retained earnings | 2,211,000 | 922,000 |
| TOTAL LIABILITIES AND SHARE EQUITY | $3,524,000 | $1,690,000 |

## Statements of Comprehensive Income
## Year Ended December 31, 20X5

|  | Par Ltd. | Sub Ltd. |
|---|---|---|
| Sales | $2,000,000 | $2,000,000 |
| Cost of sales | 1,400,000 | 1,700,000 |
| Gross margin | 600,000 | 300,000 |
| Depreciation expense | 100,000 | 90,000 |
| Interest expense | 63,000 | 44,000 |
| Income tax expense | 140,000 | 74,000 |
| Other expenses | 124,000 | 78,000 |
| Investment income | (37,000) | (60,000) |
| NET INCOME AND COMPREHENSIVE INCOME | $ 210,000 | $ 74,000 |

Required (under the entity method)

a. Prepare the consolidated statement of comprehensive income for the year ended December 31, 20X5.

b. Present the following as they would appear on the consolidated SFP at December 31, 20X5:

   i. net capital assets;

   ii. goodwill; and

   iii. retained earnings.

   [CGA-Canada, adapted]

P5-10 (75 minutes, medium)

On January 1, 20X4, Parent Ltd. purchased 90% of the shares of Sub Ltd. for $972,000. At that time Sub Ltd. had the following SFP:

## Sub Ltd.
## Statement of Financial Position
## January 1, 20X4

|  | Carrying value | Fair value |
|---|---|---|
| Cash | $ 60,000 | $ 60,000 |
| Accounts receivable | 120,000 | 160,000 |
| Inventory—FIFO | 180,000 | 220,000 |
| Capital assets, net | 1,500,000 | 1,350,000 |
| Goodwill | 100,000 | — |
|  | $1,960,000 |  |
| Current liabilities | $ 140,000 | 140,000 |
| Bonds payable | 800,000 | 850,000 |
| Common shares | 400,000 | — |
| Retained earnings | 620,000 | — |
|  | $1,960,000 |  |

The bonds were issued at par and will mature in 10 years. Sub Ltd. has a receivables and inventory turnover of greater than six times per year. The capital assets have an average of 10 years of remaining life and are being amortized straight-line. The annual tests for goodwill impairment have indicated no impairment of goodwill since the date of acquisition.

In 20X4, Sub Ltd. sold inventory to Parent Ltd. for $320,000; the inventory had cost $260,000. At the end of 20X4, 25% was still in Parent's inventory, but it was all sold in 20X5.

In 20X5, Parent Ltd. sold inventory to Sub Ltd. for $275,000; the inventory had cost $200,000. At the end of 20X5, 35% was left in Sub's inventory.

During 20X4, the subsidiary earned $875,000 and paid dividends of $50,000. During 20X5, the subsidiary incurred a loss of $172,000 and paid dividends of $60,000.

The parent company used the cost method for the investment in the subsidiary and netted almost everything to "Other expenses."

At December 31, 20X5, the following financial statements were available:

| Statements of Financial Position December 31, 20X5 | | |
| --- | --- | --- |
| | Parent Ltd. | Sub Ltd. |
| Cash | $ 400,000 | $ 75,000 |
| Accounts receivable | 850,000 | 179,000 |
| Inventory | 970,000 | 245,000 |
| Capital assets, net | 2,631,000 | 1,863,000 |
| Goodwill | — | 100,000 |
| Investment in Sub Ltd. | 975,000 | — |
| | $5,826,000 | $2,462,000 |
| Current liabilities | $ 450,000 | $ 49,000 |
| Bonds payable | — | 800,000 |
| Common shares | 1,000,000 | 400,000 |
| Retained earnings, December 31, 20X5 | 4,376,000 | 1,213,000 |
| | $5,826,000 | $2,462,000 |

| Statements of Comprehensive Income Year Ended December 31, 20X5 | | |
| --- | --- | --- |
| | Parent Ltd. | Sub Ltd. |
| Sales | $9,865,000 | $1,650,000 |
| Cost of sales | 8,040,000 | 1,140,000 |
| Gross profit | 1,825,000 | 510,000 |
| Depreciation | (106,000) | (104,000) |
| Other expenses | (369,000) | (808,000) |
| Gain on sale of building | — | 230,000 |
| Net income and comprehensive income | $1,350,000 | $ (172,000) |

## Required

**a.** Prepare a consolidated statement of comprehensive income for 20X5 under the entity method.

**b.** Calculate the amounts that would appear on the consolidated SFP at December 31, 20X5, under the entity method, for:

  **i.** goodwill;

  **ii.** capital assets, net;

  **iii.** bonds payable; and

  **iv.** NCI.

  [CGA-Canada, adapted]

### P5-11

Company Granite purchased 80% of Company Marble on January 1, 20X1, for $700,000, when the net book value of Company Marble was $900,000. The fair value of the net identifiable assets of Marble on that date was $1,000,000. The carrying (i.e., book) and fair values of the net identifiable assets and associated future expected lives of Company Marble are provided below:

| | Carrying (book) | Fair value | Future life |
|---|---|---|---|
| Inventory | $ 200,000 | $ 250,000 | |
| Land | 200,000 | 250,000 | |
| Building (net) | 470,000 | 500,000 | 10 |
| Patent | 230,000 | 250,000 | 10 |
| Bond payable | (200,000) | (250,000) | 5* |
| Total | $ 900,000 | $1,000,000 | |
| *The bonds payable is redeemable at the end of 5 years. | | | |

All amortization is charged on a straight-line basis. The retained earnings of Company Marble on the date of acquisition were $400,000.

The separate entity SFP of Granite on January 1, 20X1, after the acquisition is provided below:

| Company Granite<br>Statement of Financial Position as<br>of January 1, 20X1 | |
|---|---|
| Cash | $ 350,000 |
| Inventory | 300,000 |
| Land | 300,000 |
| Building | 400,000 |
| Investment in Company Marble | 700,000 |
| **TOTAL ASSETS** | $2,050,000 |
| | |
| Bond payable | 300,000 |
| Common stock | 800,000 |
| Retained earnings | 950,000 |
| **TOTAL LIABILITIES AND OWNERS' EQUITY** | $2,050,000 |

During 20X1, Marble sold inventory costing $100,000 to Granite for $150,000. Half of the inventory purchased from Marble remained unsold in the inventory of Granite at the end of 20X1. The remaining inventory was sold to an outside party by Granite in 20X2.

During 20X1, Marble sold land costing $100,000 to Granite for $150,000. This land remains unsold with Granite at the end of 20X2.

In 20X2, Granite sold goods costing $80,000 to Marble for $120,000. One-quarter of the inventory purchased from Granite during 20X2 remained unsold in the ending inventory of Marble at the end of 20X2.

The separate-entity balance sheets of Company Granite and Company Marble as at December 31, 20X2, are provided below.

| Separate-Entity SFPs as of December 31, 20X2 | | |
|---|---|---|
| | Granite | Marble |
| Cash | $ 510,000 | $ 540,000 |
| Inventory | 250,000 | 250,000 |
| Land | 450,000 | 100,000 |
| Building | 340,000 | 329,000 |
| Patent | | 161,000 |
| Investment in Company Marble | 700,000 | |
| TOTAL ASSETS | $2,250,000 | $1,380,000 |
| | | |
| Bond payable | $          0 | $ 200,000 |
| Common stock | 800,000 | 500,000 |
| Retained earnings | 1,450,000 | 680,000 |
| TOTAL LIABILITIES AND OWNERS' EQUITY | $2,050,000 | $1,380,000 |

Required

a. Provide the consolidated balance sheet on the date of acquisition under proportional consolidation.

b. Provide the following SFP consolidated amounts on December 31, 20X2, under the entity method:

   i. Consolidated retained earnings; and

   ii. Non-controlling interest balance.

Provide the adjusted net incomes of Granite and Marble, respectively, for 20X2 if the separate entity net incomes of Granite and Marble in 20X2 were $150,000 and $120,000, respectively, and Marble paid dividends of $30,000 in 20X2.

P5-12 (90 minutes, difficult)

Plain Ltd. acquired 80% of the voting shares of Stylish Ltd. on January 1, 20X3, for $1,200,000. The financial statement of Stylish Ltd. on the date of acquisition was as follows:

## Stylish Ltd.
### Statement of Financial Position January 1, 20X3

|  | Carrying value | Fair market value |
|---|---|---|
| Cash | $ 50,000 | $ 50,000 |
| Accounts receivable | 115,000 | 140,000 |
| Inventory | 300,000 | 280,000 |
| Land | 300,000 | 420,000 |
| Depreciable capital assets | 580,000 | 500,000 |
| Accumulated depreciation | (120,000) | |
| Total | $1,225,000 | |
| Current liabilities | 275,000 | 250,000 |
| Common shares | 450,000 | — |
| Retained earnings | 500,000 | — |
| Total | $1,225,000 | |

The inventory will be sold and the accounts receivable collected within 20X3, and the depreciable capital assets will be depreciated over 10 years, straight-line, with no salvage value.

During 20X3, Stylish Ltd. sold inventory to Plain Ltd. for $180,000, with a 20% gross profit on the sale price. At the end of 20X3, $30,000 (at sale price) of these goods were still in the inventory of Plain Ltd. Plain Ltd. sold goods at $200,000 to Stylish Ltd. during 20X3, with a 30% gross profit on the sale price, and $50,000 (at sale price) of these goods were still in inventory at the end of 20X3. All of these goods remaining in inventory were sold during 20X4.

During 20X4, Plain Ltd. sold $150,000 of goods to Stylish Ltd., with a 25% gross profit on sale price, and $50,000 (at sale price) of these goods were in inventory at the end of 20X4. In addition, Stylish Ltd. sold goods to Plain Ltd. for $250,000, with a 20% gross profit on sale price, and $100,000 (at sale price) of these goods were still in inventory at the end of 20X4.

While Plain paid dividends of $20,000 in 20X3, Stylish paid $15,000; similarly, while Plain paid dividends of $25,000 in 20X4, Stylish paid $20,000.

The retained earnings balance of Plain on January 1, 20X3, was $1,650,000.

The following are the financial statements of the two companies at December 31, 20X4:

### Statements of Financial Position
### December 31, 20X4

|  | Plain Ltd. | Stylish Ltd. |
|---|---|---|
| Cash | $ 53,000 | $ 80,000 |
| Accounts receivable | 150,000 | 251,000 |
| Inventory | 420,000 | 350,000 |
| Land | 680,000 | 385,000 |
| Depreciable capital assets | 1,200,000 | 580,000 |
| Accumulated depreciation | (300,000) | (236,000) |
| Investment in Stylish Ltd. | 1,200,000 | — |
| Total | $3,403,000 | $1,410,000 |
| Current liabilities | $ 250,000 | $ 180,000 |
| Common shares | 1,160,000 | 450,000 |
| Retained earnings | 1,993,000 | 780,000 |
| Total | $3,403,000 | $1,410,000 |

## Statements of Comprehensive Income
### Year Ended December 31, 20X4

|  | Plain Ltd. | Stylish Ltd. |
|---|---|---|
| Sales | $ 96,000 | $ 900,000 |
| Cost of goods sold | 640,000 | 550,000 |
| Depreciation | 120,000 | 58,000 |
| Other expenses | 130,000 | 162,000 |
| Total expenses | 890,000 | 770,000 |
| Net income | 106,000 | 130,000 |

**Required**

Calculate the following under the entity method, considering all dates carefully:

**a.** equity in the earnings of Stylish using the equity method for 20X3;

**b.** the adjusted earnings of Plain for 20X3;

**c.** consolidated net income for 20X4;

**d.** consolidated retained earnings balance at the end of 20X4;

**e.** nCI balance at the end of 20X4; and

**f.** investment in Stylish account balance at the end of 20X3 under the equity method.

### P5-13 (30 minutes, medium)

The consolidated statement of comprehensive income of Top Corporation (TOP) and its subsidiary Bottom Company (BTM) was prepared incorrectly by an inexperienced accounting clerk. You have been hired by TOP and are asked to prepare a corrected consolidated SCI for an upcoming meeting. TOP owns 80% of the outstanding shares of BTM, and BTM declared and paid a dividend of $25,000 on December 15, 20X6. The following is the preliminary consolidated SCI of TOP, as prepared by the accounting clerk, for the year ended December 31, 20X6:

## Statements of Comprehensive Income
### Year Ended December 31, 20X6

|  | Top Corporation | Bottom Company | Consolidated |
|---|---|---|---|
| Sales | $900,000 | $400,000 | $1,300,000 |
| Gain on sale of capital assets | — | 50,000 | 50,000 |
| Investment income | 20,000 | — | 20,000 |
|  | 920,000 | 450,000 | 1,370,000 |
| Cost of goods sold | 600,000 | 200,000 | 800,000 |
| Gross profit | 320,000 | 250,000 | 570,000 |
| **Expenses** |  |  |  |
| Selling and administrative | 120,000 | 90,000 | 210,000 |
| Amortization | 50,000 | 40,000 | 90,000 |
| Income taxes | 60,000 | 48,000 | 108,000 |
| Net income and comprehensive income | $ 90,000 | $ 72,000 | $ 162,000 |

### Additional Information

Your discussions with other management personnel provided you with the following additional information:

1. The gain on sale of capital assets resulted from BTM selling equipment to TOP on January 1, 20X6. At the time of the sale, the equipment was recorded on BTM's books with a cost of $120,000 and net carrying value of $60,000. The equipment was purchased on January 1, 20X1, and has been amortized on a straight-line basis over its estimated useful life of 10 years. There was no change in the estimated useful life of the equipment upon acquisition by TOP. Amortization in the year of acquisition/sale is based on the number of months owned, for both companies.

2. TOP and BTM had never had any intercompany sales prior to January 1, 20X6. However, on October 31, 20X6, TOP sold BTM inventory for $60,000, which originally cost TOP $40,000. By December 31, 20X6, 50% of this inventory had been resold by BTM to its retail customers.

3. TOP uses the cost method of accounting to record its investment in BTM.

4. At the date of acquisition of the common shares of BTM there was no fair value adjustment.

### Required

Prepare a corrected consolidated SCI for the year ended December 31, 20X6, under the entity method.

[CGA-Canada, adapted]

### P5-14 (45 minutes, medium)

Mallik Ltd. purchased 30,000, or 25%, of Lee Chan Inc.'s shares on January 1, 20X8, for $300,000 and classified the investment as a fair value through OCI investment. Lee Chan Inc. reported a loss of $(100,000) in 20X8 and a profit of $200,000 in 20X9, and paid dividends of $50,000 in 20X8 and $75,000 in 20X9. On December 31, 20X8, 50% of the $100,000 worth of goods sold by Lee Chan to Mallik in 20X8 still remained in Mallik's ending inventory. Lee Chan's gross margin is 50%. Lee Chan's shares traded at $15 per share on December 31, 20X8, and January 1, 20X9.

On January 1, 20X9, Mallik obtained significant influence over the operating and investing decisions of Lee Chan when the controlling shareholder sold some shares in Lee Chan in the open market. Accordingly, the investment in Lee Chan was reclassified by Mallik to a significant-influence investment. On January 1, 20X9, Lee Chan's shareholders' equity was $1,500,000, Lee Chan had inventory that was overvalued by $100,000, and the balance of the FVA was allocated to a building that had a remaining useful life of 10 years.

Mallik sold the inventory purchased from Lee Chan in 20X8 by the end of 20X9. However, $50,000 worth of inventory purchased by Mallik from Lee Chan during 20X9 remained in its ending inventory at the end of 20X9. Lee Chan's gross profit ratio continued to be 50% in 20X9 as well.

On December 31, 20X9, Mallik sold its investment in Lee Chan for $12 per share.

### Required

Prepare all journal entries relating to Mallik's investment in Lee Chan chronologically by date for 20X8 and 20X9. Show all supporting calculations.

## P5-15 (65 minutes, medium)

Penny Ltd. acquired a 75% interest in Szabo Inc., on December 31, 20X0, for $637,500. On that date Szabo had common stock of $550,000 and retained earnings of $125,000. Szabo's inventory was overvalued by $85,000 on that date, and the balance of the FVA was allocated to buildings. The carrying value of Szabo's buildings (net) on that date was $75,000. Penny's buildings had a carrying value of $150,000 on that date. While Szabo's buildings had a future life of 10 years, Penny's buildings had a future life of 15 years on December 31, 20X0.

Szabo reported net income of $50,000 in 20X1 and $65,000 in 20X2. While Szabo declared $30,000 dividends in 20X1, it declared $20,000 dividends in 20X2.

Penny, which uses the equity method, reported net income of $60,000 in 20X1 and $70,000 in 20X2. Penny declared $40,000 dividends in 20X1 and $60,000 dividends in 20X2. Penny's retained earnings under the equity method on December 31, 20X2, were $250,000.

### Required

Compute the following, showing all supporting calculations:

a. non-controlling interest in net income for years 20X1 and 20X2, respectively;

b. separate-entity net income of Penny under the cost method for 20X1 and 20X2;

c. separate-entity retained earnings of Penny under the cost method on December 31, 20X1;

d. non-controlling interest at December 31, 20X2;

e. investment in Szabo at December 31, 20X2, under the equity method; and

f. the consolidated buildings (net) at December 31, 20X2, using the investment in Szabo balance calculated in part (e) above.

## P5-16 (120 minutes, difficult)

Parent Corp. purchased 80% of the outstanding shares of Subsidiary Corp. on January 1, 20X1, for $800,000. The Statement of Financial Position (SFP) of Subsidiary Corp. and the fair values of the different accounts are provided below.

| Subsidiary Co. Statement of Financial Position as of January 1, 20X1 | | |
|---|---|---|
| | Carrying value | Fair value |
| Cash | $ 250,000 | $ 250,000 |
| Accounts receivable | 150,000 | 150,000 |
| Inventory | 175,000 | 250,000 |
| Land & buildings | 550,000 | 550,000 |
| Less accumulated depreciation | (250,000) | |
| Investments | 115,000 | 150,000 |
| Goodwill | 160,000 | |
| **TOTAL ASSETS** | **$1,150,000** | **$1,350,000** |
| | | |
| Accounts payable | $ 225,000 | $ 200,000 |
| Long-term debt | 325,000 | 325,000 |
| Shareholders' equity | | |
| Contributed capital | 450,000 | |
| Retained earnings | 150,000 | |
| **TOTAL LIABILITIES & OWNERS' EQUITY** | **$1,150,000** | **$ 525,000** |

The buildings are being depreciated using straight-line depreciation and had a future life of five years on the date of acquisition. All current assets and liabilities turned over by the end of 20X1.

The separate-entity financial statements of Parent Corp. and Subsidiary Corp. for 20X2 are provided on the following two pages.

| Parent Corp. Statement of Financial Position as of December 31, 20X2 | |
|---|---|
| Cash | $1,135,000 |
| Accounts receivable | 100,000 |
| Inventory | 300,000 |
| Land & buildings | 650,000 |
| Less accumulated depreciation | (580,000) |
| Investments | 145,000 |
| Investment in subsidiary | 800,000 |
| Goodwill | 250,000 |
| **TOTAL ASSETS** | **$2,800,000** |
| | |
| Accounts payable | $ 350,000 |
| Long-term debt | 750,000 |
| Shareholders' equity | |
| Contributed capital | 550,000 |
| Retained earnings | 1,150,000 |
| **TOTAL LIABILITIES & OWNERS' EQUITY** | **$2,800,000** |

| Parent Company Statement of Comprehensive Income Year Ended December 31, 20X2 | |
|---|---|
| Sales | $4,500,000 |
| Dividend income | 80,000 |
| Total revenues | 4,580,000 |
| Cost of goods sold | 3,600,000 |
| Depreciation expense | 90,000 |
| Interest expense | 37,500 |
| Administrative expenses | 275,000 |
| Other expenses | 55,000 |
| Income tax expense | 122,500 |
| Total expenses | 4,180,000 |
| Net income and comprehensive income | $ 400,000 |

| Parent Company Statement of Changes in Equity—Retained Earnings Section Year Ended December 31, 20X2 | |
|---|---|
| Beginning retained earnings | $ 900,000 |
| Add net income during the year | 400,000 |
| Less dividends declared | (150,000) |
| Ending retained earnings | $1,150,000 |

## Subsidiary Co.
## Statement of Financial Position
## December 31, 20X2

| | |
|---|---:|
| Cash | $ 650,000 |
| Accounts receivable | 175,000 |
| Inventory | 185,000 |
| Land & buildings | 550,000 |
| Less accumulated depreciation | (360,000) |
| Investments | 0 |
| Goodwill | **250,000** |
| TOTAL ASSETS | **$1,450,000** |
| | |
| Accounts payable | $ 275,000 |
| Long-term debt | 300,000 |
| Shareholders' equity | |
| Contributed capital | 450,000 |
| Retained earnings | 425,000 |
| TOTAL LIABILITIES & OWNERS' EQUITY | **$1,450,000** |

## Subsidiary Company
## Statement of Comprehensive Income
## Year Ended December 31, 20X2

| | |
|---|---:|
| Sales | $2,750,000 |
| Dividend income | 15,000 |
| Gain on sale of investments | 30,000 |
| Total revenues | 2,795,000 |
| Cost of goods sold | 2,150,000 |
| Depreciation expense | 55,000 |
| Interest expense | 15,000 |
| Administrative expenses | 196,000 |
| Other expenses | 24,000 |
| Income tax expense | 105,000 |
| Total expenses | 2,545,000 |
| Net income and comprehensive income | $ 250,000 |

## Subsidiary Company
## Statement of Changes in Equity-Retained Earnings Section
## Year Ended December 31, 20X2

| | |
|---|---:|
| Beginning retained earnings | $ 275,000 |
| Add net income during the year | 250,000 |
| Less dividends declared | (100,000) |
| Ending retained earnings | $ 425,000 |

Additional information:

- Subsidiary Corp. sold goods worth $300,000 at a gross profit of 25% to Parent Corp. in 20X0 (the year before 20X1). All of these goods remained unsold in Parent Corp.'s ending inventory at the end of 20X0. Half of these goods were sold in 20X1, and the remaining half were sold in 20X2 to outsiders by Parent Corp.

- Subsidiary Corp. sold goods worth $250,000 at a gross profit of 30% to Parent Corp. in 20X1. One-third of these goods remained unsold with Parent Corp. at the end of 20X1. Parent Corp. sold goods worth $300,000 at a gross profit of 25% to Subsidiary Corp. in 20X1. Half of these goods remained unsold with Subsidiary Corp. at the end of 20X1.

- Subsidiary Corp. sold goods worth $200,000 at a gross profit of 30% to Parent Corp. in 20X2. Half of these goods remained unsold with Parent Corp. at the end of 20X2. Parent Corp. sold goods worth $350,000 at a gross profit of 25% to Subsidiary Corp. in 20X2; 40% of these goods remained unsold with Subsidiary Corp. at the end of 20X2.

- Subsidiary Corp. sold all of its investments in 20X2 to Parent Corp. for $145,000.

### Required

**Note: No financial statements are required.**

a.  Show the purchase price allocation calculations required at the time of acquisition and the goodwill and NCI balances at the time of acquisition.

b.  Show all necessary consolidation adjustments required in 20X2 relating to 20X1 and 20X2 (i.e., show the remaining adjustments other than the acquisition-related adjustments required in the previous bullet, necessary under the MEAR steps).

c.  Calculate the NCI balance at the end of 20X1.

d.  Calculate the consolidated retained earnings balance at the end of 20X1.

e.  Calculate the adjusted income of Subsidiary Corp. and the adjusted income of Parent Corp. for 20X2.

f.  Calculate the consolidated income in 20X2.

g.  Calculate the NCI's share of the consolidated income in 20X2.

h.  Calculate Parent Corp.'s share of the consolidated income in 20X2.

i.  Calculate the consolidated retained earnings balance at the end of 20X2.

j.  Calculate the NCI balance at the end of 20X2.

# Chapter 6

## Subsequent-Year Consolidations: General Approach

## Learning Objectives

**After studying this chapter, you should be able to:**

LO ❶ adjust for intercompany sale of depreciable long-term assets;

LO ❷ use the general approach to consolidation in the years after founding or buying a subsidiary;

LO ❸ report non-consolidated subsidiaries and investment in associates and jointly controlled entities under the equity basis in the years after the initial investment; and

LO ❹ consolidate subsidiaries that have been recorded using the equity method.

## INTRODUCTION

The notes to the consolidated financial statements for 2011 of Porsche SE, the holding company of the Porsche group, prepared under IFRS, include the following disclosure relating to the principles followed during consolidation:

> Intragroup expenses and income as well as receivables, liabilities and provisions are eliminated. Intercompany profits from the sale of assets within the group which have not yet been resold to third parties are eliminated.

The disclosure by Porsche SE above is typical of disclosures relating to consolidation by companies following IFRS. Inventec, a Taiwanese company that manufactures notebook computers, servers, and mobile devices, provides the following additional information relating to unrealized gains on the intercompany sale of depreciable assets in its third quarter 2011 report:

> Gains and losses resulting from [intercompany] transactions involving depreciable assets are recognized rateably over their economic lives.

We discussed and illustrated the elimination of intercompany balances and unrealized gains in the previous chapters. The Inventec quote indicates an additional complication created by intercompany sales of long-term amortizable assets—amortization of long-term assets sold intercompany. In this chapter, among other issues, we will discuss the adjustments required to report intercompany sales of long-term depreciable assets in the consolidated financial statements.

# The Journey So Far

It has been a long journey since we first started our discussion of consolidations in Chapter 2. At last, in this chapter, we reach the end of our exploration of the major facets of consolidated financial statements. We do not intend to be exhaustive (even though you may feel exhausted!). There are many additional complications to preparing consolidated statements. It is easy to imagine "What if . . . ?" scenarios. But additional complications are rare and should not be your focus. Once you understand Chapters 3 through 6, you will understand all of the significant issues in consolidation.

In Chapter 6, as well as illustrating intercompany sale of long-term amortizable assets, we will also discuss:

- the MEAR steps under the general approach to consolidation in the years after founding or buying a subsidiary;
- equity-basis reporting;
- briefly, consolidation when the parent uses the equity method to record its investment in its subsidiary; and
- consolidated reporting of discontinued operations.

In addition, we provide two appendices on the Companion Website:

- Parent corporations may invest in non-voting or preferred shares in addition to voting shares. Appendix 6A will briefly discuss the impact that such investments have on control and on consolidation.
- Intercompany bond holdings also are possible. In the vast majority of cases, intercompany debt can be eliminated by a simple adjustment, as shown in earlier chapters. In rare instances (*extremely* rare in Canada, where there is no organized exchange for bonds), there may be intercompany bond holdings involving premiums and discounts. Appendix 6B illustrates the adjustments for a bond premium or discount.

Readers who are not interested in some of the more obscure aspects of consolidation are encouraged to skip online Appendices 6A and 6B and proceed directly to Chapter 7.

## 6.1 INTERCOMPANY SALE OF LONG-TERM ASSETS

**LO ①**
Adjust for intercompany sale of depreciable long-term assets

### General Concept

We have repeatedly illustrated that unrealized profits on intercompany sales must be removed from consolidated net income. The concept of eliminating unrealized intercorporate profits or gains is applicable to *any* sale between members of a group of controlled, jointly controlled, or significantly influenced companies. The sale need not involve the parent or investor corporation; sales from one subsidiary to another or from one significantly influenced investee corporation to another require elimination of unrealized profit.

However, as pointed out earlier, in Chapter 5, the extent to which unrealized gains and losses relating to downstream transactions are eliminated depends on whether such transactions are with a subsidiary or with an associate/joint venture. We will illustrate this difference later in the chapter. First, however, we will focus on unrealized gains relating to transactions with subsidiaries.

# Downstream Sales of Amortizable Assets

Suppose that at the end of 20X6, Company P (PC), buys a piece of equipment for $200,000 and sells it to its wholly owned subsidiary, Company S (SC), for $250,000$_D$. SC will depreciate the asset's cost of $250,000 (assuming zero residual value) over the remaining useful life of the asset of 10 years on a straight-line basis, beginning in 20X7.

**Adjustments at the End of the Year of the Intercompany Sale**  The cost of the asset to the consolidated entity is the original cost of the equipment to PC of $200,000. Therefore, when consolidating the financial statements for 20X6, we must reduce the reported value of the equipment from its carrying value on SC's books of $250,000 to the actual cost to the consolidated entity (that is, to PC) of $200,000. To prepare the consolidated statements, we must:

- eliminate the $50,000$_D$ gain on the intercompany sale from PC's revenue; and
- reduce the equipment account by the $50,000$_D$ unrealized gain.

The adjustment in the consolidation working papers is:

| | | |
|---|---|---|
| Gain on sale of equipment | 50,000 | |
|    Equipment | | 50,000 |

**Adjustments in the Year After the Intercompany Sale**  The adjustments in 20X6 will reduce the consolidated retained earnings balance at the end of that year by $50,000. Remember that these adjustments are not actually recorded on any company's books—neither those of PC nor those of SC. Hence, PC's separate-entity opening retained earnings balance in 20X7 will be overstated by $50,000$_D$. Therefore, the cumulative consolidation adjustment required while calculating the opening consolidated retained earnings balance in 20X7 in relation to the unrealized gain in the prior year of 20X6 is a negative adjustment of $50,000.

In 20X7, SC will begin to depreciate the equipment at the rate of $25,000 per year. From the viewpoint of the consolidated entity, depreciation expense is overstated because SC's carrying value of the equipment includes the unrealized profit of $50,000$_D$. Based on the actual cost of the equipment of $200,000, depreciation expense should be only $20,000 per year. Therefore, the excess depreciation of $5,000 in the books of SC must be reversed via a depreciation adjustment in PC's consolidated statements.

This reversal of $5,000 also represents the realization of one-tenth of the unrealized gain of $50,000$_D$ in 20X7. Thus, the unrealized gains will be realized on a straight-line basis over the 10-year useful life of the equipment. The following schedule summarizes the effect of the difference in depreciation on the unrealized gain relating to the equipment at the end of 20X7:

| | Cost | Useful life (years) | Depreciation/ realized gain per year | Carrying value/ unrealized gain at the end of 20X7 |
|---|---|---|---|---|
| In SC's books | $250,000 | 10 | $25,000 | $225,000 |
| In consolidated statements | 200,000 | 10 | 20,000 | 180,000 |
| Unrealized/realized gain | $ 50,000 | 10 | $ 5,000 | $ 45,000 |

By the end of 20X7, the consolidation adjustments will:

- reduce the cost of the equipment on the statement of financial position from $250,000 to $200,000 (to eliminate the $50,000 overstatement of equipment in SC's books);
- eliminate the unrealized gain of $50,000$_D$ in the opening retained earnings of PC, with a negative adjustment of $50,000;
- decrease depreciation expense by $5,000 (to eliminate the excess depreciation charged by SC); and
- reduce accumulated depreciation by $5,000.

The associated working paper adjustments are:

| | | |
|---|---|---|
| Beginning retained earnings | 50,000 | |
|    Equipment | | 50,000 |
| | | |
| Accumulated depreciation—equipment | 5,000 | |
|    Depreciation expense—equipment | | 5,000 |

The reduction of the *opening* retained earnings by $50,000 and the partly offsetting decrease in depreciation expense of the *current year* by $5,000 will have a net reducing effect on the *ending* retained earnings of $45,000.

On intercompany *inventory* sales, the profit is realized when the inventory is eventually *sold* to an outside party. On *depreciable assets*, the profit is realized not by direct sale to outsiders, but rather by *using* the asset to produce goods or services to be sold to outsiders.

### Adjustments in the Second Year After the Intercompany Sale

In 20X8, the *unrealized gain in prior years* must be eliminated from the opening consolidated retained earnings. So far, the unrealized gain at the end of 20X6 (and therefore at the beginning of 20X7) was $50,000$_D$. However, $5,000, one-tenth of the unrealized profit of $50,000$_D$, was realized by the end of 20X7 when we decreased the consolidated depreciation expense of that year by that amount. Therefore, the unrealized gain at the *beginning* of 20X8 of $50,000 \times 9/10 = \$45,000_D$ is adjusted via a negative cumulative adjustment to the opening consolidated retained earnings of 20X8 for that amount. To summarize, the following adjustments should be made in the consolidated financial statements of PC at the beginning of 20X8:

- reduce retained earnings by $45,000, which is $50,000 \times 9/10$;
- reduce accumulated depreciation by the $5,000 depreciation in previous years (one year, 20X7, so far); and
- reduce the equipment account by the full intercompany profit of $50,000$_D$.

The adjustment is:

| | | |
|---|---|---|
| Beginning retained earnings | 45,000 | |
| Accumulated depreciation—equipment | 5,000 | |
|    Equipment | | 50,000 |

In 20X8, SC will again recognize an excess amortization of $5,000, while another $5,000 of the unrealized gains in prior years becomes realized. Therefore, when we prepare the year-end 20X8 consolidated statements, we will make exactly the same additional adjustment for 20X8 as we made for 20X7's depreciation:

■ decrease depreciation expense by $5,000; and

■ reduce accumulated depreciation by $5,000.

The adjustment is:

| | | |
|---|---|---|
| Accumulated depreciation—equipment | 5,000 | |
| Depreciation expense—equipment | | 5,000 |

### Adjustments in the Seventh Year After the Intercompany Sale
In subsequent years, the adjustment for the remaining unrealized gain will reflect the depreciation taken to date. For example, in 20X13, we will recognize the fact that the equipment has already been depreciated for six years (20X7 through 20X12, inclusive). The situation by the end of 20X13 is summarized below:

| | Cost | Depreciation/ realized gains in prior years (20X7–20X12) | Depreciation/ realized gain in 20X13 | Carrying value/ unrealized gain at the end of 20X13 |
|---|---|---|---|---|
| In SC's books | $250,000 | $150,000 | $25,000 | $75,000 |
| In consolidated statements | 200,000 | 120,000 | 20,000 | 60,000 |
| Unrealized/realized gain | $ 50,000 | $ 30,000 | $ 5,000 | $15,000 |

Therefore, using the direct approach to consolidation, the line-by-line adjustments during 20X13 will be as follows:

■ equipment—reduce by the full unrealized profit of $50,000$_D$;

■ *opening* consolidated retained earnings (on the retained earnings section of the statement of changes in equity)—reduce by the four years' unrealized gain on the transaction that remains at the start of the year: $50,000 × 4/10 = $20,000$_D$;

■ depreciation expense—reduce by the current year's depreciation of the unrealized profit ($50,000 × 1/10) = $5,000;

■ accumulated depreciation—multiply the unrealized gain by the fraction of years elapsed since the intercompany sale (i.e., $50,000 × 7/10 = $35,000$_D$), and subtract that amount from the accumulated depreciation balance;

■ closing consolidated retained earnings—reduce by the remaining three years' unrealized gain on the transaction: $50,000 × 3/10 = $15,000$_D$—which will happen automatically when the adjustments to the opening consolidated retained earnings and current year consolidated earnings flow through to the closing retained earnings.

The adjustments are:

| | | |
|---|---|---|
| Beginning retained earnings | 20,000 | |
| Accumulated depreciation—equipment | 35,000 | |
| Equipment | | 50,000 |
| Depreciation expense—equipment | | 5,000 |

### Adjustments in the Tenth and Later Years After the Intercompany Sale

By the end of 20X16, the asset is fully depreciated and there will be no depreciation expense in subsequent years. The only consolidation adjustment that will be made in 20X17 and thereafter (until the asset is retired and written off) will be a cumulative adjustment that has no impact on either consolidated net income or consolidated retained earnings.

- equipment—reduce by the full unrealized gain of $50,000_D
- accumulated depreciation—reduce by the full realized gain of $50,000_D

The adjustment is:

| | | |
|---|---|---|
| Accumulated depreciation—equipment | 50,000 | |
| Equipment | | 50,000 |

## Upstream Sales of Amortizable Assets

When the intercompany sale of an amortizable asset is upstream or is horizontal (i.e., between two subsidiaries), the consolidation eliminations are exactly the same as those shown above *if* the selling subsidiary is 100% owned by the parent.

If the selling subsidiary is *not* wholly owned, the adjustments are complicated somewhat by the presence of the non-controlling interest (NCI). The adjustments will now affect both consolidated retained earnings and NCI to the extent of their respective ownership share in SC.

For example, assume the same situation as above except that SC sells the equipment to PC, and PC owns 75% of the shares of SC. The non-controlling interest will have a 25% interest in the $50,000^U gain.

### Adjustments in the Year of the Intercompany Sale

The full $50,000^U will be eliminated from consolidated net income in 20X6, and the annual amortization of $5,000 will also be eliminated in each of the following 10 years. However, the non-controlling interest will also have to be adjusted for elimination of the unrealized profit.

When non-controlling interest is computed for the consolidated statement of financial position, the unrealized profit *at the end of the year* must be deducted from the subsidiary's net carrying value before we calculate the non-controlling interest's share. The impact on the year-end 20X6 statement of financial position can be shown as follows:

- equipment—reduce by the full unrealized gain of $50,000^U;
- ending non-controlling interest—reduce by its share of the unrealized gain ($50,000 \times 25\%) = \$12,500^U$; and
- ending consolidated retained earnings—reduce by its share of the unrealized gain ($50,000 \times 75\%) = \$37,500^U$.

The corresponding adjustment is:

| | | |
|---|---|---|
| Retained earnings | 37,500 | |
| NCI | 12,500 | |
|   Equipment | | 50,000 |

Notice that both the retained earnings and the non-controlling interest are reduced by negative adjustments. That will always be the case, because they are simply the allocated proportions of the unrealized gain.

**Adjustments in the Year After the Intercompany Sale**   In 20X7, we make the same unrealized gain adjustment again to the opening balances, since none of the unrealized gain had been recognized by the beginning of the year. In addition, we also must make the statement of comprehensive income adjustment, including the portion allocated to the non-controlling interest. The adjustments for 20X7 are as follows:

■   equipment—reduce by the full unrealized gain of $50,000^U;

■   opening non-controlling interest—reduce by its share of the unrealized gain ($50,000 × 25%) = $12,500^U;

■   *opening* retained earnings—reduce by its share of the unrealized gain ($50,000 × 75%) = $37,500^U;

■   depreciation expense—reduce by $5,000; and

■   accumulated depreciation—reduce by $5,000.

The corresponding adjustments are:

| | | |
|---|---|---|
| Beginning retained earnings | 37,500 | |
| Beginning NCI | 12,500 | |
|   Equipment | | 50,000 |
| | | |
| Accumulated depreciation—equipment | 5,000 | |
|   Depreciation expense—equipment | | 5,000 |

The adjustments to the opening NCI and retained earnings, respectively, coupled with the reduction in the depreciation expense by $5,000 during the year, will have the net effect of reducing the *ending* NCI by $11,250 [$12,500 − (25% of $5,000)] and *ending* retained earnings by $33,750 [$37,500 − (75% of $5,000)].

**Adjustments in the Second Year After the Intercompany Sale**   Because of the above adjustments, by the end of 20X7, one-tenth of the unrealized gain (i.e., $5,000) will have been recognized. Therefore, given that consolidation-related adjustments do not carry over to the next year, the following adjustments should be made as cumulative adjustments to opening balances in 20X8:

■   equipment—reduce by the full unrealized gain of $50,000^U;

■   *opening* non-controlling interest—reduce by its share of the unrealized gain ($45,000 × 25%) = $11,250^U;

- *opening* consolidated retained earnings—reduce by its share of the unrealized gain ($45,000 × 75%) = $33,750$^U$; and

- accumulated depreciation—reduce by $5,000.

The adjustment is:

| | | |
|---|---|---|
| Beginning retained earnings | 33,750 | |
| Beginning NCI | 11,250 | |
| Accumulated depreciation—equipment | 5,000 | |
|   Equipment | | 50,000 |

During 20X8, we should make the following additional current-year adjustments:

- decrease depreciation expense by $5,000; and

- reduce accumulated depreciation by $5,000.

The associated adjustment is:

| | | |
|---|---|---|
| Accumulated depreciation—equipment | 5,000 | |
|   Depreciation expense—equipment | | 5,000 |

The decrease in depreciation expense will flow through to *ending* retained earnings and *ending* NCI in the ratio of 75:25. In summary, by the end of 20X8, the net impact on the *ending* retained earnings and *ending* NCI will be a negative adjustment of $30,000 and $10,000, respectively.

**Adjustments in the Seventh Year After the Intercompany Sale**   Jumping ahead several years, to 20X13, the adjustments will be:

1. Cumulative adjustments

   - equipment—reduce by the full unrealized gain of $50,000$^U$;

   - *opening* non-controlling interest—reduce by its share of the unrealized gain ($50,000 × 25% × 4/10) = $5,000$^U$;

   - *opening* consolidated retained earnings—reduce by its share of the unrealized gain ($50,000 × 75% × 4/10 ) = $15,000$^U$; and

   - accumulated depreciation—reduce by $30,000.

The adjustment is:

| | | |
|---|---|---|
| Beginning retained earnings | 15,000 | |
| Beginning NCI | 5,000 | |
| Accumulated depreciation—equipment | 30,000 | |
|   Equipment | | 50,000 |

2. Current-year adjustments are:

   - decrease depreciation expense by $5,000; and

   - reduce accumulated depreciation by $5,000.

The associated adjustment is:

| | | |
|---|---|---|
| Accumulated depreciation—equipment | 5,000 | |
| Depreciation expense—equipment | | 5,000 |

By year-end, the cumulative impact of the above adjustments will be to reduce *ending* consolidated retained earnings by $11,250 and *ending* NCI by $3,750.

Each year, the current operations adjustment is the same as long as depreciation is being charged. The cumulative adjustment, however, gradually shifts the total net gain from unrealized (as deductions from consolidated retained earnings and non-controlling interest) to realized (as a reduction in accumulated depreciation).

We have been explaining intercompany sales of depreciable assets outside of the broader context of the consolidation process. To isolate and highlight the effects of the unrealized profit elimination, we have shown the direct impact on the *consolidated retained earnings* and *non-controlling interest*. In practice, this adjustment is included in the overall adjustment for consolidated retained earnings and non-controlling interest, just as we did in earlier chapters for unrealized profits in intercompany inventory transactions.

The next major section of this chapter will illustrate the broader approach to calculating the non-controlling interest in earnings.

## Losses on Intercompany Sales

*Losses* on intercompany sales may or may not be eliminated. The key question is whether or not the loss reflects impairment in that asset. If there is no evidence of impairment of the value of the asset sold, then the intercompany loss on the sale should be eliminated. But if the sale price reflects impairment in the asset, then the asset should have been written down even without the sale; the loss on the sale simply reflects an impairment that should be reflected by a reduction in the carrying value of the asset anyway. Thus, the crucial question in deciding whether or not to eliminate a loss is whether the asset should have been written down even if it had *not* been sold.

Under IAS 36, *Impairment of Assets*, an impairment loss exists when the carrying value of the asset exceeds its recoverable value. The recoverable value of an asset represents the higher of its (1) fair value less costs to sell and (2) value in use. **Value in use** of an asset represents the present value of the estimated future cash flows expected to be generated from the continuing use of the unit and from its disposal at the end of its useful life. However, it is not necessary to determine *both* the fair value less costs to sell and the value in use of an asset. As long as one of these values exceeds the carrying value of the asset, there is no impairment.

## Subsequent Sale of Intercompany-Acquired Capital Assets

One company may buy a depreciable asset from another in the consolidated group, and then later sell that asset to a third party in an arm's-length transaction.

For example, suppose PC sells the equipment, previously acquired from SC, for $220,000 at the beginning of 20X10. PC will recognize a gain of $45,000, the

$220,000 proceeds from sale minus the remaining net carrying value to PC of $175,000 (i.e., $250,000 cost to PC × 70% remaining useful life). The current example is a continuation of our original example wherein PC owns 100% of SC; therefore, there is no NCI.

At the beginning of 20X10, 70% of the original gain from the intercompany sale will still remain unrealized. Therefore, the cumulative adjustment required to opening retained earnings to recognize this unrealized gain is:

■ *opening* consolidated retained earnings—reduce by $35,000[U].

Once the asset has been sold to a third party, the entire remaining unrealized gain must be recognized and added to the gain (or deducted from the loss) on the third-party sale:

■ gain on sale of equipment—increase by $45,000.

Therefore, in essence we simultaneously decreased opening retained earnings by $35,000 and increased gain on sale of equipment by $45,000. This should seem familiar, since we encountered a similar pair of adjustments in earlier chapters when the unrealized gain on intercompany sale of inventory was realized in the subsequent year on the sale of such inventory to a third party. In earlier chapters, instead of increasing gain on sale of equipment, we decreased cost of goods sold to recognize the realization of the gain on the sale of the inventory.

Thus, the gain on PC's sale will be increased by the remaining unrealized profit on SC's sale, reflecting the fact that for the consolidated entity as a whole, a profit of $80,000 was realized on the sale of the equipment to an unrelated party.

| | | |
|---|---:|---:|
| Sale price | | $220,000 |
| Consolidated carrying value: | | |
|   Cost to SC | $200,000 | |
|   Depreciation (3 years @ $20,000) | 60,000 | 140,000 |
| Gain to consolidated entity | | $ 80,000 |

### Concept Check 6-1

1. What are the different types of consolidation-related adjustments required relating to the intercompany sale of a depreciable asset in a previous period?

2. What consolidation-related adjustments are required when a depreciable asset sold intercompany in a previous year is sold to a third party in a subsequent year?

LO ❷
Use the general approach to consolidation in the years after founding or buying a subsidiary

## 6.2 SUBSEQUENT-YEAR CONSOLIDATIONS—GENERAL APPROACH

So far we have discussed the process of preparing consolidated financial statements (1) at the date of acquisition; (2) one year subsequent to acquisition; and (3) two years subsequent to acquisition. We have explored the basic concepts underlying consolidation and the treatment of non-controlling interest. The major procedural aspects of consolidation have also been presented. In this section, we discuss the general approach to preparing consolidated financial statements at any reporting date subsequent to acquisition, regardless of how long ago the business combination occurred.

# Basic Conceptual Approach and Consolidation Steps Under the Direct Method

Previous chapters have emphasized that consolidated financial statements must reflect adjustments for three types of events: (1) the acquisition transaction; (2) the cumulative effects of amortization and transactions to the beginning of the current reporting period; and (3) the effects of amortization and transactions in the current period. It doesn't matter whether the three types of adjustments are kept separate or combined.

The general nature of these adjustments is portrayed in Exhibit 6.1 with a timeline. The first point of interest on the timeline is point A, the date of acquisition of the parent's controlling interest in the subsidiary. The consolidation adjustments for this event are a constant, and have been thoroughly discussed.

**Exhibit 6.1** Overview of Consolidation Adjustments

**(1) Acquisition adjustments**

   **a)** Eliminate subsidiary's share equity accounts; establish non-controlling interest.

   **b)** Add fair value increments and goodwill.

   **c)** Offset subsidiary's accumulated depreciation against the asset account(s).

**(2) Cumulative operations adjustments** to start of the current year (i.e., affecting current year's *beginning*-of-year SFP amounts).

   **a)** Recognize the non-controlling interest's share of subsidiary retained earnings from date of acquisition to *start* of the current year.

   **b)** Recognize the cumulative amortization of fair-value increments (or decrements) and goodwill.

   **c)** Eliminate the impact of intercompany transactions that affect carrying values:

   **i)** Gains and losses from intercompany transactions that are still unrealized at the start of the year.

   **ii)** Flow-through to retained earnings of fair-valued assets and liabilities that have since been sold to third parties.

**(3) Current year operations adjustments.**

   **a)** Amortize fair-value increments (decrements) and goodwill.

   **b)** Eliminate the current year's intercompany transactions.

   **c)** Realize previously unrealized profits (losses), if they are realized or partially realized in the current year.

   **d)** Eliminate unrealized profits (losses) arising from intercompany transactions in the current year.

   **e)** Recognize the non-controlling interest in earnings.

   **f)** Eliminate year-end intercompany balances.

| **A** Date of acquisition | **B** Start of current year | **C** End of current year |

Point C on the timeline is the most recent point, which is the current SFP date. The adjustments for point C and for the year then ended (the time between point B and point C) have been reviewed several times in the previous chapters and should be reasonably clear to you by now.

The more problematic adjustment is likely to be that for the time between acquisition (point A) and the beginning of the current year (point B). We have pointed out that the consolidation adjustments for the intervening period (points A to B) are *cumulative* adjustments. We can simply accumulate the effects of each year's current operations adjustments, bearing in mind that the net effect of all adjustments to statement of comprehensive income accounts and to previous years' current nonmonetary accounts (e.g.,

**Exhibit 6.2** MEAR Steps Under the General Approach to Consolidation

| Consolidation Steps | Acquisition-Related (*Chapter 3*) | Relating to First Year Following Acquisition (*Chapter 4*) | Relating to Following Years (*Chapter 5*) | General Approach (*Chapter 6*) |
|---|---|---|---|---|
| 1. Measure | ■ Calculate cost and fair value adjustments (FVA)<br>■ Allocate FVA<br>■ Determine NCI balance | | | 1. Measure<br>■ Calculate cost and FVA<br>■ Allocate FVA<br>■ Determine NCI balance |
| 2. Eliminate and Recognize | ■ Eliminate parent's investment account and subsidiary's share equity accounts | ■ Eliminate intercompany transactions & balances<br>■ Eliminate unrealized profits | ■ Recognize realized profits | 2. Eliminate and Recognize<br>■ Eliminate parent's investment account and subidiary's share equity accounts<br>■ Eliminate intercompany transactions & balances<br>■ Eliminate unrealized profits cumulative & current<br>■ Recognize realized profits |
| 3. Amortize | | ■ Amortize FVAs<br>■ Recognize impairments | ■ Recognize cumulative amortization of FVAs<br>■ Recognize cumulative impairments | 3. Amortize<br>■ Amortize FVAs cumulative & current<br>■ Recognize impairments cumulative & current |
| 4. Recognize NCI share of earnings | | ■ Recognize NCI share of earnings<br>■ Calculate NCI SFP balance<br>■ Calculate RE balance | | 4. Recognize NCI share of earnings<br>■ Update NCI balance<br>■ Update RE balance |
| 5. Check<br>■ Independent calculation of RE balances<br>■ Independent calculation of NCI balances | | | | |

**Exhibit 6.3** Parent Corp. buys 80% of Sub Ltd.

| Fair Value Adjustments Date of Acquisition December 31, 20X4 | | Excess of fair value over carrying value [Dr/(Cr)] |
|---|---|---|
| | | 100% |
| Inventories | | $ 10,000 |
| Machinery | | 75,000 |
| Investments | | 10,000 |
| Total fair value adjustments | | $ 95,000 |
| Goodwill calculation | | |
| Purchase price | | $ 800,000 |
| Implied fair value of 100% of Sub [$800,000 × (100% ÷ 80%)] | | $1,000,000 |
| Carrying value of assets of Sub | $855,000 | |
| Plus fair value adjustments as above | 95,000 | |
| Fair value of 100% of Sub's net identifiable assets | | 950,000 |
| Goodwill at 100% | | $ 50,000 |

inventories) will usually be reflected in retained earnings. The result will then be the point A to point B adjustment when we prepare the consolidated statements for the next accounting period (point B to point C).

If we have the task of preparing only a year-end consolidated SFP, then we don't have to worry about point B but can adjust the SFP amounts directly to year-end balances. For example, there would be no reason to distinguish between fair value amortizations in the current year and those relating to prior years. Although SFP-only consolidations may be encountered in student examination situations, actual accounting practice calls for preparing a full set of financial statements and not just a non-comparative year-end SFP. In preparing a full set of financial statements, we need to isolate the adjustments relating to the current period so that we can prepare the SCI as well as the comparative SFP.

The general MEAR steps to consolidation, which accomplish the consolidation adjustments in Exhibit 6.1, and thus can be used in any year subsequent to acquisition, are provided in Exhibit 6.2.

To illustrate the preparation of consolidated financial statements in *any* year, we will use a different example than the one used in previous chapters. This example will include an intercompany sale of capital assets to illustrate the adjustments described in the first part of this chapter.

## Basic Information

On December 31, 20X4, Parent Corp. acquired 80% of the outstanding common shares of Sub Ltd. by issuing Parent shares worth $800,000. At the date of acquisition, Sub's shareholders' equity totalled $855,000, consisting of $300,000 in the common share account and $555,000 in retained earnings.

**Exhibit 6.4** Calculation of NCI

| | |
|---|---:|
| Goodwill at 100% as calculated in Exhibit 6.3 above | $ 50,000 |
| NCI's goodwill at 20% = [$50,000 × 20%] | 10,000 |
| 100% of Sub's fair value as calculated in Exhibit 6.3 above: | 1,000,000 |
| Non-controlling interest | |
| Entity method [($1,000,000) × 20%] | 200,000 |

Some of Sub's assets had a fair value that differed from carrying value as shown in Exhibit 6.3. The implied fair value of Sub Ltd. is $1,000,000 and the goodwill at 100% is $50,000 as shown in Exhibit 6.3. Exhibit 6.4 shows the calculation of the NCI's share of goodwill of $10,000 and the NCI value of $200,000 under the entity method.

Exhibit 6.5 shows the separate-entity financial statements for Parent and Sub at December 31, 20X10, six years after Parent's acquisition of its 80% interest in Sub. Other relevant information is as follows:

1. Sub's machinery had an estimated remaining useful life of 10 years from December 31, 20X4. At the date of acquisition, the balance in Sub's accumulated depreciation (on machinery) account was $575,000. Machinery is depreciated on a straight-line basis, assuming no residual value.

2. In 20X7, Sub sold its investments for a profit of $45,000 over carrying value.

3. During 20X10, intercompany sales were as follows:

    a) Parent had sales totalling $100,000$_D$ to Sub at a gross margin of 40% of selling price. On December 31, 20X10, $40,000 of the amount sold was still in Sub's inventory.

    b) Sub had sales of $700,000$^U$ to Parent at a gross margin of 40% of sales. At year-end, $70,000 was still in Parent's inventory.

4. The inventories on January 1, 20X10, contained intercompany purchases as follows:

    a) Sub held goods purchased from Parent for $20,000; and

    b) Parent held goods purchased from Sub for $100,000.

    The gross margin on intercompany sales held in the beginning inventories was 40% of selling price for both companies. All of the beginning inventories were sold to third parties during 20X10.

5. Parent collects royalties from Sub (as well as from other companies). Between January 1, 20X5, and December 31, 20X9 (that is, prior to the current year), Sub paid a total of $500,000 in royalties to Parent. During 20X10, Sub paid $90,000 to Parent for royalties.

6. In 20X8, Sub sold machinery to Parent for $91,000$^U$. The machinery had originally been acquired by Sub in 20X5 for $100,000. Sub had been depreciating the machinery on a straight-line basis over 10 years (i.e., at $10,000 per year), with a full year's depreciation in the year of acquisition and no depreciation in the year of disposal. Thus, the net carrying value of the machine to Sub was $70,000 at the time of the sale to Parent. After the sale from Sub to Parent, Parent continued to depreciate the machinery over the seven remaining years of its original useful life (i.e., at $13,000 per year beginning in 20X8).

**Exhibit 6.5** Parent Corp. and Sub Ltd. Condensed Separate-Entity Financial Statements

| Statements of Financial Position December 31, 20X10 | | |
|---|---|---|
| | **Parent** | **Sub** |
| **Assets** | | |
| Cash | $ 50,000 | $ 20,000 |
| Accounts receivable | 150,000 | 160,000 |
| Inventories | 180,000 | 100,000 |
| Machinery | 5,000,000 | 2,700,000 |
| Accumulated depreciation | (1,770,000) | (1,240,000) |
| Investment in Sub Ltd. (at cost) | 800,000 | — |
| Other investments | 100,000 | — |
| **TOTAL ASSETS** | $4,510,000 | $1,740,000 |
| | | |
| **Liabilities and shareholders' equity** | | |
| Accounts payable | $ 450,000 | $ 200,000 |
| Bonds payable | 300,000 | 500,000 |
| Total liabilities | 750,000 | 700,000 |
| Common shares | 1,200,000 | 300,000 |
| Retained earnings | 2,560,000 | 740,000 |
| Total shareholders' equity | 3,760,000 | 1,040,000 |
| **TOTAL LIABILITIES AND SHAREHOLDERS' EQUITY** | $4,510,000 | $1,740,000 |

| Statements of Comprehensive Income Year Ended December 31, 20X10 | | |
|---|---|---|
| | **Parent** | **Sub** |
| Sales revenue | $2,000,000 | $1,500,000 |
| Royalty revenue | 150,000 | — |
| Dividend income | 75,000 | — |
| Total revenue | 2,225,000 | 1,500,000 |
| Cost of sales | 1,200,000 | 900,000 |
| Other expenses | 560,000 | 411,000 |
| Total expenses | 1,760,000 | 1,311,000 |
| **NET INCOME AND COMPREHENSIVE INCOME** | $ 465,000 | $ 189,000 |

| Statements of Changes in Equity—Retained Earnings Section Year Ended December 31, 20X10 | | |
|---|---|---|
| | **Parent** | **Sub** |
| Retained earnings, beginning of year | $2,395,000 | $ 641,000 |
| Net income | 465,000 | 189,000 |
| Dividends declared | (300,000) | (90,000) |
| Retained earnings, end of year | $2,560,000 | $ 740,000 |

# A Caution for Students

Before we launch into an illustration of consolidation techniques, we would like to caution you about your problem-solving approach to complex consolidation problems.

When we prepare financial statements for a real enterprise, it is rather obvious that statements of financial position must balance, and that the full set of four financial statements must *articulate*, or tie in to each other. However, when we are attempting consolidations for learning and practice, it may well be beneficial not to worry too much if our statements of financial position don't balance! It is possible to spend many hours in an attempt to find an error (or errors) that keep our statements from balancing or from articulating properly. This particularly is a problem when we are using the direct approach, in which the *ad hoc* nature of the adjustment process denies us the self-balancing feature of the worksheet approach.

Often, the error is very minor—sometimes only a simple arithmetic error. We generally recommend, therefore, that you not get too stressed if your problem solutions don't quite work. This is especially true in examination situations, where looking for small mistakes will consume valuable time that could be better used to answer other questions and problems.

Therefore, we urge all users of this book not to get too upset if your statements don't balance. Even the authors of this text sometimes have trouble getting their solutions to balance!

# Direct Approach

We will follow the MEAR steps under the column titled "General Approach," in Exhibit 6.2.

The first step, of **M**easure, requires us to calculate the cost of the acquisition and the FVAs, allocate the FVAs to the various assets and liabilities, including goodwill, and lastly determine the NCI balance. The purchase price of $800,000 was already given. Exhibits 6.3 and 6.4 show the FVA attributable to the various assets and liabilities, with the remainder allocated to goodwill, and the calculation of the fair value of 100% of Sub at $1,000,000 and the NCI balance of $200,000.

As compared with our practice in prior chapters, Exhibit 6.3 accomplishes the goal of the **M**easure step somewhat differently. This is a result of the absence of full information in our example. The example does not provide the carrying values of the individual assets and liabilities of the subsidiary at the time of acquisition. In contrast, we are given the FVAs relating to each asset and the overall carrying value of the net assets of the subsidiary. Therefore, Exhibit 6.3 uses the provided information to calculate the parent's share of goodwill. However, the overall logic remains the same as in previous chapters.

**Eliminate**   Now, we are ready to move to the next step, of **E**liminate.

**Eliminate Intercompany Transactions and Balances**   There are four intercompany items in our example:

| | |
|---|---|
| Upstream sale by Sub Ltd. | $(700,000) |
| Downstream sale by Parent Corp. | $(100,000) |
| Royalty paid by Sub Ltd. to Parent Corp. | $ (90,000) |
| Dividends declared by Sub Ltd. | $ (90,000) |

1.  Sub Ltd. sold $700,000^U$ worth of goods to Parent Corp. We need to eliminate $700,000^U$ from both sales and cost of goods sold.

2.  Parent Corp. sold $100,000_D$ worth of goods to Sub Ltd. We must eliminate $100,000_D$ from both sales and cost of goods sold as well.

3.  Sub Ltd. paid royalties of $90,000 to Parent Corp. We must eliminate $90,000 from both royalty revenue and other expenses.

4.  Sub Ltd. declared dividends of $90,000. Of the $90,000 dividends declared by Sub Ltd., Parent Corp.'s share is only $72,000; the remaining $18,000 belongs to the NCI. Therefore, while we eliminate the dividends declared amount of $90,000, we need to eliminate only $72,000 from dividend income. The NCI's share of $18,000 will be subtracted from the NCI balance on the SFP.

**Eliminate Unrealized Profits and Realized Profits**   There are two realized gains relating to the intercompany sale of inventory in the previous year and two unrealized gains relating to the intercompany sale of inventory in 20X10.

| | |
|---|---|
| Realized profit on downstream sale of inventory in the previous year | $ 8,000 |
| Realized profit on upstream sale of inventory in the previous year | $ 40,000 |
| Unrealized profit on downstream sale of inventory in the current year | $ (16,000) |
| Unrealized profit on upstream sale of inventory in the current year | $ (28,000) |

1.  The inventory sold downstream last year is now realized. Therefore, the associated cumulative adjustment required will decrease the opening consolidated retained earnings of 20X10 by $8,000_D$, while decreasing cost of goods sold of 20X10 by $8,000_D$. We encountered similar examples in earlier chapters of realized gains relating to intercompany sales of inventory in previous periods. The associated discussion applies to our present example as well, and therefore we have chosen not to repeat it here.

2.  Since the $40,000^U$ realized gain pertains to an upstream sale of inventory in the previous year, the cumulative adjustment required in 20X10 will decrease opening consolidated retained earnings by $32,000^U$ *and* opening NCI by $8,000^U$, while decreasing cost of goods sold of 20X10 by $40,000^U$.

3.  Cost of goods sold of 20X10 should be increased by $16,000_D$ while ending inventory should be decreased by $16,000 to reflect the unrealized gain of $16,000_D$ on the unsold portion of the inventory sold downstream during the year. Only the ending consolidated retained earnings (not the ending NCI) should be adjusted by the $16,000_D$ unrealized gain, since it relates to a downstream sale of inventory.

4.  Likewise, cost of goods sold of 20X10 should by increased by $28,000^U$ while ending inventory should be decreased by $28,000^U$ to reflect the unrealized gain of $28,000^U$ on the upstream sale of inventory remaining unsold at year-end. However, both ending consolidated retained earnings and ending NCI should be adjusted by their portion of the $28,000^U$ unrealized gain, since the sale is now upstream.

Our current example also features the upstream sale of machinery, a long-lived depreciable asset, in the prior year of 20X8. This machinery was originally acquired by Sub in 20X5. Sub depreciated the machinery for three years (in 20X5, 20X6, and 20X7) prior to selling it to Parent Corp. Therefore, the following types of adjustments need to be made in 20X10 relating to the upstream sale of machinery:

1. Eliminate the unrealized gain on the upstream sale of machinery in 20X8.
2. Eliminate the excess depreciation charged by Parent Corp. and recognize the portion of the gain realized in the prior years of 20X8 and 20X9.
3. Eliminate the excess depreciation charged by Parent Corp. and recognize the portion of the gain realized in the current year of 20X10.
4. Reinstate the original cost and accumulated depreciation at the time of the upstream sale back on the machinery account.

The following schedule calculates the various unrealized and realized gains relating to the upstream sale of machinery:

| | Cost/ carrying value | Depreciation/ realized gains in prior years (20X8– 20X9 (cumulative adjustments) | Depreciation/ realized gain in 20X10 (current adjustments) | Carrying value/ unrealized gain at the end of 20X10 |
|---|---|---|---|---|
| In Parent's books | $91,000 | $26,000 | $13,000 | $52,000 |
| In consolidated statements | 70,000 | 20,000 | 10,000 | 40,000 |
| Unrealized/realized gain | $21,000 | $ 6,000 | $ 3,000 | $12,000 |

We will now elaborate on the various eliminations. The unrealized gain relating to the upstream sale of machinery in 20X8 is $21,000^U$, and thus must be eliminated. The corresponding cumulative adjustment in 20X10 will reduce the opening machinery account balance by $21,000^U$ while reducing opening retained earnings by $16,800^U$ and opening NCI by $4,200^U$.

The excess depreciation charged by Parent Corp. and the realized gains on the machinery each year is $3,000^U$. Therefore, Parent Corp. would have cumulatively charged excess depreciation of $6,000^U$ in the prior years of 20X8 and 20X9. The $6,000^U$ also represents the portion of the unrealized gain of $21,000^U$ realized in the prior years. Therefore, a cumulative adjustment for $6,000^U$ must be made in 20X10 to reverse the impact of the excess depreciation in prior years. The adjustment will increase opening consolidated retained earnings by $4,800^U$ and opening NCI by $1,200^U$, while reducing accumulated depreciation by $6,000^U$.

A current year adjustment of $3,000^U$ is also required to reverse the excess depreciation of $3,000^U$ in 20X10. This adjustment will decrease the depreciation expense of 20X10 and accumulated depreciation, respectively, by $3,000^U$. The effect of this adjustment will be to increase ending consolidated retained earnings by $2,400^U$ and ending NCI by $600^U$.

In our initial example on the intercompany sale of equipment in this chapter, the selling company sold the equipment immediately after purchase, without charging any depreciation. However, in our present example, the machinery sold by Sub Ltd. had been depreciated by it during 20X5–20X7, prior to its sale in 20X8. Sub Ltd. would therefore have eliminated from its books both the original cost and the accumulated depreciation of the machinery on its sale to Parent Corp.

However, given that the sale was not to an outside party, from the consolidated perspective, no sale of the machinery occurred. Therefore, we have to reinstate the original cost of $100,000 and accumulated depreciation of $30,000$^U$ at the time of sale of the machinery back onto the consolidation-level SFP. Specifically, we need to add back $30,000$^U$ to both the machinery account and to the accumulated depreciation account on the consolidated SFP.

You may wonder why the adjustment is only $30,000 and not $100,000, when our aim is to reinstate the original balance of $100,000. For the answer, recall that by eliminating the $21,000$^U$ unrealized gain earlier, we reduced the carrying value of the machinery from $91,000 to $70,000, the net carrying value of the machinery in the books of Sub at the time of its sale. Therefore, to increase the value of the machinery from $70,000 to $100,000, we need to adjust the machinery value further by only $30,000, not $100,000.

**Amortize FVAs**  The third step (**A**mortize) in our MEAR approach to consolidation requires us to amortize FVAs and recognize any impairment. The schedule below shows the calculations relating to the amortization of the FVAs, allocated to the various assets and liabilities at the time of acquisition.

| | 100% FVA | Amortization period | Amortization per year | Amortization/ impairment loss during previous periods (cumulative adjustments) | Amortization/ impairment loss during 20X10 (current adjustments) | Balance of FVA remaining at the end of 20X10 |
|---|---|---|---|---|---|---|
| Inventories | $ 10,000 | — | | $10,000 | — | $  — |
| Machinery | 75,000 | 10 | $7,500 | 37,500 | $7,500 | 30,000 |
| Investment | 10,000 | — | — | 10,000 | — | — |
| Goodwill | 50,000 | — | | — | — | 50,000 |
| Total | $145,000 | | | $57,500 | $7,500 | $80,000 |

Remember that even though Parent Corp. owns only 80% of Sub Ltd., under the entity method, 100% of the fair values of the assets and liabilities of Sub Ltd., including goodwill, are included in the consolidated financial statements. Therefore, the schedule above calculates the amortization of the full 100% FVA, not just the portion owned by Parent Corp.

**Inventory**  Typically in consolidation problems it is assumed that the subsidiary's inventory at the time of acquisition is fully sold by the end of the subsequent year. In our example, that would be 20X5. Sub Ltd. would have expensed only the carrying cost of the inventory in its books as cost of goods sold in 20X5. However, the FVI of $10,000 relating to inventory indicates that the cost of the inventory to the consolidated entity is $10,000 higher. Therefore, to reflect the true cost of the inventory to the consolidated entity, the FVI of $10,000 would have been amortized in the consolidated statements of 20X5. The adjustment in 20X5 would have reduced net income by $10,000 and, by extension, also reduced ending consolidated retained earnings of 20X5 by $8,000 and ending NCI of 20X5 by $2,000.

Remember that consolidation adjustments do not carry over to later years. We are now in 20X10. Therefore, to capture the impact of the prior year amortization of the $10,000 FVI relating to inventory, we need to make a cumulative adjustment in 20X10 reducing beginning inventory by $10,000 (that is, to eliminate the $10,000 FVI) while reducing opening retained earnings by $8,000 and NCI by $2,000.

**Machinery**   The machinery had a future useful life of 10 years at the time of acquisition. Therefore, the FVI relating to machinery should be amortized as additional depreciation over this 10-year period on a straight-line basis. Five years are past since the time of acquisition. Therefore, the FVI amortized in prior years must be $7,500 × 5 = $37,500. A cumulative adjustment for this amount is required in 20X10 increasing accumulated depreciation by $37,500 while reducing opening retained earnings by $30,000 and opening NCI by $7,500.

An additional $7,500 current-year depreciation expense has to be recognized in 20X10. The current year adjustment will increase accumulated depreciation by $7,500 while reducing ending consolidated retained earnings by $6,000 and ending NCI by $1,500. The unamortized balance of the FVI relating to machinery at the end of 20X10 is $30,000.

**Investment**   Sub Ltd. sold its investment in 20X7 for a profit of $45,000. However, the true cost of the investment to the consolidated entity is $10,000 higher, as reflected by the FVI of $10,000 allocated to investment. Therefore, the true profit on the sale of the investment to the consolidated entity is $10,000 lower, at $35,000. The $10,000 FVI would have been treated as part of the cost of the investment while calculating the gain on the sale of the investment at the consolidated level in 20X7. We must make a cumulative adjustment in 20X10 to recognize the decrease in the gain of $10,000 in 20X7. The adjustment will decrease the investment value by $10,000 (i.e., to eliminate the $10,000 FVI) while reducing opening consolidated retained earnings by $8,000 and opening NCI by $2,000.

**Goodwill**   Finally, there is no impairment in the acquisition-related goodwill. Therefore, the goodwill balance will continue to be at $50,000.

**Recognize NCI Share of Current Year Earnings**   The calculation of the NCI's share of the adjusted income of Sub Ltd. for 20X10 is provided in the schedule below.

| Details | Amount |
|---|---|
| Net income of Sub Ltd. for 20X10 (from separate-entity financial statement) | $189,000 |
| Add: | |
| Realized profit on upstream sale of inventory in the previous year | 40,000 |
| Excess depreciation charged by Parent Corp. on machinery purchased from Sub Ltd. | 3,000 |
| Less: | |
| Unrealized profit on upstream sale of inventory in the current year | (28,000) |
| Amortization of FVAs during the year | (7,500) |
| Adjusted net income of Sub Ltd. for 20X10 | $196,500 |
| NCI's share @ 20% | $ 39,300 |

The adjusted net income of Sub Ltd. for 20X10 after making all the above adjustments is $196,500. Therefore, the NCI's share is $39,300, while Parent Corp.'s share will be $157,200. However, note that we also need to adjust Parent Corp.'s separate-entity net income by increasing it by $8,000 and decreasing it by $16,000, which is the realized and unrealized gain, respectively, in 20X10 from the downstream sale of inventory.

**Recognize NCI Share of Prior Years' Earnings**   The change in the retained earnings of Sub Ltd. from the time of acquisition until the beginning of 20X10 is $86,000 (i.e., $641,000 beginning retained earnings balance of Sub Ltd. minus $555,000 retained earnings balance of Sub Ltd. at the time of acquisition). The NCI's share of this change at 20% is therefore $17,200. Adding the $17,200 to the NCI balance at the time of acquisition results in the NCI balance at the beginning of 20X10 of $217,200. The $217,200 is before allocating to the NCI its share of the consolidation adjustments relating to previous years.

In our current example, we must adjust the opening consolidated retained earnings and the opening NCI for the impact of the prior years' adjustments:

| | |
|---|---:|
| Amortization of FVA machinery during 20X5–20X9 | $ (37,500) |
| Unrealized profit on upstream sale of inventory in 20X9 | (40,000) |
| Unrealized gain on upstream sale of machinery in 20X8 | (21,000) |
| Realized gain on upstream sale of machinery in 20X8–20X9 | 6,000 |
| Amortization of FVI relating to inventory | (10,000) |
| Amortization of FVI relating to investment | (10,000) |
| Total | $(112,500) |
| NCI's share (20% × $112,500) | $ (22,500) |

Note that the opening retained earnings of 20X10 should also be adjusted for the unrealized gains in 20X9 of $8,000$_D$ from the downstream sale of inventory.

**Actual Consolidation**   Now we have all the information necessary to prepare the consolidated statement of income and the retained earnings section of the consolidated statement of changes in equity and consolidated SFP for Parent Corp. for the year 20X10. We can start the consolidation process by adding the carrying values of both companies and making the various adjustments identified in the previous steps. We also need to remember to eliminate the shareholders' equity of $855,000, consisting of $300,000 in the common share account and $555,000 in retained earnings, and the investment at cost of $800,000.

To do the above, following our practice in earlier chapters, we can go down the SCI, SCE/RE, and SFP and insert the correct amounts on a line-by-line basis. In Exhibits 6.6 and 6.7, we have added together the separate-entity amounts and made the required additional adjustments and eliminations. The adjustments and eliminations are listed below once again, now by each financial statement, starting with the statement of comprehensive income. Exhibits 6.6 and 6.7 illustrate consolidation under the entity method.

**Statement of Comprehensive Income and SCE/RE**   Following the practice under the direct method, the calculation of each consolidated item of revenue and expense is shown in brackets in Exhibit 6.6.

■ *Sales revenue.* The consolidated sales are reduced by the intercompany sales during 20X10 of $100,000$_D$ plus $700,000$^U$.

■ *Royalty revenue.* Royalties are reduced by the intercompany royalties of $90,000 paid by Sub to Parent during 20X10.

■ *Dividend income.* Sub paid dividends of $90,000 during 20X10. Of this amount, Parent received $90,000 × 80% = $72,000. The dividend income of Parent is reduced by the amount of the intercompany dividends of $72,000.

**Exhibit 6.6** Parent Corp.

| Condensed Consolidated Statement of Comprehensive Income<br>Year Ended December 31, 20X10 | |
|---|---:|
| **Revenues** | |
| Sales revenue [2,000,000 + 1,500,000 − **100,000**$_D$ − **700,000**$^U$] | $2,700,000 |
| Royalty revenue [150,000 − **90,000**] | 60,000 |
| Dividend Income [75,000 − **72,000**] | 3,000 |
| | 2,763,000 |
| | |
| **Expenses** | |
| Cost of sales [1,200,000 + 900,000 − **100,000**$_D$ − **700,000**$^U$ + **16,000**$_D$ + **28,000**$^U$ − **8,000**$_D$ − **40,000**$^U$] | 1,296,000 |
| Other expenses [560,000 + 411,000 − **90,000** + **7,500** − **3,000**$^U$] | 885,500 |
| | 2,181,500 |
| **Net income and comprehensive income** | $ 581,500 |
| Net income attributable to: | |
| Owners of the parent | 542,200 |
| Non-controlling interests | 39,300 |
| Statement of Changes in Equity—Retained Earnings Section<br>Year Ended December 31, 20X10 | |
| Retained earnings, December 31, 20X9 [2,395,000 − **21,200** − **8,000**] | $2,365,800 |
| Net income | 542,200 |
| Dividends declared [300,000 + 90,000 − **90,000**] | (300,000) |
| Retained earnings, December 31, 20X10 | $2,608,000 |

■ *Cost of sales.* The cost of sales of the two companies is adjusted for (1) the intercompany sales; (2) the unrealized profits in the ending inventories; and (3) the realization of the previously unrealized profits in the beginning inventories.

■ The intercompany sales are $100,000$_D$ and $700,000$^U$, which are deducted from cost of sales as the offset to the deduction from sales, above.

■ The unrealized profits in the ending inventories are $16,000$_D$ for the downstream sales ($40,000 × 40%) and $28,000$^U$ for the upstream sales ($70,000 × 40%). These amounts are added to cost of sales.

■ The now-realized profits from the beginning inventory are $20,000 × 40% = $8,000$_D$ for downstream sales (in Sub's inventory) and $100,000 × 40% = $40,000$^U$ for upstream sales (in Parent's inventory). These now-realized amounts are subtracted from cost of sales, thereby increasing consolidated net income.

■ *Other expenses.* Operating expenses are adjusted for (1) the intercompany royalty expense; (2) the amortization of the fair value adjustments; and (3) the over-depreciation of the machinery that was sold by Sub to Parent.

1. Intercompany royalty payments of $90,000 are eliminated.

2. On a straight-line basis, the $75,000 fair value increment on the machinery is amortized over 10 years at $7,500 per year.

**3.** The depreciation expense relating to the machinery sold intercompany must be adjusted. Parent recorded $13,000 of depreciation on the asset during 20X10, but the depreciation based on the cost of the machinery to Sub is only $10,000. Therefore, depreciation expense must be reduced by $3,000$^U$.

■ *Non-controlling interest in earnings of Sub Ltd.* Exhibit 6.5 shows that Sub's separate-entity net income is $189,000. Parent has equity in only 80% of this amount. The remaining 20% is equity of the non-controlling interest. Before taking the 20%, we must adjust Sub's separate-entity earnings for the realized and unrealized profits from upstream sales. There are four adjustments.

**1.** Parent's opening inventory contains $100,000$^U$ of goods that had been purchased from Sub. The gross profit percentage was 40%, which yields an unrealized gross profit at the beginning of the year of $100,000 \times 40\% = \$40,000$^U$. This amount has been sold to outsiders, and therefore has now been realized. We must add the $40,000$^U$ in now-realized profit to Sub's nominal earnings.

**2.** Parent's *ending* inventory contains unrealized profit of $70,000 \times 40\% = \$28,000$^U$. We must subtract this amount from Sub's separate-entity net income.

**3.** Parent also is depreciating the machinery that had been purchased from Sub in 20X4. Parent's depreciation is $91,000 \div 7 = \$13,000$. Depreciation based on the historical cost of the asset to Sub would have been $100,000 \div 10 = \$10,000$. Parent has charged an extra $3,000$^U$ in depreciation. Remember that amortization or depreciation constitutes recognition of the benefits of using a capital asset. Therefore, the extra $3,000$^U$ represents the realization of part of the previously unrealized intercompany profit. This $3,000$^U$ is added to Sub's nominal net income.

**4.** The fair value increment of $75,000 allocated to machinery at the time of acquisition is being amortized over 10 years. Therefore, an extra amortization expense of $7,500 should be added to the other expense line item.

After these four adjustments are made, we can simply multiply the result by 20% to find the non-controlling interest's share of the Sub earnings that are included in Parent's consolidated net income.

■ *Retained earnings.* Once the net income for the year has been determined, the ending retained earnings can be calculated. First, however, we must determine the consolidated retained earnings at the beginning of the current year, January 1, 20X10. The opening balance of retained earnings will include Parent's separate-entity retained earnings, plus Parent's share of Sub's retained earnings *since the date of acquisition*, plus and minus adjustments for amortization, unrealized profits, and sale of fair-valued assets. The opening retained earnings on January 1, 20X10, on the separate-entity financial statements of Parent Corp. is $2,395,000. It needs to be adjusted for Parent's Corp.'s share of the adjusted change in retained earnings of Sub Ltd. of $21,200. We will provide the calculations leading to the $21,200 amount accompanied by detailed explanations later in the chapter in the section titled "Check." Therefore, we will not provide the calculations or explanations here.

■ *Dividends declared.* Parent's consolidated statements show only the dividends paid by Parent Corp.

Note that there is no need to adjust for the royalties paid by Sub to Parent prior to the beginning of 20X10. The $500,000 in prior-year royalties has reduced Sub's retained earnings, but has increased Parent's retained earnings by the same amount. On consolidation, the effects are directly offsetting. No adjustment needs to be made for intercompany expenses in prior years, only for unrealized profits.

**Statement of Financial Position**   Exhibit 6.7 shows the consolidated statement of financial position for Parent Corp. at December 31, 20X10. Cash, accounts receivable, investments, and accounts payable are simply the sum of the two companies' balances. The common share amount is for Parent only, since this is Parent's statement of financial position. The calculations of the other amounts are summarized below.

- *Inventories*. The inventories are reduced by the full amount of the unrealized earnings in the ending inventories, both downstream ($16,000$_D$) and upstream ($28,000$^U$). In addition, we added and subtracted the acquisition-related FVA allocated to inventory.

- *Machinery*. First, we must offset Sub's accumulated depreciation at the date of acquisition ($575,000) against the asset account. Then we add the fair value increment of $75,000. This adjustment assumes that all of the machinery to which the fair value increment applies is still held by Sub.

   Next, we must adjust for the intercompany sale of machinery. The total upstream unrealized profit of $21,000$^U$ is deducted to reduce the carrying value of the machinery from the $91,000 reflected on Parent's books to the $70,000 net carrying value that had been on Sub's books. However, the machinery should not be shown in the consolidated machinery account at its net carrying value to Sub at the time of the intercompany sale, but rather at the full historical cost ($100,000) to Sub. Therefore, the $30,000$^U$ accumulated depreciation that existed on Sub's books at the time of the sale must be restored; $30,000$^U$ is added to the machinery account and is also added to the accumulated depreciation account, below.

- *Accumulated depreciation*. First, Sub's accumulated depreciation at the date of Parent's acquisition ($575,000) is eliminated. Next, the amortization of the fair value increment over the six years between the date of acquisition and the current statement of financial position date is added ($7,500 × 6 = $45,000). In addition, the accumulated depreciation of $30,000$^U$ that existed on the machinery sold intercompany is restored, as explained in the preceding paragraph. Deducted from accumulated depreciation is three years' annual depreciation adjustment on the intercompany machinery sale (3 years @ $3,000 per year = $9,000$^U$).

- *Non-controlling interest*. The non-controlling interest starts out as 20% of Sub's net assets (i.e., shareholders' equity) at the statement of financial position date. On December 31, 20X10, Sub's net assets amount to $1,040,000. The non-controlling interest's share of the net asset value at 20% is $208,000. From that amount we must subtract the non-controlling interest's share of the unrealized profit from the upstream sales at the end of the year: $70,000 × 40% × 20% = $5,600$^U$.

   Also, we must deduct the non-controlling interest's share of the remaining unrealized profit from the upstream sale of machinery. Three years have elapsed since the sale, leaving 4/7 of the profit unrealized: $21,000 × 4/7 × 20% = $2,400$^U$.

   Finally, we should allocate to the NCI its share of the time-of-acquisition FVAs that are still unamortized by the end of 20X10. From the **A**mortize step we know that

**Exhibit 6.7** Parent Corp.

| Condensed Consolidated Statement of Financial Position, December 31, 20X10 | |
| --- | --- |
| **ASSETS** | |
| Current assets | |
| Cash [50,000 + 20,000] | $ 70,000 |
| Accounts receivable [150,000 + 160,000] | 310,000 |
| Inventories [180,000 + 100,000 + (10,000 – 10,000) – 16,000$_D$ – 28,000$^U$] | 236,000 |
| | 616,000 |
| Capital assets | |
| Machinery [5,000,000 + 2,700,000 – 575,000 + 75,000 – 21,000$^U$ + 30,000$^U$] | 7,209,000 |
| Accumulated depreciation [1,770,000 + 1,240,000 – 575,000 + (7,500 × 6) + 30,000$^U$ – (3,000 × 3)$^U$] | (2,501,000) |
| | 4,708,000 |
| Other assets | |
| Investments [800,000 + 100,000 + 0 – 800,000 + (10,000 – 10,000)] | 100,000 |
| Goodwill | 50,000 |
| | 150,000 |
| **TOTAL ASSETS** | $ 5,474,000 |
| **LIABILITIES AND SHAREHOLDERS' EQUITY** | |
| Liabilities: | |
| Current: accounts payable [450,000 + 200,000] | $ 650,000 |
| Long-term: bonds payable [300,000 + 500,000] | 800,000 |
| Total liabilities | 1,450,000 |
| **EQUITY** | |
| Common shares [Parent Corp. shares only] | 1,200,000 |
| Retained earnings [see calculation later in text] | 2,608,000 |
| | 3,808,000 |
| Non-controlling interest in Sub Ltd. [1,040,000 – (70,000 × 40%) (21,000 × 4/7) + 80,000] × 20% | 216,000 |
| Total equity | 4,024,000 |
| **TOTAL LIABILITIES AND SHAREHOLDERS' EQUITY** | $ 5,474,000 |

the unamortized FVA balance is $80,000. The NCI share therefore is $16,000. After accounting for all the adjustments, the ending NCI balance is $216,000. Note that we will use a different calculation while checking the NCI balance later in the chapter. This has been done deliberately and is aimed at improving your understanding of the concepts underlying the consolidation process.

- *Retained earnings.* The year-end retained earnings could be obtained from Exhibit 6.6, but that would take all the fun out of our consolidation! Instead, you should attempt to derive the year-end consolidated retained earnings directly. The year-end consolidated retained earnings consists of:

1. the parent's year-end separate-entity retained earnings;
2. plus the subsidiary's year-end separate-entity retained earnings;
3. minus the subsidiary's date-of-acquisition retained earnings;
4. minus the non-controlling interests' share of the subsidiary's retained earnings *since the date of acquisition*;
5. less the cumulative amortization on fair value adjustments from the date of acquisition to the current year-end; and
6. less unrealized profits (net of non-controlling interest, where appropriate) at the *end* of the year.

We will illustrate the independent derivation of the ending consolidated retained earnings balance in the following section.

**Check**   The NCI and consolidated retained earnings balances have been calculated below to provide independent checks of our calculations of these balances on the SFP. We will first calculate the opening NCI and consolidated retained earnings and next calculate the ending NCI and consolidated retained earnings:

| NCI Balance at the Beginning of 20X10 | | |
|---|---|---|
| Balance of NCI at the time of acquisition | | $  200,000 |
| Add: NCI's share of the adjusted change in retained earnings in prior years | | |
| Retained earnings balance of Sub Ltd. at the end of 20X9 | $641,000 | |
| Retained earnings balance of Sub Ltd. at the time of acquisition | 555,000 | |
| Change in carrying value of Sub Ltd. in previous years* | 86,000 | |
| Less: | | |
| Total of cumulative adjustments pertaining to previous years | (112,500) | |
| Adjusted change in retained earnings of Sub Ltd. in prior years | (26,500) | |
| NCI's share @ 20% | | (5,300) |
| Opening balance of NCI on Jan. 1, 20X10 | | $  194,700 |

*See calculations under previous section titled "Recognize NCI Share of Prior Years' Earnings."

| Opening Consolidated Retained Earnings Balance at the Beginning of 20X10 | | |
|---|---|---|
| Opening retained earnings balance from separate-entity financial statements of Parent Corp. on Jan. 1, 20X0 | | $2,395,000 |
| Add: Parent Corp.'s share of the adjusted change in retained earnings in prior years: | | |
| Adjusted change in retained earnings of Sub Ltd. in prior years (as calculated in the section just above) | (26,500) | |
| Parent Corp.'s share @ 80% | | (21,200) |
| Unrealized gain on downstream sale of inventory in 20X9 | | (8,000) |
| Opening consolidated retained earnings balance on Jan. 1, 20X10 | | $2,365,800 |

**Exhibit 6.8** Ending NCI and Retained Earnings Balance at the End of 20X10

| NCI Balance at the End of 20X10 | |
|---|---:|
| Balance of NCI at the beginning of 20X0 | $ 194,700 |
| Add: NCI's share of Sub Ltd.'s adjusted net income in 20X10 | 39,300 |
| Less: NCI's share of dividends declared by Sub Ltd. in 20X10 | (18,000) |
| Ending balance of NCI in 20X10 | $ 216,000 |

| Consolidated Retained Earnings Balance at the End of 20X10 | | |
|---|---:|---:|
| 20X10 separate-entity ending retained earnings balance of Parent Corp. | | $2,560,000 |
| Less unrealized profit on downstream sale of inventory | | (16,000) |
| Less dividend income from Sub Ltd. | | (72,000) |
| Add realized profit on downstream sale of inventory in 20X9 | | 8,000 |
| Adjusted separate-entity retained earnings balance of Parent Corp. | | 2,480,000 |
| Add: Parent Corp.'s share of the adjusted change in retained earnings in prior years: | | |
| Adjusted change in retained earnings of Sub Ltd. in prior years | $ (26,500) | |
| Parent Corp.'s share @ 80% | | (21,200) |
| Less: Unrealized gain on downstream sale of inventory in 20X9 | | (8,000) |
| Add Parent Corp.'s share of Sub Ltd.'s adjusted Income: | | |
| Adjusted net income of Sub Ltd. for 20X10* | 196,500 | |
| Parent Corp.'s share @ 80% | | 157,200 |
| 20X10 ending consolidated retained earnings balance of Parent Corp. | | $2,608,000 |

\* See calculations in previous section titled "Recognize NCI Share of Current Year Earnings."

The calculations of the ending NCI and consolidated retained earnings are provided in Exhibit 6.8.

# Parent-Company Extension Method

The SFP under the parent-company extension method differs from the SFP under the entity method in two respects—the balances of (1) goodwill and (2) non-controlling interest. Under the parent-company extension method, only the parent's portion of the goodwill is reported on the consolidated SFP, while the NCI balance does not include its share of the goodwill. In our example, therefore, under the parent-company extension method, at the time of acquisition the goodwill balance will be $40,000 instead of $50,000 and the NCI balance will be $190,000 instead of $200,000.

Since there was no impairment in the value of goodwill during 20X10, the statements of comprehensive income under both methods will be identical. Further, since there was no impairment in the value of goodwill from the time of acquisition until the end of 20X10, the same $10,000 difference will persist at the 20X10 year-end on the SFP. Therefore, on December 31, 20X10, under the parent-company extension method the goodwill balance will remain at $40,000, while the NCI balance will be $206,000 instead of $216,000.

## Worksheet Approach

As usual, for the illustration of how the worksheet approach applies to our example, please refer to the Companion Website.

**LO ❸**

Report non-consolidated subsidiaries and investment in associates and jointly controlled entities under the equity basis in the years after the initial investment

## 6.3 EQUITY-BASIS REPORTING

To determine Parent's equity in Sub's 20X10 earnings, we start with Parent's 80% share of Sub's reported net income of $189,000, or $151,200. This amount must then be adjusted for (1) amortization of fair value adjustments; (2) previously unrealized profits now realized in 20X10; and (3) unrealized profits at the end of 20X10. The top section of Exhibit 6.9 illustrates the necessary calculations.

After making all the necessary adjustments, including the adjustment relating to the "excess" depreciation taken on the machinery that had been sold intercompany, Parent's equity in Sub's earnings is $149,200. If we take this amount and add it to Parent's net income less the dividends received from Sub, we obtain $542,200, which is exactly the same as the consolidated net income derived in Exhibit 6.6.

| | |
|---|---|
| Parent separate-entity net income (Exhibit 6.5) | $465,000 |
| Less dividends received from Sub | (72,000) |
| Plus equity in earnings of Sub (Exhibit 6.9) | 149,200 |
| Consolidated net income | $542,200 |

At the end of 20X10, Parent's investment in Sub should amount to:

1. the original purchase price to acquire the 80% share;

2. plus 80% of the increase in Sub's retained earnings since the date of acquisition;

3. less amortization and realization of fair value adjustments and goodwill between the date of acquisition and year-end 20X10; and

4. less any unrealized profits at year-end 20X10.

The lower section of Exhibit 6.9 illustrates this calculation.

The equity method is useful for double-checking the results of the consolidation process. The increase in the balance of the investment account added to the parent company's separate-entity retained earnings must equal the consolidated retained earnings. For this example:

($848,000 − $800,000) + $2,560,000 = $2,608,000.

**Exhibit 6.9** Parent Corp.'s Equity in the Earnings of Sub Ltd.

| December 31, 20X10 | | |
|---|---|---|
| **Parent Corp.'s Equity in the Earnings of Sub Ltd.** | | |
| Parent's share of Sub's reported net income [$189,000 × 80%] | | $151,200 |
| Adjustments: | | |
| Amortization of fair value adjustment: | | |
| Machinery [$7,500 × 80%] | | ($6,000) |
| Unrealized profit in opening inventories: | | |
| Downstream [$8,000 × 100%] | 8,000 | |
| Upstream [$40,000 × 80%] | 32,000 | 40,000 |
| Unrealized profit in ending inventories: | | |
| Downstream [$16,000 × 100%] | (16,000) | |
| Upstream [$28,000 × 80%] | (22,400) | (38,400) |
| Profit realized through depreciation on machinery sold inter-company [$3,000 × 80%] | | 2,400 |
| **Parent Corp.'s equity in the 20X10 earnings of Sub Ltd.** | | **$149,200** |
| **Parent Corp.'s investment in Sub Ltd.** | | |
| Initial investment (cost) | | $800,000 |
| Equity in unremitted earnings (net of dividends received from Sub): | | |
| Parent's share of the change in Sub's retained earnings since the date of acquisition [$740,000 - $555,000] × 80% | | 148,000 |
| Less amortization of fair value adjustments through 20X10: | | |
| Inventories (80% of the amount realized) | $(8,000) | |
| Investments (80% of the amount realized) | (8,000) | |
| Machinery [$75,000 × 80% × 6/10] | (36,000) | (52,000) |
| Less remaining unrealized profits, December 31, 20X10: | | |
| Inventory, downstream [$16,000 × 100%] | (16,000) | |
| Inventory, upstream [$28,000 × 80%] | (22,400) | |
| Machinery [$21,000 × 80% × 4/7] | (9,600) | (48,000) |
| **Investment in Sub Ltd. (equity basis), December 31, 20X10** | | **$848,000** |

# Equity-Basis Reporting of Investment in Associate/Interest in Joint Venture

Recall from Chapter 5 that IFRS requires application of the proprietary theory when reporting investments in associates and joint ventures under the equity method. Therefore, Parent's equity in the 20X10 earnings of Sub Ltd. and the balance in its investment in Sub Ltd. account on December 31, 20X10, will both be different if Sub Ltd. is an associate or joint venture of Parent Corp. rather than a subsidiary.

The difference will stem from the difference in treatment accorded to the realized and unrealized gains/losses arising from downstream sales. Using the entity method, 100% of downstream unrealized and realized gains/losses are attributed to Parent Corp. when Sub Ltd. is its subsidiary. In contrast, using the proprietary method, only 80% of the unrealized and realized gains/losses are attributed to Parent Corp. when Sub Ltd. is instead Parent's associate or is a joint venture. These differences and their impact on the equity in the earnings of Sub Ltd. and Parent Corp.'s investment in Sub Ltd. account, respectively, are summarized below.

| | |
|---|---:|
| Parent's equity in the 20X10 earnings of Sub Ltd. | $149,200 |
| Reversal of difference due to 100% instead of 80% adjustment relating to unrealized profit in opening inventories [$8,000 × (100% − 80%)] | (1,600) |
| Reversal of difference due to 100% instead of 80% adjustment relating to unrealized profit in ending inventories [$16,000 × (100% − 80%)] | 3,200 |
| Parent Corp.'s equity in the 20X10 earnings of associate/ joint venture | $150,800 |
| Investment in Sub Ltd. (equity basis), December 31, 20X10 | $848,000 |
| Reversal of 100% instead of 80% adjustment relating to unrealized profit in ending inventories [$16,000 × (100% − 80%)] | 3,200 |
| Investment in associate/joint venture (equity basis), December 31, 20X10 | $851,200 |

**LO ④**
Consolidate subsidiaries that have been recorded using the equity method

## 6.4 CONSOLIDATION WITH EQUITY-BASIS RECORDING

Throughout this book, we have focused on consolidation when the parent company records its investment in the subsidiary at cost. This is the normal practice, since the cost method simplifies both parent-company bookkeeping and parent-company consolidation.

If the parent *records* its investment on the equity basis instead of the cost basis, the consolidation process must be modified accordingly. This is not a big problem. The only differences in the parent's separate-entity accounts between cost-basis and equity-basis reporting are that:

■ the investment account includes the parent's share of the subsidiary's unremitted earnings to date (that is, the subsidiary's accumulated net incomes since the date of acquisition minus the dividends paid) in addition to the cost of the acquisition;

■ the parent's opening retained earnings includes the cumulative amount of unremitted earnings to the beginning of the year;

■ "Equity in earnings of subsidiary" will appear on the parent's separate-entity statement of comprehensive income; and

■ the parent will show no dividend income from the subsidiary.

To prepare consolidated statements when the parent uses the equity basis of recording the investment, we must first remove the effects of the equity basis from the parent's accounts or trial balance. Once that is done, we can consolidate the accounts exactly as we have above.

**Exhibit 6.10** Comparison of Cost-Basis Versus Equity-Basis Recording of Investment

**Parent Corp. Statement of Financial Position December 31, 20X10**

| | Cost | Equity | Difference Debit/(Credit) |
|---|---|---|---|
| ASSETS | | | |
| Cash | $ 50,000 | $ 50,000 | |
| Accounts receivable | 150,000 | 150,000 | |
| Inventories | 180,000 | 180,000 | |
| Machinery | 5,000,000 | 5,000,000 | |
| Accumulated depreciation | (1,770,000) | (1,770,000) | |
| Investment in Sub Ltd. | 800,000 | 848,000 | $ 48,000 |
| Other investments | 100,000 | 100,000 | |
| TOTAL ASSETS | $4,510,000 | $4,558,000 | |
| LIABILITIES AND SHAREHOLDERS' EQUITY | | | |
| Accounts payable | $ 450,000 | $ 450,000 | |
| Bonds payable | 300,000 | 300,000 | |
| Total liabilities | 750,000 | 750,000 | |
| Common shares | 1,200,000 | 1,200,000 | |
| Retained earnings | 2,560,000 | 2,608,000 | $ 48,000 |
| Total shareholders' equity | 3,760,000 | 3,808,000 | |
| TOTAL LIABILITIES AND SHAREHOLDERS' EQUITY | $4,510,000 | $4,558,000 | |

**Statement of Comprehensive Income**
**Year Ended December 31, 20X10**

| | Cost | Equity | |
|---|---|---|---|
| Sales revenue | $2,000,000 | $2,000,000 | |
| Royalty revenue | 150,000 | 150,000 | |
| Dividend income | 75,000 | 3,000 | $ 72,000 |
| Equity in earnings of Sub Ltd. | — | 149,200 | $(149,200) |
| Total revenue | 2,225,000 | 2,302,200 | |
| Cost of sales | 1,200,000 | 1,200,000 | |
| Other expenses | 560,000 | 560,000 | |
| Total expenses | 1,760,000 | 1,760,000 | |
| Net income and comprehensive income | $ 465,000 | $ 542,200 | |

**Statement of Changes in Equity—Retained Earnings Section**
**Year Ended December 31, 20X10**

| | | | |
|---|---|---|---|
| Retained earnings, beginning of year | $2,395,000 | $2,365,800 | $ 29,200 |
| Net income | 465,000 | 542,200 | |
| Dividends declared | (300,000) | (300,000) | |
| Retained earnings, end of year | $2,560,000 | $2,608,000 | |

Exhibit 6.10 shows Parent Corp.'s separate-entity financial statements for 20X10 using both the cost method and the equity method. The accounts that show a difference are set in boldface. All other accounts are the same regardless of which recording method is used.

The first step in consolidation when Parent uses the equity basis of recording its investment is simply to reverse the differences between the two bases by undoing the equity recording. Using the amounts in the "difference" column of Exhibit 6.10, the reversal requires us to make the following changes:

| | | |
|---|---|---|
| Equity in earnings of Sub Ltd. | Decrease by | $149,200 |
| Investment in Sub Ltd. | Decrease by | $ 48,000 |
| Dividend income | Increase by | $ 72,000 |
| Retained earnings (opening) | Increase by | $ 29,200 |

A slight variation is to leave the subsidiary's dividends received in the equity in earnings account, since they will be eliminated in the consolidation process anyway:

| | | |
|---|---|---|
| Equity in earnings of Sub Ltd. | Decrease by | $77,200 |
| Investment in Sub Ltd. | Decrease by | $48,000 |
| Retained earnings (opening) | Increase by | $29,200 |

Either adjustment will work equally well. The equity-reversal entry can be made either before starting the consolidation process by adjusting the parent's separate-entity accounts, or by entering the reversing amounts in the consolidation working papers—either direct method or worksheet approach—as the first step after entering the separate-entity amounts.

## 6.5 A FINAL WORD

Since we are now at the end of the consolidation-related chapters, it is worthwhile to see what empirical research has to say about the usefulness of consolidated statements. Reality Check 6–1 provides findings from academic studies on the usefulness of consolidated statements and the value relevance of NCI reporting.

## Relevant Standards

### IFRS

**IFRS 3**   Business Combinations
**IFRS 10**   Consolidated Financial Statements
**IFRS 11**   Joint Arrangements
**IAS 28**   Investments in Associates
**IAS 36**   Impairment of Assets

## 6.6 SUMMARY OF KEY POINTS

1. When amortizable capital assets are sold between related companies, any unrealized profit must be eliminated. Intercompany losses on unrealized sales may or may not be eliminated, depending on whether the loss reflects a true decline in the recoverable benefit of the asset. The amount of *unrealized* profit declines as the asset is amortized because amortization reflects the use of the asset and thus the realization of its benefits. **LO 1**

2. For downstream sales, the full amount of unrealized profit is eliminated if such sales are to a controlled entity and only to the extent of the investor's share if such sales are to an associate or joint venture. For upstream sales (or lateral sales between subsidiaries/associates/joint ventures), the non-controlling interest absorbs its share of

unrealized profit in the case of sales from controlled entities, and unrealized gains are eliminated only to the extent of the investor's share in the case of sales from associates or joint ventures. **LO 1**

3. An asset that was acquired via an intercompany sale may be sold to an outside third party. When that happens, any remaining unrealized gain must be combined with the recorded gain or loss on the sale. **LO 1**

4. In general, consolidation adjustments fall into three categories: (1) acquisition adjustments; (2) cumulative operations adjustments; and (3) current operations adjustments. For problems that are to be solved by a student, these three may be combined to arrive at a year-end statement of financial position or a single-year statement of comprehensive income. In practice, however, comparative statements are always required, and the distinction between beginning and ending statement of financial position amounts must be preserved. **LO 2**

5. The acquisition adjustments stay the same over time. There is no need to alter them, although they may be modified to reflect changes in asset structure, such as the disposition of fair-valued assets that were acquired but no longer held. In effect, this is a combination of acquisition and cumulative adjustments. **LO 2**

6. The theory underlying the cumulative operations adjustments is that date-of-acquisition balances must be updated to reflect amortizations and intercompany transactions to the *beginning* of the reporting year. Amounts such as opening inventories and opening retained earnings must be correctly stated. **LO 2**

7. Current operations adjustments have two basic functions: (1) to correctly state consolidated end-of-period balances and (2) to adjust the year's earnings to reflect only transactions with non-related entities. **LO 2**

8. Equity-basis reporting of subsidiaries will result in the same parent-company net income and retained earnings as will consolidation. Calculations for equity-basis earnings therefore can provide a useful check on the accuracy of consolidated results. **LO 3**

9. If the parent company records its investment on the equity basis, the first step in consolidation is to reverse the impact of the entity-basis adjustments. Then, consolidation can proceed as has been described throughout this book. **LO 4**

Visit the text's website at www.pearsoned.ca/beechy **for practice quizzes, additional problems, Excel® templates, answers to Concept Check questions, and important IFRS updates.**

# Self-Study Problems

**1.** Sparrow Limited is an 80%-owned subsidiary of Parks Corporation, a manufacturer of industrial equipment. In 20X7, Sparrow purchased a grummling machine from Parks for $100,000. Parks had manufactured the machine at a cost of $60,000. Sparrow uses straight-line depreciation over a 10-year period for its grummling machines, and follows the practice of depreciating its assets by one-half year in both the year of acquisition and the year of disposal. No residual value is assumed. Single-asset accounting (that is, not group depreciation) is used. Sparrow used the machine in its productive operations from 20X7 to 20X0, in which year it was sold for scrap for $1,000.

## Required

Prepare the adjustments that would be necessary in each of 20X7, 20X8, 20X12, 20X19, and 20X20 for the grummling machine when preparing Parks Corporation's consolidated financial statements.

**2.** On January 1, 20X5, Power Corporation purchased 80% of the outstanding shares of Spencer Corporation for $2,500,000 in cash. On that date, Spencer Corporation's common shares had a carrying value of $2,000,000 and the company had retained earnings of $1,000,000. On January 1, 20X5, all of Spencer's identifiable assets and liabilities had fair values that were equal to their carrying values except for:

**a.** a building that had an estimated fair value of $600,000 less than its carrying value; its remaining useful life was estimated to be 10 years; and

**b.** a long-term liability with a fair value of $500,000 less than its carrying value; the liability matures on December 31, 20X12.

The statements of comprehensive income of Power Corporation and Spencer Corporation for the year ended December 31, 20X9, are shown in Exhibit 6.11. Additional information is as follows:

**a.** On January 1, 20X6, Spencer sold a machine to Power for $210,000. Spencer originally paid $400,000 for the machine on January 2, 20X1. At the original date of purchase by Spencer, the machine had an estimated useful life of 20 years, with no estimated residual value. There has been no change in these estimates—the machine still retains its value in use.

**b.** Both companies use the straight-line method for all depreciation and amortization.

**Exhibit 6.11** Separate-Entity Statements of Comprehensive Income

| Year Ended December 31, 20X9 | Power | Spencer |
|---|---|---|
| Sales | $2,000,000 | $900,000 |
| Investment income | 1,000,000 | 100,000 |
| Gain on sale of land | — | 68,000 |
| Total revenue | 3,000,000 | 1,068,000 |
| Cost of goods sold | 1,300,000 | 500,000 |
| Other operating expenses | 960,000 | 320,000 |
| Total expenses | 2,260,000 | 820,000 |
| Net income and comprehensive income | $ 740,000 | $248,000 |

**c.** During 20X8, the following intercompany inventory sales occurred:

- Power sold $500,000 of merchandise to Spencer, $100,000 of which is in Spencer's inventory at 20X8 year-end.

- Spencer sold $300,000 of merchandise to Power, $70,000 of which is in Power's inventory at the end of 20X8.

**d.** During 20X9, the following intercompany inventory sales occurred:

- Power sold $400,000 of merchandise to Spencer, $90,000 of which is in Spencer's inventory at 20X9 year-end.

- Spencer sold $250,000 of merchandise to Power, $60,000 of which is in Power's inventory at the end of 20X9.

**e.** Intercompany inventory transactions are priced to provide Power with 30% gross margin (on sales price) and Spencer with 40% gross profit (on sales). Both companies use the first-in first-out inventory cost flow assumption.

**f.** On September 1, 20X9, Spencer sold a parcel of land to Power Company for $133,000 that it had originally purchased for $65,000.

**g.** During 20X9, Power declared and paid $250,000 in dividends, while Spencer declared and paid $40,000 in dividends.

**h.** Power accounts for its investment in Spencer on the cost basis.

**i.** There was no impairment of goodwill at the end of 20X9.

Required

**a.** Prepare a consolidated SCI for Power Corporation for the year ended December 31, 20X9. Show supporting calculations for each amount in the consolidated SCI.

**b.** Independently, calculate Power Corporation's net income using equity-basis reporting. [SMA, adapted]

## Review Questions

1. Under what conditions is a profit on an intercompany sale considered to be *unrealized*?

2. A capital asset is sold by a subsidiary to its parent company at the asset's fair market value, which is less than the asset's carrying value on the subsidiary's books. Would the unrealized loss on the sale be eliminated upon consolidation? Explain.

3. Company P owns 60% of Company S1 and 90% of Company S2. S1 sells inventory to S2 at a profit of $20,000. All the goods are still in S2's inventory at year-end. By what amount should consolidated net income be adjusted to eliminate the unrealized profit?

4. Company IR owns 30% of Company IE1 and 40% of Company IE2. IE1 sells inventory to IE2 at a profit of $20,000. All the goods are still in IE2's inventory at year-end. By what amount should IR's equity-basis investment income be adjusted to eliminate the unrealized profit?

5. In what way is the profit on intercompany sales of depreciable assets *realized*?

6. What happens if a company sells a long-lived asset that is part of its *inventory* to another company in the consolidated group instead of one that is shown as a *capital asset* on the books of the selling company?

7. How does the adjustment differ when there is a sale of an intangible asset, for example, a patent with limited life, instead of a capital asset from the subsidiary to the parent?

8. Explain the composition of consolidated retained earnings in terms of the parent's and subsidiary's separate-entity retained earnings.

9. When a fair-valued asset is sold by a subsidiary to its parent, how does the amount of the fair value adjustment affect the unrealized profit elimination?

10. When a fair-valued asset is sold to outsiders, what is the disposition of the fair value adjustment when the statements are consolidated in the year of the sale? What is the disposition of the increment in years following the sale?

11. Explain briefly how the process of consolidation differs when the equity method is used by the parent for recording the investment account as compared with the cost method.

12. What does the equity-basis balance of the investment account for a subsidiary represent (e.g., cost of the investment, market value of the investment)?

13. Under equity reporting, why are unrealized profits from *downstream* sales deducted from the investor's equity in the earnings of the investee instead of from the parent's own earnings?

## 6.7 CASES

## CASE 6-1 INTERNATIONAL CONSOLIDATORS INC.

Your friend is a financial analyst whose accounting knowledge is virtually nonexistent. Your friend believes that financial analysts take companies' financial statements at face value, disregarding in their analysis the implications of the consolidation-related adjustments and management's accounting choices in preparing the company's consolidated statements. Given your strong advanced accounting background, you find this purported practice naive to say the least.

Recently, you met with your friend over coffee and the conversation slowly drifted to his work. He indicated that he had been following the performance of International Consolidators Inc. (ICI). ICI had acquired 80% of the shares of Prime Target Inc. (PTI) on December 31, 20X5, for $3,220,000 by issuing shares. PTI appeared to be an ideal acquisition given that its return on year-end equity was 20.42% for 20X5. The return on equity for ICI on the same basis for 20X5 was 10.69%. The statement of financial position of PTI on December 31, 20X5, the fair values of its identifiable assets and liabilities, and their future useful lives, where applicable, were as shown in Exhibit A:

---

### Exhibit A

**International Consolidators Inc.**
**Statement of Financial Position, Fair Values, and Future Useful Lives**
**December 31, 20X5**

| | Carrying | Fair value | Future useful lives |
|---|---|---|---|
| **ASSETS** | | | |
| Cash | $ 75,000 | $ 75,000 | |
| Inventory | 75,000 | 150,000 | |
| Accounts receivables | 200,000 | 375,000 | |
| Buildings | 500,000 | 600,000 | 10 years |
| Accumulated depreciation—buildings | (300,000) | | |
| Plant & equipment | 800,000 | 700,000 | 10 years |
| Accumulated depreciation—plant & equipment | (400,000) | | |
| Land | 500,000 | 1,500,000 | |
| Patents | — | 750,000 | 10 years |
| **TOTAL ASSETS** | $1,450,000 | $4,150,000 | |
| **LIABILITIES & OWNERS' EQUITY** | | | |
| Accounts payable | $ 200,000 | $ 200,000 | |
| Long-term debt | 300,000 | 400,000 | 10 years |
| Contributed capital | 500,000 | — | |
| Retained earnings | 450,000 | — | |
| **TOTAL LIABILITIES & OWNERS' EQUITY** | $1,450,000 | $ 600,000 | |

---

## Exhibit B

### International Consolidators Inc.
### Consolidated Statement of Comprehensive Income
### Year Ended December 31, 20X7

| | |
|---|---:|
| Sales revenue | $6,668,220 |
| | (2,652,796) |
| COGS | |
| Gross profit | 4,015,424 |
| Dividend income | $ 0 |
| Amortization expense | (365,000) |
| Administrative & interest expenses | (1,109,404) |
| Selling & marketing expenses | (1,643,530) |
| Loss on goodwill impairment | (300,000) |
| Income tax expense | (209,098) |
| Net income and comprehensive income | $ 388,392 |
| Allocated to: | |
| Shareholders of ICI | $ 427,125 |
| Non-controlling interest | $ (38,733) |

### Consolidated Statement of Changes in Equity—Retained Earnings Section December 31, 20X7

| | |
|---|---:|
| Retained earnings, beginning of year | $1,386,732 |
| Net income attributable to shareholders of ICI | 427,125 |
| Dividends for the year | (200,000) |
| Retained earnings, end of year | $1,613,857 |

### Consolidated Statement of Financial Position December 31, 20X7

| Assets | |
|---|---:|
| Cash | $ 515,202 |
| Inventory | 252,000 |
| Accounts receivable | 555,000 |
| Buildings | 2,100,000 |
| Accumulated depreciation—buildings | (990,000) |
| Plant & equipment | 2,700,000 |
| Accumulated depreciation—plant & equipment | (1,540,000) |
| Land | 3,250,000 |
| Patents | 600,000 |
| Investment in Prime Target Inc. | 0 |
| Goodwill | |
| TOTAL ASSETS | $7,617,202 |

*Case Continued >*

## Liabilities & owners' equity

| | |
|---|---|
| Accounts payable | $ 422,510 |
| Long-term debt | 655,000 |
| Contributed capital | 4,220,000 |
| Retained earnings | 1,613,857 |
| NCI | 705,835 |
| **TOTAL LIABILITIES & OWNERS' EQUITY** | **$7,617,202** |

### Prime Target Inc.
### Statement of Comprehensive Income Year Ended December 31, 20X7

| | |
|---|---|
| Revenue | $3,749,200 |
| Cost of goods sold | (2,361,996) |
| Gross profit | 1,387,204 |
| Amortization expense | (50,000) |
| Administrative & interest expenses | (412,412) |
| Selling & marketing expenses | (612,500) |
| Income tax expense | (62,458) |
| Net income and comprehensive income | $ 249,834 |

### Statement of Financial Position December 31, 20X7

**Assets**

| | |
|---|---|
| Cash | $ 252,184 |
| Inventory | 80,000 |
| Accounts receivable | 225,000 |
| Buildings | 500,000 |
| Accumulated depreciation—buildings | (340,000) |
| Plant & equipment | 600,000 |
| Accumulated depreciation—plant & equipment | (360,000) |
| Land | 800,000 |
| **TOTAL ASSETS** | **$1,757,184** |

**Liabilities & owners' equity**

| | |
|---|---|
| Accounts payable | $172,510 |
| Long-term debt | 175,000 |
| Contributed capital | 500,000 |
| Retained earnings | 909,674 |
| **TOTAL LIABILITIES & OWNERS' EQUITY** | **$1,757,184** |

When ICI had acquired its controlling interest in PTI on December 31, 20X5, ICI management had touted the potential synergies between the two companies. It is now the end of 20X7, and your friend is clearly disappointed by the financial results presented in the consolidated financial statements issued by ICI under IFRS for 20X7. Your friend does not see the result of any synergy between the two companies in the consolidated financial statements, as provided in Exhibit B. He notes that the return on total year-end equity is an unimpressive 5.94%. You gently point out to him that he is disregarding the impact of accounting, especially consolidation-related accounting, on these numbers.

To this your friend counters, "Fair enough. I'd like for you to show me just what I'm overlooking. Here are the separate-entity financial statements of PTI for 20X7 and some other information that I've been able to gather about the two companies [Exhibit C]. Would you mind preparing the separate-entity financial statements of ICI

---

## Exhibit C

## ADDITIONAL INFORMATION

- On December 31, 20X5, the net identifiable assets of ICI had a fair value that was $2,275,000 greater than their net carrying value.
- Upstream sales from PTI to ICI during 20X7 = $1,499,680. Downstream sales from ICI to PTI during 20X7 = $1,472,900.
- PTI (subsidiary) declared and paid dividends of $50,000 in 20X6 and $60,000 in 20X7.
- ICI (parent) declared and paid dividends of $150,000 in 20X6 and $200,000 in 20X7.
- Inventory purchased from PTI (subsidiary) in ICI's (parent) 20X7 beginning inventory = $100,000. Inventory purchased from PTI (subsidiary) in ICI's (parent) 20X7 ending inventory = $150,000. PTI sold goods at the same gross profit percentage in both 20X6 and 20X7.
- Inventory purchased from ICI (parent) in PTI's 20X7 beginning inventory = $40,000. Inventory purchased from ICI (parent) in PTI's (subsidiary) 20X7 ending inventory = $50,000. ICI sold goods at the same gross profit percentage of 45% in both 20X6 and 20X7.
- On January 1, 20X6, PTI sold plant & equipment that on that date had an original cost of $200,000 and carrying value of $100,000 to ICI for $200,000. The plant & equipment also had a future useful life of 10 years on January 1, 20X6.
- PTI (subsidiary) purchased additional land from an outside party for $300,000 on January 1, 20X7.
- Due to impairment in 20X7, the value of goodwill relating to the purchase of PTI was worth $175,000 on December 31, 20X7.
- PTI is the sole subsidiary of ICI.
- Neither company purchased or sold any other buildings, plant and equipment, or land, or issued additional shares since ICI purchased its controlling interest in PTI.

(SCI, SFP, and statement of changes in equity—retained earnings section) under the cost method for 20X7 based on the information provided? I'd like to understand how the consolidation process affects ICI's financial results. Can you also give me some guidance as to the true economic operating results and financial position of the two companies?"

# CASE 6-2 ALRIGHT BEVERAGES LTD.

Alright Beverages Ltd. (ABL) was federally incorporated in 19X0. In the initial years, the company produced a cranberry drink that was for sale at sporting and entertainment events in eastern Canada. In 19X7, operations were expanded to include sales to bars, restaurants, and fast-food outlets. To penetrate additional markets, ABL started manufacturing a wide variety of fruit beverages and acquired the distributorship of another company's fruit concentrate. Sold under the brand name Fruit Brite, the fruit beverages were only moderately successful in terms of sales.

In 20X0, a management review indicated that while sales of the new fruit beverage line had increased, ABL's cost to manufacture the beverages was also greater than that of its competitors. Much of the profit was being made on the distribution of the fruit concentrate.

In an attempt to improve profitability, the company entered the retail market in 20X1. To finance the expansion, ABL obtained funds from two sources—namely, bank loans and its first public issue of shares. The funds were used to purchase a bottling plant in Toronto and to provide working capital during the first year of operation. The retail operation was administered by a newly incorporated, wholly owned subsidiary, Fruitbrite Flavours Ltd. (FFL). In the first year the company incurred a loss on its retail operations, but subsequent years were profitable.

FFL continued to expand until it had a nationwide bottling and distribution network. In major cities, the bottlers were wholly owned subsidiaries of FFL; in smaller cities, the bottlers were independents who bottled other products as well. In all cases, ABL sold its fruit concentrate to the bottlers.

In 20X4, ABL acquired 70% of the shares of Concentrated Vending Ltd. (CVL), a manufacturer of fruit beverage vending machines located in Windsor, Ontario. ABL purchased CVL at a price well below its proportionate carrying value, since CVL had encountered financial difficulties. ABL lent CVL funds to finance a plant modernization program. ABL contracted with the founders of CVL to continue as senior management, since ABL had no experience in the equipment manufacturing industry. The management contract stipulated that a bonus would be paid, amounting to 20% of CVL's income before taxes, in each of the next five consecutive years. Although the plant modernization was successful, CVL had difficulty selling enough machines to achieve a break-even point.

Sales of fruit beverages through vending machines were growing rapidly with the increased awareness of the importance of a healthier lifestyle. This was a segment of the market in which the ABL group did not participate. Therefore, early in 20X6, ABL created a wholly owned subsidiary, VendSell Ltd. (VSL). VSL buys the machines from CVL at regular retail price and then sells them to local operators with the condition that only ABL products be sold in the machines. The intent was to place machines in as many locations as possible.

VSL sells the majority of machines under conditional sales contracts, in which the buyer agrees to make an initial payment of $500 and payments of $75 per month for the next 48 months, for a total of $4,100. Machine maintenance is the responsibility of the operator. The payment plan was devised with three objectives in mind:

1. to place the maximum number of machines by offering an easy payment plan;

2. to defer payment of income tax by deducting the full cost of the machines when sold and deferring recognition of the revenue until the cash was collected; and

3. to ensure that only ABL products were used during the payment period, since title to the machine would not transfer until all payments had been made.

The fruit concentrate for the machines is purchased by the local operators from the bottler in the particular area, who in turn had purchased the fruit concentrate from ABL. The operator is charged an amount equal to the cost to the bottler plus 20%.

During 20X6, VSL expects to buy 8,000 machines from CVL at a price of $5,000 each. The machines currently cost CVL $3,000 each to manufacture. This cost to CVL is significantly lower than in previous years. To supply VSL, the volume of production in 20X6 is expected to be twice that of 20X5. As a result, CVL expects to show a profit in 20X6.

By the end of 20X6, VSL expects to sell 6,800 machines. The revenue from initial payments will amount to $3,400,000, and VSL expects to receive total revenues of $5,100,000 from initial payments and instalments in 20X6.

In its annual report for 20X5, ABL reported after-tax earnings of $4,575,000 on consolidated revenue of $77,970,000. Since CVL accounted for less than 10% of ABL's consolidated assets, revenues, and income, no segmented information was presented in the 20X5 annual report.

Within the management of ABL there is disagreement over the proper accounting treatment for the activities of ABL, VSL, FFL, and CVL for 20X6 and the effect on consolidation and reporting.

Required

In August 20X6, you were engaged as an independent advisor. Prepare a report in which you:

1. outline the major accounting and reporting issues faced by the company and its subsidiaries;

2. identify alternative policies to deal with the issues outlined; and

3. provide recommendations on the preferred policies.

[CICA]

# CASE 6-3 LE GOURMAND

Le Gourmand is one of Canada's most famous French restaurants. Located 20 kilometres north of Toronto, it draws diners from all over the province to enjoy its fare. One of the attractions at the restaurant is its private-label brand of wines—produced, bottled, and aged by Ombre Wines Ltd., located in the Niagara Peninsula.

The owner of Le Gourmand, Francois LeClerc, decided on New Year's Eve to increase the ties between Ombre Wines Ltd. and Le Gourmand Inc.; Le Gourmand is Ombre Wines's largest customer. On January 2, 20X5, Le Gourmand Inc. purchased 3,000 common shares of Ombre Wines Ltd. on the open market for $207,000. This left very few common shares still available to the public. The preferred shares were owned by the founders of Ombre Wines, but their children owned many of the common shares and were gradually selling them because none of them wished to take over the business.

Ombre Wines Ltd.'s owners' equity at January 2, 20X5, was:

| | |
|---|---:|
| **Preferred shares:** | |
| Cumulative, 6%, non-voting; | |
| 2,000 authorized, 1,000 issued | $ 20,000 |
| **Common shares:** | |
| 7,000 authorized, 6,000 issued | 137,000 |
| Retained earnings | 170,000 |
| | $327,000 |

At January 1, 20X5, the carrying values of Ombre Wines Ltd.'s assets approximated fair values except as follows:

| | Carrying value | Fair value |
|---|---|---|
| Two identical parcels of land, purchased in January 19X3 as an investment; each parcel cost $20,000 and the fair value of each parcel was identical | $40,000 | $60,000 |
| The land on which Ombre Wines's factory was located | $70,000 | $85,000 |
| Grape press, purchased in January 20X0 (useful life when the press was purchased was 10 years, no residual value) | $20,000 | $24,000 |

In September 20X5, Ombre Wines sold one of the parcels of land that it had been holding as an investment (both lots had been put on the market but only one had sold). The proceeds were $18,000. The real estate market had declined badly in 20X5. The purchaser, however, had also discovered that Ombre Wines had been using the vacant lots to dump some residue from the wine processing; the land would not be ready to produce crops for at least five years. The purchaser had originally been willing to offer $24,000, but reduced this to $18,000 when the land use was confirmed by its lawyer.

Sales from Ombre Wines to Le Gourmand totalled $100,000 and $120,000 in 20X4 and 20X5, respectively. At December 31, 20X4, Le Gourmand's inventory contained $45,000 of Ombre Wines's wine. A year later, the inventory included $60,000 of Ombre Wines's wine. Of the ending inventory acquired from Ombre Wines, $20,000 had not been paid for as at December 31, 20X5. In settlement of part of this payable, Le Gourmand sent some old office equipment to Ombre Wines. The equipment had cost $10,000 and had a net carrying value at December 31, 20X5, of $1,000. Ombre Wines agreed to accept the equipment and to forgive $5,000 of the receivable from Le Gourmand, leaving a balance of $15,000 due from the restaurant. Ombre Wines did not depreciate this office equipment during 20X5.

Ombre Wines's most recent dividend declaration was December 31, 20X3.

The amortization policy for all capital assets is straight-line.

Francois LeClerc is looking forward to the cash flow from dividends that he hopes his company will receive from Ombre Wines Ltd. each year.

The statements of financial position of the two companies at December 31, 20X5, and the statements of comprehensive income for the year then ended are presented in Exhibit D below.

## Exhibit D

### Statements of Financial Position
### December 31, 20X5

| | Le Gourmand Inc. | Ombre Wines Ltd. |
|---|---|---|
| **Assets** | | |
| Accounts receivable | — | 66,000 |
| Inventory | 85,500 | 134,000 |
| Investment in Ombre Wines | 207,000 | — |
| Land | 30,000 | 90,000 |
| Building | 40,000 | 60,000 |
| Equipment | 25,000 | 75,000 |
| | $389,250 | $441,400 |

### Statements of Financial Position
### December 31, 20X5

| | Le Gourmand Inc. | Ombre Wines Ltd. |
|---|---|---|
| **Liabilities and owners' equity** | | |
| Accounts payable | $ 34,000 | $ 13,000 |
| Taxes payable | 2,150 | 15,000 |
| Long-term debt | — | 10,000 |
| Deferred income taxes | 1,600 | — |
| Preferred shares | — | 20,000 |
| Common shares | 155,000 | 137,000 |
| Retained earnings | 196,500 | 246,400 |
| | $389,250 | $441,400 |

### Statements of Comprehensive Income Year Ended
### December 31, 20X5

| | Le Gourmand Inc. | Ombre Wines Ltd. |
|---|---|---|
| Sales | $400,000 | $300,000 |
| Gain on transfer of office equipment | 4,000 | — |
| Loss on sale of land | — | (2,000) |
| Cost of goods sold | (275,000) | (100,000) |
| Salaries | (78,000) | (55,000) |
| General and administration | (4,500) | (3,000) |
| Depreciation, building | (2,500) | (3,600) |
| Depreciation, equipment | (3,000) | (8,000) |
| Interest expense | — | (1,000) |
| Tax expense | (16,000) | (51,000) |
| Net income and comprehensive income | $ 25,000 | $ 76,400 |

Describe the alternative accounting treatments available to Le Gourmand Inc. for its investment in Ombre Wines Ltd. Describe why each alternative is an option and conclude which treatment is appropriate based on your description. Calculate Le Gourmand Inc.'s net income for the year ended December 31, 20X5. Show details of all calculations.

## CASE 6-4 CONSTRUCTIVE INSPIRATIONS INC.

### Overview

Jennifer Lu is a world-renowned architect. She and her husband, Johnnie Nu, are in the midst of a divorce. On the whole the separation has been amicable and civil. Jennifer and Johnnie have agreed to divide the value of their assets equally. One of these assets is her architectural consulting company, Constructive Inspirations Inc. (CI). They have agreed that Jennifer would continue to own Constructive Inspirations and that her husband would get other assets owned by them of equal value. The two of them have decided that the value of Constructive Inspirations will be based on the higher of CI's ending owner's equity, or six times its net income before taxes (but after all expenses) in 20X9. The calculation of both amounts will be guided by current IFRS standards for publicly accountable enterprises (i.e., public companies) as long as the end results are logical and fair to both parties. Both Jennifer and Johnnie are important clients of Accounting Experts LLP. They have approached Accounting Experts LLP for advice on the accounting methods to be adopted for the purpose of valuing CI in relation to their divorce settlement.

   Further details about Constructive Inspirations, including items about which the two disagree, are provided below.

### Cutting Edge Design Supplies

Constructive Inspiration purchased 40% of the shares of Cutting Edge Design Supplies (CEDS) on January 1, 20X7. The remaining 60% of CEDS's shares were purchased on that date by a group of 15 friends of Jennifer. These friends have no architectural background. Their reasons for investing in CEDS are their belief in Jennifer's vision and their conviction that their investment in CEDS will payoff handsomely in the long run. They play no part in the day-to-day operations of CEDS, and have, via a written agreement dated January 1, 20X7, given Constructive Inspirations the authority to make operating and financing decisions in relation to CEDS. One of the employees of CI is on the board of CEDS. On the date of acquisition of CEDS, the carrying values of its assets and liabilities were equal to their fair values except for inventory and a patent. The balance of the fair value adjustment of $100,000 was allocated to goodwill. The schedule below provides details on the carrying and fair values of inventory and the patent.

| | Carrying value | Fair value |
|---|---|---|
| Inventory | $150,000 | $100,000 |
| Patent | $200,000 | $300,000 |
| The patent had a remaining useful life of 10 years on January 1, 20X7. | | |

A test for impairment at the end of 20X8 indicated that the acquisition-related goodwill had a value of $80,000 at that time. There was no further impairment of this goodwill in 2009.

From the beginning, CI has not charged any management fee to CEDS for the time spent by CI's employees on CEDS operations. Johnnie estimates that the management fee that should have been charged is $100,000, $125,000, and $150,000 for 20X7, 20X8, and 20X9, respectively.

On July 1, 20X8, CI provided a loan of $100,000 to CEDS via a 10%-interest-bearing note payable. CEDS has been prompt in paying the interest on the note to CI. The loan is still outstanding at the end of 20X9.

CEDS sold a piece of equipment purchased by it on February 1, 20X7, to CI on January 1, 20X8. CEDS had recorded the full year's depreciation of $75,000 on the equipment in 20X7. No depreciation was recorded by CEDS for 20X8. The equipment was originally purchased by CEDS for $300,000 and sold to CI for $270,000. The equipment had a remaining useful life of three years with zero residual value on January 1, 20X8. CI charged a full year's depreciation in 20X8.

CEDS sold $80,000 and $90,000 worth of supplies to CI in 20X8 and 20X9, respectively; 20% of the supplies sold in 20X8 and 30% of the supplies sold in 20X9 by CEDS remained in CI's inventory at year-end. CEDS gross margin on these sales is 40%.

CI has from inception used the cost method to account for its investment in CEDS. CEDS has not declared any dividends since its acquisition by CI.

## Other Issues

- CI's employees have a bonus based on the net income of CI before taxes.

- CI uses a line of credit with a local bank for its working capital needs. The bank bases the terms of the line of credit on the financial statements of CI. CI's receivables and assets act as collateral for the line of credit.

Required

Having recently graduated with a business degree from university, you are now working for Accounting Experts LLP. The partner of Accounting Experts LLP has asked you to analyze the above case and prepare a report for him. He will be using the report to prepare himself for an upcoming meeting with Jennifer and Johnnie.

In your report, discuss how the different accounting alternatives available impact the financial affairs of CI, and support your accounting choice by discussing how it serves the users ranked by you as the most important and how it serves the objectives of those users. You should also discuss any concerns about the formula used for valuing CI and the "fairness" of using IFRS-based financial statements for determining CI's value. Ignore income taxes.

# Problems

## P6-1 (20 minutes, medium)

Dudes Outfitters Ltd. is a 70%-owned subsidiary of Trail Ltd. On January 10, 20X2, Dudes sold some display cases to Trail Ltd. for $95,000, recognizing a gain of $48,000 before tax on the transaction. Trail Ltd. depreciated the cases on a straight-line basis over six years, taking a full year's depreciation in 20X2.

On February 12, 20X5, Trail sold the display cases to an unaffiliated company for $55,000.

### Required

Prepare the appropriate consolidated adjustments relating to the display cases for each year ended December 31, 20X2, through 20X5.

[CICA]

## P6-2 (20 minutes, medium)

On January 1, 20X3, Sub Ltd., 80%-owned by Par Ltd., sold a building to Par Ltd. for $1,980,000. The building cost Sub $800,000 and was 70% depreciated (at 5% per year). Par will depreciate the building over the six remaining years, straight-line.

### Required

Give the consolidation eliminations required in relation to this transaction for the years ended

**a.** 20X3; and

**b.** 20X5.

[CGA–Canada, adapted]

## P6-3 (30 minutes, medium)

Parent Corp. owns 70% of the voting shares of Sub Ltd. During 20X4, Sub Ltd. sold inventory costing $640,000 to Parent Corp. for $800,000. At December 31, 20X4, Parent Corp. still had $400,000 of these goods in its inventory, and had not yet paid for $500,000 of the goods. All of the remaining goods were sold in 20X5.

Sub Ltd. also sold a piece of land (cost of $180,000) to Parent Corp. on July 1, 20X4, for $260,000, for which Parent Corp. had issued Sub Ltd. a five-year, 10%-per-annum note. The interest will be paid on July 1, 20X5.

### Required

**a.** Prepare the consolidation-related eliminations required in 20X4 and 20X5, respectively.

**b.** Assuming that Sub Ltd. earned $680,000 during 20X4 and $880,000 during 20X5, calculate the non-controlling interest in the earnings of Sub Ltd.

[CGA–Canada, adapted]

## P6-4 (30 minutes, medium)

Adam Ltd. owns 80% of the outstanding shares of Bob Ltd. Adam Ltd. also owns 70% of the shares of Xena Ltd. During the year 20X5, Adam sold $500,000 (cost) of goods (widgets) to Bob at a 60% markup. Xena sold $400,000 (cost) of goods (gadgets) to Adam at a 50% markup.

Adam sold a piece of land (cost $100,000) to Bob for $60,000.

On October 1, 20X5, Xena sold land (cost $80,000) and a building (cost $110,000) to Adam for $400,000; 40% of the price was allocated to land, and 60% of the price was allocated to building. The building had five years of expected life at October 1, 20X5, and was 30% depreciated at that time.

The $400,000 was unpaid at year-end and Adam had agreed to pay $10,000 interest on the unpaid amount.

An inventory count showed that 20% of the widgets that Bob had purchased from Adam were unsold at December 31, 20X5; 70% of the gadgets that Adam had purchased from Xena were also unsold.

Required

Assume that Adam Ltd. uses the cost method of keeping its accounts.

a.  Prepare the consolidation-related eliminations that would be required at December 31, 20X5, to prepare the consolidated financial statements.

b.  Calculate the effect on the non-controlling interest. By how much would the income to each non-controlling interest be changed? Keep the two subsidiaries separate.

[CGA–Canada, adapted]

P6-5 (20 minutes, medium)

On January 1, 20X2, Peter Limited purchased 70% of the outstanding voting common shares of Susan Limited at a cost of $147,000. At acquisition date, the carrying value of Susan Limited was $161,000, inventory was undervalued by $2,500, and depreciable capital assets were undervalued by $7,500. Relevant information for 20X5 is shown in the schedule below.

Required

a.  Calculate non-controlling interest in net income for 20X5 assuming consolidation is appropriate.

b.  Calculate non-controlling interest in the consolidated statement of financial position as of the end of 20X5.

c.  Calculate consolidated net income for 20X5 assuming a 10-year remaining life at acquisition date for capital assets and straight-line depreciation. Note that Peter Limited uses the cost method and that Susan Limited paid dividends during the year.

| Reported at End of 20X5 | | |
|---|---|---|
| | Peter | Susan |
| Net income and comprehensive income | $ 44,000 | $ 11,000 |
| Dividends paid | 4,000 | 1,000 |
| Current assets | $170,800 | $ 40,000 |
| Investment in Susan (at cost) | 139,200 | — |
| Capital assets (net) | 330,000 | 1 60,000 |
| | $640,000 | $200,000 |
| Liabilities | $140,000 | $ 30,000 |
| Common shares | 400,000 | 150,000 |
| Retained earnings (end) | 100,000 | 20,000 |
| | $640,000 | $200,000 |

[CGA–Canada, adapted]

## P6-6 (40 minutes, medium)

Anita Company owns a controlling interest in Brian Company and Gabriel Company. Anita purchased an 80% interest in Brian at a time when Brian reported retained earnings of $450,000. Anita purchased a 60% interest in Gabriel at a time when Gabriel reported retained earnings of $100,000. In each acquisition, the purchase price was equal to the proportionate net carrying value of the acquired company's shares, and the fair values of the assets and liabilities approximated their carrying values.

An analysis of the changes in retained earnings of the three companies during the year 20X5 gives the following results:

|  | Anita Company | Brian Company | Gabriel Company |
|---|---|---|---|
| Retained earnings, January 1, 20X5 | $ 742,000 | $686,000 | $475,000 |
| Net income for the year | 550,000 | 348,000 | 310,000 |
| Dividends paid | (250,000) | (200,000) | (150,000) |
| Retained earnings, December 31, 20X5 | $1,042,000 | $834,000 | $635,000 |

Gabriel sells some raw materials to Anita. After further processing and assembly, the parts made from those raw materials are sold by Anita to Brian, where they become a part of the finished products sold by Brian. Intercompany profits included in inventories at the beginning and end of the current year are estimated as follows:

|  | January 1, 20X5, inventory | December 31, 20X5, inventory |
|---|---|---|
| Intercompany profit included on sales from Gabriel to Anita | $70,000 | $50,000 |
| Intercompany profit included on sales from Anita to Brian | 60,000 | 80,000 |

Brian also rents a building to Gabriel. Gabriel is paying $5,000 per month according to the lease contract. Anita carries its investments on a cost basis. Ignore the impact of income taxes.

### Required

**a.** Compute the consolidated net income for 20X5.

**b.** Prepare the retained earnings section of the statement of changes in equity for 20X5.

**c.** What change would there be in consolidated net income if the three companies had engaged in the same transactions, but all purchases, sales, and lending had been with firms outside the affiliated group? Give the amount of the difference and explain how it is derived.

[SMA, adapted]

## P6-7 (45 minutes, easy)

On June 30, 20X1, Punt Corporation acquired 70% of the outstanding common shares of Slide Ltd. for $3,210,000 in cash plus Punt Corporation common shares estimated to have a fair market value of $1,200,000. On the date of acquisition, the fair market value and carrying value of each of Slide Ltd.'s assets were generally equal, except for inventory, which was undervalued by $225,000, and capital assets (net), which was overvalued by $1,000,000. The shareholders' equity of Slide at that time was $3,440,000, consisting of:

| | |
|---|---:|
| Common shares | $2,900,000 |
| Retained earnings | 540,000 |
| | $3,440,000 |

Statements of financial position at June 30, 20X5, are as follows:

| | Punt Corp. | Slide Ltd. |
|---|---:|---:|
| **Assets** | | |
| Cash and marketable securities | $ 4,548,000 | $ 321,000 |
| Accounts and other receivables | 2,153,000 | 950,000 |
| Inventory | 2,940,000 | 1,206,000 |
| Capital assets (net) | 17,064,000 | 7,161,000 |
| Other long-term investments | 3,038,000 | 2,240,000 |
| Investment in Slide Ltd. | 4,410,000 | – |
| **Total assets** | $34,153,000 | $11,878,000 |
| **Liabilities** | | |
| Current liabilities | $ 3,025,000 | $ 2,090,000 |
| Mortgage note payable | 12,135,000 | 4,000,000 |
| Total liabilities | 15,160,000 | 6,090,000 |
| **Shareholders' equity** | | |
| Common shares | 10,000,000 | 2,900,000 |
| Retained earnings | 8,993,000 | 2,888,000 |
| Total shareholders' equity | 18,993,000 | 5,788,000 |
| **Total liabilities and shareholders' equity** | $34,153,000 | $11,878,000 |

Additional Information

1. Slide Ltd. had income of $1,460,000 for the year ended June 30, 20X5. Dividends of $480,000 were declared during the fiscal year but were not paid until August 12, 20X5.

2. Slide Ltd. has had an average inventory turnover of four times per year over the past decade.

3. The capital assets that were overvalued on the date of acquisition had a remaining useful life of 20 years.

4. Slide sold goods to Punt during the year ended June 30, 20X4, at a gross profit margin of 25%. The opening inventory of Punt at July 1, 20X4, included items purchased from Slide in the amount of $160,000. There were no sales from Slide to Punt during the year ended June 30, 20X5.

5. Punt sold goods to Slide Ltd. during the current fiscal year at a gross profit margin of 30%. Of the $750,000 of sales, goods worth $200,000 were in Slide's closing inventory at June 30, 20X5. None of these intercompany sales still in inventory had been paid for at the fiscal year-end.

6. Both companies follow the straight-line method for depreciating capital assets.

7. The controller of Punt has informed you that, to date, there has been no impairment in goodwill.

**Required**

Prepare the consolidated statement of financial position for Punt Corporation and its subsidiary, Slide Ltd., at June 30, 20X5.

[SMA, adapted]

**P6-8 (20 minutes, medium)**

On January 1, 20X1, ABC Limited purchased 90% of the outstanding common shares of XYZ Limited for $150,000. At that date, XYZ Limited's condensed statement of financial position and fair values was as follows:

|  | Carrying value | Fair value |
|---|---|---|
| Cash | $ 20,000 | $20,000 |
| Land | 40,000 | 50,000 |
| Building (net) | 40,000 | 60,000 |
|  | $100,000 | |
| Liabilities | $ 20,000 | 20,000 |
| Common shares | 20,000 | |
| Retained earnings | 60,000 | |
|  | $100,000 | |

Assume a 10-year amortization period for any capital assets.

**Required**

a. Assume the following information regarding net income and dividends for XYZ Limited:

| Year | Net Income | Dividends |
|---|---|---|
| 20X1 | $20,000 | $4,000 |
| 20X2 | 24,000 | 4,000 |
| 20X3 | 18,000 | 4,000 |
| 20X4 | (20,000) | 4,000* |
| 20X5 | 20,000 | 52,000 |
| *The 20X4 dividend was a stock dividend | | |

Calculate the balance in the investment account in ABC's books at the end of 20X5 assuming that ABC uses the equity method of accounting in its books.

b. Assume that ABC uses the cost method of accounting for its investment. Prepare a journal entry or entries to reflect the information previously provided for 20X4 and 20X5.

[CGA–Canada, adapted]

**P6-9 (10 minutes, easy)**

On April 2, 20X4, Curry Ltd. acquired 40% of the outstanding common shares of Jasmine Ltd. by issuing one share of Curry plus $6 cash for each of Jasmine's shares acquired. At the time of purchase, Curry's shares were trading at $25 per share and Jasmine's shares were trading at $28. Jasmine had a total of 1 million shares outstanding.

At the date of acquisition, the shareholders' equity of Jasmine totalled $18,000,000. The fair values of Jasmine's assets and liabilities were the same as their net carrying values, except for the following capital assets:

| | Carrying value | Fair value |
|---|---|---|
| Land | $5,000,000 | $8,000,000 |
| Building | 6,000,000 | 5,000,000 |
| Equipment | 5,000,000 | 7,000,000 |

The building and equipment have estimated remaining useful lives of ten years and five years, respectively. Jasmine uses straight-line amortization.

For the year ended March 31, 20X5, Jasmine reported net income of $1,800,000. Jasmine's dividend payout was 60% for fiscal 20X5.

**Required**

For the year ended March 31, 20X5, compute:

**a.** Curry's equity in the earnings of Jasmine; and

**b.** the balance of the investment account at the fiscal year-end, using the equity method. Provide supporting calculations.

**P6-10 (20 minutes, medium)**

At the 20X5 annual meeting for Jasmine's shareholders, Curry nominated seven directors for Jasmine's 12-person board of directors. After some negotiation, five of Curry's nominees were accepted onto the board. During fiscal year 20X6, the following occurred:

**1.** Curry shifted a substantial amount of business to Jasmine. Jasmine became the major supplier of one of Curry's raw materials and had sales totalling $7,000,000 to Curry. Of that total, $1,200,000 was in Curry's raw materials inventory at year-end. The other $5,800,000 had been utilized in finished goods, of which 40% was still in inventory on March 31, 20X6.

**2.** Curry began selling some products to Cinnamon Corp., a wholly owned subsidiary of Jasmine. Fiscal 20X6 sales totalled $2,500,000, all within the last two months of the year. At year-end, 60% of the sales were still in Cinnamon's inventory.

**3.** Operating results for fiscal 20X6 were reported as follows:

| | Curry | Jasmine |
|---|---|---|
| Sales | $80,000,000 | $20,000,000 |
| Cost of sales | (56,000,000) | (12,000,000) |
| | 24,000,000 | 8,000,000 |
| Operating expenses | (6,000,000) | (4,000,000) |
| Income tax expense | (7,200,000) | (1,600,000) |
| Net income and comprehensive income | $10,800,000 | $ 2,400,000 |

**Required**

Using the information above and in P6–9, prepare a schedule(s) in which you:

**a.** Compute the amount of investment income that Curry should recognize in fiscal 20X6 from its investment in Jasmine.

**b.** Compute the balance of Curry's investment account for its investment in Jasmine at March 31, 20X6.

**P6-11 (20 minutes, easy)**

Slater Company purchased 30% of the outstanding voting shares of Rogan Company for $1,600,000 in cash on January 1, 20X3. On that date, Rogan Company's shareholders' equity was made up of common shares of $3 million and retained earnings of $1 million. There were no differences between the carrying values and the fair values of any of its net identifiable assets or liabilities. The net income and dividends declared and paid by Rogan Company for the two years subsequent to its acquisition were as follows:

|                    | 20X3         | 20X4      |
|--------------------|--------------|-----------|
| Net income (loss)  | ($200,000)   | $180,000  |
| Dividends          | 50,000       | 60,000    |

The statements of comprehensive income for the year ended December 31, 20X5, prior to the recognition of any investment income, for Slater and Rogan Companies are as follows:

|                                     | Slater       | Rogan      |
|-------------------------------------|--------------|------------|
| Sales                               | $3,000,000   | $550,000   |
| Other revenues                      | 200,000      | —          |
| Total revenues                      | 3,200,000    | 550,000    |
| Cost of goods sold                  | 1,500,000    | 300,000    |
| Other expenses                      | 300,000      | 40,000     |
| Loss                                | —            | 30,000     |
| Total expenses                      | 1,800,000    | 370,000    |
| Net income and comprehensive income | $1,400,000   | $180,000   |

During 20X5, Slater Company declared and paid dividends of $120,000, while Rogan Company declared and paid dividends of $80,000. Rogan Company declared and paid its dividends on December 31 of each year.

**Required**

**a.** Assume that Slater can exercise significant influence over the affairs of Rogan. Also assume no impairment in the value of the investment. Provide the following:

   **i.** the SCI of Slater Company, including recognition of any investment income or loss, for the year ended December 31, 20X5; and

   **ii.** the balance in the investment in Rogan Company account as it would appear on the December 31, 20X5, statement of financial position of Slater Company.

**b.** Assume that Slater cannot exercise significant influence over the affairs of Rogan. Provide the journal entry of Slater Company related to its investment in Rogan Company for 20X5.

   [SMA, adapted]

**P6-12 (60 minutes, medium)**

To maintain closer ties with associated companies in the oil business, King Oil Company decided to purchase holdings of common shares in several companies. The following is a list of activities associated with these acquisitions during 20X5.

| | |
|---|---|
| February 15 | Acquired 80,000 shares of Lub Oil Co. at $8 per share, representing 70% of the outstanding shares. At date of acquisition, carrying value of the Lub Oil Co.'s net assets was $800,000. Assets were considered to be valued at market. |
| April 13 | Acquired 140,000 shares of Richman Refineries at $11 per share, representing 60% of the outstanding shares. The purchase price corresponds to the underlying carrying value. |
| May 17 | Acquired 50,000 shares of Discovery Co. Ltd. at $5 per share, representing 2% of the outstanding shares. |
| June 30 | Lub Oil Co. announced a loss of $50,000 for the first six months of 20X5. Richman Refineries announced earnings of $120,000 for the first six months of 20X5 and declared a dividend of $0.10 per share. |
| August 15 | Dividend received from Richman Refineries. |
| October 11 | Dividend of $0.05 per share received from Discovery Co. Ltd. with a statement of earnings for the six months ended September 30 indicating net earnings of $60,000. |
| December 31 | Lub Oil Co. announced a loss of $40,000 for the year. |
| | Richman Refineries announced earnings of $200,000 for the year, including a gain of $40,000. |
| | Discovery Co. Ltd. announced earnings of $90,000 for the nine months ended December 31. |

To date, there has been no goodwill impairment.

Required

a. Investments in shares could be recorded and/or reported using either the equity method or the cost method. Distinguish between the two methods, indicating under what circumstances each method should be used.

b. Prepare journal entries to record the above transactions in the books of King Oil Company, assuming the use of the equity method of accounting where appropriate for reporting purposes.

[SMA, adapted]

P6-13 (75 minutes, medium)

On January 1, 20X2, Porter Inc. purchased 80% of the outstanding voting shares of Sloan Ltd. for $3,000,000 in cash. On this date, Sloan had common shares outstanding in the amount of $2,200,000 and retained earnings of $1,100,000. The identifiable assets and liabilities of Sloan had fair values that were equal to their carrying values except for the following:

1. Capital assets (net) had a fair value $200,000 greater than its carrying value. The remaining useful life on January 1, 20X2, was 20 years, with no anticipated residual value.

2. Accounts receivable had a fair value $75,000 less than carrying value.

3. Long-term liabilities had a fair value $62,500 less than carrying value. These liabilities mature on June 30, 20X10.

It is the policy of Porter to test all goodwill balances for impairment on an annual basis. To date, there has been no impairment in goodwill. Both Porter and Sloan use the straight-line method for depreciation. Porter Inc. is a public company.

## Additional Information

1. Between January 1, 20X2, and December 31, 20X4, Sloan earned $345,000 and paid dividends of $115,000.

2. On January 1, 20X4, Sloan sold a patent to Porter for $165,000. On this date, the patent had a carrying value on the books of Sloan of $185,000 and a remaining useful life of five years.

3. On September 1, 20X4, Porter sold land to Sloan for $103,000. The land had a carrying value on the books of Porter of $82,000. Sloan still owned this land on December 31, 20X5.

4. For the year ended December 31, 20X5, the statements of comprehensive income revealed the following:

|  | Porter | Sloan |
|---|---|---|
| Total revenues | $2,576,000 | $973,000 |
| Cost of goods sold | 1,373,000 | 467,000 |
| Depreciation expense | 483,000 | 176,000 |
| Other expenses | 352,000 | 153,000 |
| Total expenses | 2,208,000 | 796,000 |
| Net income and comprehensive income | $ 368,000 | $177,000 |

Porter records its investment in Sloan using the cost method and includes dividend income from Sloan in its total revenues.

5. Porter and Sloan paid dividends of $125,000 and $98,000, respectively, in 20X5.

6. Sloan issued no common shares subsequent to January 1, 20X2. Selected statement of financial position accounts for the two companies at December 31, 20X5, were:

|  | Porter | Sloan |
|---|---|---|
| Accounts receivable (net) | $987,000 | $133,000 |
| Inventories | 1,436,000 | 787,000 |
| Capital assets (net) | 3,467,000 | 1,234,000 |
| Patents (net) | 263,000 | — |
| Land | 872,000 | 342,000 |
| Long-term liabilities | 1,876,000 | 745,000 |
| Retained earnings | 4,833,000 | 1,409,000 |

7. During 20X5, Porter's merchandise sales to Sloan were $150,000. The unrealized profits in Sloan's inventory on January 1 and December 31, 20X5, were $14,000 and $10,000, respectively. At December 31, 20X5, Sloan still owed Porter $5,000 for merchandise purchases.

8. During 20X5, Sloan's merchandise sales to Porter were $55,000. The unrealized profits in Porter's inventory on January 1 and December 31, 20X5, were $1,500 and $2,500, respectively. At December 31, 20X5, Porter still owed Sloan $2,000 for merchandise purchases.

# Required

**a.** Compute the balances that would appear in the consolidated statement of financial position of Porter and Sloan as at December 31, 20X5, for the following:

   **i.** patent (net);

   **ii.** non-controlling interest; and

   **iii.** retained earnings.

**b.** Porter has decided not to prepare consolidated financial statements and will report its investment in Sloan by the equity method. Calculate the investment income that would be disclosed in the statement of comprehensive income of Porter for the year ended December 31, 20X5.

[SMA]

## P6-14 (25 minutes, easy)

On January 1, 19X8, Partial Company acquired 80% of the outstanding voting shares of the Sum Company for $3,900,000 in cash. On this date, Sum Company had $2,000,000 in common shares outstanding and $2,000,000 in retained earnings. Any excess of cost over carrying value is to be recorded in the consolidated financial statements as goodwill and is tested annually for impairment. On December 31, 20X5, the statements of financial position of the two companies are as follows:

| Statements of Financial Position December 31, 20X5 | | |
|---|---|---|
| | **Partial Company** | **Sum Company** |
| Cash | $ 3,000,000 | $ 1,000,000 |
| Accounts receivable | 7,000,000 | 2,000,000 |
| Inventories | 4,100,000 | 3,000,000 |
| Investment in Sum | 3,900,000 | — |
| Capital assets (net) | 7,000,000 | 5,000,000 |
| TOTAL ASSETS | $25,000,000 | $11,000,000 |
| Liabilities | $ 5,000,000 | $ 3,000,000 |
| Common shares | 7,000,000 | 2,000,000 |
| Retained earnings | 13,000,000 | 6,000,000 |
| TOTAL LIABILITIES AND EQUITIES | $25,000,000 | $11,000,000 |

## Additional Information

**1.** Sum Company sells merchandise to Partial Company at a price that provides Sum with a gross margin of 50% of the sales price. During 20X5, these sales amounted to $1,000,000. The December 31, 20X5, inventories of Partial contain $200,000 of these purchases, while the December 31, 20X4, inventories of Partial contained $100,000 in merchandise purchased from Sum.

**2.** At the end of 20X5, Partial owes Sum $60,000 for merchandise purchased on account. The account is non-interest-bearing.

**3.** On December 31, 20X2, Partial Company sold equipment to Sum Company for $550,000. At the time of the sale, the equipment had a net carrying value in Partial's records of $450,000. The remaining useful life of the asset on this date was 10 years.

**4.** There has been no impairment in goodwill since January 1, 19X8.

## Required

Prepare a consolidated statement of financial position for Partial Company and its subsidiary, Sum Company, at December 31, 20X5. Ignore the impact of income taxes.

[SMA, adapted]

**P6-15 (45 minutes, medium)**

In January 20X3, Paris Ink Company (Paris) purchased 80% of the common shares of Slade Paper Ltd. (Slade) by issuing common shares worth $800,000. At that date, Slade's common shares and retained earnings totalled $250,000 and $340,000, respectively. The net carrying values and fair values of the net identifiable assets of Slade were the same except for the following:

**1.** The fair market value of inventory was greater than carrying value by $50,000.

**2.** The FMV of capital assets had replacement cost that exceeded net carrying value (NCV) by $120,000, although net realizable value exceeded NCV by only $60,000 (management planned to retain the capital assets throughout their remaining useful life of 12 years).

**3.** Although the NCV of Slade's bonds payable was $400,000, the FMV was $460,000, due to a decline in the interest rates since the bonds were originally issued. The bonds payable mature on December 31, 20X8, and have a nominal rate of interest of 12%. The companies use straight-line amortization for bond premiums and discounts.

The financial statements for Paris and Slade for the year ended December 31, 20X5, are presented in Exhibit E. Additional information on transactions between Paris and Slade is presented in Exhibit F.

---

## Exhibit E
## FINANCIAL STATEMENTS

### Statements of Comprehensive Income
### Year Ended December 31, 20X5

|  | Paris | Slade |
|---|---|---|
| Sales | $3,850,000 | $1,650,000 |
| Cost of goods sold | 2,550,000 | 1,120,000 |
| Gross profit | 1,300,000 | 530,000 |
| **EXPENSES** | | |
| Administration; selling | 550,000 | 384,000 |
| Amortization | 136,000 | 74,000 |
| Interest | – | 56,000 |
|  | 686,000 | 514,000 |
| **OTHER INCOME** | | |
| Interest; dividends | 76,000 | 4,000 |
| Gain on sale of land | – | 100,000 |
|  | 76,000 | 104,000 |
| Income before income taxes | 690,000 | 120,000 |
| Income tax expense | 260,000 | 30,000 |
| Net income and comprehensive income | $ 430,000 | $ 90,000 |

---

## Statements of Financial Position
### December 31, 20X5

|  | Paris | Slade |
|---|---|---|
| **Assets** | | |
| **Current assets:** | | |
| Cash | $ 45,000 | $ 80,000 |
| Accounts receivable | 655,000 | 455,000 |
| Inventory | 420,000 | 350,000 |
| Marketable securities | 380,000 | 45,000 |
| Due from Slade | 200,000 | – |
| | 1,700,000 | 930,000 |
| Capital assets (net) | 1,450,000 | 690,000 |
| Investment in Slade | 800,000 | – |
| | $3,950,000 | $1,620,000 |
| **LIABILITIES** | | |
| **Current liabilities:** | | |
| Accounts payable | $ 665,000 | $ 280,000 |
| Note payable to Paris | – | 200,000 |
| | 665,000 | 480,000 |
| Bonds payable | – | 400,000 |
| **Shareholders' equity** | | |
| Common shares | 2,500,000 | 250,000 |
| Retained earnings | 785,000 | 490,000 |
| | $3,950,000 | $1,620,000 |

## Required

**a.** Calculate the carrying value of the goodwill on the consolidated financial statements of Paris Ink Company at December 31, 20X5. Paris tests goodwill for impairment on an annual basis.

**b.** Prepare a consolidated SCI for Paris Ink Company for the year ended December 31, 20X5.

**c.** Calculate the following balances for Paris Ink Company's consolidated statement of financial position as at December 31, 20X5:

   **i.** inventory; and

   **ii.** non-controlling interest.

     [ICAO]

## ADDITIONAL INFORMATION

1. On July 1, 20X5, Paris advanced Slade $200,000, due on July 1, 20X6. Interest of 8% is due at maturity.
2. Intercompany sales from Slade to Paris were as follows for 20X3–20X5:

|  | 20X3 | 20X4 | 20X5 |
|---|---|---|---|
| Sales | $200,000 | $240,000 | $250,000 |
| Gross profit margin | 32.00% | 33.33% | 30.00% |
| Amount remaining in inventory at year-end | $ 60,000 | $ 75,000 | $100,000 |

   All amounts in closing inventory at the end of each year were sold during the first four months of the following year.
3. On March 1, 20X5, Slade sold land to Paris for $300,000. The original cost of the land was $200,000. Assume this transaction was taxed at the company's normal tax rate.
4. During 20X5, Paris sold inventory to Slade for $108,000, which represented a markup of 35% above cost. At December 31, 20X5, 20% of these goods remained in inventory.
5. During 20X5, Paris paid dividends of $250,000 and Slade paid dividends of $50,000.
6. Paris and Slade pay taxes at 40% and 25% rates, respectively.

P6-16 (50 minutes, medium)

Pop Company acquired 70% of Son Limited on January 1, 20X4, for $343,000. On the acquisition date, common shares and retained earnings of Son Limited were $100,000 and $200,000, respectively. The fair market values of Son's identifiable net assets were equivalent to their carrying value except for capital assets, which were undervalued by $50,000, and long-term debt, which was overvalued by $100,000. The undervalued capital assets have a remaining life of 10 years. The long-term debt matures on December 31, 20X8. Any goodwill is tested for impairment on an annual basis. Both companies use the straight-line method of amortization.

Intercompany transactions include the downstream sale of a capital asset in 20X4, which included an unrealized profit of $30,000 to be amortized over five years. During 20X5, there was an intercompany upstream sale of land for $120,000. The original cost of the land was $95,000.

For the year ended December 31, 20X5, Pop Company had net income of $244,000 and declared dividends of $10,000. Son Limited had 20X5 net income of $85,000 and paid dividends of $10,000. All dividends have been declared and paid on December 31. Pop Company uses the cost method to account for its investment in Son Limited. Shown below are the statements of financial position for the parent company and its subsidiary on December 31, 20X5.

| Statements of Financial Position December 31, 20X5 | | |
| --- | --- | --- |
| | Pop Company | Son Limited |
| Current assets | $1,200,000 | $250,000 |
| Investment in Son Limited | 345,000 | — |
| Capital assets (net) | 900,000 | 450,000 |
| Goodwill | — | — |
| TOTAL ASSETS | $2,445,000 | $700,000 |
| Current liabilities | $1,045,000 | $ 75,000 |
| Long-term debt | 500,000 | 200,000 |
| Non-controlling interest | — | — |
| Common shares | 500,000 | 100,000 |
| Retained earnings | 400,000 | 325,000 |
| TOTAL LIABILITIES AND EQUITIES | $2,445,000 | $700,000 |

**Required**

**a.** Determine consolidated net income for the year ended December 31, 20X5. Show all your calculations.

**b.** Calculate the balances of the following accounts as they would appear in the consolidated statement of financial position on December 31, 20X5:

　**i.** capital assets, net;

　**ii.** non-controlling interest; and

　**iii.** retained earnings.

**c.** Prepare the required December 31, 20X5, journal entry to eliminate the investment in Son Limited's account.

　[CGA–Canada, adapted]

**P6-17 (50 minutes, medium)**

Note: All dollar amounts in the question are in 000s.

On December 31, 19X9, Hari Company (Hari) purchased 70% of the outstanding common shares of Amin Limited (Amin) for $7,000. On that date, Amin's shareholders' equity consisted of common shares of $250 and retained earnings of $4,500. The financial statements for Hari and Amin for 20X5 were as follows:

| Statements of Financial Position December 31, 20X5 | | |
| --- | --- | --- |
| | Hari | Amin |
| Cash | $ 1,340 | $ 780 |
| Accounts receivable | 2,800 | 1,050 |
| Inventory | 3,400 | 2,580 |
| Capital assets (net) | 4,340 | 3,010 |
| Investment in Amin | 7,000 | — |
| Total | $18,880 | $7,420 |
| Current liabilities | $ 4,200 | $ 540 |
| Long-term liabilities | 3,100 | 1,230 |
| Common shares | 1,000 | 250 |
| Retained earnings | 10,580 | 5,400 |
| Total | $18,880 | $7,420 |

### Statements of Comprehensive Income Year Ended December 31, 20X5

|  | Hari | Amin |
|---|---|---|
| Sales | $21,900 | $7,440 |
| Cost of sales | 14,800 | 3,280 |
| Gross profit | 7,100 | 4,160 |
| Other revenue | 1,620 | — |
| Amortization expense | (840) | (420) |
| Other expenses | (5,320) | (2,040) |
| Income before income taxes | 2,560 | 1,700 |
| Income tax expense | 800 | 680 |
| Net income and comprehensive income | $ 1,760 | $1,020 |

### Statements of Changes in Equity—Retained Earnings Section Year Ended December 31, 20X5

|  | Hari | Amin |
|---|---|---|
| Retained earnings, beginning | $10,420 | $5,180 |
| Net income | 1,760 | 1,020 |
| Dividends paid | (1,600) | (800) |
| Retained earnings, ending | $10,580 | $5,400 |

### Additional Information

1. In negotiating the purchase price at the date of acquisition, it was agreed that the fair values of all of Amin's assets and liabilities were equal to their carrying values, except for the following:

|  | Carrying value | Fair value |
|---|---|---|
| Inventory | $2,100 | $2,200 |
| Equipment | 2,500 | 3,000 |

2. Both companies use FIFO to account for their inventory and the straight-line method amortize their capital assets. Amin's capital assets had a remaining useful life of 10 years at the acquisition date.

3. Each year, goodwill is evaluated to determine if there has been permanent impairment. It was determined that goodwill on the consolidated statement of financial position should be reported at $1,100 on December 31, 20X4, and at $1,030 on December 31, 20X5.

4. During 20X5, inventory sales from Amin to Hari were $10,000. Hari's inventories contained merchandise purchased from Amin for $2,000 on December 31, 20X4, and $2,500 at December 31, 20X5. Amin earns a gross margin of 40% on its intercompany sales.

5. On January 1, 20X1, Hari sold some equipment to Amin for $1,000 and recorded a gain of $200 before taxes. This equipment had a remaining useful life of eight years at the time of the purchase by Amin.

6. Hari charges $50 per month to Amin for consulting services.

7. Hari uses the cost method in accounting for its long-term investment.

### Required

a. Prepare a consolidated statement of income for the year ended December 31, 20X5.

**b.** Calculate consolidated retained earnings at January 1, 20X5, and then prepare the retained earnings section of the consolidated statement of changes in equity for the year ended December 31, 20X5.

**c.** Explain how the historical cost principle supports the adjustments made on consolidation when there has been an intercompany sale of equipment.

[CGA–Canada, adapted]

**P6-18 (40 minutes, medium)**

On January 1, 20X0, Mariachi Corporation acquired 70% of the outstanding shares of Sombrero Company for $84,700 cash. On that date, Sombrero Company had $35,000 of common shares outstanding and $25,000 of retained earnings. On January 1, 20X0, the carrying values of each of Sombrero Company's identifiable assets and liabilities were equal to their fair value except for the following:

|  | Carrying value | Fair value |
|---|---|---|
| Inventory | $25,000 | $35,000 |
| Equipment | 10,000 | 30,000 |

The equipment had a useful life of 10 years as at January 1, 20X0, and all inventory was sold during 20X0. The following are the separate-entity financial statements for Mariachi and Sombrero at December 31, 20X5:

**Statements of Financial Position**
**December 31, 20X5**

|  | Mariachi | Sombrero |
|---|---|---|
| Cash | $120,000 | $ 20,000 |
| Accounts receivable | 90,000 | 65,000 |
| Inventory | 250,000 | 90,000 |
| Capital assets (net) | 225,000 | 150,000 |
| Investment in Sombrero | 85,000 | — |
| Total | $770,000 | $325,000 |
| Accounts payable | $230,000 | $180,000 |
| Deferred income taxes | 70,000 | 60,000 |
|  | 300,000 | 240,000 |
| Common shares | 200,000 | 35,000 |
| Retained earnings | 270,000 | 50,000 |
| Total | $770,000 | $325,000 |

**Statements of Comprehensive Income**
**Year Ended December 31, 20X5**

|  | Mariachi | Sombrero |
|---|---|---|
| Sales | $750,000 | $600,000 |
| Cost of goods sold | (500,000) | (450,000) |
| Gross margin | 250,000 | 150,000 |
| Dividend income | 21,000 | — |
| Gain on sale of trademark | — | 12,000 |
| Amortization expense | (35,000) | (20,000) |
| Other expenses | (86,000) | (62,000) |
| Income tax expense | (60,000) | (32,000) |
| Net income and comprehensive income | $ 90,000 | $ 48,000 |

### Statements of Changes in Equity—Retained Earnings Section
### Year Ended December 31, 20X5

| | | |
|---|---|---|
| Retained earnings, beginning of year | $ 180,000 | $ 32,000 |
| Net income | 90,000 | 48,000 |
| Dividends paid | — | (30,000) |
| Retained earnings, end of year | $270,000 | $ 50,000 |

### Additional Information

1. On January 1, 20X2, Mariachi sold Sombrero a trademark with a net carrying value of $20,000 for cash consideration of $28,000. The trademark has an indefinite useful life. On July 1, 20X5, Sombrero sold the trademark to an unrelated company for cash consideration of $40,000.

2. Sombrero sells goods to Mariachi at 25% above cost. Total sales from Sombrero to Mariachi during 20X5 were $50,000, of which $20,000 remained in Mariachi's inventory at year-end. Mariachi still owed Sombrero $18,000 for this inventory at December 31, 20X5. In 20X4, total sales from Sombrero to Mariachi were $40,000, of which $10,000 remained in Mariachi's inventory at year-end.

3. Mariachi uses the cost method to account for its investment in Sombrero.

4. Each year, goodwill is evaluated to determine if there has been permanent impairment. To date there has been no impairment in value.

### Required

a. Prepare a calculation for the purchase price discrepancy and goodwill as of January 1, 20X0.

b. Prepare a consolidated statement of income for the year ended December 31, 20X5.

c. What would the balance be for each of the following consolidated statement of financial position accounts as at December 31, 20X5?

    i. accounts receivable

    ii. inventory

    iii. equipment

    iv. non-controlling interest

      [CGA–Canada, adapted]

### P6-19 (40 minutes, medium)

Aztec Corporation purchased 70% of the outstanding shares of Inca Limited on January 1, 20X2, at a cost of $84,000. Aztec has always used the cost method to account for its investments. On January 1, 20X2, Inca had common shares of $50,000 and retained earnings of $30,000, and fair values were equal to carrying value for all of its net assets except for inventory (fair value was $9,000 less than carrying value) and equipment (fair value was $24,000 greater than carrying value). The equipment had an estimated remaining life of six years on January 1, 20X2.

The following are the separate-entity financial statements of Aztec and Inca at December 31, 20X5:

### Statements of Financial Position
### December 31, 20X5

|  | Aztec | Inca |
|---|---|---|
| Cash | $ — | $ 10,000 |
| Accounts receivable | 40,000 | 30,000 |
| Note receivable | 0 | 40,000 |
| Inventory | 66,000 | 44,000 |
| Capital assets (net) | 220,000 | 76,000 |
| Land | 150,000 | 30,000 |
| Investment in Inca | 80,000 | — |
| Total | $556,000 | $230,000 |
| Accounts payable | $140,000 | $ 60,000 |
| Notes payable | 40,000 | — |
| Common shares | 150,000 | 50,000 |
| Retained earnings | 226,000 | 1 20,000 |
| Total | $556,000 | $230,000 |

### Statements of Comprehensive Income
### Year Ended December 31, 20X5

|  | Aztec | Inca |
|---|---|---|
| Sales | $798,000 | $300,000 |
| Management fee revenue | 24,000 | — |
| Investment income | 14,000 | 3,600 |
| Gain on sale of land | — | 20,000 |
|  | 836,000 | 323,600 |
| Cost of sales | 480,000 | 200,000 |
| Amortization expense | 40,000 | 12,000 |
| Interest expense | 10,000 | — |
| Other expenses | 106,000 | 31,600 |
| Income tax expense | 80,000 | 32,000 |
|  | 716,000 | 275,600 |
| Net income and comprehensive income | $120,000 | $ 48,000 |

### Statements of Changes in Equity—Retained Earnings Section
### Year Ended December 31, 20X5

|  | Aztec | Inca |
|---|---|---|
| Retained earnings, beginning of year | $ 106,000 | $ 92,000 |
| Net income | 120,000 | 48,000 |
| Dividends paid | — | (20,000) |
| Retained earnings, end of year | $ 226,000 | $ 120,000 |

Additional Information

1. During 20X5, Inca made a cash payment of $2,000 per month to Aztec for management fees, which is included in Inca's "other expenses."

2. During 20X5, Aztec made intercompany sales of $100,000 to Inca. The December 31, 20X5, inventory of Inca contained goods purchased from Aztec amounting to $30,000. These sales had a gross profit of 35%.

3. On April 1, 20X5, Aztec acquired land from Inca for $40,000. This land had been recorded on Inca's books at a net carrying value of $20,000. Aztec paid for the land by signing a $40,000 note payable to Inca, bearing interest at 8%. Interest for 20X5 was paid by Aztec in cash on December 31, 20X5. This land was still being held by Aztec on December 31, 20X5.

4. The fair value of the consolidated goodwill remained unchanged from January 1, 20X2, to July 1, 20X5. On July 1, 20X5, a valuation was performed, indicating that the fair value of consolidated goodwill was $3,500.

Required

a. Prepare a calculation of goodwill and any unamortized fair value adjustment as at December 31, 20X5.

b. Prepare Aztec's consolidated SCI for the year ended December 31, 20X5.

c. Calculate the following balances that would appear on Aztec's consolidated statement of financial position as at December 31, 20X5:

   i. inventory;

   ii. land;

   iii. notes payable;

   iv. non-controlling interest; and

   v. common shares.

   [CGA–Canada, adapted]

P6-20 (45 minutes, difficult)

On January 1, 19X9, Apache Company purchased 80% of the outstanding voting shares of Navaho Company for $300,000. Navaho's assets and liabilities all had fair values that were equal to their carrying values. The $100,000 excess of purchase price over the carrying values of Navaho Company's net assets was allocated to goodwill. Goodwill is tested for impairment on an annual basis. Between January 1, 19X9, and January 1, 20X5, Navaho Company earned $200,000 and paid dividends of $40,000. Both companies use the straight-line method to calculate depreciation and amortization.

Additional Information

1. On January 1, 19X5, Navaho Company purchased a machine for $100,000 that had an estimated useful life of 20 years; on January 1, 20X0, Navaho Company sold the machine to Apache Company for $60,000. The estimated useful life of the machine remains unchanged at a total of 20 years (15 years from January 1, 20X0).

2. During 20X5, Navaho Company had sales of merchandise in the amount of $400,000 to Apache Company, of which $60,000 remains in the December 31, 20X5, inventories of Apache Company. Apache Company had no sales to Navaho Company during 20X5, but had sales of $200,000 to Navaho Company in 20X4. Of these sales, $40,000 remained in the December 31, 20X4, inventories of Navaho Company. Intercompany sales are priced to provide the selling company with a 40% gross profit on sales prices.

3. On September 1, 20X5, Navaho Company sold a piece of land to Apache Company for $50,000. The land had been purchased for $35,000.

4. During 20X5, Navaho Company declared dividends of $6,000 and Apache Company declared dividends of $35,000.

5. During 20X5, Navaho Company paid Apache Company $10,000 in management fees.

6. On July 1, 20X5, Apache Company lent Navaho Company $100,000 for five years at an annual interest rate of 10%. Interest is paid on July 1 of each year for which the loan is outstanding.

7. To date, there has been no impairment in the value of goodwill.

Apache Company carries its investment in Navaho Company by the cost method. On this date, the statements of comprehensive income of Apache Company and Navaho Company for the year ended December 31, 20X5, are as follows:

|  | Apache | Navaho |
|---|---|---|
| Merchandise sales | $3,000,000 | $2,000,000 |
| Investment income | 60,000 | — |
| Other revenue | 50,000 | 70,000 |
| Total revenues | 3,110,000 | 2,070,000 |
| Cost of goods sold | 1,800,000 | 1,400,000 |
| Depreciation expense | 400,000 | 400,000 |
| Selling and administrative | 500,000 | 200,000 |
| Loss on sales of investments | — | 26,000 |
| Total expenses | 2,700,000 | 2,026,000 |
| Net income and comprehensive income | $ 410,000 | $ 44,000 |

Required

a. Prepare the consolidated SCI for Apache Company and its subsidiary, Navaho Company, for the year ended December 31, 20X5.

b. Assume that Apache Company prepares separate-entity statements for its bank and uses the equity method of reporting its investment in Navaho. Provide a detailed calculation of Apache Company's investment income for the year ended December 31, 20X5.

[SMA, adapted]

# Chapter 7
## Segment and Interim Reporting

## Learning Objectives

**After studying this chapter, you should be able to:**

**LO ①** describe segmented reporting and identify and distinguish between operating segments and reportable segments;

**LO ②** state the segment information and entity-wide disclosures that are required to be reported;

**LO ③** describe the scope, content, and periods covered in interim reports;

**LO ④** explain the different theoretical approaches to recognition and measurement for interim reporting; and

**LO ⑤** apply the recognition and measurement principles for interim reporting.

## INTRODUCTION

Toronto-based Thomson Reuters Corporation is a world leader in the provision of information to businesses and professionals. The company operates in more than 100 countries around the world. In fiscal year 2011, the company reported revenue of $13.8 billion on its consolidated financial statements. Consolidated statements give a good overview of the Thomson Reuters economic entity, but they obscure information about the sources of the company's revenues and profits. Investors will want to know which market segments and which geographic markets are driving Thomson Reuters's profitability. Fortunately, securities regulators and standard-setters have recognized this shortcoming of consolidated statements. To help investors better understand where and how they were able to generate their profits, public companies are required to disclose key financial information by operating and geographic segment.

Thomson Reuters has two key lines of business—markets and professional. "Markets" is a business segment that includes revenue generated from financial services and media businesses. "Professional" includes revenue generated from services to three different types of client businesses: legal, tax and accounting, and intellectual property and science. As well as operating in North America, Thomson Reuters also operates across the globe, in the Americas, the Asia-Pacific region, and a broad "EMEA" area—Europe, Middle East, and Africa.

The previous chapters have discussed only "the big picture" in the form of annual consolidated statements. Investors also want more timely financial information; they find that annual financial reports don't provide sufficiently timely information. Therefore, public companies also supplement their annual reports with interim financial reports. For example, Thomson Reuters issues quarterly unaudited financial statements in May, August, and November in addition to its annual financial statements, which are usually issued in March.

This chapter looks at two types of information that a public company provides to its shareholders that are intended to remedy some of the shortcomings of annual consolidated information:

- disaggregated reporting for *segments* of the enterprise, as supplementary information; and

- reporting for shorter, *interim* periods of time, normally quarterly for public reporting in Canada and the United States (semi-annually in most other countries).

The requirements for segment and interim reporting are imposed by securities regulators and thus apply only to public companies. IFRS has developed standards to guide preparation of this information to enhance comparability.

## 7.1 SEGMENT REPORTING

### General Concept

LO ❶
Describe segmented reporting and identify and distinguish between operating segments and reportable segments

Consolidated statements don't disclose the financial position and results of operations for the many separate entities and activities comprising the consolidated whole. A financial statement user cannot see the relative importance and profitability of a consolidated entity's different lines of business. Nor can a user determine the company's risk exposure in its various types of activities.

Each type of business will be affected by different factors relating to markets, supply, competition, and so forth. Analysts and investors need such information to make predictions about the companies they follow, but such information is not available in the consolidated financial statements without additional disclosure.

The response of securities regulators (and securities laws) to this need has been to require segment reporting as a mandatory disclosure to accompany consolidated statements. **Segment reporting** is the disaggregation of consolidated results by the principal activities and environments of the business.

Also known as **line of business reporting**, segmented reporting helps financial statement users understand the risks and rewards inherent in different lines of business and different geographic areas. National and regional economic and political environments differ, and exchange rate fluctuations add an additional dimension to risk analysis.

Segment reporting is not the same as reporting by separate legal entity (i.e., by subsidiary). Segment reporting addresses the problems cited above for consolidated groups of companies, but it does not address the needs of financial statement users who seek to understand the operations of an individual legal entity—that is, for the parent company or for an individual subsidiary.

For example, if a bank gives a loan to a Thomson Reuters subsidiary, the bank only has claim on the assets of that subsidiary, not on those of the parent company nor of other subsidiaries. Thus, the bank needs to understand in which business segments that subsidiary operates. It is only if there is a correspondence between corporate entities and segments in the consolidated financial statements that a creditor (such as a bank) or a minority shareholder can gain insight into the viability of the individual corporation in which that creditor has a stake.

**Core Principle** Segment reporting for publicly accountable enterprises is governed by the provisions of IFRS 8, *Operating Segments*. The IFRS 8 requirements for segment reporting are quite broad and permit substantial flexibility in reporting. The *core principle* of IFRS 8 is that a company should disclose information that helps users evaluate the nature and financial results of its principal activities, as well as understand the economic environments in which it operates. Therefore, IFRS 8 requires disclosure of key business segments, as well as information relating to (1) products and services; (2) geographic areas; and (3) major customers. We will discuss the reporting of each category of information in the sections that follow.

## Applicability

IFRS 8 applies only to *publicly-accountable enterprises*. There is no equivalent requirement in Canadian accounting standards for private enterprises (ASPE). IFRS 8 can be used as a guideline for private enterprises (including subsidiaries within a corporate group) if they choose to provide segment reporting either voluntarily or at the request of major creditors.

In developing the requirements in IFRS 8, the IASB was conscious of the benefit–cost relationship in presenting segmented information. In general, the IASB preferred to recommend disclosure only of information that was already readily available within the reporting enterprise, mainly from the management accounting system. Thus, some of the variability that exists in practice is the result of differing management accounting systems.

The focus of the segment disclosure requirements is on reportable operating segments. There are two key words here—*reportable* and *operating*. Not all operating segments are reportable. We will clarify the distinction in the following discussion.

In addition to reporting on their definable operating segments, enterprises should report additional company-wide information about:

- products and services;
- geographic areas; and
- major customers.

## Operating Segments

**Identifying Operating Segments** The first step is to identify the segments to be reported. In some instances, identifying operating segments is not a problem. If a telephone company buys a gas pipeline company, it is clear that those are two distinct segments; they share no resources, markets, management expertise, or common costs, except at the top corporate level. Operationally, there is no similarity.

In other instances, however, it is more difficult to identify operating segments than one perhaps might expect. IFRS 8 cites three aspects to defining an operating segment:

1. It is a component of the enterprise that is expected to generate revenues and incur expenses. A segment need not be generating revenues currently, but should be expected to do so in the normal future course of its activity.

2. Discrete financial information on the business component is regularly available through the company's internal financial reporting system.

3. The business component's operating results are reviewed regularly by the enterprise's "chief operating decision maker," which normally will be the COO (chief operating officer), the CEO (chief executive officer), or the president; this function also could be exercised by a *group* of executive officers. This decision maker uses the various business components' financial information to make resource allocation decisions and assess performance within the enterprise.

Clearly, the guidelines focus on the decision-making process within the enterprise. The accounting system must provide the information as a matter of routine, and that information must be used by senior management for allocating resources and assessing performance within the company. Thus **identifiable operating segments** are the businesses in a company that regularly provide separate financial information for review to the chief operating decision maker, who, in turn, uses the information to allocate resources and assess performance.

Normally there will be a manager in charge of a business component, and that manager will interact and negotiate directly with the chief operating decision maker about the segment's plans, results, and resources. In a matrix organization, where one manager is responsible for geographic areas and another is responsible for products or services across the entire enterprise, IFRS recommends that the operating segments be determined by referring to the *core principle* of IFRS 8—that is, disclosing information that best enables users to understand and evaluate the entity's operating results and prospects and the environment in which it operates.

Although some operating segments may be quite separable when defined by the criteria described above, they may nevertheless be combined for segment reporting if they meet certain restrictive criteria. Separately identifiable segments may be combined only if they have similar economic characteristics. For example, it is unlikely that segments could be combined if they exhibit different long-term average gross margins or if they operate in different economic environments. The economic indicators considered by a firm in making this assessment must be disclosed.

In addition to having similar economic characteristics, the segments must also be similar with respect to all of the following *aggregation criteria*. These criteria include the nature of the product or service, the nature of the production processes, the type or class of customer, the methods of distribution, and the regulatory environment (if applicable). Finally, any combining of segments must be consistent with the *core principle* of segment reporting contained in IFRS 8.

**Judgment Issues** As you may expect, the determination of identifiable segments takes a lot of professional judgment. For example, two business components may serve the same general market, although not necessarily the same customers. If the products are complementary, or are substitutes for each other, then the enterprise may simply be horizontally integrated in the same market rather than being in two different segments.

For example, suppose that a beer company owns a winery. Beer and wine are likely to have different segment managers and distinct financial reporting, and may be viewed by senior management as two different segments. But since both beer and wine serve the same general market, it may make sense to report only one alcoholic beverages segment rather than two segments.

The degree of vertical integration may also be used as a criterion for segmentation. A company may produce a raw material, refine it, convert it into manufactured products, and sell the products through its own chain of stores. Each of these activities may have different future prospects, and therefore users may find information about each of these activities important. However, the question arises as to whether the company is in three segments (resources, manufacturing, and retailing) or in one vertically integrated segment.

The relative independence of the various levels of the business may provide an indication of the appropriate treatment. If the three levels of business operate fairly autonomously, buying materials from external suppliers and selling intermediate outputs on the open market, then the enterprise would seem to be in separate segments rather than in just one. The most important indicator, however, is the way in which they are managed. If the business component is managed as a separate segment, then the company should treat it as a separate segment even if most or all of its sales are made internally. However, it is important to remember that a segment must earn revenues and incur expenses. If almost all of the raw material goes into the enterprise's own manufacturing plants, and if the divisions are treated as cost centres or revenue centres rather than as profit centres, then it is unlikely that the business component is an operating segment (remember that this would likely cause them to fail the first criterion for identifying an operating segment—that is, the revenue/expense criterion).

Different companies with seemingly comparable operations could quite legitimately segment their results differently. One company may report several related operating segments, while another company with seemingly similar segments may choose to report the segments together as a single, dominant, integrated segment. Therefore, users should be cautious when comparing segment information of seemingly similar companies.

**Ethical Issues**  Wherever a large degree of management judgment is permitted, there also is a potential for ethical dilemmas. In some situations, management may be tempted to "hide" segments that aren't doing well by reclassifying them inside broader segments. This is not just hypothetical. When Canadian standards were changed in the pre-IFRS period, some problematic segments did magically disappear from consolidated statements.

One example was the Canadian federal government's publicly accountable airport authority. One large airport operated at huge losses for years, and every year the press came down hard on the government's support for this "white elephant." After accounting standards were changed to give management more discretion in identifying and combining segments based on the company's internal reporting structure, this problematic airport suddenly disappeared from public view because it was reclassified into a segment that included some very profitable airports. As far as the government was concerned, it was "Problem solved!"

IFRS guidelines are intended to discourage such practices, but they can be circumvented by managers.

**Reportable Segments**    There is a difference between an *identifiable* segment and a *reportable* segment. To be reportable, a segment must be separately identifiable, and must also satisfy at least one of three quantitative criteria or guidelines. The general guidelines are that a segment is considered **reportable** if it comprises 10% or more of the enterprise's:

- total revenues, including sales between segments; *or*
- operating profits; *or*
- combined assets of all operating segments.

In applying the 10% guideline for profits, a problem arises when some of the operating segments operate at a loss while others are profitable. The offsetting effect of profits and losses reduces the size of the company's total profit (or loss), and thereby reduces the level of segment profit or loss that would satisfy the 10% criterion. The approach to dealing with the offsetting effect is that the 10% profit guideline should be applied to the *larger* of the absolute value of:

1. 10% of the combined profits of all of the segments that reported profits, or
2. 10% of the combined losses of all of the segments that operated at a loss for the period.

Any segment reporting a profit or loss of which the absolute value is greater than the amount determined above is reportable.

For example, suppose that a company has six operating segments, as follows:

| Segment | Operating Profit (Loss) |
|---------|-------------------------|
| A | $25,000 |
| B | (10,000) |
| C | 9,000 |
| D | 36,000 |
| E | (35,000) |
| F | 40,000 |
| Total | $65,000 |

The total profit is $65,000, and all of the segments have profits or losses that are higher than 10% of that amount. However, the sum of the profitable segments is $110,000, while the sum of the losses is $45,000. The basis for applying the 10% guideline is the larger of those two amounts, or $110,000. Any segment that has a profit or a loss larger than $11,000 is reportable. Under that criterion, segments B and C cease to be reportable segments (although they still may meet one of the other criteria).

Only one of the 10% tests needs to be met. The 10% test prevents companies from being forced to provide segment information on those segments that have relatively insignificant operations but nevertheless are identifiable separately. After applying the quantitative criteria, if an operating segment does not meet any of these criteria (i.e., it is an immaterial segment), it can be combined with another related immaterial segment

**Exhibit 7.1** Identifying Reportable Segments

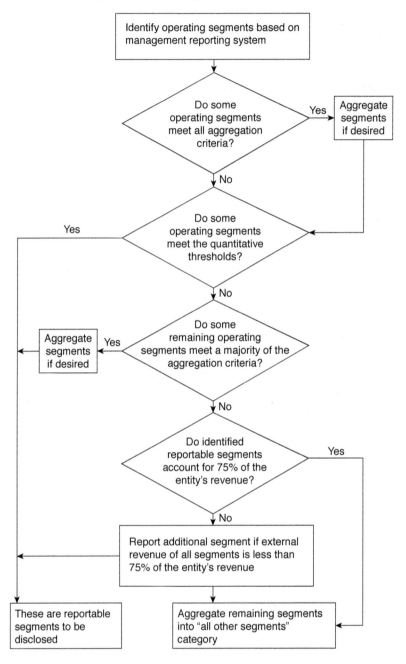

Source: IFRS 8, Operating Segments, Implementation Guidance, p. 888. Accessed September 2009 at http://eifrs.iasb.org/eifrs/files/115/ifrs08_bv2009_190.pdf.

provided the two segments have similar economic characteristics and meet a *majority* of the aggregation criteria listed earlier.

What is the minimum and maximum number of segments that should be disclosed? IFRS 8 suggests that at least 75% of the enterprise's consolidated external revenues should be disclosed by separate operating segments; only then can any remaining segments that did not meet the quantitative criteria be combined into an "other" category. If the 75% threshold is not met, additional small segments should be disclosed until the 75% threshold is met. Management, however, can choose to report additional segments even if the 75% threshold has been met. IFRS 8 suggests that 10 segments may be a reasonable upper limit for disclosure. Exhibit 7.1 presents a diagram for identifying reportable segments.

The definition of "profit" is intentionally ambiguous. The requirements make no reference as to how profit is measured. It may be pre-tax or after-tax, and it may or may not include costs, such as interest expense or allocated head office expenses. The profit measure is simply the one used by the chief operating decision maker in allocating resources to the segment and assessing its performance. In other words, segment profit is measured on the same basis as the company measures it in its internal reporting system.

If more than one measure is used by the chief operating decision maker, then the reported measure should be the one that is measured in a manner that is the most consistent with the measurement of profit in the company's financial statements. Again, a financial statement reader must be extremely cautious in trying to compare segment profits between different enterprises.

It is quite possible for an identifiable segment to satisfy one of the 10% criteria in one year and not the next, or vice versa. Therefore, the determination of reportable segments must be based on more than a one-year view. If a segment is likely to exceed a 10% guideline more often than not, or if management believes that the segment is of continuing significance, then it probably should be reported *each* year even if it may not meet the guideline every year.

The qualitative criterion of *consistency* suggests that the same segment breakdown should be reported each year until a significant shift in relative importance of lines of business causes a segment to permanently drop below the 10% guidelines. The guidelines should also be used to identify emerging segments, those that are increasing in importance in the consolidated enterprise.

## Concept Check 7-1

1. What is segment reporting?
2. What risks does segment reporting help financial statements users assess?
3. How can an operating segment be identified?

# 7.2 SEGMENT INFORMATION TO BE REPORTED

Three basic pieces of information should be reported for each segment:

- a measure of profit or loss;
- total assets, if regularly provided; and
- a measure of liabilities, if regularly provided.

Remember that the requirement is specifically for "a" measure of profit—there is no suggestion as to how profit should be measured. The profit measure is whatever the company's senior management uses to evaluate the segment.

LO ❷
State the segment information and entity-wide disclosures that are required to be reported

# Operating Segment Performance for Thomson Reuters

How does Thomson Reuters determine and report operating segment performance? The company's 2012 interim financial statements disclose the following:

> In accordance with IFRS 8, Operating Segments, the Company discloses information about its reportable segments based upon the measures used by management in assessing the performance of those reportable segments. By definition, results from the Media business and Other businesses are excluded from reportable segments as they do not qualify as a component of the Company's four reportable segments, nor as a separate reportable segment. The Company uses segment operating profit to measure the operating performance of its reportable segments. The costs of centralized support services such as technology, news, accounting, procurement, legal, human resources and strategy are allocated to each segment based on usage or other applicable measures. Segment operating profit is defined as operating profit before (i) amortization of other identifiable intangible assets; (ii) other operating gains and losses; (iii) certain asset impairment charges; and (iv) corporate-related items (including corporate expense, costs associated with the Reuters integration program that was completed in 2011, and fair value adjustments). Management uses this measure because amortization of other identifiable intangible assets, other operating gains and losses, certain asset impairment charges and corporate-related items are not considered to be controllable operating activities for purposes of assessing the current performance of the reportable segments. While in accordance with IFRS, the Company's definition of segment operating profit may not be comparable to that of other companies.

Source: Thomson Reuters Corporation, First Quarter Report (period ended March 31, 2012), p. 37.

IFRS 8 lists additional items to be disclosed for each reportable segment. However, these items are reported only *if* they are reviewed regularly by the chief operating decision maker. Regular review can be either (1) by their inclusion in the measure of segment profit that is used by senior management, or (2) by their being separately reported and reviewed. The information to be disclosed is as follows:

- revenues, separately disclosed by:
  - sales to external customers;
  - intersegment sales; and
  - interest revenue and interest expense, normally disclosed separately
- income tax expense or benefit;
- amortization and depreciation;
- significant non-cash items other than amortization and depreciation;
- nature and amount of material revenues, expenses, gains, or losses (such as discontinued operations; inventory and property, plant, and equipment write-downs or reversals; disposal of property, plant, and equipment or investments; restructuring costs or reversals; litigation settlements; other reversals of provisions);
- total expenditures for additions to non-current assets (other than financial instruments, deferred tax assets, post-employment benefit assets, and rights arising under insurance contracts);
- information about associates and joint ventures accounted for by the equity method:
  - equity in earnings; and
  - amount of investment.

In the notes, the reporting enterprise should explain the basis for determining reportable segments. Also, the company should present a general description of the products and services from which each segment derives its revenues.

The segment information reported to the chief operating decision maker may be based on non-consolidated data or, alternatively, on information that may not have an equivalent within IFRS. Therefore, a reconciliation of the segmented revenues, profits, assets, liabilities, and any other reported material item to the amounts in the consolidated financial statements is also required.

## Entity-Wide Disclosures

LO
State the segment information and entity-wide disclosures that are required to be reported

To achieve the objective of improving information through disaggregation, IFRS 8 requires that key information on products and services, geographic areas, and major customers should be provided if it is not already disclosed in the reportable segment information. These disclosures are required for the company as a whole even if the company has only one reportable segment or if the company does not have any separate reportable segments.

**Products and Services**   We stated above that the company should disclose the nature of each segment's products and services. However, a company may not have separate reportable segments but still may have a series of different product types or services. In that case, the company should disclose the external revenues from each group of similar products and services. These disclosures should be consistent with the information that form the basis for the company's reported financial statements.

**Geographic Areas**   One of the primary tasks of a financial statement reader is to assess the potential business risks that are facing an enterprise. Several aspects of business risk are related to the countries or geographic areas in which the company does business. Risks relate to both revenue potential and asset exposure.

If a Canadian company generates significant amounts of revenue in Europe, for example, European revenues (and profits) will be threatened if the euro weakens in relation to the Canadian dollar. As the euro declines, Canadian services and products become more expensive in terms of euros. Or, if the company maintains its prices in euros, the Canadian-dollar profit margin will decline as the euro declines. Similarly, assets located in certain geographic areas may be a source of risk. The risk can arise either politically (e.g., political instability) or economically (e.g., high inflation).

To help investors assess risk, companies should disclose the extent to which their sales are to foreign versus domestic customers, and also the breakdown between domestic and foreign assets. The specific required disclosures *for each geographic area* are as follows:

- revenues from external customers in foreign countries;
- revenues from external customers in the company's home country;
- non-current assets that are located in foreign countries; and
- non-current assets that are located in the company's home country.

Note that if the revenues or assets in an individual foreign country are material, they are to be disclosed separately. In many cases, the domestic–foreign breakdown is provided as part of the segment disclosure. If the segment disclosures contain all of the appropriate information, then no additional reporting is necessary. Otherwise, the company should disclose these four pieces of information for the consolidated enterprise as a whole. The information for these disclosures should be consistent with the company's reported financial statements.

**Major Customers**   Another major risk factor is the extent to which a corporation is dependent upon one or a few major customers. What will happen to the company if 45% of its services are provided to a customer that goes bankrupt?

Because of the risk inherent in relying on major customers, a reporting enterprise should disclose information about the extent of its reliance on its major customers. Not too surprisingly, the guideline is 10%. If the company relies on a single customer for 10% or more of its external revenue, the company should disclose the total amount of revenues from each such customer and the segment or segments that generate those total revenues. Customers under common control are considered to be a single customer.

Note that there is no requirement to disclose the *name* of the important customer or customers. This may be viewed as a shortcoming. If one or more companies in the retail clothing business are in financial jeopardy, it may not be terribly helpful to a financial-statement reader to know that a significant part of a clothing manufacturer's revenue comes from a retail clothing chain without knowing the name of the chain.

For entity-wide disclosures, management may be exempted from the disclosure requirements for products and services and geographic areas if the information is unavailable and it would be excessively costly to develop it. If management takes advantage of this exemption, it must be disclosed in the notes. Exhibit 7.2 presents a summary of the disclosure requirements for IFRS 8.

**Exhibit 7.2** IFRS-8 Disclosures

| Required Segment Disclosures | | |
| --- | --- | --- |
| Type | Disclosure | Reconciliation Required |
| General | Basis for determining segments | N/A |
| | Products and services of segment | N/A |
| Reportable Segments: Disclosures based on management information | Measure of profit or loss | Yes |
| | Segment assets (if reviewed) | Yes |
| | Measure of liabilities (if reviewed) | Yes |
| | Significant profit or loss items (if reviewed) | Yes |
| | Additions to non-current assets (if reviewed) | Yes |
| | Information on associates and joint ventures (if reviewed) | Yes |

| Required Entity-Wide Disclosures (only if not disclosed in segment disclosures): | |
| --- | --- |
| Type | Disclosure |
| Products and Services | External revenue |
| Geographic | External revenue |
| Areas | Non-current assets |
| Major Customers | External revenue |

# Examples of Segment Reporting

There is no prescribed format for the reporting of information by segments; the method of presentation is left entirely up to the preparers. In the following paragraphs, we will discuss two quite different examples of segment disclosure.

**Agrium Inc.**   Our first example of segmented financial reporting is shown in Exhibit 7.3, for Calgary-based Agrium Inc. Agrium is a major supplier of agricultural products and services, as well as a global producer of agricultural nutrients and industrial products. Agrium segments its operations by product or service (as opposed to geography, which we will see in our second example). It has three reportable business segments: Wholesale, Retail, and Advanced Technologies. The company gives a brief description of its segments in Note 1, and then in Note 29 reports each of the pieces of information required under segment reporting.

**Exhibit 7.3** Agrium Inc., Segmented Financial Reporting, December 31, 2011

---

### 1. Corporate information [excerpts]

Agrium (with its subsidiaries) is a major retail supplier of agricultural products and services in North and South America, Australia and Europe and a leading global producer and marketer of agricultural nutrients and industrial products. We produce and market three primary groups of nutrients: nitrogen, phosphate and potash as well as controlled-release crop nutrients and micronutrients.

Agrium operates three strategic business units:

- Retail operates in North and South America and Australia and sells crop nutrients, crop protection products, seed and services directly to growers.

- Wholesale operates in North and South America and Europe producing, marketing and distributing three primary groups of crop nutrients: nitrogen, potash and phosphate for agricultural and industrial customers around the world.

- Advanced Technologies ("AAT") produces and markets controlled-release crop nutrients and micronutrients in the broad-based agriculture, specialty agriculture, professional turf, horticulture, and consumer lawn and garden markets worldwide.

### 29. OPERATING SEGMENTS

Our operating segments are the strategic business units through which we operate and report our business: Retail, Wholesale, Advanced Technologies and Other. Each of these segments has developed its own strategy, goals and tactics in alignment with Agrium's overall corporate strategy. Segment results are reviewed internally by the senior leadership team on regular basis for the purpose of making decisions regarding resource allocations and performance assessments.

|  | 2011 | 2010 |
|---|---|---|
| **Consolidated sales** | | |
| Retail | | |
| Crop nutrients | 4,537 | 3,001 |
| Crop protection products | 3,449 | 2,703 |
| Seed | 1,085 | 877 |
| Merchandise | 629 | 158 |
| Services and other | 616 | 230 |
| | 10,316 | 6,969 |

*Exhibit Continued >*

---

| | | |
|---|---:|---:|
| Wholesale | | |
|   Nitrogen | 2,051 | 1,458 |
|   Potash | 809 | 675 |
|   Phosphate | 893 | 596 |
|   Product purchased for resale | 1,566 | 1,039 |
|   Other | 257 | 216 |
| | **5,576** | **3,984** |
| Advanced Technologies | 510 | 397 |
| Other[a] | (932) | (607) |
| | **15,470** | **10,743** |
| Consolidated inter segment sales | | |
|   Retail | 29 | 28 |
|   Wholesale | 817 | 524 |
|   Advanced Technologies | 86 | 55 |
| | 932 | 607 |
| Consolidated net earnings | | |
|   Retail | 600 | 409 |
|   Wholesale | 1,846 | 889 |
|   Advanced Technologies | (51) | 12 |
|   Other[a] | (172) | (197) |
|   Earnings before finance costs and income taxes | 2,223 | 1,113 |
|   Finance costs related to long-term debt | 101 | 88 |
|   Other finance costs | 59 | 31 |
|   Earnings before income taxes | 2,063 | 994 |
|   Income taxes | 555 | 264 |
| **Consolidated net earnings from continuing operations** | **1,508** | **730** |
| **Consolidated net loss from discontinued operations** | **(133)** | **(17)** |
| **Consolidated net earnings** | **1,375** | **713** |

(a) The Other segment is a non-operating segment for inter segment eliminations and corporate functions.

| | December 31, | | January 1, |
|---|---:|---:|---:|
| | 2011 | 2010 | 2010 |
| **Total assets** | | | |
|   Retail | 7,685 | 6,935 | 5,389 |
|   Wholesale | 2,997 | 2,633 | 3,175 |
|   Advanced Technologies | 474 | 460 | 418 |
|   Other | 1,914 | 1,360 | 692 |
|   Discontinued operations | 70 | 1,504 | – |
| | 13,140 | 12,892 | 9,674 |

## Investments in associates

| | | | |
|---|---|---|---|
| Retail | 19 | 4 | — |
| Wholesale | 279 | 274 | 270 |
| Advanced Technologies | 29 | 86 | 87 |
| Other | 28 | 41 | 13 |
| | 355 | 405 | 370 |

| | 2011 | 2010 |
|---|---|---|
| **Additions to non-current assets[a]** | | |
| Retail | 263 | 747 |
| Wholesale | 516 | 350 |
| Advanced Technologies | 61 | 18 |
| Other | 26 | 51 |
| | 866 | 1,166 |

(a) Includes property, plant and equipment, intangibles and goodwill.

| Additional information | Retail | | Wholesale | | Advanced Technologies | | Other | |
|---|---|---|---|---|---|---|---|---|
| | 2011 | 2010 | 2011 | 2010 | 2011 | 2010 | 2011 | 2010 |
| Share-based payments | — | — | — | — | — | — | (51) | 111 |
| Earnings from associates | (1) | — | (19) | (22) | (1) | (4) | — | — |
| Material non-cash items | | | | | | | | |
| Depreciation and amortization | 169 | 115 | 173 | 192 | 24 | 19 | 15 | 8 |
| Asset impairement | — | — | — | — | 61 | — | — | — |

| Key data by region | 2011 | | 2010 | |
|---|---|---|---|---|
| | Sales[a] | Non-current assets[b] | Sales[a] | Non-Current assets[b] |
| Canada | 1,957 | 1,570 | 1,393 | 1,259 |
| United States | 9,550 | 2,856 | 8,016 | 2,747 |
| Europe | 925 | 16 | 625 | 21 |
| South America | 725 | 230 | 497 | 234 |
| Australia and Asia | 2,223 | 904 | 144 | 1,004 |
| Other | 90 | 290 | 68 | 294 |
| | 15,470 | 5,866 | 10,743 | 5,559 |

(a) Sales by location of third party customers.

(b) Excludes financial instruments, deferred tax assets and discontinued operations.

No revenues from transactions with a single external customer amount to 10 percent or more of Agrium's revenues.

Source: Agrium Inc. 2011 Annual Report.

First, the company provides net sales by reportable operating segment. In addition, it also provides the net sales by major product categories for the retail and wholesale segments. The company thereby fulfills two requirements: In addition to reporting on the reportable operating segments, it also provides information about its products and services.

Note that the "other" category of sales for a negative $932 million is an elimination of intersegment sales. The resulting total segment sales ($15,470 million) is the same amount shown for net sales on the company's SCI. Thus it is reconciled to the corresponding amount on the consolidated financial statement, as required.

Second, note that the reported income number ($2,223) is defined as "Earnings before finance costs and income taxes." The total reported is the same as the relevant item on the consolidated financial statements. In addition, all items reported below this number are identical to the corresponding numbers on the consolidated financial statements.

Third, note that total assets are reported for all three segments and there are substantial assets used for corporate functions. The total asset balance of $13,140 reconciles to the total assets reported on the SFP (not shown here). Additions to non-current assets and other items, such as material non-cash items on the income statement, are also disclosed.

Finally, the company discloses its sales and non-current assets (capital assets and goodwill) by major geographic area, as required under segment reporting, in a separate table. The totals can be reconciled to the totals on the company's financial statements. (The reconciliation for non-current assets requires the use of information in Note 17 in addition to information on the SFP.) It should be noted that the company discloses additional segment information in its management discussion and analysis (MD&A). For example, gross profit by segment and product line is discussed in addition to major expenses.

**Magna International Inc.**   A more extensive example using geographic segment disclosure can be found in Magna International Inc. Magna is a major Canada-based global supplier of automobile parts and systems, generating 81% of its revenue outside of Canada. The segmented reporting note for Magna is shown in Exhibit 7.4, slightly shortened from the original.

**Exhibit 7.4** Magna International Inc.

| Segmented Financial Reporting [excerpts] |
| December 31, 2011 |

**24. SEGMENTED INFORMATION**

[a]   Magna, a diversified global automotive supplier, follows a corporate policy of functional and operational decentralization. It conducts its operations through divisions, which function as autonomous business units. As at December 31, 2011, Magna had 286 manufacturing operations and 88 product development, engineering and sales centres in 26 countries. Magna designs, develops and manufactures technologically advanced automotive systems, assemblies, modules and components, and engineers and assembles complete vehicles, primarily for sale to OEMs of cars and light trucks. The Company's capabilities include the design, engineering, testing and manufacture of automotive interior systems; seating systems; closure systems; body and chassis systems; vision systems; electronic systems; exterior systems; powertrain systems; roof systems; hybrid and electric vehicles/systems as well as complete vehicle engineering and assembly.

Given the differences between the regions in which the Company operates, Magna's operations are segmented on a geographic basis between North America, Europe and Rest of World. The Company maintains management teams in each of the Company's two primary markets, North America and Europe. The role of the North American and European management teams is to manage Magna's interests to ensure a coordinated effort across the Company's different product capabilities. In addition to maintaining key customer, supplier and government contacts in their respective markets, the regional management teams centrally manage key aspects of the Company's operations while permitting the divisions enough flexibility through Magna's decentralized structure to foster an entrepreneurial environment.

Consistent with the above, the Company's internal financial reporting separately segments key internal operating performance measures between North America, Europe and Rest of World for purposes of presentation to the chief operating decision maker to assist in the assessment of operating performance, the allocation of resources, and the long-term strategic direction and future global growth in the Company.

The Company's chief operating decision maker uses Adjusted EBIT as the measure of segment profit or loss, since management believes Adjusted EBIT is the most appropriate measure of operational profitability or loss for its reporting segments. Adjusted EBIT represents income from operations before income taxes; interest income, net; and other expense, net.

The following table shows certain information with respect to segment disclosures:

| | Total sales | External sales | Depreciation and amortization | Adjusted EBIT | Goodwill | Fixed asset additions | Fixed assets, net |
|---|---|---|---|---|---|---|---|
| | | | | 2011 | | | |
| North America | | | | | | | |
| Canada | $ 5,951 | $ 5,552 | | | | $ 115 | $ 586 |
| United States | 7,025 | 6,514 | | | | 281 | 804 |
| Mexico | 2,902 | 2,698 | | | | 162 | 477 |
| Eliminations | (1,023) | — | | | | — | — |
| North America | 14,855 | 14,764 | $358 | $1,373 | $ 644 | 558 | 1,867 |
| Europe | | | | | | | |
| Euroland [i] | 10,122 | 9,956 | | | | 292 | 1,012 |
| Great Britain | 913 | 909 | | | | 7 | 53 |
| Other European countries | 1,707 | 1,564 | | | | 124 | 537 |
| Eliminations | (186) | — | | | | — | — |
| Europe | 12,556 | 12,429 | 259 | (22) | 393 | 423 | 1,602 |
| Rest of World | 1,599 | 1,506 | 38 | 56 | 158 | 236 | 485 |
| Corporate and Other [ii], [iii] | (262) | 49 | 31 | (40) | 1 | 19 | 282 |
| Total reportable segments | 28,748 | 28,748 | 686 | 1,367 | 1,196 | 1,236 | 4,236 |
| Other expense, net | | | | (156) | | | |
| Interest income, net | | | | 6 | | | |
| | $28,748 | $28,748 | $686 | $1,217 | $1,196 | $1,236 | 4,236 |
| Current assets | | | | | | | 8,146 |
| Investments, goodwill, deferred tax assets and other assets | | | | | | | 2,297 |
| Consolidated total assets | | | | | | | $14,679 |

*Exhibit Continued >*

[i]   For purposes of segmentation, Euroland has been defined as those European countries that have adopted the euro as their common currency.

[ii]  Included in Corporate and Other EBIT are intercompany fees charged to the automotive segments.

[iii] Corporate and Other includes equity loss of $66 million [2010 - $30 million, 2009 - $nil] related to the Company's proportionate share of the net loss in E-Car. For the year ended December 31, 2010, Corporate and Other also includes sales of $8 million and an Adjusted EBIT loss of $50 million related to E-Car prior to the deconsolidation of E-Car under the Arrangement *[note 3]*.

For the year ended December 31, 2011, E-Car had sales of $92 million [2010 - $20 million, 2009 - $5 million], an Adjusted EBIT loss of $91 million [2010 - $89 million. 2009 - $45 million] and fixed assets of $77 million [2010 - $76 million, 2009 - $15 million].

[b] The following table aggregates external revenues by customer as follows:

|                      | 2011     | 2010     | 2009     |
|----------------------|----------|----------|----------|
| General Motors       | $ 6,202  | $ 4,731  | $ 3,141  |
| BMW                  | 4,191    | 3,090    | 2,850    |
| Fiat / Chrysler Group| 3,864    | 3,102    | 1,817    |
| Ford Motor Company   | 3,549    | 3,371    | 2,525    |
| Volkswagen           | 3,187    | 2,567    | 2,001    |
| Daimler AG           | 2,793    | 2,354    | 1,757    |
| Other                | 4,962    | 4,250    | 2,785    |
|                      | $28,748  | $23,465  | $16,876  |

[c] The following table summarizes external revenues generated by automotive products and services:

|                                  | 2011     | 2010     | 2009     |
|----------------------------------|----------|----------|----------|
| Exterior and interior systems    | $11,020  | $ 8,637  | $ 5,927  |
| Body systems and chassis systems | 6,056    | 4,801    | 3,374    |
| Powertrain systems               | 3,667    | 3,064    | 2,114    |
| Complete vehicle assembly        | 2,690    | 2,163    | 1,764    |
| Vision and electronic systems    | 2,066    | 1,756    | 1,315    |
| Tooling, engineering and other   | 2,065    | 2,005    | 1,625    |
| Closure systems                  | 1,184    | 1,039    | 757      |
|                                  | $28,748  | $23,465  | $16,876  |

Source: Magna International Inc. 2011 Annual Report.

You should observe several points in this exhibit.

■   In the first table, the company reports three geographic regions: North America, Europe, and Rest of World, since Magna's internal reporting system provides information at the level of these three regions for assessing performance and allocating resources. Canada is included in the "North America" region in the first table. No other region (e.g., Asia or Africa) meets the reporting criteria, and therefore Magna lumps all other regions into "Rest of World." Magna discloses total sales, both including and excluding intersegment sales. Magna's measure of segment profit is *adjusted earnings before interest and taxes (EBIT)*. Finally, the totals at the bottom all equal the corresponding accounts in the consolidated financial statements.

■ In the second table, Magna discloses its major customers *by name*. The six customers disclosed account for roughly 82% of Magna's sales in 2011. Note also that Daimler AG is still disclosed even though it is slightly less than 10% of total revenues in 2011. This is for comparative consistency, since Daimler did meet the 10% guideline in 2009 and 2010.

■ In the third table, Magna discloses its sales by similar products and services.

## Concept Check 7-2

1. What three key items of information should be reported for each segment?
2. What is the reason for requiring companies to report geographic segments?
3. What key disclosures are required for major customers?

## 7.3 INTERIM REPORTING

LO ❸
Describe the scope, content, and periods covered in interim reports

*Interim statements* are financial statements issued for any period of time of *less* than one year. One of the basic postulates of accounting is *periodicity*—that it is feasible to break the financial life of an organization into discrete time periods and to report meaningfully on financial performance during that period. All enterprises issue financial reports at least once a year. However, periodicity can also be applied to shorter periods.

## Applicability

Public companies are required by securities regulations and/or corporations acts to issue interim statements. In Canada and the United States, quarterly statements are required. In most other counties, interim statements need only be semi-annual. Interim reports of public companies must comply with IFRS, but they do not need to be audited.

For public reporting, consistency between annual and interim reports is essential. Although interim reports may be prepared in less detail than annual statements and necessarily will include more estimates, it would be a rude shock to managers and shareholders alike if the annual statements were not consonant with the operations as described by the interim statements. Thus interim statements should be prepared by using accounting and reporting approaches that are consistent with those used for preparing the annual statements.

There is no requirement or obligation for private enterprises to issue interim statements. IFRS requirements do not apply, and there is no requirement for interim statements in ASPE. Of course, private enterprises may issue interim statements (1) for their own use or (2) at the request of stakeholders such as banks or private equity investors. Internal interim reports may be monthly rather than quarterly, and will almost certainly be more detailed than those prepared for external release. Since the reports are for management's use only, they may be prepared on a basis that is

**Exhibit 7.5** Statements Required for Interim Reporting, with Sample Dates*

| Type of Statement | Current Reporting | Comparative Reporting |
|---|---|---|
| Statement of financial position | | |
| ■ At a point in time | Sep 30, 20X3 | Dec 31, 20X2 |
| Statement of comprehensive income | | |
| ■ Interim period (3 months ended) | Sep 30, 20X3 | Sep 30, 20X2 |
| ■ Year-to-date (9 months ended) | Sep 30, 20X3 | Sep 30, 20X2 |
| Statement of cash flows | | |
| ■ Year-to-date (9 months ended) | Sep 30, 20X3 | Sep 30, 20X2 |
| Statement of changes in equity | | |
| ■ Year-to-date (9 months ended) | Sep 30, 20X3 | Sep 30, 20X2 |

*Assuming that quarterly reporting is required, that the company is reporting for its third quarter, and that the fiscal year-end is December 31, 20X3.

consistent with the internal decision-making process rather than the basis on which the annual statements are prepared.

Interim reports issued at the request of other stakeholders fall under the broad category of special-purpose financial reporting. The statements may follow the general format and reporting principles that the company uses for the annual financial statements. Alternatively, the statements may be specially designed to satisfy specific needs of external users—for example, to satisfy bank covenants concerning the fair value of collateral.

# General Principles of Application

IAS 34, *Interim Financial Reporting*, specifies the minimum content of interim statements and specifies the recognition and measurement principles that are to be used in interim statements. Since the frequency for issuing interim statements is a function of national securities regulators, IFRS does not indicate how frequently they should be prepared (quarterly or half-yearly).

**Content and Consistency of Interim Reports**  IFRS requires that interim reports contain condensed statements of (1) financial position; (2) comprehensive income; (3) changes in equity; and (4) cash flows, along with selected note disclosures. What is meant by "condensed statements"? At a minimum, condensed statements should include the same headings and subtotals that the company uses in the annual financial statements. This should not be interpreted too literally. Too much aggregation will result in statements that are not useful. Some aggregation, however, is acceptable. For example, a company's SFP may have several lines for different types of depreciable capital assets, and these may be collapsed into a single line for interim statements. Further, on the interim SCI, some expenses may be collapsed into a single line titled "operating expenses."

There is also no need to repeat most note disclosures on interim financial statements. A statement reader has access to the previous year-end financial statements, and much of the information in those notes will be substantially the same for the interim periods.

Given this, the *exception reporting* principle is used for note disclosure—to the extent that there are significant changes, the company should provide note disclosure. Thus, only new or significantly changed accounting policies are disclosed.

In addition, the notes should disclose any material events or transactions that affect interpretation of the current interim period's financial results. Examples would include changes in strategic investments, restructurings, and/or discontinued operations. Subsequent-event disclosure is also required.

Finally, the notes to the interim statements should also indicate that they should be read in conjunction with the company's previous annual financial statements, since fuller information is available in the annual statements than in the interim statement.

**Periods Covered**   The period covered by the interim statements varies somewhat depending on the type of statement. Interim SCIs should report on both the individual interim period and on the year to date. For example, the third-quarter SCI will show operating results both for the third quarter and for the year-to-date cumulative amounts for the first three quarters.

The statement of changes in equity and the cash flow statement, in contrast, report only on a year-to-date basis. The SFP will be as of the reporting date, of course; there is no such thing as a year-to-date SFP, since that statement reports on financial condition at a point in time.

All financial statements need a basis for comparison. Interim statements produced for external users are normally prepared on a comparative basis. In most statements, the comparison is with the same period of the preceding year. For the SFP, however, the comparison is with the previous year-end SFP. Exhibit 7.5 summarizes these comparative requirements for external reporting. For internal reports, budgeted figures for the period may provide a more relevant basis for comparison.

**Segment Information**   Segment information should also be presented in the interim statements. Segment information should include at least the following:

- segment revenues, segregated between intersegment revenues and those to external customers;
- segment profit (loss);

- segment assets if there has been a significant change from the amounts reported in the previous annual statements;

- any changes in the basis of segmentation or the method of reporting segment profit; and

- reconciliation of segment earnings to consolidated earnings for the interim period.

The interim segment information is essentially the same as that required in the annual financial statements.

## 7.4 THE PERIODICITY PROBLEM

At first glance, it may appear that the preparation of interim statements poses no special problems. After all, interim reports use the same accounting policies that are used for the annual statements, so what's the big deal? Just use the same policies, and interim reporting is a no-brainer, right? Wrong! Interim reporting is not quite so simple.

When we prepare annual financial statements, we face many challenges of estimation and inter-period allocation. Revenue recognition can present significant difficulties, the costs of tangible and intangible capital assets must be allocated, and future costs must be estimated to achieve matching. When these accounting problems are confronted for a period shorter than a year, their significance increases proportionately.

Estimation errors will have a much larger impact on the operating income for a month or a quarter than they will on the operating income for a year. Cut-off procedures will not be as stringent for the unaudited interim statements, and interim inventories are most likely to be estimated or to be taken from perpetual inventory records whose accuracy has not been verified by a physical count.

Not only will estimation errors have a greater impact, but the materiality threshold will also be lower because the amounts on the quarterly SCI and cash flow statement will be only about one-fourth of the annual amounts. Estimation variances that might be ignored in the annual statements (with the higher materiality threshold) become significant in the quarterly statements. The result is that interim statements will be intrinsically and significantly less reliable than annual statements.

Additional estimation and allocation problems arise because of the shorter accounting period. Some costs and revenues are seasonal or annual in nature, and interim statements require allocations that are not necessary for annual statements.

For example, annual insurance costs pose no problems if the accounting period is a year, but how should the cost be allocated if the period is a month? An easy answer would be to allocate one-twelfth of the cost to each month. However, suppose that the insurance is an expensive public liability policy for an amusement park that is open all year, but that does the bulk of its business in the summer months. Should the cost be allocated by time or by volume of activity to match the cost with the revenue?

Another example is a factory that shuts down in the month of August for a vacation for all production employees. The fixed costs of the factory during August could be viewed as a cost to be allocated to all of the interim periods, or as a cost of the individual period in which August falls. Similarly, annual costs such as once-a-year major maintenance costs could either be allocated, or could be allowed to fall into the interim period in which they occur.

Some costs are determined not only on an annual basis, but also *after* the end of the year. Customer rebates, sales bonuses, and income taxes are examples of these costs. Should an attempt be made to estimate and allocate these costs, or should they be allowed to fall into the last interim period?

As the preceding examples suggest, there are two basic approaches to the preparation of interim statements. The interim period can be viewed either as a distinct and separate accounting period of its own (the *discrete approach*), or as a part of a year (the *integral approach*).

## Discrete Approach

**LO 4**
Explain the different theoretical approaches to recognition and measurement for interim reporting

**General Approach**   Under the **discrete approach** (or *separate-period approach*), each interim period is accounted for by using the company's normal accounting policies applied to the interim period as though it were a year. A company's policy may be to immediately expense all costs that may have future benefits that are difficult to measure, such as development costs. Under this accounting policy, deferred charges and credits are normally not carried on the SFP.

A company that follows this policy will also apply it to the interim periods under the discrete approach. Costs will be permitted to fall into the period in which they are incurred, even though they may be annual costs that benefit other interim periods.

The discrete approach implicitly recognizes that since revenues and expenses are likely to be "lumpy," the interim earnings are also going to be lumpy, and are not just a proportionate part of the annual earnings. This approach treats the insurance costs, vacation costs, or maintenance costs as period costs for the quarter rather than allocating them to the other periods.

**Taxes**   Under the discrete approach, income taxes are calculated for each interim period separately. If the firm is operating under a progressive tax structure, the tax expense in earlier periods will be calculated using the lower tax rate while the tax expense in later periods will be calculated using the higher tax rate.

In addition to income taxes, firms usually incur payroll taxes (e.g., Employment Insurance, Canada Pension Plan). These taxes are often only paid up to a certain maximum of employee earnings. Under the discrete approach, the payroll tax expense will be recognized as the taxes are incurred and paid. The expense to the firm therefore will be higher for the earlier periods and lower for the later periods.

## Integral Approach

**General Approach**   Under the **integral approach**, the interim period is viewed simply as a part of the longer period of a year. Expenses are allocated across the interim periods in such a way as to portray the company's likely annualized operating results. Theoretically, if a company is heading for a year in which the operating margin (net income divided by sales) is 10%, then the interim statements should reflect that fact. Under this view, the interim statements should be the best predictor available of the company's operating results for the year.

For the examples cited above, the integral approach will allocate the insurance costs proportionately to the volume of business, and will allocate the costs of the plant closing, the annual maintenance costs, and the estimated bonuses and rebates to all of the interim periods.

**Taxes**   Income taxes are viewed as an annual expense to be allocated to interim periods in proportion to the pre-tax interim net income. There will be no separate computation of income taxes for the interim period as though it were a separate taxation period. Instead, an average tax rate will be estimated and used to calculate income tax expense.

Payroll taxes will be handled similarly. An effective average rate will be used to calculate the expense to be recognized for each interim period even though the actual payroll taxes will have been paid ahead of the expense recognition.

# 7.5 RECOGNITION AND MEASUREMENT IN PRACTICE

**Internal Reporting**   For internal interim reports, the discrete approach is almost always used. The comparative amounts for internal users are likely to be budgeted figures for the period (perhaps supplemented by the previous year's figures), and budgets generally include major costs as expenses of the period in which they occur. Controllability is a concern in budgeting, and costs allocated from previous periods are not controllable in the later periods to which they are allocated. Also, internal reports frequently do not include any income tax estimates, thereby eliminating one major estimation problem.

## Public Reporting

**General Approach**   For measuring interim period operating results, IAS 34 adopts the year-to-date approach for measuring assets, liabilities, revenues, and expenses. This approach generally favours the discrete approach—a company should apply the same accounting policies to its interim statements as it used in its annual statements. However, the recommendations also contain some aspects of the integral approach because they suggest that the frequency of reporting should not affect the measurement of the annual results. That is, because the interim period is viewed as a part of a full year, the year-to-date approach allows recognition in the current interim period of amounts resulting from changes in estimates of amounts reported in earlier interim periods.

Therefore, the IAS 34 approach might be characterized as a "modified discrete" approach. As you can imagine, the presence of two differing approaches can lead to potential conflicts in the application of this standard. To assist users, IAS 34 provides some further guidance for particular revenues and costs and also provides examples of recognition and measurement applications in an appendix.

**Revenues and Costs**   As we noted earlier under the periodicity problem, revenues and costs may not be earned/incurred evenly throughout the year. Some revenues may be affected by seasons or cycles or may only be received occasionally. Further costs, such as maintenance, may be incurred unevenly throughout the year. The question arises as to how to handle these types of revenues and costs. Should they be anticipated?

For example, if maintenance is typically performed in the third quarter, should we anticipate it by accruing for it in the first quarter? IAS 34 recommends that costs and revenues should be accrued or deferred at the end of interim periods *only if those same costs or revenues would normally be accrued or deferred at the end of the fiscal year.*

## Specific Examples

**General Application**  Generally the discrete approach will be used in interim reporting for most revenues and costs. A general exception to the use of the discrete approach arises for costs that are determined only on an annual basis. IAS 34 specifically discusses year-end bonuses, contingent lease payments, employer payroll taxes, and income taxes. The section uses the terminology of "constructive obligation" to rationalize these exceptions, but the basic point is simply that companies can estimate or project the determining factors for the entire year and accrue the costs in the interim statements.

LO **5**

Apply the recognition and measurement principles for interim reporting

For example, contingent rents may be based on annual sales in excess of a contractual minimum. In a strict application of the discrete approach, no accrual for contingent rent is made until the threshold level of sales is achieved. IAS 34, however, provides for this type of cost to be spread out over several interim periods—an application of the integral approach.

As another example, consider purchases made under an annual volume rebate or discount scheme. If attainment of the required level of sales to qualify for the rebate is probable, the buyer and the seller should recognize the associated asset and liability, respectively—another application of the integral approach.

In contrast, consider major planned periodic maintenance. A company may have a policy of shutting down its manufacturing plant every August for planned maintenance. IAS 34 suggests that these costs should not be anticipated unless there is a legal or constructive obligation. The argument is that the intention or necessity to incur maintenance costs in the future cannot give rise to an obligation; therefore, no liability should be recognized.

**Income Tax Reporting**  IFRS recommends that interim income tax expense be estimated by using the estimated average annual effective income tax rate (an integral approach). The average rate will differ from the marginal rate only under a two-rate tax system or a progressive tax system, in which higher levels of income are taxed at a different rate than lower levels. Instead of accruing income tax at the lower rate in the early quarters, the average rate applicable to management's estimate of the full year's earnings should be used. The average rate should be used even if the early quarters show a loss and even if the overall earnings for the year are expected to be zero.

Canada has a flat-rate structure for corporate income taxes (except for small businesses, which are not subject to IFRS requirements anyway). However, Canadian corporations with operations in other countries may be subject to variable tax rates, and thus the issue of multiple tax rates still exists for enterprises reporting in Canada.

The benefits of an income tax loss in an interim period are recognized in that period if:

- the loss will be offset by taxable income in the other interim periods of that year;
- the loss can be used as a tax loss carryback to a prior year; or
- it is probable that the benefit of the loss will be realized as a tax loss carryforward.

For example, suppose that a company expects to earn $800,000 evenly over the year (i.e., $200,000 each quarter). Also suppose that the company pays tax at 20% on the first $300,000 of earnings and 40% on any amount above. What would be reported for income tax expense for the first quarter? Under the discrete approach, the tax would be $40,000 ($200,000 × 20%). IAS 34, however, recommends the use of the integral approach, wherein an average rate is calculated and then used to estimate income tax expense. In this scenario, an average tax rate of 32.5% ([20% × 300,000 + 40% × 500,000] ÷ 800,000) would be used and the income tax expense reported would be $65,000 (i.e., $200,000 × 32.5%).

As another example, suppose that a company has a loss of $50,000 in the first quarter but expects to earn $120,000 over the following three quarters. If the expected average tax rate is 30%, the first-quarter interim SCI will show an income tax *benefit* or recovery (i.e., a negative tax expense, or a credit) of $50,000 × 30% = $15,000. The following quarters will show a positive income tax expense totalling $120,000 × 30% = $36,000. The total income tax expense for the year will be $36,000 – $15,000 = $21,000, based on cumulative net income of $70,000 for the year (i.e., $120,000 – $50,000).

## Concept Check 7-3

1. Which condensed financial statements must be reported in interim reports under IFRS? What is meant by the term *condensed statements*?
2. What segment disclosures should be presented in interim financial statements?
3. What is the periodicity problem?
4. What is the discrete approach to interim reporting? What is the integral approach to interim reporting?

# Illustrative Interim Statement

Exhibit 7.6 shows the interim SFP and condensed SCI for North West Company Inc. These are the third-quarter statements for fiscal year 2011–2012. North West is a retailer of food and everyday products and services such as electronics, home furnishings, and clothing. The company's interim statements comply with the IAS 34 recommendations. In Exhibit 7.6, we have omitted the statement of earnings and the statement of cash flows and most of the notes for brevity, but the following points should be noted:

■ The financial statements shown in Exhibit 7.6 contain all the current and comparative information required. However, the consolidated balance sheet also presents the comparative balance sheet for the same date in the previous year. The statement of cash flows, not presented, also contains both the required year-to-date information and information on the most recent three-month interim period (not required). This additional disclosure on the statement of cash flows is common in Canada.

The notes to the financial statements are less detailed than those in the annual report. The excerpt from Note 2 points out that the interim statements should be read in conjunction with the annual statements.

**Exhibit 7.6** Interim Financial Statements [Excerpts]

### NORTH WEST COMPANY 2011–12 THIRD-QUARTER FINANCIAL STATEMENTS
### CONDENSED CONSOLIDATED BALANCE SHEETS

| (unaudited, $ in thousands) | October 31, 2011 | October 31, 2010 | January 31, 2011 |
|---|---|---|---|
| **CURRENT ASSETS** | | | |
| Cash | $ 33,981 | $ 28,769 | $ 31,231 |
| Accounts receivable | 69,897 | 68,943 | 70,180 |
| Inventories (Note 6) | 202,063 | 198,020 | 177,019 |
| Prepaid expenses | 7,271 | 7,000 | 6,359 |
| | 313,212 | 302,732 | 284,789 |
| **NON-CURRENT ASSETS** | | | |
| Property and equipment | 261,641 | 256,904 | 259,583 |
| Goodwill | 26,013 | 26,675 | 26,241 |
| Intangible assets | 14,828 | 17,585 | 17,147 |
| Deferred tax assets | 22,164 | 28,856 | 17,017 |
| Other assets | 12,914 | 12,106 | 11,811 |
| | 337,560 | 342,126 | 331,799 |
| **TOTAL ASSETS** | **$650,772** | **$644,858** | **$616,588** |
| **CURRENT LIABILITIES** | | | |
| Accounts payable and accrued liabilities | $111,411 | $ 107,886 | $116,773 |
| Current portion of long-term debt (Note 9) | 89,960 | 54,258 | 68,257 |
| Income tax payable (Note 7) | 15,583 | 540 | 347 |
| | 216,954 | 162,684 | 185,377 |
| **NON-CURRENT LIABILITIES** | | | |
| Long-term debt (Note 9) | 113,198 | 162,666 | 124,339 |
| Provisions | 3,938 | 3,741 | 3,784 |
| Defined benefit plan obligation (Note 10) | 25,568 | 10,277 | 9,000 |
| Deferred tax liabilities | 2,888 | 1,416 | 2,587 |
| Other long-term liabilities | 5,064 | 4,937 | 5,026 |
| | 150,656 | 183,037 | 144,736 |
| **TOTAL LIABILITIES** | **367,610** | **345,721** | **330,113** |
| **SHAREHOLDERS' EQUITY** | | | |
| Share capital (Note 5) | 165,133 | 165,133 | 165,133 |
| Unit purchase loan plan (Note 13) | — | (136) | — |
| Contributed surplus | 3,144 | 2,263 | 2,491 |
| Retained earnings | 115,836 | 132,422 | 119,739 |
| Accumulated other comprehensive income | (951) | (545) | (888) |
| **TOTAL EQUITY** | 283,162 | 299,137 | 286,475 |
| **TOTAL LIABILITIES & EQUITY** | **$650,772** | **$644,858** | **$616,588** |

*Exhibit Continued >*

**CONDENSED CONSOLIDATED STATEMENTS OF COMPREHENSIVE INCOME**

| (unaudited, $ in thousands) | Three Months Ended October 31, 2011 | Three Months Ended October 31, 2010 | Nine Months Ended October 31, 2011 | Nine Months Ended October 31, 2010 |
|---|---|---|---|---|
| NET EARNINGS FOR THE PERIOD | $ 17,000 | $22,409 | $44,460 | $60,490 |
| Other comprehensive income/(expense): | | | | |
| Exchange differences on translation of foreign controlled subsidiaries, net of tax | 1,438 | (84) | (63) | (545) |
| Actuarial losses on defined benefit plans, net of tax | (13,531) | — | (13,531) | — |
| Total other comprehensive income, net of tax | (12,093) | (84) | (13,594) | (545) |
| COMPREHENSIVE INCOME | $ 4,907 | $22,325 | $30,866 | $59,945 |

Note 2. Basis of Preparation

These condensed consolidated financial statements have been prepared in accordance with International Accounting Standard 34, Interim Financial Reporting, as issued by the International Accounting Standards Board (IASB) and using the accounting policies the Company expects to adopt in its annual consolidated financial statements as at and for the financial year ending January 31, 2012. These condensed consolidated financial statements should be read in conjunction with the Company's audited annual consolidated financial statements and the accompanying notes included in The North West Company Inc.'s 2011 Annual Financial Report.

(Source: The North West Company Inc., 2011–12 3rd Quarter Financial Report, p. 17.)

## 7.6 ACCOUNTING STANDARDS FOR PRIVATE ENTERPRISES

There are no standards for either segmented reporting or interim reporting in the *CICA Handbook, Part II*. Any such reporting is purely voluntary, although specific stakeholders may request (or demand) interim or segmented information. This absence is consistent with earlier Canadian standards—private enterprises also were exempt from all earlier Canadian standards on interim reporting and segmented disclosure.

Private enterprises that wish to prepare interim statements or disclose segment information may use the principles in IAS 34 and IFRS 8 as guidelines for reporting.

# Relevant Standards

**IASB**

**IFRS 8**   Operating Segments
**IAS 34**   Interim Financial Reporting

## 7.7 SUMMARY OF KEY POINTS

1. Segment reporting is the disaggregation of consolidated results by the principal activities and environments of the business. Segment reporting is intended to provide information to enable financial-statement readers to assess the risk and return that a company generates in its different lines of business. Segment information reveals performance aspects that are concealed by the aggregated nature of consolidated statements. The requirements for segment reporting apply only to public companies, with a few exceptions. **LO 1**

2. Basically, segment information is provided for reportable operating segments. An *operating* segment is one that has a separate reporting line directly to the company's chief operating officer for evaluation and resource allocation. A *reportable* segment is an operating segment that accounts for at least 10% of the consolidated company's revenues, profits, or assets. **LO 1**

3. The corporation should report a measure of profit or loss, total assets (if regularly provided), and a measure of liabilities (if regularly provided) for each reportable segment. Detail, as prescribed by IFRS 8, should be provided for specific SCI line items, additions to non-current assets, and associates and joint ventures *if* those items are reviewed regularly by the chief operating decision maker. **LO 2**

4. As well, the corporation should report certain entity-wide information on products and services, on the geographic distribution of revenues and assets, and on customers that account for 10% or more of the company's revenues. **LO 2**

5. Interim financial statements are those that are issued for any period less than a year. Public companies are required to issue interim statements—quarterly in the United States and Canada, semi-annually in most other countries. The requirement for interim reporting applies only to companies that are required to prepare interim statements by law or regulation. **LO 3**

6. Interim statements should consist of a statement of financial position, statement of comprehensive income, statement of cash flow, statement of changes in equity, and notes that explain major estimates and deviations from or exceptions to the accounting policies that are used for the annual statements. **LO 3**

7. Interim statements may be condensed, but should include all of the subtotals and headings that the company uses in its annual statements, and should include those line items specifically required by IFRS. The company should also disclose in its notes major changes, such as discontinued operations, restructurings, acquisitions, and other changes in strategic investments. **LO 3**

8. There are two basic approaches to interim reporting, the discrete approach and the integral approach. The underlying philosophy of interim reporting is the *discrete* approach, in which each interim period is treated as a distinct time period. Under the discrete approach, costs will be permitted to fall into the period in which they are incurred, even though they may be annual costs that benefit other interim periods. Expenses such as major maintenance costs are recognized in the quarter in which they are incurred. **LO 4**

9. Certain types of expenses are determinable only on an annual basis. For these items, the *integral* or *part-of-year* approach is used. The annual amount is estimated and apportioned to the interim periods. **LO 4**

10. The integral approach is used for expenses such as bonuses, contingent rent, income tax, payroll taxes, and quantity discounts that can be viewed as constructive obligations. Companies are obliged to make these payments on the basis of operations through the year and are capable of estimating the determining factors for the entire year. Given that these expenses are determined on an annual basis, these costs are estimated and allocated to the interim periods. **LO 5**

**Visit the text's website at** www.pearsoned.ca/beechy **for practice quizzes, additional problems, Excel® templates, answers to Concept Check questions, and important IFRS updates.**

# Self-Study Problems

1. The CFO for Acme Inc. has identified four segments under IFRS 8. She has gathered the following information on those segments:

| Operating segment | External sales | Operating profit (loss) | Total assets |
|---|---|---|---|
| East | 760 | 50 | 1,000 |
| West | 60 | 80 | 680 |
| North | 90 | 10 | 160 |
| South | 100 | (15) | 150 |

There were no intersegment revenues during the year.

**Required**

Identify which segments are reportable segments.

2. Tim Smith is the new controller for Widget Corporation, a company traded on the TSX venture exchange. It is his first time working for a public company. He is preparing the preliminary financial statements for the first quarter. Widget Corporation lost $100,000 in the first quarter and expects to lose $1,200,000 in the second quarter, earn $600,000 in the third quarter, and earn $900,000 in the fourth quarter. A large part of the loss in the second quarter is because of $800,000 in maintenance costs that are incurred when the factory is shut down as part of its annual maintenance program. The maintenance costs in the first quarter were $50,000 and are expected to be $50,000 for the third and fourth quarters also. The company is subject to an income tax rate of 30% on the first $100,000 of income and 50% on any income above $100,000.

**Required**

Assume that tax losses cannot be carried back or forward to another taxation year.

   **a.** How should Tim account for the maintenance costs?

   **b.** What is the income tax expense to be reported for the first quarter? What is the estimated income tax expense for each of the remaining three quarters?

# Review Questions

1. What are the objectives of segmented reporting?
2. When a corporation reports financial information by segments, do the segments correspond to specific subsidiaries?
3. What type of company is required to provide segmented reporting?
4. How does the IASB consider benefit–cost relationships for segmented reporting?
5. What is the core principle that underlies segment reporting?
6. What are the guidelines for determining whether an operating segment is *reportable*?
7. Companies L and D both operate food processing plants, and both operate a chain of retail food stores. Company L transfers all of the output from its processing plants to its stores, while Company D's processing plants produce private-label products for other retailers. How might the segment reporting of the two companies differ?
8. How is *profit* defined for determining operating segments?

9. How much of the consolidated enterprise's business activity must be reported in operating segments to satisfy IFRS requirements?

10. When some operating segments operate at a loss and others are profitable, how is the 10% reporting guideline applied?

11. What data must be reported for each geographic segment? How do these data differ from the data reported for industry segments?

12. How is the risk of relying on major customers considered in IFRS 8?

13. Explain briefly why interim reporting poses problems different from those of annual reporting.

14. What types of companies does IAS 34 apply to for interim reporting?

15. What does the *exception reporting* principle mean for note disclosure in interim reporting?

16. What comparative period(s) are used for interim financial statements?

17. What are the two basic approaches to the preparation of interim statements? Which approach is recommended by IAS 34?

18. Under the discrete, or separate-period, approach to interim statements, how would an annual, one-time expenditure such as plant maintenance be reported? How would the reporting differ under the integral, or part-of-a-year, approach?

19. How does the measurement of income tax expense differ between the two approaches to interim reporting?

# 7.8 CASES

## CASE 7-1 ERMINE OIL LIMITED

Ermine Oil Limited (Ermine) is a fully integrated Canadian oil company. Ermine commenced operations as a petroleum exploration company and was very successful in its oil field discoveries. To attain market security and improve profits, Ermine was forced to embark on a program of vertical integration. It first acquired a refining division and then marketing and transportation divisions. From the beginning, management appreciated the integrated nature of the business, and production was transferred between divisions at standard cost. The management control system recognized the exploration, refining, and transportation divisions as cost centres and the marketing division as a revenue centre. While the exploration, refining, and transportation divisions did make external sales, historically none of these divisions' external sales accounted for 10% of Ermine's total sales. However, in the last fiscal year, due to unusual world market conditions, the transportation division's sales accounted for 11% of Ermine's total sales. Over 90% of Ermine's sales were within Canada, with the balance spread over many countries worldwide. Ermine did not feel it was necessary to disclose segmented information in its annual financial statements.

Beluga Petroleum Limited (Beluga) was similar to Ermine in size and also in scope of operations except that, in addition, it had a chemical division. However, Beluga was a subsidiary of a foreign oil company and its divisions were each organized as profit centres with products transferred between divisions at world market prices. Each division purchased and sold products extensively to outside companies. In addition, about 15% of Beluga's sales were exported, almost exclusively to the United States. In its annual financial statements, Beluga showed segmented information by the five divisions (exploration, refining, transportation, chemical, and marketing), and sales were divided between domestic and export operations.

Required

Discuss how both Ermine and Beluga could report differently with respect to disclosure of segmented information, and yet be in accordance with generally accepted accounting principles.

[SMA, adapted]

## CASE 7-2 INTERIM REPORTING

In today's rapidly changing financial markets, financial-statement users are demanding more information, released more promptly than in the past. To respond to these needs, the IASB issued IAS 34.

At a professional development session, two members engaged in a lively discussion. One member is a controller of an international public company, while the other member is a senior financial analyst in a securities firm.

Financial Analyst: "My review of IAS 34 leads me to conclude that the objectives of interim reporting should be the same as those of annual reporting."

Controller: "I disagree. Interim reports are aimed at different users, serve different purposes, and must be published more quickly than annual reports. It follows that the underlying objectives should also differ."

Financial Analyst: "Regardless of the content of interim reports, the interim operating results should be measured on the same basis as the annual results because the interim period is an integral part of the annual period."

Controller: "I agree that there is a measurement problem for interim reporting, but I don't see that there is a simple solution. For example, I find it difficult to make interim estimates for various expenses given the cyclical nature of our business. After all, the interim period is only a portion of the annual period."

### Required

Prepare a memo discussing the main issues raised in the preceding conversation.
[CICA, adapted]

## CASE 7-3 SHAW NAVIGATIONAL COMPANY

The Shaw Navigational Company is a public Canadian corporation that operates a fleet of ships on the Great Lakes. In common with other Great Lakes shipping companies, rates are quoted and revenues are collected in U.S. dollars, regardless of the location or nationality of the shipper. More than 90% of Shaw's consolidated gross revenues, operating profits, and identifiable capital assets relate to the shipping business, and thus Shaw's management claims exemption from segmented reporting requirements on the grounds that shipping represents its only operating segment. In 20X3, Shaw's consolidated net income was $1,680,000.

Shaw does have two subsidiaries that are not in the shipping business. One is a bus company that operates on intercity routes in Manitoba, and that is consolidated with the shipping operation. The bus fleet has recently been modernized, and the new buses have been acquired by means of leases rather than by an outright purchase.

The other subsidiary is a casualty insurance company located in Michigan. About 20% of the insurance company's business involves Great Lakes shipping, although mainly for shipping companies other than Shaw. Shaw's earnings from the insurance company amounted to $203,000 in 20X3.

### Required

Comment on management's assertion that Shaw is exempt from segment reporting because it operates in one line of business.

# Problems

## P7-1 (10 minutes, easy)

JCN Company sells laptop computers, desktop computers, and software in more than seven countries. The company is required to file financial statements annually with a securities commission. The controller has just compiled the following information on last year's revenues:

|  | Revenue (in millions) |
|---|---|
| Laptop computers | $360 |
| Desktop computers | 48 |
| Software | 200 |
|  | $608 |
| United States | $160 |
| Canada | 180 |
| South America | 100 |
| Asia | 58 |
| Africa | 70 |
| Europe | 40 |
|  | $608 |

### Required

Which of the above should be reported as an operating segment and which as a geographic segment in a note to the financial statements?

## P7-2 (20 minutes, medium)

The Auto Corporation has internal reporting for four divisions. The following data have been gathered for the year just ended.

|  | Div. A | Div. B | Div. C | Div. D |
|---|---|---|---|---|
| Interdivisional sales | $    — | $50,000 | $    — | $ 10,000 |
| External sales | 75,000 | 5,000 | 200,000 | 100,000 |
| Direct divisional expenses | 15,000 | 25,000 | 50,000 | 60,000 |
| Allocated joint costs | 35,000 | — | 55,000 | — |
| Depreciation | 12,500 | 17,500 | 22,500 | 20,000 |
| Capital expenditures | 40,000 | 10,000 | 80,000 | 30,000 |
| Identifiable assets | 62,500 | 92,500 | 122,500 | 107,500 |
| Liabilities | 17,500 | 22,500 | 27,500 | 52,500 |

1. Divisions A and C share production facilities. Joint product costs, depreciation, capital expenditures, and much of the identifiable assets are allocated approximately one-third to Division A and the remainder to Division C.
2. Division B sells over 90% of its output to Division D on a cost-plus basis.
3. Unallocated corporate expenses not included above amount to $59,500.

## Required

**a.** From the preceding information, which of the operating segments do you recommend should be reported by the Auto Corporation? Explain your recommendation fully.

**b.** Prepare a schedule of supplementary financial information by segments, in accordance with IFRS 8 recommendations, based on the information provided above, together with a condensed consolidated SCI.

### P7-3 (15 minutes, easy)

The controller for Saskatoon Potash Inc. has determined that her company has five identifiable segments under IFRS 8. She has gathered the following information on those segments:

| Operating segment | External sales | Inter segment sales | Operating profit (loss) | Total assets |
|---|---|---|---|---|
| Red | 800 | 100 | 75 | 900 |
| Green | 600 | 200 | 60 | 680 |
| Blue | 150 | — | 5 | 200 |
| Grey | 160 | — | (11) | 140 |
| Yellow | 90 | — | (15) | 180 |

### Required

Identify which segments are reportable segments.

### P7-4 (15 minutes, easy)

The following information is available for Export Corporation's operating subsidiaries throughout the world, in thousands of Canadian dollars:

| | External sales | Sales to operating regions | Identifiable assets | After-tax profit |
|---|---|---|---|---|
| Canada | $ 60,000 | $300,000 | $ 30,000 | $ 7,500 |
| South America | 275,000 | 60,000 | 125,000 | 7,000 |
| United States | 235,000 | 30,000 | 100,000 | 13,500 |
| Asia | 55,000 | — | 22,500 | 5,000 |
| Europe | 50,000 | — | 30,000 | 7,500 |
| General Corporate | — | — | 45,000 | 4,500* |
| Consolidated | $675,000 | | $352,500 | $45,000 |

*Investment income, less general corporate expenses

### Required

Determine which regions you would suggest reporting as geographic areas, as part of the entity-wide disclosures in IFRS 8. Identify the characteristics that led to your choices.

### P7-5 (15 minutes, medium)

Alena Gallant, the vice-president of finance for Baie Comeau International, has identified seven operating segments in her company. She has compiled the following information on these operating segments:

| Operating segment | External revenue | Inter segment sales | Operating profit (loss) | Total assets |
|---|---|---|---|---|
| Segment 1 | 95 | 10 | 40 | 200 |
| Segment 2 | 25 | 6 | 6 | 69 |
| Segment 3 | 11 | 20 | 5 | 47 |
| Segment 4 | 35 | — | (19) | 38 |
| Segment 5 | 90 | 4 | (7) | 110 |
| Segment 6 | 10 | 57 | 48 | 80 |
| Segment 7 | 34 | 3 | 7 | 56 |

**Required**

Identify which segments are reportable and which segments can be combined and reported in the "Other" category under IFRS 8. (Show all work for each separate test.)

**P7-6 (25 minutes, medium)**

This year, for the first time, CTR Corporation must report supplementary information by operating segment. The controller has prepared the following note for inclusion in the annual report.

*Segmented Data*

*Your company operates in several different operating segments. Selected financial data by division are provided below, in Canadian dollars.*

| | Hardware | Tires | Other | Consolidated |
|---|---|---|---|---|
| Sales to outsiders | $400,000 | $200,000 | $300,000 | $ 900,000 |
| Sales between divisions | 50,000 | 10,000 | 60,000 | 120,000 |
| Total sales | $450,000 | $210,000 | $360,000 | $1,020,000 |
| Operating profit | 15,000 | 40,000 | 20,000 | 62,000 |
| Capital expenditures | 5,000 | 25,000 | 30,000 | 70,000 |
| Assets | 65,000 | 240,000 | 90,000 | 455,000 |

*During the year, your company had export sales that resulted in gross profit of $50,000.*

**Required**

Criticize the note as prepared by the controller. Identify any missing information, either numerical or verbal, and indicate errors in presentation.

**P7-7 (20 minutes, easy)**

Jane Jones is the controller for XYZ Corporation, a publicly traded company in Canada. XYZ Corporation made $100,000 in the first quarter and $250,000 in the second quarter. It also earned $550,000 in the third quarter and earned $100,000 in the fourth quarter. The company is subject to an income tax rate of 20% on the first $400,000 of income and of 50% on any income above $400,000.

**Required**

a. How much income tax expense would Jane recognize in each quarter assuming she follows the discrete approach to accounting for income taxes?

**b.** How much income tax expense would Jane recognize in each quarter assuming she follows the integral approach to accounting for income taxes?

**c.** Which approach should Jane use?

### P7-8 (20 minutes, medium)

Labels Ltd. experienced the following events during the first quarter of 20X3:

**1.** The annual sales catalogue was developed and provided online, at a cost of $2,500,000.

**2.** Programming and consulting fees were incurred for annual updates of the internet site, at a cost of $1,250,000.

**3.** Payroll taxes for various government programs were paid as follows: Q1–$650,000; Q2 –$600,000; Q3–$150,000; Q4–$100,000. Total salaries and wages were paid evenly over the year and amounted to $30,000,000.

**4.** A notice of assessed value for property taxes was received. The tax assessment will be received and be due in the second quarter. Taxes for 20X3 are estimated at $1,400,000.

**5.** Labels uses the declining-balance method for depreciation. The total depreciation for 20X3 on assets held at the start of the year will be $4,400,000.

**6.** The company's top management receives annual bonuses based on 10% of annual net income after taxes.

#### Required

For each event reported above, indicate what impact it would have on the first-quarter interim report under each approach to interim statements:

**a.** the integral, or part-of-year, approach; and

**b.** the discrete, or separate-period, approach.

### P7-9 (20 minutes, medium)

The Aspen Company is a retail department store chain. The company's fiscal year ends on the Saturday closest to January 31 of each year. The company is publicly held and submits quarterly financial statements to the shareholders.

Like most retail establishments, Aspen operates at a loss for most of the year, but generally recovers the losses in the fourth quarter to finish the year with a profit. In fiscal year 20X5, the company reported pre-tax net income of $3,000,000 and paid taxes at a rate of 45%.

In the first quarter of 20X6, the company suffered a loss of $2,250,000 before taxes. In the second quarter, economic conditions improved slightly, but the cumulative six-month loss was $3,900,000, the worst in the company's history. Nevertheless, management predicted that the losses would be recovered as the economy improved, and forecast a break-even per-formance for the year as a whole.

The loss did decline in the third quarter, to a cumulative loss of $1,950,000; the fourth quarter almost completely wiped out the loss, ending the year with a fiscal pre-tax loss of only $150,000.

#### Required

Assume that tax losses can be carried back for only one year. Determine the provision for income taxes that should be reported on Aspen's interim SCIs for fiscal year 20X6.

P7-10 (30 minutes, hard)

The Crouse Corporation is a publicly traded company that operates a chain of stores and online websites that sell sports memorabilia. Last year, Crouse's first year of operations, resulted in an operating loss carryforward of $150,000 for which no deferred tax asset was recognized. The average annual tax rate is normally expected to be 40%.

Required

**a.** Assume that Crouse Corporation earned $200,000 in the first quarter of this year and expects to earn a similar amount for each of the remaining three quarters. What would be the income tax expense for each quarter of the current year under IAS 34? What would be the effective annual tax rate for the current year?

**b.** Assume that Crouse Corporation earned $25,000 in the first quarter of this year and expects to earn a similar amount for each of the remaining three quarters. What would be the income tax expense for each quarter of the current year under IAS 34? (Assume that the company believes that it is now very likely that it will earn enough profits to use all of its tax loss carryforward.)

# Chapter 8
## Foreign Currency Transactions and Hedges

## Learning Objectives

**After studying this chapter, you should be able to:**

**LO ❶** describe the conceptual alternatives to account for foreign currency transactions and balances;[1]

**LO ❷** describe the practice of hedging;

**LO ❸** define and describe hedge accounting and explain when it can be used; and

**LO ❹** explain the accounting for fair-value hedges and cash-flow hedges.

## INTRODUCTION

Bombardier is a large Canadian manufacturer of railcars and of business and regional aircraft. The company operates in 25 countries, including the United States, China, Ireland, France, and Germany. In fiscal year 2011, the company had revenue of $18.3 billion, 93% of which was generated from outside Canada. With such widespread global operations, even small fluctuations in foreign currency rates can have a significant impact on Bombardier's financial results.

In its 2011 annual report, Bombardier estimates that a $0.01 change in the Canada–US exchange rate in its aerospace division can affect costs for the next 12 months by $24 million. This is potentially a major factor affecting its operations. Over the previous five years, the Canada–US exchange rate has changed by as much as 19% in a year. Clearly, this volatility has a direct impact on the company's earnings.

Fortunately there are ways to minimize or eliminate the risk posed by fluctuating exchange rates. As we will see in this chapter, a company can use currency hedges to offset these potential gains or losses. Indeed, Bombardier also reports (in the same sensitivity analysis) that after considering the effects of its hedging program, a $0.01 change in the Canada–US exchange rate is expected to have only a $5 million impact.

Many Canadian corporations engage in some form of international activity, ranging from occasional transactions to highly complex and interrelated international operations. In this chapter, we will address the two major accounting issues that arise

---

[1]Accounting for financial instruments is an intermediate accounting topic and therefore is not addressed directly in this chapter. However, it will help the reader to be familiar with the IFRS 7 reporting requirements for financial assets.

from a company's transactions in foreign currencies: (1) accounting for the transactions themselves on the company's books and (2) accounting for currency hedging activities to protect the company from the adverse consequences of exchange rate fluctuations. The next chapter will deal with situations in which a company has operating subsidiaries in foreign countries; this issue is known as *accounting for foreign operations*. Bombardier has both foreign currency transactions and foreign operations.

## 8.1 FOREIGN CURRENCY CONCEPTS

LO ❶
Describe the conceptual alternatives to account for foreign currency transactions and balances

### Definitions

Transactions that are denominated in a foreign currency are called **foreign currency transactions**. A transaction is **denominated** in a foreign currency whenever the monetary value of the transaction is specified in a currency that is *not* the company's functional currency.[2] For most Canadian companies the functional currency is the Canadian dollar; any transaction that is stated in a different currency is a foreign currency transaction. Such transactions include (1) borrowing or lending money and (2) buying or selling products at an amount stated in a foreign currency (e.g., US dollars, Japanese yen, or euros). All foreign currency transactions must be translated into the functional currency for accounting purposes, using the exchange rate in effect at the date of the transaction, known as the **spot exchange rate**.

On the other hand, if a Canadian company's functional currency is the US dollar, all of its transactions denominated in Canadian dollars are considered foreign currency transactions for financial reporting purposes. In that case, the Canadian dollar transactions must be translated to US dollars.

### Causes of Exchange Rate Changes

Why do exchange rates fluctuate? Some short-run changes in exchange rates are the result of speculation in the money markets. Over the longer run, however, exchange rates are related to differential inflation rates.

If Country A experiences inflation that is in excess of inflation in Country B, then the currency in Country A will decline in value relative to Country B's currency. The relative change in exchange rates will be approximately equal to the relative change in purchasing power of the currency; a fixed nominal amount of Country A's currency will buy less after a period of inflation than the equivalent nominal amount of Country B's currency, and therefore the relative values of the two currencies will be adjusted through the money markets to recognize the fact that Country A's currency will not buy as much any more. This is known as the **purchasing power parity (PPP)** concept.

Other theories have also been proposed to explain the changes in exchange rates, but it has been difficult to gather evidence in support of these different theories. Research

---

[2] As we will see in Chapter 9, a firm's functional currency is the currency of the primary economic environment in which the company operates.

over the past 25 years supports purchasing power parity as the best explanation of the direction of exchange rate changes over the long term. In the short term, however, this research has found that exchange rate changes are very difficult to explain. This is especially true for explaining changes between countries with low inflation rates and free capital markets.[3]

In addition, other factors often come into play. Some countries do not allow their currency to float freely. Their currencies are either pegged to a particular currency (usually the US dollar) or targeted to a narrow trading range. For example, prior to July 21, 2005, China pegged the exchange rate of its currency, the renminbi, against the US dollar. Since 2005, the Chinese government has managed the exchange rate for its currency within a very narrow band. One of the major reasons for the use of fixed or controlled exchange rates by countries such as China is that it assists their companies who are exporting into markets such as the United States's by reducing foreign currency risk. However, the management of exchange rates often fails or is ineffective when the official exchange rates bear no relationship to the underlying purchasing power parity between currencies. This leads to widespread trading of such currencies in the illicit or underground market.

## Foreign Currency Transactions

**Example: Sale Denominated in Euros**   Suppose that on December 5, 20X5, Domestic Corporation sells 100 units of its product in Germany for €100,000. To record this sale on its books, Domestic Corporation must translate the euro-denominated sale into the equivalent amount in Canadian dollars. If we assume that the exchange rate on the date of sale was €1 = C$1.25 (that is, that each euro is worth $1.25, or that one dollar is worth €0.80), then the Canadian equivalent is $125,000. The sale can be recorded as follows, assuming that it was a sale on account:

| | | |
|---|---|---|
| Accounts receivable | 125,000 | |
| Sales | | 125,000 |

The amount of the sale in its Canadian equivalent will then be added to the other domestic and foreign sales without further difficulties.

If the German customer pays the amount owing on December 21, Domestic Corporation will receive €100,000. If the exchange rate is €1 = $1.27 on the payment date, Domestic will receive $127,000 when the euros are converted to Canadian dollars. Domestic will debit cash for $127,000 and credit accounts receivable for $125,000. The $2,000 difference represents a gain that has been realized by Domestic because the value of the euro went up while Domestic was holding a receivable that was denominated in euros. If the exchange rate had gone down instead of up, Domestic would have realized a loss instead of a gain.

---

[3] Kenneth Rogoff, "Exchange Rates in the Modern Floating Era: What Do We Really Know?" *Review of World Economics* 145 (2009), p. 1–12.

**Theoretical Alternatives**   Theoretically, the gain on the exchange rate change could be treated in either of two ways: (1) by increasing the amount of revenue recognized by $2,000 or (2) by crediting a separate gain account. The difference may seem minor, since both treatments will result in an increase in net income in the same period. The alternative treatments can have a substantive impact, however, when a company buys inventory or capital assets in a foreign currency and the exchange rate changes between the date of purchase and the date of payment. Any exchange gain or loss realized by holding the liability could, in theory, be either (1) added to the cost of the assets acquired or (2) treated as a gain or loss of the period.

The first approach, to attach exchange gains and losses to the asset or the revenue that results from the initial transaction, is known as the **one-transaction theory** because the accrual and the cash settlement are viewed as a single economic event. The second approach is called the **two-transaction theory** because the accrual (i.e., the sale or purchase) is viewed as one economic event, while the eventual cash settlement (collection of the receivable or payment of the liability) is treated as a separate financing activity. Under the two-transaction theory, exchange gains and losses normally flow directly through to net income in the period in which they occur.

**Current Practice**   The two-transaction theory underlies the IFRS approach to foreign currency transactions. The financing component of a foreign currency transaction is separated from the purchase or sale itself because the cash flow is controlled by the domestic company, and the results of such essentially speculative activity should not be hidden in gross revenue or in the cost of assets. The financing component can be controlled because the company has many options—purchases can be paid for by bank drafts at the time of the transaction; receivables can be sold to banks or finance companies, or can be financed by the sale of credit "paper" denominated in the same currency; the foreign currency–denominated payable or receivable can be hedged (which is the subject of the second part of this chapter); and so forth.

Under the two-transaction approach, the collection by Domestic of the €100,000 receivable will be recorded as follows:

| | | |
|---|---|---|
| Cash (€100,000) | 127,000 | |
| Accounts receivable | | 125,000 |
| Foreign currency exchange gain | | 2,000 |

The two-transaction approach also applies to purchases. Companies frequently buy inventory or other assets at a price that is fixed in foreign currency. The cost of the asset is measured at the exchange rate in effect at the date of the purchase. If the liability is settled later at a higher or lower exchange rate, the exchange gain/loss has no impact on the carrying value of the asset.

# Foreign Currency Balances

**Monetary Balances**   Now assume instead that the receivable is not collected until June 5, 20X6, and that the fiscal year of Domestic Corporation ends on December 31. The receivable was initially recorded on Domestic's books at $125,000, but actually the receivable is for €100,000. We will also assume that the euro is worth $1.28 on December 31. The $1.28 is referred to as the **closing rate**—that is, the foreign exchange rate on the date of the SFP. On December 31, the value of the €100,000 receivable is $128,000— that is, $3,000 greater than the original recorded amount of the transaction. How should accounts receivable be reported and how should the $3,000 gain be reported in the year-end financial statements?

In theory, we could translate foreign currency-denominated monetary assets and liabilities on the SFP using either (1) the historical rate or (2) the closing rate. Use of the historical rate means translating the foreign currency amount into our functional currency at the rate in effect when the monetary balance was created. If that approach were used, gains and losses from exchange rate fluctuations would be recognized only when realized—at the settlement or payment date. The historical approach ignores objectively measurable changes in the value of assets and liabilities, and enables management to manipulate earnings through the timing of cash settlement.

Thus, accounting practice uses the closing rate as the only feasible approach for reporting foreign currency monetary assets and liabilities. IFRS defines **monetary assets and liabilities** as currency held (i.e., cash) and assets and liabilities that are to be received or paid in a fixed or determinable amount of currency. The balances of monetary assets and liabilities, both current and long-term, are translated at the exchange rate at the SFP date. Because exchange rates change over time, the change will cause a Canadian dollar translation gain or loss.

Now that we have resolved that monetary balances should be shown at the closing rate, we need to answer the related question of how the associated gains should be reported. There are two possible alternatives:

1. defer the unrealized gain or loss until the asset or liability is *settled* (that is, paid); or

2. recognize the gain or loss in 20X5 net income.

Proponents of deferral argue that exchange rates go up and down, and that the 20X5 gain may well be cancelled out by a loss in 20X6. Furthermore, long-term foreign currency-denominated monetary assets and liabilities may not be settled for years. They argue that there is no point in recognizing gains and losses that may never be realized. In addition, if it is debt-related, the old debt may well be replaced by new debt (i.e., refinanced) at the end of its term. If the debt is refinanced, these proponents argue, no gain or loss needs to be recognized.

However, exchange gains and losses don't generally bounce up and down without reason. Exchange rates are subject to longer-term trends caused by changing relative economic performance between countries. Granted, exchange rates do not always behave in accordance with economic theory in the short run, but longer-term exchange rate changes are not random events.

In the example above, the gain reflects the increase in asset value and therefore should be included in income. The exchange rate change is an economic event affecting the company in 20X5. The company's receivable is worth more (in Canadian dollars) at the end of 20X5. This change in the company's net assets therefore should be recognized in net income. Indeed, the general rule is that all gains and losses on monetary assets and liabilities should be recognized in earnings.

Now we will turn our attention to two other issues: (1) accounting for non-monetary balances and (2) practical ways of dealing with a large volume of foreign currency transactions.

**Non-Monetary Balances**   The foregoing discussion has focused on the translation of monetary balances. If the foreign currency transaction was not a sale but was, for example, a purchase of inventory, then the transaction will result in two SFP amounts—(1) an account payable and (2) inventory. The account payable is a monetary balance and will be treated exactly as the account receivable discussed above.

The inventory, however, is a *non-monetary balance*. A **non-monetary balance** is, by definition, an amount that is *not* fixed in terms of a currency and does not represent a claim against monetary resources. Therefore, non-monetary balances are not affected by changes in the exchange rate if carried at historical cost. If inventory is carried at historical cost, then the historical cost of inventory that was purchased with a foreign currency is simply the domestic currency equivalent of the foreign currency *at the date of the purchase*. Non-monetary balances are carried at historical exchange rates because that is the historical cost.

An exception arises when a non-monetary asset is reported on the SFP at fair value rather than at historical cost. For example, suppose that Domestic Corporation purchased biological assets in US dollars and that Domestic reports its inventory of biological assets at fair value. If the current fair value is quoted in US dollars, it makes no sense to take a current value and translate it at a historical rate.

To report the current value of the investment in Canadian dollars, the current value in US dollars must be converted into Canadian dollars at the exchange rate in effect on the date fair value was determined. In most cases, such as the biological asset example above, this will be the spot exchange rate at the end of the reporting period (i.e., the closing rate).

**Practical Expedients**   Usually, companies that engage in a large volume of foreign currency transactions will not use the current rate at the actual transaction date for translating *each* transaction. Instead, the sales may be accumulated for a period of time and a single rate applied to the aggregate.

If, for example, a company has thousands of sales transactions in US dollars during a year, it is impractical to check on the current exchange rate (the spot rate) every time a sale occurs. A company might use the average rate for each week or each month for that period's transactions. These approaches are expedient for accounting for a large volume of transactions. Minor differences between the actual spot rate and the rate used for translation will be adjusted when the accounts are settled, or when still-outstanding monetary account balances are adjusted to the current rate on the reporting date.

An alternative to grouping transactions is to use a pre-determined standard rate for translating foreign currency transactions. If a company uses a profit-centre approach for evaluating its managers, it may be desirable to remove the effects of uncontrollable currency fluctuations from the profit centre's operating results so that the managers are not held accountable for factors beyond their control. The total amount of current monetary balances will then be adjusted to the current rate for external reporting.

# General Accounting Principles for Foreign Exchange–Denominated Items

Consistent with our discussion above, the appropriate accounting for foreign exchange transactions and balances can be summarized by the following three simple principles:

**General Principle 1**—All *monetary items* are translated using the exchange rate on the SFP date and the associated gains and losses are recognized in earnings. The exchange gains and losses are recognized in earnings regardless of whether the monetary assets and liabilities are carried at amortized value or fair value.

**General Principle 2**—All *non-monetary items carried at historical cost* are measured using the historical exchange rate. There are no exchange gains or losses, so accounting for foreign exchange changes is not an issue.

**General Principle 3**—All non-monetary items carried at fair value are measured using the exchange rate on the date that fair value is determined. Exchange gains and losses are recognized in earnings with one exception. For non-monetary assets where the changes in fair value are recognized in other comprehensive income (i.e., investments in equity securities), the associated foreign exchange gains and losses are also recognized in other comprehensive income.

These principles are summarized in Exhibit 8.1.

## Concept Check 8-1

1.  What is the spot exchange rate?

2.  Explain the "two-transaction" theory.

3.  What options are available to handle unrealized gains and losses from changes in foreign exchange rates?

**Exhibit 8.1** General Principles for Accounting for Foreign Exchange Transactions in the Absence of Hedging

| Type of Financial Asset or Liability | Exchange Rate for Translation | Existence of Exchange Gain or Loss | Disposition of Exchange Gains and Losses | Exceptions in the Absence of Hedging |
|---|---|---|---|---|
| Monetary assets or liabilities | Exchange rate on reporting date | Yes | Profit and loss | n/a |
| Non-monetary assets and liabilities at historical cost | Historical rate | No | n/a | n/a |
| Non-monetary assets and liabilities at fair value | Exchange rate on date fair value is determined | Yes | Profit and loss | Equity investments using OCI election: foreign exchange gain/loss taken to OCI (with fair value change). |

## 8.2 NATURE AND USE OF HEDGING

LO ❷
Describe the practice of hedging

Hedging is any tactic used to reduce or eliminate commodity risk (e.g., risk of non-availability or change in value of the commodity) or financial risk (e.g., currency or interest rate risk). In this chapter, we are specifically interested in hedging related to the financial risk arising from currency or foreign exchange fluctuations. When a company holds a receivable denominated in a foreign currency, there will be a loss if the foreign currency falls in value relative to the Canadian dollar. Conversely, a loss on a foreign currency-denominated liability will occur if the foreign currency strengthens or increases in value relative to the Canadian dollar. To protect against foreign currency losses, companies frequently *hedge* their monetary foreign currency balances.

**Hedging** is the creation of an offsetting position in the same foreign currency. If a company is holding a receivable of 1 million Japanese yen, the risk of gain or loss can be neutralized, for example, by incurring a liability of 1 million Japanese yen for an equal term.

There are several ways of hedging. The most common is to enter into a *forward contract* with a bank or currency dealer. If a receivable is being hedged, then the company will contract to pay a bank an equivalent amount of foreign currency in exchange for Canadian dollars at a specified rate at a specified time in the future.

Some major currencies are also traded in a *futures* market. Futures markets for agricultural products are well known. Wheat, oats, and corn are traded on the commodities exchanges, as are cattle, cotton, copper, coffee, orange juice, plywood, and heating oil. The commodity that is of immediate concern here is money. On the Chicago Mercantile Exchange, for example, one can buy a futures contract for Canadian dollars, US dollars, euros, British pounds, or Japanese yen, among others. Futures contracts are for standard terms (e.g., 30, 60, 90, and 180 days) and for limited denominations.

*Options* are also available on most major currencies. A call option gives a holder the right to buy the currency while a put option gives a holder the right to sell the currency. The terms of the option are often standardized as to the quantity of a foreign currency, the price, and the expiry of the option. Depending on its nature, the option may be exercisable at any point during its life or only at the end of its life.

Another example of a hedging instrument is a *currency swap*, wherein corporations in two different countries agree to guarantee the payment of each other's interest and principal on foreign currency-denominated long-term debt. A Canadian company with outstanding British pound sterling debt may enter into a currency swap agreement with a British company that has outstanding Canadian dollar debt.[4] Each party to the agreement thereby converts its foreign currency exposure to a fixed domestic equivalent, effectively eliminating exchange rate risk.

There are many different types of hedging instruments (see Reality Check 8–1). In this text, we will focus on forward contracts because they are the most common in Canada and generally the most effective form of foreign currency hedge. Forward contracts are individually negotiated and thus can be tailored to suit the needs of the hedger in terms of currency type and contract duration.

---

[4] In practice, swaps are usually more complicated than this example and may involve more than two companies. Swaps normally are arranged through financial intermediaries, usually banks.

## What Derivatives Does Bombardier Use?

Derivative financial instruments are mainly used to manage the Corporation's exposure to foreign exchange and interest-rate market risks, generally through forward foreign exchange contracts, interest rate swap agreements, cross-currency interest-rate swap agreements and interest-rate cap agreements. [. . . .]

Derivative financial instruments are classified as HFT (held-for-trading), unless they are designated as hedging instruments for which hedge accounting is applied [see below].

Source: Bombardier Inc., 2011 Annual Report, p. 145.

Forward contracts, futures contracts, options, and swaps are examples of *secondary*, or *derivative, instruments*. **Derivative instruments** are contracts that derive their value from transferring one or more of the financial risks inherent in an underlying primary financial instrument. A derivative must possess three characteristics:

1. its value must change as a result of changes in a foreign exchange rate, a specified interest rate, a financial instrument price, a commodity price, and so forth;

2. it must require very little or no initial investment; and

3. it must be settled in the future.

An example of a forward contract would be an agreement by a company to pay a bank $150,000 Canadian for the delivery of €100,000 in 90 days. In this case, the contracted amount of Canadian dollars is fixed, as is the contracted amount of euros, but the value of this contract will change over the next 90 days as the exchange rate between the Canadian dollar and the euro changes. Thus, (1) the value of the forward contract changes in response to changes in the value of the euro (i.e., the underlying); (2) the forward contract has zero value when initiated (as we will see); and (3) the contract is settled in 90 days. As such, a forward contract possesses all three characteristics of a derivative instrument.

## Hedging Practice

To illustrate the practice of hedging, suppose that on November 1, 20X3, Domestic Corporation sells some of its product in Germany for €100,000. At the date of the sale, the euro is selling at a current or spot rate of $1.2717 in Canadian funds. As a result of the sale, Domestic has acquired a foreign currency monetary balance (account receivable) of €100,000 (worth $127,170).

If Domestic wishes to protect itself against a possible exchange loss caused by a fall in the value of the euro, Domestic can buy a forward contract for an equivalent amount of euros. Assuming that the receivable will be collected in 90 days (on January 30, 20X4), Domestic can buy a contract for the *payment* of €100,000 90 days hence. The commitment to pay €100,000 will offset the commitment to receive €100,000 from the German customer.

On November 1, 20X3, a 90-day forward contract for euros is available for $1.2702. Domestic contracts to deliver or pay €100,000 in 90 days and the contract will be for

$127,020. The $150 difference between the current value of €100,000 ($127,170) and the price of the forward contract ($127,020) reflects the difference in interest rates between the two countries over the next three months. In effect, Domestic is selling the euros that it will receive from the German customer. But since Domestic will not receive the euros for 90 days, the contract to deliver the euros will not be executed until then.

As a result, Domestic will have a *receivable* (from the customer) that is denominated in euros, but will also have a *payable* that is denominated in euros. The euro receivable and the euro payable are due at the same time. The two financial instruments will fluctuate in tandem as the euro exchange rate changes—a gain on one instrument will be offset by a loss on the other.

There are two ways to record the sale and associated hedge: (1) the gross method and (2) the memorandum (or net) method. The gross method gives us a clearer view of the basic underlying economics of a hedge than does the memorandum method. Therefore, we will illustrate the gross method first, followed by the same example reported by the memorandum method.

**Gross Method**   Under the **gross method of recording a hedge**, the full amounts of both the hedge and the monetary item being hedged are recorded.

Using the gross method, the entries to record (1a) the sale of the merchandise and (1b) the sale of the euros for delivery in the future are as follows:

| | | |
|---|---|---|
| *November 1, 20X3* | | |
| **(1a)** | | |
| Accounts receivable (€100,000) | 127,170 | |
| Sales | | 127,170 |
| [sale of merchandise for €100,000 on account] | | |
| **(1b)** | | |
| Forward contract receivable (in C$) | 127,020 | |
| Forward contract payable (€100,000) | | 127,020 |
| [purchase of a forward contract to deliver €100,000] | | |

In the second entry, both the receivable and the payable in the forward contract are recorded at the gross amount at the time of entering into the contract.[5] It appears that the receivable and the payable for the forward contract are offsetting. However, this is not really the case. The receivable is fixed in terms of Canadian dollars and represents the amount to be received by Domestic when Domestic delivers the euros. The payable, on the other hand, is denominated in euros; the actual dollar equivalent will change as the price of the euro changes.

As is evident from the two entries, an effective hedge now exists because the account receivable from the customer is for the same amount and denominated in the same currency (euros) as the forward contract payable. Also, the forward contract

---

[5] The memorandum alternative, as we will see, offsets the receivable with the payable and records the net amount. For financial statement presentation, only the net value of the contract is presented (i.e., the forward contract receivable is netted against the forward contract payable) even when the gross method is used.

receivable fixes the Canadian dollar value of the euros that Domestic will receive when it collects on its accounts receivable and, in turn, remits the euros to the bank to settle its forward contract.

Assume that Domestic's fiscal year ends on January 31. On January 30, 20X4, the customer pays €100,000 to Domestic, and Domestic delivers the euros in execution of the forward contract. Also assume that the spot rate for the euro is $1.2500 on the settlement date. The receipt of the €100,000 from the customer (1c) will be recorded as follows:

| January 30, 20X4 | | |
|---|---|---|
| **(1c)** | | |
| Cash (€100,000 @ 1.2500) | 125,000 | |
| Exchange gains and losses | 2,170 | |
|     Accounts receivable (€100,000 @ 1.2717) | | 127,170 |
| [receipt of €100,000 from customer, on account] | | |

There is a loss of $2,170 due to the fact that the exchange rate fell during the 90-day period.

To execute the forward contract that is now due, Domestic will (1d) deliver €100,000 and (1e) receive the contracted amount of $127,020 in return. The entries to record this transaction will appear as follows:

| January 30, 20X4 | | |
|---|---|---|
| **(1d)** | | |
| Forward contract payable | 127,020 | |
|     Exchange gains and losses | | 2,020 |
|     Cash (€100,000 @ 1.2500) | | 125,000 |
| [payment of €100,000 to fulfill the forward contract obligation] | | |
| **(1e)** | | |
| Cash | 127,020 | |
|     Forward contract receivable (in C$) | | 127,020 |
| [receipt of cash from the buyer of the forward contract] | | |

Domestic recognizes a *loss* of $2,170 on the receivable and a *gain* of $2,020 on the forward contract. The net amount is a loss of $150. The fact that we end up with a net loss may suggest that the forward contract was not completely successful at eliminating risk, but that is not correct. The $150 loss is the difference between the spot rate and the forward rate on the date of the original sale, multiplied by the amount of the foreign currency balance being hedged: €100,000 × ($1.2717 – $1.2702).

What the hedge really does is limit any possible gain or loss to a known amount, the spread between the spot rate and the forward rate. The same net loss will exist in our example regardless of the actual exchange rate at the settlement date.

For example, suppose that instead of a rate of $1.2500, the actual spot rate on the settlement date was $1.2850. The three entries to record the receipt from the customer and the settlement of the forward contract will then be as follows:

| | | |
|---|---|---|
| **(1c2)** | | |
| Cash (€100,000 @ 1.2850) | 128,500 | |
|    Exchange gains and losses | | 1,330 |
|    Accounts receivable (€100,000 @ 1.2717) | | 127,170 |
| [receipt of €100,000 from customer, on account] | | |
| **(1d2)** | | |
| Forward contract payable | 127,020 | |
| Exchange gains and losses | 1,480 | |
|    Cash (€100,000 @ 1.2850) | | 128,500 |
| [payment of €100,000 to fulfill the forward contract obligation] | | |
| **(1e2)** | | |
| Cash | 127,020 | |
|    Forward contract receivable (in C$) | | 127,020 |
| [receipt of cash from the buyer of the forward contract] | | |

Settlement of (1c2) (the customer receivable) and (1d2) (the forward contract) results in a gain of $1,330 and a loss of $1,480, respectively, for a net loss of $150, exactly as when the spot rate was $1.2500.

In the example that we have used above, the forward rate happened to be *lower* than the spot rate, resulting in a net *loss*. Forward rates may be either higher or lower than the spot rate. The spread between the spot and forward rates depends on (1) the interest rate differential between the two countries and (2) how the market predicts the rate will move.

If the forward rate is *lower* than the spot rate, the hedge of a receivable would lock the hedger into a *loss*. But the loss would be quite minor in comparison to the potential loss from an unprotected position. The day-to-day change in the spot rate can easily be larger than the spread between the spot and forward rates. Thus the small certain loss can be viewed as the cost of insurance against a possibly substantial speculative loss. Of course, hedging also eliminates the possibility of realizing a gain as well.

When the forward rate is higher than the spot rate, the contract has a premium. When the forward rate is less, then a discount exists. If the hedge is of a foreign currency *receivable*, as above, a premium results in a gain while a discount results in a loss.

Conversely, if the hedge is of a foreign currency *liability*, a premium results in a loss while a discount causes a gain. The following table summarizes this relationship:

| | Net result if a forward contract is priced at a: | |
|---|---|---|
| **Item being hedged** | **Premium** | **Discount** |
| Monetary assets | gain | loss |
| Monetary liability | loss | gain |

In the example above, the forward contract was recorded by means of a journal entry that assigned equal values to the receivable and the payable. In addition to this method of recording, we will examine one other method of recording the hedge that yields the same result and that may be more appropriate.

**Memorandum Entry, or Net, Method**   A second method of accounting for the forward contract is the **memorandum entry method**. Under this method, the forward contract is not recorded at all on November 1, 20X3. At the time of entering into the forward contract, the forward contract receivable is equal to the forward contract payable. The receivable is simply netted against the payable and, because the contract has zero value, only a memorandum entry is used. We will refer to this method as the net method.

A forward contract is an executory contract as well as a financial instrument. You already know (from previous courses) that an executory contract is an agreement by two parties to perform in the future. For accounting purposes, no liability or receivable is normally deemed to exist for an executory contract until one of the parties has actually performed, or *executed*, the contract. Usually the contract enters the accounting records only when it is settled. However, a forward contract is also a financial instrument, and as a result the accounting for forward contracts differs from the usual non-recognition of executory contracts.

Recognition for financial instruments such as forward contracts occurs when the entity becomes party to the contractual provisions of the instrument rather than when performance occurs. Conceptually, the forward contract should be recognized on November 1, 20X3. However, since there is no cost at the beginning of the contract, there is no explicit cost that we can recognize and record. Thus it can be argued that there should be no entry on November 1, 20X3.

As a result, the net method of accounting for the forward contract makes no entry for the contract on November 1, 20X3. Unlike the gross method, the liability and the receivable relating to the contract are not recorded on the day that Domestic enters into the forward contract. The journal entries are as follows:

| | | |
|---|---|---|
| *November 1, 20X3* | | |
| **(2a)** | | |
| Accounts receivable (€100,000) | 127,170 | |
| Sales | | 127,170 |
| [sale of merchandise for €100,000 on account] | | |
| **(2b)** | | |
| No entry for forward contract | | |
| | | |
| *January 30, 20X4* | | |
| **(2c)** | | |
| Cash (€100,000 @ 1.2500) | 125,000 | |
| Exchange gains and losses | 2,170 | |
| Accounts receivable (€100,000 @ 1.2717) | | 127,170 |
| [receipt of €100,000 from customer, on account] | | |
| **(2d)** | | |
| Cash (re: C$ forward contract receivable) | 127,020 | |
| Exchange gains and losses | | 2,020 |
| Cash (re: €100,000 forward contract payable) | | 125,000 |
| [settlement of forward contract @ $1.25 spot rate] | | |

The disadvantage of this approach is that since the forward contract has not been explicitly recognized on the books, it is easy to overlook when adjustments are made at year-end. At a conceptual level, however, the second approach (i.e., net method) is superior since it is difficult to record an asset (or liability) that has no cost. This is despite the fact that the forward contract meets the IFRS recognition criterion. In practice, the most common method is to treat the forward contract as an executory contract and thus not formally record it.

This example described an asset exposure. A liability exposure (e.g., a foreign currency account payable) is treated similarly. However, the company will then enter into a forward contract to *receive* instead of *deliver* the foreign currency.

The two methods of recording the hedge are shown in Exhibit 8.2. The two entries for the sale and the collection of the customer receivable are identical under both methods. The accounting for the hedge does not affect the transactions for the primary instrument.

We also saw that regardless of the spot rate on the settlement date, the hedge offsets any gains or losses in the corresponding receivable. The cost was a small exchange loss of $150 in both scenarios. The accounting reflects the economics behind management's decision to enter into the hedge. Any exchange loss (gain) is matched with the related exchange gain (loss), and this is reflected in the financial statements for the period.

There are several issues still to be addressed. The accounting for an intervening year-end will be examined next. We will also discuss how we handle accounting for hedges when normal accounting does not allow the matching of related exchange gains and losses.

**Exhibit 8.2** Alternative Recording Methods for Hedging Contracts

| | Gross Method | | Net Method | |
|---|---|---|---|---|
| **November 1, 20X3** | | | | |
| (a) Accounts receivable (euros) | 127,170 | | 127,170 | |
| Sales | | 127,170 | | 127,170 |
| (b) Forward contract receivable (C$) | 127,020 | | | |
| Forward contract payable (euros) | | 127,020 | | |
| **January 30, 20X4** | | | | |
| (c) Cash (euros) | 125,000 | | 125,000 | |
| Exchange gains and losses | 2,170 | | 2,170 | |
| Accounts receivable (euros) | | 127,170 | | 127,170 |
| (d) Cash (C$) | | | 127,020 | |
| Forward contract payable (euros) | 127,020 | | | |
| Exchange gains and losses | | 2,020 | | 2,020 |
| Cash (euros) | | 125,000 | | 125,000 |
| (e) Cash (C$) | 127,020 | | | |
| Forward contract receivable (C$) | | 127,020 | | |

Note: The gross method records the forward contract when initiated; the net method records the forward contract at settlement. A January 31 fiscal year-end is assumed.

# Intervening Year-End

The foregoing illustration dealt with the simplest situation, in which all of the related events occurred within the same accounting period. More commonly, a hedging relationship spans more than one accounting period, especially if the reporting enterprise is a public company that must report quarterly. When a foreign currency hedge spans two or more accounting periods, we continue to follow the general principles that were introduced earlier in the chapter.

When a receivable is denominated in a foreign currency, it will be translated at the year-end spot rate, and any exchange gains and losses will be included in net income. A forward contract is a derivative, and gains and losses from derivatives also are reported in earnings. Thus, forward contracts are reported at fair value at the SFP date, and changes in fair value are recognized in net income, regardless of whether the change has been realized or not. An exception arises when a forward contract is formally designated as a hedge under *hedge accounting*, a specific IFRS term that we will explain and discuss shortly.

To illustrate, we can slightly modify the previous example by assuming that Domestic's fiscal year ends on *December 31* instead of January 31. There will be a financial statement reporting date between the November 1 sale and the January 30 settlement date. Assume also that the spot rate for the euro on December 31 is $1.2600.

If the receivable was *not* hedged, the entries relating to (a) the sale at a rate of $127,170; (b) the year-end adjustment of the account receivable balance to $126,000 at the December 31 spot rate of $1.2600; and (c) the settlement at $1.2500 would be as follows:

| | | |
|---|---|---|
| (a) *November 1, 20X3* | | |
| Accounts receivable (€100,000) | 127,170 | |
|   Sales | | 127,170 |
| [sale for €100,000 when the spot rate = $1.2717] | | |
| (b) *December 31, 20X3* | | |
| Exchange gains and losses | 1,170 | |
|   Account receivable | | 1,170 |
| [reduce receivable to year-end spot rate: <br>   €100,000 × ($1.2600 − $1.2717)] | | |
| (c) *January 30, 20X4* | | |
| Cash (€100,000 @ $1.25) | 125,000 | |
| Exchange gains and losses | 1,000 | |
|   Account receivable | | 126,000 |
| [receipt of cash to settle the €100,000 receivable at the January 30 spot rate of $1.25] | | |

In the absence of a hedge, the exchange gain/loss is recognized in the period in which it occurred. Of the total $2,170 exchange loss, $1,170 occurred in 20X3 and $1,000 occurred in 20X4.

If the receivable is hedged, however, the exchange gain/loss will be offset by a loss/gain on the forward contract liability on the settlement date. These gains and losses naturally offset using "normal" accounting for both the receivable balance and the forward contract on the SFP date. The use of *hedge accounting* is not necessary. The entries are shown in Exhibit 8.3 for both methods and the following comments are provided on the journal entries.

*November 1, 20X3*

**(a)** An entry is made to record the sale and associated receivable.

**(b)** Under the gross method, the forward contract is recorded using the forward rate of $1.2702.

*December 31, 20X3*

**(c)** At year-end, accounts receivable are re-valued to $126,000 by crediting accounts receivable for $1,170 and recognizing an exchange loss of $1,170 [€100,000 × ($1.2600 – $1.2717)].

**(d)** In addition, the forward contract must be valued at fair value. The forward rate for delivery of euros in 30 days is 1.2594. We will use this rate to value the forward contract because there are 30 days remaining until delivery is required. The value of the €100,000 payable under the forward contract declined from $127,020 to $125,940, for a gain of $1,080 [€100,000 × ($1.2702 – $1.2594)].

**Exhibit 8.3** Recording Hedging Contracts with Intervening Year-End

| | Gross Method | | Net Method | |
|---|---|---|---|---|
| **November 1, 20X3** | | | | |
| (a) Accounts receivable (euros) | 127,170 | | 127,170 | |
| Sales | | 127,170 | | 127,170 |
| (b) Forward contract receivable (C$) | 127,020 | | | |
| Forward contract payable (euros) | | 127,020 | | |
| **December 31, 20X3** | | | | |
| (c) Exchange gains and losses | 1,170 | | 1,170 | |
| Accounts receivable (euros) | | 1,170 | | 1,170 |
| (d) Forward contract (payable—euros) | 1,080 | | 1,080 | |
| Exchange gains and losses | | 1,080 | | 1,080 |
| **January 30, 20X4** | | | | |
| (e) Cash (euros) | 125,000 | | 125,000 | |
| Exchange gains and losses | 1,000 | | 1,000 | |
| Accounts receivable (euros) | | 126,000 | | 126,000 |
| (f) Cash (C$) | | | 127,020 | |
| Forward contract (payable—euros) | 125,940 | | | 1,080 |
| Exchange gains and losses | | 940 | | 940 |
| Cash (euros) | | 125,000 | | 125,000 |
| (g) Cash (C$) | 127,020 | | | |
| Forward contract receivable (C$) | | 127,020 | | |

Note: The gross method formally records the forward contract when initiated; the net method formally records the forward contract only at settlement. A December 31 fiscal year-end is assumed.

*January 30, 20X4*

**(e)** When the customer's account is settled, an entry is made to record the receipt of €100,000 (at the January spot rate of $1.2500).

**(f) and (g)** The settlement of the forward contract is also recorded to reflect both the payment of €100,000 to satisfy the forward contract payable and the receipt of C$127,020 in settlement of the forward contract receivable.

In 20X3, the exchange loss of $1,170 on the customer's account is offset against the $1,080 exchange gain on the forward contract. The net result is a loss of $90 in 20X3. In 20X4, the exchange loss of $1,000 on the customer receivable is offset by the $940 gain on the forward contract and the result is a $60 loss in 20X4. The net cost of the hedge is $150, the same as above, but it is now distributed across two periods.

### Concept Check 8-2

1. What is hedging?
2. Identify three instruments that can be used for hedging.
3. What is a derivative instrument?

Define and describe hedge accounting and explain when it can be used

## 8.3 HEDGE ACCOUNTING

Hedging allows management to limit their exposure to certain risks, such as changes in currency exchange rates. In the example above, normal accounting rules reflected well the ability of a forward contract (the hedging item) to offset exchange gains and losses on monetary items, such as trade accounts receivable (the hedged item). But this is not always the case.

Assume that a company issues a purchase order to buy a machine. If the machine is priced in a foreign currency and if the lead time to delivery is several months or more, the company would be exposed to potentially large exchange losses (or gains).

To limit its exposure, the company may decide to enter into a forward contract. While this would be good business practice, normal accounting rules may not reflect the substance of this transaction. For example, if there was an intervening year-end, under normal accounting the company would be required to value the forward contract at fair value at year-end and to recognize the associated gain/loss in net income. Because we do not normally recognize the purchase order on the financial statements, there would be no offsetting loss/gain. The financial statements would not reflect the intent of the hedge because the gains and losses would not be matched.

To overcome this problem, IFRS provides special rules for hedging activities (i.e., hedge accounting). **Hedge accounting** allows gains and losses on the hedged item to be matched with losses and gains on the hedging instrument in the same period. *It is important to note that hedge accounting is optional.*

### Requirements for Hedge Accounting

*Hedge accounting* is a formal accounting designation and not simply a net result. For example, a Canadian company may have a substantial amount of receivables that are denominated in euros and may also have a large amount of payables in the same currency.

Effectively, the currency risks from the receivables and the payables should offset each other to some extent. This sort of offsetting position is sometimes called a **natural (implicit) hedge**—any gain or loss from the receivables will be offset by the loss or gain from the payables. The foreign exchange gains and losses will flow through to net income and naturally tend to offset each other. While this is a form of hedge in substance, it is not what the IFRS calls hedge accounting!

Under IFRS hedge accounting, a hedging relationship qualifies for special accounting rules only if it meets *all* of the following conditions:

1. The hedging relationship includes only eligible hedging instruments and hedged items.

2. The hedging relationship is formally designated and documented at inception within the company's overall risk management strategy. The documentation must identify the hedged item and hedging instrument. It must also discuss the nature of the risk being hedged and the assessment procedures that will be used to determine hedge effectiveness (see Reality Check 8–2).

3. The hedging relationship fulfils the hedge effectiveness criteria.

Other points that underlie the concept of hedge accounting are as follows:

- A *hedged item* can be (a) an asset or liability; (b) an unrecognized *firm commitment,* such as a purchase order; (c) a highly probable forecast transaction, such as a future revenue stream; or (d) a net investment in a foreign operation. A derivative instrument cannot normally be a hedged item.[6] Our focus in this chapter is on hedging changes in the future cash flows or fair value that result from exposure to changes in foreign currency exchange rates.

- A **hedging instrument** (that is, the offsetting risk) is normally a derivative. It can also be a non-derivative financial asset or liability that is measured at fair value through profit or loss.

- An **effective hedge** is one where the changes in the fair value or cash flows of the hedging instrument offset the changes in the fair value or cash flows of the hedged item.

Hedge accounting gives companies the ability to change the timing of recognition in net income of certain unrealized foreign currency gains and losses. Exchange gains and losses on hedging instruments (usually derivatives) are normally recognized in income in the current period. To match the gains and losses between a hedging instrument and a hedged item, a company can either:

- speed up recognition of the offsetting loss or gain on the hedged item into the current period; or

- defer recognition on the loss or gain on the hedging instrument to correspond with the hedged item.

---

[6] However, a hedged item may contain a derivative that is part of a larger aggregated exposure.

## Bombardier's Use of Hedge Accounting

Designation as a hedge is only allowed if, both at the inception of the hedge and throughout the hedge period, the changes in the fair value of the derivative and non-derivative hedging financial instruments are expected to substantially offset the changes in the fair value of the hedged item attributable to the underlying risk exposure. The Corporation formally documents all relationships between the hedging instruments and hedged items, as well as its risk management objectives and strategy for undertaking various hedge transactions. This process includes linking all derivatives to forecasted cash flows or to a specific asset or liability. The Corporation also formally documents and assesses, both at the hedge's inception and on an ongoing basis, whether the hedging instruments are highly effective in offsetting the changes in the fair value or cash flows of the hedged items.

Source: Bombardier Inc., 2011 Annual Report, pp.146–147.

Hedge accounting includes three types of hedging:

1. **Fair-value hedge**: the hedging of potential changes in fair value that result from changes in foreign exchange rates and that affect profit or loss. Fair-value hedges can be for the exposure to changes in exchange rates that affect recognized assets or liabilities and unrecognized firm commitments.

2. **Cash-flow hedge**: the hedging of the variability in cash flows that results from changes in foreign exchange rates and that affects profit or loss. Cash-flow hedges can be for the exposure to changes in exchange rates that affect recognized assets or liabilities and highly probable forecast transactions.

3. **Hedge of a net investment in a foreign operation**: we will discuss this topic in more detail in the next chapter.

In this chapter we focus on fair-value hedges and cash-flow hedges. In both cases the specific risk is potential changes in foreign currency exchange rates. It is also important to remember that hedge accounting may not be applied until and unless the company has made a formal designation of a hedging relationship. The objective of the formal declaration is to keep companies from loosely defining their hedging relationships and thereby selectively choosing how to report gains or loss at reporting dates—that is, showing a gain/loss in OCI rather than in net income, or vice versa.

### Concept Check 8-3

1. Why do companies need hedge accounting?
2. Is hedge accounting optional or required? Explain.
3. What are the three possible hedging relationships found in hedge accounting?

# 8.4 ACCOUNTING FOR FAIR-VALUE AND CASH-FLOW HEDGES

LO

Explain the accounting for fair-value hedges and cash-flow hedges

Hedge accounting can be used in a variety of circumstances. However, for our discussions of foreign currency exposure, the most relevant and practical issues concern anticipated transactions. **Anticipated transactions** are those that are expected to occur in the future but for which no asset or liability has been recognized. Companies often have a foreign currency risk exposure for anticipated transactions.

For example, a Canadian airline is exposed to risk on its anticipated purchases of aircraft fuel. The risk takes two forms: (1) a *fair-value risk* that the US dollar price will increase and (2) a *currency risk* that the US–Canadian exchange rate will change. Both types of risk can be hedged against. The airline can hedge the fair-value risk on fuel prices by buying futures options for oil. But the hedge won't solve the currency risk because the options are in US dollars. Therefore, the airline may also hedge against adverse exchange rate changes through a currency hedge. Projected future purchases of oil are one example of the type of anticipated transactions that we will concern ourselves with for the remainder of the chapter.

In discussing anticipated transactions, IFRS distinguishes between a *firm commitment* and a *forecasted transaction*:

■ A **firm commitment** is a binding agreement for the exchange of resources where the quantity, price, and dates are specified. An example of a firm commitment would be a purchase order that has been accepted by the source company.

■ A **forecasted transaction** is an anticipated transaction for which no firm commitment exists. Examples of a forecasted transaction would be a projected future revenue stream or a projected future inventory purchase.

The distinction between a firm commitment and a forecasted transaction is important. Under IFRS, the hedge of a firm commitment is accounted for as a fair-value hedge, while the hedge of a highly probable forecasted transaction is accounted for as a cash-flow hedge. However, under IFRS, a hedge of the foreign currency risk of a firm commitment can be accounted for as either a fair-value hedge or a cash-flow hedge.

Anticipated transactions do not immediately cause any financial assets or liabilities to be recorded, because by definition the transactions are *anticipated* future transactions. Nevertheless, a company often hedges the anticipated cash flow to offset the currency risk. Normal accounting for an anticipated transaction and hedge in this situation would not result in the associated exchange gains and losses being matched. The use of hedge accounting resolves this problem.

## Fair-Value Hedge

The accounting for a fair-value hedge is straightforward. The foreign currency gain or loss (i.e., the particular risk) on the hedging *instrument* is recognized in the current period's net income. The foreign currency gain or loss (i.e., the same particular risk) on the hedged *item* is also recognized in the current period net income, and the carrying value of the hedged item is adjusted. The gains and losses of the hedged item and hedging instrument will then offset one another in the same period.

In practice, hedge accounting using fair-value hedges will usually not be necessary to offset gains and losses on recognized assets or liabilities. Foreign exchange gains and losses are already recognized in current period net income for all classes of financial assets and liabilities with one exception—equity investments where the entity has elected the fair value through other comprehensive income option. Exchange gains and losses from derivatives are also included in current period net income. The exchange gains and losses, therefore, are already matched for most financial assets and liabilities.

For many businesses, it takes a lot of time and effort to go through the IFRS's necessary formal designation and documentation process for hedge accounting. It is unlikely companies will use hedge accounting if the foreign exchange gains and losses are naturally offsetting (see Reality Check 8–3).

A fair-value hedge is commonly used for a firm commitment, such as a purchase order. Because a purchase order is not normally recognized on the financial statements, there would be no foreign exchange gain/loss to offset the loss/gain on the hedging instrument. Using a fair-value hedge allows for the foreign exchange gain/loss on the purchase order to be recognized immediately so that it can offset the loss/gain on the hedging instrument.

### Example: Fair-Value Hedge of a Commitment to Purchase a Machine

To illustrate accounting for a fair-value hedge, assume that Domestic Corporation issues a purchase order to Français Ltée. on November 1, 20X7, to purchase a machine for €200,000. The machine is delivered on January 30, 20X8, and payment is made on March 1, 20X8. Domestic has a December 31 fiscal year-end.

Domestic Corp. finalized the decision to purchase the machine on November 1, based on the Canadian dollar equivalent cost of the machine at that time. If the euro appreciates significantly in value between November 1 and the payment date, Domestic will incur substantial additional cost for the machine. Therefore, it is common for a purchaser to hedge a commitment as soon as the purchase contract is signed and the foreign currency cost of the asset or service is established.

Suppose that on November 1, 20X7, the spot rate for the euro is €1 = C$1.5000. The €200,000 initial commitment is equivalent to C$300,000. Domestic Corp. hedges its euro commitment by entering into a forward contract to *receive* €200,000 on March 1, 20X8.

Assume that, on November 1, the March 1 forward rate for the euro is $1.5100. The relevant exchange rates are summarized in the table below:

| Date | Event | Spot rate | Forward rate to March 1, 20X8 |
|---|---|---|---|
| November 1, 20X7 | Purchase order issued | 1.5000 | 1.5100 |
| December 31, 20X7 | SFP date | 1.5050 | 1.5130 |
| January 30, 20X8 | Machine delivered | 1.5300 | 1.5340 |
| March 1, 20X8 | Forward contract settled | 1.5400 | n/a—settlement date |

We will also assume that this transaction qualifies as a fair-value hedge under hedge accounting. The entries to record these transactions are summarized in Exhibit 8.4, and the following comments are provided on the journal entries.

*November 1, 20X7*

**(a)** No entry is made to record the purchase order.

**(b)** Under the gross method, the forward contract is recorded using the forward rate of $1.51.

*December 31, 20X7*

**(c)** At year-end the forward contract is adjusted to (recorded at) fair value and the gain is recognized in net income. The adjustment to the forward contract ($600) is determined using the forward rate on December 31 [€200,000 × (1.513 − 1.510)].

**(d)** In addition, an exchange loss on the purchase order is recognized in net income and a liability is recognized to reflect the increase in the cost of the purchase order commitment. The amount of the loss and associated liability ($1,000) is determined using the spot rate on December 31 [€200,000 × (1.505 − 1.500)]. The net exchange loss from November 1 to December 31 is $400 ($1,000 − $600).

*January 30, 20X8*

**(e)** The forward contract is re-valued by making an entry for $4,200, the change in the value of the contract [€200,000 × (1.534 − 1.513)]. The gain is recognized in net income.

**(f)** An additional exchange loss on the purchase order is recognized in net income. The increase in the cost of the purchase order commitment is also recognized as an increased liability. The amount of the loss and associated liability ($5,000) is determined using the spot rate on January 30 [€200,000 × (1.530 − 1.505)]. The net exchange loss from January 1 to January 30 is $800 ($5,000 − $4,200).

**(g)** On delivery, accounts payable are recorded at the spot rate ($306,000 = €200,000 × 1.530) to reflect the value of the obligation to pay €200,000 to the supplier. The PO commitment liability is reversed as the increase in the liability is now captured in accounts payable. Finally, the machine is recorded at $300,000 to balance the journal entry. This results in the equipment being recorded at the spot rate (1.500) that was in effect when the purchase order was issued.

*March 1, 20X8*

**(h)** and **(i)** The forward contract is settled on March 1, 20X8. Domestic Corp. pays the $302,000 it contracted to pay (€200,000 × 1.510) and in return receives €200,000 valued at $308,000. The difference is a gain of $6,000 on the contract, of which

**Exhibit 8.4** Recording a Fair-Value Hedge

| | Gross Method | | Net Method | |
|---|---:|---:|---:|---:|
| **November 1, 20X7** | | | | |
| (a) Issue PO (purchase order)—no entry | | | | |
| (b) Forward contract receivable (euros) | 302,000 | | | |
|     Forward contract payable (C$) | | 302,000 | | |
|     [to record the forward contract using | | | | |
|     forward rate: (€200,000 × 1.51)] | | | | |
| **December 31, 20X7** | | | | |
| (c) Forward contract receivable (euros) | 600 | | 600 | |
|     Exchange gains and losses | | 600 | | 600 |
|     [€200,000 × (1.513 – 1.510)] | | | | |
| (d) Exchange gains and losses | 1,000 | | 1,000 | |
|     PO commitment liability | | 1,000 | | 1,000 |
|     [€200,000 × (1.505 – 1.500)] | | | | |
| **January 30, 20X8** | | | | |
| (e) Forward contract receivable (euros) | 4,200 | | 4,200 | |
|     Exchange gains and losses | | 4,200 | | 4,200 |
|     [€200,000 × (1.534 – 1.513)] | | | | |
| (f) Exchange gains and losses | 5,000 | | 5,000 | |
|     PO commitment liability | | 5,000 | | 5,000 |
|     [€200,000 × (1.530 – 1.505)] | | | | |
| (g) Machine | 300,000 | | 300,000 | |
|     PO commitment liability | 6,000 | | 6,000 | |
|       Accounts payable | | 306,000 | | 306,000 |
| **March 1, 20X8** | | | | |
| (h) Forward contract payable | 302,000 | | | |
|     Cash (C$) | | 302,000 | | |
| (i) Cash (euros) | 308,000 | | 308,000 | |
|     Forward contract receivable (euros) | | 306,800 | | 4,800 |
|     Exchange gains and losses | | 1,200 | | 1,200 |
|     Cash (C$) | | | | 302,000 |
| (j) Accounts payable | 306,000 | | 306,000 | |
|     Exchange gains and losses | 2,000 | | 2,000 | |
|       Cash (euros) | | 308,000 | | 308,000 |

Note: The gross method records the forward contract when initiated; the net method records the forward contract only at settlement. A December 31 fiscal year-end is assumed.

$4,800 was recognized earlier. The remaining $1,200 is the gain that occurred between January 30 and March 1 [€200,000 × (1.540 – 1.534)].

(j) Domestic Corp. uses the €200,000 (worth C$308,000) it received from its forward contract to settle the payable for the machine. As a result of the change in the exchange rate, the company incurs an exchange loss of $2,000 [€200,000 × (1.540 – 1.530)]. The net exchange loss from January 30 to March 1 is $800 ($2,000 – $1,200).

Observe the following about this transaction:

- The cost of the hedge was $2,000 [€200,000 × (1.510 – 1.500)], the difference between the spot rate and the forward rate at the time the machine was ordered; $400 was recognized as an exchange loss in 20X7, and $1,600 was recognized as an exchange loss in 20X8 ($800 between January 1 and January 30 and $800 between January 30 and March 1, 20X8).

- The cost of the machine was $300,000, which can be calculated using the spot rate (€200,000 × 1.500) at the time it was ordered. None of the cost of the hedge was included in the cost of the machine.

## Cash-Flow Hedge

The accounting for a cash-flow hedge achieves matching by deferring the recognition of the gains and losses on the hedging instrument in other comprehensive income. In addition to disclosing exchange gains/losses as a component of OCI, the cumulative gains/losses are also disclosed as a separate component of equity in the statement of changes in equity. Any ineffective portion of the hedging instrument is recognized in net income.

The accounting for the hedged item proceeds as normal. When *non-financial* assets are subsequently recognized, the gains or losses can be removed from other comprehensive income and included in the initial cost of the asset or liability. If the length of the forward contract was to the delivery date, then the terms of the hedge establish the cost of the anticipated goods or services.

Alternatively, for both *non-financial* and *financial* assets, the associated gains and losses in other comprehensive income can be left in the equity account and only reclassified into income in the same period(s) that the asset acquired or liability assumed affects net income.

### Example: Cash-Flow Hedge of a Commitment to Purchase a Machine

To illustrate accounting for a cash-flow hedge, we will reuse our Domestic Corp. example. A cash-flow hedge can be used by Domestic because, as a firm commitment, the purchase order automatically meets the criteria of being a highly probable future transaction. Further, the foreign exchange risk on the purchase order exposes Domestic to variability in cash flows. Thus cash-flow hedge accounting is appropriate. To continue our example, assume that Domestic Corporation issues a purchase order to Français Ltée. on November 1, 20X7, to purchase a machine for €200,000. The machine is delivered on January 30, 20X8, and payment is made on March 1, 20X8. Domestic has a December 31 fiscal year-end.

Domestic Corp. hedges the commitment as soon as the purchase contract is signed. We will assume that this transaction qualifies as a cash-flow hedge under hedge accounting. Of course, Domestic will not recognize a liability related to the commitment on the SFP until the machine has been delivered.

Suppose that on November 1, 20X7, the spot rate for the euro is €1 = C$1.5000. The €200,000 initial commitment is equivalent to C$300,000. Domestic Corp. hedges its euro commitment by entering into a forward contract to *receive* €200,000 on March 1, 20X8. Assume that the March 1 forward rate for the euro is $1.5100 on November 1. The relevant exchange rates are summarized in the table below:

| Date | Event | Spot rate | Forward rate to March 1, 20X8 |
|---|---|---|---|
| November 1, 20X7 | Purchase order issued | 1.5000 | 1.5100 |
| December 31, 20X7 | SFP date | 1.5050 | 1.5130 |
| January 30, 20X8 | Machine delivered | 1.5300 | 1.5340 |
| March 1, 20X8 | Forward contract settled | 1.5400 | n/a—settlement date |

The entries to record these transactions are summarized in Exhibit 8.5, and the following comments are provided on the journal entries.

*November 1, 20X7*

**(a)** No entry is made to record the purchase order.

**(b)** Under the gross method, the forward contract is recorded using the forward rate of $1.51.

*December 31, 20X7*

**(c)** At year-end the forward contract is adjusted to (recorded at) fair value and the gain is deferred in other comprehensive income. The increase in the fair value of the forward contract ($600) is determined using the forward rate on December 31 [€200,000 × (1.513 − 1.510)].

*January 30, 20X8*

**(d)** The forward contract is re-valued by making an entry for the change in the value of the contract, $4,200 [€200,000 × (1.534 − 1.513)]. The gain is deferred in other comprehensive income.

**(e)** On delivery, the machine and associated payable are recorded at the spot rate ($306,000 = €200,000 × 1.530).

**(f)** Next, the gain deferred in other comprehensive income is reclassified. We have chosen to adjust the cost of the machine. As such, the deferred gain will be amortized into income over the life of the machine through its effect on the depreciation expense of the machine. The carrying value of the machine is $301,200. This is slightly more than the $300,000 cost using the spot rate at the time the machine was ordered but is less than the $306,000 cost if there had been no hedge.

*March 1, 20X8*

**(g) and (h)** The forward contract is settled on March 1, 20X8. Domestic Corp. pays the $302,000 it contracted to pay (€200,000 × 1.510) and in return receives €200,000 valued at $308,000. The difference is a gain of $6,000 on the contract, of which $4,800 was recognized earlier. The remaining $1,200 is the gain that occurred between January 30 and March 1 [€200,000 × (1.540 − 1.534)].

**(i)** Domestic Corp. uses the €200,000 (worth C$308,000) it received from its forward contract to settle the payable for the machine. As a result of the change in the exchange rate, the company incurs an exchange loss of $2,000 × [€200,000 (1.540 − 1.530)]. The net exchange loss from January 30 to March 1 is $800 ($2,000 − $1,200).

The following can be noted about this transaction:

- No gains or losses were recognized in net income in 20X7.
- The cost of the hedge was $2,000 [€200,000 × (1.510 − 1.500)]; $800 was recognized as an exchange loss in 20X8 (between January 30 and March 1, 20X8), and $1,200 was included in the cost of the machine.

**Exhibit 8.5** Recording a Cash-Flow Hedge

| | Gross Method | | Net Method | |
|---|---|---|---|---|
| **November 1, 20X7** | | | | |
| (a) Issue PO—no entry | | | | |
| (b) Forward contract receivable (euros) | 302,000 | | | |
| Forward contract payable (C$) | | 302,000 | | |
| [to record the forward contract using forward rate: (€200,000 × 1.51)] | | | | |
| **December 31, 20X7** | | | | |
| (c) Forward contract receivable (euros) | 600 | | 600 | |
| Other comprehensive income | | 600 | | 600 |
| [€200,000 × (1.513 − 1.510)] | | | | |
| **January 30, 20X8** | | | | |
| (d) Forward contract receivable (euros) | 4,200 | | 4,200 | |
| Other comprehensive income | | 4,200 | | 4,200 |
| [€200,000 × (1.534 − 1.513)] | | | | |
| (g) Machine | 306,000 | | 306,000 | |
| Accounts payable | | 306,000 | | 306,000 |
| (h) Other comprehensive income | 4,800 | | 4,800 | |
| Machine | | 4,800 | | 4,800 |
| **March 1, 20X8** | | | | |
| g) Forward contract payable | 302,000 | | | |
| Cash (C$) | | 302,000 | | |
| h) Cash (euros) | 308,000 | | 308,000 | |
| Forward contract receivable (euros) | | 306,800 | | 4,800 |
| Exchange gains and losses | | 1,200 | | 1,200 |
| Cash (C$) | | | | 302,000 |
| i) Accounts payable | 306,000 | | 306,000 | |
| Exchange gains and losses | 2,000 | | 2,000 | |
| Cash (euros) | | 308,000 | | 308,000 |

Note: The gross method records the forward contract when initiated; the net method records the forward contract at settlement. A December 31 fiscal year-end is assumed.

- The cost of the machine was $301,200, which consists of two components: $300,000, calculated using the spot rate ($1.50) at the time it was ordered, and $1,200, which is the cost of the hedge that was allocated to the machine for the price protection it provided from November 1, 20X7, to January 30, 20X8.

This example illustrated the purchase of an asset. The same principles apply if the purchase is of services rather than of an asset. If the company were *selling* assets or services priced in a foreign currency, the same procedures would apply, except that the recognized monetary item would be a receivable instead of a payable; any discount or premium on the forward contract would be reflected in sales revenue.

Finally, because the foreign currency risk associated with a firm commitment can be accounted for as either a fair-value or cash-flow hedge, when a forecast transaction becomes a firm commitment (e.g., inventory purchases) the cash-flow hedge of the foreign currency risk does not have to be re-designated as a fair-value hedge.

## Concept Check 8-4

1. What is a firm commitment?
2. What is a forecast transaction?
3. How are gains and losses on cash-flow hedges treated?

## Effective Hedges

Earlier in the chapter, an effective hedge was defined as one where the changes in the fair value or cash flows of the hedging instrument offset the changes in the fair value or cash flows of the hedged item. The question arises as to how to assess the effectiveness of a hedge. This is important because an assessment must be done before a hedge can be designated for hedge accounting under IFRS.

A hedging relationship can be designated for hedge accounting only if it meets all of the following effectiveness requirements:

1. an economic relationship exists between the hedging instrument and the hedged item;
2. the designation is based on the relative quantities of the hedged item and hedging instrument;

### Reality Check 8–4

## Bombardier's Use of Cash-Flow Hedges

How significant are the gains and losses deferred in other comprehensive income using cash-flow hedge accounting rules?

In its 2011 second-quarter interim financial statements, Bombardier reported net income of $211 million. In its statement of comprehensive income it also reported a loss on cash-flow hedges of $143 million. These losses almost equal 70% of its reported income. Clearly, the magnitude of amounts involved using cash-flow hedge accounting can be very significant. However, it is important to remember that there are unrealized and unrecognized economic gains offsetting these losses. Cash-flow hedge accounting provides Bombardier with the ability to defer these losses and subsequently match them with the corresponding economic gains. Thus hedge accounting allows the financial reporting to reflect the original intention of management in entering into the hedges.

**Exhibit 8.6** Summary of Accounting for Fair Value and Cash Flow Hedges

| Item | Fair Value Hedge | Cash Flow Hedge |
|---|---|---|
| 1. Hedging instrument | | |
|     Measurement | Change in fair value | Change in fair value |
|     Impact on income–effective portion | Recognize in profit and loss | Deferred—recognize in OCI and accumulate in equity |
|     Impact on income–ineffective portion | Recognize in profit and loss | Recognize in profit and loss |
| 2. Hedged item | | |
|     Measurement | Change in fair value | n/a |
|     Impact on income | Recognize in profit and loss | n/a |
| 3. Offsetting of hedging instrument and hedged item | Occurs in current period | Deferred to future period |

**3.** the designation does not deliberately create hedge ineffectiveness by mismatching the relative quantities of the hedged item and the hedging instrument so as to attain an inappropriate accounting outcome; and

**4.** the value change in the hedging relationship is not dominated by the effect of credit risk.

Hedge effectiveness can be assessed through the use of either quantitative or qualitative techniques. The actual mechanics of the different possible tests are beyond the scope of this chapter, but you should be aware that this test is very important. In addition to assessing hedge effectiveness on inception of a hedge relationship, it should be assessed for each reporting date and for any significant change in circumstances related to the hedge. Hedge effectiveness is always assessed prospectively (i.e., it is forward-looking).

Hedge ineffectiveness is measured and recognized in profit or loss. If the hedge relationship does not meet the hedge effectiveness requirements, rebalancing of the hedging relationship is likely required. If, however, the risk management objective has changed, then hedge accounting should be discontinued. It is important to note that a company cannot voluntarily discontinue hedge accounting.

# 8.5 ACCOUNTING STANDARDS FOR PRIVATE ENTERPRISES

The accounting for foreign currency transactions and hedges for private enterprises is prescribed in Sections 1651 and 3856 of the *CICA Handbook, Part II.*

The general principles for accounting for foreign exchange transactions and balances for private enterprises are very similar to IFRS.

- All *monetary items* are translated using the exchange rate on the SFP date, and the associated gains and losses are recognized in net income.

- All *non-monetary items carried at historical cost* are measured using the historical exchange rate. There are no exchange gains or losses, so accounting for foreign exchange changes is not an issue.

## Proposed Change

The IASB has proposed significant changes to the standards dealing with financial instruments and hedge accounting. The purpose of the new standards is to streamline and simplify the accounting for financial instruments. The project consists of three phases: phase 1 addresses the classification and measurement of financial instruments; phase 2 addresses the impairment of financial instruments; and phase 3 addresses hedge accounting. As of the date of writing this text, IFRS 9 had been issued to address the classification and measurement of financial assets. The IASB hopes to issue final standards addressing the classification and measurement of financial liabilities and the remaining issues in phases 2 and 3, with a required adoption date likely for years beginning on or after January 1, 2015.

■  The accounting for *non-monetary items carried at fair value* is slightly different from IFRS. These items are measured using the exchange rate in effect on the balance sheet date and not the exchange rate on the date that the fair value was determined as used by IFRS. Exchange gains and losses are also recognized in net income.

A much simpler hedge accounting model with more limited application is used for private enterprises. As with IFRS, hedge accounting is optional. From the perspective of hedging foreign currency exposures, hedge accounting can be used for the hedging of (1) anticipated transactions and (2) the net investment in a foreign operation.[7]

The documentation required by ASPE for the use of hedge accounting is not as extensive as that required by IFRS, but the critical terms of the forward contract and the hedged item must be the same. For example, ASPE requires that a foreign currency forward contract must be for the same amount and the same currency as the hedged item and, further, that the forward contract must mature within 30 days of the date of the anticipated transaction. If these conditions are not met, then the hedge does not qualify for hedge accounting.

Further, under ASPE, only forward contracts can be used as hedging instruments; options and futures contracts are not allowed as hedging instruments under hedge accounting. The forward contract is only recognized at maturity, and at that time any gains and losses are used to adjust the carrying value of the hedged item.

Finally, private enterprises also have disclosure requirements to ensure that appropriate information is available about the use of hedge accounting. For example, private enterprises are required to disclose key terms of the anticipated transaction and the forward contract and the net effect of using hedge accounting.

---

[7] Additionally, hedge accounting can also be used for "a foreign currency-denominated interest-bearing asset or liability hedged with a cross-currency interest rate swap to mitigate the effect of changes in interest rates and foreign currency exchange rates" (*CICA Handbook, Part II*. Section 3856.32(d)).

**Exhibit 8.7** Foreign Currency Transactions and Hedges: IFRS and ASPE Comparison

| Item | IFRS | ASPE |
|---|---|---|
| 1. Accounting for foreign currency transactions / balances | | |
|     Monetary items | ■ Measure using closing exchange rate | ■ Measure using closing exchange rate |
| | ■ Gains/losses recognized in income | ■ Gains/losses recognized in income |
|     Non-monetary items at historical cost | ■ Measure using historical exchange rate | ■ Measure using historical exchange rate |
| | ■ No foreign exchange gains/losses | ■ No foreign exchange gains/losses |
|     Non-monetary items at fair value | ■ Measure using exchange rate on date fair value was determined | ■ Measure using closing exchange rate |
| | ■ Gains/losses recognized in income | ■ Gains/losses recognized in income |
| 2. Hedge Accounting | | |
|     Use | Optional | Optional |
|     Nature of hedge accounting model | Sophisticated, with extensive documentation required | Simple, with more limited documentation required |
|     Derivatives used as hedging instruments | Forward contracts, futures contracts, options, currency swaps (no restrictions) | Forward contracts only |
|     Assessment of effectiveness | Multiple methods | Critical terms must match |

## Relevant Standards

### IASB

| | |
|---|---|
| **IAS 21** | The Effects of Changes in Foreign Exchange Rates |
| **IAS 32** | Financial Instruments: Presentation |
| **IAS 39** | Financial Instruments: Recognition and Measurement |
| **IFRS 7** | Financial Instruments: Disclosures |
| **IFRS 9** | Financial Instruments |

### ASPE

| | |
|---|---|
| **1651** | Foreign Currency Translation |
| **3856** | Financial Instruments |

## 8.6 SUMMARY OF KEY POINTS

1. Exchange rates change for several reasons. Some changes, especially short-term fluctuations, are the result of the speculative activities of money market traders. Longer-term, the fundamental cause for changes in exchange rates is differential inflation rates between countries. Differential inflation rates cause exchange rates to change to compensate for the changing purchasing power between currencies. **LO 1**

2. Many, if not most, Canadian corporations engage in international activities to some extent. Foreign currency transactions are very common. A foreign currency transaction is one where the value of the transaction is fixed in a currency other than the enterprise's functional currency. Foreign currency transactions must be recorded on the corporation's books at their equivalent in Canadian dollars at the time of the transaction. For revenues, expenses, and non-monetary balances, the amounts that are established by the initial transaction are not changed at subsequent reporting dates. For monetary items denominated in a foreign currency, the balances are translated using the current or spot rate, and any exchange gains and losses are recognized in net income at subsequent reporting dates. **LO 1**

3. Financial assets and liabilities that are denominated in a foreign currency may be hedged. Hedging involves incurring a foreign currency liability to offset a foreign currency financial asset, or an asset to offset a liability. Derivative instruments are most commonly used for hedging. In Canada, the most common derivative instrument for foreign currency hedges is a forward contract. Futures, options, and currency swaps are other types of derivatives for hedging a foreign currency risk exposure. The accounting for hedges is usually straightforward because the normal rules for accounting for financial instruments allow the gain or loss on the hedged item to be recognized in the same period as the offsetting loss or gain on the hedging instrument. In those cases where the gains and losses do not offset, hedge accounting can be used to match the gains and losses. **LO 2**

4. *Hedge accounting* is a formal accounting designation that allows gains and losses on the hedged item to be matched with losses and gains on the hedging instrument in the same period. It is important to note that hedge accounting is optional. A hedging relationship must be specifically designated and documented by management within the company's risk management strategy. Hedge accounting may not be used prior to explicit designation and documentation of the hedge. **LO 3**

5. When hedge accounting is used, a foreign currency exposure is hedged using either a fair-value hedge or a cash-flow hedge (coverage of hedges of a net investment in a foreign operation is deferred to the next chapter). In a fair-value hedge, the foreign currency gain or loss on the hedged item and the hedging instrument are recognized in current period net income. **LO 4**

6. In a cash-flow hedge, the exchange gains/losses on the hedging instrument are deferred as a component of *other comprehensive income* on the SCI and as a separate component of shareholders' equity in the statement of changes in equity. When the asset or liability is recognized, the accumulated exchange gain/loss is removed from accumulated other comprehensive income and recognized in net income in a manner that reflects the effect of the associated asset or liability on net income. **LO 4**

7. Once the hedging relationship has been established, management must evaluate the effectiveness of the hedge. Hedge accounting can continue to be used only if the hedge continues to be effective. To the extent that a hedging relationship is not effective, gains and losses arising from the portion of the exposure that is not effectively hedged must be recognized in net income. **LO 4**

**Visit the text's website at** www.pearsoned.ca/beechy **for practice quizzes, additional problems, Excel® templates, answ.ers to Concept Check questions, and important IFRS updates.**

# Self-Study Problems

1. On December 31, 20X5, Debtor Limited issued €5,000,000 in debentures to a private investment company located in Frankfurt, Germany. The debentures are due on December 31, 20X8. Debtor Limited is a privately held Alberta company that reports to its shareholders and creditors in Canadian dollars using IFRS. Debtor did not hedge its euro-denominated debt. Over the life of the bonds, the exchange rates for the euro were as follows:

| Date | Canadian dollar equivalent |
|---|---|
| December 31, 20X5 | $1.27 |
| December 31, 20X6 | $1.30 |
| December 31, 20X7 | $1.34 |
| December 31, 20X8 | $1.35 |

**Required**

Calculate the amount of gain or loss that will appear on Debtor Limited's net income for each of 20X6, 20X7, and 20X8. Disregard any interest expense.

2. On December 2, 20X1, Domestic Corporation sold merchandise to a Taiwanese customer for 1 million Taiwan Dollars (TWD). The TWD was worth C$0.0300 on the date of the sale. On December 3, 20X1, Domestic entered into a forward contract with its bank to deliver TWD1,000,000 in 60 days at a rate of $0.0290.

    Domestic's fiscal year ended on December 31, 20X1. The TWD was worth $0.0294 at year-end, and the forward rate for settlement of a February 1 contract was $0.0287 at year-end. On February 1, 20X2, the customer paid the balance owing, and Domestic also settled the forward contract. The exchange rate on the settlement date was $0.0280.

**Required**

   **a.** In general journal form, record the entries in 20X1 and 20X2 relating to the account receivable and to the forward contract

   **b.** How would the entries relating to the account receivable differ if Domestic had not hedged the receivable?

3. On October 14, 20X7, Buycorp signed a contract with Sellco, a US company, to purchase inventory for US$200,000. The inventory was to be delivered on January 30, 20X8, with payment to be made (in US dollars) on February 28, 20X8.

    Having signed the contract, Buycorp immediately arranged a forward contract through the company's bank for US$200,000 as a hedge against the commitment. The spot rate for the US dollar was $1.200 on October 14; the February 28 forward rate was $1.220.

    On December 31, 20X7, the spot rate was $1.210 and the forward rate was $1.230. Sellco delivered the inventory to Buycorp on January 30, 20X8. The spot rate on that date was $1.222, and the forward rate was $1.235. Buycorp paid the amount due on February 28, 20X8, per the contract. The spot rate was $1.240 on February 28.

**Required**

   **a.** Assume that the hedge is designated as a cash-flow hedge. Prepare journal entries to record the acquisition of the inventory and the related hedge on Buycorp's books through February 28, 20X8. Assume Buycorp's fiscal year ends on December 31.

**b.** Assume that the hedge is designated as a fair-value hedge. Prepare journal entries to record the acquisition of the inventory and the related hedge on Buycorp's books through February 28, 20X8. Assume Buycorp's fiscal year ends on December 31.

4. On June 30, 20X4, Poplarcorp issued a purchase order to Tannenbaumcorp, a German company, to purchase inventory for €50,000. The inventory was to be delivered and payment was to be made (in euros) on February 28, 20X5.

    Poplarcorp has €50,000 in a French bank, which it designates as a hedge against the commitment. The spot rate for the euro was $1.40 on June 30, 20X4. On December 31, 20X4, the spot rate was $1.38. Tannenbaumcorp delivered the inventory to Poplarcorp and Poplarcorp paid the amount due on February 28, 20X5, per the purchase order. The spot rate was $1.35 on February 28.

Required

**a.** Assume that the hedge is designated as a cash-flow hedge. Prepare journal entries to record the acquisition of the inventory and the related hedge on Poplarcorp's books through February 28, 20X5. Assume Poplarcorp's fiscal year ends on December 31.

**b.** Assume that the hedge is designated as a fair value hedge. Prepare journal entries to record the acquisition of the inventory and the related hedge on Poplarcorp's books through February 28, 20X5. Assume Poplarcorp's fiscal year ends on December 31.

5. On September 30, 20X5, Winter Company of Saskatoon, Canada, hedges the forecasted sale on April 1, 20X6, of £2,000,000 of wheat to Scotties Cereals, a British company. Winter Company has a December 31 fiscal year-end. The following are the relevant exchange rates:

| Date | Event | Spot rate | Forward rate to April 1, 20X6 |
|---|---|---|---|
| September 30, 20X5 | Forecasted sale | 1.6000 | 1.6100 |
| December 31, 20X5 | SFP date | 1.6150 | 1.6220 |
| April 1, 20X6 | Wheat delivered and forward contract settled | 1.6300 | n/a—settlement date |

Assume that this transaction qualifies as a cash-flow hedge under hedge accounting rules.

Required

Prepare journal entries to record the above activities on Winter Company's books in 20X5 and 20X6.

## Review Questions

1. What is a foreign currency transaction?
2. What causes changes in exchange rates?
3. CarpCorp, a Canadian company, bought a machine from the United States for US$100,000 when the exchange rate was C$1.20. The liability for the machine was paid when the exchange rate was C$1.25. At what cost should the machine be recorded in the accounts, assuming (a) the one-transaction theory, and (b) the two-transaction theory?

4. CarpCorp bought inventory from the United Kingdom when the pound was worth C$1.80. When the year-end SFP was prepared, the pound was worth C$1.70. If the account payable for the inventory was unpaid at year-end, and the amount of the purchase was £5,000, how should the liability be reported on the SFP? How should the change in the value of the pound be reported (if at all)?

5. Explain the difference between a *monetary balance* and a *non-monetary balance*.

6. Why would some companies decide to use an average rate for each week or month for translating foreign currency transactions?

7. What is the purpose of *hedging*?

8. What are the three characteristics of a derivative?

9. CarpCorp has a liability of €400,000. If CarpCorp wants to hedge the liability, should the company enter into a forward contract to *buy* euros or to *sell* euros?

10. Does hedging eliminate all gains and losses arising from a foreign currency exposure? Explain.

11. Why is a forward contract viewed as an executory contract?

12. What is hedge accounting?

13. How does hedging an *anticipated transaction* differ from hedging a liability?

14. Explain the term "cash-flow hedge."

15. What is the difference between a hedged item and a hedging instrument?

16. What is a fair-value hedge?

17. What conditions must a hedging relationship meet for hedge accounting to be applied?

18. What is an effective hedge?

19. What are the requirements necessary for a hedge to be deemed effective?

## 8.7 CASES

## CASE 8-1 GRAHAM ENTERPRISES LIMITED

Graham Enterprises Limited (Graham) has just negotiated the purchase of an office build-ing for £20 million in London, United Kingdom, to be used as the head office of its newly incorporated, wholly owned European operating subsidiary, Graham Overseas Limited (GOL). Transfer of ownership to GOL is to be made on January 1, 20X6. Graham has arranged a loan for £20 million to finance the purchase through its bankers. The loan, to be dated January 1, 20X6, is at 12% and is repayable in 20 equal annual installments commencing January 1, 20X7. The loan would be made to GOL, which would make all interest and principal payments in pounds sterling.

The building will be depreciated on a straight-line basis over 20 years. Assume the following exchange rates: January 1, 20X6, £1 = $2.00; December 31, 20X6, £1 = $1.50.

Required

1. Discuss the nature of the relationship between the building and the loan, and evalu-ate the alternatives available to Graham.
2. Discuss fully the options available to Graham in structuring its relationship to GOL, and evaluate the impact of each alternative on the consolidated financial statements. Show all supporting calculations.

[SMA, adapted]

## CASE 8-2 VIDEO DISPLAYS, INC.

Video Displays, Inc. (VDI) is a privately held corporation chartered under the *Canada Business Corporations Act*. The corporation was formed in 20X1 by four engineers who found themselves jobless after their previous employer (Argo Corporation) discontinued the production of television sets in Canada.

One of the sidelines of Argo had been the assembly of video display units (VDUs). A VDU is the basic chassis containing the liquid crystal display (LCD) screen and related components that are used in computers and in video game sets. When Argo discontinued production, the four engineers purchased some of Argo's assembly and testing equipment and formed VDI.

VDI has been fairly successful because it is the only Canadian producer of VDUs. Some computer manufacturers have a policy of obtaining their components in the coun-try in which they manufacture the computers, and thus VDI has enjoyed the benefits of local-sourcing policies since it is the only Canadian producer.

In 20X4, VDI needed additional debt financing. After being refused by several Canadian banks, the executives of VDI went to New York where, on March 1, they quickly obtained a five-year, 12% term loan of $3,000,000 (US) from Citibank, with interest payable annually on the anniversary date of the loan. The US dollar was worth C$1.10 on March 1, 20X4. By the end of 20X4, the exchange rate had slipped to $1.06.

In 20X5, VDI extended its operations into the United States by contracting with an electronic component distributor in Cambridge, Massachusetts. The US distributor supplies component assemblies to small manufacturers, and saw an opportunity to sell VDI's VDUs to independent manufacturers of computers. The December 31, 20X5, VDI unadjusted trial balance showed a balance due from the US distributor of $449,000. The 20X5 shipments to and payments from the distributor are shown in Exhibit A. VDI gave the distributor US$60,000 on April 4 as an accountable advance for financing promotional expenses. By December 31, 20X5, the distributor had spent and accounted for $40,000 of this advance. At the end of 20X5, the exchange rate was C$1.15 to US$1.00.

## Required

Explain the impact of the transactions described above on VDI's financial statements on December 31, 20X5.

### Exhibit A
### CURRENT ACCOUNT WITH US DISTRIBUTOR 20X5*

|  |  | Dr | Cr | Balance |
| --- | --- | --- | --- | --- |
| Feb. 1: Shipment | (US$100,000) |  | $105,000 | $105,000 |
| April 1: Shipment | (US$180,000) |  | 189,000 | 294,000 |
| May 1: Payment | (US$100,000) | 108,000 |  | 186,000 |
| July 1: Shipment | (US$200,000) |  | 204,000 | 390,000 |
| Aug. 30: Payment | (US$150,000) | 171,000 |  | 219,000 |
| Nov. 15: Shipment | (US$200,000) |  | 230,000 | 449,000 |
| * In Canadian dollars. |  |  |  |  |

[CGA–Canada, adapted]

## CASE 8-3 CANADA COLA INC.

Canada Cola Inc. (CCI) is a public company engaged in the manufacture and distribution of soft drinks across Canada. Its primary product is CanaCola ("Fresh as a Canadian stream"), which is a top seller in Canada and generates large export sales.

You, CA, met with Jim MacNamara, the partner in charge of the CCI engagement, to commence planning for the upcoming audit of CCI.

During this meeting, the partner informed you that early this year CCI entered into an agreement with the government of Russia and has commenced the manufacture and sale of CanaCola in Russia. A short summary of the agreement is contained in Exhibit B. The partner would like you to prepare a detailed report that discusses the accounting and auditing implications of this new division of CCI for this engagement.

*Case Continued >*

*Case Continued >*

## Exhibit B
## SUMMARY OF AGREEMENT

1. The Russian government will provide the land and the building for the plant. It will make no further investment.

2. CCI will install bottling machinery costing $5 million in the Russian plant. Once installed, the machinery may not be removed from Russia.

3. CCI will be required to provide the funds for the initial working capital. CCI will sell US dollars to the Russian government in exchange for local currency (rubles).

4. CCI will be wholly responsible for the management and daily operations of the plant. Canadian managers will be transferred to Russia.

5. CCI will be permitted to export its cola syrup to Russia at CCI's Canadian cost.

6. CCI and the Russian government will share equally in the profits from the sale of CanaCola in Russia.

7. Although foreign currency can be converted into rubles, rubles cannot be converted back into any foreign currency. Therefore, the Russian government will sell vodka to CCI (at the prevailing export price in Russia) in exchange for the rubles CCI earns in profits. CCI will be permitted to export this vodka to Canada, where it may be sold in the Canadian domestic market only.

Required

Prepare the report for the partner.

[CICA]

## CASE 8-4 SPRINGFORTH INC.

It is December 1, 20X4, and you are a public accountant with a large national firm. One of your clients, Jamie Smith, the president of SpringForth, has called seeking your advice on several issues that have arisen recently.

SpringForth Inc. is a rapidly growing company in the social media space that has recently established numerous subsidiaries around the world. It is based in Toronto and was listed on the TSX exchange in early 20X4. In its most recent quarter, profits dropped significantly due to adverse changes in foreign exchange rates. Jamie notes that in the past the company has not hedged any transactions, in part because they had not been significant and movements had been favourable and in part because of the complexity and perceived cost. She is particularly concerned because of several recent transactions that have occurred and has approached you for advice on how to proceed. She would like you to provide an overview of the options available to her and the implications of each. In particular, she would like your recommendations on the following two issues that have arisen and are likely to be typical in the foreseeable future.

1.  SpringForth's growth has been primarily organic, but yesterday, after several months of negotiations, SpringForth agreed to acquire a competitor, SummerBreeze, a large privately held company based in London, United Kingdom. The acquisition closes on February 1, 20X5. The purchase price agreed to was £225 million.

2.  SpringForth's subsidiaries are growing rapidly, and its foreign currency transactions/balances are increasing. For example, Jamie recently met with the management team of SpringUp, an Italian subsidiary, and noted that it now has significant exposure to the US dollar at $5 million in receivables. Another subsidiary, EverSpring, located in Australia, has $2 million in payables and $1 million in purchase orders that are denominated in US dollars.

Given SpringForth's rapid growth, Jamie sees a future with even greater exposure to foreign currency fluctuations for her company. Further, given its leadership position in the social media space, she believes that its is also likely to be a consolidator in the industry.

Required

Prepare the report for Jamie Smith.

# Problems

## P8-1 (10 minutes, easy)

NWT Ltd. is an outfitter based in Yellowknife that caters mainly to American clients. On January 1, 20X1, NWT Ltd. borrows US$300,000 from Norsebank of St. Paul, Minnesota. The annual interest rate is 5%, the term of the loan is four years, and interest is payable annually on December 31. Principal is to be repaid on December 31, 20X4. The relevant foreign exchange rates for 20X1 and 20X2 are:

| | |
|---|---|
| January 1, 20X1 | C$1.10 = US$1.00 |
| December 31, 20X1 | C$1.13 = US$1.00 |
| December 31, 20X2 | C$1.07 = US$1.00 |

### Required

Calculate the exchange gain/loss on the loan principal for 20X1 and 20X2 that will appear on the financial statements of NWT Ltd.

## P8-2 (15 minutes, easy)

Weyburn Corp., a Canadian company, sells its products to customers in the United Kingdom at prices quoted in pounds sterling. On November 14, 20X1, Weyburn sold and shipped goods that had cost $65,000 to produce to a UK company for £100,000. On December 20, Weyburn received an international draft for part of the amount due, £40,000. At year-end (December 31), the remaining £60,000 was unpaid.

On February 12, 20X2, Weyburn received payment of the remaining £60,000.

### Required

In general journal form, prepare journal entries to record the above events and any adjustments necessary at year-end. Exchange rates (Canadian dollar equivalent to £1) are as follows:

| | |
|---|---|
| November 14 | $1.51 |
| December 20 | $1.56 |
| December 31 | $1.58 |
| February 12 | $1.55 |

## P8-3 (15 minutes, easy)

At the end of the fiscal year, December 31, 20X2, Avonlea Ltd. finds itself with two accounts receivable in pesos:

1. from a sale on July 1, 20X2, and due to be collected on December 1, 20X3, for 1,000,000 pesos; and

2. From a sale on September 1, 20X2, and due to be collected on February 1, 20X4, for 2,000,000 pesos.

Exchange rates (spot):

| | |
|---|---|
| July 1, 20X2 | $1 = 16 pesos |
| September 1, 20X2 | $1 = 17 pesos |
| December 31, 20X2 | $1 = 18 pesos |
| December 1, 20X3 | $1 = 11 pesos |
| December 31, 20X3 | $1 = 9 pesos |

**Required**

Prepare the journal entries for December 31, 20X2, and December 31, 20X3, assuming that the foreign exchange risk is *not* hedged.

    [CGA–Canada, adapted]

**P8-4 (20 minutes, easy)**

Polar Limited is a Canadian company that recently completed two large transactions with companies based in Germany.

**1.** On July 1, 20X4, Polar acquired equipment at a cost of €500,000 from Bier Ltd. Polar received reasonable terms regarding this purchase acquisition. The €500,000 was in the form of a note payable on June 30, 20X7, at an interest rate of 6% per year, the interest to be paid semi-annually on December 31 and June 30.

**2.** On October 1, 20X4, Polar also sold inventory that cost C$100,000 to another German company, Wein Ltd., for €87,500. Payment is due from Wein on March 1, 20X5. Polar uses a perpetual inventory system. The spot rates for the euro were as follows:

| | |
|---|---|
| July 1, 20X4 | C$1.00 = €0.650 |
| October 1, 20X4 | C$1.00 = €0.750 |
| December 31, 20X4 | C$1.00 = €0.800 |
| Average rate July 1–December 31, 20X4 | C$1.00 = €0.770 |
| Average rate 20X4 | C$1.00 = €0.700 |
| March 1, 20X5 | C$1.00 = €0.850 |

**Required**

**a.** Prepare all journal entries regarding Polar's notes payable and interest-related transactions on July 1, 20X4, and December 31, 20X4.

**b.** Prepare all journal entries regarding Polar's sales, cost of sales, and accounts receivable transactions on October 1, 20X4, December 31, 20X4, and March 1, 20X5.

    [CGA–Canada, adapted]

**P8-5 (15 minutes, easy)**

FX Corporation provides special effects for movies filmed in Manitoba. The company needs a sophisticated piece of equipment that can only be sourced from the United States. FX submitted a purchase order for US$50,000 for the equipment on July 1, 20X8, and received the equipment on October 31, 20X8. The company paid US$30,000 to the supplier on December 1, 20X8. The company will amortize the equipment starting in the month of acquisition. The equipment has an expected useful life of five years, and the company uses the straight-line method for amortization. FX Corporation has a December 31 year-end.

    The relevant exchange rates are:

| | |
|---|---|
| July 1, 20X8 | C$1.00 = US$0.9500 |
| October 31, 20X8 | C$1.00 = US$0.9600 |
| December 1, 20X8 | C$1.00 = US$0.9900 |
| December 31, 20X8 | C$1.00 = US$1.0000 |

**Required**

**a.**  Prepare all relevant journal entries for 20X8 relating to the above activities.

**b.**  Calculate the carrying value of FX's equipment and accounts payable on its December 31, 20X8, SFP.

### P8-6 (25 minutes, medium)

Refer to P8-5 and assume that the remaining payment of US$20,000 is due on January 1, 20X9. FX enters into a forward contract with a bank on December 1, 20X8, to buy US$20,000 for delivery on January 1, 20X9. The relevant forward rate on December 1, 20X8, was C$1 = US$0.9950. Assume that the forward rate and spot rate on December 31, 20X8, and the spot rate on January 1, 20X9, were the same (i.e., US$1.0000).

**Required**

**a.**  Should FX Corporation use hedge accounting in this situation? Why or why not?

**b.**  Prepare all relevant journal entries related to the purchase of the equipment and the hedge for 20X8 and 20X9.

### P8-7 (30 minutes, medium)

On November 7, 20X5, Labrador Limited signed a contract to buy equipment from a US manufacturer. The equipment was to be delivered on January 15 and paid for on February 15, 20X6. The price of the equipment was US$500,000. On the same date that Labrador signed the contract, it made a 20% deposit as part of the terms of the contract. It also immediately entered into a forward contract with the bank to buy US$400,000 on February 15, 20X6.

Labrador designated the forward contract as a hedge of the outstanding purchase commitment on the equipment. The equipment is delivered on January 15, 20X6. The exchange rates are:

|  | Spot | Forward |
|---|---|---|
| September 7, 20X5 | C$1.00 = US$0.92 | C$1.00 = US$0.91 |
| December 31, 20X5 | C$1.00 = US$0.90 | C$1.00 = US$0.893 |
| January 15, 20X6 | C$1.00 = US$0.88 | C$1.00 = US$0.875 |
| February 15, 20X6 | C$1.00 = US$0.85 | n/a |

Labrador paid the manufacturer and closed out the forward contract on February 15, 20X6.

**Required**

**a.**  Assume the hedge was designated as a fair-value hedge. Record the journal entries to record the purchase and the related hedge for 20X5 and 20X6. Labrador's fiscal year ends on December 31. Ignore amortization of the equipment.

**b.**  Assume the hedge was designated as a cash-flow hedge. Record the journal entries to record the purchase and the related hedge for 20X5 and 20X6. Labrador's fiscal year ends on December 31. Ignore amortization of the equipment.

## P8-8 (20 minutes, medium)

Diamond Limited began purchasing parts from China. The Chinese currency is the renminbi (RMB). Diamond entered into the following transactions in 20X1 and 20X2:

| | |
|---|---|
| November 1, 20X1 | Ordered machine parts from the Chinese supplier for RMB2,000,000. The supplier promised to deliver the machine parts at the beginning of December, and payment is expected on January 15, 20X2. |
| December 1, 20X1 | Received shipment of the machine parts. |
| December 31, 20X1 | Acquired a forward contract to receive RMB2,000,000 on January 15, 20X2, as a hedge of the account payable to the Chinese supplier. The forward contract rate was RMB1 = C$0.16. Diamond treats all forward contracts as executory contracts. |
| January 15, 20X2 | Received RMB2,000,000 on the forward contract; paid RMB2,000,000 to the Chinese supplier in settlement of the payable. |

Spot rates were as follows:

| | |
|---|---|
| November 1, 20X1 | RMB1 = C$0.15 |
| December 1, 20X1 | RMB1 = C$0.18 |
| December 31, 20X1 | RMB1 = C$0.17 |
| January 15, 20X2 | RMB1 = C$0.19 |

### Required

Prepare the journal entries for these transactions, including any adjusting entries needed at the December 31, 20X1, fiscal year-end. Specify if no entry is required on any specific date(s).
[CGA–Canada, adapted]

## P8-9 (20 minutes, medium)

At the beginning of 20X2, Skeena Industries Ltd. obtained a four-year loan of US$400,000 from a bank in New York City. At the time of the loan, the US dollar was worth C$1.10. At the end of 20X2, the exchange rate had changed to US$1.00 = C$1.14. By the end of 20X3, the US dollar was worth C$1.20.

During 20X3, Skeena Industries Ltd. sold goods to a French customer for €800,000. At the time of the sale, the euro was worth C$1.50. The customer paid one-fourth of the amount due later in the year, when the euro was worth C$1.41. By the end of 20X3, the euro had declined in value to C$1.35.

### Required

Determine the impact of the transactions described above on Skeena Industries's financial statements for the year ended December 31, 20X3.

## P8-10 (20 minutes, easy)

Salluit Limited purchased a capital asset from a French company for €200,000. The asset was delivered to Salluit Limited on November 1, 20X7. Salluit Limited agreed to pay the supplier in full on February 1, 20X8. The payment was made as agreed. The exchange rates were as follows:

| | |
|---|---|
| November 1, 20X7 | C$1.00 = €0.70 |
| December 31, 20X7 | C$1.00 = €0.60 |
| February 1, 20X8 | C$1.00 = €0.62 |

## Required

**a.** Prepare journal entries for 20X7 and 20X8 to record the above information.

**b.** Assume that Salluit Limited hedged the obligation on November 1, 20X7. The forward rate was C$1.00 = €0.64 on November 1, 20X7, and C$1.00 = €0.63 on December 31, 20X7. Prepare the appropriate journal entries for 20X7 and 20X8.
[CGA–Canada, adapted]

### P8-11 (20 minutes, easy)

On May 5, 20X5, Sugluk Corp. purchased inventory from a Japanese supplier and gave the supplier a 90-day note for ¥40,000,000. On the same date, Sugluk entered a forward contract with its bank to receive ¥40,000,000 in 90 days. The spot rate for the yen was $0.0095. The forward rate was $0.0100.

### Required

Prepare general journal entries to record the purchase, the hedge, and final settlement of both the note and the hedge, assuming each of the following spot rates at the settlement date:

**a.** $0.0095

**b.** $0.0100

**c.** $0.0093

**d.** $0.0102
[CGA–Canada, adapted]

### P8-12 (25 minutes, medium)

On October 15, 20X1, Nahanni Limited sold merchandise to two companies in Sweden. In the first transaction, the price was 3,000,000 kronor and was to be paid in 90 days. Worried about the exposure to the exchange risk, the company hedged the receivable for a 90-day period with a forward contract.

In the second transaction, the price was 3,600,000 kronor and the date of payment was November 15, 20X4. Due to the difficulty of getting a forward contract to match the date payment was due, the company decided to remain in an "unhedged" position on this receivable.

Exchange rates:

| | |
|---|---|
| October 15, 20X1, spot rate | $1 = 8.00 kronor |
| October 15, 20X1, forward 90-day rate | $1 = 9.26 kronor |
| December 31, 20X1, spot rate | $1 = 9.10 kronor |
| December 31, 20X1, forward rate to January 13, 20X2 | $1 = 9.30 kronor |
| January 13, 20X2, spot rate | $1 = 9.45 kronor |
| December 31, 20X2, spot rate | $1 = 7.75 kronor |

### Required

Ignoring closing entries,

**a.** Prepare all the related journal entries required for the first sale in each of 20X1 *and* 20X2.

**b.** Assuming instead that the company had not hedged the receivable from the first sale in any way, prepare the appropriate journal entries for 20X1 *and* 20X2 to record this situation.

**c.** Prepare all the related journal entries for the *second* sale in each of 20X1 *and* 20X2.
[CGA–Canada, adapted]

## P8-13 (25 minutes, medium)

Pinware Wholesalers Inc. (Pinware) imports high quality goods from select European countries. On May 1, 20X3, Pinware purchased Swiss watches from a supplier in Switzerland for 400,000 Swiss francs (CHF). Payment of the invoice was due on August 31, 20X3. On May 1, 20X3, Pinware also entered into a forward contract that was a perfect hedge of the full amount of the invoice price at a rate of CHF1 = C$0.945. Pinware's year-end is June 30, and on June 30, the August 31, 20X3, forward rate is CHF1 = C$0.925. On August 31, 20X3, the forward contract was settled and the Swiss supplier was paid. The relevant spot rates were as follows:

| | |
|---|---|
| May 1, 20X3 | CHF1 = C$0.930 |
| June 30, 20X3 | CHF1 = C$0.920 |
| August 31, 20X3 | CHF1 = C$0.915 |

### Required

Prepare all relevant journal entries to record the transactions related to the purchase of the watches. Be sure to include any year-end adjustments required on June 30, 20X3.
[CGA–Canada, adapted]

## P8-14 (40 minutes, hard)

Assume that Pinware Wholesalers Inc. (Pinware) must order the watches three months in advance of expected delivery. On May 1, 20X3, Pinware ordered Swiss watches from a supplier in Switzerland for 400,000 Swiss francs (CHF) when the spot rate was CHF1 = C$0.930. Delivery is to be made on July 30, and payment is to be made on August 31, 20X3. On May 1, 20X3, Pinware also entered into a forward contract with a bank to hedge the commitment by agreeing to purchase CHF400,000 on August 31, 20X3, at a rate of CHF1 = C$0.935. Pinware takes delivery of the watches on July 30, 20X3, and pays the invoice on August 31, 20X3. The relevant exchange rates are as follows.

| Date | Spot Rate | Forward Rate |
|---|---|---|
| May 1, 20X3 | 0.930 | 0.935 |
| June 30, 20X3 | 0.938 | 0.942 |
| July 30, 20X3 | 0.945 | 0.948 |
| August 31, 20X3 | 0.950 | n/a |

### Required

a.  Prepare journal entries to record all of the transactions, including any adjustments required on June 30, 20X3, assuming that Pinware does not use hedge accounting.

b.  Prepare journal entries to record all of the transactions, including any adjustments required on June 30, 20X3, assuming that Pinware designates the hedge a fair-value hedge.

c.  Prepare journal entries to record all of the transactions, including any adjustments required on June 30, 20X3, assuming that Pinware designates the hedge a cash-flow hedge.

P8-15 (30 minutes, medium)

Following are transactions of L'Anse Ltd., a company engaged in importing products into Canada.

| September 1, 20X3: | Incurred a liability for 1,000,000 pesos, due February 1, 20X4, for purchasing inventory. |
|---|---|
| October 1, 20X3: | Incurred a liability for 6,000,000 yen, due November 1, 20X4, for purchasing inventory. |
| November 1, 20X3: | Incurred a liability for 22,000 Brazilian reals, due March 1, 20X5, for purchasing inventory. |

Exchange rates:

| | |
|---|---|
| September 1, 20X3 | |
| $1 = 15 pesos | Spot rate |
| $1 = 12 pesos | Forward contract rate |
| October 1, 20X3 | |
| $1 = 80 yen | Spot rate |
| $1 = 95 yen | Forward contract rate |
| November 1, 20X3 | |
| $1 = 1.80 reals | Spot rate |
| $1 = 1.60 reals | Forward contract rate |
| December 31, 20X3, spot rates: | |
| $1 = 10 pesos | |
| $1 = 100 yen | |
| $1 = 1.50 reals | |
| Relevant December 31, 20X3, forward rates: | |
| $1 = 9 pesos | |
| $1 = 105 yen | |
| $1 = 1.45 reals | |

Required

Parts (a) and (b), below, are based on different policies regarding hedging. Answer each part as an independent problem.

a. L'Anse Ltd. did not hedge or cover its exchange risk position. Prepare the journal entries for 20X3. The company has a December 31 year-end.

b. At the time of each transaction, L'Anse Ltd. entered into a forward contract, which was a perfect and complete hedge against the foreign exchange risk. Prepare the journal entries for 20X3. The company has a December 31 year-end.
   [CGA–Canada, adapted]

P8-16 (30 minutes, medium)

Muskoka Furniture Inc. (Muskoka) imports pine furniture from factories around the world for sale to retailers in Canada. On November 1, 20X4, Muskoka bought a bedroom furniture set from a supplier in the United States for US$2,000. The invoice called for payment to be made on February 28, 20X5. On November 1, 20X4, Muskoka entered into a forward contract with a bank to hedge the existing monetary position by agreeing to buy US$2,000 on February 28, 20X5, at a rate of US$1 = C$1.150. Muskoka's year-end is December 31. On February 28, 20X5, Muskoka settled the forward contract with the bank and the US supplier was paid.

Spot rates were as follows:

| | |
|---|---|
| November 1, 20X4 | US$1 = C$1.140 |
| December 31, 20X4 | US$1 = C$1.160 |
| February 28, 20X5 | US$1 = C$1.190 |

The February 28, 20X5, forward rate on December 31, 20X4, was US$1 = C$1.165.

Required

Prepare journal entries to record all of the transactions, including any adjustments required on December 31, 20X4. Show your supporting calculations.

[CGA–Canada, adapted]

P8-17 (40 minutes, hard)

Muskoka Furniture Inc. (Muskoka) can also import custom pine furniture, but it must be ordered several months in advance as it is only manufactured after a specific request is made. Assume that on November 1, 20X4, Muskoka orders custom bedroom furniture from a supplier in the United States for US$2,000. The invoice calls for delivery and payment to be made on February 28, 20X5. On November 1, 20X4, Muskoka entered into a forward contract with a bank to hedge the commitment by agreeing to buy US$2,000 on February 28, 20X5, at a rate of US$1 = C$1.150. Muskoka's year-end is December 31. On February 28, 20X5, Muskoka received the furniture, settled the forward contract with the bank, and paid the US supplier.

Spot rates were as follows:

| | |
|---|---|
| November 1, 20X4 | US$1 = C$1.140 |
| December 31, 20X4 | US$1 = C$1.160 |
| February 28, 20X5 | US$1 = C$1.190 |

The February 28, 20X5, forward rate on December 31, 20X4, was US$1 = C$1.165.

Required

a. Prepare journal entries to record all of the transactions for 20X4 and 20X5, including any adjustments required on December 31, 20X4, assuming that Muskoka does not use hedge accounting. Show your supporting calculations.

b. Assume that Muskoka Furniture Inc. designates the hedge as a fair-value hedge of a commitment, documents the relationship, and assesses the hedge as effective. Prepare journal entries to record all of the transactions for 20X4 and 20X5, including any adjustments required on December 31, 20X4, assuming that Muskoka can use hedge accounting.

c. Assume that Muskoka Furniture Inc. designates the hedge as a cash-flow hedge of a commitment, documents the relationship, and assesses the hedge as effective. Prepare journal entries to record all of the transactions for 20X4 and 20X5, including any adjustments required on December 31, 20X4.

**P8-18 (30 minutes, medium)**

Terrace Ltd., a manufacturer of motorcycles located in Burnaby, British Columbia, successfully negotiated a contract to sell 100 small motorcycles to the police department of Fairbanks, Alaska. The contract price for the cycles was US$10,000 each. The contract was signed on May 12, 20X6, with payment to be made by October 1. Terrace then entered into a forward contract to hedge against changes in the US dollar exchange rate.

Delivery of the motorcycles began on July 5 and continued in 20-cycle lots at two-week intervals until the last delivery, on August 30, 20X6. The buyer then paid the US$1,000,000 contract price when due, and Terrace settled with the bank.

The exchange rates were as follows:

| Canadian equivalent of US$1.00: | Spot rate | Forward rate |
|---|---|---|
| May 12, 20X6 | $1.15 | $1.18 |
| May 31–August 30, 20X6 | 1.10 | 1.08 |
| October 1, 20X6 | 1.12 | n/a |

**Required**

**a.** What amounts relating to the sale and the hedge would appear on Terrace's SCI and SFP for the year ended December 31, 20X6?

**b.** Assume instead that Terrace's year-end was May 31. What amounts would appear on Terrace's financial statements at May 31, 20X6?

**c.** Assume that Terrace's year-end was May 31 and Terrace designated the hedge as a cash-flow hedge. What amounts would appear on Terrace's financial statements at May 31, 20X6?

**P8-19 (30 minutes, medium)**

Espanola Corporation, a Canadian corporation, engaged in the following transactions in late 20X7 and early 20X8:

| | |
|---|---|
| December 2 | Purchased sheet aluminum from a US subsidiary of a Canadian aluminum company for US$160,000, payable in 60 days. |
| December 2 | Acquired a forward contract to receive US$160,000 in 60 days, as a hedge of the account payable. The forward contract rate was C$1.10. |
| December 20 | Sold large cans to a Buffalo canner for US$200,000, due in 60 days. |
| January 31 | Received US$160,000 on the forward contract; paid US$160,000 to the aluminum company. |
| February 18 | Received US$200,000 from the Buffalo canner. |

Spot rates for the US dollar were as follows:

| | |
|---|---|
| December 2 | $1.07 |
| December 20 | $1.12 |
| December 31 | $1.14 |
| January 31 | $1.20 |
| February 18 | $1.17 |

The January 31, 20X8, forward rate on December 31, 20X7, was $1.15.

## Required

Prepare journal entries for these transactions, including any adjusting entries needed at the December 31, 20X7, year-end.

### P8-20 (30 minutes, medium)

On November 1, 20X3, Blue Mussels Company issued a purchase order to Rainy Company, a Spanish company, to purchase equipment for €100,000. The equipment was to be delivered and payment was to be made (in euros) on February 1, 20X4.

Blue Mussels Company has a €100,000 receivable due on February 1, 20X4, from Bonbon Company, a French company, which it designates as a hedge against the commitment. The spot rate for the euro was $1.42 on November 1, 20X3. On December 31, 20X3, the spot rate was $1.40. Rainy Company delivered the equipment to Blue Mussels Company and Blue Mussels Company collected the receivable and paid the amount due on February 1, 20X4, per the purchase order. The spot rate was $1.37 on February 1.

### Required

a. Assume that the hedge is designated as a cash-flow hedge. Prepare journal entries to record the acquisition of the equipment and the related hedge on Blue Mussels Company's books through February 1, 20X4. Assume Blue Mussels Company's fiscal year ends on December 31.

b. Assume that the hedge is designated as a fair-value hedge. Prepare journal entries to record the acquisition of the equipment and the related hedge on Blue Mussels Company's books through February 1, 20X4. Assume Blue Mussels Company's fiscal year ends on December 31.

### P8-21 (20 minutes, medium)

On November 30, 20X5, P&P Company of Nova Scotia, Canada, hedges the forecasted sale on February 1, 20X6 of €1,000,000 of blueberries to Compagnie Souris, a company head-quartered in France. P&P Company has a December 31 fiscal year-end. The following are the relevant exchange rates:

| Date | Event | Spot rate | Forward rate to February 1, 20X6 |
|------|-------|-----------|----------------------------------|
| November 30, 20X5 | Forecasted sale | 1€=$1.4500 | 1.4600 |
| December 31, 20X5 | SFP date | 1€=$1.5150 | 1.5210 |
| February 1, 20X6 | Blueberries delivered and forward contract settled | 1€=$1.5300 | n/a—settlement date |

Assume that this transaction qualifies as a cash-flow hedge under hedge accounting rules.

### Required

Prepare journal entries to record the above activities on P&P Company's books in 20X5 and 20X6.

# Chapter 9
## Reporting Foreign Operations

## Learning Objectives

**After studying this chapter, you should be able to:**

**LO ❶** describe the conceptual alternatives to translate the financial statements of foreign operations;

**LO ❷** distinguish between accounting exposure and economic exposure to exchange rate changes;

**LO ❸** explain the conceptual alternatives for reporting translation gains and losses;

**LO ❹** determine a company's functional currency after considering the relevant factors identified by IFRS; and

**LO ❺** translate a company's financial statements and properly handle any translation gain or loss in preparation for consolidation.

## INTRODUCTION

Montreal-based CGI Group Inc. (CGI) is a large Canadian provider of information technology (IT) services such as outsourcing, business process services, and systems integration and consulting to companies around the world. CGI operates in 16 countries, including the United States, India, Poland, and Australia, either directly or through its subsidiaries. In fiscal year 2011, the company had revenues of $4.3 billion, 53% of which was generated from outside Canada. The company's strategy is to grow both organically and through acquisitions. Currently, it sees future growth coming from international markets such as the United States and Europe.

The company conducts its international business through operating entities in foreign countries. These entities are likely to be companies that were either created or purchased by CGI. Subsidiaries operating abroad keep their books in the local currency of the country in which they are operating. The problem is that these foreign-currency subsidiary financial statements need to be translated into Canadian dollars to enable CGI to consolidate them. This issue of how to do this is known as accounting for foreign operations.

The previous chapter illustrated how a Canadian company accounts for its foreign-currency transactions. A somewhat different problem arises when a Canadian corporation actually has one or more active, self-contained operations located in a foreign country.

In that case, the company is not merely selling its products in US dollars or buying inventory in Japanese yen; instead the company has a foreign operation that will likely have to prepare financial statements in the operation's host-country currency.

This chapter examines the problems of accounting for foreign *operations* rather than foreign *transactions*. We begin with a brief discussion of the possible forms of organization for a foreign operation. Then, we discuss:

- the reasons for preparing separate financial statements for foreign operations and why that presents a problem for the parent corporation;

- the two methods that can be used for translating foreign operations—(1) the temporal method and (2) the current-rate method—and their relationship to foreign-currency transaction accounting;

- the competing concepts of foreign exchange risk exposure—(1) accounting exposure and (2) economic exposure;

- the alternative treatments of gains and losses that arise from translating a foreign operation;

- the determination of a foreign operation's functional currency as a necessary condition for deciding which method to use; and

- a final summary comparison of the two translation methods.

Of course, we will provide illustrations as we proceed through the discussion.

## 9.1 FORMS OF ORGANIZATION FOR FOREIGN OPERATIONS

LO ❶
Describe the conceptual alternatives to translate the financial statements of foreign operations

Theoretically, a Canadian parent company could organize its foreign operations in any way that it wants. Possible options are:

- branch office of the parent;

- unincorporated partnership involving officers or directors of the parent corporation;

- unincorporated partnership with an unrelated partner;

- incorporated joint venture with one or more unrelated corporate co-venturers;

- incorporated subsidiary, with minority shareholdings by unrelated shareholders; or

- wholly owned incorporated subsidiary.

The most common approach is the last one—to incorporate its foreign operations as a wholly owned subsidiary. A foreign operation is subject to the laws of its host country, including its tax laws. An incorporated subsidiary is best able to comply with host-country regulations and tax law. In addition, if the foreign operation gets into financial difficulty, an incorporated subsidiary can be kept separate from the parent and can be sold or liquidated without endangering the health of the parent. Unincorporated branches, partnerships, and joint ventures, on the other hand, may leave the parent company much more vulnerable to adverse situations in the host country.

Some foreign subsidiaries are *not* wholly owned by the parent. This may be either by choice or by law. A local shareholder can provide local knowledge, political contacts, access to capital, or intellectual capital. It is foolish for a parent company to venture

# Unincorporated Joint Venture

Modelo Molson Imports, L.P., is a partnership formed on January 1, 2008, between Grupo Modelo S.A.B. de C.V. (the producer of well-known Mexican brands of beer such as Corona) and Molson "to import, distribute, and market the Modelo beer brand portfolio across all Canadian provinces and territories." Each company owns 50% of the partnership, which makes it an unincorporated joint venture. In the news release the following was noted:

The joint venture board will consist of 6 directors, half from Grupo Modelo and half from Molson. [. . .] The 50/50 joint venture will be headquartered in Toronto and led by Robert Armstrong, previously CEO for Modelo's office in Canada.

Source: Molson Coors, "Grupo Modelo and Molson Create a Joint Venture for Beer Importation Into Canada," press release, January 2, 2008, http://www.molsoncoors.com/newsroom/press-releases/article/155.

into a market that it does not understand, and a local "partner" can be very valuable. In some host countries, foreign companies are *required* to have local participation. These mandatory legal arrangements are often called "joint ventures," but be careful here—the arrangement often is not a joint venture in an accounting sense.

Generally speaking, unincorporated foreign operations are not practical. An exception that occasionally arises is an unincorporated joint venture between two corporations—one foreign and one Canadian. These are often either marketing or production arrangements. The two companies pool their resources to operate in either or both countries.

The accounting for foreign operations is not affected by the form of organization. The accounting standards that we discuss in the remainder of this chapter are applicable to all forms of organization.

## 9.2 THE TRANSLATION PROBLEM

To illustrate the nature of the problem, assume that Domestic Corporation decides to establish a sales subsidiary in the country of Pantania. Domestic's legal representatives in Pantania draw up the papers for a corporation in that country, to be named Forsub Ltd. Domestic Corporation nominates the founding board of directors of Forsub and Forsub begins operations. Forsub issues 100 common shares to Domestic Corporation for 500 pants per share, the pant being the local currency of Pantania. Forsub will record the investment *in Pantanian pants* (P) as follows:

| Cash | P50,000 | |
|------|---------|---------|
| Common shares | | P50,000 |

If the pant is worth C$2 at the time of the transaction, P50,000 will be worth C$100,000. Domestic will record the investment on its books at cost, as it would any initial investment:

| Investment in Forsub Ltd. | $100,000 | |
|------|---------|---------|
| Cash | | $100,000 |

Now, suppose that after receiving the cash, Forsub buys inventory for P20,000 (P5,000 on account) and land for P40,000. To finance this purchase, Forsub issues five-year bonds amounting to P25,000. The transactions will be recorded as follows on Forsub's books:

| | | |
|---|---|---|
| Cash | P25,000 | |
| Bonds payable | | P25,000 |
| Inventory | P20,000 | |
| Cash | | P15,000 |
| Accounts payable | | P 5,000 |
| Land | P40,000 | |
| Cash | | P40,000 |

At the time of these transactions, the exchange rate is still P1 = C$2. Forsub's SFP will then appear as follows:

| | | | |
|---|---|---|---|
| Cash | P20,000 | Accounts payable | P 5,000 |
| Inventory | 20,000 | Bonds payable | 25,000 |
| Land | 40,000 | Common shares | 50,000 |
| Total assets | P80,000 | Total liabilities and share-holders' equity | P80,000 |

A short while later, Domestic Corporation's fiscal year ends. Since Forsub is a subsidiary of Domestic, Domestic will consolidate Forsub. As with any subsidiary that is consolidated, the investment account is eliminated and Forsub's assets and liabilities are added to those of the parent company in Domestic's SFP.

However, Forsub's assets and liabilities are expressed in pants, not dollars. We can't add pants to dollars, and therefore we must translate all of Forsub's financial statement elements from pants to Canadian dollars.

In the previous chapter, we translated individual foreign-currency *transactions*. When we are trying to consolidate a foreign *operation*, however, we need to translate the whole set of foreign-currency financial statements before we can consolidate. The problem is how to translate the financial statements. IFRS adopts a *functional currency* approach to solve the translation problem.

In the **functional currency approach**, each entity in a reporting group must ascertain its own functional currency and use that currency to measure the results of its operations and its financial position. In effect, the functional currency is the measurement currency of an economic entity. In most cases, the functional currency is the currency of the host country. In some situations, however, a majority of the subsidiary's transactions may be in a different currency (e.g., US dollars), in which case that dominant transaction currency becomes the subsidiary's functional currency.

If an economic entity reports in a currency that is not its functional currency, the entity must re-measure its transactions using the functional currency. If an economic entity reports in its functional currency and it is not the same as the reporting entity, then the entity must translate its statements to the currency of the reporting entity. However, before we learn more about the functional currency approach, we need to understand several other concepts:

1. the two methods of translation used under the functional currency approach:
   a. temporal method; and
   b. current-rate (or closing rate) method;
2. the difference between *accounting exposure* and *economic exposure* to currency fluctuations; and
3. the alternatives available for reporting the gains and losses arising from foreign exchange translations.

After discussing these concepts, we will explain how to determine the functional currency of a subsidiary and how to use that information to translate the financial statements.

One observation before we begin: The terms "temporal method" and "current-rate method" don't actually appear in the standards, neither in IFRS nor in ASPE. However, over many decades of use, they have become the widely accepted "shorthand" describers of the two basic techniques for translating foreign-currency financial statements. Theoretically, there are a couple of other methods that could be used, but these are no longer seriously discussed. Now we shall plunge ahead into the sometimes bewildering world of foreign-currency financial statement translation.

## Temporal Method

*Temporal* means "related to time." The temporal method uses multiple rates for translating a foreign operation's financial statement elements:

- *Monetary* assets and liabilities are translated at the year-end spot rate or closing rate; *non-monetary* assets or liabilities *reported at fair value* are translated at the rate at the date on which the fair value is determined (usually the SFP closing rate on the SFP date).

- *Non-monetary* assets and liabilities reported at historical cost are translated at the exchange rate that existed when the element was first recognized.

On the SFP, the year-end spot rate (i.e., the closing rate) is used to translate cash, accounts receivable, accounts payable, long-term debt, and all other monetary items. The closing rate on the date fair value is determined is used for non-monetary assets or liabilities that are reported on the SFP at fair value. For example, some inventories (such as precious metals) and some held-for-sale assets may be reported on the subsidiary's SFP at fair value rather than at historical cost. These balances are reported at the closing rate because their carrying value represents an amount that can be converted to cash.

On Forsub's SFP, the monetary items are cash, accounts payable, and long-term debentures. These three elements are translated at the closing rate. If the closing rate at the SFP date is P1 = C$2.30, the P20,000 cash balance is translated to C$46,000 for consolidation.

Non-monetary items that are reported at historical cost are translated at the exchange rate in effect at the date of the transaction that created the non-monetary items. The rate on the date of the transaction is known as the **historical rate**. In essence, the temporal approach uses the same translation rules as we described in the previous chapter for monetary and non-monetary balances arising from foreign-currency transactions.

For Forsub Ltd., the non-monetary items are inventory and land, both purchased when the rate was P1 = C$2.00. Thus, these two assets will be translated at the $2.00 historical rate, while the cash, payables, and bonds will be translated at the $2.30 closing rate.

Note that the historical rate is $2.00 because that was the rate existing at the time that the inventory and land were purchased. The fact that the rate was also $2.00 when the original investment in Forsub was made by Domestic is coincidental. If the land had been purchased when the rate was $2.10 and the inventory bought when the rate was $2.15, then those would be the historical rates used for translating each account balance.

The only account on the Forsub SFP that we have not yet discussed is the common shares. Since this is a non-monetary item, it is logical that it should be translated at the historical rate of $2.00. This account will be eliminated when Forsub is consolidated. Since the offsetting account in Domestic's SFP is the investment in Forsub account, the subsidiary's common share account should be translated at the historical rate to facilitate the elimination on consolidation.

In summary, the accounts on Forsub's SFP will be translated as follows under the temporal method:

| Item | Rate |
| --- | --- |
| Cash | Closing |
| Inventory | Historical |
| Land | Historical |
| Accounts payable | Closing |
| Bonds payable | Closing |
| Common shares | Historical |

Since the various accounts are not being translated with a uniform measurement approach, the translated SFP will not balance until we allow for a *translation gain or loss*. The total gain or loss will be the amount needed to balance the translated SFP. It is a loss of $3,000 in this example. With this addition to the SFP, the translated SFP of Forsub Ltd. will appear as shown in the last column of Exhibit 9.1.

**Composition of Translation Loss**   The $3,000 translation loss may appear to be a "plug"—just an amount necessary to balance the SFP. However, the translation loss is not a random event. It can be derived directly from the information given about Forsub's transactions. There are three components to the $3,000 translation loss:

1. **A gain of $6,000 on the balance of cash.** Forsub originally received P50,000 in cash when the exchange rate was $2.00, and obtained another P25,000 from the issuance of bonds. While the rate was still $2.00, the company purchased land and inventory, thereby reducing the cash balance to P20,000. The company then held this balance of cash while the exchange rate rose to $2.30. The increase in the exchange rate meant that the P20,000 balance was worth $46,000 at the end of the fiscal year

(P20,000 × $2.30) as compared with only $40,000 (P20,000 × $2.00) when the cash was received. Thus, holding a cash balance when the exchange rate rose resulted in an increase in the equivalent amount in Canadian dollars, a gain of $46,000 − $40,000 = $6,000.

2.  **A loss of $1,500 on the accounts payable.** Forsub still owes P5,000 to its trade creditors, but the dollar equivalent of this amount has changed from $10,000 (P5,000 × $2.00) to $11,500 (P5,000 × $2.30). In Canadian dollar terms, the value of the debt has risen, thereby resulting in a loss.

3.  **A loss arising from the bonds payable.** The P25,000 in bonds were issued when the exchange rate was $2.00, or a Canadian dollar equivalent of $50,000. At year-end, the equivalent of the bond indebtedness is $57,500, because the year-end exchange rate is $2.30. Therefore, a loss of $7,500 ($50,000 − $57,500) has arisen as a result of holding a liability that is denominated in pants, as the Canadian dollar equivalent increased because of changes in the exchange rate.

By breaking the translation loss down into its component amounts, we can see that the loss of $3,000 is really a net amount arising from a loss of $9,000 ($1,500 + $7,500) on monetary liabilities minus a gain of $6,000 on holding cash, a monetary asset. This information is summarized at the bottom of Exhibit 9.1. We will examine the nature of this loss and its accounting implications more extensively later in the chapter. For the moment, however, note that *the only items that give rise to translation gains or losses are those account balances that are translated at the closing rate*.

**Exhibit 9.1** Translation of Statement of Financial Position, Temporal Method

| Forsub Ltd. December 31, 20X5 | | | |
|---|---|---|---|
| Exchange rate, December 31, 20X5: P1.00 = C$2.30 | | | |
| | Balance on Forsub's books | Exchange rate | Translated amount |
| Cash | P 20,000 | 2.30 | $ 46,000 |
| Inventory | 20,000 | 2.00 | 40,000 |
| Land | 40,000 | 2.00 | 80,000 |
| Total assets | P 80,000 | | $166,000 |
| | | | |
| Accounts payable, current | P 5,000 | 2.30 | $ 11,500 |
| Bonds payable, long-term | 25,000 | 2.30 | 57,500 |
| Common shares | 50,000 | 2.00 | 100,000 |
| Translation gain (loss) | — | | (3,000) |
| | P 80,000 | | $166,000 |

Calculation of net translation loss:

| | | | | |
|---|---|---|---|---|
| Cash | P 20,000 | asset × ($2.30 − $2.00) = | $ 6,000 | gain |
| Accounts payable | (5,000) | liability × ($2.30 − $2.00) = | (1,500) | loss |
| Bonds payable | (25,000) | liability × ($2.30 − $2.00) = | (7,500) | loss |
| Net | P (10,000) | liability × ($2.30 − $2.00) = | $ (3,000) | loss |

The net amount of balances that are translated at the closing rate is called the foreign operation's **accounting exposure** to currency rate fluctuations. In Exhibit 9.1, the *accounting exposure* is a net monetary liability balance of P10,000: (P20,000 − P5,000 − P25,000). The translation loss is:

P10,000 × ($2.30 − $2.00) = $3,000

Balances that are translated at historical rates do not give rise to translation gains or losses because the rate at which they are translated does not change. The net amount of the exchange gain or loss can be calculated by looking only at the net changes in those balances that are translated at the closing rate.

**Relationship of Temporal Method to Transaction Accounting**   In Exhibit 9.1, we translated Forsub's year-end balances by using the temporal method, and we calculated a gain on the balance of cash and a loss on the balance of bonds and accounts payable. An important characteristic to note about the temporal method is that *it yields exactly the same results in terms of the translated amounts as would have resulted from translating each transaction separately,* as we discussed in Chapter 8. In substance, the temporal method views the operations of the foreign company as though the transactions had been carried out directly by Domestic Corporation operating from its home base in Canada.

Exhibit 9.2 illustrates the individual transactions as they would have been recorded by Domestic if they had been direct transactions. The first transaction shows the deposit of $100,000 in the Bank of Pantania—this amount is translated to P50,000 by the bank. The remaining transactions record the issuance of the bonds and the purchase of the inventory and land, recorded in the equivalent amount of Canadian dollars.

At year-end, it is necessary to record the monetary foreign currency-denominated balances at their current equivalents. These adjustments (for cash, accounts payable, and bonds payable) result in a net foreign-currency loss of $3,000. The impact of these individual transactions on Domestic Corporation's SFP would be exactly the same as translating Forsub's SFP by the temporal method and consolidating.

# Current-Rate Method

An alternative approach to the translation of the results of foreign operations is to translate *all* of the asset and liability balances at the current rate, which for the SFP is the closing rate. The historical rate is used only for the shareholders' equity accounts. The current-rate SFP is shown in Exhibit 9.3.

Under the current-rate method, the total assets of Forsub translate to $184,000, as compared with $166,000 under the temporal method. The much larger amount is due to the fact that under the temporal method, the large non-monetary assets were translated at the lower historical rate. Conversely, if the exchange rate had declined during the period, the translated total assets would be less under the current-rate method than under the temporal method.

Every solvent corporation has more assets than liabilities. When all the assets and liabilities are translated at the current rate, the translated assets will always exceed the translated liabilities. As a result, the translated net assets will always be positive—the

**Exhibit 9.2** Direct Transactions Equivalent to Forsub's Transactions

| | | |
|---|---:|---:|
| If the parent company had engaged in the transactions directly instead of through Forsub, the transactions would have been recorded on Domestic's books as follows: | | |
| a. Cash (in Bank of Pantania) | 100,000 | |
|     Cash (in Canadian bank) | | 100,000 |
|     [to record transfer of cash for Pantanian bank account] | | |
| b. Cash (in Pantania) | 50,000 | |
|     Bonds payable | | 50,000 |
|     [to record issuance of bonds in Pantania] | | |
| c. Inventory (cost = P20,000) | 40,000 | |
|     Cash (in Pantania) | | 30,000 |
|     Accounts payable (P5,000) | | 10,000 |
|     [to record purchase of inventory in Pantania, paid in pants] | | |
| d. Land (cost = P40,000) | 80,000 | |
|     Cash (in Pantania: P40,000) | | 80,000 |
|     [to record purchase of land in Pantania, paid in pants] | | |
| **Year-end adjusting entries, December 31, 20X5:** | | |
| e. Cash [P20,000 × (2.30 − 2.00)] | 6,000 | |
|     Foreign-currency gains/losses | | 6,000 |
|     [to adjust the cash balance to the year-end closing rate] | | |
| f. Foreign-currency gains/losses | 1,500 | |
|     Accounts payable [P5,000 × (2.30 − 2.00)] | | 1,500 |
|     [to adjust the accounts payable balance to the year-end closing rate] | | |
| g. Foreign-currency gains/losses | 7,500 | |
|     Bonds payable [P25,000 × (2.30 − 2.00)] | | 7,500 |
|     [to adjust the bonds payable balance to the year-end closing rate] | | |

excess of assets over liabilities. Thus, when the current-rate method is used, the net balance of those SFP accounts that are translated at the current rate will always be a net *asset* balance.

## Comparison of Translation Methods

The two different methods yield different accounting exposures and different amounts of gain or loss. Indeed, as we will demonstrate shortly, a translation loss that arises under one method often becomes a gain under the other method. The accounting exposure to foreign-currency fluctuations under the two methods can be summarized as follows:

■ Using the temporal method, the accounting exposure can be either a net asset or net liability balance, depending on whether monetary assets and non-monetary assets measured at fair value exceed monetary liabilities and non-monetary liabilities measured at fair value (for a net asset exposure) or vice versa (for a net liability exposure).

**Exhibit 9.3** Translation of Statement of Financial Position, Current-Rate Method

Forsub Ltd.
December 31, 20X5

Exchange rate, December 31, 20X5: P1.00 = C$2.30

|  | Balance on Forsub's books | Exchange rate | Translated amount |
|---|---|---|---|
| Cash | P20,000 | 2.30 | $ 46,000 |
| Inventory | 20,000 | 2.30 | 46,000 |
| Land | 40,000 | 2.30 | 92,000 |
| Total assets | P80,000 | | $184,000 |
| Accounts payable, current | P 5,000 | 2.30 | $ 11,500 |
| Bonds payable, long-term | 25,000 | 2.30 | 57,500 |
| Shareholders' equity | 50,000 | 2.00 | 100,000 |
| Translation gain (loss)* | — | | 15,000 |
| | P80,000 | | $184,000 |

*Calculation of net translation gain:

Translation gain = net asset position × change in exchange rate

$$= P50,000 \times (\$2.30 - \$2.00)$$

$$= \$15,000 \text{ gain}$$

■ Under the current rate method, the accounting exposure to currency fluctuations is always measurable as the net assets of the foreign subsidiary—almost always a positive net asset value.

A distinct characteristic of the current rate method is that the proportionate amounts of the various asset and liability accounts do not change when the SFP is translated. For example, bonds are 31% of Forsub's total assets in pants (P25,000 ÷ P80,000), and they continue to be 31% of total assets in dollars ($57,500 ÷ $184,000). Under the temporal method, however, the proportion changes from 31% to 35% ($57,500 ÷ $166,000).

Many people feel that this characteristic is an advantage of the current rate method—the "true" financial position of Forsub is that shown by the SFP in pants, and the process of currency translation should not change this picture of the foreign operation.

We can summarize the two translation methods as follows:

1. Temporal method
   a) translates all monetary items at the closing rate and fair-value items at the exchange rate on the date the fair value is determined; translates all non-monetary historical cost items at their individual historical rate;
   b) yields an accounting exposure to exchange rate fluctuations of the net balance of monetary and fair-value assets and liabilities, depending on the financial structure of the company; and
   c) does not give effect to implicit hedges of monetary and fair-value items by offsetting non-monetary items.

2. Current-rate method
   a) translates all assets and liabilities at the closing rate, whether current or non-current and whether monetary or non-monetary;

**b)** yields an accounting exposure to exchange rate changes that is always a net asset position, equivalent to the owners' equity in the foreign operation;[1] and

**c)** preserves the proportionate relationships between the various SFP items and does not "distort" the statement as compared with the way it would appear in local currency.

So far, we have been treating the net translation gain or loss under each of the methods as a SFP item. However, there actually are various treatments possible *under each method* of translation. Before we consider these alternative treatments of the translation gain or loss, however, we should further address the concept of *exchange rate exposure*.

### Concept Check 9-1

**1.** What is usually the best way to structure a company's operations in a foreign country? Why?

**2.** How are foreign-currency-denominated non-monetary assets that are carried at fair value translated under the temporal method?

**3.** What characteristic of translation is the main advantage of the current-rate method?

**LO ❷**

Distinguish between accounting exposure and economic exposure to exchange rate changes

## 9.3 ACCOUNTING EXPOSURE VERSUS ECONOMIC EXPOSURE

Throughout the foregoing discussion, we have pointed out that under each translation method, we can anticipate the nature of the translation gain or loss. We know which items will be translated at the current exchange rate, and only those amounts will give rise to a translation gain or loss. If we know which way the exchange rate is moving, then we can predict whether the translation will result in a gain or a loss for the current period.

We have also observed that since the different methods translate different accounts at the current exchange rate, a given movement in the exchange rate may cause a gain under one method but may cause a loss under another method. In the case of Forsub, above, we calculated a loss of $3,000 under the temporal method and a gain of $15,000 under the current-rate method.

The net balance of those SFP amounts that we translated at the current exchange rate is the *accounting exposure* to fluctuations in the foreign exchange rate. This exposure arises as the result of the accounting method of translation that we are using at the time. If a translation gain or loss is to be reported on the financial statements of the parent corporation, then the qualitative characteristic of "faithful representation" should be present. In other words, is there really an *economic* gain to the parent when an accounting gain is reported?

It might seem that when a Canadian company holds an asset that is denominated in a foreign currency and that currency rises in value against the Canadian dollar, the company experiences an economic gain because the asset increases in value as measured in dollars. Since a Canadian company's equity in a foreign operation is almost always a net asset position, one could argue that an increase in the exchange rate will result in a gain to the parent because that net investment will be worth more as a result of the change in the rate.

---

[1] This is true unless the foreign operation has more liabilities than assets, in which case the owners' equity will be a deficit and there will be a net liability position rather than a net asset position.

Such an argument, however, does not consider the impact of exchange rate changes on the earnings ability of the foreign subsidiary. In most instances, the foreign operation exists as a going concern that is expected to contribute favourably to the profits of the parent. Therefore, it makes sense to evaluate the impact of currency realignments on the earnings ability of the foreign operation. This impact is known as the **economic exposure** of the foreign operation. The economic exposure is much more complicated than the accounting exposure because many more factors are involved than simply the mechanical aspects of the translation method and the direction of change in the exchange rates.

## Example of Economic Exposure

Suppose, for example, that the business of Forsub Ltd. is to import a product from Canada and to sell it in Pantania. The cost to produce the product is $10.00, and it is sold in Pantania at P6. When the exchange rate is P1 = $2.00, the value of the sale is $12.00 (P6 × $2), resulting in a gross profit of $2.00 ($12 − $10) to Domestic Corporation.

If the exchange rate goes up to P1 = $2.30, the value of each sale will then be $13.80, for an increased gross profit of $3.80. In such a situation, the increase in the value of the pant is a real gain in economic terms. Forsub will either have a larger profit on its sales (if it maintains the same selling price in pants), or it may decrease its price and increase its volume of sales in Pantania (owing to the price elasticity of demand). Either way, Domestic may be better off as a result of the increase in the value of the pant.

Now, suppose instead that the business of Forsub is to produce a product from materials in Pantania and then to transfer the product to Domestic Corporation for sale in Canada. The product costs P10 to produce in Pantania, and sells for $25 in Canada. When the exchange rate is P1 = $2.00, the cost of production is the equivalent of $20, yielding a gross margin of $5. An increase in the value of the pant to $2.30 will cause the production cost to rise to $23 in Canadian dollars, thereby lowering the gross margin to $2.00. In this situation, an increase in the value of the pant is disadvantageous to Forsub and Domestic Corporation. Instead of being a gain, a rise in the value of the pant is actually a loss in earnings ability.

Of course, things are not really all that simple. Exchange rates do not change autonomously, but are the result of other economic factors, such as relative rates of inflation and interest rate differentials in the various countries. If the value of the pant increased because of high inflation in Canada, then Domestic may be able to charge a higher price for the product and maintain or possibly even increase its relative gross margin.

The economic impact of changes in exchange rates is quite complex and will vary from company to company and situation to situation.

## Past Versus Future

Economic exposure is a result of the economic characteristics of the foreign operation, such as the sources of its raw materials, the sources of its debt financing, the market in which its products are sold, the price elasticity of demand for its products, and much more. *Economic exposure is the impact of an exchange rate change on the present value of future cash flows*—it is forward-looking.

In contrast, accounting exposure is historically oriented. It measures the mechanical impact of translating the results of past transactions. The economic exposure is not determinable from the accounting exposure, since the accounting exposure is mechanical in origin and has no relationship to the future earnings impact of a change in exchange rates.

However, application of the concept of faithful representation leads to the conclusion that, in any situation, the preferred accounting translation method is the one that yields an accounting exposure that best reflects the economic exposure. If an increase in the exchange rate is likely to have a beneficial economic impact on the foreign operation and the consolidated subsidiary, then the accounting translation method should yield a translation gain when the exchange rate goes up, rather than a loss.

### Concept Check 9-2

1. Does an increase in the value of a foreign currency always increase the value of a subsidiary in the same foreign country?

2. Why are reported translation gains and losses said to be focused on the past?

LO ❸

Explain the conceptual alternatives for reporting translation gains and losses

## 9.4 ALTERNATIVES FOR REPORTING TRANSLATION GAINS AND LOSSES

So far in this chapter, we have treated the gain or loss arising from the translation of the SFP of a foreign operation simply as a balancing figure on the subsidiary's translated SFP. However, several theoretical alternatives are available for reporting these gains or losses on the parent's consolidated statements. The broad alternatives are:

1. immediate recognition of the net gain or loss in consolidated net income (applied to all companies);

2. limited recognition of gains and losses in a manner that is consistent with the treatment of similar types of *transaction* gains or losses; and

3. deferred recognition of gains and losses until realized, the deferral to be shown as a balancing amount in the consolidated SFP (e.g., as a separate component of shareholders' equity).

    Each of these alternatives can be applied under either method of translation. However, some of the alternatives are more logical under one method than the other, as we shall see later.

### Immediate Recognition

Once upon a time, US standards required immediate recognition of all translation gains and losses. For many companies, immediate recognition had a significant effect on net income from operations and therefore affected earnings per share, dividend payout ratios, and profit-sharing and bonus calculations, as well as certain debt-covenant calculations such as times-interest-earned.

As a result, the managers of some of these companies engaged in massive hedging operations to offset possible losses from an accounting exposure in a foreign operation. Others reorganized the financial affairs of their foreign subsidiaries to reduce the accounting exposure. In the process, the companies incurred significant "real" economic risks in an attempt to eliminate "fictional" accounting losses.

In response to this undesirable economic impact of immediate recognition, US standards were changed so that, in certain circumstances, the translation gains and losses would instead be reported on a cumulative basis as a separate component of shareholders' equity.

The experience in the United States clearly indicated the practical inadvisability of mandating the current recognition of translation gains and losses in all cases. Those instances in which current recognition seems particularly inappropriate are when the foreign operation is substantially autonomous in its activities. If a foreign operation functions independently of its parent, then recognition of a translation gain or loss is apt to be misleading because the accounting exposure is not at all indicative of the economic exposure.

## Limited Recognition

The second broad approach to the disposition of translation gains and losses is to limit recognition only to gains and losses arising from monetary items, so that they are treated in the same manner as foreign-currency *transactions*, as described in the preceding chapter.

This approach probably works best if it is limited to certain types of companies. Some foreign operations operate in the same primary economic environment as the parent. These operations are often extensions of the parent's domestic business. Examples include foreign sales offices and foreign production centres that have no real economic autonomy. Since the parent is directly involved in the foreign operation, the parent is, in effect, using the subsidiary as a facilitating mechanism for a series of foreign-currency transactions. Therefore, it is logical to apply the same recognition principles to foreign operations that are interdependent with the parent as would be applied to foreign-currency transactions.

The limited recognition alternative is inappropriate for foreign operations that operate in a different primary economic environment from the parent as relatively autonomous operations. Recognition implies that the parent will be directly affected by the subsidiary. However, it is not clear that future operating cash flows will be affected by exchange rate changes if the subsidiary is operating independently.

## Deferred Recognition

The third alternative is to defer recognition of the translation gain or loss *indefinitely* so that it doesn't affect earnings at all. The cumulative translation gain or loss will be reported as an SFP item. The gain or loss would be recognized only if it is realized if the parent sells the subsidiary (or a significant enough portion to lose control).

This alternative seems appropriate for subsidiaries that essentially operate autonomously. The main argument for deferral of cumulative translation gains and losses is that a gain or loss is the result of a mechanical process of translating from a foreign currency into the parent's functional currency, and thus has little direct effect on the present and future cash flows from operations. Recognition of these gains and losses in income may not be reflective of the economic exposure to exchange rate changes.

Translation gains and losses clearly do not fit within the current definitions of assets and liabilities. To be shown on the SFP, they can only be placed directly in shareholders' equity. Thus the cumulative foreign-currency adjustment is treated as a separate component of consolidated shareholders' equity under this alternative.

### Concept Check 9-3

1. What are three alternatives for handling translation gains and losses?
2. When is the recognition of translation gains and losses in current year net income inappropriate?

LO **4**

Determine a company's functional currency after considering the relevant factors identified by IFRS

## 9.5 THE FUNCTIONAL CURRENCY APPROACH

To summarize, we have discussed two possible methods to convert foreign currency-denominated financial statements into another currency—the temporal method and the current-rate method. To apply the two different approaches, we must define the circumstances under which they are used. The determination is essentially made on the basis of the foreign operation's functional currency.

The **functional currency** is the currency of the primary economic environment in which the entity operates, which is normally the country in which it generates and expends cash. If Canada is the primary economic environment in which the parent operates, then the parent's functional currency is the Canadian dollar. The functional currency of an entity is not necessarily the same as the presentation currency. The functional currency is the currency used to measure the transactions of an entity. The **presentation currency** is the currency used to present an entity's results on its financial statements. If an entity's presentation currency is different from its functional currency, then the statements will have to be translated from the functional currency to the presentation currency.

Let us continue our example regarding Domestic Corporation and its subsidiary, Forsub. We will assume that the Canadian dollar is the *functional currency* of Domestic Corporation and that it is also the *presentation currency* on its financial statements. If it is determined that Canada is the primary economic environment in which Forsub operates, then the Canadian dollar will also be the functional currency of Forsub. For example, this would be the case if Forsub buys most of its materials in Canadian dollars and also sells its output in Canadian dollars, such as an off-shore manufacturing subsidiary that imports parts from the parent for assembly and then sells the finished product back to the parent or to other customers in Canadian dollars.

Because Forsub's transactions have been recorded in terms of pants, the local currency, the goal will be to re-measure them in terms of its functional currency—that is, the Canadian dollar. Since the subsidiary is operating in the same economic environment as the parent, the results should be the same as if the parent had engaged in the transactions. Further, the goal is to produce the same financial statements that would have resulted if we had used the functional currency to record all the transactions. To accomplish this re-measuring, the temporal method will be used to translate the financial statements. With the temporal method, only translation gains and losses on monetary items (and fair-value non-monetary items) are recognized in net income.

If, however, it is determined that Pantania is the primary economic environment in which Forsub operates, then the pant will be the functional currency of Forsub. There will be no need to re-measure the transactions, but the statements will still need to be translated to Canadian dollars, the presentation currency, before they can be consolidated. To accomplish this translation, the current-rate method will be used.

With the current-rate method, translation gains and losses are not recognized in earnings but instead are reported on the SCI as a component of other comprehensive income. The cumulative amount is reported as a separate component of shareholders' equity, as mentioned above. The decision to defer gains and losses is a reflection of the ambiguity surrounding the economic impact of exchange rate changes.

The above illustrations are the two basic scenarios encountered in translating financial statements and therefore are the focus of our discussions in this chapter. Other scenarios are possible.

For example, Forsub, although a Pantanian subsidiary of a Canadian parent, may nonetheless identify the United States as its primary economic environment because most of its revenue and some of its expenses are in US dollars. In this case its functional currency would be the US dollar. If Forsub's transactions are recorded in pants, they will first have to be re-measured in terms of its functional currency, the US dollar, using the temporal method. Next, since the presentation currency for the group is the Canadian dollar, the re-measured transactions will have to be translated into Canadian dollars using the current-rate method.

An interesting aspect of dual concepts of *functional* currency and *presentation* currency is that the reporting (for consolidation purposes) may not reflect the geographic location of the subsidiary at all. However, never lose sight of the fact that we're talking only about statements prepared for consolidation. The Pantanian subsidiary will almost certainly prepare its separate-entity financial statements in pants for reporting to stakeholders in Pantania, such as to bankers, tax authorities, regulators, and local "joint venture" partners or local minority shareholders.

Exhibit 9.4 should help you identify the steps to be followed during translation when the accounting records are maintained in a currency other than the Canadian dollar.

## Determining the Functional Currency

As we have noted, the functional currency is the currency of the primary economic environment in which the company operates. This environment is normally the one where it generates and spends its cash. The determination of a company's functional currency is not always easy. To assist companies in determining their functional currency, IFRS discusses several primary and secondary indicators.

**Primary Indicators**   The first two primary indicators are the currency "influences" on the subsidiary's (1) costs of the goods and services acquired and (2) selling prices for goods and services sold. In many cases, this will simply be the currency in which prices are denominated (and settled), which may or may not be the local currency of the foreign subsidiary.

The third primary indicator relates to the source of the competitive forces and regulations that affect the selling prices of the company's goods and services. Selling prices may be strongly affected by competitive forces from another country, such as competition in the parent's home country. Another type of competitive force arises when a particular type of product is priced and sold worldwide in a single currency, such as the

**Exhibit 9.4** Translation Decisions Where Accounting Records Are Maintained in a Currency Other Than Canadian Dollars

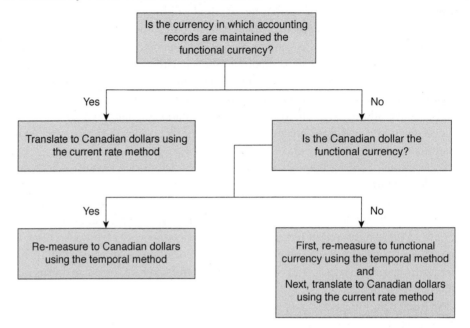

worldwide market for aircraft, which is priced internationally in US dollars. For example, Bombardier Inc., a Canada-based manufacturer of aircraft and rail transportation systems, states in its financial statements that it financial statements "are expressed in U.S. dollars, the functional currency of Bombardier Inc."[2]

Regulations from another country may also influence selling prices, such as limitations on prices that the buying country will permit. For example, suppose that a Canadian province limits the Canadian dollar price that its health service will pay for prescription drugs. A pharmaceutical company has a subsidiary in Mexico that sells most of its product to Canada. The Canadian regulations are a strong influence on the Mexican subsidiary's selling prices, which may effectively make the Canadian dollar the subsidiary's functional currency, even though the subsidiary's nominal selling prices may be stated in Mexican pesos.

**Secondary Indicators**  If the functional currency is not easily determined from the primary factors, the following factors should also be considered in determining the functional currency:

1. the currency in which financing activities are conducted, including the issuance of debt and equity instruments;

2. the currency in which cash from operating activities is kept. That is, if currencies from operating activities are routinely converted to another currency before being held in the bank, then that other currency may be the company's functional currency;

3. whether the activities of the foreign operation are conducted independently of the parent or as an extension of the parent;

---

[2] Bombardier Inc., Annual Report, (2011), p. 143.

## Accounting with the Same Functional Currency

CGI Group Inc. offers the following explanation of its accounting for foreign operations that have the same functional currency as the parent—the Canadian dollar:

> The Company's consolidated financial statements are presented in Canadian dollars, which is also the parent company's functional currency. Each entity in the Company determines its own functional currency and items included in the financial statements of each entity are measured using that functional currency. Functional currency is the currency of the primary economic environment in which the entity operates. [...] For the accounts of foreign operations with the same functional currency as the Company, monetary assets and liabilities are translated at the exchange rate in effect at the balance sheet date and non-monetary assets and liabilities are translated at historical exchange rates. Revenue and expenses are translated at average rates for the period. Translation exchange gains and losses of such operations are reflected in the consolidated statement of earnings.

Notice that the disclosure does not refer to the technical accounting name "temporal method" but broadly explains this accounting method for the benefit of readers who are not fortunate enough to be professional accountants.

Source: CGI Group Inc., 2012 First Quarter Condensed Consolidated Financial Statements, p. 14.

4. whether the foreign operation conducts a low or high proportion of its activities with the parent;

5. whether the cash flows of the foreign operation directly affect the cash flows of the parent and are readily available to the parent; and

6. whether the cash flows of the foreign operation are sufficient to service its debt obligations without the need for funds from the parent.

Often, the functional currency is not obvious. Selecting a functional currency in these situations is a matter of professional judgment. The choice should be the one that most faithfully represents the economic impact of the activities of the company. In the following section, we will briefly review the nature of foreign operations that typically have a functional currency that is the same as or different from that of the parent.

## Entities with the Same Functional Currency as the Parent

If an entity has the same functional currency as the parent, it typically operates as an extension of the parent company in the foreign country. Such operations are usually treated as revenue centres or cost centres from a management accounting standpoint. These operations are largely or entirely dependent on the parent, either for a source of product or for disposition of production. Interdependent foreign operations are a direct arm of the parent, and the parent controls the assets and liabilities of the subsidiary.

Therefore, their operations are viewed simply as a series of foreign-currency *transactions*. If the financial statements are prepared in the local currency, they will have to be re-measured into the functional currency to be consolidated with the parent. The results obtained by re-measuring the financial statements of the foreign operation should appear as though the parent had engaged in the foreign-currency transactions directly, rather than through a foreign subsidiary.

The method used for re-measuring such integrated operations should be the same as the method used by the parent for reporting the results of its foreign-currency *transactions*. The method that accomplishes this objective is the *temporal method*. The translation gains and losses that arise from re-measuring foreign operations using the temporal method are treated in the same manner as for foreign-currency transactions. That is, the gains or losses on monetary transactions and balances are reported in the current year's net income.

We will demonstrate the application of this method in the following sections.

## Entities with a Different Functional Currency from the Parent

An entity with a different functional currency from the parent is often viewed as being an individual, autonomous foreign business entity. The parent company's accounting exposure to exchange rate changes is limited to the net investment of the parent in the foreign subsidiary. Therefore, under IFRS, closing rates are used for translating the SFP, which is the current-rate method.

The net gain or loss that arises from translating these operations is not recognized in net income, but is reported as other comprehensive income. As we explained above, this treatment is recommended because:

1. the accounting exposure may not be indicative of the economic exposure, and

2. this exchange gain or loss has no direct effect on the cash flows of the parent.

The cumulative gain or loss is reported as a separate component of consolidated shareholders' equity. The cumulative gain or loss would be brought into comprehensive income only by the sale of the subsidiary or by other loss of control of the subsidiary, such as being taken over by its host country's government.

The parent may choose to hedge its net investment in a foreign entity. The use of hedge accounting is only available for entities that have a different functional currency from the parent. Any gains or losses from the hedge will be deferred (similar to a cash-flow hedge) and offset against the cumulative translation loss or gain in equity.

---

### Reality Check 9–3

## Accounting with a Different Functional Currency

How does CGI account for subsidiaries that have a different functional currency than the parent company?

For foreign operations that have functional currencies different from the Company, assets and liabilities denominated in a foreign currency are translated into Canadian dollars at exchange rates in effect at the balance sheet date. Revenue and expenses are translated at average exchange rates prevailing during the period. Resulting unrealized gains and losses are reported as net unrealized gains and losses on translating financial statements of foreign operations in other comprehensive income.

Source: CGI Group Inc., 2012 First Quarter Condensed Consolidated Financial Statements, p. 14.

---

Although IFRS permits hedge accounting for a parent's net investment in a foreign subsidiary, it is rather difficult to find a rationale for actually engaging in such a hedge. It would make sense only if both of two conditions exist:

1. the net investment is a reasonable approximation of the fair value of the investment, which is highly unlikely, and

2. the parent intends to sell the subsidiary in the near future and wants to guard against value loss through currency fluctuations.

The second condition can arise when one company buys another with the intent of reselling (also known as *flipping*) the acquired company to another buyer.

## Operations in Hyperinflationary Economies

An exception to the general recommendations given above occurs when a subsidiary's functional currency is that of a country that is experiencing hyperinflation. Some countries historically have had very high rates of inflation, sometimes well over 100% per year. This creates a problem because historical-cost financial statements will show long-term non-monetary assets at a historical cost that is expressed in currency of a far different purchasing power than the current exchange rate suggests.

The solution recommended in IFRS is to adjust the foreign operation's financial statements for changes in the price level of the foreign currency. The adjusted statements are then translated using the closing rate for all amounts (assets, liabilities, equities, revenues, and expenses). IAS 29 provides several guidelines as to what constitutes a "highly inflationary" economy. It suggests that an inflation rate of 100% over a three-year period (that is, averaging 26% per year, compounded) would be highly inflationary. In addition, the standard provides several behavioural guidelines based on the actions of the general population and businesses that would be indicative of hyperinflation. We will not discuss this issue any further in this text.

### Concept Check 9-4

1. What are the three primary indicators that a company should use to determine its functional currency?

2. Why are the translation gains and losses resulting from the use of the current-rate method not recognized in net income?

LO **5**

Translate a company's financial statements and properly handle any translation gain or loss in preparation for consolidation

## 9.6 APPLICATION OF IFRS RECOMMENDATIONS

Let's return to the introductory example of Domestic Corporation and its Pantanian subsidiary, Forsub Ltd. We determined earlier in the chapter that under the temporal method of translation, there was a net translation loss of $3,000 in the first year. If Forsub's functional currency is the Canadian dollar, the temporal method is used to re-measure the operations of Forsub in Canadian dollars. The net re-measurement, or translation loss, of $3,000 will be included *in Domestic Corporation's net income*. (For convenience, we will use the more common term "translate" instead of "re-measure" from here on.)

Instead, suppose that Forsub's functional currency is the pant. Then the current-rate method is appropriate—the entire translation gain or loss will be reported as a separate component of Domestic Corporation's shareholders' equity. Exhibit 9.3 shows that the current-rate method yields a net translation gain of $15,000, none of which is included in net income.

Obviously, a key facet of applying the IFRS recommendations is the determination of the functional currency of the foreign operation. Bear in mind, however, that if the foreign operations are relatively minor or if the parent is not otherwise constrained to follow GAAP for publicly accountable enterprises, it may be simpler and no less informative to apply the current-rate method across the board to all foreign subsidiaries and to report the translation gains or losses in other comprehensive income.

### Extending the Example

Earlier in this chapter, we described the initial transactions for the establishment of Forsub Ltd. by Domestic Corporation. After Forsub was established, the subsidiary purchased land and inventory and issued bonds. Exhibits 9.1 and 9.3 illustrate translation of Forsub's SFP accounts under two different translation methods. For simplicity, we assumed that Forsub had no operating revenues or expenses for the first year, 20X5 (even though, strictly speaking, there should have been some bond interest accrued). While we did point out that the translation gain or loss may be taken into income in 20X5, it is taken into income by the *parent* company and reported on the consolidated SCI.

Now let us make the example more realistic by looking at Forsub's financial statements for the next year, 20X6. Forsub Ltd.'s separate-entity SFP and SCI are shown in Exhibit 9.5. Additional information is as follows:

1. At the beginning of 20X6, Forsub purchased some equipment for P30,000; the equipment has an expected useful life of six years.

2. The ending inventory was purchased in the last quarter of the year, when the exchange rate was $2.45.

3. The exchange rate at December 31, 20X6, was $2.50; the average rate during the year was $2.40.

**Current-Rate Method**   The translation of Forsub's account balances using the current-rate method is shown in Exhibit 9.6. All of the assets and liabilities are translated at the closing rate of $2.50. The shareholders' equity accounts are translated at the historical rates as follows:

■   common shares at the rate that existed at the time of the initial investment, and

■   retained earnings at the rate that existed at the time the earnings were recognized.

**Exhibit 9.5** Forsub Ltd. Financial Statements, 20X6

### Statement of Financial Position
### December 31, 20X6

| Assets | | Liabilities and shareholders' equity | |
|---|---|---|---|
| Cash | P 15,000 | Accounts payable, current | P 22,000 |
| Accounts receivable | 15,000 | Bonds payable, long-term | 25,000 |
| Inventory | 10,000 | | 47,000 |
| Land | 40,000 | Common shares | 50,000 |
| Equipment | 30,000 | Retained earnings* | 8,000 |
| Accumulated depreciation | (5,000) | | 58,000 |
| Total assets | P105,000 | | P105,000 |

*No revenues or expenses were recognized in 20X5, the only previous year.

### Statement of Comprehensive Income
### Year Ended December 31, 20X6

| | | |
|---|---|---|
| Sales revenue | | P 60,000 |
| Cost of sales: | | |
| Beginning inventory | P 20,000 | |
| Purchases | 30,000 | |
| Ending inventory | (10,000) | 40,000 |
| Gross margin | | 20,000 |
| Operating expenses: | | |
| Depreciation | 5,000 | |
| Interest expense | 3,000 | |
| Other expenses | 4,000 | 12,000 |
| Net income | | P 8,000 |

In this example, the only amount in retained earnings ($19,200) is the current earnings for 20X6, and thus the translated amount is the same as that shown on the translated SCI. The balancing figure for the SFP is the cumulative translation gain of $25,800.

Under a pure application of the current-rate method, the SCI would also be translated at the year-end closing rate. However, Exhibit 9.6 shows the SCI being translated at the average rate for the year rather than at the year-end rate. This is known as the *average-rate approach to the current-rate method*, and is used because this method results in the same amounts in the presentation currency regardless of how a foreign subsidiary is translated into the presentation currency.

For example, this method will provide the same results if the subsidiary is directly translated into the presentation currency or if the subsidiary is first translated into its functional currency and then into the presentation currency. In addition, this method ensures the additivity of the interim earnings figures of the parent company. IFRS recommends the use of exchange rates at the dates of the transactions rather than the year-end rate for SCI amounts. For practical reasons, a rate that approximates the dates of the transactions rates (i.e., an average rate) can be used if the exchange rates do not fluctuate significantly.

**Exhibit 9.6** Translation by Current-Rate Method, 20X6

Exchange rate, December 31, 20X6: P1.00 = C$2.50
Average exchange rate for 20X6: P1.00 = C$2.40

**Statement of Financial Position**
**December 31, 20X6**

| | Local currency (pants) | Exchange rate | Translated amounts (C$) |
|---|---|---|---|
| **Assets** | | | |
| Cash | P 15,000 | 2.50 | $ 37,500 |
| Accounts receivable | 15,000 | 2.50 | 37,500 |
| Inventory | 10,000 | 2.50 | 25,000 |
| Land | 40,000 | 2.50 | 100,000 |
| Equipment | 30,000 | 2.50 | 75,000 |
| Accumulated depreciation | (5,000) | 2.50 | (12,500) |
| Total assets | P105,000 | | $262,500 |
| **Liabilities and shareholders' equity** | | | |
| Accounts payable, current | P 22,000 | 2.50 | $ 55,000 |
| Bonds payable, long-term | 25,000 | 2.50 | 62,500 |
| | 47,000 | | 117,500 |
| Common shares | 50,000 | 2.00 | 100,000 |
| Retained earnings | 8,000 | (below) | 19,200 |
| Cumulative translation gain (loss)* | — | | 25,800 |
| | 58,000 | | 145,000 |
| Total liabilities and shareholders' equity | P105,000 | | $262,500 |

**Statement of Comprehensive Income**
**Year Ended December 31, 20X6**

| | Local currency (pants) | Exchange rate | Translated amounts (C$) |
|---|---|---|---|
| Sales | P 60,000 | 2.40 | $144,000 |
| Cost of sales: | | | |
| Beginning inventory | 20,000 | | |
| Purchases | 30,000 | | |
| Ending inventory | (10,000) | | |
| | 40,000 | 2.40 | 96,000 |
| Gross margin | 20,000 | | 48,000 |
| Operating expenses: | | | |
| Depreciation | 5,000 | 2.40 | 12,000 |
| Interest expense | 3,000 | 2.40 | 7,200 |
| Other expenses | 4,000 | 2.40 | 9,600 |
| | 12,000 | | 28,800 |
| Net income | P 8,000 | | $ 19,200 |
| OCI—20X6 Translation Gain | | | $ 10,800 |
| Comprehensive Income | | | $ 30,000 |

*Cumulative exchange gain:
  2005 gain on P50,000 net investment: P50,000 × ($2.30 − $2.00) = $15,000
  2006 gain on P50,000 net investment: P50,000 × ($2.50 − $2.30) =  10,000
  2006 gain on retained earnings: P8,000 × ($2.50 − $2.40) =      800
  Cumulative translation gain                                  $25,800

On the SCI, all items are translated at the average rate, regardless of the type of revenue or expense, assuming that the revenue and expense accrued evenly through the year. Allocations of past costs, such as depreciation and amortization, are translated the same as are current costs such as interest expense. As a result, the translated amount of net income is also equal to the average rate times the net income as expressed in pants.

The cumulative translation gain of $25,800 that arises under the current-rate method can be broken down into three components:

1. the $15,000 gain arising from the first year's change in the exchange rate from $2.00 to $2.30 (Exhibit 9.3);

2. an additional $10,000 gain in the current year, 20X6, caused by a further increase in the exchange rate from $2.30 to $2.50; and

3. an $800 gain on the retained earnings from the period of their generation (mid-20X6) to the end of 20X6, during which period the exchange rate changed from $2.40 to $2.50.

These components of the cumulative gain are summarized at the bottom of Exhibit 9.6. In addition, the gain for the current year can also be calculated directly by examining the change in net assets for the year. Starting with the beginning of year balance of these net assets, we can add the inflows (usually net income) and subtract the outflows (usually dividends) to arrive at the year-end balance of net assets expressed in pants. We then need only convert each balance or flow at the exchange rate in effect at the time of the balance or flow, and find the difference at year-end between the balance in foreign currency and the derived amount in domestic currency. Such a statement is shown in Exhibit 9.7.

Translation of Forsub Ltd.'s accounts to dollars results in total assets of $262,500, as compared with total liabilities and equities of $262,500. The cumulative translation gain is $25,800. In Exhibit 9.6, the cumulative translation gain can be thought of as a single amount pending disposition. The reason is that when the foreign operation's statements are translated, the translation gain or loss is not part of the statements of the subsidiary, but is an amount that must be allocated or assigned *on the parent's consolidated statements*.

**Exhibit 9.7** Current-Rate Method—Analysis of Cumulative Translation Gain, 20X6

| | Local currency (pants) | Exchange rate | Translated amounts (C$) |
|---|---|---|---|
| Amounts arising in 20X6: | | | |
| Net assets: | | | |
| Balance January 1, 20X6 | P50,000 | 2.30 | $115,000 |
| Changes during 20X6 | | | |
| Net income | 8,000 | 2.40 | 19,200 |
| Dividends | n/a | | — |
| Derived balance | | | 134,200 |
| Actual balance | P58,000 | 2.50 | 145,000 |
| Net translation gain for 20X6 | | | 10,800 |
| Amounts relating to previous periods | | | |
| Gain from 20X5 | | | 15,000 |
| Cumulative translation gain, December 31, 20X6 | | | $ 25,800 |

The consolidation process is straightforward:

- The portion of the cumulative translation gain or loss that relates to *prior years* is included in opening accumulated other comprehensive income.

- The portion of the gain or loss that relates to the *current year* is reported as a separate component of share equity in the consolidated SCI.

For Domestic, the $25,800 year-end 20X6 cumulative translation loss will be reported as follows:

- The $15,000 gain that arose in 20X5 will be included in consolidated accumulated OCI for January 1, 20X6.

- The $10,800 gain pertaining to 20X6 will be reported as other comprehensive income in Domestic's consolidated SCI for the year ended December 31, 20X6.

- As a result, a cumulative translation gain of $25,800 will appear as accumulated translation gains/losses in the equity section of the consolidated SFP at December 31, 20X6.

**Temporal Method**   If, instead, the accounts of Forsub Ltd. are translated by using the temporal method, then the procedure is somewhat more complicated. Exhibit 9.8 illustrates the application of the temporal method for 20X6.

The monetary assets and liabilities are translated by using the current rate. The non-monetary assets are translated at their historical rates. It is assumed that the ending inventory was purchased when the exchange rate was $2.45, and thus that is the historical rate for inventory. The specific historical rate for land is $2.00 and for the equipment is $2.30. The accumulated depreciation must be translated at the same rate as was used for the gross asset cost.

On the SCI, the revenues and expenses are translated at the rates that were in effect at the time that the revenues were realized or the costs were incurred. For many revenue and expense items, realization coincides with recognition, so that the historical rate is essentially the same as the average rate for the period as was used in the current-rate method. Although the result is the same for some SCI items, the concept is quite different.

Under the current-rate method, cost of sales could be translated simply by taking the cost of sales in pants and multiplying it by the average exchange rate for the period. Under the temporal method, however, the cost of sales amount must be derived by multiplying the beginning inventory by its historical rate of $2.00, adding the purchases at the historical/average rate of $2.40, and subtracting the ending inventory at its historical rate of $2.45. The resulting figure for cost of sales, $87,500, *cannot be derived directly by multiplying any exchange rate by the cost of sales in pants, P40,000.*

Similarly, any depreciation or amortization expense must be translated at the exchange rates that existed at the time the original costs were incurred. In this example, the only such expense is the depreciation of the equipment. Since the equipment was purchased when the rate was $2.30, the depreciation expense must be translated at $2.30. Other expenses are translated at the rate that existed when they were *accrued*. It does not matter whether they have been paid in cash. Thus interest expense and other expenses have been translated at the average rate for the year.

The net income that results from using the temporal method amounts to $28,200 before considering any components of the translation loss. This amount cannot be derived directly from the original net income of P8,000—it must be obtained by working

**Exhibit 9.8** Translation by Temporal Method, 20X6

Exchange rate, December 31, 20X6: P1.00 = C$2.50
Average exchange rate for 20X6: P1.00 = C$2.40

### Statement of Financial Position
### December 31, 20X6

| | Local currency (pants) | Exchange rate type* | Exchange rate | Translated amounts (C$) |
|---|---|---|---|---|
| **Assets** | | | | |
| Cash | P 15,000 | C | 2.50 | $ 37,500 |
| Accounts receivable | 15,000 | C | 2.50 | 37,500 |
| Inventory | 10,000 | H | 2.45 | 24,500 |
| Land | 40,000 | H | 2.00 | 80,000 |
| Equipment | 30,000 | H | 2.30 | 69,000 |
| Accumulated depreciation | (5,000) | H | 2.30 | (11,500) |
| Total assets | P105,000 | | | $237,000 |
| **Liabilities and shareholders' equity** | | | | |
| Accounts payable, current | P 22,000 | C | 2.50 | $ 55,000 |
| Bonds payable, long-term | 25,000 | C | 2.50 | 62,500 |
| | 47,000 | | | 117,500 |
| Common shares | 50,000 | H | 2.00 | 100,000 |
| Retained earnings—Operations | 8,000 | | | 28,200 |
| Retained earnings—Cumulative translation gain (loss) [Exhibit 9.9] | | | | (8,700) |
| | 58,000 | | | 119,500 |
| Total liabilities and shareholders' equity | P105,000 | | | $237,000 |

### Statement of Comprehensive Income
### Year Ended December 31, 20X6

| | Local currency (pants) | Exchange rate type* | Exchange rate | Translated amounts (C$) |
|---|---|---|---|---|
| Sales | P 60,000 | H/A | 2.40 | $144,000 |
| Cost of sales: | | | | |
| Beginning inventory | 20,000 | H | 2.00 | 40,000 |
| Purchases | 30,000 | H/A | 2.40 | 72,000 |
| Ending inventory | (10,000) | H | 2.45 | (24,500) |
| | 40,000 | | | 87,500 |
| Gross margin | 20,000 | | | 56,500 |
| Operating expenses: | | | | |
| Depreciation | 5,000 | H | 2.30 | 11,500 |
| Interest expense | 3,000 | H/A | 2.40 | 7,200 |
| Other expenses | 4,000 | H/A | 2.40 | 9,600 |
| | 12,000 | | | 28,300 |
| Net income before translation loss | P 8,000 | | | 28,200 |
| 20X6 translation loss | | | | (5,700) |
| Net income | | | | $ 22,500 |

*Exchange rate types:
  C   = current, year-end rate
  H   = historical rate for the individual item
  H/A = historical rate, assumed to be the average for the year

through the SCI and translating all of its individual components by the appropriate historical rates. Note that the temporal method net income of $28,200 is quite different from the current-rate method net income of $19,200. This difference is due to the lags in expense recognition of two types of costs: inventory and depreciable capital assets.

Translation of Forsub Ltd.'s accounts to dollars results in total assets of $237,000, and total liabilities and equities of $237,000. The cumulative translation loss included in total liabilities and equities is $8,700. In Exhibit 9.8, the cumulative translation loss is shown as a single amount pending disposition, separate from retained earnings from operations. The reason is that when the foreign operation's statements are translated, the translation gain or loss is not part of the statements of the subsidiary, but is an amount that must be allocated or assigned *on the parent's consolidated statements*.

### Allocating the Accumulated Translation Loss—Temporal Method

We know from Exhibit 9.1 that $3,000 of the $8,700 cumulative translation loss arose in 20X5, and therefore that the loss arising in 20X6 must be the remainder, or $5,700.

The gain or loss from holding monetary assets and liabilities can be computed by analyzing the flow of these items. Unlike the bonds payable in this example, monetary assets and liabilities may not be constant throughout the year. The impact of the exchange gains and losses must be measured only for the period of time that the current monetary items are in the enterprise.

For example, sales revenue increased monetary assets, either as cash or as accounts receivable, by P60,000. Assuming that the sales were even throughout the year, we can measure the gain from holding monetary assets resulting from the sales by multiplying the P60,000 by the change in the exchange rate from the average for the year ($2.40) to the end of the year ($2.50). Similarly, the current expenses (or expenditures) that caused either a decline in monetary assets or an increase in monetary liabilities must be taken into account.

The easiest way, however, to measure the net gain or loss from the monetary assets and liabilities is to construct a funds-flow statement, with funds defined as net monetary assets. Starting with the beginning-of-year balance of these net monetary assets, we can add the inflows and subtract the outflows to arrive at the year-end balance of net monetary assets expressed in pants. We then need only to convert each balance or flow at the exchange rate in effect at the time of the balance or flow, and find the difference at year-end between the balance in foreign currency and the derived amount in domestic currency.

Such a funds-flow statement is shown at the top of Exhibit 9.9. The ending balance in pants is a P17,000 net monetary liability, as can be verified by referring to Exhibit 9.5. The year-end balance is equivalent to a $42,500 net monetary liability at the SFP date. The sum of the inflows and outflows, however, when translated at the rates in effect during the year, amounts to a $36,800 net monetary liability.

In effect, the $36,800 shows what the ending balance of the net monetary liabilities would have been if Domestic Corporation had maintained all of its Pantanian balances in dollars rather than in pants, and had converted to and from dollars only on the transaction dates. Since the actual dollar-equivalent balance of the accounts in pants is $42,500, Domestic Corporation has suffered a loss of $5,700 by having Forsub Ltd. hold balances in pants.

The remainder of Exhibit 9.9 summarizes the remaining amounts included in the $8,700 cumulative translation loss at December 31, 20X6. As we stated above, a total of $3,000 of the loss pertains to 20X5, while the remaining loss of $5,700 pertains to 20X6.

When Domestic Corporation consolidates Forsub Ltd., the total cumulative translation loss of $8,700 must be included somewhere in Domestic's consolidated financial statements. The temporal method is intended to yield the same result as if Domestic had carried out the foreign transactions directly. Therefore, the *translation* loss must be reported in Domestic's consolidated statements in a way that duplicates the treatment of gains and losses from foreign-currency *transactions*.

The consolidation process is quite straightforward:

■ The portion of the cumulative translation gain or loss that relates to *prior years* is included in opening consolidated retained earnings.

■ The portion of the gain or loss that relates to the *current year* is reported in the consolidated SCI, along with any foreign-currency gains and losses of the parent.

For Domestic, the $8,700 year-end 20X6 cumulative translation loss will be reported as follows:

■ The $3,000 loss that arose in 20X5 will be included in consolidated retained earnings for January 1, 20X6.

■ The $5,700 loss pertaining to 20X6 will be reported as an expense (i.e., foreign exchange loss) in Domestic's consolidated SCI for the year ended December 31, 20X6.

**Additional Considerations**  The discussion above implicitly assumed a 100%-owned, parent-founded subsidiary. Additional considerations arise when a subsidiary is purchased (see OLP 9-1 for a comprehensive example that addresses these considerations). The question arises as to how to handle the goodwill and fair value adjustments that arise when a subsidiary is purchased. Given that these items are most properly viewed as assets

**Exhibit 9.9** Temporal Method—Analysis of Cumulative Translation Loss, 20X6

| | Local currency (pants) | Exchange rate | Translated amounts (C$) |
|---|---|---|---|
| **Amounts arising in 20X6:** | | | |
| Monetary items: | | | |
| Balance January 1, 20X6 | P(10,000) | 2.30 | $ (23,000) |
| Changes during 20X6 | | | |
| Sales revenue | P 60,000 | 2.40 | 144,000 |
| Inventory purchases | (30,000) | 2.40 | (72,000) |
| Interest expense | (3,000) | 2.40 | (7,200) |
| Other expenses | (4,000) | 2.40 | (9,600) |
| Purchase of equipment | (30,000) | 2.30 | (69,000) |
| Derived balance | | | (36,800) |
| Actual balance | P(17,000) | 2.50 | (42,500) |
| Net translation loss for 20X6 | | | 5,700 |
| **Amounts relating to previous periods** | | | |
| Loss from 20X5 on monetary items | | | 3,000 |
| **Cumulative translation loss, December 31, 20X6** | | | $ 8,700 |

and liabilities of the subsidiary and not the parent, then the solution is relatively simple. If the items would be translated at the historical rate on the SFP of the subsidiary, then the historical rate is used to translate the fair value adjustments or goodwill, and no additional translation gains and losses will occur. If, however, the items are translated at the year-end current rate (i.e., closing rate) on the subsidiary's SFP, then a translation gain or loss is calculated; it is treated in a manner similar to our earlier discussions of translation gains and losses.

The appropriate historical rate for purchased subsidiaries is the historical rate from the consolidated entity's perspective. For an item on the subsidiary's financial statements at the date of the acquisition, the historical rate is the exchange rate on date of acquisition; it is not the exchange rate on the date the subsidiary acquired the item. For items acquired subsequent to the date of acquisition by the subsidiary, the historical exchange rate is the rate on the date of acquisition because this rate is also the historical rate from the consolidated entity's perspective.

The presence of a non-controlling interest presents no particular difficulties. The non-controlling interest is assigned its share of any translation gains and losses whether related to the translation of the financial statements of the subsidiary or to the translation of the fair value adjustments and goodwill.

## Comparison of Accounting Implications

Exhibit 9.10 compares the reporting implications of using the current-rate or temporal method. The decision to use a particular translation method will depend on the functional currency of the entity. The translation method used, in turn, will decide (1) whether the

**Exhibit 9.10** Comparison of Methods for Translating Foreign Operations

|  | Current-Rate Method | Temporal Method |
|---|---|---|
| When to use | Use when presentation currency differs from functional currency | Use when functional currency differs from currency in which accounts are maintained |
| Extent of accounting exposure | Net asset position (usually) or net liability position | Net monetary & non-monetary items carried at fair value (most often a net liability position) |
| Most likely translation gain/loss: |  |  |
| If foreign currency is strengthening | Exchange gain | Exchange loss |
| If foreign currency is weakening | Exchange loss | Exchange gain |
| Accounting treatment of gain/loss: |  |  |
| Arising from previous years | Report in equity | Include in opening consolidated retained earnings |
| Arising in the current year | Report in consolidated other comprehensive income | Report in consolidated net income |
| Indication of true economic exchange risk exposure? | No relationship | No relationship |

translation effect will be a gain or a loss and (2) how that gain or loss will be reported in the parent's consolidated financial statements.

Remember, however, that the accounting exposure does not reflect the economic exposure. There is no necessary relationship between the direction of change in a foreign currency and its impact on the economic contribution of the foreign operation to its parent's welfare.

### Concept Check 9-5

1. Explain briefly how the translation gain or loss can be calculated directly when the current-rate method is being used.

2. How would revenue be translated under the current-rate method and the temporal method? How would unearned revenue be translated under both methods?

## 9.7 ACCOUNTING STANDARDS FOR PRIVATE ENTERPRISES

Canadian private-entity accounting standards use the same two methods of translating financial statements as IFRS—the temporal method and the current-rate method. However, there are differences:

- Canadian standards do not use the concept of functional currency to determine which method to use. Instead they look at the nature of the foreign operation's relationship to its parent—the foreign operation is either integrated with the parent or is independent of the parent (i.e., self-sustaining). Integrated operations use the temporal method to translate their financial statements and self-sustaining operations use the current-rate method.

- The factors used to determine whether an operation is either integrated or self-sustaining are similar to the factors used to determine the functional currency of an operation. As a result, it is unlikely that there will be major translation differences for most foreign operations under ASPE as compared with IFRS.

- There is no statement of comprehensive income for Canadian private enterprises, and thus no such category as "other comprehensive income" in which to report translation gains or losses. The translation gains or losses on "self-sustaining" operations (i.e., using the current-rate method) flow directly into the "cumulative translation gains/losses" separate component of shareholders' equity, and therefore will appear on the statement of changes in equity.

- The translation of financial statements for operations in highly inflationary environments is also different for private enterprises. ASPE recommends the use of the temporal method for translating these operations and does not allow the adjustment of the foreign operation's financial statements for changes in the general price level of the foreign country.

## Relevant Standards

### IASB

**IAS 21** The Effects of Changes in Foreign Exchange Rates
**IAS 29** Financial Reporting in Hyperinflationary Economies

### ASPE

**Section 1651** Foreign Currency Translation

## 9.8 SUMMARY OF KEY POINTS

1. A foreign operation is a subsidiary based in a country other than the parent's home country. The separate-entity financial statements of the foreign operation normally will be stated in terms of the host country's local currency. To prepare consolidated financial statements, the subsidiary's foreign-currency statements must be translated into the currency of the consolidated entity (normally Canadian dollars). **LO 1**

2. There are two methods for translating foreign operations: the temporal method and the current-rate method. The temporal method translates all monetary assets and liabilities at the exchange rate at the SFP date, known as the current rate or closing rate. Non-monetary assets and liabilities are translated at historical rates, except for those that are carried at fair value. For fair-valued non-monetary assets, the rate at the date on which such fair value is determined is used under IFRS. The temporal method achieves the same translated amounts as would have arisen if the parent corporation had carried out the foreign operations directly, as a series of foreign-currency transactions, instead of through a foreign subsidiary. **LO 1**

3. The current-rate method translates all assets and liabilities at the current rate. For the SFP, current rate is the closing exchange rate at the fiscal year-end. For the SCI, the current rate usually is the average rate for the reporting period. **LO 1**

4. In a world of fluctuating exchange rates, all translation methods will yield a translation gain or loss. The gain or loss that arises from the translation is not a real economic gain or loss, however. Accounting gains and losses are the result of the *accounting exposure* to foreign-currency fluctuations, and are a mechanical result of the translation method used. **LO 2**

5. Economic exposure to foreign-currency fluctuations is the result of real economic impacts on the foreign subsidiary's operations, and cannot be measured by accounting methodologies. Any correspondence between accounting exposure and economic exposure is purely coincidental. **LO 2**

6. Translation gains and losses can be accorded (1) immediate recognition; (2) limited recognition in accordance with the treatment given to *transaction* gains and losses; or (3) deferred recognition. Immediate recognition of all translation gains and losses has been tried (in the United States) and subsequently rejected. The two remaining methods are both in use, even though they give diametrically opposed results. The limited recognition approach is applied to foreign operations that have the same functional currency as the parent. The deferral approach is used for foreign operations that have a different functional currency from the parent. **LO 3**

7. The IFRS defines functional currency as the currency of the primary economic environment in which the entity operates, which is normally the environment in which it generates and expends cash. If the functional currency of the subsidiary is the same as the parent's, and if the foreign subsidiary's transactions have been recorded in a currency other than the functional currency, then the goal will be to re-measure them in terms of the functional currency. If the subsidiary is operating in the same economic environment as the parent, the results should be the same as if the parent had engaged in the transactions. This is best accomplished by the temporal method. **LO 4**

8. If the currency of the primary economic environment in which the foreign subsidiary operates is a foreign currency, then that foreign currency will be the functional currency of the subsidiary. There will be no need to re-measure the transactions, but the statements will still need to be translated to Canadian dollars before they can be consolidated. The current-rate method is used to translate these statements. **LO 4**

9. Using the temporal method, the items in the SCI of a subsidiary are translated using the historical rates for all items. For many items the historical rate is essentially the same as the average rate for the period. Using the current-rate method, IFRS recommends the use of exchange rates at the dates of the transactions. For practical reasons, the items in the SCI of a subsidiary are translated using an average rate that approximates the relevant exchange rates for the period. **LO 5**

10. The treatment of the translation gain or loss depends on whether the foreign operation has the same functional currency as the parent. If it has the same functional currency as the parent (i.e., the temporal method is being used), the translation gain or loss is reported in the consolidated statements in net income—that is, in a manner that is consistent with reporting foreign-currency transactions. **LO 5**

11. If the foreign operation has a different functional currency from the parent (i.e., the current-rate method is being used), the annual translation gain or loss is reported as an item of other comprehensive income in the consolidated SCI under IFRS and in the statement of changes in equity under ASPE. The cumulative translation gain or loss is reported as a separate component of shareholders' equity under both IFRS and ASPE. **LO 5**

---

**Visit the text's website at** www.pearsoned.ca/beechy **for practice quizzes, additional problems, Excel® templates, answers to Concept Check questions, and important IFRS updates.**

# Self-Study Problems

1. Early in 20X1, Irene Corporation established a subsidiary in Simonia. The subsidiary was named Gordon Limited, and Irene's investment was $1,250,000. When this investment was translated into Simonian frasers (SF), the currency of Simonia, the initial capitalization amounted to SF500,000.

    Gordon Limited negotiated a three-year bank loan of SF200,000 from a Simonian bank when the exchange rate was 2.40. The company purchased depreciable capital assets for SF600,000 (exchange rate = 2.30).

    The company then began operations. Due to an accumulation of cash through operations, Gordon invested SF200,000 in land during 20X2. The exchange rate at the time of the investment was 1.90. At the end of 20X2, Gordon's comparative SFP and SCI are as shown in Exhibit 9.11. Assume that any dividends are declared and paid at year-end.

**Exhibit 9.11** Gordon Limited

## Statement of Comprehensive Income
### Years Ended December 31

|  | 20X2 | 20X1 |
|---|---|---|
| Revenue | SF300,000 | SF220,000 |
| Depreciation expense | 60,000 | 60,000 |
| Interest expense | 40,000 | 40,000 |
| Other expenses | 120,000 | 80,000 |
|  | 220,000 | 180,000 |
| Net income | SF 80,000 | SF 40,000 |

## Statement of Financial Position
### December 31

|  | 20X2 | 20X1 |
|---|---|---|
| **Assets** |  |  |
| Cash | SF 30,000 | SF160,000 |
| Accounts receivable | 40,000 | 30,000 |
| Land | 200,000 | — |
| Tangible capital assets | 600,000 | 600,000 |
| Accumulated depreciation | (120,000) | (60,000) |
| Total assets | SF750,000 | SF730,000 |
| **Liabilities and shareholders' equity** |  |  |
| Accounts payable, current | SF 10,000 | SF 20,000 |
| Notes payable, due January 1, 20X4 | 200,000 | 200,000 |
|  | 210,000 | 220,000 |
| Common shares | 500,000 | 500,000 |
| Retained earnings | 40,000 | 10,000 |
|  | 540,000 | 510,000 |
| Total liabilities and shareholders' equity | SF750,000 | SF730,000 |

Other exchange rate information for the Simonian fraser is as follows:

| | |
|---|---|
| 20X1 average | 2.20 |
| 20X1 year-end | 2.00 |
| 20X2 average | 1.70 |
| 20X2 year-end | 1.50 |

**Required**

Assume that Gordon Limited's functional currency is the Simonian fraser. Determine how the financial statement amounts shown in Gordon's SFP and SCI will affect Irene Corporation's consolidated statements for *each* of 20X1 and 20X2, including disposition of the cumulative translation gain or loss.

2.  Refer to the information in Problem 9.1 above and Exhibit 9.11. Assume instead that Gordon Limited's functional currency is the Canadian dollar.

**Required**

  **a.** Translate Gordon's 20X1 financial statements.

  **b.** Determine the amount of translation gain or loss for 20X1.

  **c.** Translate Gordon's 20X2 financial statements.

  **d.** Determine the amount of translation gain or loss for 20X2.

# Review Questions

1.  Distinguish between foreign-currency *transactions* and foreign-currency *operations*.

2.  Explain the differences between these two translation methods:
    **a.** temporal; and
    **b.** current-rate.

3.  Which translation method views the foreign subsidiary's operations as though they were foreign-currency transactions of the parent?

4.  Why is the common share account of a foreign subsidiary translated at the historical rate under both translation methods?

5.  What is meant by the *accounting exposure* of a foreign operation? How is the accounting exposure measured?

6.  How does the accounting exposure under the temporal method differ from the accounting exposure under the current-rate method?

7.  For a given foreign operation for a given accounting period, is it possible for the accounting exposure under the temporal method to result in a translation loss, while the accounting exposure under the current-rate method results in a translation gain? Explain.

8.  Define *economic exposure*. Distinguish between economic exposure and accounting exposure.

9.  Forop Ltd. is a foreign subsidiary of Domop Inc. Domop's accounting exposure to exchange rate changes when translating the accounts of Forop is a substantial net liability exposure. Domop's management expects the foreign currency in which Forop operates to increase in value relative to the Canadian dollar; such an increase will result in a large

translation loss. The management of Domop proposes to enter into a forward contract to receive an equivalent amount of foreign currency to hedge against the potential translation loss. Would you recommend that Domop's management follow their proposed course of action? Explain.

10. What is meant by the term *functional currency*?

11. What translation method is recommended for foreign operations with the same functional currency as the parent? Why is this method recommended?

12. What recommendation is made regarding the financial statement disposition of translation gains or losses for foreign operations with the same functional currency as the parent? Why?

13. How can management determine the functional currency of a foreign operation?

14. Mammoth Corporation has subsidiaries in 13 different countries, operating in 10 different currencies. Do all 13 have to be viewed the same way? Explain.

15. What translation method is recommended for foreign operations with a different functional currency from the parent?

16. Under the current-rate method, why are the revenue and expense accounts translated at average exchange rates, rather than at the closing rate at the SFP date?

17. How does the translation of cost of goods sold differ between the current-rate method and the temporal method?

18. How does the translation of depreciation and amortization differ under the current-rate method as compared with the temporal method?

19. Explain how the translation gain or loss on monetary items can be computed. Is the amount of gain or loss affected by the translation method used?

20. What is the impact of hyperinflation on the translation method for a foreign operation with a functional currency different from its parent?

## 9.10 CASES

## CASE 9-1 GLOBAL CORP.

Global Corp. is a large, publicly traded firm headquartered in Toronto. The company has substantial Canadian operations and is also invested in a number of businesses in different countries around the world. The functional currency of Global, the parent company, is the Canadian dollar, and the presentation currency of the consolidated entity is also the Canadian dollar.

One Global investment is Indogold Inc., an Indonesian gold producer. The gold produced is priced and sold in US dollars. Approximately 50% of its costs for supplies and labour are denominated in the Indonesian rupiah, 40% of its costs for supplies and labour are denominated in US dollars, and the remaining 10% are depreciation charges related to monies spent to acquire and develop the property.

Global also has oil drilling and producing operations in Canada. Global acquired its drilling equipment in Germany. To finance the purchase, Global created a structured entity (SE) in Germany. Global lent the SE the euros it required to finance the purchase of the equipment. The SE has no direct employees or management, and all the directors are Global employees.

Global has an investment in Northern Patriots, a US company that sells products imported from Global. The products are sold in the northeastern United States at prices determined by local competition. Northern Patriots's costs are also determined locally, except for the products it sells, which are costed in Canadian dollars. Global financed the subsidiary with a small equity investment and a substantial long-term Canadian dollar loan. Northern Patriots pays all excess funds to Global via intercompany dividends.

Global also invested a substantial sum of Japanese yen in East Asia Holdings Corporation. East Asia in turn invested the monies into Japan Manufacturing, a company that operates in Japan. Japan Manufacturing acquires all of its materials and labour from sources in Japan and sells all of its manufactured goods in Japan. The management of Japan Manufacturing is responsible for obtaining any future financing and makes all dividend decisions. East Asia Holdings acts only as a holding company and remits all dividends to Global.

### Required

What are the functional currencies of the five entities described above? Discuss the factors that you considered in making your decision and specify any additional information that you would like to have.

# CASE 9-2 ELITE DISTRIBUTORS LIMITED

Elite Distributors Limited is a Canadian public company that has been undergoing rapid expansion. The company is based in a major Canadian seaport, and several years ago found it necessary to open a sales office in the United States to transact business directly in that country.

Elite also has a wholly owned subsidiary, located in Singapore, that manufactures one of the main products that Elite sells in Canada. Substantially all of the Singapore subsidiary's sales are to Elite. There is a second (80%-owned) subsidiary in the Republic of Ireland that was acquired in an attempt to diversify. This company sells exclusively through its own sales offices throughout northern Europe and has very few transactions with Elite, except for the regular payment of dividends.

### Required

Recommend the appropriate accounting policies for Elite to follow with respect to each of these foreign operations. Support your recommendations.

[SMA, adapted]

# CASE 9-3 CARE INC.

Care Inc. (CI), a national manufacturer and retailer of women's shoes, purchased 100% of the common shares of ShoeCo, a footwear manufacturing company located in a foreign country. CI financed the purchase of ShoeCo's shares through a loan from a Canadian bank. To obtain this financing, CI had to offer one of its Canadian manufacturing plants as security. ShoeCo will continue to be managed and operated by locals and be responsible for obtaining operational loans.

ShoeCo sells most of its production to its domestic market. Previously a supplier of CI's, ShoeCo will continue to supply about 10% of its production to CI. CI has established a contract with ShoeCo that guarantees both a minimum quantity and a fixed price in Canadian dollars.

### Required

1. What is ShoeCo's functional currency? Explain how you reached your conclusion.

2. Describe both the temporal and current-rate translation methods. Which method would CI use?

[CICA]

# CASE 9-4 MULTI-COMMUNICATIONS LTD.

Multi-Communications Ltd. (MCL) is a Montreal-based public company with operations throughout North America. Its core business is communications media, including newspapers, radio, television, and cable. The company's year-end is December 31.

You, CA, have recently joined MCL's reporting office as a finance director, reporting to the chief financial officer, Robert Allen. It is October 20X8. Mr. Allen has asked you to prepare a report discussing the accounting and auditing issues that may arise with the auditors during their visit in November.

MCL's growth in 20X8 was achieved through expansion into the United States by acquiring a number of newspaper, television, and cable operations. Since the US side of MCL's operations is now significant, management will be reporting its financial statements in US dollars. Shareholders' equity at the beginning of the period was $220 million, including a separately disclosed cumulative foreign exchange gain of $45 million. Management merged this balance with retained earnings because "the operations it relates to are no longer considered foreign for accounting purposes, and as a result no foreign-currency exposure will arise."

With recent trends in international free trade, MCL decided to position itself for future expansion into the South American market. Therefore, in 20X8 MCL bought a company that owns a radio network in a country in South America that has high inflation. MCL was willing to incur losses in the start-up since it was confident that in the long run it would be profitable.

The government's objectives are to open the country's borders to trade and to lower its inflation rate. The government was rather reluctant to let a foreign company purchase such a powerful communication tool. In exchange for the right to buy the network, MCL agreed, among other conditions, not to promote any political party, to broadcast only pre-approved public messages, and to let the government examine its books at the government's convenience. Management has recorded its investment in the books using the cost method.

In 20X8, MCL acquired a conglomerate, Peter Holdings (PH), which held substantial assets in the communications business. Over the past three months, MCL has sold off 80% of PH's non–communications-related businesses. In the current month, MCL sold PH's hotel and recreational property business for $175 million, realizing a gain of $22 million ($14.5 million after tax). The assets related to the non-communications businesses were scattered throughout the United States, and MCL lacked the industry expertise to value them accurately. Management therefore found it difficult to determine the net realizable value of each of these assets at the time PH was acquired.

In 20X8, MCL decided to rationalize its television operations. Many of PH's acquisitions in the television business included stations in areas already being served by other stations operated by MCL. MCL systematically identified stations that were duplicating services and did not fit with MCL's long-range objectives. These assets have been segregated on the SFP and classified as current. The company anticipates generating a gain on the disposal of the entire pool of assets, although losses are anticipated on some of the individual stations. Operating results are capitalized in the pool. Once a particular station is sold, the resulting gain or loss is reflected in income.

*Case Continued >*

Nine stations are in the pool at the present time. In 20X8, three were sold, resulting in gains of $65,000 after tax. Losses are expected to occur on several of the remaining stations. Although serious negotiations with prospective buyers are not underway at present, the company hopes to have disposed of them by early 20X9. To facilitate the sale of these assets, MCL is considering taking back mortgages.

In 20X8, MCL estimated the fair market value of its intangible assets at $250 million. Included as intangibles are newspaper and magazine circulation lists, cable subscriber lists, and broadcast licences. Some of these assets have been acquired through the purchase of existing businesses; others have been generated internally by operations that have been part of MCL for decades.

Amounts paid for intangibles are not difficult to determine; however, it has taken MCL staff some time to determine the costs of internally generated intangibles. To increase subscriptions for print and electronic media, MCL spends heavily on subscription drives by way of advertisements, cold calls, and free products. For the non-acquired intangibles, MCL staff have examined the accounting records for the past 10 years and have identified expenditures totalling $35 million that were expensed in prior years. These costs relate to efforts to expand customer bases. In addition, independent appraisers have determined the fair market value of these internally generated intangibles to be in the range of $60 million to $80 million. To be conservative, management has decided to reflect these intangibles on the December 31, 20X8, SFP at $60 million.

The market values of companies in the communications industry have been escalating in the past few years, indicating that the value of the underlying assets (largely intangibles) is increasing over time. MCL management stated that these licences do not lose any value, and in this industry, actually increase in value over time.

MCL has invested in the installation of fibre optic cable, which can transmit far more, far faster than conventional cable. The cost of the cable itself is negligible. MCL will be using it for transmission between its stations in two major Canadian cities. MCL needed only six cables to link all its television and radio stations between the two cities, but it decided to put in 36 cables since it was doing the digging anyway. To date, MCL has sold six cables and charges a monthly fee to new owners to cover their share of maintenance expenses. MCL is leasing 10 other cables for 15-year periods.

Required

Prepare the report.

[CICA]

## CASE 9-5 JOHNSTON CO. LTD.

Johnston Co. Ltd. is a medium-sized Canadian company, incorporated in 20X1; its shares are traded on the Toronto Stock Exchange. The company began operations as a processor and distributor of frozen herbs, but quickly branched out until it provided a full line of Canadian specialty foods under the Johnston name. Some of these products were processed by Johnston itself, while others were processed for Johnston by other Canadian companies under contract.

The company's strategic plan calls for steady growth in sales and earnings. Accordingly, expansion into the lucrative United States market in 20X7 is under serious consideration. A major concern is fluctuations in the exchange rate between the Canadian and American dollars; various analysts have given the company quite substantially different forecasts regarding the long-term exchange rate outlook.

Johnston is considering two different proposals. The first involves setting up sales offices in the United States with orders filled from Johnston's Canadian warehouses. The sales offices would be responsible for sales, billing, and collections. All transactions would be in US dollars.

Alternatively, Johnston is considering establishing a wholly owned subsidiary in the United States to process and distribute a full line of specialty foods. It has not yet determined how the company would finance the purchase of the plant and equipment for this subsidiary.

The president has asked you, the controller, to prepare a report for possible use at a meeting of the board of directors. Specifically, he wants you to recommend which of the above proposals is preferable with respect to the impact of each on current and future income. He wants you to fully support your recommendation and to limit your discussion to foreign-currency translation issues, ignoring hedging and income tax considerations.

## Required

Prepare the report for the president.

[SMA, adapted]

# CASE 9-6 BUY CARTIER LTD.

Buy Cartier Ltd. (BCL) is a Canadian public company that operates primarily in the commercial and recreational transportation sector. Worldwide, the commercial transportation business is growing strongly, fuelled in part by rapid rates of urbanization. Traffic congestion, pollution, and commuting times are rising in major cities. Rail transportation represents an efficient, cost-effective solution to these problems. Analysts expect that the global passenger rail equipment market will grow at a compounded annual rate of more than 5%. Constraints on government's ability to finance new transportation systems have resulted in the contracting of services to private companies such as BCL.

BCL has three divisions. The rail and transit operation offers a full range of urban, suburban, and intercity vehicles, as well as complete rail transit systems. The recreational products division designs, builds, and distributes personal recreational transportation vehicles such as snowmobiles and watercraft. The capital services division oversees the financing activities for the company and provides secured financing for customer purchases of recreational product inventories and railcar leasing and management services for commercial customers.

Despite an uneasy economy, BCL has expanded its operations considerably in fiscal year 20X5. This expansion is consistent with management's published objective to double the corporation's revenues, profits, and earnings per share over the next five years.

*Case Continued >*

*Case Continued >*

It is now June 20X5, and BCL's fiscal year ends on September 30. You, CA, have recently accepted the position of assistant to the chief financial officer of BCL, Dave Butler. Your duties at BCL include overseeing the external reporting process and coordinating the external audit function.

BCL is an audit client of Rankin & Rankin (R&R), your previous employer. Mr. Butler has scheduled a meeting with the R&R audit partner and manager. In preparation for this meeting, Mr. Butler has asked you to prepare a report that discusses the major accounting and audit issues that might arise during the meeting with respect to the rail and transit division. Mr. Butler has provided you with information about new developments in this division (see Exhibit A). Mr. Butler would also like to know what information should be gathered to help the audit go as smoothly as possible. He is hopeful that your previous experience as an auditor at R&R will help reduce disagreements (which have been a problem between management and the auditors) and the current year's audit fee.

**Required**

Prepare your report for Mr. Butler.

---

### Exhibit A

### CURRENT ACTIVITIES IN RAIL AND TRANSIT DIVISION

1. On May 1, 20X5, BCL announced that it had signed an agreement to purchase all of the shares of Alltrans Rail Systems Inc., a US transportation company, for US$300 million (approximately C$500 million). A summary of the SFP items of Alltrans at April 30, 20X5 (in thousands of US$), is as follows:

| Assets | |
|---|---:|
| Receivables | $ 80,500 |
| Inventories | 100,200 |
| Capital assets | 500,100 |
| Goodwill | 20,000 |
| Other assets | 50,000 |
| | $750,800 |
| **Liabilities** | |
| Short-term borrowings | $ 20,500 |
| Accounts payable and accrued liabilities | 62,300 |
| Long-term debt | 330,000 |
| Deferred income taxes | 80,200 |
| | $493,000 |

Alltrans has a contract with a US city to provide inter-city bus transit until December 1, 20X9. To ensure adequate continuation of services, key members of

Alltrans have been retained under management contracts, which provide bonuses for the next two years based on Alltrans' operating results. The fiscal year-end of Alltrans is June 30. Management of Alltrans does not want to change the year-end and wishes to retain its current auditors, Patterson & Cole.

The Alltrans purchase is the single largest acquisition in BCL's history. As a result of this acquisition, US operations are now the largest part of BCL's global operations. Management has decided to report its financial statements in US dollars. The existing cumulative foreign exchange gain on other US operations of $16 million was transferred to retained earnings because reporting in US dollars means there is no longer any exposure to the Canadian/US dollar exchange rate.

2. In accordance with its intention to position itself in the growing international markets, BCL incorporated a company in Peru, called Transcom SA. The intent is to develop a citywide transit system in this South American country's capital city, Lima. To secure government approval and licences for the system, BCL agreed to invest C$50 million in the company. The government has agreed to provide subsidies for the purchase of the transit vehicles. These subsidies will become repayable if Transcom SA does not meet government-imposed quotas for hiring local employees to service the rail system.

BCL engineers will design the transit system, and BCL will provide the transit vehicles. BCL engineers have been seconded to oversee the design stage of the project. The engineers are working with local government officials, and construction of the rail system and manufacture of the transit vehicles is expected to commence in February 20X6. The local government must approve all stages of the rail system design and will also approve the design of the transit vehicles. Once the system is complete, Transcom SA will operate it; however, the services provided would be rate-regulated by local government. The local government will also approve transit schedules. BCL agreed to allow government officials to review all books and records of Transcom SA at the convenience of the government. BCL expects that Transcom SA will incur losses in the start-up of the operations. Management of BCL has recorded its $50 million investment in Transcom SA using the cost method.

[ICAO adapted]

## Problems

**P9-1 (30 minutes, easy)**

Crete Ltd. is a foreign subsidiary of a Canadian parent and is located in the country of Hatos. The SFP accounts of Crete are as follows, stated in hats (H):

| | |
|---|---|
| Cash | H 40,000 |
| Accounts receivable | 20,000 |
| Inventory (at market) | 120,000 |
| Capital assets | 400,000 |
| Accumulated depreciation | (160,000) |
| Long-term note receivable | 100,000 |
| Total assets | H520,000 |
| Accounts and notes payable | H 80,000 |
| Bonds payable | 300,000 |
| Common shares | 140,000 |
| Total liabilities and equities | H520,000 |

### Additional Information

1. Crete Ltd. is wholly owned by Gialea Corp. Gialea established Crete when the hat was worth $1.10.
2. The capital assets were purchased when the hat was worth $1.30.
3. The bonds payable were issued when the hat was worth $1.25.
4. The long-term note receivable arose when the hat was worth $1.40.
5. The inventory was purchased when the hat was worth $1.50.
6. The current exchange rate for the hat is $1.60.

### Required

a. Translate the SFP accounts of Crete Ltd. into Canadian dollars, using each of the following methods:
    i) current-rate; and
    ii) temporal.

   In each case, treat the translation gain or loss as a single, balancing figure.

b. For each method, calculate the:
    i) accounting exposure; and
    ii) additional gain or loss that would result if the exchange rate one year hence were 1.85, assuming no change in the SFP accounts in hats.

## P9-2 (15 minutes, easy)

The SCI for 20X3 for Hilary Co., expressed in Coker francs (CF), is as follows:

| | |
|---|---:|
| Sales revenue | CF3,000,000 |
| Cost of goods sold: | |
| Beginning inventory | 200,000 |
| Purchases | 1,000,000 |
| | 1,200,000 |
| Ending inventory | 400,000 |
| | 800,000 |
| Depreciation | 300,000 |
| Other operating expenses | 900,000 |
| Interest expense | 200,000 |
| Total expenses | 2,200,000 |
| Net income | CF 800,000 |

Hilary Co. is 100% owned by Bryan Inc., a Canadian corporation.

Sales revenue, purchases of inventory, and operating expenses (except depreciation) all occurred evenly through the year. Interest expense accrued throughout the year, but was all paid at the end of the year. The beginning inventory was purchased on October 1, 20X2, when the exchange rate was 0.74; the ending inventory was purchased on November 1, 20X3, when the exchange rate was 0.85. The capital assets were acquired when the exchange rate was 0.62. Other exchange rate information is as follows:

| | |
|---|---|
| December 31, 20X2 | 0.77 |
| Average for 20X3 | 0.82 |
| December 31, 20X3 | 0.87 |

### Required

Translate the SCI into Canadian dollars, using the:

**a.** current-rate method; and

**b.** temporal method.

## P9-3 (40 minutes, medium)

Investco Ltd. is a Canadian real estate and property developer that decided to hold a parcel of land in downtown Munich, Germany, for speculative purposes. The land, costing €12,000,000, was financed by a five-year bond (€9,000,000), which is repayable in euros, and an initial equity injection by Investco of €3,000,000. These transactions took place on January 1, 20X5, at which time a German subsidiary company was created to hold the investment. Investco plans to sell the land at the end of five years and use the euro proceeds to pay off the bond. In the interim, rent is being collected from another company, which is using the land as a parking lot.

The 20X5 year-end draft financial statements of the German subsidiary company are shown below (assume that rental revenue is collected and interest and other expenses are paid at the end of each month).

```
                        German Subsidiary
                  Statement of Comprehensive Income
                          For the Year Ended
                         December 31, 20X5
```

| | | |
|---|---:|---:|
| Rental revenue | | € 1,000,000 |
| Interest expense | € 990,000 | |
| Other expenses | 10,000 | 1,000,000 |
| Net income | | €        0 |

```
                    Statement of Financial Position
                         December 31, 20X5
```

| | |
|---|---:|
| Cash | — |
| Land | € 12,000,000 |
| | € 12,000,000 |
| Bond (due December 31, 20X9) | €  9,000,000 |
| Common shares | 3,000,000 |
| | € 12,000,000 |

Assume the following exchange rates:

| | |
|---|---|
| January 1, 20X5 | €1 = $1.20 |
| December 31, 20X5 | €1 = $1.65 |
| Average, 20X5 | €1 = $1.40 |

**Required**

a. Prepare the translated 20X5 SCI and SFP at December 31, 20X5, following GAAP and assuming the German subsidiary's functional currency is the:
   i) Canadian dollar; and
   ii) euro.
b. Which translation method better reflects Investco's *economic exposure* to exchange rate movements? Explain.
c. Which translation method would Investco be required to use? Explain.

   [SMA, adapted]

P9-4 (15 minutes, easy)

Birch Limited is a 100%-owned foreign subsidiary with operations in England. Birch was acquired by its Canadian parent on January 1, 20X7. The financial records of Birch are maintained in pounds sterling (£) and provide the following information related to its equipment:

| Date of purchase | Cost of purchase |
|---|---|
| January 1, 20X7 | £3,000 |
| January 1, 20X8 | £4,500 |

The equipment is being amortized on a straight-line basis over its estimated useful life of 10 years.

Foreign exchange rates were as follows:

| | |
|---|---|
| January 1, 20X6 | £1 = C$1.50 |
| Average for 20X6 | £1 = C$1.51 |
| January 1, 20X7 | £1 = C$1.55 |
| Average for 20X7 | £1 = C$1.58 |
| January 1, 20X8 | £1 = C$1.63 |
| Average for 20X8 | £1 = C$1.47 |
| December 31, 20X8 | £1 = C$1.40 |

Birch's financial statements must be translated into Canadian dollars so that they can be consolidated with the financial statements of the Canadian parent.

Required

a. Assume that Birch's functional currency is the pound sterling. Calculate the translated Canadian-dollar balances for the following accounts for 20X8:
   i) equipment;
   ii) accumulated amortization—equipment; and
   iii) amortization expense.
b. Assume that Birch's functional currency is the Canadian dollar. Calculate the translated Canadian-dollar balances for the following accounts for 20X8:
   i) equipment; and
   ii) accumulated amortization—equipment.
      [CGA–Canada, adapted]

P9-5 (35 minutes, medium)

On December 31, 20X3, Oak Company (Oak), a Canadian corporation, purchased 100% of the outstanding common shares of Maple Limited (Maple). Maple was incorporated on January 2, 20X0, and began operations immediately in the southwestern United States. Common shares were issued on the date of incorporation, and no more common shares have been issued since then. The SFP for Maple at December 31, 20X9, was as follows:

| Maple Limited<br>Statement of Financial Position<br>December 31, 20X9 | |
|---|---|
| Cash | US$ 100,000 |
| Accounts receivable (note 1) | 200,000 |
| Inventory (note 2) | 300,000 |
| Equipment—net (note 3) | 1,100,000 |
| | US$1,700,000 |
| Accounts payable | US$ 250,000 |
| Bonds payable (note 4) | 700,000 |
| Common shares | 100,000 |
| Retained earnings | 650,000 |
| | US$1,700,000 |

## Additional Information

1. The accounts receivable relating to sales occurred evenly throughout the month of December 20X9.

2. Maple uses the FIFO method to account for its inventory. The inventory available for sale during the year was purchased as follows:

| Date of purchase | Cost of purchase | Exchange rate |
|---|---|---|
| December 31, 20X8 | US$100,000 | US$1.00 = C$1.31 |
| March 1, 20X9 | 1,000,000 | US$1.00 = C$1.35 |
| November 1, 20X9 | 180,000 | US$1.00 = C$1.38 |

3. The equipment was purchased on May 26, 20X3.

4. Bonds of US$700,000 were issued on May 26, 20X3, to finance the purchase of the equipment.

5. Maple reported net income of US$200,000, which was earned evenly throughout the year, and paid dividends of US$160,000 on July 1, 20X9.

6. Foreign exchange rates were as follows:

| January 2, 20X0 | US$1.00 = C$1.05 |
|---|---|
| May 26, 20X3 | US$1.00 = C$1.15 |
| December 31, 20X3 | US$1.00 = C$1.17 |
| December 31, 20X8 | US$1.00 = C$1.31 |
| July 1, 20X9 | US$1.00 = C$1.36 |
| December 31, 20X9 | US$1.00 = C$1.40 |
| Average for December 20X9 | US$1.00 = C$1.39 |
| Average for 20X9 | US$1.00 = C$1.34 |

## Required

a. Translate the SFP of Maple at December 31, 20X9, into Canadian dollars using the temporal method. Assume that the translated SFP will be consolidated with Oak's SFP. For retained earnings, simply use the amount required to balance your SFP.

b. Calculate the foreign exchange gain or loss on the bonds payable for the year ended December 31, 20X9.

c. Prepare an independent calculation of the translation gain or loss for 20X9, assuming that Maple's functional currency is the US dollar.

d. "Since the current-rate method uses the current rate to translate capital assets, the translated amount should represent the current value of the capital assets in Canadian dollars." Is this a valid statement? Briefly explain.

[CGA–Canada, adapted]

### P9-6 (75 minutes, difficult)

On January 1, 20X5, Pierre Company of Sherbrooke, Quebec, purchased 80% of the outstanding shares of Simon Limited of Switzerland for CHF200,000. Simon's statements of financial position as at December 31, 20X4, and December 31, 20X5, and Simon's 20X5 statement of comprehensive income and retained earnings follow.

| Simon Ltd.<br>Statement of Financial Position<br>December 31 | | |
| --- | --- | --- |
| | 20X5 | 20X4 |
| **Assets** | | |
| Cash | CHF120,000 | CHF 50,000 |
| Accounts receivable | 85,000 | 75,000 |
| Inventory | 80,000 | 60,000 |
| Equipment, net | 250,000 | 300,000 |
| | CHF535,000 | CHF485,000 |
| **Liabilities and shareholders' equity** | | |
| Accounts payable | CHF 60,000 | CHF 90,000 |
| Bonds payable | 200,000 | 200,000 |
| Common shares | 100,000 | 100,000 |
| Retained earnings | 175,000 | 95,000 |
| | CHF535,000 | CHF485,000 |

| Simon Ltd.<br>Statement of Comprehensive Income and Retained Earnings<br>Year Ended December 31, 20X5 | |
| --- | --- |
| Sales | CHF500,000 |
| Cost of sales | (280,000) |
| Amortization | (50,000) |
| Other expenses | (20,000) |
| Net income | 150,000 |
| Retained earnings, January 1, 20X5 | 95,000 |
| | 245,000 |
| Dividends paid | 70,000 |
| Retained earnings, December 31, 20X5 | CHF175,000 |

Additional Information

1. Simon was incorporated on January 1, 20X2, at which time it acquired all of its equipment and issued its 10-year bonds.

2. Simon's purchases and sales occurred evenly during 20X5. Simon's December 31, 20X4, and December 31, 20X5, inventory was acquired evenly over the final six months of 20X4 and 20X5, respectively.

3. Dividends were paid on July 1, 20X5.

4. The carrying values of Simon's identifiable assets and liabilities approximated fair values. Any purchase price discrepancy should be assigned to goodwill. Ignore income taxes.

5. Foreign exchange rates were as follows:

| | |
|---|---|
| January 1, 20X2 | CHF1 = C$0.90 |
| Average for July–December 20X4 | CHF1 = C$0.92 |
| December 31, 20X4/January 1, 20X5 | CHF1 = C$0.94 |
| July 1, 20X5 | CHF1 = C$0.98 |
| December 31, 20X5 | CHF1 = C$1.02 |
| Average for July–December 20X5 | CHF1 = C$1.00 |
| Average for 20X5 | CHF1 = C$0.99 |

**Required**

**a.** Translate the financial statements of Simon as at December 31, 20X5, assuming that Simon's functional currency is the Swiss franc. Include a separate calculation of any translation gain or loss on the fair value increment related to goodwill.

**b.** Translate the financial statements of Simon for the year ended December 31, 20X5, assuming that Simon's functional currency is the Canadian dollar.

[CGA–Canada, adapted]

**P9-7 (80 minutes, difficult)**

On December 31, 20X14, Pride Company of Vancouver acquired 100% of the outstanding shares of Soul Company of Switzerland for CHF300,000. On this date, the fair values of Soul's identifiable assets and liabilities were equal to their carrying value. Soul's statements of financial position as at December 31, 20X14, and December 31, 20X15, and Soul's 20X15 statement of comprehensive income and retained earnings follow.

| Soul Co. Statement of Financial Position December 31 | | |
|---|---|---|
| | **20X15** | **20X14** |
| **Assets** | | |
| Cash | CHF 80,000 | CHF 60,000 |
| Accounts receivable | 140,000 | 80,000 |
| Inventory | 110,000 | 80,000 |
| Equipment, net | 250,000 | 280,000 |
| | CHF 580,000 | CHF 500,000 |
| **Liabilities and shareholders' equity** | | |
| Accounts payable | CHF 150,000 | CHF 115,000 |
| Bonds payable | 120,000 | 120,000 |
| Common shares | 140,000 | 140,000 |
| Retained earnings | 170,000 | 125,000 |
| | CHF 580,000 | CHF 500,000 |

## Soul Co.
### Statement of Comprehensive Income and Retained Earnings
### Year Ended December 31, 20X15

| | |
|---|---:|
| Sales | CHF 850,000 |
| Cost of sales | (500,000) |
| Gross margin | 350,000 |
| Amortization expense | (30,000) |
| Other expenses | (245,000) |
| Net income | 75,000 |
| Retained earnings, January 1, 20X5 | 125,000 |
| | 200,000 |
| Dividends paid | (30,000) |
| Retained earnings, December 31, 20X5 | CHF 170,000 |

## Additional Information

1. Inventory on hand at December 31, 20X14, and December 31, 20X15, was purchased evenly over the final three months of 20X14 and 20X15, respectively, from suppliers in Switzerland. Sales and purchases occurred evenly throughout the year.

2. The plant and equipment on hand at December 31, 20X14, was originally acquired for CHF450,000 on January 1, 20X8, the date of Soul's incorporation. No plant and equipment was acquired or sold during fiscal 20X15.

3. Dividends were declared and paid on September 30, 20X15.

4. The bonds were issued on January 1, 20X10, and mature on December 31, 20X19. The Swiss franc has changed over time relative to the Canadian dollar, but the foreign exchange trend has little effect on Soul's sales prices, which are largely determined by local competition. Foreign exchange rates were as follows:

| | |
|---|---|
| January 1, 20X8 | CHF1 = C$0.66 |
| January 1, 20X10 | CHF1 = C$0.76 |
| December 31, 20X14/January 1, 20X15 | CHF1 = C$0.86 |
| July 1, 20X15 | CHF1 = C$0.92 |
| September 30, 20X15 | CHF1 = C$0.94 |
| December 31, 20X15 | CHF1 = C$0.96 |
| Average for October–December 20X14 | CHF1 = C$0.84 |
| Average for October–December 20X15 | CHF1 = C$0.95 |
| Average for 20X15 | CHF1 = C$0.91 |

## Required

a. Determine Soul's functional currency. State three facts from the problem to support your conclusion.

b. Ignore your answer in part a) and assume that Soul's functional currency is the Canadian dollar. Translate the statement of comprehensive income and the statement of financial position for the year ended December 31, 20X15, to Canadian dollars. Include an independent calculation of any translation gains/losses.

c. Ignore your answers to parts a) and b) and assume that Soul's functional currency is the Swiss franc. Translate the statement of comprehensive income and the statement of financial position for the year ended December 31, 20X15, to Canadian dollars. Include an independent calculation of any translation gains/losses that Pride must include in its consolidated statements.

[CGA–Canada]

P9-8 (45 minutes, difficult)

On December 31, 20X5, KTR Corporation acquired 80% of the outstanding shares of SJC Limited for $5,000,000. Assume US$1,000,000 of the purchase price discrepancy related to unrecorded patents (useful life of five years) and the remainder was due to goodwill. KTR is a Vancouver-based company, while SJC is based in Las Vegas, in the USA. SJC's financial statements follow.

| SJC Ltd. Statement of Financial Position December 31 | 20X6 | 20X5 |
|---|---|---|
| **Assets** | | |
| Cash | US$ 300,000 | US$ 250,000 |
| Accounts receivable | 1,350,000 | 1,100,000 |
| Inventory | 2,100,000 | 1,800,000 |
| Equipment, net | 3,250,000 | 3,000,000 |
| | US$7,000,000 | US$6,150,000 |
| **Liabilities and shareholders' equity** | | |
| Accounts payable | US$ 560,000 | US$ 400,000 |
| Bonds payable | 3,000,000 | 3,000,000 |
| Common shares | 1,500,000 | 1,500,000 |
| Retained earnings | 1,940,000 | 1,250,000 |
| | US$7,000,000 | US$6,150,000 |

| SJC Ltd. Statement of Comprehensive Income and Retained Earnings Year Ended December 31, 20X6 | |
|---|---|
| Sales | US$5,000,000 |
| Cost of sales | (3,200,000) |
| Amortization expense | (350,000) |
| Bond interest expense | (240,000) |
| Other expenses | (470,000) |
| Net income | 740,000 |
| Retained earnings, January 1, 20X6 | 1,250,000 |
| | 1,990,000 |
| Dividends paid | (50,000) |
| Retained earnings, December 31, 20X6 | US$1,940,000 |

Additional Information

1. Inventory on hand as at December 31, 20X5, and December 31, 20X6, was purchased when the exchange rates were US$1.00 = C$1.10 and US$1.00 = C$1.28, respectively. Sales and purchases occurred evenly throughout 20X6.

2. Of the $3,000,000 plant and equipment (net) recorded on the December 31, 20X5, SFP, $2,000,000 (net) was purchased on December 31, 20X1, and $1,000,000 (net) was purchased on December 31, 20X5. Plant and equipment costing an additional $600,000 was purchased on December 31, 20X6. The plant and equipment purchased in 20X1 and 20X5 is being amortized at $250,000 per year and $100,000 per year, respectively.

3. Dividends were declared and paid on October 31, 20X6.

4. The bonds were issued at par on December 31, 20X1, with an 8% interest rate, and they mature on December 31, 20X11. They pay interest semi-annually.

5. Ignore the impact of income taxes in the question.

6. Foreign exchange rates were as follows:

| | |
|---|---|
| December 31, 20X1 | US$1.00 = C$1.00 |
| December 31, 20X5 | US$1.00 = C$1.20 |
| October 31, 20X6 | US$1.00 = C$1.27 |
| December 31, 20X6 | US$1.00 = C$1.30 |
| Average for 20X6 | US$1.00 = C$1.25 |

Required

a. You are the controller of KTR. Assuming that SJC's functional currency is the Canadian dollar, translate the SCI for the year ended December 31, 20X6, into Canadian dollars. Include an independent calculation of any foreign exchange gains/losses.

b. Assuming that SJC's functional currency is the Canadian dollar, translate the following SFP accounts for SJC into Canadian dollars as at December 31, 20X6:
   i) accounts receivable;
   ii) plant and equipment (net); and
   iii) bonds payable.

c. Assuming that SJC's functional currency is the US dollar, translate the following SFP accounts for SJC into Canadian dollars as at December 31, 20X6:
   i) plant and equipment (net);
   ii) common shares; and
   iii) retained earnings.

d. Assuming SJC's functional currency is the US dollar, calculate the translation gain or loss arising from the fair value increments.

e. Assume that you have just been hired at KTR and you are discussing the operations of SJC with the chief executive officer. List two questions about the operations of SJC that you could ask the CEO to help you establish SJC's functional currency.

[CGA–Canada]

P9-9 (90 minutes, medium)

SuperSpan Corporation is a foreign subsidiary of Port Corporation, a Canadian company. SuperSpan was acquired on January 1, 20X6. On this date, there was no purchase price discrepancy and the fair values of SuperSpan's identifiable assets and liabilities were equal to their carrying values. SuperSpan manufactures furniture for sale based on sales prices determined by worldwide competition. The chief financial officer of SuperSpan emailed the following December 31, 20X7, financial statements, stated in euros (€), to you, the CFO of Port:

| SuperSpan Corporation Statement of Financial Position | | |
| --- | --- | --- |
| | December 31, 20X7 | December 31, 20X6 |
| **Assets** | | |
| Cash | €  300,000 | €  250,000 |
| Accounts receivable | 350,000 | 325,000 |
| Inventory | 500,000 | 425,000 |
| Equipment, net | 575,000 | 300,000 |
| | €1,725,000 | €1,300,000 |
| **Liabilities and shareholders' equity** | | |
| Accounts payable | €  145,000 | €  200,000 |
| Bonds payable | 400,000 | 400,000 |
| Common shares | 900,000 | 500,000 |
| Retained earnings | 280,000 | 200,000 |
| | €1,725,000 | €1,300,000 |

| SuperSpan Corporation Statement of Comprehensive Income Years Ended December 31 | | |
| --- | --- | --- |
| | 20X7 | 20X6 |
| Sales | € 2,100,000 | € 2,000,000 |
| Cost of goods sold | 1,600,000 | 1,500,000 |
| Gross profit | 500,000 | 500,000 |
| Selling and administrative | 145,000 | 120,000 |
| Bond interest expense | 30,000 | 30,000 |
| Amortization | 125,000 | 100,000 |
| Income before income taxes | 200,000 | 250,000 |
| Income taxes | 80,000 | 100,000 |
| Net income | €   120,000 | €   150,000 |

Additional Information

**1.** The following exchange rates were noted:

| January 1, 20X1 | €1 = C$1.55 |
| --- | --- |
| January 1, 20X6 | €1 = C$1.52 |
| Average for October 1–December 31, 20X6 | €1 = C$1.48 |
| Average for 20X6 | €1 = C$1.50 |
| December 31, 20X6 | €1 = C$1.45 |

| | |
|---|---|
| July 1, 20X7 | €1 = C$1.44 |
| Average for October 1–December 31, 20X7 | €1 = C$1.43 |
| November 1, 20X7 | €1 = C$1.41 |
| Average for 20X7 | €1 = C$1.42 |
| December 31, 20X7 | €1 = C$1.40 |

2. On January 1, 20X1, SuperSpan acquired equipment for €900,000 with an expected useful life of nine years. On July 1, 20X7, it acquired €400,000 of new equipment with an expected useful life of eight years. SuperSpan amortizes its equipment on a straight-line basis, calculated monthly.

3. SuperSpan partly financed its acquisition of equipment on January 1, 20X1, by issuing €400,000, eight-year, 5% bonds payable. Similarly, SuperSpan financed its acquisition of equipment in 20X7 by issuing €400,000 of common shares on July 1, 20X7.

4. Inventory on hand on December 31, 20X6, and December 31, 20X7, includes a significant amount of wood imported from western Canadian timber firms. It was purchased evenly over the last three months of 20X6 and 20X7.

5. Dividends of €40,000 were declared and paid on November 1, 20X7. No dividends were paid in 20X6.

6. All other sales, purchases, and expenses occurred evenly each year.

Required

a. Should SuperSpan's financial statements be translated into Canadian dollars using the temporal method or the current-rate method? Provide two facts from the question to support your answer.

b. Disregard your response to part a). Using the current-rate method, translate SuperSpan's 20X7 financial statements into Canadian dollars.

c. Disregard your responses to parts a) and b). Using the temporal method, translate SuperSpan's 20X7 financial statements into Canadian dollars. (The retained earnings of €200,000 on December 31, 20X6, should be translated as $288,750.)

   [CGA–Canada, adapted]

P9-10 (35 minutes, medium)

On January 2, 20X2, EL Limited established a subsidiary in Mexico City, Mexico. The subsidiary was named GC Company, and the cost of EL's investment was C$500,000. When this investment was translated into Mexican pesos, the cost of the investment was p5,000,000. On January 2, 20X2, GC obtained long-term debt of p1,000,000 from a bank in Mexico City when the exchange rate was p1.00 = C$0.10. The long-term debt must be repaid at the end of four years. The opening SFP for GC on January 2, 20X2, is shown below.

| GC Company<br>Statement of Financial Position<br>January 2, 20X2 | |
|---|---:|
| Current monetary assets | p 6,000,000 |
| Long-term debt | 1,000,000 |
| Common shares | 5,000,000 |
| | p 6,000,000 |

The December 31, 20X2, SFP and SCI for GC are shown below.

| GC Company Statement of Comprehensive Income December 31, 20X2 | |
|---|---|
| Revenues | p 3,200,000 |
| Amortization expense | 300,000 |
| Operating expenses | 2,200,000 |
| Total expenses | 2,500,000 |
| Net income | p 700,000 |

| GC Company Statement of Financial Position December 31, 20X2 | |
|---|---|
| Current monetary assets | p 2,800,000 |
| Capital assets | 4,900,000 |
| Accumulated amortization | (300,000) |
| | p 7,400,000 |
| Current monetary liabilities | p 900,000 |
| Long-term debt | 1,000,000 |
| Common shares | 5,000,000 |
| Retained earnings | 500,000 |
| | p 7,400,000 |

The relevant exchange rates for the Mexican peso were as follows:

| January 2, 20X2 | p1.00 = C$0.10 |
|---|---|
| Average for 20X2 | p1.00 = C$0.12 |
| December 31, 20X2 | p1.00 = C$0.14 |

During 20X2, GC purchased capital assets when the exchange rate was p1.00 = C$0.11. Dividends were declared and paid when the exchange rate was p1.00 = C$0.13. Revenues and other expenses were incurred evenly throughout the year.

Required

a. Calculate the exchange gains/losses for the temporal and current-rate methods to be disclosed on the December 31, 20X2, SFP and SCI.

b. Translate the 20X2 SFP and SCI for GC, assuming GC's functional currency is the:
   i) Mexican peso; and
   ii) Canadian dollar.
   [CGA–Canada]

P9-11 (20 minutes, medium)

On January 1, 20X6, Woods Ltd. formed a foreign subsidiary that issued all of its currently outstanding common shares on that date. Selected captions from the SFPs, all of which are shown in local currency units (LCU), are as follows:

| | 20X7(LCU) | 20X6(LCU) |
|---|---|---|
| Accounts receivable, net of allowance for uncollectable accounts of 2,200 LCU at December 31, 20X7, and 2,000 LCU at December 31, 20X6 | 40,000 | 35,000 |
| Inventories, at cost | 80,000 | 75,000 |
| Capital assets, net of accumulated depreciation of 31,000 LCU at December 31, 20X7, and 14,000 LCU at December 31, 20X6 | 163,000 | 150,000 |
| Long-term debt | 100,000 | 120,000 |
| Common stock, authorized shares par value 10 LCU per share, issued and outstanding 5,000 shares at December 31, 20X7, and December 31, 20X6 | 50,000 | 50,000 |

Additional Information

| Exchange Rates | |
|---|---|
| January 1 to July 31, 20X6 | 2.1 LCU = $1 |
| August 1 to October 31, 20X6 | 1.9 LCU = $1 |
| November 1, 20X6, to June 30, 20X7 | 1.8 LCU = $1 |
| July 1 to December 31, 20X7 | 1.6 LCU = $1 |
| Average rate for 20X6 | 2.0 LCU = $1 |
| Average rate for 20X7 | 1.7 LCU = $1 |

| Accounts Receivable—Analysis | 20X7 (LCU) | 20X6 (LCU) |
|---|---|---|
| Balance beginning of year | 37,000 | — |
| Sales (36,000 LCU per month in 20X7 and 31,000 per month in 20X6) | 432,000 | 372,000 |
| Collections | (423,600) | (334,000) |
| Write-offs (May 20X7 and December 20X6) | (3,200) | (1,000) |
| | 42,200 | 37,000 |

| Allowance for Uncollectable Accounts | 20X7 (LCU) | 20X6 (LCU) |
|---|---|---|
| Balance beginning of year | 2,000 | — |
| Provision for uncollectables | 3,400 | 3,000 |
| Write-offs | (3,200) | (1,000) |
| | 2,200 | 2,000 |

| Inventory, FIFO Basis | | |
| --- | --- | --- |
| | 20X7 (LCU) | 20X6 (LCU) |
| Balance beginning of year | 75,000 | — |
| Purchases (June 20X7 and June 20X6) | 335,000 | 375,000 |
| Less: Inventory at year-end | (80,000) | (75,000) |
| Cost of goods sold | 330,000 | 300,000 |

On January 1, 20X6, Woods's foreign subsidiary purchased land for 24,000 LCU and capital assets for 140,000 LCU. On July 1, 20X7, additional equipment was purchased for 30,000 LCU. Capital assets are being depreciated on a straight-line basis over a 10-year period with no salvage value. A full year's depreciation is taken in the year of purchase.

On January 15, 20X6, 7% bonds with a face value of 120,000 LCU were sold. The bonds pay interest on July 15 and January 15 each year. The first payment was made on July 15, 20X6.

### Required

Prepare a schedule translating the selected captions above into Canadian dollars at December 31, 20X6, and December 31, 20X7, using the temporal method. Show supporting computations in good form.

[CGA–Canada, adapted]

### P9-12 (60 minutes, medium)

Refer to P9-2. The comparative year-end SFPs for Hilary Co. were as follows:

| | 20X3 | 20X2 |
| --- | --- | --- |
| Cash | CF 200,000 | CF 500,000 |
| Accounts receivable | 400,000 | 300,000 |
| Inventory | 400,000 | 200,000 |
| Land | 500,000 | — |
| Equipment (net) | 1,700,000 | 2,000,000 |
| Total assets | CF3,200,000 | CF3,000,000 |
| Accounts payable | CF 500,000 | CF 400,000 |
| Bonds payable | 1,800,000 | 1,800,000 |
| Common shares | 500,000 | 500,000 |
| Retained earnings | 400,000 | 300,000 |
| Total liabilities and equities | CF3,200,000 | CF3,000,000 |

The common shares were issued when the exchange rate was CF1 = C$0.52.

The land was purchased at the end of 20X3. The bonds were issued at the end of 20X1, and they mature at the end of 20X7. The exchange rate at the end of 20X1 was 0.62. Dividends are declared and paid at the end of each year. The retained earnings at the end of 20X2 were earned at an average exchange rate of 0.67.

### Required

a. Translate the 20X2 and 20X3 SFPs using the current-rate method. (Note that each year's SFP is translated at the current rate *at that year's SFP date*.)

**b.** Translate the 20X2 and 20X3 SFPs using the temporal method.

**c.** Calculate the translation gain or loss for 20X3 under each translation method.

### P9-13 (45 minutes, difficult)

SEQEA Company was incorporated on January 2, 20X4, and commenced active operations immediately. Common shares were issued on the date of incorporation and no new common shares have been issued since then. On December 31, 20X12, RST Company purchased 70% of the outstanding common shares of SEQEA for 1,500,000 Swedish kronor (SEK). The purchase price discrepancy was SEK1,000,000 and was wholly assigned to goodwill.

SEQEA's main operations are located in Sweden. It manufactures and sells fine Swedish furniture. Approximately 40% of its sales are to RST, 40% to companies throughout Western Europe, and 20% to China. To satisfy the extra demand from RST, SEQEA built a new manufacturing plant in Sweden in 20X14. The plant was financed with retained earnings and a loan from a Swedish bank. Most of the material and labour for the manufacturing operation are obtained from local sources in Sweden.

For the year ended December 31, 20X15, the SCI for SEQEA was as follows:

| | |
|---|---:|
| Sales and other revenue | SEK 8,500,000 |
| Cost of goods sold | 4,000,000 |
| Amortization expense | 150,000 |
| Other expenses | 3,850,000 |
| Net income | SEK 500,000 |

The comparative SFP in condensed form for SEQEA was as follows:

| | 20X15 | 20X14 |
|---|---:|---:|
| Inventory (Note 1) | SEK 200,000 | SEK 180,000 |
| Property, plant, and equipment—net (Note 2) | 1,700,000 | 1,850,000 |
| Monetary assets | 2,400,000 | 2,170,000 |
| | SEK 4,300,000 | SEK 4,200,000 |
| Monetary liabilities | SEK 2,400,000 | SEK 2,500,000 |
| Non-monetary liabilities (Note 3) | 195,000 | 170,000 |
| Common shares | 100,000 | 100,000 |
| Retained earnings | 1,605,000 | 1,430,000 |
| | SEK 4,300,000 | SEK 4,200,000 |

### Additional Information

1. The ending inventory for 20X14 and 20X15 was manufactured evenly throughout the last month of each year. The additions to inventory, sales and other revenue, and other expenses occurred evenly throughout the year.

2. The property, plant, and equipment on hand at the end of 20X12 had been purchased by SEQEA on January 10, 20X9. The new manufacturing plant was completed on December 31, 20X14, for a total cost of SEK100,000. The amortization on the new plant in 20X15 was SEK5,000. There have been no other purchases or sales of capital assets since 20X12.

3. The non-monetary liabilities represent obligations for SEQEA to provide services over the next 12 months. The obligations arose evenly throughout the last six months of 20X15.

4. Dividends were declared and paid on December 31, 20X15.

5. There has been no impairment of goodwill since RST purchased SEQEA.

6. SEQEA's financial statements must be translated to Canadian dollars so that they can be consolidated with the financial statements of RST.

Foreign exchange rates were as follows:

| | |
|---|---|
| January 2, 20X4 | SEK1 = C$0.30 |
| January 10, 20X9 | SEK1 = C$0.25 |
| December 31, 20X12 | SEK1 = C$0.24 |
| Average for 20X14 | SEK1 = C$0.23 |
| Average for December 20X14 | SEK1 = C$0.21 |
| December 31, 20X14 | SEK1 = C$0.20 |
| Average for 20X15 | SEK1 = C$0.18 |
| Average for July–December 20X15 | SEK1 = C$0.17 |
| Average for December 20X15 | SEK1 = C$0.16 |
| December 31, 20X15 | SEK1 = C$0.15 |

Required

a. The CFO is wondering whether SEQEA's financial statements should be translated into Canadian dollars using the current-rate or the temporal method. What is your recommendation? Why?

b. Ignore your answer to part a) and determine the Canadian dollar amount for the following items on the financial statements for the year ended December 31, 20X15, under the current-rate method:
   i)  other expenses;
   ii) inventory at end of year;
   iii) common shares; and
   iv) the translation gain or loss for 20X15 from all sources.

c. Ignore your answers to parts a) and b) and determine the Canadian dollar amount for the following items on the financial statements for the year ended December 31, 20X15, under the temporal method:
   i)  cost of goods sold;
   ii) amortization expense;
   iii) monetary assets;
   iv) non-monetary liabilities; and
   v)  the translation gain or loss for 20X15 from all sources.
      [CGA–Canada, adapted]

# Chapter 10
## Financial Reporting for Not-for-Profit Organizations

## Learning Objectives

**After studying this chapter, you should be able to:**

LO **1**    identify the characteristics of not-for-profit organizations (NFPs) and explain how NFPs differ from business enterprises;

LO **2**    explain the primary reporting issues that arise from the special characteristics of NFPs;

LO **3**    describe two GAAP reporting methods for NFPs: the deferral method when fund accounting is not used and the restricted-fund method when fund accounting is used; and

LO **4**    describe the application and use of budgetary control accounts and encumbrance accounting.

## INTRODUCTION

The Canadian Cancer Society (CCS) is a national organization dedicated to finding a cure for cancer and to supporting people living with cancer. CCS is a registered charity that operates through a national office and 10 provincial and territorial divisions. In its 2011 annual report, CCS reported revenue in excess of $212 million. Significant sources of this revenue include well-known campaigns, such as the "Relay for Life" campaign, and a more traditional annual giving campaign.

Not-for-profit organizations such as the Canadian Cancer Society differ significantly from profit-oriented business organizations. For example, the Canadian Cancer Society is a corporation "without share capital." Since there are no shareholders, the typical primary user of a business's financial statements is non-existent. Another difference is that there are legal restrictions on how some of CCS's revenues can be used. The donors of CCS's restricted funds have needs that differ from the needs of users of business financial statements. The different needs of different users of an organization like CCS lead to different reporting objectives. Different reporting objectives lead to different accounting issues. In this chapter, we will examine the unique accounting issues that arise for not-for-profit organizations.

Most study of accounting focuses on business enterprises. However, there are many organizations in Canada that are not businesses. The non-business sector includes not-for-profit organizations and the government—that is, the entire public sector. Schools, universities, hospitals, social service agencies, performing arts organizations, museums, trade associations, unions, political parties, and philanthropic foundations are a few examples of *not-for-profit organizations* that have an important place in our society. The different levels of *governments* that exist in Canada include those at the municipal, territorial, provincial, and federal level.

Overall, close to 20% of all Canadian employment is in not-for-profit organizations or governments. The larger segments are health care, education, and the various levels of government and government services. Indeed, *non-business organizations* comprise a larger component of the Canadian economy than manufacturing.

Given the importance of non-business organizations, not only in Canada but worldwide, it is somewhat surprising that so little attention is given to this important segment of the economy in accounting courses. Generally, it is only when students reach the advanced level that they are introduced to the particular problems faced by not-for-profit organizations and by governments. Well, better late than never! In this chapter, we discuss not-for-profit organizations. Governmental accounting is discussed in Chapter 11, "Public Sector Financial Reporting."

## 10.1 OVERVIEW OF NON-BUSINESS ORGANIZATIONS

As a first step, we must make a distinction between *non-business* and *not-for-profit* organizations. A **non-business organization** is any organization that is not a private enterprise operating for profit. Non-business organizations can be roughly divided into three groups: (1) governments; (2) governmental units; and (3) not-for-profit organizations.

**Governments** are the governing bodies (legislatures, councils, ministries, etc.) at the federal, provincial, territorial, and municipal levels. **Governmental accounting** is the body of principles and practices that has been developed for recordkeeping and reporting by these various levels of government.

Governmental accounting is usually regulated by law. The underlying accounting and reporting principles were developed by governments and by professional organizations. In Canada, the pronouncements of the CICA's Public Sector Accounting Board influence financial reporting by governments. As we will see in the next chapter, the financial statement objectives of governments are quite different from those of private enterprises because of the sources of their funds, their ability to tax, and their legal reporting obligations.

**Governmental units** are organizations that are set up by governments to carry out some aspect of their policy. Governmental units include school boards, public housing authorities, parking authorities, public cemeteries, water systems, and electric utilities. Such units may be incorporated, but they are corporations without share capital. *Governmental units* are not the same as **crown corporations**, such as VIA Rail Canada or the Liquor Control Board of Ontario, which are business corporations *with share capital* but that have the government as the only shareholder. Some governmental units do carry on some type of business (e.g., local transportation systems), but they are public-sector organizations rather than private enterprises. Therefore, they fall within the general classification of non-business organizations.

**Not-for-profit organizations (NFPs)** function as educational, scientific, charitable, artistic, or social agencies. They can be incorporated or unincorporated—if incorporated, they are *corporations without share capital*, such as the Canadian Cancer Society cited above. The term "social agency" covers a lot of ground, since a social agency can range anywhere from an amateur baseball club to a major hospital, with the Salvation Army, the Liberal Party of Canada, and the Kiwanis Club in between.

NFPs can be classified as private sector NFPs or government NFPs. The only difference between the two is that government NFPs are organizations controlled by the government. Government NFPs must have an equivalent counterpart in the private sector and, further, must possess the same purpose or intent as any NFP.

Terms other than *not-for-profit organization* are often used to describe the widely diverse types of organizations that are in this sector of the economy. The most popular alternative term is **non-profit** organization, usually abbreviated as **NPO**.[1] Another alternative is "volunteer organization," because they frequently use the services of volunteers for delivering the organization's services. Also, the directors of not-for-profit organizations are generally prohibited from being paid, and thus are volunteer directors. In this book we will use the term *not-for-profit organization*.

## 10.2 ACCOUNTING STANDARDS FOR NOT-FOR-PROFIT ORGANIZATIONS

Accounting for NFPs has been a concern among accounting standard-setters across the world. There have been attempts to create international standards, but those have come to naught. Instead, NFP accounting has been addressed by each nation (or region, in the case of the European Union) individually. This "go it alone" approach is largely due to national differences in NFP economic environments and legislation.

In Canada, GAAP for private sector (non-government) NFPs is contained in the *CICA Handbook, Part III*. Generally speaking, the *CICA Handbook* requires private sector NFPs to comply with ASPE reporting—*CICA Handbook, Part II*, except as otherwise specified in *Part III*. Private sector NFPs also have the option of adopting IFRS as contained in the *CICA Handbook, Part I*. GAAP for government NFPs is contained in the *PSAB Handbook*. Generally speaking, the *PSAB Handbook* requires government NFPs to comply with the public sector accounting standards in the handbook *except* as otherwise specified in the PS 4200 series. Government NFPs also have the option of following only the public sector accounting standards used by governments (i.e., ignoring the PS 4200 series). Because the PS 4200 series is similar to the *CICA HB Part III* 4400 series, the discussions in this chapter will refer to private sector NFPs. The principles, however, are equally applicable to government NFPs.

In practice, NFPs are "required" to follow Canadian GAAP, but this is an effective requirement only when the NFP is audited and is required to get a "clean" audit opinion. An audit usually is required by federal or provincial legislation for large NFPs such as universities and hospitals. Smaller NFPs seldom have an audit unless it is required by a funding organization, such as a government ministry.

NFPs often provide special-purpose financial statements for specific users. For example, provincial ministries of social services usually require an NFP to submit both its

---

[1] This is the more traditional term for a not-for-profit organization and is in common use (e.g., government departments such as the Canada Revenue Agency still use the term "non-profit organization").

budget request and its financial statements in a format that complies with ministry regulations (which may differ from CICA standards); from the ministry's point of view, the main purpose of an audit is to provide assurance that the NFP has an effective internal control system and that the managers aren't subverting the money for unauthorized (or personal) purposes.

NFPs are quite different from business enterprises. The following sections will explain the many fundamental differences. Once you understand just how different NFPs can be from businesses, we then can examine NFP accounting options.

**LO 1**

Identify the characteristics of not-for-profit organizations (NFPs) and explain how NFPs differ from business enterprises

## 10.3 CHARACTERISTICS OF NOT-FOR-PROFIT ORGANIZATIONS

Canada's not-for-profit sector, as a proportion of the country's total workforce, is the second largest in the world—the largest is the Netherlands. Not-for-profit organizations employ approximately 2 million individuals, representing 11.1% of the economically active population in Canada. The not-for-profit sector represents $79.1 billion, or 7.8%, of Canada's gross domestic product (GDP).[2] A recent study estimated that there were 161,000 not-for-profit organizations in Canada. The distribution of these organizations is skewed to many small organizations and very few large organizations (see Exhibit 10.1). As Exhibit 10.1 shows, 41% of organizations in the not-for-profit sector had less than $30,000 in revenue, 88% had less than $500,000 in revenue, and only 1% had more than $10 million in revenue.

**Exhibit 10.1** Distribution of Organizations and Not-for-Profit Sector Revenues by Organization Size

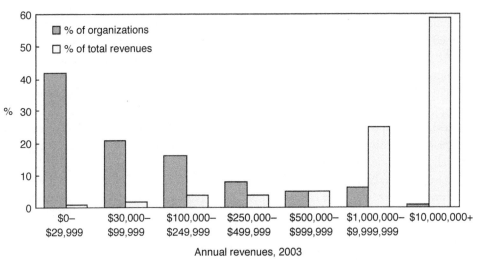

Source: Adapted from Statistics Canada, Cornerstones of Community: Highlights from the National Survey of Nonprofit and Voluntary Organizations 61-533-XIE2004001 2003, Revised, Released June 30, 2005.

---

[2] Imagine Canada, *The Canadian Nonprofit and Voluntary Sector in Comparative Perspective*, 2005.

The not-for-profit sector can be divided into two groups: (1) a core group consisting of a large number of relatively small organizations and (2) a smaller group consisting of a few relatively large organizations. The primary constituents of this second group are hospitals, colleges, and universities.

Clearly there will be differences between these two groups. For example, it is estimated that government funding makes up more than 70% of the revenue of hospitals, colleges, and universities but makes up only about 20% of the funding of small NFPs.[3] These organizations will also differ in terms of need for and understanding of sophisticated accounting.

With this in mind we will first examine how NFPs differ from business enterprises. Later, we will consider how the differences among NFPs may affect the accounting choices made by NFPs.

There are four very fundamental ways in which not-for-profit organizations (NFPs) differ from business enterprises:

1.  NFPs have *members* instead of owners; there are no residual economic interests.

2.  The organization has a different "bottom line." The organization's objectives may be to serve the common good rather than to maximize net income or generate a return on investment.

3.  The nature of revenues and the relationship between revenues and costs differs significantly from those of businesses. As well, the sources of revenue often sharply restrict the flexibility of the organization to use that revenue.

4.  The suppliers of funds (who are the primary users of the financial statements) are not providing capital to earn a return on their investment. Therefore, financial reporting objectives often differ significantly from those of the profit sector.

These four characteristics profoundly affect the nature of NFP financial reporting. We will expand upon each of these characteristics in the following sections.

## No Owners

Not-for-profit organizations have no owners. Regardless of whether an NFP is incorporated or unincorporated, no one has a right to the residual earnings or assets of the organization. As we have already mentioned, incorporated NFPs are legally defined as *corporations without share capital*. Since NFPs have no owners, they have no transferable ownership interest.

Although NFPs have no shareholders, they do have *members*, who elect the board of directors.[4] The constitution of the organization specifies the conditions for membership. Membership may be either *open* or *closed*.

In an open membership, the conditions for membership are clearly specified in the constitution or bylaws of the organization, and membership is available to anyone who is able to fulfill the membership requirements. A closed membership exists when the members are designated by the board of directors. Membership is *closed* in the sense that it is not automatically open to all otherwise-qualified individuals who apply, and because the

---

[3] *Satellite Account of Not-for-Profit Institutions and Volunteering*, Statistics Canada, December 2008.

[4] In some NFPs, the members elect only some of the directors, while other directors are appointed by stakeholder groups, such as government or constituency groups.

board has the power to change the requirements for membership at any board meeting. In some not-for-profit organizations, the directors are the *only* members of the organization—in effect, the board elects itself.

## A Different "Bottom Line"

NFPs exist to perform a service. Since there are no residual economic interests, financial performance on its own is not a primary objective. Obviously, an NFP must remain financially viable to continue to operate and to fulfill its service objectives, but financial viability is a *means to an end* rather than being the end itself, as is the case with business enterprises.

Businesses provide goods and services to individuals (or to organized groups such as other businesses) at a price. Price is the rationing mechanism, but it also provides the revenue that finances the cost of providing the goods and services. Goods and services that are consumed by individuals (and thus unavailable to others) and that are rationed are referred to as **private goods and services**.

Not-for-profit organizations may also provide private goods and services. This is particularly true in NFPs such as sports or social clubs, wherein the primary objective of the organization is to provide services to its members. Private goods are also provided by organizations such as trade unions and professional organizations.

However, an NFP may provide goods and services that are not intended to benefit specific individuals but instead to benefit groups within society at large, or the common welfare. Greenpeace, for example, is engaged in environmental awareness activities that benefit society as a whole. The Canadian Cancer Society is engaged in supporting cancer research and in increasing public awareness of cancer (and understanding for those who are afflicted with it). The benefits of the activities of organizations such as Greenpeace and the Canadian Cancer Society are available to all individuals within the "target" group either free or at a nominal charge—these benefits are known as **collective goods and services** or **public goods and services**. Other examples of collective goods include accounting standard-setting, cancer awareness programs, anti-racism campaigns, and museum exhibitions.

Business enterprises do not provide collective goods; collective goods are provided *only* by governments and not-for-profit organizations. Because there is no parallel in the private sector, proprietary accounting is of little help in designing financial reports for providers of collective goods. Accounting standard-setters have implicitly acknowledged this fact in providing for different accounting principles for governments (as we will discuss in Chapter 11) as well as for some types of NFPs.

The accounting policies of an NFP are not driven foremost by a need to determine residual interest, as is the case with shareholders in a business corporation. NFPs also have recognized costs, but the residual "bottom line" of revenues minus recognized costs is more of a true *residual, what is left over*, rather than a business-type net income measure.

## Relationship Between Revenue and Costs

In business enterprises, the providers of revenue are the beneficiaries of the businesses' goods and services. There is a direct link between the service performed, the beneficiary of the service, and the generation of revenue. Therefore, much of business accounting focuses on *matching* to revenue the costs incurred to generate that revenue.

In some NFPs, there is a similar link. Clubs, private societies, and religious organizations generate revenue primarily from their members and spend that revenue primarily on activities and services that benefit their members. For convenience, we can refer to those organizations wherein the members are the primary (or only) beneficiary of the organization's goods and services as being **self-beneficial organizations**. The members provide the primary revenues, and they receive the benefits of the goods and services.

However, many other types of NFPs do not derive their primary revenues from the beneficiaries of their services. Instead, most social service agencies and arts organizations obtain the bulk of their revenue from governments or private donors, or both. When the beneficiaries of the goods and services are different from the providers of the resources, the NFP is a **public-beneficial organization**.[5]

A key aspect of public-beneficial NFPs is that their revenue is largely independent of the costs. The revenue comes from one group, but the money is spent on serving a different group. This is very different from businesses, where the costs are incurred to earn the revenue. Therefore, not-for-profit organizations (and governments) need expenditure controls that are markedly different from those normally encountered in private enterprise.

Businesses measure their expenses in relation to revenue, thereby using the cost–revenue relationship as a control device. In contrast, when revenues are received by an NFP from individual donors or as a block grant from government, the relationship between costs and revenues is broken and costs must be controlled directly. Therefore, the budgetary and management reporting system of NFPs is often designed to prevent managers from exceeding their *spending* authority—*expenditures* become more of a focus than *expenses*.

Some or all of the donations or grants received by a not-for-profit organization may be restricted for particular uses or programs. The donor wants assurance that the funds were used for the intended purpose. The accounting and reporting system must be able to match expenditures to specific programs or purposes. Funds are not transferable from one program to another; therefore, it may not be meaningful to combine revenues and expenditures relating to different programs into a single operating statement for the NFP as a whole.

For example, a school or university will have a large amount of operating funds (grants from government and fees received from students) that are specifically designated for operating specified educational programs. The operating funds cannot be used for buildings or for ancillary activities such as providing free parking for faculty or low-cost meals for students. The school will receive separate capital grants that can be used only for capital projects, such as new buildings or substantial renovations, and there will also be scholarship funds that must be used only for student aid. Therefore, the accounting and financial reporting system of many NFPs must be able to distinguish between the various funds and be able to show that the various restrictions have been observed.

## Objectives of Financial Reporting

The primary users of the financial statements of a not-for-profit organization are the suppliers of its funds. Funds are derived from (1) members; (2) granting agencies; (3) the general public; and (4) creditors. The objectives of financial statements for not-for-profit

---

[5] Charitable organizations are sometimes called "beneficial organizations," which is the same idea.

organizations are focused on the needs of users. In general, the financial reporting objectives for not-for-profit organizations are:

- stewardship;
- measuring the cost of services rendered;
- cash-flow prediction; and
- management evaluation.

The first two are the primary objectives; the others tend to flow from satisfying the first two objectives. The relevance and priority of the primary objectives depends on the characteristics of the not-for-profit organization.

If a public-beneficial organization provides collective goods and services using funds donated by the public, *stewardship reporting* of the resources provided by the contributors is most likely to be the primary objective. Greenpeace is a good example. Measurement of the cost of Greenpeace's environmental protection activities is of limited usefulness; there is no meaningful measure of output and thus no useful cost of providing services can be determined. The emphasis in NFP reporting often is on disposition of the resources provided for specific purposes or programs rather than on the costs of services provided. This is an *input* basis of reporting rather than the *output* basis that we are accustomed to in business reporting.

On the other hand, a public-beneficial organization may provide private goods and services on a *cost recovery basis*. An overnight hostel for homeless people may be supported by reimbursement on a fee-for-service basis from the city government. The city is the source of funds, and the city will want to know the cost per bed per night; the city may support several such programs and will want to compare the efficiency of the services provided. In such a case, measuring the cost of service becomes the primary reporting objective, and an output-based system of reporting (similar to that used by business enterprises) is appropriate.

A distinctive feature of NFP financial reporting is a strong commonality of interests among the various users of the statements. Members, managers, directors, and creditors need to see the organization and its programs in the same light as do the major providers of the resources. Managers and directors are accountable to the resource providers for the disposition of resources entrusted to their care. Creditors are also aware that future cash flows may be coming from the suppliers of resources (e.g., government ministries) rather than from the sale of goods and services.

Therefore, there often is a strong dominant influence by the providers of the resources in shaping financial reporting objectives and thereby determining accounting policies. This is particularly true of public-beneficial organizations that are providing goods and services (either private or collective) with a fixed revenue base.

## Concept Check 10-1

1. Describe four ways in which NFPs differ from business enterprises.
2. What are *collective goods and services*? What types of organizations offer collective goods and services?
3. What is a *public-beneficial organization*? Explain how a public-beneficial organization differs from a *self-beneficial organization*.
4. What are the financial reporting objectives for NFPs?

## 10.4 PRIMARY REPORTING ISSUES

LO

Explain the primary reporting issues that arise from the special characteristics of NFPs

There are several important reporting issues that shape the financial reporting of not-for-profit organizations. The primary reporting issues for an NFP are:

1. expense versus expenditure reporting;

2. revenue recognition and segregation of resources;

3. capital assets;

4. expense allocations; and

5. defining the reporting entity.

We will discuss these issues first, and then we will examine the basic reporting options that are available to NFPs. An NFP should choose the option that best suits the nature of its operations and meets its users' needs.

## Expense Versus Expenditure Reporting

There are three different bases on which the resource outflows of any organization can be recognized in the statement of operations:

- *Disbursement* basis: outflows are recognized only when the cash is paid out or disbursed (i.e., a strict cash basis of reporting).

- *Expenditure* basis: outflows are recognized when liabilities are incurred or cash is paid out (i.e., accrual accounting applied to liabilities).

- *Expense* basis: outflows are recognized when goods and services are used in the operations (i.e., a "full accrual" basis of reporting).

Not-for-profit organizations must decide whether they are going to recognize their costs on the basis of disbursements, expenditures, or expenses. If they have a GAAP constraint,[6] the *CICA Handbook* requires the expense basis. However, many small NFPs may not have a GAAP constraint. Also, their members may not have the expertise to prepare or understand GAAP-compliant statements. Therefore, it is worthwhile to undertake a brief examination of alternatives to GAAP.

**Disbursement Basis** A disbursement (i.e., strict cash) basis may be suitable for small organizations with few accrued expenses or payables. The use of a strict cash basis, however, may result in reported expenditures that do not properly reflect the commitments made by the organization during the reporting period. Strict cash basis reporting can cause an organization to lose control of its resource management and to lose track of what it owes.

The real choice therefore is between recognizing costs in the statement of operations on the basis of *expenditures* or of *expenses*. The expenditure basis has little equivalency in the private sector, where we normally think in terms of expenses. But the notion of expenses is related to the concept of profit, which generally does not exist in the not-for-profit sector.

---

[6] Some not-for-profit organizations may have a GAAP constraint imposed by their funding body. Most not-for-profit organizations, however, will only have a GAAP constraint if they voluntarily choose to follow GAAP.

**Expenditure Basis**  An expenditure occurs when a liability is incurred or cash (or other asset) is paid out to obtain goods or services. Note that the emphasis is on *obtaining* goods and services instead of on *using* goods and services, which is the focus of expense.

The expenditure basis means that costs are recorded in operations when incurred, either by disbursing cash or by incurring a liability. Supplies, for example, would be recognized in the statement of operations when acquired rather than when used—no supplies inventory would appear on the SFP. In contrast, the expense basis means that goods and services are recognized in the statement of operations when they are used in performing the organization's service.

An expenditure basis is most appropriate when service and program outputs are difficult to measure and therefore there is no clear basis for allocating expenses or measuring efficiency. A clear example would be any form of public or collective good wherein there is no specific beneficiary and no revenue derived from the costs incurred. Specific activities may be clearly defined but the general operations of the organization cannot be specifically related to programmatic goals with measurable outputs. An expenditure basis is also appropriate for programs wherein fixed-grant revenues are intended to finance variable-cost services, as in public-beneficial organizations that derive their primary revenues from block grants by government ministries or foundations.

**Expense Basis**  In contrast, the expense basis is likely to be most appropriate when the NFP is delivering goods or services to individuals and the organization needs to measure the cost of providing those goods or services. For example, hospitals may use an expense basis so that they know the cost of specific services. Revenue providers, such as the provincial governments, often use comparative cost information (that is, from many different hospitals) to evaluate the efficiency of individual hospitals.

On the other hand, it may be useful to exclude certain costs from the cost-of-services calculation when those costs fall outside of the funding guidelines that have been established by the funding agency (i.e., the provincial Ministry of Health). The most notable such cost is the cost of capital assets.

## Revenue Recognition and Segregation of Resources

Contributions are a major source of revenue for most NFPs. A **contribution** is defined as a non-reciprocal transfer of cash (or other assets) to the NFP. Typical examples would include donations, bequests, grants, and government subsidies. They are non-reciprocal transfers because the individuals or organizations providing the contribution do not receive anything back in exchange for the contribution.

The nature of the relationship between revenues and costs is important. In a business enterprise, an individual gives money to the business in exchange for a product or service. Thus the focus of accounting is on the exchange (or reciprocal transfer). Revenue is recognized when the earnings process is complete (for example, upon delivery of the good). Furthermore, performance is measured by matching costs to the revenue generated.

With contributions, the connection between revenues and expenses is severed because the contribution is non-reciprocal. Therefore contribution revenue is not recognized when earned (because it is never *earned*)—it simply is received. Since there is no "earning," the contribution is recognized when received. Thus revenue recognition for contributions is relatively easy when compared with revenue recognition for businesses.

There is one exception. Contributions are sometimes received with restrictions on how the money is to be spent. In these cases, to help ensure that the money is spent appropriately (i.e., to meet the stewardship objective), the revenue may be recognized by matching it to the related expense, where possible. This of course is the exact opposite of businesses, where expenses are matched to the revenue. We will explore when and how this occurs in more detail below.

The *AcSB* recommends two alternative methods of accounting for contributions: (1) the *deferral method* or (2) the *restricted-fund method*. Before we demonstrate these two methods, we must first discuss the use of fund accounting by NFPs. We then will explain the three different types of contributions that NFPs may receive.

## Fund Accounting
An NFP may or may not segment its operations and resources by fund. **Fund accounting** is a set of accounting procedures that are used in a particular fund to record the transactions of that fund and that result in a set of self-balancing accounts. The focus of fund accounting is on keeping track of resources that are designated for specific purposes. The purpose is to avoid mixing up resources that are intended for diverse purposes and to ensure that management fulfills its stewardship responsibility for proper disposition of the resources.

A single non-business organization can have several (or many) such accounting enti-  ties. The extent to which an organization's funds need to be segregated is largely a matter of common sense, based on the types of contributions they receive and the users' needs. Appendix 10A on the Companion Website provides more detail on fund accounting.

An organization that uses fund accounting will typically create funds on the basis of either (1) the restrictions placed by donors or (2) the programs it offers. An organization may create separate funds to track resources that are restricted for specific purposes by its donors. For example, a university could have a building fund (to account for donations received to build new residences), a research fund (to account for grants received for research), and an endowment fund (to account for donations received to fund scholarships).

Alternatively, an organization may create separate funds for each program that it offers. For example, a homeless shelter could have a food program fund (to track resources and activities related to its meals for the homeless program), a shelter fund (to track resources and activities related to its temporary or overnight accommodations), and a housing fund (to track resources and activities related to its long-term accommodations program).

Each fund in an organization is a self-balancing set of accounts. A fund has its own revenues, expenses, assets, and liabilities. The "equity" section of a fund is referred to as the fund balance (i.e., net assets). The use of fund accounting by an organization assists users in assessing whether monies are being spent for the purpose intended by external donors or whether the organization is achieving its program objectives.

The accounting for contribution revenue depends on whether an organization uses fund accounting, and if it does, how it uses fund accounting. Three options are possible:

- If the organization does not use fund accounting, it will use the *deferral method* to account for contribution revenue.

- If the organization uses fund accounting and creates and groups its funds based on externally imposed restrictions, it will use the *restricted-fund method* to account for contribution revenue in each fund.

- If the organization uses fund accounting and creates and groups its funds based on the programs it offers (or on any basis other than externally imposed restrictions), it will use the deferral method in each fund to account for contribution revenue. The deferral method is used because each fund could have both unrestricted and restricted contributions.

For our purposes, we will focus on the first two options to illustrate the two methods of accounting for contribution revenue. The principles in the third option are the same as those discussed in the first two options, applied fund-by-fund rather than for the organization as a whole.

**Three Categories of Contributions**  Contributions can be classified into three different categories: restricted contributions, endowment contributions, and unrestricted contributions. NFPs often receive revenue grants that are earmarked for specific purposes. When the use of the revenue is specified by the donor, the revenue is called a **restricted contribution** or **grant**. To maintain proper control over restricted funds, the NFP must have a way of segregating restricted funds from its other resources. This is important for two reasons:

- the donor and other external users need to see that the funds are being used for the donor-designated purposes; and
- the NFP needs to show financial-statement users that restricted funds are not available for general purposes and cannot be transferred to general operations.

Externally restricted contributions are contributions *restricted by the donor* for specific purposes or uses. They may not be used for other purposes, and the system of accounts must maintain the integrity of the donation and its purpose. Externally restricted contributions must be distinguished from board-designated funds (internally restricted), which are funds that the board of directors has earmarked for a specific purpose. The board can decide to reverse its internal restriction, and therefore internal restrictions do not have the same importance for financial reporting as do true restricted funds.

An **endowment contribution** is a special type of restricted contribution. Not only is the contribution restricted in purpose, but also the principal amount of the contribution cannot be spent. The contribution must be invested in an endowment fund, and only the earnings on the investment can be spent for the intended purposes. An example is a scholarship fund within a university. The principal amount to establish the scholarship is maintained, and interest earned on that principal is used to provide scholarships.

An **unrestricted contribution** is provided without any restrictions on its use by the organization. Basically, it is any contribution that does not meet the definition of either a restricted contribution or an endowment contribution.

It is critical to remember the differences between these types of contributions as we discuss the NFP reporting options. The recognition and presentation of different types of contributions on the financial statement differ among these methods.

## Reality Check 10–1

## Deferral Method

The Canadian Cancer Society uses the deferral method to account for externally restricted contributions that relate to its regular operations. For deferred contributions that arise, it states in the financial statement notes that:

"Deferred contributions are recognized as revenue when the related expenses are incurred."

Source: Canadian Cancer Society, Financial Statements for the Year Ended January 31, 2011, p. 8

**Deferral Method: Business-Type Accounting** This method is conceptually similar to that used by business enterprises, at least on the surface. The concept behind this method is to match the revenues with the associated expenses. The revenue is recognized as the related expenses are incurred, at least for restricted contributions.

Unrestricted contributions are recognized as revenues in the current period. They are available for any use by the organization.

The treatment of *restricted contributions* depends on the purpose for which they have been restricted by the donor. If the contribution is for expenses of the current period, the contribution should be recognized as revenue in the current period. If the contribution is for expenses of a future period, it is recorded as *deferred contributions or deferred revenue* until the related expense is recognized.

Note that this matching process is reversed from our normal expectation in business enterprise accounting. For businesses, the usual focus is on recognizing revenue first, and then matching expenses to that revenue. If there are related costs that will be incurred in the future (e.g., warranty expense), those future costs are estimated and recognized in the period in which the revenue has been recognized to achieve matching.

Under the deferral method of NFP accounting, first the expenses are recognized, and then the revenue is matched. If revenue is received prior to the expense, the revenue must be deferred until the expense is recognized. Note that the deferral is until the *expense* is recognized, not the *expenditure*. If a restricted contribution is for a capital asset, the treatment depends on whether or not that asset will be amortized. If the asset is amortized, the revenue will be deferred and recognized on the same basis as the amortization of the specific asset that has been purchased.

**Example: Deferral Method** For example, suppose that a donor contributes $30,000 to a social agency on December 13, 20X5. The donation is restricted for the purchase of a new van. The van will be purchased in 20X6. The van will be depreciated over three years, straight-line. When the contribution is received, the credit will be to deferred contribution revenue:

| December 13, 20X5 | | |
|---|---|---|
| Cash | 30,000 | |
| Deferred contribution revenue (restricted—van) | | 30,000 |

If the van is purchased on January 27, 20X6, the transaction will have no immediate impact on the statement of operations:

| January 27, 20X6 | | |
|---|---|---|
| Capital asset—van | 30,000 | |
| Cash | | 30,000 |

At the end of 20X6, the agency will record $10,000 in depreciation. Simultaneously, the same amount of revenue will be recognized:

| December 31, 20X6 | | |
|---|---|---|
| Depreciation expense | 10,000 | |
| Accumulated depreciation | | 10,000 |
| Deferred contribution revenue (restricted—van) | 10,000 | |
| Contribution revenue | | 10,000 |

Under the deferral method, all revenues are added together in the statement of operations. If the restricted revenue were recognized when it is received or when the van is purchased, the agency would show restricted revenue that is not matched by an expense—and any unmatched revenue will lead financial statement readers to believe that the NFP has more revenue available for unrestricted purposes than it really does.

To avoid showing revenue without any related expenses, *endowment contributions* are recognized as direct increases in net assets in the current period because they will never be available to meet expenses of the organization. This is also true for assets that are not amortized (e.g., land). If a contribution is received that is restricted for the purchase of land, the revenue will be shown as a direct increase in net assets. These kinds of contributions are shown on the statement of changes in net assets, which may be in a separate statement or combined with the statement of operations.

**Example: Deferral Method**  Suppose that another donor contributes $1,000,000 to a social agency on June 30, 20X6. The money is to be perpetually invested in Government of Canada bonds. The interest earned can be spent as the agency sees fit. On July 1, 20X6, a $1,000,000, 4% government bond is purchased at par. Interest is paid semi-annually on June 30 and December 31. The contribution is an endowment; therefore the credit will be to net assets:

| June 30, 20X6 | | |
|---|---|---|
| Cash | 1,000,000 | |
| Net assets (endowment) | | 1,000,000 |

The bond is purchased on July 1, 20X6:

| July 1, 20X6 | | |
|---|---|---|
| Bond Investments | 1,000,000 | |
| Cash | | 1,000,000 |

At the end of 20X6, the agency will record $20,000 in interest revenue:

| December 31, 20X6 | | |
|---|---|---|
| Cash | 20,000 | |
| Interest revenue | | 20,000 |

**Restricted-Fund Method**  The second method is based on the concepts of fund accounting that have been used in not-for-profit organizations for many years. A number of separate funds (i.e., self-balancing sets of accounts) are used to segregate the three basic different types of contributions: (1) restricted funds; (2) endowment funds; and (3) the general fund (or operating fund) for unrestricted contributions.

Unrestricted contributions are recognized as revenue in the general fund. The accounting for restricted contributions depends on whether or not there is a separate restricted fund for that contribution. If there is a separate restricted fund, it is recognized as revenue in the current period in that fund. If there is no separate fund, it is *recognized in the general fund using the deferral method* of accounting for contributions. Therefore, restricted contributions are treated differently depending on whether they are shown in a separate fund.

**Example: Restricted-Fund Method**  Using our previous example, suppose that a donor contributes $30,000 to a social agency on December 13, 20X5. The social agency has a general fund, a capital asset fund, and an endowment fund. The donation is restricted for the purchase of a new van. The van will be purchased in 20X6. The van will be depreciated over three years, straight-line. When the contribution is received, the credit will be to revenue of the capital asset fund:

| December 13, 20X5 | | |
|---|---|---|
| Capital asset fund | | |
| Cash | 30,000 | |
| Contribution revenue | | 30,000 |

The van is purchased on January 27, 20X6:

| January 27, 20X6 | | |
|---|---|---|
| Capital asset fund | | |
| Capital asset—van | 30,000 | |
| Cash | | 30,000 |

At the end of 20X6, the agency will record $10,000 in depreciation (assuming that it is recorded in the capital asset fund):

| December 31, 20X6 | | |
|---|---|---|
| Capital asset fund | | |
| Depreciation expense | 10,000 | |
| Accumulated depreciation | | 10,000 |

Endowment contributions are recognized as revenues in the *endowment fund* in the current period. Note the difference here between the two reporting methods. The restricted-fund method shows the contributions as *revenue* in a separate fund. In contrast, the deferral method shows endowment contributions as a direct increase in net assets— there is no revenue recognition on the statement of operations.

**Example: Restricted-Fund Method**  Suppose that another donor contributes $1,000,000 to a social agency on June 30, 20X6. The money is to be perpetually invested in Government of Canada bonds. The interest earned can be spent as the agency sees fit. On July 1, 20X6, a $1,000,000, 4% government bond is purchased at par. Interest is paid semi-annually on June 30 and December 31. The contribution is an endowment; therefore the credit will be to revenue of the endowment fund:

| June 30, 20X6 | | |
|---|---|---|
| Endowment fund | | |
| Cash | 1,000,000 | |
| Contribution revenue | | 1,000,000 |

The bond is purchased on July 1, 20X6:

| July 1, 20X6 | | |
|---|---|---|
| Endowment fund | | |
| Bond investments | 1,000,000 | |
| Cash | | 1,000,000 |

At the end of 20X6, the agency will record $20,000 in interest revenue in the general fund since the use of the interest revenue is unrestricted:

| December 31, 20X6, | | |
|---|---|---|
| General fund: | | |
| Cash | 20,000 | |
| Interest revenue | | 20,000 |

Notice also that under the restricted-fund method, contributions in separate restricted and endowment funds are recognized currently. When restricted funds are shown separately, there will be no confusion about whether excess revenue is available for general use. The use of a restricted fund makes it clear to users that those resources are not available for general operations. Matching of revenues to expenses is not of concern in this reporting framework, and therefore there is no need to defer recognition of the revenue.

The restricted-fund method of accounting tends to result in a higher level of revenue than does the deferral method. The reasons are that (1) restricted revenues often are recognized earlier because there is no need to defer recognition of the revenue until the expense has been recognized and (2) contributions to endowment funds are recognized as revenue under the restricted-fund method but not under the deferral method. Therefore, the selection of accounting method may place an organization over the size test for capitalizing capital assets (i.e., average revenues of less than $500,000) if the restricted-fund method is used, but not if the deferral method is used. The accounting for the different types of contributions under the two systems is summarized in Exhibit 10.2.

**Pledges**   How should pledges be recognized in the financial statements of NFPs? A **pledge** is a promise to give cash (or other assets) to the NFP. A promise to pay could be viewed as a receivable. However, a donor may give a pledge, but may subsequently decide not to actually give the money. Unlike a business transaction, for an NFP donor, there is no exchange—an NFP donor is making a one-way promise that can later be rescinded, retracted, or completely ignored by the donor.

## Reality Check 10–2

## Accounting for Pledges

The accounting policy note on pledges for the Canadian Cancer Society is consistent with the practices of most NFPs.

Source: Canadian Cancer Society, Financial Statements for the Year Ended January 31, 2011, p. 10.

> Revenue from donations is recognized on a cash basis, with no accrual being made for amounts pledged but not received.

**Exhibit 10.2** Summary of Revenue Recognition of Contributions

| Method | Type of contribution | Accounting |
|---|---|---|
| Deferral method | Unrestricted | Recognize as revenue in the current period |
| | Restricted | |
| | ■ To pay for (or repay debt incurred for) current-period expenses | Recognize as revenue in the current period |
| | ■ To pay for (or repay debt incurred for) future-period expenses | Defer, match revenues to expenses |
| | ■ To pay for (or repay debt incurred for) capital asset—amortizable | Defer, match revenues to expenses (amortization) |
| | ■ To pay for (or repay debt incurred for) capital asset—non-amortizable | Recognize as direct increase to net assets |
| | Endowment | Recognize as direct increase to net assets |
| Restricted-fund method | Unrestricted | Recognize as revenue in the general fund |
| | Restricted | |
| | ■ Appropriate restricted fund exists | Recognize as revenue in restricted fund |
| | ■ No appropriate restricted fund | Recognize as revenue in general fund using the deferral method |
| | Endowment | Recognize as revenue in the endowment fund |

An NFP can recognize a pledge as a receivable on its SFP if both of two criteria are met: (1) the amount can be reasonably estimated, and (2) ultimate collection is reasonably assured.

The amount is not usually in doubt. Most pledges are for cash, and are payable within a fairly short period of time. Cash pledges may be uncertain in amount, however, if they depend on future events. For example, a business may promise to contribute 1% of its revenue from sales of a certain product. Even though the contribution will be in cash, the amount will not be known until the sales results are known.

The estimation criterion may also not be met when the pledge is not in cash but in the form of a non-cash asset. It may be impossible to get a reasonable estimate of the value of the asset until it is in the NFP's hands and can be reliably assessed. As well, the donation may be contingent on some future event, such as the donor's death, which makes both the timing *and* the value of the donation uncertain.

The dual criteria of measurability and collectability often are difficult to achieve for many not-for-profit organizations. Most NFPs prefer not to count their cash before it has been received. Therefore, revenue is usually recognized only when the amount is collected.

**Donated Goods and Services**   It is not unusual for people and businesses to donate goods and services. Indeed, the very nature of most NFPs and volunteer organizations means that much of the work is being carried out by volunteers through contributed services. As well, companies often choose to donate goods or services, such as an airline that provides free transportation to a sports organization to fly athletes to major competitions. An accounting issue arises from non-monetary donations—should the donated goods and services be assigned a value and reported in the statements?

In some cases, goods or services are donated as a way of helping the organization raise money. The goods or services are sold or auctioned off, and the organization ultimately receives cash in exchange for the donated goods or services. In such instances, the inflow of cash determines the value of the donation, and the amount of cash received must be recorded as a donation by the not-for-profit organization.

More commonly, however, the goods and services are donated to help the organization achieve its objectives. The United Way, for example, receives substantial donations of executive time from businesses to help manage its campaigns. Should the United Way record the value of the donated time?

**To Record or Not?**   When donated goods or services are assigned a value and recorded by the organization, the credit to revenues offsets the debit to expenditures and there is no impact on the net operating results. However, the absolute values of the revenues and expenses are affected, and it is possible that management's performance could be evaluated differently.

For example, one measure of the performance of a fundraising organization is the proportion of funds raised that are consumed as fundraising expenses. An organization that spends only 10% of the donations to obtain those donations is perceived as doing a better job than one that spends 40% of the funds it raises. But if the 40% organization is paying for all of the services it receives, while the 10% organization is using enormous amounts of volunteer effort, are the financial results of the two organizations really comparable? If the 10% organization were to record the value of its donated effort, its cost ratio may rise to 60%. Thus the recording of donated goods and services can have an impact on the perceptions of the readers of the statements, at least in terms of performance evaluation.

For stewardship reporting, the advantages of reporting the value of donated goods and services are not clear. If the primary objective of the statements is to report on how management used the funds at its disposal, then reporting donated services on the statements may only impair the reporting objective, because it will appear that management had more funds at its disposal than was actually the case.

**Guidance from Canadian Accounting Standards**   Practice has varied considerably. Recording and reporting the value of *donated goods and services* seems to have been the exception rather than the rule in the past. The requirements to record donated goods and services are:

■   the value can be reasonably estimated; and

■   the goods and services would otherwise have been purchased in the normal course of business.

While the general recommendation for donated goods and services is permissive (i.e., "may"), the suggested recommendation for *donated capital assets* is stronger. The CICA

*Handbook* requires that donated capital assets "should" be recorded at fair value. When the fair value cannot be reasonably determined, the capital asset should be recorded at nominal value.

## Capital Assets

Capital-asset accounting is controversial largely because of the various methods that NFPs use to finance asset acquisitions. Some NFPs must fund their asset acquisitions through operating revenue, while others may acquire major long-term assets only by special grants or donations. As a result, three different approaches used for accounting for capital assets have developed:

1.  charge to operations immediately (an expenditure basis);
2.  capitalize and depreciate (an expense basis); or
3.  capitalize but *not* depreciate.

**Expenditure Basis**   Charging the cost of capital assets to operations when incurred is the expenditure basis as applied to capital assets. It is possible to use an expenditure basis for capital assets while using an expense basis for other costs. In the past, this approach was by far the most commonly used. The main reason for its popularity relates to the nature of the revenue used to acquire the assets.

Many funding organizations (especially government granting agencies and ministries) restrict NFPs' use of operating revenues to operating expenditures, *excluding* capital-asset acquisition. Separate grants are given as capital grants for the acquisition of capital assets, and the funding organizations usually prohibit the inclusion of depreciation in the operating accounts. When a capital grant is given, the revenue from the grant is matched to the cost of acquiring the asset in the period of acquisition, and no capitalization or depreciation occurs.

Sometimes capital grants are given only for major assets such as buildings, while smaller acquisitions (such as furniture or computers) must be financed through the operating grants. In that case, different accounting policies sometimes have been used for the two types of assets due to the differing relationship to revenues.

Even in organizations where revenue comes from general donations rather than from government grants, expenditures for major depreciable capital assets may be financed by means of special capital fundraising campaigns. There is no intent on the part of either

---

**Reality Check 10–3**

## Accounting for Donated Goods and Services

The accounting policies of the Canadian Cancer Society for donated time and donated capital assets are:

> The Society's programs benefit substantially from services in the form of volunteer time. The value of these services is not recorded in these financial statements.[a] [...] Capital assets [...] donated to the Society are recorded at their fair market value at the date of acquisition when fair market value can be reasonably estimated.[b]

[a] Canadian Cancer Society, Financial Statements for the year ended January 31, 2011, p. 13.

[b] Canadian Cancer Society, Financial Statements for the year ended January 31, 2011, p. 7.

the organization or the donors that part of the cost of assets be charged against operations. If depreciation expense is charged in periods following the acquisition, then the organization will show a deficit in those periods even if fundraising activities are sufficient to cover the expenditures for the period (or, conversely, if expenditures are held to the level of the revenue raised).

It can be argued that when an organization receives separate funding for its capital acquisitions and replacements, it is a form of double-counting to deduct depreciation from operating funds. The usual approach in such circumstances is to charge the full cost of the acquisition against the capital grant when it is received; this approach achieves matching of the revenues and related expenditures. However, the disadvantage of immediate write-off is that the assets do not appear on the SFP.

**Expense Basis**   The argument for the expense approach is that depreciation is a cost of providing services and that depreciation should therefore be recorded regardless of the way in which the assets were financed. For example, the FASB has argued that "using up assets in providing services [...] has a cost whether those assets have been acquired in prior periods or in the current period and whether acquired by paying cash, incurring liabilities, or by contribution."[7] Similarly, the CICA *Handbook* recommends that capital assets of limited life should be amortized, and that amortization should be included in the NFP's operating statement as an expense.

Depreciation accounting makes sense under either of two circumstances:

1.   the cost of replacing capital assets must be recovered from general revenues, or
2.   evaluation of efficiency requires that the cost of *all* inputs, including capital assets, be included in the measurement of outputs.

The expense basis would seem to be appropriate for hospitals, colleges, and universities (HCU), which account for 64% of the value of activity in the NFP sector. Users of HCU financial statements, such as governments, would be very interested in being able to evaluate the efficiency of the HCUs' operations to aid them in their resource allocation decisions. An expense basis that includes depreciation also seems appropriate for self-beneficial organizations and for private goods that are paid for on a fee-for-service basis, regardless of whether the payer is the direct beneficiary or is an outside funder (e.g., a hostel that receives reimbursement from a city for overnight accommodation of homeless people).

**Capitalization Only**   The third approach to reporting capital assets is to capitalize the assets and never charge the cost to operations. This approach makes sense when (1) asset replacement or renewal is separately funded or (2) the assets do not decline in value or in usefulness.

**Canadian Standards for Capital Assets**   Canadian NFP GAAP requires that NFPs capitalize and amortize all capital assets (although land is not amortized, of course). Smaller NFPs need not comply with this recommendation. The exemption applies to any organization whose average gross annual consolidated revenues of the preceding and current years is less than $500,000. From our review of the NFP sector earlier in the chapter it appears that over 85% of organizations in the NFP sector could take advantage of this exemption.

---

[7] Statement of Financial Accounting Standard No. 93, Recognition of Depreciation by Not-for-Profit Organizations (FASB, 1987), 20.

**Collections—A Special Issue** A related issue is the capitalization of collections in museums and galleries. Collections are worth a great deal of money, and they are acquired through the use of donors' funds. Since the AcSB requires the capitalization of capital assets, it also would like to see collections capitalized. However, the Board realizes that this is impractical in most situations because the cost of valuing the collections would be greater than any benefit gained by it.

Thus, for collections, capitalizing the cost of collections is *permissible* but not *required*. To assist preparers in determining whether their assets qualify as a collection of works of art or historical treasures, the CICA requires that the following three criteria be met:

1. The asset(s) must be available to be seen or used (e.g., for education or research) by the public.

2. The collection needs to be maintained and protected.

3. If an asset from the collection is sold, the proceeds from its sale cannot be used for the operations of the NFP. The funds must be used to acquire new pieces for the collection or to help in meeting the second criterion—to care for the collection.

Classification as a *collection* is important because the recommendation to capitalize capital assets does not apply to collections. Instead, the NFP has three options:

- capitalize with no depreciation;
- capitalize and depreciate; or
- disclose only.

The most common alternative is simply to disclose the *existence* of a collection. Although reporting or disclosing the *value* of a collection may be desirable, the practice is not generally followed. Estimates of the value of assets inevitably are unreliable, are difficult to verify, and may not be free from bias. In addition, there is a cost associated with having independent appraisals made, and most institutions would prefer not to incur that cost.

## Expense Allocations

Donors often are interested in the efficiency of the organization in accomplishing its mission. In particular, donors often focus on the costs reported for fundraising and general support (i.e., non-program costs). NFPs are acutely aware of the fact that they are often evaluated on their ability to control the costs of these two functions. As a result, they have an incentive to minimize the costs reported in these two functions.

One practice is to reallocate the costs from one of these two functions to an unrelated function such as education. To help ensure that these allocations are legitimate, the AcSB introduced a standard that requires disclosure of allocated expenses by NFPs.

If amounts are allocated from fundraising and general support to other areas, the standard requires the following disclosures:

- explanation of allocation policies;
- explanation of the nature of the expenses allocated;
- the allocation basis;

- the amounts allocated from fundraising and general support; and
- the amounts and areas the expenses are allocated toward.

The standard also provides three specific criteria that must be met before an amount can be allocated to the education function. The information (1) must be targeted at specific individuals or groups; (2) must provide advice that is specific enough to allow an individual to act in an informed manner; and (3) must be related to the educational objectives of the organization.

Changes to the bases for allocations are to be reported as changes in accounting policy.

# Defining the Reporting Entity

There are many types of relationships that may exist between legally distinct but operationally similar NFPs that are under common control. As a result, the definition of the reporting entity is not as simple as it is for business enterprises.

For example, some arts organizations and social service organizations have a *foundation* that serves primarily to raise money for the main organization. The foundation usually has a board of trustees that is drawn directly from the board of directors of the principal operating arts or social service organization that it controls. Therefore, both the foundation and the operating agency are under common control.

Since the foundation is a legally separate organization, it could report separately from the operating agency. If reporting were done on this basis, it would be difficult to evaluate the operations of the operating agency because a large part of the revenues (or the expenses) would be "hidden" in the foundation's statements. Unless the reader of the operating agency knows that the foundation exists, he or she will have difficulty evaluating the agency's financial position or the results of its operations.

**Control and Significant Influence**   To reduce this problem, the CICA recommends that an organization report each controlled NFP either by consolidating that entity or by providing specific disclosures of key financial statement information of that entity. The issue here is what constitutes **control**.

The most common indicator that control exists is when one organization has the right to appoint the majority of another NFP's board of directors. However, there may be other factors that indicate control for an NFP, including (1) significant economic interest; (2) provisions in the organization's charter or bylaws; or (3) common or complementary objectives. Clearly, professional judgment is required for determining whether control exists.

An NFP may also exercise significant influence over another NFP. In these cases the reporting NFP should describe its relationship with the entity and disclose the nature and extent of its economic interest. Finally, the reporting NFP may not exercise control or significant influence, but may still have an economic interest in another NFP. In these cases the reporting NFP should disclose the nature and extent of its economic interest in the notes to the financial statements.

It is important to note that the nature of the economic interest can range from a level of economic dependence that gives de facto control to another organization to very limited economic dependence that provides neither control nor significant influence.

## Economic Interest

The Canadian Cancer Society had a close relationship with the National Cancer Institute of Canada (NCIC). In fact, subsequent to the 2009 fiscal year, the operations and related assets and liabilities of the NCIC were integrated with the CCS. The CCS disclosed its economic interest in NCIC in the following note in its 2009 financial statements:

> The Society has an economic interest in the activities of the NCIC by virtue of significant funds contributed

to the NCIC for research in support of the Society's mission. The Society contributed 22% (2008 – 24%) of its revenue to the NCIC. The contribution for the fiscal year was $45,413 (2008 – $48,046).

Source: Canadian Cancer Society, Financial Statements for the Year Ended January 31, 2009, p. 19.

**Investments in Profit-Seeking Enterprises**   An NFP may also own shares in a profit-oriented enterprise. If the NFP controls the enterprise, then it has two options: It can consolidate the enterprise or it can account for the enterprise using the equity method; additional disclosure is required when the equity method is used. If the NFP can exercise significant influence over the enterprise, then the equity method is used. Finally, if no significant influence can be exerted, the cost method is used to account for the investment in the profit-oriented enterprise. These requirements are summarized in Exhibit 10.3.

**Related-Party Transactions**   Our discussion above focused on the issue of consolidation of related entities, which is the usual connotation of consolidation, as we have seen in Chapters 2 through 7 of this text. However, there are two other issues that we need to address briefly. The first is the concept of related parties and related-party transactions. To the extent that control, significant influence, or an economic interest exists, the parties are related. In this case, if there are transactions between the related parties, the financial statements must contain disclosure on the relationship, and the nature and amount of the transaction(s).

**Exhibit 10.3**  **Summary of Accounting for Economic Interests in NFPs and Investments in Profit-Oriented Enterprises**

| Type of Organization | Extent of Influence | Recommended Accounting |
|---|---|---|
| Not-for-profit organization | Control | Consolidate; or provide specific and extensive disclosure |
| | Significant influence | Describe relationship and disclose nature and extent of economic interest |
| | Economic interest | Disclose nature and extent of economic interest |
| Profit-oriented enterprise | Control | Consolidate; or use equity method with supplemental disclosure |
| | Significant influence | Use equity method |
| | No significant influence | Use cost method |

**Consolidation versus Combination**   There is another aspect of consolidation that is unique to non-business organizations: If an organization has restricted funds and is using fund accounting, to what extent should separate funds and restricted resources be *consolidated* or *combined* on the organization's financial statements?

If there is a large number of separate funds under control of management, separate reporting of the operations and SFP of each fund would result in quite a voluminous report, even though columnar formats could be used for conciseness. Separate reporting by funds may clarify the status of each individual fund for stewardship reporting purposes, but may obscure the overall financial position of the organization and the results of its operations.

On the other hand, consolidation of the various funds may hide important characteristics of individual funds, and may impede stewardship reporting.

The AcSB supports consolidated reporting. The AcSB recommends that the *statement of financial position* show a total for each financial statement item that includes all funds. The recommendation for a consolidated total does not rule out separate reporting of funds (or of programs), but simply states that everything should be added together at the end.

Note that the requirement for a total applies only to the statement of financial position. The operating statement need not have a "total" column under the restricted-fund approach because to provide a total for the operating statement would suggest that the money is interchangeable between funds, which clearly is not the case when restricted funds exist.

While this recommendation for aggregating all of the resources on the SFP may seem relatively innocuous, reporting of organization-wide totals implicitly suggests that resources can be moved from fund to fund or program to program. Many NFPs oppose the recommendation for consolidated reporting for that reason.

There is a middle ground between fully detailed fund reporting and full consolidation. Similar types of funds or funds with similar objectives can be combined for reporting purposes. All of the ancillary, self-supporting activities of a university—such as the bookstore, food services, parking, and residences—can be grouped together because they are similar types of funds. Also, all the student aid funds can be combined for reporting purposes since they serve a similar objective.

The funds do not need to have the same treatment for reporting on all the financial statements. Funds (or groups of funds) can be reported separately on the statement of operations, but combined on the statement of financial position. Conversely, the funds may be combined on the statement of operations, but reported separately on the statement of financial position and the cash flow statement. An NFP may account in different ways for different funds or programs. When such is the case, it may be impossible to meaningfully consolidate the various funds or programs.

## Concept Check 10-2

1. When should the expense basis of reporting for capital assets be used?
2. What disclosures are required for expense allocations?
3. What indicators of control can be used to determine if one NFP controls another NFP?
4. Briefly explain how the recognition of contribution revenue by NFPs differs from the recognition of revenue by businesses.

## 10.5 FINANCIAL REPORTING FOR NOT-FOR-PROFIT ORGANIZATIONS

LO **3**

Describe two GAAP reporting methods for NFPs: the deferral method when fund accounting is not used and the restricted-fund method when fund accounting is used

In the sections above we have briefly described the substantial differences between NFPs and businesses. These differences include the nature of the organizations, the financial reporting objectives, and the specific reporting issues. Due to these differences, it is not surprising that GAAP for NFPs developed quite differently from that for business enterprises.

Many NFPs are not constrained by GAAP and do not need to comply with the *CICA Handbook* recommendations. These organizations may use a reporting method that is mandated by their primary funding agency, such as the Ministry of Health or the Ministry of Social Services. Alternatively, they may follow a more traditional expenditure-based reporting system.

In the following sections we will further explain three methods of reporting:

1. expenditure-based or "traditional" method;

2. deferral method; and

3. restricted-fund method.

The first method is the one most commonly used by smaller NFPs. The second and third methods are those recommended by the AcSB and usually are used by large organizations such as universities and hospitals. Some organizations use a dual-reporting approach. They may use one of the AcSB's recommended methods to obtain a clean audit opinion, and then use an expenditure-based set of statements to satisfy their primary user's needs. Such an approach is somewhat costly, since it involves extensive year-end adjustments to get from an expenditure approach to one of the CICA–recommended expense approaches.

## Types of Financial Statements

The *CICA Handbook* recommends that NFPs prepare the following four financial statements:

1. statement of financial position;

2. statement of operations;

3. statement of changes in net assets; and

4. cash-flow statement.

The second and third statements will often be combined into a single statement of operations and changes in net assets or fund balances. The statements should be in a comparative format, with comparisons to the previous year. There may also be comparisons to budgeted amounts. In addition to the statements themselves, there should be notes to the financial statements.

This list of statements looks deceptively simple. The statements do not look much different from those that we are accustomed to seeing for businesses. The differences can be great, however. As we will discuss shortly, the presentation will depend on which one of the three reporting methods the NFP has chosen to use.

# Reporting Options

**Expenditure-Based Method**   In the sections above on reporting issues, we outlined the basic nature of NFP financial reporting as it developed throughout the twentieth century. Many NFPs use the following reporting practices:

- Revenues are recognized when received; accruals are rare.

- Resource *outflows* are recognized when the cost is incurred or when the liability is incurred. Accruals are seldom made for items such as pensions, leases, or vacation pay. The general tendency is to report on a flow-of-funds accrual basis, without inter-period allocations.

- Capital assets may or may not be recorded on the SFP, but depreciation is used only for funds that conduct activities that are expected to be self-supporting on a cost-recovery or profit-making basis.

- Funds are segregated on the SFP, and separate statements of operations are used for different funds (or for different groups of funds of similar nature).

- Funds rarely are totalled on the statement of operations; the SFP more often shows a total for all funds.

- Related organizations are not consolidated.

Many NFPs follow these practices, usually because their donors or funding agencies want to see what the organization's managers have done with the resources placed at their disposal during the year—a classic instance of applying the stewardship objective of financial reporting.

***CICA Handbook* Methods**   As mentioned previously, we will explore two options consistent with the CICA recommendations: the *deferral method* (when the organization does not use fund accounting) and the *restricted-fund method* (when the organization creates funds based on donor restrictions).[8] The two methods can be briefly described as follows:

**Deferral Method**   The deferral method can be used by any NFP. Under this method:

- no distinction is made between different funds or groups of resources in the SFP or the statement of operations;

- "full accrual" accounting is used, including the possible accrual of pledges and full inter-period allocation of revenues and expenses (including amortization and depreciation of capital assets) in accordance with the recommendations of the *CICA Handbook* for business enterprises; and

- restricted revenues are deferred and matched to the expenses that they were intended to fund.

**Restricted-Fund Method**   The restricted-fund method *may* be used by any NFP that has at least one fund that is restricted by an outside donor. Under this method:

- The NFP presents a separate operating statement for each fund (or group of similar funds)—no totals for the organization need to appear on the statement of operations because the funds are not interchangeable.

---

[8] It is possible for NFPs to use the deferral method and fund accounting concurrently. We do not explore this option here although the principles would be the same.

- The statement of financial position should present totals for the organization as a whole.

- Accrual accounting is applied and capital assets are capitalized.

- Amortization and depreciation may or may not be charged to general operations; amortization/depreciation can be charged to a separate capital fund instead.

- Revenue is usually recognized in the appropriate fund when it is received (or accrued) rather than when the expenses are incurred.

Each organization decides how many restricted funds it wishes to have on its statements—there is no general rule except that their distinct nature should be preserved. Restricted donations and endowments must not be combined with unrestricted donations. Unrestricted contributions are recognized as revenue in the *general fund* in the current period. This treatment of unrestricted contributions is similar to their treatment in the deferral method.

An NFP may decide not to have a separate fund for smaller restricted contributions. Instead, smaller funds can be combined into a single larger restricted fund. For example, the many different scholarship and bursary endowments typically present in a college or university are combined into a single "financial aid endowment fund."

The whole point of this method of accounting is to recognize that restricted and endowed funds are not interchangeable with unrestricted funds, and that a deficit in the operating fund cannot be remedied by transferring money from the restricted funds to the operating fund.

**Comparison of Methods**    The deferral method requires total columns for both the statement of financial position and the statement of operations. All funds, by implication, may be perceived as transferable between activities or programs.

In contrast, under the restricted-fund method, the resources and liabilities of the various funds are added together for a "total" column on the statement of financial position. However, the various funds do not need to be added together on the statement of operations.

## Reality Check 10–5

## Comparison of Methods

In 1998, York University began using the deferral method for financial reporting. The university previously had used the traditional method, which in most regards is similar to the restricted-fund method. To prepare its comparative 1998 statements, the university had to restate its 1997 statements from restricted-fund to deferral, which gave a rare opportunity to compare the two methods. In the original (restricted-fund) statements, the university reported an operating surplus of $3.5 million, and a total surplus in all funds of $27.5 million. The difference was largely due to surpluses in restricted trust and endowment funds. When restated, the total surplus of $27.5 million became a deficit of $4.1 million. A major cause was the provision of $19.8 million of depreciation. No results were reported for operating funds, since they were no longer separately reported. The performance of the restricted trust and endowment funds disappeared from view, as did the losses on ancillary services such as the bookstore and student residences. After 1998, the reader had no way of understanding the underlying causes of any deficit or surplus, whether from operations, restricted trust funds, ancillary services, or sponsored research.

Source: T. H. Beechy, "Turning a Surplus into a Deficit—'Improved' Accounting for Universities?" Paper presented at the International Symposium on Public Sector Management, Universität Klagenfurt, Austria, June 25, 2007.

Another important distinction between the deferral method and the restricted-fund method is that, under the restricted-fund method, depreciation and amortization on capital assets does not need to be charged to the operating fund. Depreciation and amortization can be segregated in the capital asset fund instead. This eliminates one of the major objections that many NFPs have to the idea of business-style accounting—that depreciation is charged against operations that are not intended to recover the costs of capital assets, if the assets have been acquired through special grants or fundraising drives.

The choice of method depends primarily on the users and their needs. If the organization wants the simplest financial statements it may select the expenditure-based method. If the primary purpose is to show information on specific activities or programs, or if there is a large number of external users who have imposed restrictions, the restricted-fund method may be more appropriate.

Exhibit 10.4 compares some of the fundamental characteristics of these two methods, as well as comparing them to the traditional method.

**Exhibit 10.4** Alternative Approaches to NFP Financial Reporting

| Accounting Practice | Expenditure-Based Approach | CICA Handbook Recommendations | |
| --- | --- | --- | --- |
| | | Deferral Method | Restricted-Fund Method |
| Accrual of pledges | Not done | Recognition if criteria met | Recognition if criteria met |
| Revenue recognition | Recognize when realized | Match to expense recognition | Recognize when realized |
| Expense or expenditure basis | Expenditure | Expense | Expense |
| Capital assets: | | | |
|   Capitalize | Sometimes | Required* | Required* |
|   Charge to operations | Seldom | Required* | Not required (may use separate fund) |
| Combine funds in "total" column: | | | |
| Statement of operations | Seldom | Required | Not required |
| Statement of financial position | Seldom | Required | Required |
| Consolidation of related organizations | Not done | Required | Required |
| General application of *CICA Handbook* (e.g., pensions, leases, expense accruals) | Not done | Required | Required |
| *Not required for NFPs that are less than the $500,000 gross revenue test. | | | |

# Illustration of GAAP Reporting Methods[9]

**Deferral Method**   Exhibit 10.5 gives an illustration of a simple set of NFP financial statements prepared by using the deferral method. This organization receives three types of contributions—endowment, restricted, and unrestricted—but the statements do not have to be prepared on the restricted-fund method. Any NFP can use the deferral method.

There are three statements:

- statement of financial position;
- statement of operations; and
- statement of changes in net assets.

In the first two statements, no distinction is made between the resources in the various funds.

However, notice that on the statement of financial position, there is not just one amount for the capital or equity of the NFP, shown here as "net assets" (other often-used headings are *fund balances, net resources available,* or *accumulated surplus*). Instead, five different types of net asset balances are shown. This is an important option in NFP accounting. Even when the deferral method is used, the different types of net assets balances may be shown separately on the statement of financial position. By using this approach, users can see that, although the total net assets amount to $1,490, only $390 of that amount is unrestricted and is available for future operations.

The third statement reconciles the beginning and ending balances of each of the different net asset balances shown on the SFP. If the statement of financial position shows more than one net asset balance, then the beginning balance must be reconciled to the ending balance for each.

On the statement of changes in net assets, observe that the total column shows a surplus of $190 (i.e., excess of revenues over expenses). In addition, this statement reveals that:

- the surplus in the unrestricted net assets actually was $220;
- the contributions to the endowment net assets of $370 were not included in revenues on the statement of operations;
- capital assets of $110 were purchased from unrestricted funds during the year; and
- the board reversed an internal restriction by $100, releasing those funds for general unrestricted use.

**Restricted-Fund Method**   Exhibit 10.6 shows the same organization, but this time using the restricted-fund method of reporting. Only two statements are presented—a statement of financial position and a combined statement of operations and changes in net assets or fund balances. In this approach, detailed statements of financial position are presented for the operating fund, for each restricted fund (research and capital assets), and for the endowment fund. We can see, for example, that of the total current assets of $830, only $680 is for unrestricted use.

---

[9] For brevity of exposition, the statements of cash flows are omitted under both approaches.

**Exhibit 10.5** Sample NFP Financial Statements—Deferral Method

### Statement of Financial Position
### December 31, 20X5
### (in thousands)

| Assets | 20X5 | 20X4 |
|---|---|---|
| Current assets: | | |
| Cash and term deposits | $ 520 | $ 280 |
| Accounts receivable | 150 | 160 |
| Supplies | 160 | 60 |
| | 830 | 500 |
| Investments | 570 | 200 |
| Capital assets, net | 1,000 | 1,100 |
| Total assets | $2,400 | $1,800 |
| Liabilities, deferred contributions, and net assets | | |
| Current liabilities: | | |
| Accounts payable and accrued liabilities | $ 80 | $ 20 |
| Current portion mortgage payable | 10 | 10 |
| | **90** | **30** |
| Mortgage payable | 110 | 120 |
| | 200 | 150 |
| Deferred contributions: | | |
| Capital | 600 | 720 |
| Other deferred contributions | 110 | — |
| | 710 | 720 |
| Net assets: | | |
| Externally restricted | 150 | 100 |
| Invested in capital assets | 280 | 250 |
| Internally restricted | 100 | 200 |
| Endowments | 570 | 200 |
| Unrestricted | 390 | 180 |
| | 1,490 | 930 |
| Total liabilities, deferred contributions, and net assets | $2,400 | $1,800 |

### Statement of Operations
### Year Ended December 31, 20X5
### (in thousands)

| | 20X5 | 20X4 |
|---|---|---|
| **Revenues** | | |
| Grants and contributions | $2,140 | $2,400 |
| Amortization of capital contributions | 120 | 100 |
| Other revenue | 1,400 | 1,200 |
| | 3,660 | 3,700 |
| **Expenses** | | |
| Salaries | 2,790 | 2,800 |
| Amortization of capital assets | 200 | 260 |
| Other expenses | 480 | 460 |
| | 3,470 | 3,520 |
| **Excess of revenues over expenses** | $ 190 | $ 180 |

## Statement of Changes in Net Assets
### Year Ended December 31, 20X5
#### (in thousands)

| Net assets | Externally restricted | Invested in capital assets | Internally restricted | Endowments | Unrestricted | Total |
|---|---|---|---|---|---|---|
| Balance, January 1 | $100 | $250 | $200 | $200 | $180 | $930 |
| Excess (deficiency) of revenues over expenses | 50 | (80) | | | 220 | 190 |
| Investment in capital assets | | 110 | | | (110) | — |
| Endowment contribution | | | | 370 | | 370 |
| Internally imposed restrictions | | | 100 | | 100 | — |
| Balance, December 31 | $150 | $280 | $100 | $570 | $390 | $1,490 |

Revenue recognition also is quite different between the two methods. Notice that in the SFP in Exhibit 10.6, there is no liability for deferred revenue. That is because revenue is recognized when realized in the restricted-fund method. The endowment is in a separate fund, and therefore the contributions to the endowment fund are recognized as revenue *for that fund* in the restricted-fund method. In the deferral method, the endowment contributions are not recognized as revenue.

Since revenue recognition is different, the total fund balances are different between the two methods. Notice that the total fund balances (or "net assets") shown in Exhibit 10.5 are $1,490, while in Exhibit 10.6 the total fund balances amount to $2,200. The difference between the two methods of $710 is reflected in the balance for deferred contributions of $710 as shown in Exhibit 10.5.

To avoid complicating the presentation, we have omitted the 20X4 comparative data for the statement of operations in Exhibit 10.6. In practice, comparative information would be presented either by putting more columns in the statement or by providing another statement in identical format for the prior year. The restricted-fund approach tends to present a lot of numbers. But the numbers are necessary to try to grasp the real operating situation of the organization.

# The Chore of Users: Unravelling GAAP

We pointed out earlier in the chapter that the users of NFP financial statements often are interested in the organization's use of the resources given to help the organization accomplish its mandate. There are two aspects to this interest—(1) stewardship over the resources themselves, and (2) effectiveness in accomplishing the organization's objectives. Unfortunately, the annual financial statements of an NFP usually do not satisfy either goal very well.

**Exhibit 10.6** Sample NFP Financial Statements—Restricted-Fund Method

Statement of Financial Position
December 31, 20X5
(in thousands)

| | Operating fund | Research fund | Capital asset fund | Endowment fund | 20X5 total | 20X4 total |
|---|---|---|---|---|---|---|
| **Current assets** | | | | | | |
| Cash and term deposits | $370 | $150 | | | $ 520 | $ 280 |
| Accounts receivable | 150 | | | | 150 | 160 |
| Supplies | 160 | | | | 160 | 60 |
| Cash and term deposits | 680 | 150 | | | 830 | 500 |
| Investments | | | | $570 | 570 | 200 |
| Capital assets, net | 200 | | $800 | | 1,000 | 1,100 |
| Total assets | $880 | $150 | $800 | $570 | $2,400 | $1,800 |
| **Current liabilities** | | | | | | |
| Accounts payable and accrued liabilities | $ 80 | | | | $ 80 | $ 20 |
| Current portion, mortgage payable | | | $ 10 | | 10 | 10 |
| | 80 | | 10 | | 90 | 30 |
| Mortgage payable | | | 110 | | 110 | 120 |
| Total liabilities | 80 | | 120 | | 200 | 150 |
| **Fund balances** | | | | | | |
| Externally restricted | 110 | $150 | | | 260 | 100 |
| Invested in capital assets | 200 | | 680 | | 880 | 970 |
| Internally restricted | 100 | | | | 100 | 200 |
| Endowments | | | | $570 | 570 | 200 |
| Unrestricted | 390 | | | | 390 | 180 |
| Total fund balances | 800 | 150 | 680 | 570 | 2,200 | 1,650 |
| Total liabilities and fund balances | $880 | $150 | $800 | $570 | $2,400 | $1,800 |

Stewardship is difficult to assess because the expense basis of reporting that is recommended by the AcSB is often in conflict with users' interest in how the organization *spent* the money given to it—expenditures rather than expenses. Sometimes the organization tries to help users by pointing out the impact of major unfunded accruals.

The deferral method makes it especially difficult to unravel the financial performance of any NFP that has restricted funds. As we pointed out in Reality Check 10–5, some universities, for example, have chosen to use the deferral method, adding together unrestricted funds, restricted funds, endowment funds, and enterprise accounts into a

| Statement of Operations and Changes in Fund Balances<br>Year Ended December 31, 20X5<br>(in thousands) | | | | |
|---|---|---|---|---|
| | Operating fund | Research fund | Capital asset fund | Endowment fund |
| **Revenues** | | | | |
| Grants and contributions | $1,650 | $640 | | $370 |
| Other revenue | 1,400 | ____ | | ____ |
| | 3,050 | 640 | | 370 |
| **Expenses** | | | | |
| Salaries | 2,300 | 490 | | |
| Amortization of capital assets | 200 | | | |
| Other | 480 | ____ | | |
| | 2,980 | 490 | | |
| Excess (deficiency) of revenues over expenses | 70 | 150 | | 370 |
| Fund balance, January 1 | 640 | | $770 | 200 |
| Interfund transfers | 90 | ____ | (90) | ____ |
| Fund balance, December 31 | $ 800 | $150 | $680 | $570 |

single set of numbers. The "bottom line" in such a situation is meaningless. Any reported surplus (or deficit) is not necessarily available for use in (or "paid" by) future operations (i.e., unrestricted). Further, given the level of aggregation, it is impossible to unravel the reasons for either a surplus or a deficit when the deferral method is used in an NFP that has restricted donations.

**Supplementary Information**    The difficulty of evaluating *efficiency* in an NFP has led to a demand for a greater volume of non-financial data as supplementary information in non-business financial statements. Data on the level of services performed or activities accomplished, membership levels, contributors, etc., can be provided. For example, a CICA research study on NFPs recommended that not-for-profit organizations provide the following information along with their annual financial statements:[10]

- the nature and objectives of the organization;
- plans for the future;
- significant events during the year and their relationship to or impact on the financial results;
- any unusual or important items or trends in the financial statements; and
- important non-financial information.

---

[10] Canadian Institute of Chartered Accountants, *Financial Reporting for Not-for-Profit Organizations* (Toronto: CICA, 1980), pp. 41–42.

It would be most useful if quantitative supplementary information were audited. Sometimes the audit opinion does cover at least some such information, but normally the supplementary information is outside the scope of the audit opinion. Auditors find it difficult to independently verify most non-financial data unless it is directly tied into the accounting and reporting system. Therefore, financial statement readers have to accept supplementary information largely on trust.

Unfortunately, there have been instances of overenthusiastic managers issuing inflated performance data to enhance the apparent efficiency or effectiveness of the organization. For example, one Canadian film festival was alleged to have announced attendance figures that were in excess of the combined maximum seating capacities of its theatres! But this type of behaviour is undoubtedly the exception rather than the rule.

### Concept Check 10-3

1. Explain the distinction between the *restricted-fund method* and the *deferral method*.
2. What types of financial statements will an NFP normally issue?
3. Why is stewardship difficult to assess in an NFP?

**LO ❹**

Describe the application and use of budgetary control accounts and encumbrance accounting

## 10.6 BUDGETARY CONTROL AND ENCUMBRANCE ACCOUNTING

By now, you will have seen that accounting for not-for-profit organizations is quite different from accounting for business enterprises. But we are not done yet. There are two other special aspects of NFP accounting. We will conclude this chapter with an overview of these two special accounting techniques—*budgetary control accounts* and *encumbrance accounting*.

### Budgetary Control Accounts

A unique characteristic that is often used in fund accounting is the practice of formally incorporating budgetary accounts into the accounting system. **Budgetary accounts** enable managers to keep a running comparison of budgeted with actual amounts of revenue and expenditure as well as to monitor expenditure levels.

It is quite possible to accomplish the same result without formally including the budget in the accounting system—many businesses routinely have budget vs. actual comparisons on their *internal* statements. The difference in non-business organizations, and especially in governments, is that when strict expenditure limits are in effect, a formalized system acts as an internal control so that managers are not permitted to issue purchase orders that will push the expenditure total above the budgeted limit. The comparison between the budget and the combined total of expenditures is constant and routine, rather than being occasional and special.

We will not go into the technical aspects of budgetary control accounts here. There are many books that explain the mechanics of fund accounting and budgetary accounts in exquisite detail. It will be sufficient to say simply that the nature of the budgetary accounts is to create a self-balancing set of accounts *within* the regular accounting system, normally within the general or operating fund.

In general, the bookkeeping approach that is used for budgetary accounts is as follows:

- Budgeted revenues are *debited* to an account that serves as an offset to actual revenues (which are credits). The difference between the budgeted and actual revenues is automatically shown within the system by netting the actual against the budgeted amounts. A net debit balance indicates that actual revenues are falling short of the budget, while a net credit balance shows that revenues are exceeding budget.

- Budgeted *expenditures* (not *expenses*) are shown as credits. The level of detail matches the level of expenditure control that has been mandated by the board of directors (or by the legislature, for governments). The budget balance is the upper limit of permitted expenditures. Managers and employees will not be permitted to make additional commitments once the budget limit has been met.

The system can automatically enforce the budget limits on expenditures by using an encumbrance system.

## The Encumbrance System

The **encumbrance system** records the estimated cost of commitments in the formal accounting system when the commitments are made rather than when a legal liability has arisen. For example, purchase orders for supplies are recorded as an *encumbrance* at the estimated cost of the supplies when the purchase order is issued, even though no liability (in either a legal or an accounting sense) exists until the supplier delivers the supplies.

In theory, an encumbrance system could be used in private enterprise accounting. In practice, encumbrance accounting is unique to governments and NFPs.

**Example: Encumbrance Accounting**    Assume that on June 15, 20X6, a social agency issues a purchase order of $7,500 to a printer for pamphlets to be used in its upcoming public educational campaign. The pamphlets are delivered on July 28, 20X6, and are invoiced at $7,457. If the social agency is using an encumbrance system, then the following entry will be made on June 15, 20X6:

| | | |
|---|---|---|
| Encumbrances—education expense | 7,500 | |
| Estimated commitments | | 7,500 |

The encumbrance is like an expense or expenditure account while estimated commitments is like a liability account. These accounts ensure that the commitment of resources and associated liability are recorded in the accounts at the time the purchase order is issued. Subsequently, on July 28, 20X6, when the goods are received, the following entries will be made:

| | | |
|---|---|---|
| Estimated commitments | 7,500 | |
| Encumbrances—education expense | | 7,500 |
| Education expense | 7,457 | |
| Accounts payable | | 7,457 |

These entries reverse the original encumbrance and record the expense and associated liability in the normal fashion. Appendix 10A on the Companion Website provides more detail on encumbrance accounting.

The objective of using an encumbrance system is to keep track of the commitments that an organization's managers have made for the acquisition of goods and services. If there is a budgetary or legislative limit on the expenditures that a manager can make during the year, then use of the encumbrance system keeps the manager from over-committing the organization and running up a large deficit.

Even in the absence of fixed budgetary limits, encumbrances can be used simply as an aid to planning and control. This is particularly true when commitments on the same budget amount can be made by several people within the organization. When control is decentralized, an encumbrance system improves regulation and communicates to managers and to the people making the expenditures just what the actual level of commitment is.

The encumbrance system is widely used in governmental accounting; budget amounts are legislated maxima that must not be exceeded. In NFPs, however, whether or not an encumbrance system is used depends on the nature of the organization and its operations. In fact, encumbrance accounting can be used in some parts of an organization and not in others, and for some types of expenditure (such as for supplies) and not for others (such as salaries). The system is most appropriate when the following conditions are present:

1. The organization, fund, or activity is a cost centre with a maximum expenditure limit *or* has no relationship between costs and revenues.

2. Goods and services acquired discretionally are a significant part of the total budget.

3. There is a significant lag between the commitment (e.g., purchase order) and the receipt of the purchased items.

4. Levels of activity (and expenditure) within the organizational unit are not affected in the short run by an autonomous demand, either external to the organization or from other parts of the organization.

5. Reporting is on an expenditure basis rather than an expense basis.

6. Responsibility for making commitments and expenditures is decentralized throughout a large organization.

If, in contrast, a small organizational unit (1) must vary its level of activity in response to market demand for its services; (2) is able to generate revenues to cover expenses; and (3) considers externally acquired goods and services of little consequence or receives them very shortly after ordering, then there is little reason to use an encumbrance system.

Encumbrance systems are used to control costs when expenditure limits are basically fixed and are not tied to revenue or activity levels. If these conditions do not exist, then encumbrances are of limited usefulness. Also, if only a very small part of expenditures is discretionary rather than being tied to longer-term employment or supply contracts, then there is little point to using encumbrances.

## Concept Check 10-4

1. Explain the purpose of recording budgetary amounts in the accounts.

2. When is the use of an encumbrance system most appropriate for NFPs?

## 10.7 A FINAL EXAMPLE

We will end this chapter with an example of NFP financial statements. Exhibit 10.7 shows the basic 2011 statements for the Canadian Cancer Society. As is common in NFP reporting, the CCS takes a slightly eclectic approach. The SFP has only one column (for each year), which suggests that the statements are prepared on the deferral method.

**Exhibit 10.7** 2011 NFP Financial Statements, Canadian Cancer Society

### Statement of Resources (In thousands of dollars)
### January 31, 2011, with comparative figures for 2010

|  | 2011 | 2010 |
|---|---|---|
| **Assets** | | |
| Current assests: | | |
| Cash | $ 38,433 | $ 35,765 |
| Short-term investments (note 4) | 80,795 | 98,189 |
| Accounts receivable | 4,135 | 3,800 |
| Prepaid expenses and supplies | 4,711 | 3,336 |
|  | 128,074 | 141,090 |
| Long-term investments (note 5) | 33,287 | 28,105 |
| Intangible assets (note 6) | 1,419 | 1,448 |
| Capital assets (note 7) | 31,633 | 28, 011 |
|  | $194,413 | $198, 654 |
| **Liabilities and Resources** | | |
| Current Liabilities: | | |
| Accounts payable and accrued Liabilities | $ 16,023 | $ 18,456 |
| Research grants payable | 9,697 | 6,564 |
| Deferred contributions (note 8) | 5,954 | 6,157 |
| Credit facility (note 9) | 739 | 1,400 |
|  | 32,413 | 32,577 |
| Accrued pension benefit liability (note 10(a)) | 4,515 | 2,941 |
| Liability for post-retirement benefits other than pensions (note 10(b)) | 17,325 | 15,521 |
| Resources: | | |
| Externally restricted (note 11) | 8,797 | 7,101 |
| Invested in capital assets (note 12) | 32,313 | 28,087 |
| Internally restricted (note 13) | 81,299 | 92,337 |
| Unrestricted | 17,751 | 20,090 |
|  | 140,160 | 147,615 |
| Commitments (note 15) | | |
| Guarantees and contingencies (note 17) | | |
|  | $194,413 | $198,654 |

*Exhibit Continued >*

*Exhibit Continued >*

## Statement of Financial Activities—Operations and Externally Restricted Resources (In thousands of dollars)
### Year ended January 31, 2011, with Comparative Figures for 2010

| | Operations | | Externally restricted | |
| --- | --- | --- | --- | --- |
| | 2011 | 2010 | 2011 | 2010 |
| Revenue: | | | | |
| Relay For Life | $ 54,263 | $ 53,004 | $ — | $ — |
| Annual giving | 48,317 | 48,539 | — | 13 |
| Major and planned gifts | 33,419 | 31,855 | 778 | 1,496 |
| Special events | 23,649 | 23,166 | — | 4 |
| Tributes | 9,846 | 11,395 | — | 1 |
| Lotteries (note 16) | 23,869 | 9,514 | — | — |
| | 193,363 | 197,473 | 778 | 1,514 |
| Government and other sponsored projects | 9,301 | 10,208 | — | (67) |
| Investment income | 3,678 | 5,435 | 538 | 453 |
| Other income | 6,365 | 7,035 | 1,793 | 1,421 |
| | 212,707 | 220,151 | 3,109 | 3,321 |
| Expenditures: | | | | |
| Cancer Control: | | | | |
| Research | 48,886 | 48,364 | 8 | 22 |
| Support for people living with cancer | 36,240 | 36,545 | 281 | 77 |
| Prevention | 21,196 | 22,815 | — | — |
| Information | 14,424 | 15,149 | — | 2 |
| Advocacy | 6,462 | 6,533 | — | — |
| | 127,208 | 129,406 | 289 | 101 |
| Supporting: | | | | |
| Fundraising | 63,522 | 67,516 | 688 | 667 |
| Fundraising lotteries (note 16) | 22,988 | 26,719 | — | — |
| Management and general (note 19) | 8,565 | 9,245 | 11 | 24 |
| | 95,075 | 103,480 | 699 | 691 |
| | 222,283 | 232,886 | 988 | 792 |
| Increase (decrease) in resources | $ (9,576) | $(12,735) | $2,121 | $2,529 |

**Statement of Cash Flows (In thousands of dollars)**
**Year ended January 31, 2011, with Comparative Figures for 2010**

|  | 2011 | 2010 |
|---|---|---|
| Cash provided by (used in): | | |
| Operating activities: | | |
| Decrease in resources | $ (7,455) | $(10,206) |
| Non-cash items: | | |
| Amortization of capital assets | 3,373 | 4,921 |
| Amortization of intangible assets | 29 | 28 |
| Gain on disposal of capital assets | — | (88) |
| Post-retirement benefits expense | 2,470 | 1,570 |
| Defined benefit pension expense | 4,947 | 2,738 |
| Unrealized losses on investments | 1,799 | 3,907 |
| Employer post-retirement benefits contributions | (666) | (556) |
| Employer defined benefit pension contributions | (3,373) | (3,295) |
| Change in non-cash operating working capital | (1,213) | 13,192 |
| | (89) | 12,211 |
| Financing activities: | | |
| Decrease in credit facility | (661) | (28) |
| Investing activities: | | |
| Capital asset additions | (6,995) | (4,607) |
| Proceeds from disposal of capital assets | — | 416 |
| Decrease in short-term investments | 17,394 | 688 |
| Decrease (increase) in long-term investments | (6,981) | 938 |
| Cash transferred from the National Cancer Institute of Canada | — | 3,388 |
| | 3,418 | 823 |
| Increase in cash | 2,668 | 13,006 |
| Cash, beginning of year | 35,765 | 22,759 |
| Cash, end of year | $38,433 | $ 35,765 |

**Statement of Changes in Resources**
**Year ended January 31, 2011, with Comparative Figures**
**for 2010 (In thousands of dollars)**

| | Externally restricted | Invested in capital assets | Internally restricted | Unrestricted | 2011 Total | 2010 Total |
|---|---|---|---|---|---|---|
| Resources, beginning of the year | $7,101 | $28,087 | $92,337 | $20,090 | $147,615 | $105,869 |
| Transfer from the National Cancer Institute of Canada (note 1) | — | — | — | — | — | 51,952 |
| Increase (decrease) in resources | 2,121 | (3,381) | (11,505) | 5,310 | (7,455) | (10.206) |
| Invested in capital assets | (482) | 6,157 | (4,367) | (1,308) | — | — |
| Appropriations (note 14) | 57 | 1,450 | 4,834 | (6,341) | — | — |
| Resources, end of year | $8,797 | $32,313 | $81,299 | $17,751 | $140,160 | $147,615 |

See accompanying notes to financial statement.

However, the statement of operations has two columns for each year—operations and externally restricted. There is no total column. Therefore, the CCS must be using the restricted-fund method. This is confirmed in the accounting policy note (not reproduced in Exhibit 10.7), which states that "the Society follows the restricted-fund method of accounting for contributions." The SFP, however, also presents "deferred contributions" of $5,954. The CCS must also be using the deferral method of accounting for some of the restricted contributions. This is also confirmed in the notes.

The consolidated statement of changes in resources contains the reconciliation of beginning fund balances (called "Resources" in the CCS statements) with the ending balances. In this statement, there are four columns for the current year, as contrasted with two columns in the operating statement. The four-column reconciliation in the statement of changes corresponds with the four balances shown under "resources" on the statement of financial position.

Finally, in the CCS 2011, cash flow statement, the adjustments decrease the accrual-basis deficit of $7,455 to a cash flow surplus of $2,668.

## Relevant Standards

### CICA Handbook, Part III

4410    Contributions—revenue recognition
4420    Contributions receivable
4430    Capital assets held by not-for-profit organizations
4440    Collections held by not-for-profit organizations
4450    Reporting controlled and related entities by not-for-profit organizations
4460    Disclosure of related party transactions by not-for-profit organizations
4470    Disclosure of allocated expenses by not-for-profit organizations

## 10.8 SUMMARY OF KEY POINTS

1. A non-business organization is any organization other than a private enterprise operating for profit. Non-business organizations can be roughly divided into three groups: (1) governments; (2) governmental units; and (3) not-for-profit organizations. **LO 1**

2. The primary differences between not-for-profit organizations and business enterprises are that (1) they have members, but no owners; (2) they do not exist to generate a return on investment; (3) expenses are not usually incurred to generate revenue; and (4) the suppliers of funds usually do not receive the benefits of an NFP's activities. **LO 1**

3. The objectives of NFP financial reporting tend to emphasize (1) stewardship and (2) measuring the cost of services. Most NFPs obtain their funding from members, external donors, and public or government granting agencies. These donors need to see how the organization used the resources that were given to it during the year. Therefore, there often is a heightened interest in stewardship reporting—what did the managers do with the funds entrusted to their care? **LO 1**

4. Accounting for expenditures becomes an important reporting objective for many NFPs. Some NFPs provide goods and services to individuals on a cost-recovery basis. In such cases, a primary reporting objective is to measure the cost of providing those services. The emphasis then falls on expense accounting rather than on expenditure accounting. **LO 1**

5. There are many reporting issues that are unique to NFPs. One of the first issues is to determine which of three different bases to use to recognize the resource outflows of any organization in the statement of operations: disbursement basis, expenditure basis, or expense basis. Second, NFPs must account for contributions from donors and funding partners. Unlike business enterprises, these contributions may be restricted for specific uses. NFPs also receive donated goods and services and donated capital assets. Third, because the majority of NFPs qualify for an exemption from the capitalize-and-amortize approach in the CICA *Handbook*, there is often an issue of how to account for capital assets. Fourth, determining the necessary disclosure required when an organization allocates costs from administrative and fundraising efforts to other expenses such as education is a new issue that many organizations are facing. Finally, there is often a problem in simply identifying the reporting entity, identifying possible related-party transactions, and implementing consolidated reporting. **LO 2**

6. Many NFPs, particularly the large number of small NFPs, use a traditional expenditure-based accounting approach on a modified accrual basis. This approach recognizes expenses when incurred and revenues when received. Long-term assets are not capitalized, and no depreciation or amortization is used. **LO 2**

7. For GAAP-constrained NFPs, the *CICA Handbook* allows an organization to account for its activities with or without fund accounting. It also requires an organization to choose one of two alternative methods of recognizing contribution revenue: the deferral method or the restricted-fund method. In this chapter, we explore these two alternatives: (1) the deferral method, assuming fund accounting is not used, and (2) the restricted-fund method, assuming fund accounting is used. The deferral method can be used by any NFP. The restricted-fund method can be used only by an NFP that has at least one externally restricted fund. The deferral method does not segregate assets by restrictions, except to separate net asset balances on the statement of financial position. The individual reported balances for different classifications of net assets are then reconciled in a statement of changes in net assets. The restricted-fund method permits segregated reporting for restricted and endowment funds. The funds do not need to be added together on the statement of operations, although a total column should be provided on the statement of financial position. **LO 3**

8. An accounting procedure that is unique to NFPs and governments is the use of budgetary accounts within the formal set of accounts. The purpose of budgetary accounts is to control the level of expenditure and also to permit an automatic comparison of budget versus actual amounts at every reporting date. Expenditure limits are enforced by means of encumbrance accounting. Encumbrance accounting records an obligation as soon as a purchase order is issued, thereby reducing the amount of available funds that can be committed to other purchases. **LO 4**

**Visit the text's website at** www.pearsoned.ca/beechy **for practice quizzes, additional problems, Excel® templates, answers to Concept Check questions, and important IFRS updates.**

# Self-Study Problems

1.  You have been recruited to act as the treasurer on the board of directors of a not-for-profit organization. The board of directors has very limited accounting experience. The organization, Rose Plants Forever (RPF), receives an estimated $800,000 per year in regular contributions from the federal government.

    RPF uses the deferral method of accounting for contributions and has no separate fund for restricted contributions. On January 1, 20X6, RPF received its first restricted cash contribution—$200,000 for the purchase and maintenance of land and a greenhouse building for its rare rose plant collection. On July 1, 20X6, RPF acquired land and a building for $44,000 and $120,000 cash, respectively. The building has an estimated useful life of 20 years and zero salvage value. On December 31, 20X6, the remaining $36,000 cash was paid to KJ Maintenance Ltd. for a three-year maintenance contract that requires KJ personnel to provide maintenance services four days per month until December 31, 20X9.

    **Required**

    Prepare the journal entries for the following dates:

    **a.** January 1, 20X6;

    **b.** July 1, 20X6; and

    **c.** December 31, 20X6.

    [CGA–Canada, adapted]

2.  The OPI Care Centre (OPI) is a not-for-profit organization funded by government grants and private donations. It prepares its annual financial statements using the deferral method of accounting for contributions, and it uses only the operations fund to account for all activities. It uses an encumbrance system as a means of controlling expenditures.

    **Required**

    The following summarizes some of the transactions that were made during 20X2. Assuming a GAAP constraint, prepare the journal entries to reflect the transactions.

    **a.** The founding member of OPI contributed $100,000 on the condition that the principal amount be invested in marketable securities and that only the income earned from the investment be spent on operations.

    **b.** During the year, purchase orders were issued to cover the budgeted cost of $1,400,000 for goods and contracted services.

    **c.** During the year, a public campaign was held to raise funds for daily operations for the current year. Cash of $800,000 was collected, and pledges for an additional $100,000 were received by the end of the year. It is estimated that approximately 95% of these pledges will be collected early in the new year.

    **d.** The provincial government pledged $600,000 for the year to cover operating costs and an additional $1,000,000 to purchase equipment and furniture. All of the grant money was received by the end of the year, except for the last $50,000 to cover operating costs for December.

    **e.** OPI used the $1,000,000 received from the provincial government to purchase equipment and furniture for the care facility. The amortization of these assets amounted to $100,000 for the year. A purchase order has not been issued for this purchase.

**f.** Invoices totalling $1,450,000 were received for goods and contracted services. Of these invoices, 90% were paid by the end of the fiscal year. Purchase orders in the amount of $1,375,000 had been issued for these services.

[CGA–Canada, adapted]

## Review Questions

1. Who owns not-for-profit organizations?

2. What is the difference between *non-business* organizations and *not-for-profit* organizations?

3. Describe the population of NFPs in Canada. Are there any financial reporting implications given the skewness of the size distribution?

4. Distinguish between an *open membership* not-for-profit organization and a *closed membership* not-for-profit organization.

5. What types of organizations offer *private goods and services*?

6. Describe the ways in which the nature of revenue in not-for-profit organizations can differ from the nature of revenue in business enterprises.

7. Who are the primary users of the financial statements of not-for-profit organizations?

8. If the emphasis in accounting for many not-for-profit organizations is on the control of cash flows, why is the accrual basis recommended?

9. Explain the difference between the *expense basis*, the *expenditure basis*, and the *disbursements basis* of reporting.

10. What alternative approaches are there to accounting for capital assets in not-for-profit organizations?

11. What is a *pledge* and what are the criteria for recognizing pledges?

12. What is a *collection* and what criteria are required to be met for a group of items to be defined as a collection?

13. Explain the differences between an *externally restricted contribution*, a *board-designated (internally restricted) fund*, an *endowment contribution,* and an *unrestricted contribution*.

14. How are *externally restricted contributions* recognized in the deferral method compared with the restricted-fund method? What is the difference if there is no separate fund in the restricted-fund method for that contribution?

15. Which method of accounting tends to result in a higher level of revenues, the restricted-fund method or the deferral method?

16. How should an NFP account for a business enterprise that it controls?

17. Why is the allocation of expenses an issue for NFPs?

18. When budgetary accounts are used, why is the amount for estimated revenues a debit instead of a credit?

19. What is an *encumbrance*?

20. What is the purpose of an *encumbrance system*?

# 10.9 CASES

## CASE 10-1 HOPE

Myesha Kind is the executive director of HOPE (Homes, Opportunity, and Peace for Everyone). HOPE is a non-profit organization with two key mandates. First, it provides food and shelter to the homeless. Second, it attempts to educate the public and lobby government for programs to assist the homeless.

Myesha is preparing her organization's year-end financial statements, and several issues have arisen. She has approached you, as a professional accountant, for advice on how to address these issues. She informs you that HOPE has a December 31 year-end and uses the deferral method for accounting for contributions.

1. HOPE received a $100,000 donation on December 3 from a wealthy benefactor. The donor clearly did not expect the monies to be spent in the current year and did not impose any restrictions on the funds. HOPE also did not have the time to spend the unexpected funds. These monies, if recognized in the current year, would likely create a sizable surplus. Myesha would like to know if they can be considered restricted for financial reporting purposes so that they could be recognized in the following year, when they will be spent.

2. HOPE has an endowment fund, the income of which is used to fund its soup kitchen. As part of its fundraising efforts, HOPE started targeting wealthy seniors two years ago and requesting their support of this program. The promotional material by HOPE has indicated that all bequests received by the organization will automatically be used to fund the soup kitchen endowment fund unless otherwise specified by the donor. The fundraising effort has been very successful, as HOPE has already received six bequests that specifically directed funds to the soup kitchen endowment fund. Recently, HOPE received a significant bequest ($200,000), but there were no specific directions on how the funds were to be used. Myesha would like to know if she can record the donation as an endowment contribution.

3. In June of the current year, HOPE received a $10,000 contribution that was restricted to funding HOPE's government lobbying program. HOPE had already budgeted sufficient funds ($17,000) for the program and used these operating funds to pay for the program in the current year. Myesha would like to know if she can defer the $10,000 until next year, when it will be used.

4. HOPE had planned on launching an educational campaign early in the following year on the problems faced by homeless youth and had received a $50,000 donation from one of its past directors specifically to fund the campaign. At its most recent board meeting, in early December, the board decided not to proceed with the campaign because another organization had initiated a similar campaign. Myesha contacted the donor to let her know of the board's decision and the donor indicated that she was willing to let HOPE keep the donation. Myesha would like to know what the implications are for HOPE's year-end financial statements.

Required

Prepare a report addressing Myesha Kind's concerns.

# CASE 10-2 REPORTING OBJECTIVES

You have recently been appointed auditor of three different organizations. The first organization is a mining company that was formed a year ago to develop a gold mining site in northern Ontario. The largest single part of the initial investment was provided by a major, publicly held mining company in exchange for 36% of the common shares. The remaining shares were issued publicly in the over-the-counter market, where they are very thinly traded. The company is still in the development stage and does not expect to commence production for at least another year.

The second organization is a not-for-profit secondary school that provides courses for students who intend to pursue a career in one of the performing arts. The school is fully recognized by the provincial Ministry of Education, which provides about 50% of the school's operating budget. Another 20% of the operating funds are provided by the Ministry of Culture and Recreation, while the remainder is derived from student fees and by fundraising in the private sector. The school occupies an old public high school building that was no longer being used by the city; the school acquired the building on a 20-year lease from the city's board of education.

The third organization is a labour union for the graduate students at a major university. The union receives its funding from dues that are mandatorily deducted by the university from the earnings of all members of the bargaining unit, whether they are members of the union or not. A portion of the funds is sent to the union's parent national organization, and another part is set aside for the strike fund, which is held and invested by a trustee until such time as it is needed to pay striking union members.

## Required

Explain how the objectives of financial reporting would likely differ for these three organizations.

# CASE 10-3 GOLD DEVELOPMENT

Gold Development (GD), a newly incorporated not-for-profit organization with a December 31 year-end, will offer low-rent housing services for people with low income.

GD reports to Logimex, a government agency that requires audited annual financial statements to be filed. Mr. Bilodeau, the project originator and administrator of GD, is not familiar with the preparation of financial statements.

GD received a non-repayable grant from Logimex in February 20X2 for the construction of an eight-storey apartment building. Construction began in April 20X2.

Residents will start to move into the apartment building between October and December 20X2, although it will not be entirely completed until the end of December 20X2. By December 20X2 all the apartments should be rented.

GD receives donations from companies and individuals in the region. It has received pledges from large, well-known companies for the next five years, and pledges from individuals for the current and next year. Pledge amounts have been set out in writing on forms signed by the donors.

For a nominal salary, Mr. Bilodeau manages the organization with the help of his wife and the local priest, both of whom are volunteers.

Required

1. Explain to Mr. Bilodeau what is meant by "reporting on a restricted-fund accounting basis" according to the *CICA Handbook*.

2. Advise Mr. Bilodeau on the appropriate accounting for the above issues assuming that GD decides to report on a restricted-fund accounting basis.

# CASE 10-4 PERTH HOUSING

Perth Housing Corporation (PHC) is a community-sponsored not-for-profit organization that was incorporated on September 1, 20X5. Its purpose is to provide residential accommodation for adults with physically disabilities in the town of Perth, Ontario.

The nature of PHC's operations is described in Exhibit A. The sources of funding are described in Exhibit B.

The executive director has asked for your assistance in establishing accounting policies for PHC for its general-purpose year-end financial statements. The accounting policies should comply with GAAP.

Required

Provide recommendations for accounting policies for PHC for the year ended August 31, 20X6. Assume that PHC would want to set up two funds for reporting purposes—a general fund and a capital fund—and that annual revenues exceed $1,050,000.

---

**Exhibit A**
**NATURE OF OPERATIONS**

In October 20X5, PHC purchased a 15-unit apartment building in downtown Perth for $1,125,000. It then spent $375,000 in renovations to upgrade the building and make it accessible for adults with physically disabilities.

PHC offers 24-hour non-medical attendant care. Support care services are provided through a combination of staff members and volunteers. The staff members receive a monthly salary. As an inducement to recruit and retain qualified support care workers, each staff member is allowed 15 sick days per year. The employee can bank the sick days not used in any one year. Upon termination or retirement, the employee is paid for banked sick days at the wage rate in effect at that time.

Rental payments are due the first day of each month and are geared to tenant income. Most of the tenants are very good about making their rent payments on time. Some rental payments are received late. On August 31, 20X6, there was $19,500 of unpaid rent.

PHC plans to install central air conditioning in the building in April 20X7 at an expected cost of $75,000. This expenditure is being financed by a special fundraising drive, which, by August 31, 20X6, had raised $30,000 in cash and $22,500 in pledges from citizens in the local community.

---

*Case Continued >*

*Case Continued >*

## CASE 10-5 YOUTH SINGERS

Youth Singers (YS) is a not-for-profit organization that was formed in 20X1 by Nancy, a retired professional singer. Members of the choir range in age from 8 to 20. The choir has won a number of major singing competitions across North America and is producing its first CD next month. The choir plans to record an annual CD of its Christmas concert.

Nancy is in charge of YS's daily operations. All major decisions need to be approved by the board of directors. Initial financing for YS came solely from private donations, and a fundraising committee was recently formed to raise funds for special projects. Last year, YS qualified for two government grants that require audited financial statements to be submitted on an annual basis. YS has attached a set of financial statements to government grant applications in the past. The Canada Revenue Agency also requires financial statements to provide tax receipts for donors.

Your CA firm has a policy of supporting its staff in volunteering their time to NFP activities. You have recently joined YS as a member of its board of directors and have volunteered to assist with all accounting issues. Details on past accounting policies are provided in Exhibit C.

You have been asked to prepare a report identifying any changes you would make to the current accounting policies for the next board of directors' meeting.

Required

Prepare the draft report to the board of directors.

### Exhibit C
### ACCOUNTING POLICIES AND OTHER INFORMATION

1. Donation—Original Historic Sheet Music
   A donor recently died, leaving in her will a large selection of sheet music to YS. It is impossible to verify the value of this donation due to its historical value. The music will be performed by the choir during concerts. The original sheet music will be displayed in a glassed-in case.

2. Annual Pledges

   Every Christmas, YS holds an annual benefit concert. At this time, YS holds a major fundraising drive and asks all concert guests to provide a donation or pledge an amount. All pledges are recognized when the pledge is made by the donor.

3. Fundraising Costs

   YS is committed to having fundraising costs not exceed 5% of donation revenue. Nancy reviews all amounts expended for fundraising each year. Part of the advertising and promotion costs for fundraising are allocated to education each year because part of the purpose of these campaigns is to educate the public on the goals of YS.

4. Capital Assets

   All capital assets are recorded at their market value as determined by the finance director. During 20X7, a local music store provided sheet music stands at manufacturer's direct costs of $20,000. Purchasing these stands at retail prices would have cost $40,000.

5. Revenues

   Individual choir members started providing singing lessons during 20X7 as a source of fundraising. The revenue during 20X7 from lessons was $50,000. Annual revenue from all sources was $200,000 in 20X6 and $280,000 in 20X7.

6. Amortization

   Capital assets are not amortized.

## CASE 10-6 FINEST ART GALLERY

Finest Art Gallery (Finest) is a major art gallery in Toronto. Finest has the largest collection of art in Canada and has five major exhibits a year. Finest is a not-for-profit organization with funding received primarily from private contributors and government grants.

The board of directors turns over its members every three years. A new board just announced for 20X3–20X5 has a number of younger members who have rejuvenated a previous idea to expand a new section of the gallery for the work of children. This would require major fundraising over the next few years. It is anticipated that this addition would attract a wider audience to the gallery and encourage young children to become interested in art at an early age.

The new board, although energetic and ambitious, lacks knowledge of accounting. Board members were recruited for their marketing skills and love of art. They have asked you, CA, to assist them over the next few months in selecting accounting policies and providing recommendations for changes to their existing policies. They want to comply with any CICA *Handbook* recommendations for not-for-profit organizations, but are not familiar with the *Handbook*'s content. You have committed to preparing a report for the next board meeting outlining specific accounting policies. If you recommend any changes, they must be fully supported. The board is concerned with the costs involved with preparing financial statements and wants to minimize these costs.

After the meeting with the board of directors, you sat down and reviewed the financial statements for 20X3. Notes from your review are included in Exhibit D.

*Case Continued >*

*Case Continued >*

A set of financial statements has been provided to any donors who requested them in the past. In addition, government agencies require a set of audited financial statements as a requirement for government grants.

Required

Prepare the report for the board of directors.

---

## Exhibit D
## NOTES TAKEN FROM A REVIEW OF THE 20X3 FINANCIAL STATEMENTS

1. The financial statements include a statement of income and expenditures and a statement of financial position. A cash flow statement was not prepared since it was felt that it does not provide meaningful information.

2. Revenues for 20X3 included the following:

| | |
|---|---:|
| Memberships | $600,000 |
| Admission fees | 800,000 |
| Government grants | 2,000,000 |
| Contributions | 450,000 |
| Endowment fund revenue | 950,000 |

3. Admission fees are recognized as money is collected. Contributions are recognized when a pledge is made by the donor. Notes to the financial statements segregate the number of restricted and unrestricted contributions. Restricted funds include any amounts donated for a specific purpose and amounts segregated by the board for future expansion or special projects.

4. All capital assets are recorded at a dollar value to have a nominal amount provided on the financial statements. No amortization is taken on these assets. A recent review of the capital assets indicated the following items. The amounts were estimated by a member of the board of directors:

| | |
|---|---:|
| Office equipment | $ 500,000 |
| Automobiles | 70,000 |
| Facilities | 10,000,000 |
| Artwork | unable to estimate |

5. During 20X3, the roof was replaced on the art gallery at a cost of $260,000. This amount was expensed. In addition, a new air-conditioning unit was installed to protect the artwork from damage due to temperature changes. The cost was $300,000. To finance the purchase of the new air-conditioning system, a piece of artwork was sold.

6. Volunteer services are not recorded.

7. For fundraising, a portion of the advertising and promotion costs incurred are allocated to education expenditures each year.

# CASE 10-7 CKER–FM ETHNIC RADIO

In the fall of 20X1, eight wealthy businesspeople from the same ethnic background formed a committee (CKER committee) to obtain a radio licence from the Canadian Radio-television and Telecommunications Commission (CRTC). Their goal is to start a not-for-profit, ethnic community radio station for their area. They plan to call the station CKER–FM Ethnic Radio (CKER). It will broadcast ethnic music, news, and sports from their country of origin, cultural information, programs on ethnic cooking, and other such programs seven days a week.

The station's capital requirements are to be financed by memberships, donations, and various types of loans. It is expected that the ongoing operations will be supported by advertising paid for by businesspeople from that ethnic community and by the larger business community targeting that ethnic audience, as well as by donations and memberships.

It is now March 20X2, and the CRTC has announced that hearings will start in one month on a number of broadcasting licence applications, including the CKER committee's application. The CKER committee members are fairly confident about the viability of their proposal; however, they have decided to seek the advice of a professional accounting firm to assist with the endeavour. The CKER committee has engaged Maria & Casano, Public Accountants, for the assignment, as three of the five partners of the firm are from the same ethnic community. The partner in charge of the assignment has stated that the firm will donate half its fee for the work.

You are a public accountant who works for Maria & Casano and have been put in charge of the assignment. You have met with the CKER committee and various volunteers associated with the project. Information gathered on station start-up is contained in Exhibit E. Exhibit F provides other information on the CKER committee's proposal. The partner has asked you to prepare a draft report to the committee members discussing the viability of the proposed radio station over the initial three-year period. Since the committee members are fairly confident that they will receive the licence, the partner has asked you to recommend accounting policies for the transactions that CKER is contemplating. Your report must also cover other significant issues that the station will face after it commences operations.

Required

Prepare the draft report.

---

## Exhibit E
## INFORMATION ON STATION START-UP

1.  Costs to date have totalled $50,000 and are mostly transportation and meeting costs, as well as postage. These costs have been paid for personally by the CKER committee members.

2.  To approve the licence application, the CRTC must see written commitments to finance the station's start-up costs and operating losses in the first two years. Remaining costs to obtain the licence, excluding donated legal work, are expected to be about $8,000, and will be paid by CKER committee members.

*Exhibit Continued >*

*Exhibit Continued >*

3.  If the CRTC approves the licence application, the CKER committee will immediately set up a not-for-profit organization and apply to the Canada Revenue Agency (CRA) for charitable status, which it will likely receive.

4.  Fairly exhaustive efforts to obtain commercial financing have failed. As a result, four wealthy individuals have volunteered to provide CKER with the financing for the start-up. They will each personally borrow $25,000 from financial institutions and give the funds to the station. These individuals expect the loan to be cost-free to them, as the station will make the interest and principal payments.

5.  A "Reverse Lifetime Contribution" program will be instituted. Under this program, a donor will pay the station a capital sum of at least $50,000. The station can do whatever it wants with the funds, but it will repay the donor an equal annual amount calculated as the capital sum divided by 90 years less the individual's age at the time of contribution. Upon the death of the donor, the station will retain the balance of the funds. Currently, a 64-year-old station supporter has committed $78,000, and seven other individuals are considering this method of assisting the station.

6.  Initially the station is to broadcast with a 2,500-watt signal. Within three to four years it hopes to obtain commercial financing for a second transmitter that will boost the power of the signal and the broadcast range.

---

## Exhibit F
## OTHER INFORMATION ABOUT PLANS FOR THE STATION

1.  The CKER committee has analyzed census and other data to determine the potential market for the station. Engineering studies have mapped out the area that will be covered by the broadcast signal. There are about 1.1 million people in the target listening area. The latest Canadian census shows that 14% of the population comes from the target ethnic group. By applying a conservative factor of 40% to these findings, the CKER committee has arrived at a listenership figure of about 5.6%, or about 62,000 people. The CKER committee has found that about one in five of the businesses in the area are run by members of the ethnic community, many of whom would like a medium for reaching their own people through direct advertising.

2.  The amount of time expected to be devoted to commercials per hour is four minutes in year one, five minutes in year two, and six minutes in year three. Advertising cost per minute, discounted to 25% below the current market rate, will be:

| | |
|---|---|
| Prime time (6 hours a day) | $40 |
| Regular time (10 hours a day) | $30 |
| Off-peak (8 hours a day) | $25 |

Advertising time will be sold by salespeople whose remuneration will be a 15% commission.

3. Miscellaneous revenue from renting out the recording studio when not in use by CKER could approach $3,000 per month in year three, but will start out at about $2,200 per month.

4. At least 120 people have committed to pay a $125 annual membership fee. Membership carries no special privileges other than to be identified as a supporter of the station. Membership is expected to grow by 20% per year.

5. Start-up capital expenditures are as follows: transmission equipment $61,000, broadcast studio equipment $62,000, and production studio equipment $40,000. Administration and other costs, including rent, are expected to total about $1,237,000 per year and will not increase when advertising sales increase.

6. The committee believes that there are no GST implications related to running the station, since it is a not-for-profit venture.

7. About one-third of the person-hours needed to run the station are expected to come from volunteers.

[CICA]

# CASE 10-8 SAFETY NET

Safety Net (SN) is a not-for-profit organization operating in Big Town, Canada. SN runs a shelter for the homeless, operates a soup kitchen, and provides counselling services to runaway teenagers and street kids. The demand for SN's services has expanded rapidly over the past few years, as has its operating budget. Exhibit G describes SN's operations.

SN's operations have changed substantially in the past year (Exhibit G). Fundraising has been much more aggressive, two government grants have been obtained, and the "bequest on death" campaign begun several years ago yielded one large bequest during the year. In dealing with these changes, the board of directors of SN realized that they need financial advice to ensure they are making informed business decisions. Accordingly, they recently approached your firm, Fortin & Larose, Public Accountants, to advise them on the reporting requests they should be making of management to provide relevant information. Where appropriate, the board would like advice on the selection of accounting policies and on financial statement disclosure and other matters of importance. In the past, SN has recorded revenue and expenses on a cash basis.

The board has asked your firm to perform an audit to meet the requirements of one of the government grants and to provide the certified documentation for both grants, for the year ended March 31, 20X8 (see Exhibit H).

It is now January 22, 20X8. The senior partner of Fortin & Larose has asked you to draft a report to the board of directors of SN providing them with the requested information. The partner has also requested a memo highlighting the various engagement issues.

*Case Continued >*

*Case Continued >*

He believes that there are additional service opportunities, and he wants you to note in the memo the services that the firm could perform for SN.

Required

Prepare the report and the memo.

---

### Exhibit G
### DESCRIPTION OF SAFETY NET'S OPERATIONS

SN has three core operations: a shelter for the homeless, a soup kitchen for the needy, and a drop-in counselling service for runaways and street kids. There are also administrative and fundraising activities.

#### SHELTER FOR THE HOMELESS

The shelter operates out of a former university residence. The residence was donated to SN several years ago when the university was closed as part of the provincial government's plan to rationalize higher education. No amount was recorded on SN's books for the donated residence. The shelter is run by a very small number of staff.

#### SOUP KITCHEN

The soup kitchen operates out of leased facilities—namely, a former church in a run-down part of town. The signing of a 20-year lease on this property resulted in the dismissal of the previous executive director of SN after the board discovered the lease costs exceeded the fair-market-value rent for similar properties and that the remaining useful life of the church, at the signing of the lease, was only 15 years.

Paid staff and volunteers prepare two meals a day. Volunteers include chefs from local restaurants, university food-service providers, and students from a local university's food sciences program.

Donated food supplies are a major component of operations, and the level of donations remains relatively constant. Corporations make donations throughout the year, and individuals donate large volumes of fresh produce in the summer and fall months. None of these donated goods or services is currently recorded.

#### COUNSELLING SERVICES FOR RUNAWAYS AND STREET KIDS

The drop-in centre has two paid counsellors who work closely with the kids and provide referrals to other programs, such as drug rehabilitation.

The centre has entered into several innovative arrangements to provide assistance to runaways needing transportation back home. A major airline has begun a frequent-flyer grant program whereby the members of its frequent-flyer program are asked to donate some or all of their frequent-flyer points to the drop-in centre. The centre can then use the donated points to acquire a plane ticket. Counsellors attempt to identify the kids most likely to benefit from free transportation back home.

## ADMINISTRATION

The administrative staff consists of the executive director, a full-time fundraiser, a manager for each of the three operating areas, a bookkeeper, and an accounting clerk/receptionist. There is a relatively large number of volunteer fundraisers. In the past, fundraising consisted mainly of a door-to-door campaign by volunteers seeking donations and selling "I care" SN memberships. In SN's financial statements, the costs of the campaign are netted against total funds raised to present a single door-to-door fundraising total.

The bookkeeper handles all accounting and banking duties except for verifying accounts payable invoices for accuracy and filing documents. The two tasks are handled by a receptionist. The bookkeeper has a desktop computer system and uses an off-the-shelf computerized accounting package.

The executive director orally promised the full-time fundraiser a bonus of 10% of funds raised in excess of $500,000.

## Exhibit H
## CHANGES TO SAFETY NET'S OPERATIONS

### FUNDRAISING

The full-time fundraiser aggressively pursued fundraising opportunities. Among the new fundraising efforts was a Safety Net charity golf tournament put on by a local golf club. The net proceeds of the tournament received from the golf club were recorded on SN's books.

SN's annual telethon was held on a local cable television station during December 20X7. Its success was greatly enhanced when a country music superstar, in town for a series of concerts, saw the broadcast and volunteered to do a one-hour personal appearance as soon as five companies pledged $20,000 each. Five local car dealers responded by making pledges, although payment has yet to be received. News of this commitment increased the number of personal pledges by viewers. Even though the number of personal pledges increased, only a small percentage of them have been honoured to date. As a result, the bookkeeper is not sure how to record the pledges.

The "bequest on death" program began several years ago. There was one large bequest during the year, which left SN with a cash fund to be used for capital acquisitions only. During the year, some of the money from the fund was used to acquire furniture for the shelter, at a cost substantially below fair market value.

Two grants were negotiated during the year. The first provides for the recovery of 50% of operating costs for the shelter and soup kitchen and 30% of other operating costs. The second government grant was a lump sum contribution of $200,000 to assist with capital costs related to the shelter for the next five years. SN must provide a minimum number of beds at the shelter during that period and create at least one full-time position or 33% of the grant becomes payable. Both grants include a clause that states, "Safety Net will provide certified documentation annually to support its claim of government funds." The second grant also requires annual audited financial statements to be submitted to the government.

*Exhibit Continued >*

*Exhibit Continued >*

During the year, SN began a campaign to raise funds to build a new shelter for runaway children. The shelter is expected to begin operations in three years. Thus far, $2 million in pledges has been raised, and construction of the building is scheduled to begin sometime in July 20X8. SN plans to apply most of the $200,000 grant from the government to the capital costs of the new shelter. The funds have therefore been set aside for this use.

[CICA]

## CASE 10-9 ART GALLERY

You have been hired to prepare a report for the board of directors of a large art gallery. The board has just reviewed the annual financial statements of the art gallery, and is dissatisfied with the financial information provided in the statements. You have been provided with the following information.

The principal activity of the art gallery is the acquisition and exhibition of modern and contemporary pieces of art. The gallery is open to the general public on a daily basis, and has special exhibits for specific interest groups. Each year the gallery has a number of fundraising activities to help defray operating costs and make the acquisition of art possible. These activities are organized by the support staff, but rely on volunteers to staff the various functions. The major fundraising activity is an Annual Rennaise Telethon (ART), which solicits pledges from corporations and individuals and has been very successful.

Capital assets, in addition to the pieces of artwork, include a building, maintenance equipment, office furniture, and fixtures. The building that houses the art gallery is a large Victorian mansion that was donated by a prominent local family several years ago. Because the building has been designated a heritage property, utilities are provided by the local utility companies for a nominal fee of one dollar a year. As well, the municipal government has exempted the gallery from paying property taxes. Funding for capital asset acquisitions comes from various granting agencies and from fundraising activities of the gallery.

The gallery also operates a gift shop on a break-even basis, with the objective of attracting visitors to the gallery. The gift shop has a small staff of salaried employees, but also operates with the assistance of a number of volunteers. The gift shop has an annual inventory of $175,000, and annual sales of approximately $1 million.

The gallery has a support staff of 17 employees, a curator, and a director who is responsible for the overall operation of the gallery. The total operating budget for the gallery is $4.2 million.

### Required

Prepare a report addressing the concerns of the board of directors of the art gallery. Your report should include a brief description of the purpose and objective of a fund accounting system. As well, you have been asked to recommend the different types of funds that would be most appropriate for the gallery. A discussion of relevant accounting policies is also required.

[CGA–Canada]

# Problems

## P10-1 (35 minutes, medium)

It has been a hectic year at Westside Lodge. In January 20X4, Charlene Karing incorporated Westside as a not-for-profit organization. Its mandate is to provide counselling services for troubled youth. During the year, the organization organized a fundraising drive, signed a 10-year lease for office space, and commenced offering services to the public. The organization looks forward to many years of improving the lives of troubled youths in the community.

The office space was found in a rundown building in an older area of Centreville. Most of the town's poorest people live in this area of town. Westside took possession of the space on April 1, 20X4, and completed leasehold improvements by June 30, 20X4, at a cost of $45,000. On July 2, 20X4, Charlene opened the doors for business. She took on the job of director of the organization at an annual salary of $72,000. However, she worked July and August of 20X4 for free. On September 1, 20X4, two social workers were hired to meet the demands of the growing organization.

It is now December 20X4. You, CGA, have been asked by Charlene to prepare the financial statements for Westside for the 10-month period ending October 31, 20X4. Charlene provided the following schedule of cash receipts and disbursements:

| | |
|---|---:|
| Cash receipts | |
| Donations from individuals and businesses | $ 90,000 |
| Grant from provincial government | 105,000 |
| | 195,000 |
| | |
| Cash disbursements | |
| Leasehold improvements | 45,000 |
| Furniture and equipment | 36,000 |
| Rent | 15,750 |
| Office supplies | 7,500 |
| Wages and benefits | 42,000 |
| Other expenses | 12,750 |
| | 159,000 |
| Cash on hand at October 31, 20X4 | $ 36,000 |

Of the $90,000 received from individuals and businesses, $15,000 was designated for the purchase of furniture and equipment and $22,500 was designated for the purpose of hiring a program director in 20X5. The remaining funds were unrestricted. The provincial government agreed to provide an annual grant equal to 70% of all expenses to a maximum of $300,000 a year. To maximize the grant received from the provincial government, Charlene wants to record the value of all donated goods and services and to claim the full cost of the leasehold improvements and furniture and equipment in the year when these assets are acquired.

The furniture and equipment is expected to have a useful life of five years. Revenue is to be recognized using the deferral method. At the end of October 20X4, $4,500 of wages and benefits had been earned but not yet paid for and $1,500 was owing for other expenses.

## Required

Prepare a statement of operations and a statement of financial position for the 10-month period ending October 31, 20X4. Show supporting calculations.
[CGA–Canada]

## P10-2 (40 minutes, medium)

You have been appointed to the board of directors for a local not-for-profit organization called "Friendship Corner" (FC). This organization has been in operation for 12 months and has never prepared a set of financial statements. Operations started on July 1, 20X3, and FC's first set of financial statements is now being prepared for the year just ended (at June 30, 20X4). A volunteer bookkeeper has done his best to keep track of the organization's financial affairs. Although he has taken an introductory accounting course, he has limited knowledge of reporting requirements for not-for-profit organizations. You have tried to explain the accounting for NFPs to him, but he still needs your help.

### Required

Prepare the journal entries in response to each of the following questions from the bookkeeper:

**a.** On January 1, 20X4, a local business donated a van to FC. This saved us from having to rent a van twice per week. The van has a fair market value of $40,000, but we obtained it for $1. It is expected to last four years. I want to record it and amortize it on a straight-line basis, if this is acceptable.

  i) What journal entries would I make for the year ended June 30, 20X4, related to this van, using the deferral method?

  ii) What journal entries would I make for the year ended June 30, 20X4, related to this van, using the restricted-fund method of accounting and assuming we have a separate capital fund?

**b.** In September 20X3, one of our "friends" won $20 million in a lottery. She was so grateful to have been helped in her time of need that she provided us with a $4 million endowment on September 30, 20X3, with the requirement that the purchasing power of the endowment be maintained. We invested it in a government bond on October 1, 20X3 (at par). The bond pays 5% interest annually, with the first payment to be received on September 30, 20X4. We are happy with this investment as it is quite secure and it protects us against inflation, which has been steady at 2% for years.

  i) What journal entries would I make for the year ended June 30, 20X4, for these transactions using the deferral method of accounting?

  ii) What journal entries would I make for the year ended June 30, 20X4, for these transactions using the restricted-fund method, assuming FC has both a general fund and a separate endowment fund?

  [CGA–Canada, adapted]

## P10-3 (35 minutes, medium)

You have recently received an accounting designation and, to celebrate, you are out for dinner with a long-time friend, Jamie. Jamie feels that "the key to success is networking, because getting to know influential people can help your career." However, Jamie may be taking this a little too far.

Jamie recently joined the board of directors for two not-for-profit organizations (NFPs). United Rays ("Rays") has annual revenues of $1,700,000, 40 paid employees, and separate funds for its key activities (a capital fund, an endowment fund, and a general fund). Shining Foundation ("Shining") has average annual revenues of $150,000 and only one paid employee. It uses the deferral method of accounting. Jamie has been appointed as the treasurer at both organizations. "A great way to network!" says Jamie. Unfortunately, Jamie barely passed her high school accounting course and has not taken any accounting courses since that time. She knows that the boards of directors of both organizations want to comply with GAAP to ensure key donors will be confident about the NFP's financial statements. However, Jamie is not sure what the specific guidelines are for NFPs under GAAP.

**Required**

Address each of Jamie's concerns, making sure your advice complies with GAAP.

**a.** Jamie stated that "Shining received a piece of equipment on January 1, 20X8, valued at $64,000, which was donated by a friend of the charity. We want to record the $64,000 as contribution revenue and amortize the equipment on a straight-line basis over four years."

Prepare the journal entries required for the contribution and amortization for the year ended December 31, 20X8.

**b.** "Shining also received its first pledge ever, and it is a big one," said Jamie. "A local high-technology company has promised to pay us $60,000 per year for the next three years, starting July 1, 20X9. It put no restrictions on how we use the donation."

Explain how the not-for-profit organizations should account for pledges. In particular, would the accounting for pledges differ for Shining because this is its "first pledge ever"?

**c.** "Rays received a $1,200,000 endowment donation on January 1, 20X8, to be used as follows: The principal is to remain intact but any interest earned can be used for charity for whatever purpose it chooses."

Prepare the journal entries for the $1,200,000 and $60,000 interest earned and received in 20X8 on the endowment donation.

**d.** "I convinced the board of directors of Rays to hold a vote next week to change our accounting for our head office building. It was acquired for $4,000,000 on January 1, 20X1, and was amortized over 25 years at $160,000 per year. However, buildings similar to ours are selling for close to $10,000,000 now. Therefore, I want to stop amortizing the building. Since we are an NFP, this is acceptable, isn't it?" asks Jamie.

State whether this would be acceptable and briefly explain.

[CGA–Canada, adapted]

**P10-4 (40 minutes, medium)**

Evergreen Chalet (Chalet) is a seniors' residence operated as a not-for-profit organization. During 20X2, Chalet built a new bingo hall on its property at a cost of $600,000. The bingo hall was financed with $300,000 of donations from private individuals and a $300,000 grant from the provincial government. In addition, a $25,000 donation was received specifically to cover the cost of future maintenance of the bingo hall. The bingo hall commenced operations on September 1, 20X2. In the last four months of the year, $7,500 was spent on maintenance of the bingo hall. The estimated useful life of the bingo hall is 40 years. Chalet amortizes its capital assets using the straight-line method.

Among other things, Chalet has an excellent reputation for its bingo nights. Most of the callers and runners for the bingo nights are unpaid volunteers.

**Required**

**a.** Based on the information provided, prepare a partial SFP to capture all activities related to the bingo hall, assuming Chalet uses the deferral method and does not have a separate capital fund for the bingo hall.

**b.** Differentiate between expenditure accounting and expense accounting as they apply to the $600,000 cost of the bingo hall.

**c.** Identify the conditions that must be met to recognize the value of volunteers' time in the financial statements of a not-for-profit organization.

**d.** Prepare the journal entry that would be made under the deferral method if volunteers' services were to be recorded at a value of $5,000.

[CGA–Canada, adapted]

## P10-5 (35 minutes, medium)

Youth Opportunities Unlimited (YOU) is a not-for-profit organization that provides sporting equipment for inner-city children who cannot otherwise afford it. YOU has been in operation since 20X1 and operated on a break-even basis from 20X1 to 20X4. In 20X5, YOU spent $240,000 on sporting equipment, similar to previous years. However, donations were reduced and YOU ended up with cash disbursements exceeding cash receipts by $60,000. In 20X6, YOU decided it needed to make some changes. You have recently obtained your professional accounting designation and have volunteered to provide advice on the following matters related to the December 31, 20X6, year-end financial statements.

### Required

**a.** The directors of YOU have heard of encumbrance accounting, but are not sure how it works.

    i) Briefly explain the difference between encumbrance accounting and a budgetary accounting system.

    ii) Briefly explain the difference between an encumbrance and a liability.

    iii) If an encumbrance system is used, what journal entries would be made to record purchase orders issued for $260,000 for goods and services and the subsequent invoices of $259,200 received that related to those purchase orders?

**b.** You has decided to follow Canadian GAAP in 20X6 for the first time. The directors have heard about the deferral method of accounting for contributions, but are not sure how to implement it. Provide journal entries to record the following transactions under the deferral method for the December 31, 20X6, financial statements.

    i) A former teacher donated $20,000 on July 1, 20X6, with the condition that 50% of it be spent on supplies to be provided to children by December 31, 20X6, and 50% to be spent on supplies to be provided to children in 20X7.

    ii) Another donor donated land to YOU for a future warehouse site in 20X6. The land originally cost $100,000 in 20X1, but had a fair value of $200,000 in 20X6.

**c.** As a small not-for-profit organization, YOU would like to simplify its accounting for capital assets.

    i) Briefly explain under what circumstances YOU would *not* have to capitalize and amortize its capital assets.

    ii) How would capital assets be reflected on YOU's financial statements and notes to financial statements if YOU chose *not* to capitalize and amortize?

    iii) One benefit of not capitalizing would be to simplify the preparation of YOU's financial statements. List *three* other arguments that support the adoption of a policy of *not* capitalizing and amortizing capital assets.

[CGA–Canada, adapted]

## P10-6 (45 minutes, medium)

Island College is a private boys' school and is operated as a not-for-profit organization. During 20X1 the school received $1,000,000 in private donations from individuals to establish a scholarship fund for its students. The principal amount of the fund must be invested in government bonds. The interest on the fund can only be used to provide scholarships to students. For the year ended December 31, 20X1, the fund earned interest of $60,000, and scholarships totalling $40,000 were awarded to students in need. At the end of the year, the balance in the scholarship fund was $1,020,000.

On January 1, 20X1, a local businessperson donated a small bus to the school. The bus seats 20 people and was worth approximately $80,000 at the time of the donation. It has an estimated useful life of six years with a residual value of $20,000. The school amortizes its capital assets using the straight-line method.

### Required

a. Prepare the journal entries to capture all activities related to the scholarship fund, assuming the school uses the deferral method and it does not have a separate endowment fund for the scholarship.

b. Prepare the journal entries to capture all activities related to the scholarship fund, assuming the school uses the restricted-fund method and records all entries in a separate endowment fund for the scholarship.

c. Assume the school wishes to record the value of the donated bus. Prepare journal entries for 20X1 to capture all activities related to the donated bus, assuming the school uses the deferral method and does not have a separate capital asset fund for the donated bus.

d. Assume the school wishes to record the value of the donated bus. Prepare journal entries for 20X1 to capture all activities related to the donated bus, assuming the school uses the restricted-fund method and has a separate capital asset fund for the donated bus.

[CGA–Canada, adapted]

## P10-7 (30 minutes, easy)

You have been hired as a consultant to provide accounting advice for a not-for-profit organization that wishes to improve its accounting system. In particular, the organization, Stop Global Warming (SGW), is considering changing its method for contributions and implementing a new budgeting and encumbrance accounting system. SGW has a December 31 year-end.

### Required

a. In November 20X4, SGW issued a $3,000 purchase order for key chains to be provided as an incentive to donors who contribute to its Spring 20X5 fundraising drive. In December 20X4, the key chains were shipped to SGW with an invoice price of $3,285. Prepare the journal entries for November 20X4 and December 20X4 using encumbrance accounting.

b. Briefly explain the difference between an encumbrance and a liability.

c. SGW has always used the restricted-fund method of accounting for contributions, but other similar organizations have been using the deferral method. Briefly explain how SGW would account for the following restricted contributions using the deferral method:

i) restricted contributions for expenses of future periods;

ii) restricted contributions for the acquisition of amortizable capital assets; and

iii) restricted contributions for expenses of the current period.

[CGA–Canada, adapted]

P10-8 (40 minutes, medium)

Ark Care is a not-for-profit organization set up for famine relief. Ark has been operating for 25 years and has a December 31 year-end. Ark's policy with respect to capital assets is to capitalize and amortize the capital assets over their expected useful lives.

On June 30, 20X3, Ark received three donations from a former director:

- $45,000 cash for famine relief.

- $75,000 to be used solely for construction of the new administrative building. Of the $75,000, 70% was received in cash, with the remainder promised in February 20X4. (Note: Construction is expected to commence in October 20X4.)

- $900,000 cash, which was invested on July 1, 20X3, in long-term Government of Canada bonds, with 6% interest to be paid semi-annually on December 31 and June 30. The $900,000 donation was given with the stipulation that it be invested in interest-bearing securities with the principal maintained by Ark, although interest earned on the securities is not restricted.

Required

a. Briefly explain (do not provide journal entries) how each of the three donations should be accounted for using the deferral method of accounting. In particular, should each of the donations be recognized as revenue for the year ended December 31, 20X3?

b. Despite the recent donations from its former director, Ark is increasingly faced with severe budgetary constraints. Ark is considering implementing encumbrance accounting in the coming year.

i) Briefly describe the process of encumbrance accounting.

ii) Briefly describe how encumbrance accounting might serve as a device to help control spending when it is used in conjunction with a formal budgeting system.

[CGA–Canada, adapted]

# Chapter 11

## Public Sector Financial Reporting

## Learning Objectives

**After studying this chapter, you should be able to:**

LO **1** identify the characteristics of governments and governmental units;

LO **2** discuss the objectives of financial reporting for the public sector and how they are reflected in government financial statements; and

LO **3** discuss the major reporting and measurement issues.

## INTRODUCTION

Nova Scotia is a small province of approximately 940,000 people on the east coast of Canada. In its 2011 public accounts (i.e., annual report), Nova Scotia reported revenue of almost $10 billion and a surplus of $569 million. The most significant revenue sources were income taxes (25%) and sales taxes (20%). Other sources included petroleum royalties (2%) and net income from government business enterprises (4%). The major expenses for the province were health (39%), education (17%), community services (11%), and debt servicing costs (10%). These types of revenues and expenses are typical for many provincial governments.

Governments such as the Province of Nova Scotia are different from the traditional business organization. Their objective is not to make a profit but rather to provide services to the public. In addition, much of their revenue is derived not from exchange transactions, but from their ability to impose and collect taxes. Given differences like these, it is easy to understand why financial reporting for governments differs from that for businesses. In this chapter we will examine exactly how the financial reporting for government differs from business. In the process, we will explore many unique issues that arise in governmental accounting.

It is important to note at the outset that governmental accounting standards are *not* set by the Accounting Standards Board but are set by the Public Sector Accounting Board (PSAB), as contained in the CICA *Public Sector Accounting Handbook (PSA Handbook)*.[1]

---

[1] The *PSA Handbook* does not have the authority to force governments to adopt its recommendations. In this chapter, however, we will refer to the recommendations of the *PSA Handbook* as the necessary requirements for governments to comply with GAAP.

LO **1**

Identify the characteristics
of governments and
governmental units

# 11.1 THE NATURE OF GOVERNMENT

## Characteristics of Government

To comprehend public sector reporting, it is important to first understand the nature of government. In Canada, there are one national government, ten provincial governments, three territorial governments, and approximately 4,000 municipal governments. The federal, provincial, and territorial governments are often referred to collectively as the *senior* levels of government.

Governments are elected as part of a democratic process. As a result, all public sector entities (i.e., governments and government organizations) are accountable to the public. **Public accountability** means that entities operating in the public sector must explain and justify the collection and spending of monies and other resources. Members of the public should be able to assess the government's stewardship over the resources entrusted to it.

Governments possess rights and powers that businesses and NFP organizations do not. For example, governments can make laws and regulations, tax, fine, and set monetary or fiscal policy. Although these rights and powers differ with different levels of governments, they allow governments to affect their environment directly and indirectly.

The governing process usually starts with the government preparing a budget that reflects its spending priorities for the year. The budget must be approved by the elected members of the legislature or council, which thereby provides the authority for funds to be spent.[2] Compliance with the priorities set out in legislation is key to good public sector reporting and proper governance. Because the budget portrays public policy, it forms a key part of the government's financial report and, as we will see, is explicitly incorporated into two of the financial statements. Including the budget in the financial report allows for a better evaluation of the government's fiscal management and thus serves to improve accountability.

Governments are generally characterized by a much broader user group than either businesses or NFP organizations. The main users are the public (either directly or as represented by legislators and councillors), the civil service, other governments, debt investors such as pension funds, and analysts. People are often surprised to learn that the market for debt is substantially larger than the market for equities and, further, that governments, as a group, are by far the largest issuers of debt. Therefore analysts are often very interested in the financial statements of government.

Most governments generate the majority of their revenues from taxes. The ability to assess and collect taxes gives governments a much more stable foundation than any business or NFP could ever attain. Because of this, going concern issues are not as important for governments. Thus there is very little emphasis on working capital in government financial statements.

There is, however, a major emphasis on debt. Due to their taxing authority, governments have a tremendous capacity to borrow. Debt, however, contains an obligation to make interest and principal payments in the future. A burden of rising debt servicing

---

[2] Given the political nature of legislatures and councils, arrangements are often in place that provide the authority to allow the government to function even if a budget has not been approved. For example, in Nova Scotia, if a budget has not passed, departments automatically have 50% of the previous year's budget to conduct ongoing business (but not new program spending).

costs will affect a government's ability to provide future services to the public. As we will see, this lack of emphasis on working capital and increased emphasis on debt significantly affects the structure of government financial statements.

Governments, like NFPs, do not have equity ownership and do not have profit as their primary objective. Instead, their objectives are to provide services to the public, to redistribute wealth to meet legislated social goals, and to develop policies to address relevant issues that may arise. Given these objectives, governments generally do not engage in exchange transactions as a primary function. Like NFPs, the link between revenue and costs is severed. The provision of a service does not normally lead to revenue, and, furthermore, the payment of taxes does not entitle the taxpayer to a pre-determined level of service. This separation of revenue from expenses has implications in the accounting for many (but not all) government activities.

The objective to provide services rather than make a profit has implications for how tangible capital assets are viewed. These assets are seen as representing future service capability and not as a source of future cash flows (as in a business). The carrying value of these assets represents the unexpired service potential of the assets.

The distinction between non-financial and financial assets is important because non-financial assets are used only for providing services, while financial assets can be used for both future services and debt payment. As well, the lack of a profit motive means that spending on capital assets usually is not focused on the financial return but rather on other objectives, such as stimulating economic activity (e.g., providing incentives for private sector employment). This suggests that the impact of capital spending on debt in the current period should be highlighted because increases in debt will affect future service potential.

In designing the government reporting model, the CICA's Public Sector Accounting Board (PSAB) identified these and other unique characteristics of governments. PSAB cites nine key characteristics of public sector entities:[3]

1.  public accountability;
2.  multiple objectives;
3.  rights, powers and responsibilities (constitutional or devolved);
4.  lack of equity ownership;
5.  operating and financial frameworks set by legislation;
6.  the importance of the budget;
7.  governance structures;
8.  nature of resources; and
9.  non-exchange transactions.

We have already addressed most of these characteristics in our earlier discussion. We should note that governments often own assets because they "came with the territory," so to speak, such as Crown land held by the government, because it *is* the government. Crown property has no acquisition cost and is difficult to value; thus it is not recognized in the financial statements. Nevertheless, governments should disclose the *existence* of these assets.

---

[3] Characteristics of Public Sector Entities, prepared by the Conceptual Framework Task Force, August 2011, http://www.psab-ccsp.ca/documents-for-comment/item52207.pdf, accessed April 29, 2012.

In addition, governments should strive to disclose the costs of the services provided. While this information often is not sufficient to evaluate the efficiency or effectiveness of the service, it is necessary information in an environment of limited resources—the spending on one item in a budget will affect what is available for spending on other items in the same budget.

Finally, consistent with the theme of increased disclosure and a higher standard of accountability, governments often need to provide additional non-financial disclosures to allow for an effective evaluation of their programs and services, similar to the non-financial measures that NFPs make.

## Types of Government Organizations

The **public sector** is defined in the *PSA Handbook* as consisting of (1) the federal, provincial, territorial, and local governments; and (2) government organizations. The *PSA Handbook* refers to any entity within one of these groups as a **public sector entity**.

The widely diverse nature and variety of government organizations makes accounting for government organizations quite complex. Organizations are included as *government organizations* in the government reporting entity only if they are controlled by the government. Further, the accounting for government organizations depends on the underlying characteristics of the organization. In general, there are three types of government organizations:

- government business enterprises (GBEs);
- government not-for-profit organizations (GNFPOs); and
- other government organizations (OGOs).

**Government Business Enterprises**   PSAB defines a GBE as one that:

- is a separate legal entity that can contract in its own name and can sue or be sued;
- has the financial and operational authority to operate as a business;
- engages in external exchange transactions (i.e., sells goods and services to parties outside of the government reporting entity) as its principal activity; and
- is capable of maintaining its operations and meeting its liabilities from external revenues through the normal operation of its business.

GBEs are deemed to be publicly accountable enterprises and as such are directed by PSAB to follow the recommendations of the *CICA Handbook, Part I,* and thus are expected to follow International Financial Reporting Standards (IFRS).

**Government Not-for-Profit Organizations**   A GNFPO is an organization controlled by the government that possesses the following four characteristics:

1. It has not-for-profit counterparts in the private sector.
2. It does not have a transferable ownership interest.
3. It is operated exclusively for the not-for-profit purpose.
4. It does not provide financial returns to its members or contributors.

GNFPOs have two choices. They can follow the *PSA Handbook*, including the sections specific to NFPs (PS 4200 to PS 4290), or they can follow the *PSA Handbook* without the sections specific to NFPs.

**Exhibit 11.1** Financial Reporting Requirements for Governments and Government Organizations[4]

| Organization | Source of Accounting |
|---|---|
| Governments (federal, provincial, territorial, local) | *PSA Handbook* |
| Government business enterprises (GBE) | IFRS (as directed by PSAB) |
| Government not-for-profit organizations (GNFPO) | *PSA Handbook* |
| Other government organizations (OGO) | *PSA Handbook* or IFRS (choose best option based on organization's objectives) |

**Other Government Organizations**   Finally, an OGO is any organization not included in the first two categories. As a general rule, OGOs will base their accounting on the *PSA Handbook*. However, PSAB recognizes that there may be situations in which IFRS may be more appropriate. To help OGOs determine whether they are eligible to use IFRS, PSAB suggests that OGOs consider a number of factors, including (1) whether they possess the characteristics of a publicly accountable enterprise, (2) the nature of their operations, assets, and mandate, and (3) their dependence on government funding.

The accounting for governments and government organizations is summarized in Exhibit 11.1. Our concern in the remainder of the chapter will be with the governments and OGOs that are subject to the *PSA Handbook*.

### Concept Check 11-1

1. Why is there very little emphasis on working capital in government financial statements?
2. How are tangible capital assets viewed in government financial statements?
3. Why is the distinction between financial and non-financial assets important?
4. What is a government business enterprise (GBE)?

## 11.2 FINANCIAL REPORTING FOR GOVERNMENTS

### The Compliance Issue

LO ❷

Discuss the objectives of financial reporting for the public sector and how they are reflected in government financial statements

PSAB recommendations are just that: *recommendations*, not *requirements* for most levels of government. Other types of organizations may have compelling reasons to comply with recommendations of the *CICA Handbook* (such as the requirements of securities acts), but such is not the case with governments and the PSAB recommendations. Nevertheless, the quality of government reporting has improved in line with the PSAB recommendations despite lacking the "clout" that the CICA's Accounting Standards Board has for public for-profit enterprises.

For senior levels of government especially, there is no mechanism to compel compliance with the PSAB recommendations. Governmental financial reporting is governed by legislation, which may be either extensive or virtually non-existent at different levels

---

[4] Adapted from PSAB website.

and in different provinces and territories. Senior governments are not audited by external auditors, but by the governments' Auditors General. Auditors General are often not required to report in accordance with the recommendations of the PSAB, but rather in accordance with that government's legal reporting requirements.

Local governments usually are audited by external auditors, although some major cities have their own city auditor. Local government auditors are required to report in accordance with provincial legislation governing municipal reporting. Many local governments are now required by provincial legislation to report in compliance with the PSAB recommendations.[5,6]

While there is no compliance mechanism for the PSAB accounting recommendations for senior levels of government, the recommendations serve as a useful guide to Auditors General. The recommendations give the auditors an authoritative lever for persuading government authorities to improve their financial reporting. Ultimately, the PSAB recommendations can guide provincial legislatures in stipulating requirements for local and provincial governmental reporting.

A standard-setting body such as the PSAB can make progress only if its recommendations are accepted by its users. Changes or improvements in existing practice must be "eased" into practice. This process will result in a greater likelihood of acceptance, even when there is no legal compliance requirement. Part of the process of introducing a new standard must be to convince users of the benefits of the standard. For example, the change from cash accounting to accrual accounting was successful because it was perceived as providing three benefits:

- improved efficiency, transparency, quality of information, and priority setting;
- improved cash management, asset management, and financial management; and
- improved accountability.[7]

It is interesting to note that although no senior governments are *required* to follow PSAB recommendations, it is now very unlikely that a government would not follow PSAB. Progress continues to be made by PSAB through persuasion and consensus among governments.

## Objectives of Governmental Reporting[8]

What are the objectives of government financial statements? What are the information needs of the users? Several research studies have examined the users and uses of financial statements.[9] As a result of these studies, the PSAB issued PS 1100, "Financial Statement

---

[5] Beauchamp, Tim, "Municipalities on the move." CA *Magazine* (September 2009), p. 50.

[6] It appears that almost all municipalities are effectively compelled to comply with PSAB recommendations. All provinces either have a legislative requirement for municipalities to comply with PSAB or require compliance for the municipality to receive specific funds from the province. The result will likely be very high compliance with PSAB recommendations.

[7] Roy, J. Paul-Emile, "Accounting bases used in Canadian government budgeting." CA *Magazine*, (January/February 2005), p. 19.

[8] The PSAB has a project underway that is examining key concepts underlying financial performance. The project is expected to be completed in September 2015, and its results may impact some of the discussion in the next couple of sections.

[9] For example, see "Financial Reporting by Governments" (CICA, 1980).

Objectives," which is applicable to all levels of government. PS 1100 provides the following four objectives for financial statements:

1. to provide an accounting of financial affairs and resources under the government's control;

2. to demonstrate government's ability to finance activities, meet liabilities, and provide future services;

3. to account for sources, allocation, and use of government resources; to evaluate how activities affect net debt; and to show how activities were financed and how cash requirements were met; and

4. to display the state of a government's finances and evaluate if the finances are in accordance with legislative requirements.

**Objective 1: Defining the Entity**   The first objective defines the broad scope of government financial statements. The statements should capture the full extent of the activities undertaken by the government. The statements should therefore include not only government departments but also all the agencies, organizations, and enterprises that it controls. Only then will users be able to properly assess a government's policies and service delivery.

**Objective 2: Statement of Financial Position**   The second objective suggests that government financial statements should allow users to assess a government's finances. This is accomplished through a statement of financial position (SFP).

Remember that debt is a very important issue for governments. The inability to pay their debt has forced governmental entities to file for bankruptcy or seek bankruptcy protection in the past, such as in the famous US case of Orange County, California, in 1994 and more recently in the case of the city of Vallejo, California, in 2008. Recently, the financial markets worldwide have expressed doubts about the ability of some European Union nations to meet their debt obligations. While such cases do not exist in recent memory in Canada, to help users assess a government's ability to finance its activities and meet its liabilities, the government's "net debt" is presented in the SFP. **Net debt** is the total of government liabilities less the total of its financial assets. Net debt is important because debt has to be serviced and repaid and therefore will impact a government's ability to deliver programs and services in the future. For users, net debt is an important indicator of a government's financial position.

In addition, you will also recall that we said that tangible capital assets (and other non-financial assets) are viewed in terms of their unexpired or future service potential and not in terms of future cash flows. Thus, the total of tangible capital assets will help users assess a government's ability to deliver its services and programs in the future.

Net debt is thought of as *claims that could reduce future services*, while tangible capital assets can be thought of as *prepaid future service potential*. The two items are combined on the SFP to produce an **accumulated deficit or surplus.** The accumulated surplus or deficit consists of two components: (1) the portion attributable to the accumulated revenues and expenses recognized in the statement of operations and (2) the portion attributable to the accumulated unrealized gains and losses recognized in the statement of remeasurement gains and losses.

For users, accumulated deficit or surplus is an important indicator of a government's financial position because it shows the recognized economic resources that a government has available.

**Objective 3: Changes in Financial Position**   The third objective suggests that government financial statements should allow users to assess changes in a government's financial position. Government financial statements should focus on explaining the changes in three items: (1) the change in the accumulated deficit or surplus; (2) the change in net debt; and (3) the change in cash. We already discussed the importance of the first two items above and, of course, understanding the change in cash is important for any organization, whether business, not-for-profit, or government. The need for users to assess these changes in financial position requires four additional financial statements:

- statement of operations;
- statement of remeasurement gains and losses;
- statement of changes in net debt; and
- statement of cash flows.

The change in the accumulated deficit or surplus is explained by two statements: (1) the statement of operations, which explains the changes in the accumulated deficit or surplus caused by revenues and expenses, and (2) the statement of remeasurement gains and losses, which explains the changes in the accumulated deficit or surplus caused by unrealized gains and losses.

**Statement of Operations**   The **statement of operations** explains (1) the source and nature of a government's revenues and (2) the purpose and nature of a government's expenses. Measuring the cost of services is important to users because it will help them assess the efficacy of government programs (with the aid of additional non-financial information).

The relationship between revenues and expenses is also important. The purpose of government is not to make money but to provide services. To the extent that there may be excess revenues, it may allow a government to budget more for particular programs. To the extent that there is a deficiency of revenues, it may mean that a government has to raise taxes to cover the costs. In addition, the deficit or surplus indicates how successful the government was in maintaining its economic resources. If the economic resources declined (e.g., the accumulated deficit increased), then it is an indication that future services may be curtailed.

**Statement of Remeasurement Gains and Losses**   The **statement of remeasurement gains and losses** reconciles the accumulated remeasurement gains and losses at the beginning of the period with the accumulated remeasurement gains and losses at the end of the period. The accumulated remeasurement gains and losses balance on this statement is increased as unrealized gains or losses are recognized and reduced as the gains and losses are realized.

The statement captures unrealized gains and losses that arise from the changes in value of items denominated in a foreign currency and from the changes in value of financial instruments carried at fair value. These changes in fair value are relevant to users to help them assess how well the government has maintained its economic resources.

The purpose of this statement is to remove these items and the volatility associated with them from the statement of operations. Including gains and losses arising from fluctuating exchange rates or from fair value remeasurements would increase the apparent volatility of reported operations and affect the comparison of actual to budget.

The statement also includes OCI arising from the reporting of GBEs in the summary government financial statements.

**Statement of Changes in Net Debt**   The **statement of changes in net debt** reconciles the deficit or surplus for the period with the change in net debt. A difference exists between the two items because the cost of goods and services in a period will not exactly equal the expenditures on goods and services. A simple statement of net debt will start with the deficit or surplus for the period, subtract the cost of non-financial assets acquired (which will be mostly tangible capital assets), and add back the amortization of tangible capital assets to arrive at the **change in net debt**. This is an important indicator of performance for users because it will allow them to determine the capital expenditures for the period and the extent to which these expenditures were covered by the revenues of the period.

**Statement of Cash Flows**   The rationale for the **statement of cash flows** is the same as it is for business—it is important to understand an organization's sources and uses of cash for the period. This statement is very similar to the statement of cash flows for a business with one major difference—the statement has a section for *capital transactions* to capture the effect of the acquisition or sale of capital assets on cash flows. To understand why these transactions are not included under investing activities (as in a business), recall our discussion of the nature of tangible capital assets for a government. Capital assets are seen as representing future service capability and not future cash flows (as in a business). Because they are not evaluated in terms of future cash flows, there is no financial "return," and therefore they are not an investment in the classic sense. In fact, for governments, the only items that will appear under investing activities will be the buying and selling of financial assets.

**Objective 4: Budget Comparison**   The fourth objective suggests that government financial statements should allow users to evaluate the financial results of the period. This is best accomplished if the results can also be compared with the budget that was initially approved by the legislature. This requirement reflects the principle that governments should be accountable for their spending. It is achieved by including the budget in the statement of operations and the statement of changes in net debt. Then, users can compare actual results to planned results, thereby improving the user's ability to evaluate the government's performance for the period.

# Qualitative Characteristics

Standard-setters have conducted research on the qualitative characteristics that the information in government financial reports should possess to be useful. An early study that interviewed various categories of users of governmental reports found a wide diversity of needs. Four qualities were stressed by the interviewees: (1) comparability among governments; (2) consistency between years; (3) completeness; and (4) timeliness. The users were particularly emphatic about *comparability*:

> Almost above everything else, users wanted to compare the reports of various governments. This meant they wanted consistency among governments in the basis for:
>
> ■ defining the reporting entity to make clear what kinds of government organizations were included and excluded;
>
> ■ classifying and reporting revenues, expenditures, assets and liabilities; and
>
> ■ reporting government debt including contingent debt.
>
> They also wanted consistency, to the extent possible, between the Public Accounts and various statistical compilations of government figures (e.g., the National Accounts) and the ability to reconcile two sets of figures where differences in basis are justified by the different purposes served by the two sets of figures.[10]

The PSAB incorporated qualitative criteria into PS 1000 that reflected these needs of users:

> Financial statements should communicate information that is relevant to the needs of those for whom the statements are prepared, reliable, comparable, understandable and clearly presented in a manner that maximizes its usefulness. [PS 1000.24]

We will not review the qualitative characteristics in detail because they are *similar to those in both Parts I and II* of the CICA *Handbook*. However, the characteristic of *accountability value* contained in this section is not in the CICA *Handbook*. The addition of **accountability value** reflects the importance of stewardship in governments. It is manifested in the inclusion of budget figures in the financial statements. This additional information characteristic reflects the unique nature of governments.

## Illustration of Government Financial Statements

Following the government reporting model, the *PSA Handbook* recommends presentation of information on five issues about government finances:[11]

■ accumulated surplus/deficit;

■ annual surplus/deficit;

■ net debt/net financial assets;

■ change in net debt; and

■ change in cash and cash flows that contributed to the change.

This information can be found in the following five statements required by PSAB:

■ statement of financial position;

■ statement of operations;

■ statement of remeasurement gains and losses;

---

[10] "Financial Reporting by Governments" (CICA, 1980), p. 31.

[11] CICA, "20 Questions About Government Financial Reporting," January 2003, p. 21.

- statement of changes in net debt; and
- statement of cash flows.

Exhibit 11.2 gives a simple illustration of government financial statements for New Province. In these financial statements, *net debt* is an important indicator of the government's finances. Net debt provides an indication of future revenues required to pay for past transactions. In the SFP, net debt is reported as $650, the difference between financial assets of $750 and liabilities of $1,400. Non-financial assets of $450 are then deducted from the $650 of net debt to measure the government's accumulated deficit of $200. The *accumulated deficit* is an indication of the government's ability to provide future services. Notice that, unlike statements for NFPs and businesses, current and noncurrent assets and liabilities are not segregated.

The financial statements also contain a statement of operations that shows an excess of revenues over expenses of $44. These expenses are shown by program or function (e.g., health or education) in the body of the financial statements and by object or type (e.g., wages or supplies) in the notes to the financial statements. To help evaluate how well the government has done, the budget is also included in the statement of operations. We can see that the government's surplus was $34 higher than forecast ($44 versus $10) and that this was entirely due to revenues being higher than forecast ($894 versus $860). This statement is prepared under "full accrual" accounting, including depreciation, not under a simple accrual (without interperiod allocation) or an expenditure basis of accounting.

As we noted earlier in the chapter, unrealized gains and losses from fair value investments and items denominated in a foreign currency are not recognized in the statement of operations. If these investments and foreign currency items are reported at fair value on the SFP, then the associated gains and losses must be reported somewhere. PSAB recommends that these gains and losses be reported on a separate statement, the statement of remeasurement gains and losses (SRGL).

In New Province's 20X5 SRGL, the accumulated unrealized remeasurement loss at the beginning of the year was $46. During the year, investments were sold and the earlier unrealized gains related to those investments ($4) were removed from the SRGL and recognized in the statement of operations as "other revenue." In addition, at year-end, the value of the portfolio investments had appreciated by $10. As a result, the carrying value of the portfolio investments was written up by $10 and the resulting unrealized gain was shown on this statement.

The accumulated deficit of $200 shown on the statement of financial position therefore arises from two sources. First, $160 of the accumulated deficit is the result of items recognized in the statement of operations. The remaining $40 is items whose recognition in the statement of operations had been deferred until the gains or losses are realized. These unrealized gains and losses were recognized in the SRGL.

You may notice from these statements that, despite the surplus of $44, the net debt on the SFP increased $100 from $550 in 20X4 to $650 in 20X5. To understand why, we need to examine the statement of changes in net debt, which reconciles a government's total expenses for the period to its spending on operations (i.e., expenditures) for the period.

The statement reports that capital spending in the period was $220. This expenditure of $220 was only partly financed by operations. Operations provided $114 (surplus of $44 plus non-cash expenses of $70 added back), which would have resulted in an increase in net debt of $106.

**Exhibit 11.2** Sample Government Financial Statements

New Province
Consolidated Statement of Financial Position
As at December 31, 20X5
($ millions)

| | 20X5 | 20X4 |
|---|---|---|
| Financial assets | | |
| Cash | $ 200 | $ 230 |
| Receivables | 150 | 170 |
| Portfolio investments | 400 | 380 |
| | 750 | 780 |
| Liabilities | | |
| Payables | 400 | 380 |
| Unmatured debt | 1000 | 950 |
| | 1400 | 1330 |
| Net debt | (650) | (550) |
| Non-financial assets | | |
| Tangible capital assets | 400 | 250 |
| Prepaids | 50 | 50 |
| | 450 | 300 |
| Accumulated deficit | (200) | (250) |
| Accumulated deficit is composed of: | | |
| Accumulated operating surplus (deficit) | (160) | (204) |
| Accumulated remeasurement gains (losses) | (40) | (46) |
| | $ (200) | $(250) |

New Province
Consolidated Statement of Operations and Accumulated Deficit
for the Fiscal Year Ended December 31, 20X5
($ millions)

| | 20X5 Budget | 20X5 Actual | 20X4 Actual |
|---|---|---|---|
| Revenue | | | |
| Income tax | $540 | $550 | $500 |
| Sales tax | 280 | 300 | 260 |
| Other revenue | 40 | 44 | 35 |
| Total revenue | 860 | 894 | 795 |
| Expenses | | | |
| Health | 355 | 360 | 350 |
| Education | 245 | 240 | 200 |
| Debt service | 50 | 50 | 40 |
| Other | 200 | 200 | 240 |
| Total expenses | 850 | 850 | 830 |
| Surplus (deficit) | 10 | 44 | (35) |
| Accumulated deficit, beginning | (204) | (204) | (169) |
| Accumulated deficit, end | $(194) | $(160) | $(204) |

## New Province
### Consolidated Statement of Remeasurement Gains and Losses
### For the Fiscal Year Ended December 31, 20X5
### ($ millions)

|  | 20X5 Actual | 20X4 Actual |
|---|---|---|
| Accumulated remeasurement gains and losses at beginning of year | $ (46) | $ (51) |
| Unrealized gains attributable to portfolio investments | 10 | 5 |
| Gain on portfolio investments reclassified to statement of operations | (4) | 0 |
| Accumulated remeasurement gains and losses at end of year | $ (40) | $ (46) |

## New Province
### Consolidated Statement of Change in Net Debt
### For the Fiscal Year Ended December 31, 20X5
### ($millions)

|  | 20X5 Budget | 20X5 Actual | 20X4 Actual |
|---|---|---|---|
| Net debt, beginning of year | $(550) | $(550) | $ (570) |
| Surplus | 10 | 44 | (35) |
| Acquisition of tangible capital assets | (200) | (220) | (10) |
| Amortization of tangible capital assets | 70 | 70 | 60 |
|  | (120) | (106) | 15 |
| Net remeasurement gain (loss) | 0 | 6 | 5 |
| (Increase) / decrease in net debt | (120) | (100) | 20 |
| Net debt, end of year | $(670) | $(650) | $(550) |

## New Province
### Consolidated Statement of Cash Flows
### For the Fiscal Year Ended December 31, 20X5
### ($ millions)

|  | 20X5 Actual | 20X4 Actual |
|---|---|---|
| Cash from operations | $150 | $ 35 |
| Cash received from (used for) capital | (220) | (15) |
| Cash received from (used for) investing | (10) | 50 |
| Cash received from (used for) financing | 50 | (50) |
| Increase (decrease) in cash | (30) | 20 |
| Cash, beginning of year | 230 | 210 |
| Cash, end of year | $ 200 | $ 230 |

We must also look to the SRGL to see if there are any other items that may affect the carrying value of financial assets or liabilities. In this example, we should note that to the extent that portfolio investments increase in value, the amount of net debt decreases. The net unrealized gain on portfolio investments of $6 from the statement of remeasurement gains and losses, therefore, is recognized in the statement of changes in net debt. The result is that net debt increased by $100 ($220 − $114 − $6), from $550 to $650.

The budget information is also included. In evaluating the performance of government, we can see that the increase in net debt was less than budgeted. It appears that the larger-than-budgeted surplus allowed the government to spend slightly more on capital assets and still keep the net debt below the budgeted figure.

The final statement is the statement of cash flows. This statement calculates the cash flows from operating activities ($150) using either the direct method or the indirect method. If the indirect method is used, the surplus or deficit for the accounting period will be adjusted to the amount of cash used or available from operations. The details of each section are not provided in this simple example. Note that the cash used to purchase capital assets ($220) is shown under a separate capital transactions section, which reflects the government's view of capital assets as representing future *service potential* and not necessarily future cash flows.

This model of financial reporting applies to all governments. The format of the statement of financial position and the inclusion of a statement of changes in net debt reflect the unique characteristics of government. The inclusion of the budget on the statement of operations and the statement of changes in net debt provides accountability—a measure of the government's achievement of its objectives.

### Concept Check 11-2

1. What five messages about government finances are contained in the government reporting model?
2. How does the SCF for governments differ from the SCF for businesses?
3. Why is the statement of changes in net debt important to users?

Discuss the major reporting and measurement issues

## 11.3 MAJOR REPORTING ISSUES

There are many reporting issues that are either unique to governments or sufficiently different from business accounting issues as to warrant separate discussion. We will discuss only the major issues and will highlight any that are similar to NFPs. The primary issues that we will discuss are:

- defining the reporting entity;
- revenue recognition;
- financial instruments and foreign currency translation;
- tangible capital assets;
- liability measurement;
- accrual accounting; and
- international harmonization.

We will briefly address these issues in the following sections.

## Defining the Reporting Entity

In Chapter 10, we discussed the problem of defining the reporting entity for not-for-profit organizations. This problem actually is much more severe for governmental reporting.

PSAB defines a government organization as "an organization that is controlled by the government" (PS 2500.04(d)). It further defines a governmental unit as any government organization that is *not* a government business enterprise.

Government activities are carried out through a very complex set of ministries, agencies, Crown corporations, quasi-business enterprises, and not-for-profit organizations formed by government for the purpose of carrying out parts of government's policies. When financial statements are prepared for a government, which of the many bodies that are directly or indirectly related to the government are to be included in the statements? PSAB recommends that the **government reporting entity** include all organizations that are *controlled* by government (PS 1300).

Persuasive evidence of **control** may be indicated by the government having:

1. the power to appoint a majority of the members of a governing body;
2. access and control over the assets of the organization;
3. the majority of the voting shares; or
4. unilateral power to dissolve the organization.

These are not the only potential indicators. The *PSA Handbook* identifies seven other possible indicators of control.[12] While these indicators are not as persuasive as the four above, in combination with other indicators they may suggest that control is present.

It also is important to understand when control is *not* present. An organization that is financially dependent on the government is not necessarily controlled by the government. Further, an organization that is regulated by the government is also not considered to be controlled by virtue of the regulation. The regulated organization chooses to participate in the industry and is free to cease those operations or expand its operations in areas beyond the regulated operation. Finally, a government's constitutional responsibility for a sector does not mean that it controls organizations in that sector.[13] While the government may have influence over these organizations, it does not necessarily exercise *control*. These organizations are often instruments of government or are dependent on government, but if they are not directly accountable to government, they are excluded from the reporting entity. The criteria for control must be applied carefully. Decisions should be based on the preponderance of the evidence after considering all relevant factors.

For example, in some provinces, school boards are elected directly by the public. However, this is not sufficient evidence to conclude that they are *not* controlled by the province. The province may have control over revenue and may also be able to restrict expenditure, either by type (e.g., teachers' salaries) or by purpose (e.g., early childhood education). If the school boards were created by provincial legislation, they also can be dissolved the same way.

Another example is an art gallery that has 11 of its 18 board members appointed by the provincial government. The gallery was created by a special act, and although a majority of the board members are appointed by government, the gallery functions completely independently of government. Despite the fact that the directors are *appointed* by the province, they do not *represent* the province and therefore control may not be present.

---

[12] See PS1300.19 for the list of the other possible indicators of control.

[13] PSAB, 20 Questions About the Government Reporting Entity, p. 17.

Finally, consider how universities should be reported. Although they are an instrument of government (to assist in educating the public) and usually are financially dependent on government for the majority of their financing, in most situations they still would not be considered to be *controlled* by the government.

PSAB also addresses the question of how organizations that constitute parts of the reporting entity should be reported in the financial statements. In general, the conclusions of the statement are that:

1. investments in entities that are not controlled by the government[14] (portfolio investments) should be reported on the *cost basis*;

2. investments in GBE (government business enterprises), such as a public utility, should be reported on a *modified equity basis*; and

3. the financial statements of all other organizations or agencies that are part of the reporting entity should be *consolidated* with the government's own financial statements.

Under the *modified equity method*, the net profit or loss of the business enterprise is included in the government's statement of operations (net of dividends or distributions) and is added to the investment account related to that enterprise. It is called a **modified equity method** because the accounting principles for the GBE are not changed to government accounting principles. The GBE's results are reported in the government's financial statements using GAAP for publicly accountable enterprises (i.e., IFRS). Exhibit 11.3 summarizes the reporting requirements for the different parts of the reporting entity.

**Exhibit 11.3** Summary of Accounting for Government Organizations and Investments

| Entity type | Control present | Accounting |
| --- | --- | --- |
| Governmental unit | Yes | Consolidate |
| Government business enterprise | Yes | Modified equity method |
| Portfolio investment | No | Cost method |

# Revenue Recognition

Revenue recognition for governments has been the source of considerable debate. As we noted earlier, revenues for governments are often characterized as non-exchange transactions. Government transfers and taxes are the two largest sources of non-exchange revenue. The accounting for government transfers is found in PS 3410 and the accounting for tax revenue is found in PS 3510.

**Government Transfers**   Section PS 3410 deals with revenue recognition by the recipient government and expense recognition by the transferring government (transferor). We will begin our discussion by first examining the nature of transfers. Then we will examine transfers from the perspective of the transferor and finally from the perspective of the recipient government.

---

[14] It should be noted that the concept of significant influence does not exist for public sector entities. Organizations are either controlled or not controlled.

A **government transfer** is the provision of either monetary or tangible capital assets by a government entity to another entity (i.e., government, organization, or individual). The transferor does not receive any goods or services in return, or expect to be repaid or expect a financial return. The transfer is a non-exchange transaction.

The government transferring the resources can, however, impose **transfer terms**. There are two types of terms that can be imposed: *eligibility criteria* and *stipulations*. If a term of the transfer can be met before the transfer occurs, it is an **eligibility criterion**. Typically an eligibility criterion will specify who can receive the transfer or what must be done to receive the transfer.

If a term of the transfer can only be met after the transfer occurs, it is a **stipulation**. Typically, a stipulation describes how the resources must be used or what must be done to keep the transfer. The distinction between the two is important. Eligibility criteria will affect the timing of the recognition of the transfer (by both parties), while stipulations will affect the timing of the recognition of revenue by a recipient government.

**Transferor Accounting**   The accounting for transfers for the transferor is straight-forward regardless of whether the transfer is of an operating or capital nature. The transferring government (transferor) will recognize an expense when the transfer is fully authorized and the *eligibility criteria* have been met. The transfer is fully authorized when it has been approved by the legislature or council. In rare cases, the transferor may recognize the expense before it is fully authorized if two conditions are met. First, the preponder-ance of the evidence must suggest that the government is committed to the transfer and, second, the transfer must receive approval from the legislature or council in the "stub" period (i.e., the period after the government's year-end but before it issues its financial statements). Finally, if the transferor transfers a tangible capital asset, its recorded expense will equal the net book value of the asset.

**Recipient Accounting**   The accounting for the recipient government is a bit more involved.

The first question that arises is, when should the transfer be recognized? It is recog-nized when the transfer has been fully authorized by the transferor and the *eligibility criteria* have been met.

Often revenue recognition will correspond with the receipt of cash or other asset from the transferor government, but, if both criteria are present, the revenue and a related receivable could be accrued. Revenue is not recognized, however, if *stipulations* attached to the transfer create a liability for the recipient government. In this case, the transfer would be recognized as deferred revenue and then recognized as revenue as the *stipulations* are met. This will allow the recipient government to match its transfer revenue with the related costs to satisfy the stipulations.

The accounting for government transfers for the recipient government is summarized in Exhibit 11.4.

**Exhibit 11.4** Summary of Accounting for Recipient Government Transfers

| Transfer type | Holding account | Revenue recognition |
|---|---|---|
| Operating or capital transfer | None | Immediate |
| Operating or capital transfer with stipulations that create a liability | Deferred revenue | Recognize as stipulations are met |

**Tax Revenues**  Tax revenue is measured using accrual accounting concepts. According to PS 3510, tax revenue and the related asset (cash or receivable) should be recognized in the government statements if three conditions are met:

1. it meets the definition of an asset;
2. the taxes are authorized by the legislature or council; and
3. the taxable event has occurred.

Examples of taxable events would be (1) the earning of income by an individual in regards to personal income taxes or (2) the sale of a taxable good in regards to sales tax. The resulting asset is measured at its net realizable value.

The issue that arises with regards to taxes is, what should or should not be included in tax revenue? The answer is that it depends on the nature of the items being discussed. The two items that have received the most attention are (1) transfers made through the tax system and (2) tax concessions. **Transfers made through the tax system** are amounts paid to entities through a reduction in taxes but which the taxpayer would have been able to receive even if that individual had not paid taxes. For example, some governments give so-called child tax benefits to all individuals who have children of a particular age and who meet the conditions required for the benefit. While it is administered through the tax system, it is available to an individual even if that individual did not pay taxes. PSAB recommends that these transfers should be shown as an expense and not as a reduction in tax revenue.

**Tax concessions** are amounts that affect the amount that an entity currently owes or previously owed. They are provided only to taxpayers and only through the tax system. They reduce the taxes that would otherwise be owed and result in forgone revenue for the government. As an example, a province may provide a property tax credit to resident landowners. The credit is available only to property tax payers and it directly reduces the property tax revenue of the government. As such it would qualify as a tax concession.

PSAB recommends that tax revenue be shown net of tax concessions—that is, tax revenue should not be shown at its gross amount before the tax concessions. In contrast, any costs related to tax collection (administrative costs or commissions) should be shown as expenses and not netted against tax revenues.

**Restricted Revenue**  The reporting of restricted revenues by governments is similar to the reporting of restricted revenues by NFPs. Governments may also have restrictions by external parties that limit the use of revenues. PS 3100 makes similar distinctions to

---

### Reality Check 11–1

## Government Transfers

The accounting for government transfers for the province of Nova Scotia is summarized in the following excerpt:

> Government transfers are recognized as revenue in the period during which the transfer is authorized and any eligibility criteria are met. Transfers are recorded as deferred revenue if they are restricted for a stated purpose, such as a specific program or the purchase of tangible capital assets.

Source: 2011 Nova Scotia Public Accounts, Volume 1, p. 70.

NFPs between external restrictions that are imposed by an external party and internal restrictions or internally restricted entities.

The recommended method for external restrictions is similar to the deferral method of recognizing contributions. PS 3100.11 states that revenue subject to external restrictions should be recognized in the period in which the resources are used for the purpose specified. Internal restrictions are treated differently, since the government can change its mind by changing legislation. To provide information to the users, disclosure is required of all internal restrictions.

## Financial Instruments and Foreign Currency Translation

In 2011, the PSAB introduced new standards in Section PS 3450 for reporting financial instruments. PSAB also made changes in the accounting for foreign currency translations (PS 2601), portfolio investments (PS 3041), and financial statement presentation (PS 1201). The changes in these four sections are mandatory for government organizations for fiscal years beginning on or after April 1, 2012, and for governments for fiscal periods beginning on or after April 1, 2015.

The principles contained in these standards are similar to those contained in the *CICA Handbook,* but there are several significant differences. The PSAB adopted an approach that, in general, attempted to simplify the accounting for financial instruments and foreign currency.

The financial instruments section (PS 3450) identifies two measurement categories: (1) cost or amortized cost and (2) fair value. Cost or amortized cost is the default category for all items covered by Section PS 3450—that is, all items are measured at cost or amortized cost unless they are required or allowed to be measured at fair value. Under Section PS 3450, only two items must be measured at fair value:

- derivatives; and
- portfolio investments (must be equity instruments that are quoted in an active market).

In addition, a government has the option of carrying a third item at fair value, those financial instruments that it manages and evaluates on a fair value basis.

The use of fair value measurements could introduce potentially significant volatility into the statement of operations. Concerns were expressed about how the unrealized gains and losses from remeasuring financial instruments could affect the budget-to-actual comparisons that are made on the statement of operations.

In response to these concerns, the PSAB introduced the statement of remeasurement gains and losses. A government would report any unrealized remeasurement gains and losses in this statement. On derecognition of the financial instrument (e.g., sale of a portfolio investment), the total remeasurement gains and losses related to that instrument are reversed or removed from the accumulated balance of remeasurement gains and losses. The total realized gain or loss, calculated in relation to the financial instrument's cost or amortized cost, is then recognized on the statement of operations.

The standard also contains significant disclosure requirements. The fair values and remeasurement gains and losses associated with each fair value category must be separately disclosed. In addition, the organization should prepare and report qualitative and quantitative disclosures about the nature and extent of the risks to which it is exposed from its financial instruments.

Changes were also made to the standard for foreign currency translations. The new standard (Section PS 2601) is very similar to the CICA *Handbook* section for measuring foreign currency transactions. The major difference between PS 2601 and the CICA *Handbook* is that PS 2601 requires that unrealized foreign exchange gains and losses be reported as remeasurement gains and losses in the SRGL rather than in the statement of operations. They are subsequently transferred to the statement of operations when they are realized.

The PSAB also eliminated the use of hedge accounting because adopting the new statement of remeasurement gains and losses meant that unrealized exchange gains and losses would not affect the statement of operations. In addition, the PSAB noted that the hedge accounting model had been criticized for its arbitrariness and complexity. The PSAB believes that the concept of remeasurement gains and losses is more meaningful and easier to understand for users than concepts such as other comprehensive income (OCI) and hedge accounting.

## Tangible Capital Assets

Historically, Canadian governments almost universally reported tangible capital assets on an expenditure basis, except for enterprise activities that operated on a cost-recovery basis. In general, tangible capital assets were seldom capitalized and were almost never depreciated. This method of accounting created several problems, an important one being that the modified accrual or "expenditure" model created a bias against spending on tangible capital assets. If a government wanted to balance the budget, it would simply defer spending on tangible capital assets. This led to the problem of an "infrastructure deficit" in Canada.[15]

The government reporting model now requires that tangible capital assets be recorded as assets and depreciated (PS 3150). The principles in PS 3150 are very similar to those espoused in the CICA *Handbook*. A major difference is the fact that governments may have significant unrecorded tangible capital assets. Governments often own assets such as Crown land or natural resources that have no purchase cost. Further, they may also own such other assets as art or historical treasures. These assets are not recognized in the financial statements because they have no acquisition cost and are difficult to value. The standard, however, recommends that governments should disclose the *existence* and *nature* of these assets.

Section 3150 also has a slightly different view of tangible capital assets than does the CICA *Handbook*. Given that one of government's objectives is to provide services (rather than to maximize profits), tangible capital assets are seen as representing future service capability and not as representing a source of future cash flows (as in a business). The carrying value of these assets therefore represents the unexpired service potential of the assets. This difference has a direct impact on any impairment testing. Write-downs will be based on the impairment of future service potential and not on the impairment of future cash flows.

---

[15] CICA, 20 Questions About Government Financial Reporting, January 2003, p. 20.

The accounting for tangible capital assets has proven to be a major issue for municipalities in particular. Municipalities provide many services that are capital intensive—water, sewer, public transit, garbage collection, sporting venues, and so forth. Because of the importance of tangible capital assets in service delivery, financial statement users need to have an understanding of the physical condition of these assets. The condition of the assets will have direct implications for the need for or use of future revenues.

The problem is that traditional accounting information does not provide sufficient information to fully assess the government's stewardship of these assets. To assist preparers and users, PSAB has issued a statement of recommended practice (SORP) (SORP 3 – *Assessment of tangible capital assets*) to provide guidance to governments in disclosing the condition of their various categories of assets. It is important to note that the SORP entails voluntary disclosure.

## Liability Measurement

As a result of recent changes, the accounting for liabilities in the *Public Sector Accounting Handbook* is very similar to that in the *CICA Handbook*. Both short- and long-term liabilities should be measured identically under either framework. Disclosure, however, may differ slightly between the two. For example the current portion of long-term debt is not required to be reported separately for public sector entities. Also, the disclosure of the fair value of financial instruments that are carried at cost is not required for public sector entities.

The reporting of government liabilities may be a bigger problem than is apparent on the surface. A major issue is the debate over what constitutes a government liability. PS 3200 suggests that liabilities can arise from a number of different kinds of obligations. In addition to the standard agreements or contracts and liabilities arising from legislation (issued by the reporting government or another level of government), liabilities can also arise from constructive obligations and equitable obligations.

The thorny issue in recognizing a liability is determining whether the government has little or no discretion to avoid the obligation. This issue can be especially difficult for certain constructive and equitable obligations, and the determination will often require estimates based on weak or modest evidence. If it is determined from the preponderance of the evidence that the government has little or no discretion to avoid the obligation, then it is recognized as a liability.

PSAB has also addressed the important issue of contingencies. Contingencies are important because users such as rating agencies tend to add outstanding guarantees to unmatured debt to assess the total debt capacity utilized by an entity. Senior governments often guarantee others' debts to achieve important policy objectives. Examples are legislated programs that offered guarantees for small-business loans or student loans. The accounting for general contingencies is similar to that found in the *CICA Handbook*.

## Accrual Accounting

The cash versus accrual debate in government accounting was similar to that for NFPs. The choice was between cash, modified cash or modified accrual, and full accrual. *Modified accrual* means accrual of assets and liabilities without necessarily allocating the costs on an expense basis (usually called *full accrual*).

In previous years, the vast majority of governments used a modified accrual basis. Gradually, there has been a shift to full accrual. An example was the introduction of PS 3250, in which PSAB recommended pension accounting that was consistent with the recommendations of Section 3461 of the CICA *Handbook*, an expense-basis recommendation.

The present government reporting model uses a full accrual basis. As we have seen, this model analyzes the characteristics of governments and reporting implications, and stresses the importance of identifying the net cost of services, net debt, and capital spending.

## International Harmonization

We will conclude our section on accounting issues by commenting briefly on the international harmonization of public sector accounting standards. Although PSAB has no official policy regarding harmonization or convergence with international standards, the Board notes that international standards have become increasingly important. The PSA Board has stated:

> In the absence of clearly demonstrated unique Canadian public sector circumstances, PSAB will endeavour to adopt a new accounting standard in Canada that reflects that of its international colleagues. Consequently, the activities of international groups such as the International Public Sector Accounting Standards Board (IPSASB) can affect Canadian public sector standard setting.[16]

Clearly, the direction of international standards will be important for those interested in government accounting in Canada.

### Concept Check 11-3

1. What is the modified equity method of accounting?
2. When can a recipient government recognize a transfer?
3. Under what conditions should tax revenue and the related asset be recognized on government financial statements?
4. What measurement categories are available to public sector entities under PS 3450?

## A Final Example

We will end this chapter with an example of a provincial government's financial statements. Exhibit 11.5 shows the consolidated statements for the Province of Nova Scotia. We will briefly highlight several of the items that we have discussed in this chapter.

The first statement is the consolidated statement of financial position. It reveals that the government's net debt decreased from $13.0 billion to $12.8 billion and that the accumulated deficit decreased slightly, from $8.4 billion to $7.9 billion. Note that a line item "Investment in Government Business Enterprises" is presented under financial assets. You should recall that this item is unique in that it is accounted for by using the modified equity method. In addition, note that a line item for deferred revenue is shown under liabilities. The details can be found in Note 4 (not included).

---

[16] PSAB website, http://pre.cica.ca/index.cfm/ci_id/1053/la_id/1.htm, accessed November 1, 2009.

**Exhibit 11.5** Financial Statements of the Province of Nova Scotia

Province of Nova Scotia
Consolidated Statement of Financial Position
As at March 31, 2011
($ thousands)

|  | 2011 | 2010 |
|---|---|---|
|  |  | *(as restated)* |
| **Financial Assets** |  |  |
| Cash and Short-Term Investments (Note 3) | 1,183,863 | 781,554 |
| Accounts Receivable and Advances | 922,518 | 913,988 |
| Inventories for Resale | 8,969 | 3,824 |
| Loans Receivable (Schedule 3) | 1,915,664 | 1,639,249 |
| Investments (Schedule 3) | 86,765 | 63,202 |
| Investment in Government Business Enterprises (Schedule 6) | 62,948 | 52,728 |
|  | 4,180,727 | 3,454,545 |
| **Liabilities** |  |  |
| Bank Advances and Short-Term Borrowings | 536,862 | 442,573 |
| Accounts Payable and Accrued Liabilities | 1,720,751 | 1,603,756 |
| Deferred Revenue (Note 4) | 395,560 | 671,251 |
| Accrued Interest | 208,522 | 198,189 |
| Unmatured Debt of Governmental Units (Schedule 4) | 12,447,250 | 11,372,026 |
| Unamortized Foreign Exchange Translation Gains and Losses, Premiums and Discounts | 150,069 | 172,227 |
| Federal Equalization Repayable Loan (Note 6) | 60,161 | 72,193 |
| Pension, Retirement, and Other Obligations (Note 7) | 1,488,883 | 1,967,476 |
|  | 17,008,058 | 16,499,691 |
| **Net Debt** | (12,827,331) | (13,045,146) |
| **Non-Financial Assets** |  |  |
| Tangible Capital Assets (Schedule 7) | 4,876,924 | 4,522,719 |
| Inventories of Supplies | 56,732 | 62,430 |
| Prepaid Expenses | 33,402 | 30,623 |
|  | 4,967,058 | 4,615,772 |
| **Accumulated Deficits** | (7,860,273) | (8,429,374) |

*Exhibit Continued >*

## Province of Nova Scotia
## Consolidated Statement of Operations and Accumulated Deficits
### For the fiscal year ended March 31, 2011
### ($ thousands)

| | Adjusted Estimate 2011 | Actual 2011 | Actual 2010 |
|---|---|---|---|
| | | | *(as restated)* |
| **Revenue (Schedule I)** | | | |
| Provincial Sources | | | |
| Tax Revenue | 4,239,802 | 4,677,158 | 4,060,509 |
| Other Provincial Revenue | 1,260,387 | 1,471,890 | 1,374,314 |
| Net Income from Government Business Enterprises (Schedule 6) | 348,573 | 357,219 | 358,731 |
| Investment Income | 182,553 | 181,741 | 149,899 |
| | 6,031,315 | 6,688,008 | 5,943,453 |
| Federal Sources | 3,355,820 | 3,208,876 | 3,287,309 |
| Total Revenue | 9,387,135 | 9,896,884 | 9,230,762 |
| **Expenses (Schedule 2)** | | | |
| Agriculture | 62,950 | 65,403 | 71,321 |
| Community Services | 1,046,440 | 923,433 | 941,186 |
| Economic and Rural Development | 130,704 | 120,540 | 128,824 |
| Education | 1,651,442 | 1,682,212 | 1,654,478 |
| Assistance to Universities | 60,643 | 93,545 | 450,359 |
| Energy | 41,063 | 34,828 | 31,282 |
| Environment | 102,080 | 95,662 | 82,588 |
| Finance | 52,959 | 74,048 | 62,943 |
| Fisheries and Aquaculture | 13,231 | 13,087 | 8,930 |
| Health | 3,734,245 | 3,763,124 | 3,560,083 |
| Health Promotion and Protection | 50,311 | 63,396 | 43,695 |
| Justice | 289,420 | 277,587 | 276,187 |
| Labour and Workforce Development | 167,033 | 148,019 | 127,268 |
| Natural Resources | 98,425 | 95,398 | 93,949 |
| Public Service | 194,492 | 161,103 | 173,102 |
| Seniors | 1,902 | 1,734 | 1,903 |
| Service Nova Scotia and Municipal Relations | 313,541 | 292,471 | 278,499 |
| Tourism, Culture, and Heritage | 62,851 | 61,915 | 63,793 |
| Transportation and Infrastructure Renewal | 401,618 | 405,710 | 378,834 |
| Restructuring Costs | 111,423 | 69,391 | 133,967 |
| Pension Valuation Adjustment | 8,448 | (25,696) | 86,410 |
| Tax Credits and Rebates | 54,800 | 48,860 | — |
| Net Loss on Disposal at Crown Assets | — | 609 | — |
| Debt Servicing Costs (Note 10) | 959,197 | 861,404 | 849,675 |
| Total Expenses (Note 9) | 9,609,218 | 9,327,783 | 9,499,276 |
| **Provincial Surplus (Deficit)** | (222,083) | 569,101 | (268,514) |
| **Accumulated Deficits, Beginning of Year** | | | |
| As Previously Reported | | (8,402,784) | (8,160,860) |
| Accounting Changes (Note 2) | | (26,590) | — |
| As Restated | | (8,429,374) | (8,160,860) |
| **Accumulated Deficits End of Year** | | (7,860,273) | (8,429,374) |

## Province of Nova Scotia
## Consolidated Statement of Changes in Net Debt
### For the fiscal year March 31, 2011
### ($ thousands)

| | Adjusted Estimate 2011 | Actual 2011 | Actual 2010 |
|---|---|---|---|
| | | | *(as restated)* |
| **Net Debt, Beginning of Year** | | | |
| As Previously Reported | (13,045,146) | (13,018,556) | (12,318,239) |
| Accounting Changes (Note 2) | — | (26,590) | — |
| As Restated | (13,045,146) | (13,045,146) | (12,318,239) |
| **Changes In the Year \*** | | | |
| Provincial Surplus (Deficit) | (222,083) | 569,101 | (268,514) |
| Acquisition and Transfers of Tangible Capital Assets | (579,894) | (702,639) | (774,988) |
| Amortization of Tangible Capital Assets | 249,871 | 345,291 | 312,578 |
| Disposal of Tangible Capital Assets | — | 3,143 | 10,071 |
| Increase in Inventories of Supplies | — | 5,698 | (5,926) |
| Increase in Prepaid Expenses | — | (2,779) | (128) |
| **Total Changes In the Year** | (552,106) | 217,815 | (726,907) |
| **Net Debt, End of Year** | (13,597,252) | (12,827,331) | (13,045,146) |

*Exhibit Continued >*

**Province of Nova Scotia**
**Consolidated Statement of Cash Flow**
**For the fiscal year March 31, 2011**
**($ thousands)**

|  | 2011 | 2010 |
|---|---|---|
|  |  | *(as restated)* |
| **Cash Inflow (Outflow) from the following activities:** |  |  |
| **Operating** |  |  |
| Provincial Surplus (Deficit) | 569,101 | (268,514) |
| Sinking Fund and Public Debt Retirement Fund Earnings | (102,234) | (92,188) |
| Amortization of Premiums and Discounts on Unmatured Debt | (6,245) | (4,685) |
| Amortization of Tangible Capital Assets | 345,291 | 312,578 |
| Net Income from Government Business Enterprises | (357,219) | (358,731) |
| Profit Distributions from Government Business Enterprises | 346,999 | 346,523 |
| Loss on Disposal of Tangible Capital Assets | 1,116 | (13,137) |
| Net Change in Other Items (Note 11) | (543,423) | (193,808) |
|  | 253,386 | (271,962) |
| **Investing** |  |  |
| Repayment of Loans | 200,201 | 185,663 |
| Advances and Investing | (521,782) | (582,681) |
| Write-offs | 21,603 | 50,162 |
|  | (299,978) | (346,856) |
| **Capital:** |  |  |
| Acquisition of Tangible Capital Assets | (702,639) | (774,988) |
| Proceeds from Disposal of Tangible Capital Assets | 2,027 | 23,208 |
|  | (700,612) | (751,780) |
| **Financing:** |  |  |
| Debentures Issued | 2,265,042 | 1,881,165 |
| Repayment of Federal Equalization Repayable Loan | (12,032) | (12,032) |
| Foreign Currency Swaps and Adjustments | (28,082) | (32,855) |
| Sinking Fund (Installments) Withdrawals | (88,128) | (99,681) |
| Repayment of Debentures and Other Long-term Obligations | (987,287) | (752,725) |
|  | 1,149,513 | 1,183,234 |
| **Cash (Outflows) Inflows** | 402,309 | (187,364) |
| Cash Position, Beginning of Year | 781,554 | 968,918 |
| **Cash Position, End of Year** | 1,183,863 | 781,554 |
| Cash Position Represented by: |  |  |
| Cash and Short-Term Investments | 1,183,863 | 781,554 |

The second statement is the consolidated statement of operations and accumulated deficits. It contains three columns: two columns present the actual results for 2010 and 2011, while the third column presents the budgeted numbers (called "Estimate") for 2011. The income from GBEs is included in the provincial sources of revenues. Recall that this income would have been calculated using the modified equity method.

The third statement is the consolidated statement of changes in net debt. The surplus was higher than budgeted and the net debt was lower than budgeted. Despite the surplus of $569 million, the government's debt decreased only $217 million for 2011. The main reason is apparent when we examine this statement. The acquisition of tangible capital assets was considerably higher than the amortization of tangible capital assets.

The final statement is the consolidated statement of cash flows. The item of interest is the section on capital transactions. The same $703 million that was present in the statement of change in net debt is also present under the section on cash flows used for capital transactions. It should be noted that the statement of remeasurement gains and losses is not included in this example. This statement is not required for governments until the 2015–16 fiscal year.

## Relevant Standards

### Public Sector Accounting Handbook

**PS 1000**   Financial Statement Concepts
**PS 1100**   Financial Statement Objectives
**PS 1201**   Financial Statement Presentation
**PS 1300**   Government Reporting Entity
**PS 2500**   Basic Principles of Consolidation
**PS 2601**   Foreign Currency Translation
**PS 3041**   Portfolio Investments
**PS 3100**   Restricted Assets and Revenues
**PS 3150**   Tangible Capital Assets
**PS 3200**   Liabilities
**PS 3410**   Government Transfers
**PS 3450**   Financial Instruments
**PS 3510**   Tax Revenue

## 11.4 SUMMARY OF KEY POINTS

1. Public sector reporting differs from private sector reporting in nine unique characteristics. The most important are: the objective of government, which is to provide a service rather than make a profit; the higher standard of accountability to a larger potential user group; and the ability to raise large amounts of money through taxes. These characteristics play an important role in shaping the public sector reporting model. **LO 1**

2. The public sector consists of the federal, provincial, territorial, and local governments and government organizations. There are three types of government organizations: government business enterprises (GBEs); government not-for-profit organizations

(GNFPOs); and other government organizations (OGOs). This chapter focused on the financial reporting for governments and other government organizations. **LO 1**

3. The Public Sector Accounting Board (PSAB) sets the standards for accounting in the public sector. The *PSA Handbook* (PS 1100) identifies the objectives of financial statements for governments. These objectives are the need to define (1) the entity—that is, what is under government's control; (2) the types of financial information needed by users—that is, the financial statements that will be required; and (3) if the results are in accordance with what was authorized by the legislature or council. Four qualitative characteristics of good financial reports for governments are also identified: comparability among governments; consistency between years; completeness; and timeliness. **LO 2**

4. PSAB recommendations require five financial statements: statement of financial position; statement of operations; statement of remeasurement gains and losses; statement of changes in net debt; and statement of cash flows. These statements will communicate five key messages: accumulated surplus or deficit; annual surplus or deficit; net debt or net financial assets; change in net debt; and change in cash and cash flows that contributed to the change. **LO 2**

5. Public sector entities have a number of reporting issues, some of which are unique to governments. The major reporting issues are defining the reporting entity, revenue recognition, financial instruments, tangible capital assets, and liability measurement. The major issue in defining the reporting entity is determining whether the government controls an organization. Revenue recognition is concerned with two sources of revenue that are unique to governments: transfers and taxes. For financial instruments, the major issue is how to recognize unrealized gains and losses on derivatives, portfolio investments, and fair value investments. The issues for tangible capital assets and liabilities are similar to those for for-profit organizations, although there are several subtle differences. Finally, the position of such international bodies as the International Public Sector Accounting Standards Board (IPSASB) will likely influence PSAB's position on government accounting issues in Canada. **LO 3**

**Visit the text's website at** www.pearsoned.ca/beechy **for practice quizzes, additional problems, Excel® templates, answers to Concept Check questions, and important IFRS updates.**

## Review Questions

1. Why is the budget important in public sector reporting?
2. How does the primary user group for government financial statements differ from that for NFP financial statements?
3. Why is the focus on debt important for government accounting?
4. What are the nine unique characteristics of government that influence the government reporting model?
5. How is the public sector defined by PSAB?
6. What are the three types of government organizations and where should each look for guidance in accounting?
7. What is the Public Sector Accounting Board? What is its role?
8. Are government auditors required to report in accordance with the PSAB's recommendations?
9. Are municipalities required to report in compliance with PSAB recommendations?
10. What are the objectives of governmental reporting?
11. Briefly explain the two key messages on a government's statement of financial position.
12. What additional element is included in the qualitative characteristics by PSAB? Why was it included?
13. What types of financial statements does the government reporting model recommend for governments?
14. What indicators provide persuasive evidence of control by governments?
15. How should a government business enterprise be reported?
16. What is a government transfer? Describe the two kinds of transfer terms a government may impose.
17. When can the transferring government (transferor) recognize a transfer as an expense?
18. How should the recipient government account for the transfer of a tangible capital asset?
19. What is a tax concession, and how does it differ from a transfer made through the tax system?
20. Why did PSAB introduce the statement of remeasurement gains and losses?

# 11.5 CASES

## CASE 11-1 PROVINCE OF MAJESTIC LAKES

You are a staff member in the finance department for the Province of Majestic Lakes. You have just completed a meeting with a new member of the provincial legislature. As part of the background material in preparing for this position, the member had been provided with a detailed reading on the "Government Reporting Model." At your meeting, the member asked for a quick written briefing on the following questions:

- What characteristics are unique for governments, and what are the reporting implications?
- What are the five key messages in the model?
- What are the required financial statements, and what are they like?
- What key information should I look for in each of the statements?
- What is the key impact of the change to "accrual" accounting?
- Why is it important to have a comparison with budgeted numbers?
- Why is it important to account for capital assets?

### Required

Provide the requested briefing for the member.

## CASE 11-2 COMPARISON OF OBJECTIVES

William Witherspoon III is executive vice-president of Marble Industries Ltd., a publicly held industrial company. Mr. Witherspoon has just been elected to the city council of Turnwater, a major industrial city. Prior to assuming office as a city councillor, he asks you, as his accountant, to explain the major differences that exist in accounting and financial reporting for a large city when compared with a large industrial corporation.

### Required

Describe the major differences that exist in the purpose of accounting and financial reporting and in the types of reports of a large city when compared with a large industrial corporation.

[CGA-Canada, adapted]

# CASE 11-3 TOWN OF EVERGREEN

Ms. Hannah Morse is a councillor for the growing town of Evergreen. She has approached you, as a friend and a public accountant, with her concerns over the draft financial statements of Evergreen for its most recent year-end, March 31, 20X2. She is concerned by the dramatic increase in revenue shown in the financial statements for the town.

Her suspicions are based on her work on the town compensation committee over the past year. She informs you that the town controller had requested a raise, which had yielded a lot of discussion at the committee. He had indicated that his compensation had not kept up with his increased workload that had resulted from the growth that the town was experiencing. After considerable discussion, the compensation committee agreed to a modest raise to the base salary. In addition, to avoid falling behind again, it agreed to the controller's request to pay a bonus based on town revenues. The bonus would be based on the town's consolidated revenue, as it was the best figure to use to track the town's growth. Each year the bonus would be paid on revenues in excess of 20X1's level of revenue.

Ms. Morse believes that the apparent increase in revenue may not be legitimate but is not sure where to look to determine what has occurred. To assist you, she provides you with a copy of the draft annual report for the town. She also informs you that last year the town's auditor had informed the audit committee that Evergreen's statements were conservative, high-quality financial statements.

Your review of the financial statements finds a substantial increase in property tax revenues and transfers from the provincial government. You find the following in the notes:

- Property taxes are recorded at their gross amount when the taxable event has occurred. Costs related to tax collection are recorded as expenses and not as a reduction in tax revenue.

- Government transfers from the province are recognized in Evergreen's financial statements only when the province has also recognized the transfer.

   Further, in the discussion accompanying the statements you also note the following:

- Town revenues: The major sources of revenue for the town are property taxes and government transfers from the province. Transfers from the province are received to help subsidize the town's recreational programs and to assist in the capital costs of constructing new streets. Substantial funds are received in advance of construction projects.

- Town expenses: The town incurred a number of expenses in the operation of the town. Several of these expenses were to encourage business to set up and stay in the town. The major components of this program were an advertising campaign and a rebate on property taxes.

## Required

Prepare your notes for your discussion with Ms. Morse on what you think may have happened. Also include any recommendations that you deem appropriate based on your preliminary review.

# CASE 11-4 HARVEST PROVINCE

The following is the trial balance for Harvest Province for the current year:

| Harvest Province Trial Balance | | |
|---|---|---|
| Account | Dr. | Cr. |
| Accumulated deficit | $ 1,250 | |
| Cash | 1,000 | |
| Education expense | 1,200 | |
| GBE income | 50 | |
| Health expense | 1,800 | |
| Income tax | | $2,750 |
| Investment in GBEs | 500 | |
| Investments | 1,500 | |
| Unmatured debt | | 5,000 |
| Other expenses | 1,200 | |
| Payables | | 2,000 |
| Prepaids | 250 | |
| Receivables | 750 | |
| Sales tax | | 1,750 |
| Tangible capital assets | 2,000 | — |
| | $11,500 | $11,500 |

Required

Prepare the consolidated statement of financial position and consolidated statement of operations and accumulated deficit for Harvest Province assuming that it has not adopted the recommendations of PS 3450 and related sections.

# CASE 11-5 GREEN PROVINCE

The following is the trial balance for Green Province for the current year:

| Green Province Trial Balance | | |
|---|---|---|
| Account | Dr. | Cr. |
| Accumulated operating deficit | $ 306 | |
| Accumulated remeasurement losses | 69 | |
| Cash | 300 | |
| Debt service | 75 | |
| Education expense | 360 | |
| Health expense | 540 | |
| Income tax | | $ 825 |
| Investments | 600 | |
| Investment gains reclassified | 6 | |
| Other expenses | 300 | |
| Other revenue | | 66 |
| Payables | | 600 |
| Prepaids | 75 | |
| Receivables | 225 | |
| Sales tax | | 450 |
| Tangible capital assets | 600 | |
| Unmatured debt | | 1,500 |
| Unrealized gains on investments | — | 15 |
| | $3,456 | $3,456 |

## Required

Prepare the consolidated statement of financial position, the consolidated statement of operations and accumulated deficit, and the statement of remeasurement gains and losses for Green Province assuming that it has adopted the recommendations of PS 3450 and related sections.

# CASE 11-6 DISTRICT OF MAPLE RIDGE

The District of Maple Ridge is well known in Canada for its high-quality financial reporting, which has won many awards over the years. Maple Ridge prepares two reports every year: an annual report and a citizen's report. The following excerpts referencing these reports are taken from its website:

## Annual Report

In accordance with the Community Charter, an Annual Report must be prepared and made available to the public before June 30 each year.

The report provides information on the District's financial position and results of operations, and must include the following information:

- the municipality's audited annual financial statements for the previous year;
- a list of the permissive tax exemptions provided by council, and for each exemption, the amount of property tax that would have been imposed during the previous year if the exemption had not been granted;
- a report on the municipality's services and operations for the previous year;
- a progress report on the performance of the municipality with respect to established objectives and measures;
- a statement of objectives and measures that will be used as the basis for determining the municipality's performance during the current year and following year;
- the details of any declarations of disqualification made against individual council members during the previous year; and
- any other information Council considers advisable.

Once completed, the annual report must be made available for public inspection. After making the report public, Council must wait a minimum of two weeks before holding an annual meeting on the report. This provides citizens with time to review the report, ask questions, and prepare submissions. Council must give notice of the date, time, and place of the annual meeting in accordance with the Community Charter's requirements for public notice.

**Note:** The District's annual reports for the years 1991 through 2010 received the Canadian Award for Financial Reporting from the Government Finance Officers Association. The award recognizes excellence in governmental accounting and financial reporting, and represents a significant accomplishment by the District of Maple Ridge and its staff.

## Citizen's Report

This award-winning report is the "Reader's Digest" version of our Comprehensive Annual Financial Report, summarized for readability and perspective. It presents the District's financial situation in the context of the larger economic picture and highlights many of the district's accomplishments.

**Note:** The District's Citizens Reports for the years 1996 through 2010 received the Award for Outstanding Achievement in Popular Annual Financial Reporting from the Government Finance Officers Association. The award recognizes conformation to program standards in the areas of creativity, presentation, understandability, and reader appeal, and represents a significant accomplishment by the District of Maple Ridge and its staff.

Source: http://www.mapleridge.ca/EN/main/municipal/2300/reports.html, accessed April 30, 2012.

Required

Visit the website for the District of Maple Ridge at http://www.mapleridge.ca/EN/main/municipal/2300/reports.html. Examine the financial statements and notes for the most recent annual report and citizen's report. Identify five strengths of Maple Ridge's reporting.

# Solutions to Self-Study Problems

## SSP 2-1

### Direct Method
Archie Corp. Consolidated Financial Statements

| Statement of Financial Position<br>December 31, 20X6 | |
|---|---:|
| **ASSETS** | |
| **Current assets** | |
| Cash and current receivables [200,000 + 400,000 – **80,000** – **200,000**] | $   320,000 |
| Inventories [900,000 + 500,000] | 1,400,000 |
| | 1,720,000 |
| | |
| **Property, plant, and equipment** | |
| Furniture, fixtures, and equipment, net of accumulated depreciation [2,000,000 + 1,700,000] | 3,700,000 |
| Buildings under capital leases, net of related amortization [6,000,000 + 3,000,000] | 9,000,000 |
| | 12,700,000 |
| | |
| **Other assets** | |
| Investment in Bunker Ltd. [1,000,000 – 1,000,000] | — |
| **TOTAL ASSETS** | **$14,420,000** |
| **LIABILITIES AND SHAREHOLDERS' EQUITY** | |
| **Liabilities** | |
| Current liabilities [1,500,000 + 400,000 – **80,000** – **200,000**] | $ 1,620,000 |
| Long-term liabilities [4,000,000 + 2,000,000] | 6,000,000 |
| | 7,620,000 |
| | |
| **Shareholders' equity** | |
| Common shares [1,500,000 + 1,000,000 – 1,000,000] | 1,500,000 |
| Retained earnings [3,100,000 + 2,200,000] | 5,300,000 |
| | 6,800,000 |
| | |
| **TOTAL LIABILITIES AND SHAREHOLDERS' EQUITY** | **$14,420,000** |
| Statement of Comprehensive Income<br>Year Ended December 31, 20X6 | |
| Sales revenue [13,000,000 + 5,000,000 – **4,000,000**] | $14,000,000 |
| Dividend income [500,000 – **500,000**] | — |
| | 14,000,000 |
| | |
| **Operating expenses** | |
| Cost of sales [7,000,000 + 3,200,000 – **4,000,000**] | 6,200,000 |
| Other operating expenses [3,500,000 + 700,000] | 4,200,000 |
| | 10,400,000 |
| | |
| **NET INCOME** | **$ 3,600,000** |

| | | | Statement of Changes in Equity—Retained Earnings Section | | | |
|---|---|---|---|---|---|---|

### Statement of Changes in Equity—Retained Earnings Section
### Year Ended December 31, 20X6

| | |
|---|---:|
| Retained earnings, December 31, 20X5 [2,100,000 + 1,600,000] | $ 3,700,000 |
| Net income | $ 3,600,000 |
| Dividends declared [2,000,000 + 500,000 − **500,000**] | (2,000,000) |
| Retained earnings, December 31, 20X6 | $ 5,300,000 |

## Worksheet Method
### Archie Corp. Consolidation Worksheet

| | Trial balances | | | | Archie Corp. |
|---|---|---|---|---|---|
| | Archie Corp. Dr/(Cr) | Bunker Ltd. Dr/(Cr) | Adjustments Dr/(Cr) | Notes | consolidated trial balance* |
| Cash and current receivables | $ 200,000 | $ 400,000 | $ (80,000) | b | |
| | | | (200,000) | c | $ 320,000 |
| Inventories | 900,000 | 500,000 | | | 1,400,000 |
| Furniture, fixtures, and equipment (net) | 2,000,000 | 1,700,000 | | | 3,700,000 |
| Buildings under capital leases (net) | 6,000,000 | 3,000,000 | | | 9,000,000 |
| Investment in Bunker Ltd. (at cost) | 1,000,000 | — | (1,000,000) | a | — |
| Current liabilities | (1,500,000) | (400,000) | 80,000 | b | (1,620,000) |
| | | | 200,000 | c | |
| Long-term liabilities | (4,000,000) | (2,000,000) | | | (6,000,000) |
| Common shares | (1,500,000) | (1,000,000) | 1,000,000 | a | (1,500,000) |
| Retained earnings, December 31, 20X5 | (2,100,000) | (1,600,000) | | | (3,700,000) |
| Dividends declared | 2,000,000 | 500,000 | (500,000) | d | 2,000,000 |
| Sales revenue | (13,000,000) | (5,000,000) | 4,000,000 | e | (14,000,000) |
| Dividend income | (500,000) | — | 500,000 | d | — |
| Cost of sales | 7,000,000 | 3,200,000 | (4,000,000) | e | 6,200,000 |
| Other expenses | 3,500,000 | 700,000 | | | 4,200,000 |
| | $ — | $ — | $ — | | $ — |

*The SFP and SCI must be prepared from the amounts in this column.

This worksheet does **not** constitute a set of financial statements!

# SSP 2-2

## Direct method (000 omitted)

Brad Corp. Consolidated Financial Statements

| Statement of Financial Position<br>December 31, 20X7 | | |
|---|---:|---:|
| **ASSETS** | | |
| Cash and investments (1,500 + 450) | $ 1,950 | |
| Current rec. and accruals (3,400 + 1,890 – 200 – 100 – 30) | 4,960 | |
| Inventories (10,640 + 5,210) | 15,850 | $ 22,760 |
| Loan receivable (1,000 + 0 – 1,000) | 0 | |
| Land (18,000 + 0) | 18,000 | |
| Buildings and equipment (net) (37,700 + 22,450) | 60,150 | |
| Investment in Pitt (20,000 + 0 – 20,000) | 0 | 78,150 |
| **TOTAL ASSETS** | | **$100,910** |
| **LIABILITIES AND SHAREHOLDERS' EQUITY** | | |
| Current payables and accruals (2,820 + 1,540 – 200 – 100 – 30) | $ 4,030 | |
| Income tax payable (180 + 85) | 265 | $ 4,295 |
| Long-term debt payable (33,750 + 1,000 – 1,000) | 33,750 | |
| Deferred tax liability (2,650 + 375) | 3,025 | 36,775 |
| Total liabilities | 41,070 | |
| Common shares (13,000 + 20,000 – 20,000) | 13,000 | |
| Retained earnings (39,840 + 7,000) | 46,840 | 59,840 |
| **TOTAL LIABILITIES AND SHAREHOLDERS' EQUITY** | | **$100,910** |

| Consolidated Statement of Comprehensive Income<br>Year Ended December 31, 20X7 | |
|---|---:|
| Sales revenue (7,100 + 3,400 – 1,400) | $ 9,100 |
| Other income (235 + 840 – 100 – 30) | 945 |
| Total revenue | 10,045 |
| Operating expenses | |
| Cost of goods sold (4,175 + 1,900 – 1,400) | 4,675 |
| Selling expenses (435 + 560) | 995 |
| General and administrative expenses (995 + 770) | 1,765 |
| Interest and other expenses (1,015 + 30 – 30) | 1,015 |
| Total operating expenses | 8,450 |
| Earnings before income taxes | 1,595 |
| Income tax expense (215 + 290) | 505 |
| Net earnings | $ 1,090 |

| Statement of Changes in Equity—Retained Earnings Section |  |
|---|---|
| Year Ended December 31, 20X7 | |
| Retained earnings, December 31, 20X6 (39,500 + 6,410) | $45,910 |
| Net earnings | $ 1,090 |
| Dividends declared (160 + 100 − 100) | (160) |
| Retained earnings, December 31, 20X7 | $46,840 |

### Worksheet method (000 omitted)

| | Trial balances Dr/(Cr) | | Adjustments Dr/(Cr) | Notes | Consolidated trial balance |
|---|---|---|---|---|---|
| | Brad | Pitt | | | |
| Cash and temp. investment | 1,500 | 450 | | | 1,950 |
| Receivables & accruals | 3,400 | 1,890 | (200) | c | |
| | | | (100) | d | |
| | | | (30) | f | 4,960 |
| Inventories | 10,640 | 5,210 | | | 15,850 |
| Loan receivable | 1,000 | — | (1,000) | e | — |
| Land | 18,000 | — | | | 18,000 |
| Buildings and equipment | 37,700 | 22,450 | | | 60,150 |
| Investment in Pitt | 20,000 | — | (20,000) | a | — |
| Current payables and accruals | (2,820) | (1,540) | 200 | c | |
| | | | 100 | d | |
| | | | 30 | f | (4,030) |
| Income tax payable | (180) | (85) | | | (265) |
| Long-term debt payable | (33,750) | (1,000) | 1,000 | e | (33,750) |
| Deferred tax liability | (2,650) | (375) | | | (3,025) |
| Common shares | (13,000) | (20,000) | 20,000 | a | (13,000) |
| Ret. earn., December 31, 20X6 | (39,500) | (6,410) | | | (45,910) |
| Sales revenue | (7,100) | (3,400) | 1,400 | b | (9,100) |
| Other income | (235) | (840) | 100 | d | |
| | | | 30 | f | (945) |
| Cost of goods sold | 4,175 | 1,900 | (1,400) | b | 4,675 |
| Selling expenses | 435 | 560 | | | 995 |
| G&A expenses | 995 | 770 | | | 1,765 |
| Interest and other exp. | 1,015 | 30 | (30) | f | 1,015 |
| Income tax expense | 215 | 290 | | | 505 |
| Dividends | 160 | 100 | (100) | d | 160 |
| Totals | $ — | $ — | $ — | | $ — |

Notes:

a. Acquisition adjustment
b. Eliminate intercompany sales
c. Eliminate intercompany receivable and payable
d. Eliminate intercompany dividends, including intercompany dividend payable/receivable
e. Eliminate intercompany loan
f. Eliminate intercompany interest accrual: $1,000,000 × 6% × 1/2 year = $30,000

# SSP 3-1

## Analysis of Fair Value of Net Assets Acquired

| | Carrying value | Fair value | Fair value adjustment | FVA allocated |
|---|---|---|---|---|
| Cash and cash equivalents | $ 1,200,000 | $ 1,200,000 | $      — | $      — |
| Accounts receivable | 1,800,000 | 1,800,000 | — | — |
| Machinery and equipment, net | 8,400,000 | 11,000,000 | 2,600,000 | 2,600,000 |
| Deferred development costs | 3,100,000 | 4,000,000 | 900,000 | 900,000 |
| Accounts payable | (1,100,000) | (1,100,000) | — | — |
| Notes payable, long-term | (1,000,000) | (900,000) | 100,000 | 100,000 |
| | $12,400,000 | $16,000,000 | $3,600,000 | $3,600,000 |

## 1. Direct purchase of Blue's net assets for $20,000,000:

| | Ace's carrying value | + FV of Blue assets acq'd | + Cost of purchase = | Ace SFP after purchase |
|---|---|---|---|---|
| Cash and cash equivalents | $ 2,350,000 | $ 1,200,000 | $ (2,000,000) | $ 1,550,000 |
| Accounts receivable | 2,000,000 | 1,800,000 | | 3,800,000 |
| Land | 5,000,000 | — | | 5,000,000 |
| Machinery and equipment (net) | 13,500,000 | 11,000,000 | | 24,500,000 |
| Deferred development costs | 600,000 | 4,000,000 | | 4,600,000 |
| Goodwill* | | 4,000,000 | | 4,000,000 |
| | | | | $43,450,000 |
| Accounts payable | (650,000) | (1,100,000) | | $ 1,750,000 |
| Notes payable, long-term | (2,000,000) | (900,000) | (18,000,000) | 20,900,000 |
| Common shares | (15,000,000) | | | 15,000,000 |
| Retained earnings | (5,800,000) | | | 5,800,000 |
| | $      — | $20,000,000 | $(20,000,000) | $43,450,000 |

*$20,000,000 purchase price $16,000,000 fair value of net assets = $4,000,000 goodwill.

## 2. Purchase of 100% of Blue's shares by issuance of Ace shares worth $20,000,000:

| | Ace's carrying value | Blue's carrying value | Adjustments | Ace consolidated SFP |
|---|---|---|---|---|
| Cash and cash equivalents | $ 2,350,000 | $1,200,000 | | $ 3,550,000 |
| Accounts receivable | 2,000,000 | 1,800,000 | | 3,800,000 |
| Land | 5,000,000 | — | | 5,000,000 |
| Machinery and equipment, net | 13,500,000 | 8,400,000 | $ 2,600,000 | 24,500,000 |
| Investment in Blue* | 20,000,000 | | (20,000,000) | — |
| Deferred development costs | 600,000 | 3,100,000 | 900,000 | 4,600,000 |
| Goodwill | | | 4,000,000 | 4,000,000 |
| | | | | $45,450,000 |
| Accounts payable | (650,000) | (1,100,000) | | $ 1,750,000 |
| Notes payable, long-term | (2,000,000) | (1,000,000) | 100,000 | 2,900,000 |
| Common shares* | (35,000,000) | (6,950,000) | 6,950,000 | 35,000,000 |
| Retained earnings | (5,800,000) | (5,450,000) | 5,450,000 | 5,800,000 |
| | $      — | $      — | $      — | $45,450,000 |

*These accounts are after recording the purchase of Blue's shares. The common shares account is increased by $400,000 × $50 = $20,000,000.

**3. Purchase of 100% of Blue's shares by shares and cash worth $14,500,000:**

**Note:** In this scenario, the purchase price is less than the fair value of Blue's net assets. Therefore, negative goodwill is $1,500,000. Negative goodwill is recognized as a gain on a bargain purchase in the consolidated financial statements issued by Ace.

| | Ace's carrying value* | Blue's carrying value | Adjustments | Ace consolidated SFP |
|---|---|---|---|---|
| Cash and cash equivalents* | $ 1,350,000 | $ 1,200,000 | | $ 2,550,000 |
| Accounts receivable | 2,000,000 | 1,800,000 | | 3,800,000 |
| Land | 5,000,000 | — | | 5,000,000 |
| Machinery and equipment, net | 13,500,000 | 8,400,000 | $ 2,600,000 | 24,500,000 |
| Investment in Blue* | 14,500,000 | | (14,500,000) | 0 |
| Deferred development costs | 600,000 | 3,100,000 | 900,000 | 4,600,000 |
| | | | | $40,450,000 |
| Accounts payable | (650,000) | (1,100,000) | | $ 1,750,000 |
| Notes payable, long-term | (2,000,000) | (1,000,000) | 100,000 | 2,900,000 |
| Common shares* | (28,500,000) | (6,950,000) | 6,950,000 | 28,500,000 |
| Retained earnings | (5,800,000) | (5,450,000) | $\left\{\begin{array}{c}5,450,000\\(1,500,000)\end{array}\right\}$ | 7,300,000 |
| | $ — | $ — | $ — | $40,450,000 |

*These accounts are after recording the purchase of Blue's shares. Cash is reduced by $1,000,000.

Common shares is increased by $270,000 × $50 = $13,500,000; investment in Blue is increased by $14,500,000.

# SSP 3-2

| 100% Purchase of Shelley Inc., January 1, 20X6 | | | | | |
|---|---|---|---|---|---|
| Purchase price | | | | | $ 850,000 |
| Less carrying value of Target's net identifiable assets (100%) | | | | | (450,000) |
| = Fair value adjustment, allocated below | | | | | 400,000 |

| | Carrying value (a) | Fair value (b) | Fair value adjustment (c) = (b) – (a) | FVA allocated | |
|---|---|---|---|---|---|
| Cash | $ 55,000 | $ 55,000 | — | | |
| Accounts receivable | 135,000 | 135,000 | — | | |
| Inventories | 90,000 | 90,000 | — | | |
| Land | 180,000 | 300,000 | $ 120,000 | $120,000 | |
| Buildings (net) | 430,000 | 450,000 | 20,000 | 20,000 | |
| Equipment | 120,000 | 180,000 | 60,000 | 60,000 | |
| Accounts payable | (140,000) | (140,000) | — | | |
| Long-term debt payable | (420,000) | (420,000) | — | | |
| Total fair value increment | | | | | $ (200,000) |
| Net asset carrying value | $450,000 | | | | |
| Fair value of assets acquired | | $650,000 | | | |
| Balance of FVI allocated to goodwill | | | | | $ 200,000 |

## Patricia Ltd.
## Consolidated SFP
## January 1, 20X6

### ASSETS

| | |
|---|---|
| Cash (80,000 + 55,000) | $ 135,000 |
| Accounts receivable (220,000 + 135,000) | 355,000 |
| Inventories (100,000 + 90,000) | 190,000 |
|   Total current assets | 680,000 |
| Land (800,000 + 180,000 + **120,000**) | 1,100,000 |
| Buildings (net) (1,100,000 + 430,000 + **20,000**) | 1,550,000 |
| Equipment (net) (720,000 + 120,000 + **60,000**) | 900,000 |
| Investment in Shelley Inc. (850,000 + 0 − **850,000**) | — |
| Goodwill (+**200,000**) | 200,000 |
| **TOTAL ASSETS** | **$4,430,000** |

### LIABILITIES AND SHAREHOLDERS' EQUITY

| | |
|---|---|
| Accounts payable (120,000 + 140,000) | $260,000 |
| Long-term debt payable (400,000 + 420,000) | 820,000 |
|   Total liabilities | 1,080,000 |
| Common shares (1,000,000 + 850,000 + 200,000 − **200,000**) | 1,850,000 |
| Retained earnings (1,500,000 + 250,000 − **250,000**) | 1,500,000 |
|   Total shareholders' equity | 3,350,000 |
| **TOTAL LIABILITIES AND SHAREHOLDERS' EQUITY** | **$4,430,000** |

**Note:** The bolded amounts are adjustments that must be made to:
- recognize fair value increments;
- recognize goodwill;
- eliminate Patricia's investment account; and
- eliminate Shelley's date-of-acquisition shareholders' equity.

# SSP 4-1

## Situation A:

Journal entries required:

| Books of Primary | | |
|---|---|---|
| Cash | 200,000 | |
| Sales | | 200,000 |
| | | |
| Cost of goods sold | 100,000 | |
| Inventory | | 100,000 |

## Sales, cost of goods sold, and gross profit amounts:

| | |
|---|---|
| Sales | 200,000 |
| Cost of goods sold | 100,000 |
| Gross profit | 100,000 |

## Situation B:

Journal entries required:

| Books of Primary | | |
|---|---|---|
| Cash | 150,000 | |
| Sales | | 150,000 |
| | | |
| Cost of goods sold | 100,000 | |
| Inventory | | 100,000 |
| | | |
| Books of Secondary | | |
| Cash | 200,000 | |
| Sales | | 200,000 |
| | | |
| Cost of goods sold | 150,000 | |
| Inventory | | 150,000 |
| | | |
| Consolidation-related entries | | |
| Sales | 150,000 | |
| Cost of goods sold | | 150,000 |

**Sales, cost of goods sold, and gross profit amounts:**

|  | Primary | Secondary | Con. adj. | Con. amounts |
|---|---|---|---|---|
| Sales | $150,000 | $200,000 | ($150,000) | $200,000 |
| Cost of goods sold | 100,000 | 150,000 | (150,000) | 100,000 |
| Gross profit | 50,000 | 50,000 |  | 100,000 |

The consolidated sales, cost of goods sold, and gross profit amounts in situation B are identical to their corresponding amounts in situation A. The consolidation adjustments made in situation B eliminate all intercompany transactions; therefore, after these adjustments are made, only those accounting entries that reflect transactions between the consolidated entity and outside parties remain to be reported on the consolidated financial statements. These remaining entries are identical to the ones made in situation A. Thus, the consolidation adjustments remove the accounting veil that exists between the parent and the subsidiary, leading to the result that would have been obtained if all the transactions had instead taken place in the hands of the parent, with the subsidiary being absent as an intermediary.

## SSP 4-2

### Situation A:

Journal entries required:

| Books of Primary | | |
|---|---|---|
| Cash | 80,000 | |
| Sales | | 80,000 |
| | | |
| Cost of goods sold | 40,000 | |
| Inventory | | 40,000 |

**Sales, cost of goods sold, and gross profit amounts:**

| Sales | 80,000 |
|---|---|
| Cost of goods sold | 40,000 |
| Gross profit | 40,000 |

### Situation B:

Journal entries required:

| Books of Primary | | |
|---|---|---|
| Cash | 150,000 | |
| Sales | | 150,000 |
| | | |
| Cost of goods sold | 100,000 | |
| Inventory | | 100,000 |

Books of Secondary

| | | |
|---|---|---|
| Cash | 80,000 | |
|   Sales | | 80,000 |
| | | |
| Cost of goods sold | 60,000 | |
|   Inventory | | 60,000 |

Consolidation-related entries

| | | |
|---|---|---|
| Sales | 150,000 | |
|   Cost of goods sold | | 150,000 |
| | | |
| Cost of goods sold | 30,000 | |
|   Ending inventory | | 30,000 |

## Sales, cost of goods sold, and gross profit amounts:

| | Primary | Secondary | Con. adj. | Con. adj. | Con. amounts |
|---|---|---|---|---|---|
| Sales | 150,000 | 80,000 | (150,000) | | 80,000 |
| Cost of goods sold | 100,000 | 60,000 | (150,000) | 30,000 | 40,000 |
| Gross profit | 50,000 | 20,000 | 0 | (30,000) | 40,000 |

    The consolidated sales, cost of goods sold, and gross profit amounts in situation B are identical to their corresponding amounts in situation A. The consolidation adjustments made in situation B eliminate all intercompany transactions, as well as any unrealized profits present in the inventory purchased from Primary by Secondary during the year and remaining unsold at the end of the year. Therefore, after these adjustments are made, only those accounting entries that reflect transactions between the consolidated entity and outside parties remain to be reported on the consolidated financial statements. These remaining entries are identical to the ones made in situation A. Thus, the consolidation adjustments remove the accounting veil that exists between the parent and the subsidiary, leading to the result that would have been obtained if all the transactions had instead taken place in the hands of the parent, with the subsidiary being absent as an intermediary.

# SSP 4-3

## Analysis of the purchase transaction:

| | | |
|---|---|---|
| Purchase price | | $10,000,000 |
| Net assets acquired: | | |
|   Carrying value of Subco's net assets | $7,000,000 | |
|   Fair value increment on buildings | 1,400,000 | |
| | | 8,400,000 |
| Goodwill | | $ 1,600,000 |

### a. Consolidated net income:

| | | |
|---|---|---|
| Separate-entity net incomes: | | |
| Parco | $ 680,000 | |
| Subco | 350,000 | |
| | | $1,030,000 |
| Adjustments: | | |
| Eliminate dividend income from Subco | $ (150,000) | |
| Unrealized profit from upstream sales [200,000 × 20%] | (40,000) | |
| Amortization of fair value increment [1,400,000/14] | (100,000) | |
| | | 290,000 |
| Consolidated net income, year ended December 31, 20X5 | | $ 740,000 |

### b. Consolidated retained earnings:

| | Parco | Subco | Consolidated |
|---|---|---|---|
| Separate-entity retained earnings, January 1, 20X5 | $3,450,000 | $1,250,000 | |
| Separate-entity net incomes for 20X5 | 680,000 | 350,000 | |
| Dividends declared in 20X5 | (200,000) | (150,000) | |
| Carrying value of retained earnings, December 31, 20X5 | $3,930,000 | $1,450,000 | $5,380,000 |
| Consolidation adjustments: | | | |
| Eliminate Subco date-of-acquisition retained earnings | | | (1,250,000) |
| Unrealized profit from upstream sales [200,000 × 20%] | | | (40,000) |
| Amortization of fair value increment [1,400,000/14] | | | (100,000) |
| | | | (1,390,000) |
| Consolidated retained earnings, December 31, 20X5 | | | $3,990,000 |

### c. Parco's equity-basis earnings in Subco:

| | | |
|---|---|---|
| Subco's unadjusted separate-entity net income | | $ 350,000 |
| Equity-basis adjustments: | | |
| Unrealized profit from upstream sales [200,000 × 20%] | $ (40,000) | |
| Amortization of fair value increment [1,400,000/14] | (100,000) | |
| | | (140,000) |
| Subco's adjusted equity-basis earnings | | $ 210,000 |

# SSP 4-4

**Measure step at the time of acquisition:**

### 100% Purchase of Subsidiary Inc., January 1, 20X8

| | | | | | |
|---|---|---|---|---|---|
| Purchase price | | | | | $1,084,000 |
| Less carrying value of Target's net identifiable assets (100%) | | | | | (687,000) |
| = Fair value increment (FVI), allocated below | | | | | $ 397,000 |

| | Carrying value (a) | Fair value (b) | Fair value increment (c) = (b) – (a) | FVI allocated | |
|---|---|---|---|---|---|
| Cash | $ 80,000 | $ 80,000 | — | | |
| Accounts receivable | 99,000 | 99,000 | — | | |
| Inventory | 178,000 | 195,000 | $ 17,000 | $ 17,000 | |
| Property, plant, and equipment | 800,000 | 740,000 | (200,000) + 140,000 | 140,000 | |
| Accumulated depreciation | (200,000) | — | 200,000 | | |
| Accounts payable | (70,000) | (70,000) | — | | |
| Long-term notes payable | (200,000) | (200,000) | — | | |
| Total fair value increment | | | | | 157,000 |
| Net asset carrying value | $ 687,000 | | | | |
| Fair value of assets acquired | | $844,000 | | | |
| Balance of FVI allocated to goodwill | | | | | $240,000 |

---

## Eliminate and Recognize steps:

### Intercompany transactions and balances:

| | |
|---|---|
| Upstream sale by Subsidiary Inc. | $(150,000) |
| Downstream sale by Parent Ltd. | (390,000) |

### Unrealized and realized profits:

| | |
|---|---|
| Realized profit on upstream sale of inventory in the previous year | $ 12,000 |
| Unrealized profit on upstream sale of inventory in the current year | (20,000) |
| Unrealized profit on downstream sale of inventory in the current year | (18,000) |
| Unrealized gain on sale of land by Subsidiary Inc. to Parent Ltd. | (210,000) |

---

## Amortize FVIs

| | FVI allocated | Amortization period | Amortization per year | Amortization/ impairment loss during previous periods | Amortization/ impairment loss during 20X9 | Balance of FVI remaining at the end of 20X9 |
|---|---|---|---|---|---|---|
| Inventory | $17,000 | — | | $17,000 | — | — |
| Property, plant, and equipment | 140,000 | 10 | $14,000 | 14,000 | $14,000 | $112,000 |
| Total | $157,000 | | | $31,000 | $14,000 | $112,000 |

We also need to remember to eliminate the subsidiary's share equity account balances at the time of acquisition, as well as the investment in the subsidiary account during consolidation.

---

**Consolidated Financial Statements (direct method)**

**Parent Ltd.**

**Statement of Comprehensive Income**

**Year Ended December 31, 20X9**

| | |
|---|---:|
| Sales revenue [1,200,000 + 987,000 − 390,000 − 150,000] | $1,647,000 |
| Cost of goods sold [800,000 + 650,000 − 390,000 − 150,000 − 12,000 + (90,000 × 20%) + (50,000 × 40%)] | 936,000 |
| Gross profit | 711,000 |
| Other operating expenses [235,000 + 147,000 + 210,000 + 14,000] | 606,000 |
| NET INCOME | $ 105,000 |

**Parent Ltd.**

**Statement of Changes in Equity—Retained Earnings Section**

**Year Ended December 31, 20X9**

| | |
|---|---:|
| Retained earnings, December 31, 20X8 [1,153,000 + 330,000 − 437,000 − 17,000 − 12,000 − (140,000/10 × 1)] | $ 1,003,000 |
| Net income | 105,000 |
| Retained earnings, December 31, 20X9 | $1,108,000 |

**Parent Ltd.**

**Statement of Financial Position**

**December 31, 20X9**

ASSETS

Current assets:

| | |
|---|---:|
| Cash [120,000 + 110,000] | $ 230,000 |
| Accounts receivable [150,000 + 135,000] | 285,000 |
| Inventory [240,000 + 195,000 − (90,000 × 20%) − (50,000 × 40%)] | 397,000 |
| | 912,000 |
| Property, plant, and equipment [1,400,000 + 910,000 − 60,000 − 210,000] | 2,040,000 |
| Accumulated depreciation [510,000 + 320,000 − 200,000 + (140,000/10 × 2)] | (658,000) |
| | 1,382,000 |
| Goodwill [76,000 + 240,000] | 316,000 |
| TOTAL ASSETS | $2,610,000 |

LIABILITIES AND SHAREHOLDERS' EQUITY

Liabilities:

| | |
|---|---:|
| Accounts payable [142,000 + 60,000] | $ 202,000 |
| Long-term notes payable [600,000 + 200,000] | 800,000 |
| | 1,002,000 |

Shareholders' equity:

| | |
|---|---:|
| Common shares | 500,000 |
| Retained earnings [1,318,000 + 520,000 − 437,000 − 17,000 − 210,000 − (90,000 × 20%) − (50,000 × 40%) − (140,000/10 × 2)] | 1,108,000 |
| | 1,608,000 |
| TOTAL LIABILITIES AND SHAREHOLDERS' EQUITY | $2,610,000 |

# SSP 4A-1

## 100% Purchase of T Ltd., January 1, 20X2

| | | | | |
|---|---|---:|---:|---:|
| Purchase price | | | | $260,000 |
| Less carrying value of Target's net identifiable assets (100%) | | | | (130,000) |
| = Fair value adjustment, allocated below | | | | 130,000 |

| | Carrying value (a) | Fair value (b) | Fair value adjustment (c) = (b) – (a) | FVA allocated | |
|---|---:|---:|---:|---:|---:|
| Buildings (net) | $150,000 | $250,000 | $100,000 | $100,000 | |
| Deferred tax liability @ 40% | | (40,000) | (40,000) | (40,000) | |
| Total fair value increment | _____ | | | | ($ 60,000) |
| Net asset carrying value | $150,000 | _____ | | | |
| Fair value of assets acquired | | $210,000 | | | _____ |
| Balance of FVA allocated to goodwill | | | | | $ 70,000 |

| *E*liminate & *R*ecognize: | |
|---|---:|
| Investment in T Ltd. and share capital of T Ltd. & recog. FVA [130 + 130] | ($260,000) |
| Upstream sale by T Ltd. to P Ltd. | (100,000) |

| Unrealized profit on intercompany sale of inventory: | |
|---|---:|
| Intercompany sale of inventory | $ 100,000 |
| Gross profit percentage | 20% |
| Gross profit | $ 20,000 |
| Percentage unsold | 50% |
| Unrealized profit | $ 10,000 |
| Tax @ 40% | 4,000 |
| After-tax unrealized profit | $ 6,000 |

## Amortize:

| | FVA Jan. 1, 20X2 | Useful Life | Amort./ year | FVA amort. in 20X2 | FVA balance Dec. 31, 20X2 |
|---|---:|---:|---:|---:|---:|
| Buildings and equip. | $100,000 | 10 | $10,000 | $10,000 | $ 90,000 |
| Deferred tax liability @ 40% | (40,000) | | (4,000) | (4,000)* | (36,000) |
| Goodwill | 70,000 | | | | 70,000 |
| Total | $130,000 | | $ 6,000 | $ 6,000 | $124,000 |

| Eliminate after-tax amounts: | | | |
|---|---|---|---|
| For 20X2 | | | |
| | *Before-tax* | *Tax @ 40%* | *After-tax* |
| Additional amortization: | | | |
| Buildings and equipment | ($10,000) | $4,000* | ($6,000) |

*The $4,000 reduction in the deferred tax liability amount reduces the income tax expense of 20X2 by $4,000.

# SSP 5-1

## Situation A:

| Sale price | $150,000 |
|---|---|
| Less cost of goods sold | 100,000 |
| Gross profit | 50,000 |
| Portion remaining unsold in Secondary's inventory | 60% |
| Unrealized profit in ending inventory of Secondary | $ 30,000 |

| Required adjustments/eliminations: | |
|---|---|
| Elimination of downstream sale | (150,000) |
| Elimination of unrealized gain in ending inventory of Secondary | (30,000) |

## Situation B:

| Sale price | $150,000 |
|---|---|
| Less cost of goods sold | 100,000 |
| Gross profit | 50,000 |
| Portion remaining unsold in Secondary's inventory | 60% |
| Unrealized profit in ending inventory of Secondary | $ 30,000 |
| Primary's 80% share of unrealized profit | $ 24,000 |

| Required adjustments/eliminations: | |
|---|---|
| Elimination of unrealized gain in ending inventory of Secondary | (24,000) |

## Situation C:

| Sale price | $150,000 |
|---|---|
| Less cost of goods sold | 100,000 |
| Gross profit | 50,000 |
| Portion remaining unsold in Primary's inventory | 60% |
| Unrealized profit in ending inventory of Primary | $ 30,000 |
| Primary shareholders' 80% share of unrealized profit | $ 24,000 |
| NCI's 20% share of unrealized profit | $ 6,000 |

| Required adjustments/eliminations: | |
|---|---|
| Elimination of upstream sale | (150,000) |
| Elimination of unrealized gain in ending inventory of Secondary | (30,000) |
| Primary shareholders' 80% share of unrealized profit | (24,000) |
| NCI's 20% share of unrealized profit | (6,000) |

## Situation D:

| | |
|---|---:|
| Sale price | $150,000 |
| Less cost of goods sold | 100,000 |
| Gross profit | 50,000 |
| Portion remaining unsold in Primary's inventory | 60% |
| Unrealized profit in ending inventory of Primary | $ 30,000 |
| Primary's 80% share of unrealized profit | $ 24,000 |

| | |
|---|---:|
| Required adjustments/eliminations: | |
| Elimination of unrealized gain in ending inventory of Primary | (24,000) |

# SSP 5-2

Measure step under entity method:

### 60% Purchase of Dakota Ltd., January 10, 20X5

| | | | | |
|---|---:|---:|---:|---:|
| Purchase price | | $150,000 | | |
| 100% fair value based on purchase price [$150,000 (100%/60%)] | | | | $250,000 |
| Less carrying value of Dakota's net identifiable assets | | | | (165,000) |
| = fair value increment, allocated below | | | | $ 85,000 |

| | Carrying value (a) | Fair value (b) | Fair value increment (c) = (b) – (a) | FVI allocated |
|---|---:|---:|---:|---:|
| Cash | $ 10,000 | $ 10,000 | — | — |
| Accounts and other receivables | 20,000 | 20,000 | — | — |
| Inventories | 30,000 | 30,000 | — | — |
| Land | 45,000 | 80,000 | $ 35,000 | $ 35,000 |
| Buildings | 150,000 | 130,000 | (20,000) | (20,000) |
| Accumulated depreciation | (50,000) | | 50,000 | 50,000 |
| Equipment | 130,000 | 10,000 | (120,000) | (120,000) |
| Accumulated depreciation | (80,000) | | 80,000 | 80,000 |
| Current accounts payable | (40,000) | (40,000) | — | — |
| Long-term liabilities | (50,000) | (50,000) | — | — |
| Total fair value increment | | | 25,000 | 25,000 |
| Net asset carrying value | $165,000 | | | |
| Fair value of assets acquired | | $190,000 | | |
| Balance of FVI allocated to goodwill @ 100% | | | | $60,000 |

**Notes:**

1.  Under the entity method the NCI balance will be equal to 40% of the full fair value of Dakota Ltd., i.e., 40% of $250,000, or $100,000.

2.  Under the parent-company extension theory, only the parent's share of the goodwill of $60,000 × 60%, or $36,000, is reported on the consolidated financial statements. Consequently, under this method, the NCI is valued at only its 40% share of the net identifiable assets of Dakota, or $190,000 × 40% = $76,000.

```
┌─────────────────────────────────────────────────────────────────────┐
│                          Regina Ltd.                                   │
│                  Consolidated SFP (direct method)                      │
│                        January 10, 20X5                                │
│  ASSETS                                                                │
│  Current assets                                                        │
│   Cash [50,000 + 10,000]                              $ 60,000         │
│   Accounts and other receivables [70,000 + 20,000]      90,000         │
│   Inventories [80,000 + 30,000]                        110,000         │
│                                                        260,000         │
│                                                                        │
│  Capital assets                                                        │
│   Land [0 + 45,000 + 35,000]                            80,000         │
│   Buildings [260,000 + 150,000 – 20,000]               390,000         │
│   Accumulated depreciation [40,000 + 50,000 – 50,000]  (40,000)        │
│   Equipment [175,000 + 130,000 – 120,000]              185,000         │
│   Accumulated depreciation [70,000 + 80,000 – 80,000]  (70,000)        │
│                                                        545,000         │
│  Goodwill [250,000 – 190,000]                           60,000         │
│  TOTAL ASSETS                                         $865,000         │
│  LIABILITIES AND SHAREHOLDERS' EQUITY                                  │
│  Liabilities                                                           │
│   Current accounts payable [80,000 + 40,000]          $120,000         │
│   Long-term liabilities [0 + 50,000]                    50,000         │
│                                                        170,000         │
│                                                                        │
│  Shareholders' equity                                                  │
│   Common shares [220,000 + 150,000]                    370,000         │
│   Retained earnings                                    225,000         │
│   Non-controlling interest [250,000 × 40%]             100,000         │
│                                                        695,000         │
│  TOTAL LIABILITIES AND SHAREHOLDERS' EQUITY           $865,000         │
└─────────────────────────────────────────────────────────────────────┘
```

Note that the total for each asset and liability is arrived at is: Regina carrying value + Dakota carrying value + Dakota FVI.

Goodwill is the difference between the 100% fair value of Dakota of $250,000, arrived at based on the purchase price of $150,000 paid by Regina for its 60% share and the fair value of the net identifiable assets of $190,000—i.e., $60.000.

The Investment in the Dakota account and the share equity accounts of Dakota need not be eliminated, since they were not included in the calculation to start with.

# SSP 5-3

**For the Measure step, see SSP 5-2.**

| Eliminate and Recognize Steps | |
|---|---|
| *Intercompany transactions and balances:* | |
| Upstream sale by Dakota Ltd. | $(400,000) |
| Downstream sale by Regina Ltd. | (200,000) |
| Dividend declared by Dakota Ltd. | (40,000) |
| Interest expense of Dakota Ltd. and revenue of Regina Ltd. and interest receivable/payable at year-end. | (2,500) |
| Note receivable of Regina Ltd. and note payable of Dakota Ltd. | (50,000) |
| *Unrealized and realized profits:* | |
| Unrealized profit on upstream sale of inventory in the current year | $ (40,000) |
| Unrealized profit on downstream sale of inventory in the current year | (20,000) |

### Amortize FVIs

| | FVI allocated | Amortization period | Amortization per year | Amortization impairment loss during 20X5 | Balance of FVI remaining at the end of 20X5 |
|---|---|---|---|---|---|
| Land | $ 35,000 | | | | $ 35,000 |
| Building | 30,000 | 10 | $ 3,000 | $ 3,000 | 27,000 |
| Property, plant, and equipment | (40,000) | 5 | (8,000) | (8,000) | (32,000) |
| Goodwill | 60,000 | | | | 60,000 |
| Total | $(85,000) | | $(5,000) | $(5,000) | $ 90,000 |

### Recognize NCI share of earnings

| Details | Amount |
|---|---|
| Net income of Dakota Ltd. for 20X5 (from separate-entity financial statement) | $110,000 |
| Add amortization of FVI during the year | 5,000 |
| Less unrealized profit on upstream sale of inventory in the current year | (40,000) |
| **Adjusted net income of Dakota Ltd. for 20X5** | $ 75,000 |
| **NCI's share @ 40%** | $ 30,000 |
| **NCI balance at the end of 20X5** | |
| Balance of NCI at the beginning of 20X5 | $100,000 |
| Add NCI's share of Dakota Ltd.'s adjusted net income in 20X5 | 30,000 |
| Less NCI's share of dividends declared by Dakota Ltd. in 20X5 | (16,000) |
| Ending balance of NCI in 20X5 | $114,000 |

**Regina Ltd.**

**Consolidated Statement of Comprehensive Income (direct method)**

**Year Ended December 31, 20X5**

| | |
|---|---:|
| Sales [2,000,000 + 1,000,000 − **400,000** − **200,000**] | $2,400,000 |
| Dividend income [24,000 + 0 − **24,000**] | — |
| Other income [7,000 + 0 − **2,500**] | 4,500 |
| | 2,404,500 |
| Cost of sales [1,000,000 + 600,000 − **400,000** − **200,000** + **40,000** + **20,000**] | 1,060,000 |
| Other operating expenses [886,000 + 280,000 + **3,000** − **8,000**] | 1,161,000 |
| Interest expense [2,000 + 10,000 − **2,500**] | 9,500 |
| | 2,230,500 |
| Net income and comprehensive income | $ 174,000 |
| **NET INCOME ATTRIBUTABLE TO** | |
| Owners of the parent | $ 144,000 |
| Non-controlling interest | $ 30,000 |

**Regina Ltd.**

**Statement of Changes in Equity—Retained Earnings Section**

**Year Ended December 31, 20X5**

| | |
|---|---:|
| Retained earnings, December 31, 20X4 | $ 225,000 |
| Net income | 144,000 |
| Dividends declared [20,000 + 40,000 − **40,000**] | (20,000) |
| Retained earnings, December 31, 20X5 | $ 349,000 |

**Regina Ltd.**

**Consolidated Statement of Financial Position (direct method)**

**December 31, 20X5**

| | |
|---|---:|
| **ASSETS** | |
| **Current assets** | |
| Cash [28,000 + 10,000] | $ 38,000 |
| Accounts and other receivables [110,000 + 30,000 − **50,000** − **2,500**] | 87,500 |
| Inventories [160,000 + 60,000 − **40,000** − **20,000**] | 160,000 |
| | 285,500 |
| **Capital assets** | |
| Land [0 + 135,000 + **35,000**] | 170,000 |
| Buildings [300,000 + 150,000 − **20,000**] | 430,000 |
| Accumulated depreciation [45,000 + 60,000 − **50,000** + **3,000**] | (58,000) |
| Equipment [200,000 + 130,000 − **120,000**] | 210,000 |
| Accumulated depreciation [80,000 + 90,000 − **80,000** − **8,000**] | (82,000) |
| | 670,000 |
| Goodwill [**250,000** − **190,000**] | 60,000 |
| **TOTAL ASSETS** | $1,015,500 |

| LIABILITIES AND SHAREHOLDERS' EQUITY | | |
|---|---|---|
| **Liabilities** | | |
| Current accounts payable and accrued liabilities [40,000 + 80,000 – **50,000 – 2,500**] | $ | 67,500 |
| Long-term liabilities [65,000 + 50,000] | | 115,000 |
| | | 182,500 |
| **Shareholders' equity** | | |
| Common shares | | 370,000 |
| Retained earnings [348,000 + 135,000 – **65,000** – 40,000 – 20,000 + 8,000 – **3,000** – (**35,000 × 40%**)] | | 349,000 |
| Non-controlling interest [(**235,000 – 40,000 + 90,000**) × **40%**] | | 114,000 |
| | | 833,000 |
| TOTAL LIABILITIES AND SHAREHOLDERS' EQUITY | | $1,015,500 |

# SSP 5-4

**For the Measure step, see SSP 5-2.**

1. **Non-controlling interest in earnings:**

| | |
|---|---|
| Dakota's separate-entity net income for 20X6 (Exhibit 5.15) | $130,000 |
| Plus unrealized upstream profit in opening inventory: | |
| $100,000 × 40% gross margin | 40,000 |
| Less unrealized upstream profit in ending inventory: | |
| $160,000 sales × 50% remaining in inventory × 40% gross margin | (32,000) |
| Add amortization of FVI during the year | 5,000 |
| Adjusted Regina net income | 143,000 |
| Non-controlling interest share | × 40% |
| | $ 57,200 |

2. **Non-controlling interest:**

| | |
|---|---|
| Dakota's shareholders' equity, December 31, 20X6 (Exhibit 5.15) | $305,000 |
| Less unrealized upstream profit at year-end: | |
| Ending inventory, $160,000 × 50% × 40% gross margin | (32,000) |
| Add balance of FVI remaining at the end of 20X6 | 95,000 |
| | 368,000 |
| | × 40% |
| Non-controlling interest share | $147,200 |

### 3. Consolidated retained earnings:

**Alternative 1**

| | | |
|---|---:|---:|
| Regina's separate-entity retained earnings, December 31, 20X5 (Exhibit 5.15) | | $ 348,000 |
| Dakota's retained earnings, December 31, 20X5 | $205,000 | |
| Less Dakota's retained earnings at date of acquisition | (65,000) | |
| Change in Dakota's retained earnings since acquisition | 140,000 | |
| Regina's ownership share | × 60% | |
| Regina's share of Dakota's cumulative earnings | | 84,000 |
| Less unrealized profits at December 31, 20X6: | | |
| Upstream: $160,000 × 50% × 40% gross margin × 60% share | | (19,200) |
| Downstream: $40,000 × 50% gross margin | | (20,000) |
| *Amortization of FVI* | | |
| Less building ($30,000 ÷ 10 × 2) × 60% | $ (3,600) | |
| Plus equipment ($40,000 ÷ 5 × 2) × 60% | 9,600 | 6,000 |
| Regina consolidated retained earnings | | $ 398,800 |

**Alternative 2**

| | |
|---|---:|
| Total retained earnings (348,000 + 205,000) | $ 553,000 |
| Less Dakota's retained earnings at acquisition date | (65,000) |
| Less NCI's share of Dakota's cumulative earnings since acquisition (205,000 − 65,000) × 40% | (56,000) |
| *Less unrealized gains on intercompany sales* | |
| 60% of upstream sales $160,000 × 50% × 40% gross margin | (19,200) |
| 100% of downstream sales $40,000 × 50% gross margin | (20,000) |
| *Amortization of FVI* | |
| Less building ($30,000 ÷ 10 × 2) × 60% | (3,600) |
| Plus equipment ($40,000 ÷ 5 × 2) × 60% | 9,600 |
| Regina's consolidated retained earnings | $398,800 |

# SSP 6-1

**Note:** This is a *downstream* sale; NCI is not affected, except by the gain from sale as scrap in 20X16.

| | | |
|---|---|---|
| **20X7** | | |
| Sales | 100,000 | |
| Cost of sales | | 60,000 |
| Equipment | | 40,000 |
| Accumulated depreciation | 2,000 | |
| Depreciation expense (40,000 ÷ 10 × 1/2 year) | | 2,000 |
| **20X8** | | |
| Retained earnings [40,000 – (40,000 ÷ 10 × 1/2 year)] | 38,000 | |
| Accumulated depreciation | 2,000 | |
| Equipment | | 40,000 |
| Accumulated depreciation | 4,000 | |
| Depreciation expense (40,000 ÷ 10) | | 4,000 |
| **20X2** | | |
| Retained earnings [40,000 – (40,000 ÷ 10 × 4.5 years)] | 22,000 | |
| Accumulated depreciation | 18,000 | |
| Equipment | | 40,000 |
| Accumulated depreciation | 4,000 | |
| Depreciation expense | | 4,000 |
| **20X9** | | |
| Accumulated depreciation | 40,000 | |
| Equipment | | 40,000 |
| **20X0** | | |
| The NCI's share of $200 on the sale of the equipment as scrap will be attributed to it as part of its share of the adjusted earnings of Sparrow Ltd. | | |

# SSP 6-2

| Measurement: | | | | |
|---|---|---|---|---|
| **80% Purchase of Spencer Corp., January 1, 20X5** | | | | |
| Purchase price | | | $2,500,000 | |
| 100% fair value based on purchase price [$2,500,000 × (100%/80%)] | | | | $3,125,000 |
| Less carrying value of Spencer's net identifiable assets | | | | (3,000,000) |
| = fair value adjustment, allocated below | | | | 125,000 |

| | Fair value adjustment (c) = (b) – (a) | FVA allocated | |
|---|---|---|---|
| Buildings | $(600,000) | $(600,000) | |
| Long-term liabilities | 500,000 | 500,000 | |
| Total fair value adjustment | | | (100,000) |
| Balance of FVA allocated to goodwill @ 100% | | | $ 225,000 |

Eliminate and Recognize steps:

*Intercompany transactions and balances:*

| | |
|---|---|
| Upstream sale by Spencer Ltd. | $ (250,000) |
| Downstream sale by Power Ltd. | (400,000) |
| Dividends declared by Spencer Ltd. | (40,000) |

*Unrealized and realized profits:*

| | |
|---|---|
| Unrealized gain from upstream sale in ending inventory | $ (24,000) |
| Unrealized gain from downstream sale in ending inventory | (27,000) |
| Unrealized gain from upstream sale of land | (68,000) |
| Realized gain from downstream sale in beginning inventory | 30,000 |
| Realized gain from upstream sale in beginning inventory | 28,000 |

**Notes:** Unrealized gains have to be eliminated, while realized gains have to be recognized.

Amortize FVAs:

| | FVA allocated | Amortization period | Amortization per year | Amortization/ impairment loss in prior years | Amortization/ impairment loss during 20X9 | Balance of FVA remaining at the end of 20X9 |
|---|---|---|---|---|---|---|
| Building | $(600,000) | 10 | $(60,000) | (240,000) | $(60,000) | $(300,000) |
| Long-term liability | 500,000 | 8 | 62,500 | 250,000 | 62,500 | 187,500 |
| Goodwill | 225,000 | | | | | 225,000 |
| Total | $ 125,000 | | $ 2,500 | $ 10,000 | $ 2,500 | $ 112,500 |

**Note:** The FVA amortization on buildings will reduce the overall amortization per year on buildings, while the FVA amortization on long-term liabilities will be an additional expense/loss on SCI.

Unrealized loss on intercompany sale of machine:

| | Cost/carrying value | Depreciation/ realized losses in prior years (20X6–20X8) (cumulative adjustments) | Depreciation/ realized loss in 20X9 (current adjustments) | Carrying value/ unrealized loss at the end of 20X9 |
|---|---|---|---|---|
| In Power's books | $210,000 | $ 42,000 | $14,000 | $154,000 |
| In consolidated statements | 300,000 | 60,000 | 20,000 | 220,000 |
| Unrealized/realized loss | $ (90,000) | $(18,000) | $(6,000) | $ (66,000) |

**Note:** Since the loss of $90,000 is being realized over the remaining useful life of the asset, the $6,000 per year realized loss will increase the amortization on the machine over its useful life.

| Non-controlling interest in earnings | |
|---|---|
| Spencer's separate-entity net income for 20X9 (Exhibit 6.11) | $248,000 |
| Adjustments for gains/losses on upstream transactions: | |
| Add unrealized gain on upstream sale of land | (68,000) |
| Add realized gain on upstream sale of inventory in previous year (20X8) | 28,000 |
| Less unrealized gain on upstream sale of inventory in current year | (24,000) |
| Less realization of unrealized loss on upstream sale of machine in 20X6 | (6,000) |
| Amortization of FVA allocated to buildings | 60,000 |
| Amortization of FVA allocated to long-term liability | (62,500) |
| Spencer net income adjusted for realized and unrealized gains | $175,500 |
| Non-controlling interest share | ×20% |
| | $ 35,100 |

1. **Consolidated statement of comprehensive income:**

| Power Corporation Consolidated Statement of Comprehensive Income Year Ended December 31, 20X9 | |
|---|---|
| Sales (2,000,000 + 900,000 − 400,000 − 250,000) | $2,250,000 |
| Investment income (1,000,000 + 100,000 − 32,000) | 1,068,000 |
| Gain on sale of land (68,000 − 68,000) | — |
| Total revenues | 3,318,000 |
| Cost of goods sold [1,300,000 + 500,000 − 400,000 − 250,000 − 30,000 − 28,000 + 27,000 + 24,000] | 1,143,000 |
| Other operating expenses [ 960,000 + 320,000 + 6,000 − 60,000 + 62,500] | 1,288,500 |
| Total expenses | 2,431,500 |
| Net income and comprehensive income | $ 886,500 |
| Net income attributable to: | |
| Owners of the parent | $ 851,400 |
| Non-controlling interest | $ 35,100 |

## 2. Check via equity-basis income:

| | | |
|---|---:|---:|
| Power Corporation separate-entity net income | | $740,000 |
| Equity in earnings of Spencer Corporation: | | |
| Spencer separate-entity net income (248,000 × 80%) | $198,400 | |
| Unrealized upstream profit from land sale (68,000 × 80%) | (54,400) | |
| Unrealized downstream profit, ending (90,000 × 30%) | (27,000) | |
| Unrealized upstream profit, ending (60,000 × 40% × 80%) | (19,200) | |
| Realized downstream profit, beginning (100,000 × 30%) | 30,000 | |
| Realized upstream profit, beginning (70,000 × 40% × 80%) | 22,400 | |
| Under-depreciation on intercompany sale of machine (6,000 × 80%) | (4,800) | |
| Amortization of FVA on building (600,000 ÷ 10) × 80% | 48,000 | |
| Amortization of FVA on long-term liabilities (500,000 ÷ 8) × 80% | (50,000) | |
| Spencer adjusted net income | | 143,400 |
| Less dividends received from Spencer (40,000 × 80%) | | (32,000) |
| Net income attributable to Power Corporation's shareholders | | $851,400 |

## SSP 7-1

A segment is reportable if it comprises 10% or more of an enterprise's total revenues, operating profits, or combined assets. Only one of the 10% tests needs to be met.

1. Reportable segments under revenue test:

$$\text{Test:} \frac{\text{Segment revenues (including intersegment)}}{\text{Total revenues (including intersegment)}}$$

**East**    = 760/1010 = 75.2%
**West**    = 60/1010 = 5.9%
**North**   = 90/1010 = 8.9%
**South**   = 100/1010 = 9.9%

East is a reportable segment. The remaining segments are less than 10% and are not reportable under this test.

2. Reportable segments under profit test:

Total profits (50 + 80 + 10) = $140

Total losses = $15

Apply 10% criteria to larger of total profits or total losses. Larger is total profits: $140 × 10% = $14. Therefore any segment reporting a profit or loss of $14 or more is reportable. East, West, and South are reportable under this test.

3. Total assets are $1,990. Any segment reporting assets of $199 (= 1,990 × 10%) or more is reportable. Segments East and West both have assets greater than $199 and are reportable under this test.

Other test: External revenues disclosed in separate operating segments must be at least 75% of consolidated external revenues. The three tests above identified East,

West, and South as the reportable segments. External revenues for the three segments are (760 + 60 + 100 =) $920, which is 91% of total external revenues of $1010.

**Conclusion:** Reportable segments are East, West, and South.

## SSP 7-2

a. Widget Corporation is a public company and therefore must comply with IAS 34. Under IAS 34, costs such as maintenance are recognized in the interim period in which they occur (consistent with the discrete approach). As such, the costs in the second quarter will be expensed in the second quarter (and cannot be accrued and allocated to other interim periods).

b. Under IAS 34, the integral approach is used to accrue income taxes. As such, an estimate is made of the weighted average annual tax rate, and this tax rate is used to accrue the income tax expense for the interim periods. The average tax rate is calculated as follows:

   i. The estimated income for the year is $200,000 (= 900,000 + 600,000 – 1,200,000 – 100,000).

   ii. The tax payable on the $200,000 is $80,000, calculated as follows: [(100,000 × 30%) + (100,000 × 50%)]

   iii. The average tax rate is 40% (i.e., 80,000 ÷ 200,000).

   Using the average tax rate, the income tax expense for each quarter is as follows:

   ■ first quarter: (100,000) × 40% = (40,000)

   ■ second quarter: (1,200,000) × 40% = (480,000)

   ■ third quarter: 600,000 × 40% = 240,000

   ■ fourth quarter: 900,000 × 40% = 360,000

   ■ Solutions to Self-Study Problems

## SSP 8-1

| Fiscal year | Year-end FX rate | C$ value of bonds | FX gain (loss) |
|---|---|---|---|
| 20X5 | 1.27 | $6,350,000 | n/a |
| 20X6 | 1.30 | $6,500,000 | (150,000) |
| 20X7 | 1.34 | $6,700,000 | (200,000) |
| 20X8 | 1.35 | $6,750,000 | (50,000) |

## SSP 8-2

**1. Receivable is a hedged solution:**

| | Gross method | | Net method | |
|---|---|---|---|---|
| December 2, 20X1 | | | | |
| Accounts receivable (TWD) | 30,000 | | 30,000 | |
| Sales | | 30,000 | | 30,000 |
| [TWD1,000,000 × 0.0300] | | | | |

*Continued >*

*Continued >*

| | Gross method | | Net method | |
|---|---|---|---|---|
| December 3, 20X1 | | | | |
|   Forward contract receivable (C$) | 29,000 | | | |
|   Forward contract payable (TWD) | | 29,000 | | |
| [TWD1,000,000 × 0.0290] | | | | |
| December 31, 20X1 | | | | |
| Exchange gains and losses | 600 | | 600 | |
|   Accounts receivable (TWD) | | 600 | | 600 |
| [TWD1,000,000 × (0.0294 − 0.0300)] | | | | |
| Forward contract (payable - TWD) | 300 | | 300 | |
| Exchange gains and losses | | 300 | | 300 |
| [TWD1,000,000 × (0.0287 − 0.0290)] | | | | |
| February 1, 20X2 | | | | |
| Cash (TWD) | 28,000 | | 28,000 | |
| Exchange gains and losses | 1,400 | | 1,400 | |
|   Accounts receivable (TWD) | | 29,400 | | 29,400 |
| [TWD1,000,000 × (0.0280 − 0.0294)] | | | | |
| Cash (C$) | | | 29,000 | |
| Forward contract (payable - TWD) | 28,700 | | | 300 |
| Exchange gains and losses | | 700 | | 700 |
| Cash (TWD) | | 28,000 | | 28,000 |
| [TWD1,000,000 × (0.0280 − 0.0287)] | | | | |
| Cash (C$) | 29,000 | | | |
| Forward contract receivable (C$) | | 29,000 | | |

## 2. Receivable is not a hedged solution:

| | | |
|---|---|---|
| December 2, 20X1 | | |
|   Accounts receivable (TWD) | 30,000 | |
|   Sales | | 30,000 |
| [TWD1,000,000 × 0.0300] | | |
| December 31, 20X1 | | |
| Exchange gains and losses | 600 | |
|   Accounts receivable (TWD) | | 600 |
| [TWD1,000,000 × (0.0294 − 0.0300)] | | |
| February 1, 20X2 | | |
| Cash (TWD) | 28,000 | |
| Exchange gains and losses | 1,400 | |
| Accounts receivable (TWD) | | 29,400 |
| [TWD1,000,000 × (0.0280 − 0.0294)] | | |

# SSP 8-3

1. **Cash-flow hedge accounting:**

| | Gross method | | Net method | |
|---|---|---|---|---|
| **October 14, 20X7** | | | | |
| Forward contract receivable (US$) | 244,000 | | | |
| Forward contract payable (C$) | | 244,000 | | |
| [US$200,000 × 1.22] | | | | |
| | | | | |
| **December 31, 20X7** | | | | |
| Forward contract (receivable) | 2,000 | | 2,000 | |
| OCI | | 2,000 | | 2,000 |
| [Gain is (200,000 × 1.23) – (200,000 × 1.22)] | | | | |
| | | | | |
| **January 30, 20X8** | | | | |
| Forward contract (receivable) | 1,000 | | 1,000 | |
| OCI | | 1,000 | | 1,000 |
| [Gain is (200,000 × 1.235) – (200,000 × 1.23)] | | | | |
| Inventory | 241,400 | | 241,400 | |
| OCI (2,000 + 1,000) | 3,000 | | 3,000 | |
| Accounts payable (US$) | | 244,400 | | 244,400 |
| (200,000 × 1.222) | | | | |
| | | | | |
| **February 28, 20X8** | | | | |
| Forward contract payable | 244,000 | | | |
| Cash (C$) | | 244,000 | | |
| ($200,000 × 1.220) | | | | |
| Cash (US$) | 248,000 | | 248,000 | |
| Forward contract (receivable) | | 247,000 | | 3,000 |
| FX gains and losses | | 1,000 | | 1,000 |
| Cash (C$) | | | | 244,000 |
| [$200,000 × (1.235 – 1.240)] | | | | |
| | | | | |
| Accounts payable | 244,400 | | 244,400 | |
| FX gains and losses | 3,600 | | 3,600 | |
| Cash (US$) | | 248,000 | | 248,000 |
| [$200,000 (1.222 – 1.240)] | | | | |

**Notes:**

- No entry is made to record the purchase order, and under the gross method, the forward contract is recorded using the forward rate of $1.22.

- At year-end, the forward contract is adjusted to (recorded at) fair value and the gain is deferred in other comprehensive income. The increase in the fair value of the forward contract ($2,000) is determined using the forward rate on December 31 [$200,000 × (1.23 − 1.22)].

- On January 30, the forward contract is re-valued by making an entry for the change in the value of the contract, $1,000 [$200,000 × (1.235 − 1.230)]. The gain is deferred in other comprehensive income.

- On delivery, the payable is recorded at the spot rate ($244,400 = $200,000 × 1.222). The $3,000 gain deferred in other comprehensive income is reclassified. We have chosen to adjust the cost of the inventory. Therefore, the deferred gain will affect income when the inventory is sold through its effect on cost of goods sold. The carrying value of the inventory is $241,400. This is slightly more than the $240,000 cost using the spot rate at the time the inventory was ordered but is less than the $244,400 cost if there had been no hedge. Hedge accounting is no longer needed as the exchange gains and losses on the US-denominated accounts payable naturally offset the exchange losses and gains on the forward contract.

- The forward contract is settled on February 28, 20X8. Domestic Corp. pays the $244,000 it contracted to pay ($200,000 × 1.220) and in return receives US$200,000 valued at C$248,000. The difference is a gain of $4,000 on the contract, of which $3,000 was recognized earlier. The remaining $1,000 is the gain that occurred between January 30 and February 28 [$200,000 × (1.235 − 1.240)]. Domestic Corp. uses the US$200,000 (worth C$248,000) it received from its forward contract to settle the payable for the inventory. As a result of the change in the exchange rate, the company incurs an exchange loss of $3,600 × [$200,000 (1.222 − 1.240)] on the payable. The net exchange loss from January 30 to March 1 is $2,600 ($3,600 − $1,000).

- The following can be noted about this transaction. No gains or losses were recognized in net income in 20X7. The cost of the hedge was $4,000 [US$200,000 × (1.20 − 1.22)]; $2,600 was recognized as an exchange loss in 20X8 (between January 30 and February 28, 20X8), and $1,400 was included in the cost of the inventory. (Note: If the hedge had covered the period to the point of delivery only, then the total cost of the hedge would have been included in the cost of the inventory and thus the forward rate would determine the cost of the inventory.)

## 2. Fair-value hedge accounting:

| | Gross method | | Net method | |
|---|---|---|---|---|
| **October 14, 20X7** | | | | |
| Forward contract receivable (US$) | 244,000 | | | |
| Forward contract payable (C$) | | 244,000 | | |
| [US$200,000 × 1.22] | | | | |
| | | | | |
| **December 31, 20X7** | | | | |
| Forward contract (receivable) | 2,000 | | 2,000 | |
| | | | | |
| FX gains and losses | | 2,000 | | 2,000 |
| [Gain is (200,000 × 1.23) − (200,000 × 1.22)] | | | | |
| FX gains and losses | 2,000 | | 2,000 | |
| Commitment liability | | 2,000 | | 2,000 |
| [Loss is $200,000 × (1.21 − 1.20)] | | | | |
| | | | | |
| **January 30, 20X8** | | | | |
| Forward contract (receivable) | 1,000 | | 1,000 | |
| FX gains and losses | | 1,000 | | 1,000 |
| [Gain is (200,000 × 1.235) − (200,000 × 1.23)] | | | | |
| | | | | |
| FX gains and losses | 2,400 | | 2,400 | |
| Commitment liability | | 2,400 | | 2,400 |
| [Loss is $200,000 × (1.222 − 1.210)] | | | | |
| | | | | |
| Inventory | 240,000 | | 240,000 | |
| Commitment liability (2,000 + 2,400) | 4,400 | | 4,400 | |
| Accounts payable (US$) | | 244,400 | | 244,400 |
| (200,000 × 1.222) | | | | |
| | | | | |
| **February 28, 20X8** | | | | |
| Forward contract payable | 244,000 | | | |
| Cash (C$) | | 244,000 | | |
| ($200,000 × 1.220) | | | | |
| | | | | |
| Cash (US$) | 248,000 | | 248,000 | |
| Forward contract receivable | | 247,000 | | 3,000 |
| FX gains and losses | | 1,000 | | 1,000 |
| Cash (C$) | | | | 244,000 |
| [$200,000 × (1.235 − 1.240)] | | | | |

*Continued >*

*Continued >*

| | Gross method | | Net method | |
|---|---|---|---|---|
| Accounts payable | 244,400 | | 244,400 | |
| FX gains and losses | 3,600 | | 3,600 | |
| Cash (US$) | | 248,000 | | 248,000 |
| [$200,000 (1.222 – 1.240)] | | | | |

**Notes:**

- No entry is made to record the purchase order. Under the gross method, the forward contract is recorded using the forward rate of $1.22.

- At year-end, the forward contract is adjusted to (recorded at) fair value and the gain is recognized in net income. The increase in the fair value of the forward contract ($2,000) is determined using the forward rate on December 31 [$200,000 × (1.23 – 1.22)]. In addition, an exchange loss on the purchase commitment is recognized in net income and a liability is recognized to reflect the increase in the cost of the purchase commitment. The amount of the loss and associated liability ($2,000) is determined using the spot rate on December 31 [$200,000 × (1.21 – 1.20)]. The net exchange loss from November 1 to December 31 is $0 ($2,000 – $2,000).

- On January 30, the forward contract is re-valued by making an entry for $1,000, the change in the value of the contract [$200,000 × (1.235 – 1.230)]. The gain is recognized in net income. An additional exchange loss on the purchase commitment is recognized in net income. The increase in the cost of the purchase commitment is also recognized as an increased liability. The amount of the loss and associated liability ($2,400) is determined using the spot rate on January 30 [$200,000 × (1.222 – 1.210)]. The net exchange loss from January 1 to January 30 is $1,400 ($2,400 – $1,000).

- On delivery, accounts payable are recorded at the spot rate (244,400 = 200,000 × 1.222) to reflect the value of the obligation to pay US$200,000 to the supplier. The PO commitment liability is reversed as the increase in the liability is now captured in accounts payable. Finally, the inventory is recorded at $240,000 to balance the journal entry. This results in the inventory being recorded at the spot rate (1.200) that was in effect when the purchase commitment was made.

- The forward contract is settled on February 28, 20X8. Domestic Corp. pays the $244,000 it contracted to pay [US$200,000 × 1.22] and in return receives US$200,000 valued at $248,000. The difference is a gain of $4,000 on the contract, of which $3,000 was recognized earlier. The remaining $1,000 is the gain that occurred between January 30 and February 28 [$200,000 × (1.235 – 1.240)]. Domestic Corp. uses the US$200,000 (worth C$248,000) it received from its forward contract to settle the payable for the inventory. As a result of the change in the exchange rate, the company incurs an exchange loss of $3,600 [$200,000 (1.222 – 1.240)] on the payable. The net exchange loss from January 30 to March 1 is $2,600 ($3,600 – $1,000).

- Observe the following about this transaction. The cost of the hedge was $4,000 [US$200,000 × (1.22 – 1.20)], the difference between the spot rate and the forward rate at the time the inventory was ordered; $0 was recognized as an exchange loss in 20X7, and $4,000 was recognized as an exchange loss in 20X8 ($1,400 between January 1 and January 30 and $2,600 between January 30 and February 28, 20X8). The cost of the inventory was $240,000, which can be calculated using the spot rate (US$200,000 × 1.20) at the time it was ordered. None of the cost of the hedge was included in the cost of the inventory.

## SSP 8-4

1. **Cash-flow hedge:**

| June 30, 20X4 | | |
| --- | --- | --- |
| | No entry | |
| | | |
| December 31, 20X4 | | |
|   OCI | 1,000 | |
|     Cash (euros in France) | | 1,000 |
| [Loss is (50,000 × 1.40) – (50,000 × 1.38)] | | |
| | | |
| February 28, 20X5 | | |
|   OCI | 1,500 | |
|   Cash (euros in France) | | 1,500 |
| [Loss is (50,000 × 1.38) – (50,000 × 1.35)] | | |
| | | |
| Inventory | 70,000 | |
|   OCI (1,000 + 1,500) | | 2,500 |
|   Cash (euros) (50,000 × 1.35) | | 67,500 |

**Notes:**

■ Because we are using a non-derivative as the hedging instrument, the designated risk for this hedge was spot rate risk. The loss deferred in other comprehensive income is reclassified. We have chosen to adjust the cost of the inventory. As such, the deferred loss will be recognized in profit and loss when the inventory is sold. The carrying value of the inventory is $70,000. It is the cost of the inventory using the spot rate at the time it was ordered [€50,000 × 1.40 = $70,000].

2. **Fair-value hedge:**

| June 30, 20X4 | | |
| --- | --- | --- |
| | No entry | |
| | | |
| December 31, 20X4 | | |
|   Commitment Liability | 1,000 | |
|   Exchange gains | | 1,000 |
| [Gain is (50,000 × 1.40) – (50,000 × 1.38)] | | |
| | | |
| Exchange losses | 1,000 | |
|   Cash (euros in France) | | 1,000 |
| [Loss is (50,000 × 1.40) – (50,000 × 1.38)] | | |

*Continued >*

*Continued >*

| February 28, 20X5 | | |
|---|---|---|
| Commitment Liability | 1,500 | |
| Exchange gains | | 1,500 |
| | | |
| [Gain is (50,000 × 1.38) – (50,000 × 1.35)] | | |
| Exchange losses | 1,500 | |
| Cash (euros in France) | | 1,500 |
| [Loss is (50,000 × 1.38) – (50,000 × 1.35)] | | |
| | | |
| Inventory | 70,000 | |
| Commitment liability (1,000 + 1,500) | | 2,500 |
| Cash (euros) (50,000 × 1.35) | | 67,500 |

**Notes:**

- On delivery, the inventory is recorded at the spot rate ($70,000 = €50,000 × 1.40) that was in effect when the purchase order was issued. The PO commitment liability is reversed as the decrease in the liability is now captured in the payment to the supplier.

## SSP 8-5

1. **Cash-flow hedge accounting:**

| | Gross method | | Net method | |
|---|---|---|---|---|
| September 30, 20X5 | | | | |
| Forward contract receivable (C$) | 3,220,000 | | | |
| Forward contract payable (£) | | 3,220,000 | | |
| [£2,000,000 × 1.61] | | | | |
| | | | | |
| December 31, 20X5 | | | | |
| OCI | 24,000 | | 24,000 | |
| Forward contract payable | | 24,000 | | 24,000 |
| [Loss is 2,000,000 × (1.622 – 1.610)] | | | | |
| | | | | |
| April 1, 20X6 | | | | |
| OCI | 16,000 | | 16,000 | |
| Forward contract payable | | 16,000 | | 16,000 |
| [Loss is 2,000,000 × (1.630 – 1.622)] | | | | |
| | | | | |
| Cash (£) | 3,260,000 | | 3,260,000 | |
| OCI | | 40,000 | | 40,000 |
| Revenue | | 3,220,000 | | 3,220,000 |

| | | | |
|---|--:|--:|--:|
| Cash (C$) | | 3,220,000 | |
| Forward contract payable | 3,260,000 | 40,000 | |
| Cash (£) | | 3,260,000 | 3,260,000 |
| | | | |
| Cash (C$) | 3,220,000 | 3,220,000 | |
| Forward contract receivable (C$) | | 3,220,000 | 3,220,000 |

**Notes:**

■ The loss deferred in other comprehensive income (OCI) is released when the sale occurs. We have chosen to net it against revenue; therefore the deferred loss will now reduce earnings through its impact on revenue. Revenues are "recorded" at the spot rate when they occur (1.63) and then reduced by the amount of the loss released from OCI (i.e., 3,260,000 – 40,000 = 3,220,000). The result is that revenues are shown at $3,220,000; in effect, they are translated at the forward contract rate of 1.61.

# SSP 9-1

SCI translated at average rate for the year:

| | 20X2 @ $1.70 | 20X1 @ $2.20 |
|---|--:|--:|
| Revenue | $510,000 | $484,000 |
| Depreciation expense | 102,000 | 132,000 |
| Interest expense | 68,000 | 88,000 |
| Other expenses | 204,000 | 176,000 |
| | 374,000 | 396,000 |
| **Net income** | $136,000 | $ 88,000 |

SFP translated at year-end rate (except for shareholders' equity):

| | 20X2 @ $1.50 | 20X1 @ $2.00 |
|---|--:|--:|
| **ASSETS** | | |
| Cash | $ 45,000 | $ 320,000 |
| Accounts receivable | 60,000 | 60,000 |
| Land | 300,000 | — |
| Tangible capital assets | 900,000 | 1,200,000 |
| Accumulated depreciation | (180,000) | (120,000) |
| | $1,125,000 | $1,460,000 |
| **LIABILITIES AND SHAREHOLDERS' EQUITY** | | |
| Accounts payable, current | $ 15,000 | $ 40,000 |
| Notes payable, long term | 300,000 | 400,000 |
| | 315,000 | 440,000 |
| Common shares (note 1) | 1,250,000 | 1,250,000 |
| Retained earnings (note 2) | 89,000 | 28,000 |

*Continued >*

*Continued >*

|  | 20X2 @ $1.50 | 20X1 @ $2.00 |
|---|---|---|
| Translation loss, cumulative (note 3) | (529,000) | (258,000) |
|  | 810,000 | 1,020,000 |
|  | $1,125,000 | $1,460,000 |

**Notes:**

- SF500,000 × 2.50 = $1,250,000

- The retained earnings are translated at the historical rate at which the subsidiaries earnings were included in the parent's net income.

| 20X1 | |
|---|---|
| Beginning balance | $ — |
| Net income (40,000 × 2.20) | 88,000 |
| Less dividends (30,000 × 2.00) | (60,000) |
| Ending balance | $28,000 |
| 20X2 | |
| Beginning balance | $28,000 |
| Net income (80,000 × 1.70) | 136,000 |
| Less dividends (50,000 × 1.50) | (75,000) |
| Ending balance | $89,000 |

**3. The translation loss can be calculated independently as follows:**

|  | Local currency (SF) | Exchange rate | Translated amounts (C$) |
|---|---|---|---|
| Amounts arising in 20X1: | | | |
| NET ASSETS: | | | |
| Balance, January 1, 20X1 | SF500,000 | 2.50 | $1,250,000 |
| Changes during 20X1 | | | |
| Net Income | 40,000 | 2.20 | 88,000 |
| Dividends | (30,000) | 2.00 | (60,000) |
| Derived balance | | | 1,278,000 |
| Actual balance | SF510,000 | 2.00 | 1,020,000 |
| Net translation loss for 20X1 | | | 258,000 |
| Amounts relating to previous periods | | | 0 |
| Cumulative translation gain, December 31, 20X1 | | | $258,000 |

|  | Local currency (SF) | Exchange rate | Translated amounts (C$) |
|---|---|---|---|
| Amounts arising in 20X2: | | | |
| NET ASSETS: | | | |
| Balance, January 1, 20X2 | SF510,000 | 2.00 | $1,020,000 |
| Changes during 20X2 | | | |

| | | | |
|---|---|---|---|
| Net Income | 80,000 | 1.70 | 136,000 |
| Dividends | (50,000) | 1.50 | (75,000) |
| Derived balance | | | 1,081,000 |
| Actual balance | SF540,000 | 1.50 | 810,000 |
| Net translation loss for 20X2 | | | 271,000 |
| Amounts relating to previous periods | | | |
| 20X1 | | | 258,000 |
| Cumulative translation gain, December 31, 20X2 | | | $529,000 |

# SSP 9-2

1. **Translated 20X1 financial statements (temporal method):**

### Statement of Comprehensive Income

| | Local currency | Exchange rate | Canadian dollars |
|---|---|---|---|
| Revenue | SF220,000 | 2.20 | $484,000 |
| Depreciation expense | 60,000 | 2.30 | 138,000 |
| Interest expense | 40,000 | 2.20 | 88,000 |
| Other expenses | 80,000 | 2.20 | 176,000 |
| | 180,000 | | 402,000 |
| Net income | SF40,000 | | $82,000 |

### Statement of Financial Position

| | Local currency | Exchange rate | Canadian dollars |
|---|---|---|---|
| **Assets** | | | |
| Cash | SF160,000 | 2.00 | $320,000 |
| Accounts receivable | 30,000 | 2.00 | 60,000 |
| Tangible capital assets | 600,000 | 2.30 | 1,380,000 |
| Accumulated depreciation | (60,000) | 2.30 | (138,000) |
| | SF730,000 | | $1,622,000 |
| **Liabilities and shareholders' equity** | | | |
| Accounts payable, current | SF20,000 | 2.00 | $ 40,000 |
| Note payable, long-term | 200,000 | 2.00 | 400,000 |
| | 220,000 | | 440,000 |
| Common shares | 500,000 | 2.50 | 1,250,000 |
| Retained earnings | 10,000 | (Note 1) | 22,000 |
| Translation gain (loss) | — | | (90,000) |
| | 510,000 | | 1,182,000 |
| | SF730,000 | | $1,622,000 |

*Continued >*

*Continued >*

| | Local currency | Exchange rate | Canadian dollars |
|---|---|---|---|
| **Note 1** | | | |
| Net income, per income statement | SF40,000 | (as above) | $ 82,000 |
| Less dividends declared and paid at year-end 20X1 | (30,000) | 2.00 | (60,000) |
| Retained earnings | SF10,000 | | $ 22,000 |

2. **Translation Loss for 20X1**

| | Local currency (SF) | Exchange rate | Translated amounts (C$) |
|---|---|---|---|
| Amounts arising in 20X1: | | | |
| MONETARY ITEMS: | | | |
| Balance, January 1, 20X1[1] | SF500,000 | 2.50 | $1,250,000 |
| Changes during 20X1 | | | |
| Sales revenue | 220,000 | 2.20 | 484,000 |
| Interest expense | (40,000) | 2.20 | (88,000) |
| Other expenses | (80,000) | 2.20 | (176,000) |
| Payment of dividends | (30,000) | 2.00 | (60,000) |
| Purchase of tangible capital assets | (600,000) | 2.30 | (1,380,000) |
| Derived balance | | | 30,000 |
| Actual balance (160 + 30 − 20 − 200) | SF(30,000) | 2.00 | (60,000) |
| Net translation loss for 20X1 | | | (90,000) |
| Amounts relating to previous periods | | | 0 |
| Cumulative translation loss, December 31, 20X1 | | | $ (90,000) |

**Note:**

■ The initial investment was treated as the beginning balance. An alternative approach would be to set the beginning balance to zero and treat the initial investment as a sale of common shares that increased the monetary balance.

3. **Translated 20X2 financial statements (temporal method):**

| Statement of Comprehensive Income | | | |
|---|---|---|---|
| | Local currency | Exchange rate | Canadian dollars |
| Revenue | SF300,000 | 1.70 | $510,000 |
| Depreciation expense | 60,000 | 2.30 | 138,000 |
| Interest expense | 40,000 | 1.70 | 68,000 |
| Other expenses | 120,000 | 1.70 | 204,000 |
| | 220,000 | | 410,000 |
| NET INCOME | SF 80,000 | | $ 100,000 |

## Statement of Financial Position

| | Local currency | Exchange rate | Canadian dollars |
|---|---|---|---|
| **Assets** | | | |
| Cash | SF  30,000 | 1.50 | $    45,000 |
| Accounts receivable | 40,000 | 1.50 | 60,000 |
| Land | 200,000 | 1.90 | 380,000 |
| Tangible capital assets | 600,000 | 2.30 | 1,380,000 |
| Accumulated depreciation | (120,000) | 2.30 | (276,000) |
| | SF 750,000 | | $ 1,589,000 |
| **Liabilities and shareholders' equity** | | | |
| Accounts payable, current | SF  10,000 | 1.50 | $    15,000 |
| Note payable, long-term | 200,000 | 1.50 | 300,000 |
| | 210,000 | | 315,000 |
| Common shares | 500,000 | 2.50 | 1,250,000 |
| Retained earnings | 40,000 | (Note 1) | 47,000 |
| Translation gain (loss) | — | | (23,000) |
| | 540,000 | | 1,274,000 |
| | SF 750,000 | | $1,589,000 |

| Note 1 | | | |
|---|---|---|---|
| Balance, January 1, 20X2 | SF  10,000 | | $    22,000 |
| Net income, per income statement | 80,000 | (as above) | 100,000 |
| Less dividends declared and paid at year-end 20X2 | (50,000) | 1.50 | (75,000) |
| Retained earnings | SF40,000 | | $    47,000 |

## 4.  Translation gain for 20X2

| | Local currency (SF) | Exchange rate | Translated amounts (C$) |
|---|---|---|---|
| Amounts arising in 20X2: | | | |
| **MONETARY ITEMS:** | | | |
| Balance, January 1, 20X2 | SF (30,000) | 2.00 | $(60,000) |
| Changes during 20X2: | | | |
| Sales revenue | 300,000 | 1.70 | 510,000 |
| Interest expense | (40,000) | 1.70 | (68,000) |
| Other expenses | (120,000) | 1.70 | (204,000) |
| Payment of dividends | (50,000) | 1.50 | (75,000) |
| Purchase of land | (200,000) | 1.90 | (380,000) |

*Continued >*

*Continued >*

| | Local currency (SF) | Exchange rate | Translated amounts (C$) |
|---|---|---|---|
| Derived balance | | | (277,000) |
| Actual balance (30 + 40 − 10 − 200) | SF(140,000) | 1.50 | (210,000) |
| Net translation gain for 20X2 | | | $67,000 |
| Amounts relating to previous periods | | | |
| 20X1 | | | (90,000) |
| Cumulative translation loss, December 31, 20X2 | | | $(23,000) |

# SSP 10-1

### 1. January 1, 20X6:

| Cash | 200,000 | |
|---|---|---|
| Deferred contribution revenue | | 200,000 |

### 2. July 1, 20X6:

| Land | 44,000 | |
|---|---|---|
| Building | 120,000 | |
| Cash | | 164,000 |
| Deferred contribution revenue | 44,000 | |
| Net assets invested in capital assets | | 44,000 |

### 3. December 31, 20X6:

| Amortization expense | 3,000 | |
|---|---|---|
| Accumulated amortization | | 3,000 |
| ($120,000/20) × 6 ÷ 12 = $3,000 | | |
| Deferred contribution revenue | 3,000 | |
| Contribution revenue | | 3,000 |
| Prepaid maintenance | 36,000 | |
| Cash | | 36,000 |

# SSP 10-2

| | | | |
|---|---|---|---|
| 1. | Cash or marketable securities | 100,000 | |
| | Net assets | | 100,000 |
| 2. | Encumbrances | 1,400,000 | |
| | Estimated commitments | | 1,400,000 |
| 3. | Cash | 800,000 | |
| | Pledge receivable | 95,000 | |
| | Donation revenue | | 895,000 |

| 4. | Cash | 1,550,000 | |
| | Grant receivable | 50,000 | |
| | Deferred revenue | | 1,000,000 |
| | Grant revenue | | 600,000 |
| 5. | Equipment and furniture | 1,000,000 | |
| | Cash | | 1,000,000 |
| | Amortization expense | 100,000 | |
| | Accumulated amortization | | 100,000 |
| | Deferred revenue | 100,000 | |
| | Revenue | | 100,000 |
| 6. | Goods and services expense | 1,450,000 | |
| | Cash | | 1,305,000 |
| | Accounts payable | | 145,000 |
| | Estimated commitments | 1,375,000 | |
| | Encumbrances | | 1,375,000 |

# Index